.₃ a m
.₁, if ponderᵒ ᵣ
.ᵧ, though students prob. ᵧ wiᶦ
ᵤₐn wade through the whole. ɒaroᵢ
college libraries should own encyclopedia.
tainly will not appear for a long time, if o ᵤₐ
want to do it. (For reviews of earlier volumeᵣ
1966; Sept. 1967).

A SOCIAL AND RELIGIOUS HISTORY OF THE JEWS

Late Middle Ages and Era of European Expansion 1200–1650

VOLUME XV

RESETTLEMENT AND EXPLORATION

About the Author

After 33 years as a member of the Columbia University Faculty of Political Science, Salo Wittmayer Baron became Professor Emeritus of Jewish History, Literature, and Institutions on the Miller Foundation in 1963. Since that time he has served as Philip J. Levin Visiting Professor at Rutgers University, Gottesman Visiting Professor at Brown University, and Alexander Marx Visiting Professor at the Jewish Theological Seminary of America. He is President of the American Academy for Jewish Research; a Fellow of the American Academy of Arts and Sciences; a corresponding member of the International Commission for a Scientific and Cultural History of Mankind; and has been editor of the quarterly *Jewish Social Studies* since its founding in 1939. He has recently been made Knight of the Order of Merit of the Republic of Italy.

Other books by Professor Baron include *The Jewish Community* (3 vols.), *Modern Nationalism and Religion*, *The Russian Jew Under Tsars and Soviets*, *History and Jewish Historians: Essays and Addresses*, *Ancient and Medieval Jewish History: Essays*, and *Steeled by Adversity: Essays and Addresses on American Jewish Life*. He is co-editor, with Joseph Blau, of *The Jews of the United States, 1790-1840: A Documentary History* (3 vols.).

A SOCIAL
AND RELIGIOUS
HISTORY OF
THE JEWS

By SALO WITTMAYER BARON

Second Edition, Revised and Enlarged

Late Middle Ages and Era of European Expansion
1200–1650

VOLUME XV

RESETTLEMENT AND EXPLORATION

Columbia University Press
New York and London 1973

The Jewish Publication Society of America
Philadelphia 5733

CONTENTS

CONTENTS

A SOCIAL AND RELIGIOUS HISTORY

OF THE JEWS

PUBLISHED VOLUMES

Late Middle Ages and Era of European Expansion

RESETTLEMENT AND EXPLORATION

DUTCH JERUSALEM

D EVELOPMENTS in Hamburg and Glückstadt before and during the Thirty Years' War were merely part of a momentous process which, hardly realized by contemporaries, was to initiate a new epoch in Jewish history. These were the incipient stages of the Resettlement Era, when Jews began reentering the West-European countries from which they had been forced to leave at various times during the Late Middle Ages. Since these countries now assumed the leadership of the Western world, such reentry opened untold new paths for the economic advancement and cultural creativity of the Jewish people. Simultaneously, these countries embarked upon the large-scale colonization of the New World, as well as of their growing possessions in Africa and Asia. With that Western expansion also went a vast enlargement of the geographic and economic basis for Jewish settlement.

In the transformation of Jewish history, even more than in the general Western developments, Holland assumed a leading role. Emerging from an eighty-year war of liberation against the overwhelming power of Spain, a war which was not formally concluded until the Peace Treaties of Westphalia of 1648, the Dutch could make a fresh start. Because they also had completely severed their medieval legal ties with the Holy Roman Empire, they were far less heavily burdened by tradition than their neighbors in England, northwestern Germany, or France. The medieval heritage of the Low Countries, to be sure, continued to influence all walks of Dutch life. But the very fact that it was a revolutionary country, which achieved its independence by defying the ruling powers of the Spanish Church and state, made it amenable to major innovations which the tradition-bound neighboring states were far more hesitant to adopt.

SPANISH NETHERLANDS

Before achieving its leading position in the European commercial and political world, Holland had to sever its age-old connections with Flanders, Brabant, and the other parts of the Spanish Netherlands which remained both Catholic and Habsburg dependencies. Here, the position of New Christians largely continued to resemble that of their counterparts in the Spanish homeland, or in such European dependencies of Spain as Sicily and Naples—except perhaps in regard to the Inquisition, which was even less effective in ferreting out heresies in the Netherlands than it was in southern Italy. Nonetheless, because of its speedy economic decline during the eighty years of the Dutch struggle for independence, the southern part of the formerly united Netherlands no longer attracted as many Jews or Judaizers as it had during the regime of Charles V until his banishment of all New Christians in 1549–50.

Needless to say, not all New Christians were secret Jews. Many of them undoubtedly could have echoed the tenor of a petition their predecessors had submitted to Charles about 1541:

Sire, we are being put to work, molested, and hanged [*patibulés*] by your officials, particularly by your agent [*receveur*] of Zeeland, in defiance of your privilege. We are accused without reason of being Jews, Marranos, heretics, or apostates. Our persons, wives, children, and families, as well as our goods and funds are taken, seized, and despoiled—all that exclusively because of the great disorder, the [officials'] avarice and covetousness of our possessions. Sire, if unwittingly we should have transgressed your ordinances we beg your gracious permission that we be judged by the burgomasters and aldermen of Antwerp in accordance with the written law.

Although this argument would not have carried much weight with Charles and his advisers after 1550, it appears to have been persuasive enough with the municipal administration of Antwerp, which had vigorously, if unavailingly, protested the decrees of 1549–50. The city, which in the short span of a few decades had become a major emporium of trade and finance for all of western Europe, knew well enough how much the Portuguese New Christians had contributed to its prosperity; it therefore closed its eyes to their possible religious transgressions. This trend, which had already begun in the Late Middle Ages, has been perhaps too sharply characterized by one modern scholar in his analysis of religious feeling in Flanders at the end of the Middle Ages. He exclaimed: "Goodbye to the green meadows of medieval piety. One gets lost in the beautiful jungle of cupidity." [1]

In reality it often was extremely difficult for the Antwerp clergy, without the support of an efficient Spanish-style Inquisition with its far-flung espionage net and full support by the majority of the population, to ascertain whether a particular individual was a practicing Catholic. This may be deduced from the testimony (as yet unpublished) of one Jaspar Nuñez on October 18, 1608. According to his own account, Nuñez had lived in Lisbon, where he traded in diamonds, rubies, and other Indian imports, but had left Portugal for the Low Countries, for he had heard "that these lands are free, wrong no one, and accept no false testimonies as they do in Portugal." (He evidently had in mind false denunciations concerning heterodox beliefs or practices.) After some twenty months in Amsterdam, Nuñez moved to Antwerp with his wife, three sons, and two daughters. Now aged sixty-five, he claimed to have attended the Spanish church on major holidays, to have confessed and received communion, although he admitted that he had not done so since the departure, some six months before, of his favorite priest, a friar of the Order of St. Peter. Most remarkably, he testified that "he believed" that his wife, sons, and daughters were good Christians.[2]

Not surprisingly, therefore, Philip II complained, on November 25, 1564, that "countless [*infinité*] Jews live there [in Antwerp], assemble in their synagogues, have themselves circumcised, and publicly observe their rites. There they perform these ceremonies very boldly and, it is said, speak evil of my person. I would not make an issue of it if, at the same time, they were not making a mockery of our holy Catholic faith and observances." Philip's complaint was echoed two years later by Provost Maximilien Morillon in his letter of September 29, 1566, to Cardinal Antoine Perrenot de Granvella: "They say that the Portuguese are badly infected [by Calvinism] and that, for this reason, they are so well accepted by the Antwerp people, while the Spaniards are hated. But I believe that they are Jews and do not care about our religion, and yet they prefer to appear as such [Catholics], in order the better to stir up dissension within our holy faith." Granvella did not have to be told that such camouflage was facilitated by the relative ineffectiveness of the Netherlands Inquisition in the face of widespread popular resistance, and the ensuing "softness" of the Belgian inquisitors, about which Fray Lorenzo de Villaviçencio was complaining in 1564–66. True, in submitting (on September 30, 1564) the name of Licentiate Peter Titelmann of Hasselt, the Flanders Inquisitor, as one of six possible candidates for an episcopal see, Bishop Martin Baldwin Rithorius claimed that Margaret of Austria, duchess of Parma, and regent of the Netherlands (1559–67), had praised Titelmann as an experienced official and a meritorious worker in the defense of Catholicism. Rithorius added: "Although among some people he [the inquisitor] has the reputation of being harsh and cruel, he is in fact sufficiently compassionate toward penitents." Nonetheless, another Spanish official, in explaining to Philip II, on December 25, 1565, the difficulties of persuading the Flemish public to accept the appointment of new bishops, described "the desire for heresy and dread of the Inquisition among the people" as the most odious aspect of the entire situation. Ultimately, Philip himself—in his letter of August 12, 1566, to the Spanish ambassador at Rome, Count Luis de Zuñiga y Requésens— expressed his readiness to replace the papal Inquisition in Flanders with the more traditional episcopal courts, provided additional bishops were installed and would supervise them adequately.[3]

It was because of that popular resentment of inquisitorial searches that an Antwerp record of 1571 could list by name 102 Portuguese, most of whom very likely were secret Jews. This document, signed by the two consuls of the "Portuguese Nation," enumerates 85 heads of families, a figure which probably reflects the presence of a secret Jewish community of some 400–500 souls. It should have come as no surprise to anyone familiar with the local conditions that a clandestine synagogue was discovered in Antwerp in 1564. Even after the "iconoclastic troubles" of 1566, which caused the exodus of some 2,000–3,000 residents; the "Spanish Fury" of 1576, in which some 7,000 inhabitants were slaughtered by the duke of Alba's soldiery; and Antwerp's surrender to the

Spanish general Alessandro Farnese in 1585, which likewise brought about the departure of at least 5,000 Protestants and Marranos to the growing commercial center of Amsterdam, a sizable New Christian community continued to reside in the city. Another list, prepared on February 23, 1591, by one J. Moutinho, probably a secretary of the group, still counted 57 men (doubtless heads of families) and 20 widows by name. The chances are that in the following years of slow recovery from the wounds inflicted on the city of Antwerp by the underpaid and undisciplined Spanish soldiers the number of such dubious New Christians increased, although the roll extant from the year 1604 listed only 27 names.[4]

We must not lose sight of the fact that Antwerp's entire population suffered severely during the Dutch uprising. Its sharp demographic decline came to the fore in 1589, when the total number of inhabitants amounted to only 42,000, as against 90,000 in 1556. To be sure, commercially, the city (including its "Portuguese" merchants) was able to carry on. Remarkably, in some areas, such as the importation and distribution of sugar from both São Thomé Island and Brazil, Antwerp maintained its leading position in western Europe until the Dutch conquests of parts of Brazil. But its financial strength was sapped, not only by the general wartime dislocations but also by the three royal bankruptcies of 1557, 1575, and 1596. The Portuguese and other bankers were also adversely affected by the cessation in 1574–1603 of the formerly very lucrative loans to the English Crown (the creditors had collected interest at the rate of 12–14 percent and had profited from delivery to the borrowers of parts of the loan in commodities at inflated prices). Yet many of them tenaciously persevered.[5]

Their struggle for survival was facilitated by some weakening in the severity of inquisitorial prosecutions. Despite his autocratic proclivities, even Philip II had to tread lightly in his support of the local Inquisition, which was left to the bishops' courts, rather than to a special Spanish-type tribunal. On principle, however, he rejected the city's plea for moderation in religious policies. It was Philip's intransigence which caused Alessandro Farnese, the famous general-diplomat of the Spanish army fighting the Dutch, to reject the pathetic, if outspoken, appeal of the Antwerp city council of November 23, 1584. Here the city fathers had argued that they, too, would like to end the War, which they insisted had been provoked by self-seeking royal advisers submitting slanted reports to the king. But the only way they saw to terminate the hostilities was for the administration to proclaim full liberty of conscience. They knew, they resignedly added, that "Farnese was not the master able to arrange that matter. Even the king of Spain is subject to the Spanish Inquisition and to orders from the pope in Rome. He has no right to accord that freedom to his subjects, although the pope and many Italian potentates grant it to Jews and Turks." [6]

A novel situation arose in 1609 as a result of the twelve-year truce between Spain and Holland. In that treaty, largely forced on Spain by its chronic financial crises and dependence on Flemish loans, the contracting parties had promised not to discriminate against each other's citizens residing in the northern and southern Low Countries, respectively. Under the provisions of these treaties, an Amsterdam Jew, in his capacity as a Dutch subject, demanded admission to Antwerp for trade purposes. Although the Spanish Netherlands were at that time under the control of Archduke Albert of Austria and his wife Isabella (Philip II's daughter), as joint sovereigns, neither were they personally willing to grant this request, nor did they wish to antagonize the king of Spain, who was still the real monarch of the country. The authorities resorted, therefore, to a legal subterfuge. They rejected the application of the would-be visitor by explaining that Jews had been barred from all Flemish lands in 1370 because of their flagrant crime against the Catholic Church. Hence they were excluded from residence in Brabant not because of the recent hostilities between the North and the South but because of a previous condition. If they tried to return, they would face severe penalties.[7]

Albert and Isabella, who had long been under the influence of the Church (they had voraciously read much of the Catholic literature recommended to them by their spiritual advisers), were eager to refuse toleration to such questionable Catholics. Not only Isabella, who had grown up in the stifling atmosphere of Philip II's autocratic court and growing Spanish racialism, but also her Austrian husband betrayed considerable personal animosity toward Jews. In a letter to Philip III on December 1, 1614, Albert wrote:

"I believe . . . that all the Portuguese residing in Holland are infidels; they have become Jews. They moved there in order to live freely [as Jews]." He also mentioned the case of one António Martínez de Figueredo who, after serving as a soldier in the Portuguese Indies, had been arrested by the Lisbon Inquisition. Subsequently he had settled as a professing Jew in Amsterdam. There he was in contact with the Dutch East India Company, supplying it with valuable information about the local conditions in the Indies. A year and a half later (May 28, 1616), the archduke reported to Philip III about a proposal by Fray Gregorio de Valencia that he secure the services of the Moroccan-Dutch merchant-diplomat Samuel Pallache; after the latter's intervening death the arrangement was to be made with Pallache's nephew Moses. Regrettably, the dispatch, at least as summarized in the published *regesta,* does not specify the purpose and the conditions of that agreement, except for a hint that it might serve to transfer some places in the Barbary States to Spanish control. Albert expressed his distrust of the entire scheme, and added that "the Jews are scarcely dependable people; there is nothing in the whole affair but a means of extracting some money." [8]

Albert and Isabella's resolve to oppose the admission of Jewish visitors to Antwerp must have been reinforced by the attitude of the contemporary papal Curia and its representatives in the Low Countries. Had not, as early as October 7, 1600, the papal nuncio Ottavio Mirto Frangipane complained to the papal secretary of state Cardinal Pietro Aldobrandini about the presence in Antwerp of many heretics and unbelievers who "simulated" being Catholic? Fifteen years later another papal secretary of state, Cardinal Scipione Borghese, learning about the projected admission of some English merchants to Antwerp (an admission supported by the curious argument that residence in the Catholic city might persuade the men to adopt the Catholic faith), wrote on October 23, 1615, to Nuncio Ascanio Gesualdo, archbishop of Bari, urging him to exercise great caution in discussing the proposal with the archduke. Borghese argued:

Heresy is like a contagious disease, and the few sick persons can infect many healthy ones, particularly in connection with mercantile exchanges. Nor ought the temporary benefits for one city outweigh the spiritual damage to all these states. Moreover, the example of that city might move other localities to make the same request. Without any real *raison d'état* for the good of the political government, it would introduce more than one religion into the state.

Borghese repeated similar instructions at two-year intervals (June 27, 1617, and June 2, 1619) to Gesualdo's successors in the office of nuncio. Albert and Isabella seem not to have offered any serious resistance to such papal interventions, which in many ways reflected Paul V's new drive to reestablish medieval papal controls over many temporal matters throughout the Catholic world.[9]

All of this did not prevent the municipal administration of Antwerp from sheltering many New Christian as well as English merchants. Two extant lists, dated in 1611 and 1619, during the period of Albert's administration, record the presence of 75 and 46 Portuguese, respectively. It goes without saying that such lists were never complete. Undoubtedly some Jewish visitors from Amsterdam never called themselves Portuguese. Perhaps they hoped, as had some of their predecessors during the period after 1549, that, because the first decree by Charles V had specifically banished Portuguese New Christians, and the public generally associated secret judaizing with the "Portuguese" group, they might more readily escape detection if they were classified as Spaniards or Dutch. Many Portuguese had indeed moved into Spain after the unification of the two countries in 1580, and could now legitimately register as Spaniards. In any case, life in Flanders had again become so acceptable to the New Christians that in 1610, as we shall see, Jacob Tirado was unable to implement the agreement he had made with the city of Rotterdam to bring in 30 Jewish families for settlement in the then rapidly developing Dutch port.[10]

After the expiration of the truce in 1621, hostilities between Holland and Spain were resumed. The Flemish New Christians and the Dutch Jews suffered along with the other inhabitants of the two countries, which again had been turned into battlefields. The small Marrano community must have shared in the "catastrophic mortality" of the Flemish population during the war and its aftermath. The Marranos may, indeed, have suffered even more than their fellow-citizens, because of the strong anti-Jewish animus of the Spaniards. This bias came clearly to the fore toward the end of the Thirty Years' War, when Holland and Spain began arranging for exchanges of war prisoners. According to a dispatch from the governor of Flanders, Manuel de Maura y Cortereal, marquis of Castel Rodrigo, to Philip IV on May 1, 1645, the Dutch prisoners to be exchanged included a Dutch lieutenant-major (Eustache Piecq) and four Jews: Jacob and Abraham Bueno, and David and Moses Cohen. The governor advised the king that this exchange would be highly advantageous to the Spaniards—doubtless because there were more Spanish prisoners-of-war in Dutch hands than Dutch soldiers in Spanish captivity—and urged him speedily to implement it. From subsequent dispatches by the governor, dated July 4, 1646, and March 28, 1647, we learn that, while some exchanges had taken place in which the Dutch showed themselves particularly generous, the four Jews, held prisoner in Spanish monasteries, had not yet been released.[11]

In 1648 the Treaty of Münster ended the eighty-year Dutch-Spanish war by forcing Spain to recognize Holland's independence and thereby finalizing the separation between the Low Countries' Protestant North and Catholic South. This treaty once again solemnly provided for mutual toleration of the citizens of Holland and what was to become Belgium. On the basis of this treaty, Dutch Jews renewed their demand for admission to Antwerp, Brussels, and other cities. In 1650 Philip IV roundly rejected their interpretation of the treaty provisions, but the Dutch Jews persisted. Thereupon Archduke Leopold William, then the Spanish governor of Flanders, appointed a Commission to review the newly created legal situation. In a lengthy memorandum submitted to the archduke on December 11, 1653, the Commission tried to resolve the following five points: (1) From the standpoint of canon and civil law, were Christian princes allowed to admit Jews and to tolerate their free practice of religion? (2) Did the province of Brabant not possess particular constitutional provisions or customs which would bar such toleration? (3) Would the admission of Jews not result in a great inconvenience and scandal for the population at large, even if they were to be assigned a special quarter either in some enclosed town or in the open country? (4) Would such admission, as might be expected, bring a notable increase in the Crown's much-needed revenue, a benefit which would outweigh the anticipated inconveniences? (5) If it were decided that such a concession could be granted to the Jews, under what conditions and legal requirements should it be carried into effect?

The Commission felt that it could answer the first point in the affirmative by citing both canon law and St. Augustine and by referring to the existing practices in Rome, other Italian cities, and many parts of Germany. As to the second query, the only pertinent regulations, those of 1550 and 1559, were originally enacted by the Crown and might easily be abrogated by a royal decree. On the third question, different persons doubtless held different opinions, but in the Commissioners' view, formal admission would merely legalize a long-existing practice. "In fact, no one doubts that a large number of Jews now live in the city of Antwerp. By great hypocrisy they imitate the Christians and the Catholics, go to confession and communion, marry and mix with Catholics in public. Yet in the secrecy of their homes they obstinately practice their Judaism." The fourth question was left to the superior judgment of the archduke, who alone could decide how urgent was the need to improve the state's financial position. On their part, the Commissioners felt that the admission of Jews would have no more untoward consequences than that of Frenchmen, "among whom that pest [of atheism] is far advanced." Moreover, soldiers of various nationalities and denominations had often been recruited by the administration for the defense of the country. Finally, in answer to the fifth question, the Commissioners suggested the enactment of a constitution modeled after the one issued by St. Carlo Borromeo for the state of Milan; that document included basic provisions for separate Jewish quarters, badges, nonemployment of Christian servants by Jews, and a limitation of the maximum interest rates. The Commission's cogent arguments ran counter, however, to the wishes of the Church. On the direct intervention of Pope Innocent X, Philip IV instructed the archduke on February 19, 1654, to reject the Jewish application and to insist upon keeping professing Jews out of the country. To justify the violation of the pertinent clause in the Treaty of Münster, the administration used the argument advanced after the truce of 1609; namely, the specific outlawry of Judaism in 1370.[12]

Enterprising Amsterdam Jews evidently were not completely

discouraged by this Spanish negativism. In 1653, while the Commission was still debating the issue, one Samuel Pinto suggested to the Spanish envoy in The Hague, Antoine Brun, that he knew of ways to increase Spain's revenues considerably, without cost to its subjects. Philip IV was sufficiently impressed to ask (on November 3, 1653) his ambassador in France, Count Fuensaldaña, for his opinion on the merits of this proposal. The count was also to consult Archduke Leopold William. Since Pinto's proposal doubtless presupposed the granting of residential rights in Flanders to himself or his Jewish agents, it was evidently rejected after the royal instruction of February 19, 1654. Eleven years later another Amsterdam Jew, Andrés de Belmonte, made a bolder proposal. In the memorandum he submitted sometime before November 30, 1665, to the new Spanish ambassador in Holland, Esteban de Gamarra, Belmonte pointed out the numerous frauds plaguing Spain's trade with the Indies and promised to help suppress them if he were appointed Spanish agent in Amsterdam. This proposal, too, called forth a royal inquiry: the queen regent, on November 30, 1665, asked the marquis of Castel Rodrigo, then interim governor of Flanders, for his opinion. Needless to say, the tradition of intolerance was too profoundly ingrained in Spain to be overcome by such dubious approaches. How deeply rooted anti-Jewish feeling had become was demonstrated six years later, when some Dutch Jews, undeterred by the failure of previous negotiations, again submitted a formal request for admission to the Spanish Netherlands. They specifically asked to be assigned living quarters in the small locality of Vilvorde. For that concession they offered the huge amount of 5,000,000 florins, as well as a substantial annual contribution thereafter. Because of opposition from the archbishop of Malines, the bishop of Antwerp, and other churchmen, even this highly advantageous offer was roundly rejected.[13]

Nonetheless, Portuguese New Christians continued to live in the Spanish Netherlands. A list dated December 10, 1666, and prepared by Francisco Henriques, secretary of the "Portuguese Nation," named 38 men and 27 women (for the most part widows). Although, technically, no Jews were yet allowed to live in Antwerp, when in 1682 the Portuguese merchant Diego Curiel refused to have his newborn son baptized, and the child was seized by a priest under the excuse that any child born in a Catholic country belonged to the Church, the court overruled the priest, and the father was acquitted. Needless to say, as in the preceding century, some New Christians were genuine Christians, but the majority doubtless were secret Jews. For example, Don Garcia de Yllan, who entertained Queen Christina of Sweden in his Antwerp home in 1654, was considered by many contemporaries a secret Judaizer. That he more or less regularly attended church services, and that he was later buried in a Catholic cemetery after leaving a testament couched in Catholic terms, need not have been more than the usual camouflage used by Marranos in all the Spanish possessions. Neither is his marriage to Doña Gracia Brandon de Mesquita, supposedly a member of the Portuguese noble family Brandão or Brandon, conclusive evidence of his Catholicism, since she may have been among the descendants of the English adventurer Sir Edward Brampton or Brandon, who, as we recall, tried to claim Old Christian ancestry by preferring adulterous Christian to legitimate Jewish ancestors. Moreover, in 1694 another Jewish "synagogue" was discovered in the city, without evoking any major punitive reaction. Thus the Marrano population in Belgium led an essentially clandestine religious life until the country was finally occupied by the French Revolutionary armies in 1792.[14]

HESITANT DUTCH BEGINNINGS

In contrast to the stationary, often retrogressive, policies of the three Philips in the southern provinces, which remained under Spanish control, Holland's meteoric rise in economic and military power during its struggle for liberation (1564–1648) was one of the historic "miracles" of the early modern period. After long playing a secondary role to their southern compatriots in Flanders and Brabant, the Dutch speedily became the leading mercantile nation of Europe. As early as 1601, the Englishman John Keymor contended, the Dutch Republic commanded a mercantile fleet of 20,000 "ships and other vessels," and had more shipping at its disposal than the combined merchant marines of England, Scotland, France, Spain, Portugal, Italy, Denmark, Sweden, Poland, and Russia. He also claimed that the Dutch were adding 1,000 ships to that fleet every year. The Dutch East India Company under the able leadership of such governors as Jan Pieterszoon Coen, who in 1619 founded the company's headquarters in Batavia (now Jakarta, Indonesia)—as well as the slower-growing West India Company, extended Dutch shipping and maritime power (including piracy, then viewed as a legitimate sideline of navigation) over the seven seas. At the same time, the growth of the Amsterdam Stock Exchange and other commercial institutions, operating with far greater competitive freedoms than elsewhere, speedily turned that Dutch city into the banking and commercial metropolis of the Western world. Certainly, the grandiose project conceived by some advisers of Philip IV of Spain to destroy Dutch shipping and maritime trade was but a belated, futile attempt to turn back the clock of European history.[15]

Not surprisingly, the pioneering efforts of the New Christians in the early stages of their settlement in the Low Countries, could now be continued in the North by professing Jews; that is, in the main, by New Christians publicly reverting to Judaism. The dominant Protestant circles viewed Catholic Spaniards or even Portuguese, who since 1580 were subjects of the Spanish king, with greater suspicion than they regarded Jews, whose hostility to Spain's inquisitorial regime could be taken for granted. True, anti-Jewish feelings were still much alive in Holland, as in the other Western countries. But under the pressure of the new economic developments, the powerful democratic trends characteristic of the revolutionary era (which, for a while, lent much vigor to Anabaptist propaganda), the secularization of politics, and the dominance of *raison d'état* in international relations, those feelings gradually receded, and in time were greatly toned down in the light of actual experiences in intergroup symbiosis.[16]

Ironically, the new center of Jewish life developed in those parts of the Low Countries which in the Middle Ages had attracted relatively few Jews. Amsterdam, especially, which was to play such a great role in later Jewish history, seems to have harbored very few Jews during the Middle Ages. Even a widely discussed "miracle of the host" in 1346 had no anti-Jewish implications, which doubtless would have been the case if a Jewish community had been present in the city. Certainly, the relative insignificance of the

Amsterdam "miracle," and the few vestiges it left in the memory and fantasy of the local populace, sharply contrasted with the long-enduring impact of the "miracle of Sainte-Gudule" of 1370 in Brussels. The provinces of Utrecht and Gelderland, which had temporarily harbored Jews in the cities of Utrecht, Zwolle, and Deventer, had lost them after a brief sojourn. An agreement reached by some New Christians with the authorities of the duchy of Gelderland and the county of Zutphen was nullified by Charles V's order of January 20, 1545, with severe threats against any New Christians found in the area after a month. The emperor also ordered his officials in Utrecht to remove such persons from the city and to refuse admission to any would-be New Christian settlers in the future. Nijmegen alone had a more durable, if small, Jewish settlement in the Late Middle Ages. In 1391 it counted three Jewish families; their number increased to five in 1410. Individual Jews were recorded there sporadically until 1491, but we hear no more about them until the arrival of the Marranos in the sixteenth century.[17]

Under the stresses and strains of the Dutch War of Liberation, however, the settlement of New Christians, and later Jews, endowed with commercial skills, capital, and far-flung international contacts, was a welcome accretion to the country's resources. True, dislike of professing Jews extended even to so enlightened a humanist as Erasmus of Rotterdam. In his glorification of France, Erasmus counted among her virtues her "not being corrupted like the Italians by the Jews' commerce." He repeated this sentiment in a private letter to Richard Bartholinus on March 10, 1516 (1517), in which he wrote: "France alone is not infected by heretics, Bohemian schismatics, Jews, or half-Jewish Marranos." On other occasions, the sage of Rotterdam attacked the leading Catholic spokesman, Girolamo Aleandro (Aleander), who later served as cardinal and papal legate, by calling him a Jew and mordantly adding, "I do not know whether he was baptized." In his repudiation of Johann Pfefferkorn's attacks on Johannes Reuchlin, a fellow-humanist, Erasmus knew of no better wish than "if he [Pfefferkorn] only were a whole Jew, or else if, just as he had his foreskin cut off, he had also had his tongue and both hands amputated!" The Protestant clergy, among both the so-called Arminians or

Remonstrants and the Counter-Remonstrants, continued to oppose the admission of Jews, and subsequently fought inch by inch against the enlargement of their civil and religious rights. Ultimately, the defeated Arminians bitterly complained that they were being treated more cruelly than Jews, who denied the very fundamentals of Christianity.[18]

In contrast, the secular powers, starting with the first recognized leader of the Dutch revolt in 1574–84, William "the Silent" of Orange, entered early negotiations with Jews. First informally, and then through the legislation of the States General, they sanctioned the presence of professing Jews, although they left the detailed regulation of Jewish status to the respective municipalities. Like Antwerp and the other great cities of the South—which, as we recall, staunchly defended their "liberties" against the Spanish regime—Amsterdam and the other large centers of the upsurging North now insisted upon their municipal autonomy in controlling all their internal affairs, including those pertaining to Jews. In vain did Philip II, an autocrat in his home country, try to "modernize"; that is, to centralize and firmly control the administration of the Low Countries. "At every turn," correctly observes Charles Wilson, "Philip found himself faced by a complex protective tangle of traditional 'liberties,' noble, ecclesiastical, municipal, that seemed cunningly contrived to defeat the process of 'government' and reform." Ultimately, Jews, too, were granted extensive religious and communal self-determination and were even allowed to erect synagogues, although for a time they were expected to avoid any public display of Jewish worship.[19]

With the spread of the Protestant Reformation and the serious internal cleavages it created in the Netherlands, the religious issue assumed vital significance, however. Almost immediately after his accession to the Spanish throne in 1556, Philip II abandoned his father's more cautious policy. He and his officials in the Low Countries became ever more intolerant of the slightest religious deviation and were particularly suspicious of the influential New Christian community. Quite early in his reign (November 25, 1564), the king warned the local authorities about the Antwerp population's heretical leanings and the presence in the city of numerous Judaizers. He ordered speedy remedial action. Before long the duke of Alba began suppressing all nonconformist trends with utmost cruelty. Many burghers as well as nobles now saw no alternative to an open revolt.[20]

Facing the strong and well-led Spanish army, William had to obtain support wherever he could find it. He needed both manpower and funds. At first he persuaded John Casimir of the Palatinate to send him a force of 10,000 mercenaries; but when he was unable to pay their wages, these men were withdrawn. At this point the initiative may have come from some Jews. A somewhat ambiguous resolution of the Antwerp city council, dated August 20, 1576, reads in part: "Concerning the proposition of the Jews who are desirous of residing in Antwerp, as in former days, it has been decided that Baron [Georges?] de Vile, who has initiated this matter, should submit certain points and articles in writing, so that negotiations may be started with them." Evidently, residence was no longer based on a clear denial of the petitioners' Jewish allegiance, such as had been constantly reiterated by the Marranos themselves and their protectors among the Antwerp municipal councilors. Probably in some connection with these deliberations, William decided to enlist the financial assistance of Jewish bankers. In 1577, through the Antwerp city council, he instructed two burghers, Pieter Verleth and Daniël van Gele, who happened to be traveling to Cologne and Frankfort, to get in touch with the Jewish financiers of that area and to try to secure large loans from them. Since there were no professing Jews in Cologne at that time, William must have had in mind bankers like Wendel of neighboring Deutz and his brother-in-law Joseph zum Goldenen Schwan of Frankfort, with whom the Dutch had negotiated a loan of 20,000 florins at 5 percent interest for six years, in 1563–64. The Gottschalk mentioned as an intermediary in William's instruction is perhaps identical with the illegal Jewish resident of Cologne by that name who in 1584 was expelled from the city and settled in Mayence. More, having learned about the great influence exercised by some Constantinople Jewish leaders at the Porte, William endeavored to persuade them through his German Jewish collaborators to think of means by which "the Spanish and Italian troops could be kept away" from Holland. The Dutch ruler evidently hoped that the Jews might influence the sultan (and also some of the Muslim

Barbary States) to open a southern front against Spain and thus reduce the pressures of the Spanish armies on the Dutch revolutionaries. This diversion, the Jews were to be told, "would accrue to their [the Jews'] and our mutual advantage." In return, the negotiators were to hold out to the Jews prospects of formal admission to settlement in the Low Countries. Clearly, the Dutch remembered Don Joseph Nasi's role in the Turko-Spanish War of 1571-72, the conflict which, despite the disaster of Lepanto, had ended in the Ottoman conquest of Cyprus.[21]

Perhaps to demonstrate their good will toward New Christians and, indirectly, toward professing Jews as well, the States General issued on October 22, 1597, a new charter in favor of "the Portuguese Nation residing in these lands." Although still pretending that its provisions related exclusively to professing Christians, the legislators clearly sought to expunge the anti-Marrano statute enacted by Charles V and to discontinue its enforcement by the Spanish administrators. In time the very term "Portuguese Nation," frequently used in Amsterdam's official documents, became almost synonymous with the Jewish communities, without necessarily implying special privileges, as it did in Antwerp. In all these liberalizing endeavors, William and his successors encountered the stiff resistance of many conservatives among the Middelburg clergy and other staunchly Protestant circles, notwithstanding the long-time association of these groups with numerous New Christians in their midst. Among the very leaders were Marcus Pérez (1527-72), who headed the Calvinist consistory of Antwerp, and Philip de Bernuy, one of the most influential Lutherans of that city. In 1613, another member of the Bernuy family was even involved in the Fettmilch uprising against both patricians and Jews in Frankfort. Pérez, it may be noted, had played a major role in the 1566 Antwerp offer to Philip II of the huge sum of 3,000,000 guilders in exchange for the proclamation of religious liberty—of course, in vain. As late as 1598, in extending to the Portuguese merchants the privilege of acquiring burghers' rights, the burgomasters of Amsterdam made it clear that the applicants were expected to be "sincere Christians" because "no practice of religion is allowed, except one which is publicly performed in churches." Nevertheless, William's overtures to the German Jews were not forgotten. They certainly helped pave the way for the subsequent admission of professing Jews for settlement in Holland. The newcomers' fears of inquisitorial trials were greatly mitigated by Article xiii of the Union of Utrecht of 1579, which united the northern provinces in their revolt against Spanish oppression. Though not specifically referring to Jews, this article provided that no one would be persecuted for religious reasons. It thus promised immunity to Marranos and also, ultimately, to professing Jews.[22]

Obviously, the prince of Orange and his associates greatly overestimated the Jews' financial resources and political influence. Moreover, these hoped-for allies had to proceed rather cautiously so long as the outcome of the war was undecided. In the event of a Spanish victory, all Marranos (whether Spanish or Portuguese) who were convicted of supporting the rebels would have been doomed as both apostates and traitors to their country (since Portugal had become part of Spain in 1580). Remarkably, many New Christians never overcame their deep sentimental attachment to their native lands. In Amsterdam most of them continued to speak Spanish or Portuguese, to such an extent that in 1622 they persuaded the local authorities to allow them to conduct their wedding ceremonies in their accustomed way, without the use of Dutch interpreters. The newlyweds had merely to register their marriage with the municipal officials. The community as a whole long continued to conduct its business in Spanish and Portuguese. More strikingly, when one Samuel Beneviste, participating in a Dutch attack on a Spanish flotilla, helped set fire to a Spanish ship, he was censured for it by the eminent poet and chronicler of Amsterdam's Jewish intellectual life, Daniel Levi (Miguel) de Barrios. The poet (himself a former Spanish army officer) doubtless voiced a fairly widespread feeling among his coreligionists when he exclaimed: "Much as he may feel rejected by his native country, no Spanish-born Hebrew should commit such an outrage against his fatherland." During the Thirty Years' War, even more remote and independent Hamburg —despite its neutrality and intensive trade relations with the Iberian Peninsula and the Low Countries, north and south—did not appear, to many New Christians wishing to return to the overt profession of Judaism, to be a wholly secure haven of refuge. In general, German Jews could not afford openly to antagonize their

Habsburg emperors, who not only were allied with Spain but until 1648 claimed for the Empire nominal overlordship of the Netherlands, because the entire Jewish status, particularly in the imperial cities, greatly depended on the good will of the imperial authorities. Both professing and secret Jews proceeded, therefore, with great caution, at least until 1609, when the twelve-year armistice between the Dutch States General and Spain seemed temporarily to guarantee the independence of Holland, although full sovereignty was not formally recognized until the Treaty of Münster of 1648.[23]

Unlike their German coreligionists, the Portuguese secret Jews in the Low Countries had little choice, however. They tried to maintain their residence in Antwerp as long as possible. To be sure, after its bloody conquest by the duke of Parma in 1585, many Marranos joined the thousands of Protestant merchants who hurriedly left the city for the northern provinces under the control of the Dutch "rebels." But many others braved the Spanish soldiers, lulling themselves into a feeling of relative security under their Catholic Iberian veneer, which was more easily maintained in the Low Countries away from the efficient investigations conducted by the Spanish or Portuguese Holy Offices. Some went north later, after the southern provinces had definitely cast their lot with the Spanish regime and joined the Counter Reformation.[24]

AMSTERDAM'S LEAP FORWARD

In those years began the epic story of the Jewish settlement in Amsterdam, a settlement which, in a few generations, was to develop into the largest Jewish community in Christian Europe. Like most of the new arrivals at the beginning of the seventeenth century, the majority of these "Portuguese" came from the embattled southern Netherlands. But many had recently left Portugal or Spain and had proceeded, sometimes indirectly, to the Dutch metropolis, which increasingly attracted settlers from many lands. Foreigners, like Andrew Marvell, were soon to comment, with a mixture of hostility and envy:

> Hence *Amsterdam*—Turk—Christian—Pagan—Jew,
> Staple of Sects, and Mint of Schisme grew;

That *Bank of Conscience,* where not one so strange
Opinion, but finds Credit and Exchange.
In vain for Catholicks our selves we bear,
The Universal Church is only there.

In 1653, when these words were written, the Jewish community's influence had begun to be felt even in neighboring lands. It was to play an ever greater role in the socioeconomic, political, and cultural destinies of the whole Jewish people. Here the Jews performed their own great historical miracle in the framework of the general "miracle of Amsterdam" so eloquently described by Jan Romein.[25]

As usual, the beginnings of the Jewish settlement are still shrouded in the mist of legend. The pertinent records of the Amsterdam Jews themselves date from many decades after the events, having been written between 1673 and 1769. They include (1) the story told in 1711 by Uri Phoebus b. Aaron ha-Levi, scion of Moses Uri b. Joseph ha-Levi, the Sephardic community's first rabbi, whose arrival in Amsterdam can now be dated precisely at 1602; (2) an enthusiastic poem by Daniel Levi (Miguel) de Barrios which uses more than a grain of poetic license; and (3) a few additional data supplied by David Franco Mendes, a late descendant of one of the earliest settlers, in a tract composed in 1769. Although some dates mentioned in these sources still are under debate and many colorful accretions to the accounts are definitely unhistorical, the story of the arrival in Holland in 1593 of a shipload of Marranos who had previously sought refuge in the German port of Emden seems to reflect an actual occurrence. In Emden, we are told, the refugees were persuaded by the local rabbi and *mohel* (circumciser), Moses Uri ha-Levi, to proceed instead to Amsterdam; they were subsequently joined there by the rabbi and his son Aaron. The leader of that expedition, Jacob Tirado (or Tyrado, known in Christian circles as Jennes or James Lopes da Costa), established the first Jewish congregation in the city (*ca.* 1597); it was named *Beth Yaacob* (House of Jacob) in his honor. Upon Moses Uri's arrival, Tirado underwent formal circumcision; in the course of later years, the ritual was allegedly performed by that *mohel* on 930 other individuals.[26]

Less certain is the story of a different shipload, which reputedly arrived in London in 1593. This group is said to have included a beautiful girl, Maria Nuñez, whose presence was reported to Queen Elizabeth. Apparently the queen was so greatly captivated by the visitor's charm that she traveled with her in an open carriage through the streets of London and tried to persuade her to marry one of the English dukes. This story is not as farfetched at it appears at first glance. Some New Christian women did indeed marry into the high aristocracy, both in Iberia and abroad. We recall the Habsburg efforts to marry off Doña Reina Mendes to Don Alphonso de Aragón in Antwerp. In 1524, Doña Mencia de Mendoza, a New Christian, married Count Hendrik van Nassau, one of Charles V's intimate counselors. The wedding, performed with great pomp, was attended by the flower of Flemish and Iberian nobility. The queen of Portugal, the emperor's sister, presided over the ceremony, leading the bride, then her house guest, to the altar. We also remember the numerous relationships between Hamburg Marranos and high dignitaries and noble families in Spain. However, the staunchly Jewish Maria Nuñez allegedly rejected the English queen's suggestion, moved to Amsterdam, and in 1598, at the age of twenty-three, married there a fellow-Marrano, Emanuel Lópes Homem of Oporto, four years her senior.[27]

In any case, the Amsterdam community was definitely established by the 1590s. One of its early leaders, Emanuel Rodrigues Vega, is mentioned in connection with various business transactions, in several notarial documents of 1595–96. His name then appears in some 93 such documents extant from the years 1597–1613. He also was the first member of the "Portuguese Nation" to secure burgher's rights in the city of Amsterdam, in 1597. The Jewish settlement slowly grew to embrace some 200 persons by 1609; it is said to have numbered 1,000 members, in a total population of about 115,000, in 1630. Two decades later, Menasseh ben Israel claimed that it consisted of 400 families (owning no less than 300 houses), or more than 2,000 souls. Most of these arrivals came, directly or indirectly, from Portugal, the policies of which, during the six decades of Spanish domination (1580–1640), forced a great many Marranos to emigrate. The temporary relaxation, under Philip III, of the prohibition against their leaving the country further stimulated their departure. It is noteworthy that of the 129 male Jews recorded in the Amsterdam registry as having married in the years 1598–1630 no fewer than 95 were born in Portugal. Only 3 were natives of Spain, while the 10 born in Antwerp, 3 in France, 2 in Venice, and 1 each in Jerusalem and Salonica may well have been of Portuguese parentage. No more than 9 had been born in Amsterdam.[28]

Sooner or later the Amsterdam authorities had to take cognizance of these new arrivals. Action was accelerated when a number of Portuguese émigrés successfully applied for admission to several neighboring cities, and Amsterdam feared that it might lose out in its competition for commercial leadership. Enlightened leaders of the burghers' class realized, to cite a 1662 statement by Pieter de la Court (a statement wrongly attributed to the influential regent Johan de Witt): "We may safely say that *Holland* cannot in any wise subsist of it self, but of necessity it must fetch its Food elsewhere, and continually invite new Inhabitants from Foreign Parts." This author asserted: "as to freedom of religion, it is certain that having till this time been greater in *Holland* than any where else, it hath brought in many Inhabitants, and driven out but few." He also argued that such freedom proves beneficial to the Reformed religion, which may and ought to depend on its own evidence and veracity. Nonetheless, because of the resistance of some conservative burghers who, according to De la Court's observation, selfishly wished "to keep the best solely for themselves," as well as of the Dutch Reformed clergy, the city for a while pretended to ignore the presence of the Jewish settlers and refrained from taking any official action concerning them until 1615. In that year, when the persecuted sect of Remonstrants (or Arminians) argued, along lines long pursued by denominational minorities, that they ought not be subjected to more severe repression than were the "alien" Jewish settlers, the provincial authorities of Holland, the most populous and wealthiest province, had to abandon the fiction that they had tolerated only professing Christians. They expressly forbade Jewish *public* worship, threatening that any synagogue erected by Jews would be mercilessly destroyed. However, their policy of toleration of Jews remained otherwise unaltered. In 1616, a rabbi, Abraham b. Joseph ha-Levi, discussing the legal validity of a testament written by Isaac ibn

Yaqar (known to Gentiles as Manuel Pimentel, a former playmate of King Henry IV of France), observed:

Interested in the city's growth, its people adopted laws and regulations including guarantees of religious freedom for all. Everyone is permitted to live according to his faith, but he must not make it publicly manifest that he belongs to a religious group at variance with the rest of the population.

This ambiguous situation evidently became untenable, since two Jewish congregations (*Beth Yaacob* and, from 1608 on, *Neve Shalom*) were already functioning in the city, and a Jewish cemetery, after a first frustrated attempt in 1602–1605, had been established in neighboring Ouderkerk in 1614. During the same period, such charitable societies as those for visiting the sick (*Biqqur Holim*) and for marrying off orphans and young girls (*Santa Companha de dotar orphas e donzellas*) had been established, in 1609 and 1615, respectively. They were speedily followed by that eminent institution of self-help for an immigrant community, the charitable loan bank (*Chonen Dalim*), founded in 1625 by the communal rabbi David Pardo and several associates.[29]

No longer able to ignore the issue, the Amsterdam municipality in 1615 appointed a committee of two, consisting of Adriaan van Pauw, son of Reinier van Pauw, the city's renowned burgomaster, and Hugo Grotius (Huigh de Groot; 1583–1645), then a young man of thirty-two, who was to become the father of international law. The council may have hoped that the two experts, representing the conservative and liberal wings, would advance a joint set of proposals. But apparently they were unable to agree, and each man submitted an independent memorandum on the best ways of permanently admitting Jews to residence in Amsterdam. While Van Pauw's proposal, evidently rather intolerant, has hitherto remained unpublished, Grotius' *Remonstrantie* has long been the subject of extensive research and has, more recently, appeared in a new critical edition.[30]

Grotius' memorandum is a curious mixture of Roman jurisprudence, medieval scholasticism, and Protestant theology. In his letter of June 28, 1640, to his lifelong friend Gerhard Johann Vos (Vossius), the famous jurist himself ranked theology ahead of both jurisprudence and history as the deepest concern of his entire intellectual career. (He wrote this letter five years before his demise.) Clearly, even as a jurist he could not fall back on any real experience, since he had had but sporadic contacts with Jews, and there existed no living memory of their treatment in Amsterdam. His effort was, therefore, a pure *Bildungserlebnis,* based upon considerable reading in the existing literature, for which he was well prepared by his extensive classical erudition and close familiarity with the juridical and theological writings of his age. He also had more than a nodding acquaintance with Hebrew. True, following the fashion of the age in his quotation of Hebrew sources, he gave the impression of greater firsthand acquaintance with them than he really possessed. His citations from the Talmud and rabbinic letters were, for the most part, borrowed from the ever growing accumulation of passages translated into Latin and incorporated into works by Christian Hebraists and such Jewish writers in Western languages as Menasseh ben Israel. But from his early years, Grotius came under the influence of several eminent Hebraists, including Joseph Justus Scaliger and Franciscus Junius, a friend and collaborator of Immanuel Tremellius. In his theological writings he at least made a conscious effort to familiarize himself with the rabbinic views, if only at times in order to refute them more effectively.[31]

Knowledge of Hebrew, to be sure, did not necessarily make a man a Jewish sympathizer. While most Christian Hebraists, including Scaliger and Junius, entertained more balanced views on Jews and Judaism than most other Protestant ecclesiastical leaders, one of Grotius' friends, Hugh Broughton, minister of the Middelburg English congregation, who allegedly corresponded with Queen Elizabeth in Hebrew, probably shared the anti-Jewish prejudices of his confreres among the Middelburg clergy. As we recall, these pastors had vigorously protested against William of Orange's early negotiations with the German Jews. Broughton himself, a good Bible student and a translator of the Prophets, though unsuccessful in securing membership in the select group of scholars appointed by King James in 1604 to issue the Authorized Version of Scripture, had long engaged in religious disputations with Jews in Frankfort and elsewhere. In 1606 he published in Amsterdam a conversionist tract in Hebrew, entitled *Parshegen ha-nishtevan ish 'ibri* or *yehudi* (Copy of a Letter to a Hebrew [or Jewish] Man) and provided Greek and Latin translations of it.[32]

Yet among more liberal scholars the study of Hebrew often did serve as an argument for Judeo-Christian coexistence. Grotius, who was a spokesman for religious toleration—particularly since his return from a diplomatic mission to England two years earlier—contended that only through association with Jews could non-Jews improve their knowledge of Hebrew. Needless to say, such a plea for toleration by no means interfered with his personal Christian piety. Yet even in his theological works he refrained from those sharp, frequently crude attacks on Jews or Judaism which were the fashion of the age. In his main apologetic work, *De veritate religionis christianae,* he invoked Judaism's testimony for the authenticity of the ancient miracles, since the Jewish religion, "though it has been a long time destitute of human assistance, nay exposed to contempt and mockery, yet it remains to this very day, in almost all parts of the world." While trying to confute the Jewish doctrines, his familiarity with which he asserted had come to him from reading works "written by the Jews in behalf of the ancient Jewish dispensation," he insisted, "I desire the Jews, that they would not look upon us as adversaries." [33]

However, the main weight of Grotius' *Remonstrantie* rests with his juridical brief arguing the merits or demerits of toleration of Jews and stating the conditions under which they might be admitted. Beginning with arguments on the negative side, Grotius cited as precedents the medieval expulsions of Jews, and even calmly discussed the Blood Accusations. As a jurist, he did not here dismiss the medieval court proceedings on this subject out of hand, although in 1636, when ritual libels in Polish Lublin came to his attention, he clearly expressed his disbelief that such practices existed among Jews. He now argued, however, that the "hospitality" of the Reformed Church demanded humane treatment of all aliens, including Jews.

Thus we have to practice natural love for every person without excluding anybody. Expulsion is against nature because it cuts off the communion established by nature. Therefore it is a punishment which should only be enforced for a violation of the law. With respect to Jews there are special considerations which are not applicable to other infidels. They are the children of Abraham, Isaac, and Jacob, the Israelites who have received the pledge to be accepted as children and are to partake of the glory, the covenants, the laws, the religion, and the promises; theirs are the forefathers from whom Christ Himself descended in the flesh, the direct relatives of the Apostles and the first teachers of our religion; yea, they are the ones to whom God's oracles have been entrusted. When discussing what books of the Old Testament must be considered canonical, we refer to Jews. As the Apostle says, they ought to be our enemies as regards the Gospel, but beloved for the sake of the forefathers, who were specially chosen by God.

These theological arguments were, in Grotius' opinion, much more important than either the practical need of Christian scholars to secure the advice of learned Jewish neighbors in the investigation of Hebrew sources or the economic considerations which had heretofore guided the elders of the various municipalities in admitting Jews. He mentioned the old Hessian metaphor (he may or may not have read the Hessian clergy's memorandum of 1538) likening the Jews to a sponge used to suck up the wealth of the population and then be squeezed dry by their rulers. Without minimizing the Jews' hatred of Christians, Grotius insisted that it was the inescapable result of their mistreatment by their Christian masters and that it would vanish under more tolerant conditions. For these reasons Grotius was decidedly in favor of admitting Jews. He felt that Amsterdam had only three alternatives: to force them to adopt Christianity, to allow them to practice no religion whatsoever, or to tolerate Judaism. The first possibility he peremptorily rejected as being morally unsound, since "it is more sinful to God to simulate the profession of true religion and to accept it against one's conscience, than to hold an erroneous opinion out of ignorance." Atheism, too, was "incomparably worse than Judaism," which could not be classified as idolatry (the suppression of which had been ordained by the Bible), because the Jews worshiped the same Deity, although they mixed with that worship some "unbelief." In short, Grotius favored the toleration of both the Jews and their faith.[34]

As a realist, Grotius advocated at the same time certain specific safeguards for the interests of the Church and the Christian burghers. Here, too, we find a curious mixture of medievalism and modernity. He proposed that Jews be made to listen to Christian sermons and generally be persuaded to accept baptism voluntarily, while Christians should be prohibited from attending synagogue services. He was adamantly opposed to intermarriage or free sexual relations between members of the two faiths, and even wished to outlaw the employment of Christian servants by Jews, except in the case of Christian midwives attending Jewish women in childbirth. On the other hand, he rejected legal segregation, including both the ghetto and the badge. He was also quite outspoken about the Jews' obligation to adhere closely to the fundamentals of their own faith. He was familiar with the three basic "principles" to which Joseph Albo had reduced the thirteen cardinal beliefs originally formulated by Maimonides—in his letter of March 23, 1633, to Gerhard Johann Vos (Vossius), Grotius was to suggest that the learned convert Michael Gellingus be induced to translate Albo's *De fundamentis ('Iqqarim)* into Latin. The jurist-theologian actually proposed that upon reaching the age of fourteen, every Amsterdam Jew be made solemnly to declare that he believes "in one God, creator and ruler of everything . . . that Moses and the prophets have revealed the truth under divine inspiration, and that there is another life after death in which the good will receive their reward and the evildoers their punishment." Economically, Grotius wanted to restrict the Jews' right to engage in retail trade and certain crafts, which might injure Christian shopkeepers and artisans. But he fully favored the Jews' constantly expanding wholesale trade and their entry into the professions. The forty-nine articles of his memorandum, containing these and other legal proposals, may reflect his opinion of what was realistically attainable, rather than his ideal goal of ultimate theoretical justice.[35]

NOVEL LEGAL APPROACH

Because of its persuasive realism and its author's growing prestige, Grotius' *Remonstrantie* exerted considerable influence on Amsterdam's ruling circles, and beyond. Hence A. K. Kuhn did not grossly exaggerate when he saw in it an important step toward Jewish emancipation. Grotius' approach was in so far more modern than medieval as, in lieu of considering the Jewish status as that of

a corporate group apart, endowed with special privileges and subject to special duties, he started from the assumption that Jews were
basically citizens, enjoying the same rights as non-Jews, save for
specific exceptions stated by law. The forty-nine articles recommended by him aimed at enumerating such exceptions, beyond
which one ought not to infringe on the principle of basic
equality.[36]

Although the ensuing 1619 ordinance of the Amsterdam city
council, doubtless reflecting a compromise between the Van Pauw
and the Grotius proposal, was considerably more restrictive, in
practice the Jewish status in most Dutch cities was even more favorable than that suggested by the great jurist. Indeed, from the
beginning of their settlement in 1593 a number of Marranos were
granted "burghers' rights" in Amsterdam and other cities, a practice which was soon extended to professing Jews as well. To be
sure, there was some residual discrimination in the admission of
Jews to citizenship. Ashkenazic peddlers were generally excluded,
and Portuguese merchants were granted these rights only on a
selective individual basis. A resolution adopted by the city council
on June 29, 1656, clearly stated: "Jews shall not be admitted to
citizenship except in so far as they are merchants of importance . . .
this status of citizen is conferred only on a particular person and
cannot be inherited by his offspring." Nor did the Jewish
"burgher" have the right to open a retail shop, since retailing
was to be restricted to Christians. According to a city ordinance of
March 29, 1632, Jewish burghers were also expressly forbidden to
sell wine or beer or generally infringe in any way on the monopolistic preserves of Christian guilds. At the same time, any new
"burgher" had to pay the regular fees associated with such rights;
these were raised from a total of 8 guilders at the beginning of the
seventeenth century to 50 guilders half a century later. Jews were
not entitled to occupy any public office, nor were they permitted to
serve in the army (they had to pay a special tax instead). But otherwise they suffered from few disabilities. Some of the prohibitions,
moreover, were observed in their breach. For example, we have occasional references to illicit sexual relations between Jews and
Christian women, but we have no record of major prosecutions
and condemnations on this score. Some typically medieval sur-

vivals like the oath *more judaico,* which was later to outlast even the full emancipation of Jews by the French Revolution, were greatly modified in Holland. One early formula of this kind, included in the *Handvesten* of November 8, 1606, reads:

You swear by the Almighty and living God, who has created Heaven and Earth, and who has given His Laws through Moses, to be upright and true concerning the matter which is herewith asked and presented to you: and so, if you declare anything false or untrue, either in whole or in part, that you submit yourself to all temporal and eternal curses, plagues, and punishments which the God of Israel has put upon those of Sodom and Gomorrah and also upon Korah, Dathan, and Abiram, or according as He has threatened all those who have called upon and used His name falsely and thoughtlessly. So truly help or punish you the Almighty and Omniscient God, Creator of Heaven and Earth.

To which the respondent was supposed to answer: Amen.[37]

A major concern of the Amsterdam legislation was to protect the Christian faith against possible attacks by Jews. In that religiously volatile age, when disputations between adherents of different Christian sects frequently threatened domestic peace, the authorities were fearful that some of the intellectually alert Portuguese arrivals might inject further elements of discord by the defense of their religion, be it Catholic or Jewish. As a matter of fact, controversial tracts published by Amsterdam Jews during the seventeenth century became cherished parts of the Jewish apologetical literature. A number of other such treatises remained unpublished, but circulated widely in manuscript copies. Grotius had suggested, therefore, that Jews be allowed to keep and even print Hebrew books, "except those which contained blasphemous or defamatory statements" with respect to Christianity. Here, again, the famed jurist referred to the Code of Justinian and, with reference to the well-known Novella 146, recommended that Jews not be allowed to print copies of the Talmud. Characteristically, he made no mention of the burnings of the Talmud that had occured in the past on orders of medieval popes. Doubtless the Dutch Reformed Church could not quite favor the enforcement of papal censorship or anything that smacked of the papal Index, which outlawed most Protestant writings as well. On the other hand, no allowance was made by Grotius as was done by the Council of Trent and some later popes, for the possibility of merely expurgating the incriminated passages from the Talmud. In practice, however, Grotius' suggestion was largely disregarded, and as early as 1644–48, Emanuel Benveniste was able to publish in Amsterdam his famous unexpurgated Talmud edition. Other provisions along these lines concerned the prohibition forbidding Jews to circumcise Christians or otherwise to propagate their faith among non-Jews; nor were they to prevent their own members from joining the dominant faith. Reference has already been made to the outlawry of intermarriage and free sexual relations among Jews and Christians, as well as to the ban on employment of Christian servants by Jews, all of which was considered prejudicial to the true belief of those Christians who thus came into intimate contact with Jews. At the same time, the authorities refused to follow the lead of some churchmen who wished to outlaw any public manifestation of Judaism. The resolution of December 13, 1619, also specifically forbade compelling Jews to wear any kind of distinguishing marks. Similarly, a later attempt to segregate Jews in a special quarter failed completely, although in Amsterdam as elsewhere Jews voluntarily concentrated for the most part around their communal institutions. When a Pastor Wachtendorp complained to the burgomasters on October 5, 1645, that on his walks "he had noticed that streets and bridges were decorated with large branches in honor of the Jewish Feast of Tabernacles," he was supported therein by the Dutch Reformed Church Council of Amsterdam. But the burgomasters merely promised to investigate, and apparently did nothing until the festival was over. Nor do we hear anything about similar complaints in the following years.[38]

Despite their numerous restrictions, Grotius' proposals and the general Amsterdam practice marked a considerable advance over the earlier attitudes of the city's authorities, which as late as May 1612 had threatened to tear down any synagogue which Jews might erect. In fact, the Sephardic synagogue of Amsterdam was so well established by 1638 that it became a sufficient tourist attraction for Queen Mother Marie de Médicis of France to visit it. Four years later (May 22, 1642), it received a formal visit from the stadholder of the Netherlands, Frederick Henry (1625–47), accompanied by Queen Henrietta Maria, wife of Charles I of England.

On this occasion the congregational rabbi, Menasseh ben Israel, delivered a flowery oration, which he speedily published in Latin, Dutch, and Portuguese.[39]

Most significantly, no one, on either the Protestant or the Catholic side, seems to have advocated the forcible conversion of Jews. The very question, so heatedly debated in the early sixteenth century by Ulrich (Udalricus or Uldericus) Zasius and others, as to whether Jewish minors might, or should, be converted against their parents' wishes, appears never to have been raised in Dutch Reformed ecclesiastical circles. Only a Dutch expatriate, Cornelius Callidius Loos, who had apparently served as canon at the Catholic church of his native Gouda but was later employed as a librarian of the Cathedral Library of Mayence, discussed that challenge to elementary parental rights. In a treatise published in 1585, he conceded the Church's right to compel Christian heretics to conform with all demands of the Catholic faith, but he inserted a special chapter insisting that "infants of infidels must not be baptized against the will of their parents." [40]

COMMUNITY CONTROLS

As a counterpart to this religio-legal differentiation, the Jewish community was granted an extensive measure of self-government, somewhat akin to the "liberties" enjoyed by the cities. While the municipal authorities tried to reserve ultimate control to themselves and indeed exercised general supervision over the management of Jewish communal affairs, they simultaneously endeavored to strengthen the hand of the communal elders. To be sure, in such borderline cases between Jewish and civic concerns as marriage, they wished at least to possess complete records of the Jewish marriages. In an ordinance issued in 1622, they demanded that Jewish marriages be confirmed before the civil authorities and registered in the municipal records, even after they had been celebrated according to Jewish rites. In fact, retroactively, all couples previously married were supposed to register at the pertinent municipal office. However, this outwardly stringent regulation seems to have been largely disregarded, Jewish unions continuing as a rule to be entered "according to the law of Moses and Israel" under rabbinic authority only. Similarly, the rabbinate was given full leeway in enforcing its will, through the instrumentality of bans. True, on a few occasions individuals successfully appealed to the municipal authorities over the heads of their communal elders and secured some mitigation of the anathemas, not by legally enforceable orders from the burgomasters but rather by the city elders' pressure on the rabbis "voluntarily" to modify their original proclamations. Such appears to have been the case when two Jews quarreling over a testamentary disposition were, through a ban, prevented from attending synagogue services. When they appealed to the authorities against what they called an infringement of their personal religious right to participate in the divine services of their faith, the municipal authorities seem to have had little difficulty in persuading the Jewish leaders to moderate their disciplinary action. On the other hand, public officials sometimes took the initiative in suggesting Jewish bans against heterodox Jews, as happened in the famous cases of Uriel (Gabriel) da Costa and Baruch (Benedict) Spinoza.[41]

More effective, and apparently legally enforceable, were appeals of sentences rendered by Jewish courts in civil litigations. In principle, the legislation provided for the right of Jewish parties to submit their controversies directly to the general courts, which also enjoyed exclusive authority in adjudicating breaches of penal law. However, here, too, in practice the rabbinic courts had no difficulty in enforcing the provisions of Jewish law on recalcitrant members. As we shall see in later chapters, both the Sephardic and the Ashkenazic communities of Amsterdam in time developed into closely knit and highly efficient organizations. The power of their elders paralleled, or even exceeded, that of their opposite numbers in Germany, Italy, or Poland. Although the individual term of office was only one year, the board as a whole was self-perpetuating. It semiannually replaced three of its six members, usually recruited from the same leading families, while the other members meekly followed their orders. At times the *parnasim* ruled their communities with an iron hand. Simultaneously, they assumed such obligations as providing the members with ritually slaughtered meat at reasonable prices, through a contract concluded with local Christian butchers in 1610.[42]

Much less is known about the early stages of the Ashkenazic

community in Amsterdam. Because of their proximity to the Holy Roman Empire, of which they had originally been a part, the northern provinces had sporadically attracted German Jewish settlers. Such individuals were recorded during the Middle Ages and, despite the intervening waves of total intolerance after 1348, they reappeared in the early seventeenth century. A German Jewish magician, for example, came to Amsterdam in 1610; and a wedding of two Ashkenazim took place there in 1617. One Jacob Sampson, who later served as a Jewish butcher, was actually born in Amsterdam in 1626. Three years earlier, a Christian visitor from Germany, Philip Ziegler, claimed to have found a number of German Jews in the city. However, the first community of Ashkenazic Jews seems not to have been organized until 1635, when Ashkenazic services were held in a rented hall on the Day of Atonement. Not surprisingly, in that very year a serious quarrel broke out between members of the congregation and its elders, a quarrel which had to be settled by the burgomasters after consultation with the heads of the Portuguese community. The subsequent rapid growth of the Ashkenazic group, mainly through immigration from Germany, is well illustrated by the municipal marriage records. No less than 252 Ashkenazic Jews registered their unions with the municipal authorities in the years 1635–70. Of these, only 35 persons had been born in Amsterdam, 3 more in other Dutch cities; 9 each in Charleville and Metz, France (probably for the most part the offspring of German Jewish parents); 28 in Poland and Lithuania, and 7 more in the province of Poznań; 4 in Prague; and the rest in various German localities. The largest contingent (15) stemmed from Frankfort. This list may not be complete. In particular, the new arrivals from Poland and Lithuania had long been accustomed to having their marriages solemnized exclusively in religious ceremonies, and often must have failed to go through with the cumbersome (and, to them, perhaps costly) new ceremony before the secular authorities.[43]

Differences between the two communities in economic standing, manners, education, and general outlook on life were so great that the very presence of the German Jewish congregation, whose membership was rapidly expanding through the immigration of victims of the Thirty Years' War, was sufficient inducement for the three existing Sephardic congregations to merge into a single body. Since the new German arrivals usually preferred to join the Ashkenazic congregation, the Spanish-Portuguese community could readily keep aloof from the unwelcome German immigrants. Although the traditional religious postulates of charity toward fellow Jews could not be ignored, and the wealthy Portuguese extended much aid to their penniless Ashkenazic coreligionists, socially the Sephardic community tried to maintain a thick wall of separation. For generations they employed German and Polish Jews in their businesses and, less frequently, for menial services in their homes, but more rigidly than their Sephardic confreres in Italy or the Balkans they tried staunchly to uphold their endogamous traditions and to prevent "intermarriage" with the Ashkenazic group. As late as 1762, Isaac de Pinto, a famous banker and economist, in a letter (of May 20) to the duke of Richelieu, marshal of France and governor of the Guienne, vigorously asserted: "The Portuguese and the Spanish, who have the honor of being descendants of the tribe of Judah or believe to be such, have never mixed, through marriage, association, or in any other way, with the children of Jacob known under the name of German [*Tudesques*], Italian, or Avignonese Jews." [44]

In the early stages of Polish immigration after 1648 the Portuguese leaders actually made efforts to resettle many of the new arrivals in Germany, where, after the Peace of Westphalia, life was returning to a measure of "normalcy." For example, in 1656 when some 300 (there are differing contemporary accounts) Polish and Lithuanian Jews arrived in Amsterdam in three ships, they were immediately provided with food and clothing and were generally cared for by their Portuguese brethren. But whether because—as we are told by the distinguished rabbi Moses b. Zvi Naphtali Rivkes (Rebecca's), himself a recent refugee from the Polish-Muscovite War in Vilna—they found life in Amsterdam too expensive, or because they were "persuaded" by the Portuguese elders to leave, many of them accepted the Portuguese offer of passage to Frankfort. As it turned out, however, the Frankfort Jewish community, greatly impoverished at the end of the Thirty Years' War, was unable to support them. Moreover, renewing a xenophobe resolution of 1550, when the city's Jewish population was still very small, the municipal elders warned that only a few new-comers would be allowed permanently to settle in Frankfort, if they pledged not to engage in any trade or lend money, nor to peddle within the city limits without a special license from the city council. It appears that none of the new arrivals applied for a residence permit under these conditions, and that all preferred to look for more hospitable locations. We do not know whether any of them returned to Amsterdam. Nonetheless, the Amsterdam German Jewish community continued to expand. It was joined in the 1650s by a new Polish Jewish congregation. Before long, the Ashkenazim actually outnumbered their Sephardic coreligionists. According to some estimates, as early as 1674 Amsterdam embraced 2,500 Sephardic and 5,000 Ashkenazic Jews. This disproportion increased in subsequent generations: in 1795, on the eve of Jewish Emancipation in the Netherlands, the 2,400 Sephardic residents were greately outnumbered by some 21,000 Ashkenazim. This rapid increase of German and Polish Jewry is the more remarkable as it sharply contrasted with an overall slowdown in Dutch population growth. It has been estimated that, after participating in the general European population explosion of the sixteenth century, Holland actually sustained a loss of some 6 percent in the number of its inhabitants between 1660 and 1730, to resume its increase at a slower rate thereafter.[45]

PROVINCIAL COMMUNITIES

Because of the overwhelming importance of Amsterdam in the Dutch economy and culture the story of the provincial communities has often been neglected. Yet in time these provincial centers assumed independent importance and greatly contributed to the socioeconomic and cultural life of West-European Jewry. Some of the provincial cities actually pioneered in attracting Jews and arranging for their new sociopolitical status; on occasion, they served as models for, and offered incentives to, the very leaders of the Amsterdam municipality.

It even appears that, in preparing his *Remonstrantie*, Grotius consulted the available legal materials from other cities, particularly Haarlem and Rotterdam. A good case has been made for the contention that Amsterdam was impelled in 1615–19 formally to admit Jews and to adopt a fairly favorable regulation of their status because it feared that the smaller cities might otherwise divert the stream of Portuguese Jewish immigrants to the provinces. One gets the impression that in those crucial years Jews seeking admission to Holland and northwestern Germany sometimes played one city against another in order to secure better terms for settlement. A few years later, the Amsterdam authorities doubtless were aware that the Portuguese community had received a very flattering invitation from Christian IV of Denmark. Dated November 25, 1622, and addressed to the "Honorable, Beloved, and Distinguished Deputies of the Portuguese Nation in Amsterdam," the royal letter stated:

We have been informed that several Powers and Lords have written to you that, if any one of your Nation should wish to establish himself under their domination and jurisdiction, he need but apply to them and expect an answer. We have already accorded to your Nation all sorts of advantageous privileges regarding liberty of religion and commerce in Our city of Glückstadt. We are also inclined by Our grace to augment and amplify these privileges in the future, dependent on the circumstances and exigencies of each case, as Our beloved and faithful Albert Dionys [Dinis], Director of Our Mint, may more fully explain to you. Therefore, it is Our gracious desire to attest to you through the present letter, that if any one or several of your Nation should desire to settle in Our said city, they have merely to send one or two persons from their midst to examine the situation; they will doubtless find it wholly satisfactory.

Amsterdam's municipal elders certainly could not afford to lose many such desirable subjects to the competition.[46]

Haarlem's decree of November 10, 1605, is among the most remarkable documents of the period. In response to a petition from several Iberian Jews, stating that they were maintaining business relations with both Oriental and Western Jews residing in Italy and Turkey, the Haarlem authorities gave express consent to the admission of that "Nation." Their decree included the following noteworthy concessions: Jews were to be exempt from serving in the municipal guard; they were to have a synagogue and a burial place where they would be able to observe their Jewish ceremonies undisturbed; they were not to be summoned to courts on the Sabbath or on Jewish holidays; their clothing was not to display any distinguishing marks, nor was it to differ in any other way from that of Christians; they were to be allowed to have their own butchers, selling ritually prepared meats. True, the charter also provided that Jews be "obliged to observe and keep Sundays and all other official [Christian] prayer and fast days in this country by closing their shops, doors, and windows and to abstain from all work." But by implication this paragraph allowed Jews to keep shops open during the rest of the week and to engage in retail trade, which they were later expressly forbidden to do in Amsterdam. Another, more liberal, provision read: "that they may also within their dwellings keep and make use of the services, for the convenience of their families, of Christian servant girls and wet nurses; however, without inducing, forcing, or corrupting them to Judaism, nor having carnal intercourse with them, under the penalties provided by the law." Of course, Jews were not to blaspheme against the name of Jesus Christ or to conduct themselves in any way injurious to, or contemptuous of, the Christian faith. It was also stated that Jews had to promise to pay respect to the Haarlem authorities, obey the local statutes, ordinances, and customs, carry burdens and perform services on a par with the city's other inhabitants, and submit to the civil and penal jurisdiction of the local law-enforcement officials. This provision was not intended, however, to undermine the authority of the Jewish elders (here styled *Parnacim* and *Mamonim*) in civil affairs or their right to issue bans. On the contrary, the community was generally to enjoy a vast measure of self-determination. The decree concluded by pledging the authorities, in cases of differences of opinion about the interpretation of certain articles, to adjust them "according to the rules of equity and justice." This decree was hailed by such a liberal Christian Hebraist as the Leiden professor, Joseph Justus Scaliger, who commented that "the Jews will come to Haarlem, will have there a synagogue and a privilege from the States [General]. This will be a great advantage [*commoditas*] for that region." In another passage he made it clear that he hoped in that way to find there a learned Jew who could teach him rabbinic literature. Remarkably, however, despite Haarlem's concessions, for their time extremely liberal, the Jews seem not to have found the city's economic opportunities sufficiently attractive compared with those of Amsterdam. Not until several decades later was a regular community organized there.[47]

Rotterdam was another major Dutch city to which Jews were admitted early. In fact, like Haarlem, the great Dutch harbor city was so anxious to attract Jews that it was prepared to concede to them greater privileges than Amsterdam. In 1610, when Emanuel Rodrigues Vega's silk contract with Amsterdam expired and he was looking for another place of settlement, he negotiated a charter with the Rotterdam city council for a new Jewish community and induced some members of his family to settle there. The breadth of that charter was indicated in the introductory provision, which read:

First, we grant these men [merchants of the Portuguese Nation] liberty and freedom of conscience in the best form, both inside and outside their homes. For this purpose we consent that they should be able to live in the fashion of the Hebrews and that on their Sabbaths, as well as during their three great holidays, they should not be summoned to courts in this city. We also allow them to acquire a piece of land outside the city which they may use for a burial place.

Other stipulations permitted the Jews to organize a distinct community under their own "consuls"; promised them immunity from special taxes, billeting, standing guard, and the like; and extended to them a variety of commercial privileges. Most important, as Jacob Zwarts points out, Rotterdam was the first Dutch city to grant a privilege explicitly permitting Jews to build a synagogue, under the protection of the authorities and as a fully legal institution. Although this charter was supposed to expire after two years, the very provision for erecting a synagogue and the parallel concession for establishing a cemetery indicated that both parties had in mind a long-term arrangement. In 1612 the charter was indeed renewed. It also was in that year that Gracia Rodrigues Vega, Emanuel's sister, acquired the burial ground for the community. Their brother Pedro also moved to Rotterdam. Nonetheless, in the long run Rotterdam, could no more than Haarlem, compete effectively with Amsterdam. While before long it accommodated a small Jewish community, it played no significant role in the history of Dutch Jewry until much later.[48]

Neither Haarlem nor Rotterdam, however, was the first Dutch city to negotiate a charter for Jews. That honor belongs to Alkmaar, a city famed in the annals of the Dutch War of Liberation because the Dutch victory in its vicinity (long extolled in Dutch literature as the *Alkmaar Victorie*) marked a decisive turning point in favor of the "rebels." As early as May 10, 1604, the Alkmaar city council arranged a charter with Moses Uri ha-Levi for the admission of Jews under favorable conditions. It was this Alkmaar charter which was used by the rabbi to urge the Amsterdam authorities to follow suit. Another record, dated October 20, 1613, relates to the attempt of one Francisco Fernandes to secure residence permits there for a number of members of the "Portuguese Nation." Subsequent records mention incidents relating to Jews in the years 1620, 1623, 1632, and 1641. On the other hand, the city of Maarsen at first refused admission to a group of Jewish refugees who had left Emden because of the resistance of the local clergy. But in time the city council relented. Similarly, Middelburg, originally the center of ecclesiastical opposition to the admission of Jews to the country, later accommodated a sizable Jewish settlement. Nijmegen, too, which had had an important Jewish community before the Black Death and again in the fifteenth century, seems at first to have resisted the resettlement of Jews. But a small Jewish community existed there again by 1683; it became quite significant in the eighteenth century. Other early Dutch communities worthy of mention were Amersfoort, Overijsel, Oldenzaal, and possibly Nijkerk. Some Jews seem to have settled quite early also in smaller localities. But the real history of these provincial communities for the most part begins only after the middle of the seventeenth century.[49]

SOCIOECONOMIC ADVANCES

Holland's dynamic economy enabled many Jewish businessmen to accumulate great wealth and to play a significant role in society. From the beginning they participated in the traditional Levant trade, both through the Levantine Trading Company, formed in 1625, and as independent merchants. They were aided therein by their numerous, affluent coreligionists in the main commercial centers of the eastern Mediterranean. They were doubly welcome to the Dutch in helping to develop the Dutch East and West India Companies. Two Amsterdam Jews are in fact recorded as shareholders in the East India Company at its foundation in 1602. True, they were a tiny minority of the 1,143 stockholders, and their investment of 4,800 guilders (in a total of 3,674,915 guilders raised in Amsterdam and of 6,459,840 guilders collected in the country as a whole) compared unfavorably even with those of an Italian and a French investor, who subscribed for shares of 12,000 and 5,400 guilders, respectively. But it is possible that, both because of their ambiguous status in Amsterdam and the spying by Iberian inquisitors, some Portuguese Jews were among those subscribers who preferred to enter their initials only. Eleven such unidentifiable stockholders, with a total investment of 83,500 guilders, are listed in the record. Five more Jewish names appear in the following two years; one of them, Melchior Mendes, with the substantial amount of 13,500 guilders. Even some Hamburg "Portuguese" participated in the early stages of the Company's financing and, in 1610, negotiated with the Amsterdam representatives about organizing a group to equip three ships for the direct route to the East Indies. This particular enterprise, however, was nipped in the bud by Spanish intervention. These data, derived only from Jewish-sounding names, are undoubtedly incomplete, as are those recorded in the following years. On the other hand, some of the New Christian and Jewish merchants, who had long cooperated with the Portuguese state monopoly in the distribution of eastern spices, preferred the helter-skelter competition which had prevailed in this branch of trade before 1602 to the newly established corporate monopoly. Moreover, it was an open secret that the new company would be as much a legally chartered pirating enterprise, preying on Spanish and Portuguese shipping, as a corporation devoted to the legitimate exchange of goods. Since the former Marranos were still technically classed as "Portuguese" traders, whose cargoes on the open seas were regarded by many Dutch captains as legitimate prizes, they must have feared that the greater efficiency of the government-chartered corporation would result in grave losses to their own shipping.[50]

Nevertheless, Portuguese Jewish merchants not only bought

shares in the East India Company but probably proved helpful to it through their long experience in overseas trade, as well as through their far-flung international contacts. Discounting some evident exaggeration, Philip III's complaint in 1607 to the Spanish viceroy of the Indies doubtless contained a kernel of truth. According to the king's informants, two New Christians of Colombo, Ceylon, had actively corresponded with the Dutch, and four or five others in Malacca had allegedly divulged Portugal's military plans. As early as 1568, such suspicions seem to have induced the Portuguese government to forbid Marrano emigration to the Indies altogether and to order ship captains to return any Marrano passengers to Portugal or at the least to land them in Goa. These conditions were further aggravated after Portugal's incorporation into the Spanish empire in 1580. In his memorandum to the Suprema of the Spanish Inquisition in 1634, Esteban de Ares Fonseca complained with considerable bitterness about the significant role which Jews were playing in both the East and West India Companies. Not surprisingly, the old Jewish community of Cochin assisted the Dutch in their conquest of the Malabar coast in 1662. Thenceforth until 1795 Cochin remained under direct Dutch domination, and the local Jews actively cooperated with their coreligionists in Amsterdam. On their part, many Amsterdam Jews greatly benefited from their lucrative membership in the Company. According to a later French observer, after a few years the Company paid annual dividends of 25–30 percent and, notwithstanding these large disbursements, increased its capital in six years from the initial 6,500,000 to 30,000,000 guilders. Despite the usual ups and downs concomitant with business cycles and other domestic and foreign developments, the Company generally prospered well into the eighteenth century, when the Jews' aggregate ownership of its shares allegedly reached a peak of 25 percent.[51]

The West India Company, dealing with a new and slowly developing area, was far less prosperous. Its main founder, Willem Usselinx, actually conceived it as a humanitarian, rather than purely commercial, enterprise. Moreover, as Charles Ralph Boxer observed, the Company was "essentially a creation of the militant Calvinist or Contra-Remonstrant Party whose adherents regarded any toleration of Popery as pandering to the Whore of Babylon."

Nevertheless, here, too, soon after the Company's foundation in 1621, after two decades of fruitless preliminary efforts (Usselinx' success coincided with the expiration of Holland's twelve-year armistice with Spain), some Amsterdam Jews are recorded in an obviously incomplete list to have subscribed for 36,100 guilders of the required 7,108,000 guilders of original capital (1623–26). Among them, Bento (Baruch) Osorio contributed 6,000 guilders. In the following years, Jewish participation increased sharply. To judge from certain data extant from 1656 to 1671, the ratio of Jewish shareholders jumped from 4 to 10 percent in fifteen years. Menasseh ben Israel was not wrong in assuring Oliver Cromwell that the Amsterdam Jews "enjoy a good part of the West and East Indian Compagnies." As is well known, this factor was to play a decisive role in the admission of the first group of Jewish settlers to New Amsterdam (later New York) in 1654. Even if they were not shareholders, many Amsterdam and other Dutch Jews collaborated with the Company in its perennial struggle with Spain. Some of them may have entertained more-or-less venturesome schemes to come to the rescue of their persecuted coreligionists in Iberia and the New World. At least according to a report the Portuguese official Esteban de Ares Fonseca submitted to the Spanish Inquisition in 1634, Amsterdam Jewry, ever hostile to Spanish interests,

also laid a plan whereby the Hollanders, while on their way to Pernambuco, were to turn aside to Buarcos where their men were to land and go to Coimbra, which is only seven leagues away, to sack the inquisition, set its prisoners at liberty and to plunder the convent of Santa Cruz. . . . To meet the expenses of this expedition the Jews of Amsterdam and Hamburg have given a large sum of money amounting, if what I have been told is true, to twelve or thirteen thousand ducats. This amount has been raised by subscription among all the Jews and has been on deposit for two years, for up to the present time there has been no opportunity to use it. Its use has been restricted solely to this expedition, which with this notice it will be easy to prevent.

Whether the expedition was indeed prevented, or the entire undertaking was but the product of Esteban's or his informer's febrile imagination, nothing of the kind did happen. With even greater abandon, Esteban had added: "The West India Company, which is a Brazilian company and composed of pirates, is governed entirely by Jews of Amsterdam, for all the rich ones give their money for the said company." Yet the credibility often given to such reports shows to what lengths the Dutch Jews were expected to go in order to rescue their imperiled brethren. We shall see that, after Portugal regained its independence in 1640, Dutch Jewish leaders, in collaboration with the Jesuit preacher-diplomat António Vieira, undertook formal diplomatic negotiations with the Portuguese government to relieve the Portuguese Marranos from the relentless prosecutions of the Holy Office.[52]

Overseas trade formed but a part of the ever-growing commerce of Dutch Jews. Many continued to ply their traditional occupations in the various branches of the money trade, but conditions in Amsterdam were in many ways different from those prevailing in other Jewish communities. To begin with, there was no commercial branch, including the growing variety of monetary transactions, in which the Christian burghers were not strongly represented; sometimes they far overshadowed the Jewish segment. Secondly, with the growth of the Jewish population, the money trade could provide a livelihood for only a small minority. An extant list of 1743, for example, listed only 5 Jewish bankers and 40 moneychangers, as contrasted with 23 jewelers, 10 brewers, 20 tobacco merchants and tobacconists, and the like. At the same time, among both Jews and non-Jews there were many rentiers living from interest on capital invested in loans and securities. No fewer than 110 Jews are thus designated in the 1743 list. Of course, this vague category may have included some part-time moneylenders. It is likely that, after the German and Polish Jews had settled in larger numbers and found their bearings in the new environment, they had a higher ratio of petty lenders than their Portuguese coreligionists. Before 1650, however, it was chiefly the wealthy Portuguese Jewish bankers who were active in this field, after transferring their monetary transactions from Antwerp, Lisbon, and other great centers of the credit trade to the Dutch metropolis. To be sure, the going rate of interest in Amsterdam was generally low; on large loans it often averaged only 3–4 percent, and it sometimes fell to as little as 2 percent. This rate contrasted with the customary 12 percent, specifically permitted in Antwerp by Charles V in

1540, and actually paid by his son Philip to the Christian bankers. Some Amsterdam capitalists found it profitable to engage in a sort of monetary arbitrage by borrowing funds at home at 3 or 4 percent and lending them to clients in England and elsewhere at 6 to 8 percent or more. As before, outstanding bankers were able to extend substantial credit to their own, as well as to foreign, governments. Before long, Amsterdam became the greatest banking center in Europe, and many crowned heads sought credit from both Jewish and non-Jewish lenders in the Dutch metropolis. In time the Jews became wealthy and influential enough not only to participate in such international relief activities as those connected with the redemption of Polish-Lithuanian captives, especially during the catastrophic years 1648–56, but also later to exert pressure on the government of Empress Maria Theresa to rescind her decree of expulsion of the Jews from Prague in 1744.[53]

Moneychanging, on the other hand, became far less lucrative. True, with the growth of international trade and visits by foreign merchants and tourists, coins of various denominations (including many either of inferior metallic content or else clipped on the way to, or in, Amsterdam) appeared in the market in large quantities. However, the Dutch authorities tried to stem the numerous abuses concomitant with that trade and, in 1609, helped to establish the Exchange Bank of Amsterdam and endowed it with a legal monopoly of currency exchange. This exclusive right also enabled it gradually to withdraw deficient coins from circulation. In 1758, when a burgher submitted a collection of defective coins to the Exchange Bank, he received them back cut in half so as to ensure their withdrawal; he accepted this decision without demurrer.

Understandably, from the outset, Jews had dealings with the Exchange Bank, since many of them were also engaged in their traditional trade (and related craftsmanship) in precious metals. In the very first year, a list of the bank's clients included 25 Portuguese Jewish names, in a total of 731. By 1620, there were 106 Portuguese Jewish accounts among 1,202 carried on the bank's books. According to Johannes Gerard van Dillen, among the major clients (*rekeninghouters*) of the Exchange Bank in that year were no fewer than 46 Portuguese Jews, together with 320 Northern (Dutch) and 297 Southern (Belgian) Netherlanders, as well as 16 Germans, 11

Englishmen, 7 Frenchmen, and 2 Italians. The Jewish ratio increased further in the following decades, with respect to both the number and the size of individual accounts. In 1661, for example, when Portuguese Jews had 265 of 2,031 accounts appearing on the bank's ledgers, the account of the Jewish banking firm of Moses and David Juda Lion alone covered ten folios. Nonetheless, in their restrictive decree of December 5, 1661, the authorities singled out the Jews, forbidding them "to peddle from house to house with goods made from gold or silver, or with species. Nor are they to sell secretly or trade in these goods, under the penalty of a fine of 10 ducats for the first offense, to be paid to the officers of the Gold- and Silversmiths Guild, and a double amount for the second offense." Such provisions were among the general guild restrictions, which still operated strongly against the Amsterdam Jews.[54]

Even more far-reaching was the Jewish contribution to the establishment and development of the Amsterdam Stock Exchange. Although appearing on the world scene later than the sixteenth-century centers of Antwerp and Lyons and having to compete with the upsurging London market, the Amsterdam Exchange quickly assumed leadership of the Western world for the rest of the seventeenth and early eighteenth centuries. Jews, who had developed considerable experience in stock transactions while in Antwerp (we recall that some of them had also had extensive dealings in Lyons and in the lesser markets of Cologne and Hamburg), were able to play a prominent role here as well. By the eighteenth century, Jewish participation in the purchase and sales of shares on the Amsterdam Exchange was so conspicuous that it gave rise to the rumor that Jews had originally invented the trade in shares as a means of large-scale corporate financing.[55]

The high position of the Jewish traders was graphically demonstrated in the seating arrangement on the Exchange floor, which accommodated some 500 persons in its new headquarters, built in 1611. Here "Portuguese Jews" were assigned front seats, together with "sugar refiners" and "dealers in securities." Moneychangers in minted and unminted gold and silver, many of whom were German Jews, had to take back seats. The Exchange, which combined the activities of a securities and a produce market, even had seats for real estate brokers, as well as separate sections for English,

French, Bremen, Hamburg, and Scandinavian merchants and skippers. It offered many opportunities for brokers of all kinds, a service in which Jews were strongly represented. At the beginning, in 1612, there were 10 Jews among 300 brokers; by 1645 the Jewish ratio increased to 30 out of 430. There also were many unlicensed brokers, later for the most part recruited from among the Ashkenazic Jews. In Amsterdam as elsewhere, the Stock Exchange stimulated speculation, in addition to permanent investments. It has been observed that in the mid-sixteenth century the speculative fever in Antwerp seized large segments of the population, including widows, soldiers, and even officials handling other people's funds. In time, many wealthy Jewish and Christian capitalists in Amsterdam likewise preferred to devote themselves to speculation, while neglecting their traditional lines of business, which required more time and effort.[56]

Because of their international contacts, Jews had, so to say, a private intelligence service which enabled them to buy and sell in the Amsterdam market on the basis of more solid information about business trends in other countries than was available to their non-Jewish competitors. This fact did not escape the attention of unfriendly observers. As early as 1618, a French diplomat in the Netherlands (possibly, the Ambassador De Beaurepas himself) attributed the Jews' extraordinary prosperity not only to their general commercial talents and communal solidarity but also to the fact

that they are numerous and influential in Amsterdam and have exceedingly intimate relations with the State, because they are equally attentive to foreign news and to commerce. . . . In both matters they obtain their information from the other Jewish communities with which they are in close contact. The most important of these is that of Venice, although it is less wealthy and less large, because it unites the West with the East and the South through the community of Salonica, which is the leading center for these other parts of the world. Together with Venice, the community of Amsterdam reigns supreme in the North, for it keeps in touch with the tolerated Jews of London and the secret associations of France. By this means the Jews in Amsterdam are the first and the best informed about foreign commerce and news of what is going on in the world. On this information they adopt plans for every week when they come together on Sundays to discuss the news . . . at a time when Christians of all denominations attend to their religious duties. In this way their Jewish brokers and agents, the most adroit persons of this kind in the world, are able each separately to spread the news to their advantage at the market on Monday mornings. . . . These practices are the source of their riches.

Exaggerated though these comments may be, they undoubtedly contain a grain of truth.[57]

Nor is it surprising that an Amsterdam Jew wrote the first major theoretical treatise on stock exchange transactions. Joseph Penso de la Vega (*ca.* 1650–92), who combined humanist learning, playwriting, and extensive poetic creativity with active dealings at the Amsterdam Stock Exchange, wrote his masterpiece *Confusión de Confusiones* in Spanish, for wider international distribution. He gave it the shape of a semi-Platonic dialogue between "a keen-witted philosopher, a discreet merchant, and an erudite stock dealer." First published in 1688, and more recently made available in Dutch, German, and partial English translations, this treatise is generally considered one of the classic works on the subject.[58]

Other Dutch Jewish businessmen who made a deep impression upon their community were the Moroccan brothers Samuel and Joseph Pallache. Samuel had enjoyed so high a standing in his native country that even the intolerant Philip II of Spain was forced to carry on diplomatic negotiations with him until 1597. From 1605 to 1608, under Philip III, Samuel and Joseph were permitted to live in the French embassy in Madrid, despite the Spanish prohibition forbidding professing Jews to enter the country, under penalty of death. Nonetheless, in 1608 Samuel Pallache was refused admission by the Amsterdam authorities, though they had at first granted it. But he managed to overcome Holland's resistance by persuading the Moroccan government to appoint him as its deputy ambassador, and later virtually as ambassador, to the Netherlands. Most of our records concerning his activities in Holland derive from the years 1612–16, when he was finally accepted by the States General as the North-African country's accredited envoy, perhaps because on December 24, 1610, he had arranged a favorable commercial treaty between the two countries. This pact opened their respective ports to Dutch and Moroccan shipping, and pledged both parties mutually not to enslave the other's subjects. This was a natural form of cooperation between two states equally threatened by Spanish imperialism. Samuel Pallache was a shrewd, and at times ruthless, businessman, but he was also dedicated to helping his coreligionists, and was very influential in the establishment of the burgeoning community. Although formerly rather prosperous, on his deathbed he found himself short of funds, and the States General had to advance him a loan of 600 guilders. The Netherlands stadholder Maurice of Nassau, prince of Orange (1587–1625), distinguished statesman and victor in the War of Liberation, marched behind the bier at Samuel's funeral.[59]

Samuel's brother Joseph succeeded him as Moroccan ambassador until 1637. During this time Joseph also helped to organize a Moroccan fleet to attack Spanish shipping, and thus effected a significant diversion of Spanish forces after the renewal of the Dutch hostilities with Spain in 1621. Apart from serving as admiral of that pirate fleet, he developed an important business in saltpeter, which on one occasion he contracted to sell to the Dutch government at the price of one ducat per quintal. His sons, Isaac, Moses, and David, continued in both their father's business and the diplomatic service in behalf of Morocco. Isaac made a living as an Amsterdam broker, as well as an instructor in Hebrew at the University of Leiden. He visited Hamburg and Lübeck in 1642, trying to persuade those cities, together with Bremen, to exchange envoys with Morocco, to have their ships call at the Moroccan ports of Salé, Safi, and Santa Cruz, and ultimately to conclude an alliance with Morocco which was to lead to the liberation of all Hanseatic prisoners held in Algeria and Tunis as well. In the following year, he visited Brandenburg and Poland with similar proposals. Regrettably, Herman Kellenbenz, who disclosed these facts from Lübeck, Gdańsk (Danzig), and Simancas archival data, was unable to ascertain the outcome of these negotiations or their possible connection with the Spanish-Portuguese War, which followed Portugal's declaration of independence in 1640.[60]

It would take us too far afield to discuss in detail the great variety of other occupations which furnished a livelihood to both Portuguese and German-Polish Jews. Among the pioneering services they rendered to their new homeland were those connected with their traditional jewelry trade and industry. There is little question that, together with other arrivals from the Spanish Netherlands, Jews were among the first diamond polishers and cutters in Amsterdam, helping to make that city, next to Antwerp, a world center of diamond cutting and trading. Reminiscent of medieval Jewish contributions, New Christian immigrants from the southern Netherlands also greatly influenced the city's growing silk industry. If Marcus Pérez, the well-known New Christian Calvinist leader in Antwerp, had helped to establish the silk industry in Basel, other Marranos promoted it in Holland. As early as 1604, Emanuel Rodrigues Vega suggested to the Amsterdam burgomasters that the city invest in a regular supply of raw silk for the manufacture and wide distribution of the final product. In that year, he was indeed given a privilege to operate two silk mills in a municipally owned building. As frequently happened with Jews, however, when his privilege expired in 1610, it was not renewed, his place being taken in part by Christian manufacturers whom he had trained. Nevertheless, he and other Jews continued in that line of business at least until 1654, when it was taken over by a monopolistic-minded Christian guild.[61]

Emanuel Rodrigues Vega pioneered also in various branches of sugar refining and trade. As early as 1596, he possessed two large storehouses in Amsterdam to accommodate his sugar imports from the island of St. Michel and the Portuguese colonies. In 1602, for example, he issued a power of attorney for his brother Pedro Rodrigues to take over 63 chests of sugar, as well as shipments of brazilwood, brought from Brazil on three Portuguese ships which had defied the order of the Portuguese authorities to unload in Lisbon, and had unloaded the merchandise in Hamburg instead (allegedly because Lisbon was besieged by the English). As a result, the Rodrigues brothers became involved in a protracted lawsuit. Jews could the better operate as sugar refiners and merchants as they had early pioneered in developing sugar-cane plantations and refineries in Brazil. In fact, in 1610 Emanuel and Pedro themselves acquired a large sugar mill in Bahia. This trade was further promoted by New Christians and Jews during the brief occupation of parts of Brazil by the Dutch West India Company (1630–54). Matters became somewhat complicated when, after the successful Portuguese uprising of 1640, Portugal and the Netherlands became allied against Spain in Europe, but continued to be belligerents in Brazil.

During the Thirty Years' War the Amsterdam Jewish traders greatly benefited from their often close familial contacts with the Jews of Hamburg. As shown by Ernst Baasch, in a twelve-month period in 1647–48 only 95 ships left Hamburg for Spanish and Portuguese ports, and 25 went to France, but no less than 956 had Dutch destinations. At both ends Jewish merchants must have derived substantial profits from that intensive exchange. These examples can be readily multiplied, for there hardly was a branch of business, international or local, in which Jews were not represented. However, a full analysis of these, in part novel, achievements of Amsterdam Jewry must be relegated to a future chapter, which will deal with the rapidly changing economic trends of the early modern period.[62]

Because of their love of public display, the Iberian exiles often created the impression of commanding far greater wealth than they really possessed. The contrast between the luxury-loving Portuguese and Spaniards, who had brought with them from their home countries an inordinate appetite for costly garments and conveyances, and the sturdy Calvinist Dutchmen was striking. The Venetian envoy Giorgio Giorgi reported home in 1626 that the Dutch "abhor luxury and gorging." In contrast, a member of the Cortes had complained to Philip IV three years earlier that Spanish subjects "spend and waste great sums in the abuse of costly garb, with so many varieties of trimmings that the work costs more than the materials; as soon as the clothes are made there is a change of fashion, and the money has to be spent all over again." Popular fancy in Amsterdam naturally exaggerated similar manifestations among the Spanish and Portuguese Jews. It was said that, on one occasion, the combined wealth of forty Jewish guests assembled at a wedding amounted to over 40,000,000 guilders. The fortune of Isaac de Pinto alone was estimated at 8,000,000 guilders. Notwithstanding the tremendous risks involved, Anthony Lopez (Isaac) Suasso purportedly financed William III's expedition to England in 1688 with an interest-free loan of 2,000,000 guilders. It may be noted, however, that at a later date some Dutch, as well as English, economists came around to recognizing luxury as a major vehicle of economic advancement. Bernard de Mandeville, a Dutchman living in London, strongly argued in *The Fable of the Bees; or, Private Vices, Public Benefits* (1714) that luxury was a mainstay of Dutch prosperity. This point of view was adopted by Samuel Johnson and a number of economists down to John Maynard Keynes.[63]

Popular rumors of this kind were, of course, vastly magnified. Certainly, in the first half of the seventeenth century the capital accumulated by the few leading Amsterdam Jews was quite modest, while the majority of their coreligionists were small merchants and craftsmen. A careful study, on the basis of official tax records for the years 1631, 1674, and 1743, has shown that, even in the prosperous year of 1674, Amsterdam's Portuguese Jewish taxpayers averaged a per-capita taxable property of but 1,448 guilders, an amount not greatly exceeding the per-capita average of 828 guilders for the general population. The Ashkenazic community, then already twice as large as the Sephardic, boasted only twelve individuals who reached the Portuguese average (just one taxpayer had 3,000 guilders), whereas the mass earned far below the city's general average. In 1743, Amsterdam's population paid an average per-capita income tax of 1.63 guilders; the 3,000 Sephardim averaged 6 guilders each; but the 10,000 German and Polish Jews averaged the mere pittance of 0.32 guilders each. The 1674 tax of the renowned banker Anthony Lopez Suasso was computed on an estimated property of 231,000 guilders; at the same time, four Christian burghers owned taxable property of from 360,000 to 650,000 guilders each. One can see how little credence can be given to the report that Lopez Suasso lent 2,000,000 guilders to William III fourteen years later! On the other hand, there also were very poor members of the community, living on private or communal charity. While we have no statistical data for the middle of the seventeenth century, the contention of a Jewish newspaper correspondent two centuries later (1849) may not be too far off the mark for the earlier conditions as well. He wrote:

In the city of Amsterdam there are twenty-two thousand Israelites, two thousand of whom are enabled to provide for themselves, without being able to extend any help to others; four thousand who give alms, and the rest, amounting to the number of sixteen thousand, are wholly or partially sustained by their more fortunate coreligionists.

We shall see in a later chapter that the Amsterdam Jewish community always managed to care for vast numbers of poverty-stricken coreligionists, even outright mendicants, without resorting to such harsh methods of repression as the "houses of correction" established by the city of Amsterdam in 1595, Antwerp in 1613, and Brussels in 1625. In short, there is little question that, from the outset, many Sephardim belonged to the upper bourgeoisie of that capitalistically rapidly advancing country.[64]

It is possible, however, that the Dutch Jews' propensity for conspicuous consumption was the result of greater prosperity achieved by them in later years and was not yet quite so pronounced in the first half of the seventeenth century. At least, in expressing his regrets about the contemplated departure of Menasseh ben Israel (whom "I have consulted from time to time, never without profit for me") for Brazil in 1640, Hugo Grotius commented: "I had imagined that the members of the Amsterdam Synagogue were both wealthy and liberal. Now, I realize that I was mistaken. However, I am not sure whether to believe that they tell the truth, or that they wish to appear poorer than they are in reality, in order to evade taxes [capitationes]." In fact, though prominent as an apologist and communal leader, Menasseh was treated as a mere preacher, receiving but 150 guilders a year for monthly sermons, which contrasted with the 600 and 450–500 guilders respectively paid his two rabbinically better-trained colleagues Saul Levi Morteira and David Pardo. (As early as 1626, the congregation was able to offer a salary of 500 guilders to the distinguished visitor Joseph Solomon Delmedigo.) Hence, as Menasseh himself explained, he had to supplement his income through earnings from printing and publishing. Needless to say, there also were many commercial crises, which doubtless were harder on Jewish businessmen than on their longer-established neighbors. While we possess no detailed records concerning the Jewish share in the insolvencies of those years, it must have been quite high. At times Jewish businessmen faced specific hazards of their own. That Rafael Jessurun (João de Haro) went bankrupt in 1634, just three years after he had been assessed on property valued at 10,000 guilders, may have been connected with the intervening arrest of his Lisbon agent by the Inquisition. Be this as it may, on the whole, while still suffering from some legal disabilities, the Jews, at least in business, were basically treated as citizens equal before the law.[65]

CULTURAL INTERPLAY

Among the various branches of industrial and mercantile endeavor, printing and the book trade had a particular Jewish significance. Hebrew printing, to be sure, had existed in the Spanish Netherlands even before the formal admission of Jews to Holland. Under the leadership of Christophe Plantin, its high-quality output, as exemplified by the Antwerp Polyglot, achieved an international reputation. Because of the uprising against the Spanish overlords, Plantin himself temporarily settled in Leiden, where he established a publishing and printing firm in 1583 which was continued by his son-in-law Franciscus Raphelengius (Frans van Ravelingen) and the latter's sons until 1616. But after settling in Amsterdam, some Portuguese Jews, before long followed by their Ashkenazic coreligionists, established many printing presses of their own, from which emerged numerous Hebrew, Ladino, and Yiddish, as well as Spanish, English and other Western-language, books of all kinds. They helped to make Amsterdam a world center of printing, which gave vast employment to the local population. It has been estimated that in the mid-seventeenth century some 30,000 persons, or well over a tenth of the total population, earned their livelihood from the book industry. As early as 1612, Ishak Franco published the first Sephardic prayerbook for the Sabbath and holidays in Spanish, for use by Marranos returning to Judaism. Some fragments of two such editions were preserved by the Portuguese Inquisition, which seized them in 1618 from one David Mexia (formerly a New Christian, known as Francisco Rodrigues de Olivença), who had dared to bring them to Lisbon concealed in his hat, perhaps in order to give them to some local Marranos. In 1617, even the Jewish communal school, Talmud Torah, established a printing press of its own, the equipment of which included both Hebrew and Latin type. However, the first Hebrew book from a Jewish press did not appear until 1627, when it was issued by Menasseh ben Israel. Before long, Amsterdam displaced Venice as the major center of Hebrew printing, in both quantity and quality. The Amsterdam books achieved so high a reputation in the Jewish world that many a Hebrew book later printed in Germany or Poland bore next to its real place of publication the name Amsterdam in larger letters. This identification often was intended to indicate merely that the volume was typographically equal to an Amsterdam edition. In fact, however, it rarely was.[66]

Some enterprising Jewish printers specialized in providing other countries with vernacular books, particularly Bibles. One of the famous Amsterdam printers and publishers of Hebrew and vernacular books was Joseph b. Abraham Athias (1633–1700). The following advertisement, which appeared in a local paper in 1667, well typifies Athias' ambitious program:

Joseph Athias, living in the St. Anttonis Breestraet, has printed with much labor and expense and is going to publish the long awaited Hebrew Bible in large Octavo, on fine Mediaen paper with Hebrew notes and Roman numbers on the margin, dividing the contents of the text for the greater comfort of all nations, in order that they may investigate everything easily. This Bible has never before been printed in this correct manner, not a single error can be found in the entire Bible (which is indeed wonderful). It has also been entirely read through and examined by the Rabbis of the Jewish Synagogue and approved by them and the professors of the Universities of Leiden, Utrecht, Groningen, and Franeker. The entire work, revised by Johannes Leusden, professor in Utrecht, is dedicated to the States General and has been accepted by the Honorable Sirs because of the worthwhileness of this work. It is honored with a large gold chain and medal.

We may discount some of this grandiloquence as characteristic of the advertising methods of the time. Nor do we have to take at face value the assertion of the States General which, in granting Athias, in 1670, a fifteen-year monopoly on the printing and sale of English Bibles, claimed that "he has undertaken this work not to make profit for himself, but only to serve the inhabitants in and outside the country." Of course, the book trade was not without perils. In 1667, Athias himself complained that during the Anglo-Dutch War, then raging, his cargo of 100 packages of English Bibles had been seized by the British before reaching its destination. On the whole, Athias could later boast (in the Introduction to a Hebrew-Yiddish Bible of 1687): "For several years I, myself, printed more than one million Bibles for England and Scotland. There is not a ploughboy or servant girl there without one." Like other overexpansive businessmen, Athias often found himself short of cash to meet his obligations. On one occasion, the heirs of a major supplier of printing paper staged a public auction of many books pledged by him as security. This auction, held on March 17, 1688, included Hebrew and Latin works, some in numerous copies, and yielded a considerable sum, though individual items were sold well below their market price. But this was only a part of the great epic of Hebrew printing, which, beginning in 1475, made a tremendous impact upon Jewish culture, first in the Mediterranean lands, and subsequently in the rest of the world.[67]

Otherwise, too, the transition from business to intellectual pursuits was very easy, and many persons engaged simultaneously in both. The Jewish community was at first too small to allow for intensive specialization. Whatever legal and guild restrictions still persisted also forced many enterprising persons to engage in the mercantile or industrial activities open to them and to pursue their intellectual interests on the side. At times, the reverse was true, and business was but the side line. We recall the manifold activities of Joseph Penso de la Vega, the Pallache family, and Menasseh ben Israel. Menasseh's numerous preoccupations are well illustrated by his Spanish letter of January 31, 1648, to an unnamed correspondent. Explaining the relative brevity of his reply to some questions relating to biblical chronology, Menasseh described his daily work schedule as follows: "Two hours are spent in the Temple every day; six in the school; one and a half in the public Academy and the private one of the Pereyras, in which I hold the office of president; two in proofreading for my printing press, where everything passes through my hands; from eleven to twelve I have appointments with all those who need assistance in their affairs or pay me visits." At the same time, he still managed to steal some hours for his literary work, although he found the constant interruptions quite discouraging. His rabbinic confrere David Pardo engaged on the side in the jewelry trade. In 1621, for example, he gave a power of attorney to a Hamburg correspondent to collect 125 guilders from Juda Jana of that city for five pounds of turquoise. We also remember that Uriel da Costa had spent some time in Hamburg as a merchant. In Amsterdam, too, he actively traded with Portugal under the assumed name of Adam Romez. Nor should we lose sight of the background and activities of the great philosopher Baruch (Benedict) Spinoza, who had not only grown up in a typical upper-middle-class Jewish family but himself made a living principally as a lens grinder and optician. His father, Michael d'Espinosa, who in 1633 owned a house in the Jewish section, did extensive business with both Jews and Gentiles. In the five months from August 21, 1651, to January 28, 1652, his deals with various firms involved the substantial amount of 61,883 guilders, as reflected in his account with the Exchange Bank alone. He also devoted much time to communal affairs, serving on several occasions as elder of the Spanish-Portuguese Congregation and of the Academy Ets Haïm, and being in charge of the charitable Jewish loan bank in 1651.[68]

Such aliases as were used by Uriel da Costa did not escape the attention of the Iberian authorities. In a noteworthy dispatch of 1655, Jacques Richard, the Spanish consul in Amsterdam, informed his ambassador in The Hague:

The president of the Synagogue signs his name Cortez instead of Corticos, which is his real name, as I have been assured by several members of his nation. There is a mystery [hidden purpose] in this change of names. It is a custom among the members of his nation to assume as many names as they please, either for purposes of deceit or in order not to jeopardize their relatives who still bear their [true] name in Spain.

It took the consul several months before he was able to supply the embassy with a list of such aliases. This list, which also noted the names of the Iberian correspondents of these businessmen, was forwarded by the ambassador on October 16 to King Philip IV, who in turn sent it on to the Spanish Inquisition. The king received thanks for that service, the inquisitor-general encouraging him to continue with his efforts, which would contribute to "the augmentation of our sacred Catholic faith, so that your realm may retain its purity and the unity of religion, and preserve it from the heresies which others practice." [69]

Amsterdam's new opportunities attracted many Jewish intellectuals. Among the early settlers was Jacob Israel Belmonte, a native of Madeira. He was not only a distinguished communal leader, who took an active part in the acquisition of the Jewish cemetery in Ouderkerk in 1614; he also wrote poetry. One of his poems, entitled *Job*, described (in one hundred octaves) the sufferings of the victims of the Inquisition. Upon his death in 1629, he was honored by the establishment of a new academy. When the Marranos were expelled from Nantes in 1615, most of them moved to Amsterdam. Two years later, seventy-three persons arrived from Saint-Jean-de-Luz in southwestern France. Among these new-comers was Alonso Nuñez Herrera, who in 1596 had been carried away from Cadiz by the English fleet under the command of the earl of Essex. In Amsterdam he publicly professed Judaism and, under the name Abraham Cohen Herrera, wrote several impor-tant kabbalistic treatises in Spanish. There also was Pablo de Pina, who stopped in Leghorn in 1599 on his way to Rome, where he in-tended to join a monastic order, and was dissuaded from that in-tent by the eminent Marrano physician Elijah Montalto. Via Brazil and Lisbon he came to Amsterdam, where he became a pro-fessing Jew and took the name Reüel (Rohel) Jesurun. His drama *El Dialogo dos Montes* was performed at the *Beth Yaacob* Syna-gogue during the Festival of Weeks in 1624. The new arrivals in-cluded several friars—among them, Henriques Solis, who in Am-sterdam became Eleazar de Solis, a distinguished physician. The Dominican Fra Vicente de Rocamora, who had served as father confessor to the Infanta Maria of Spain, later empress of Germany, suddenly appeared in Amsterdam under the name of Isaac, en-gaging in the study of medicine. Even the important playwright Antonio Enríquez Gómez (Enrique Enríquez de Paz, *ca.* 1600–1662), whose twenty-odd comedies had competed with those of Pedro Calderón de la Barca in attracting vast audiences in Madrid and who had been named knight of the Order of St. Miguel for his valiant services in the Spanish army, likewise suddenly disap-peared from Madrid to emerge in Amsterdam as a professing Jew. The Inquisition, unable to lay its hands upon all the "culprits," burned some of them in effigy; and it is, indeed, largely from in-quisitorial records that we learn much about their Christian ante-cedents.[70]

Extraordinary mobility of this kind was not limited to haunted refugees of the Inquisition. Other Jews, too, moved by a desire for economic betterment, by temporary local difficulties, or by a spirit of adventure, often changed their places of residence in rapid suc-cession. The well-known rabbi Jacob b. Aaron Sasportas (1610–98), for instance, a native of Algerian Oran, first served as rabbi in the Moroccan communities of Tlemçen, Fez, and Salé. Imprisoned in 1646 in connection with a conflict among the local Muslim authorities, he escaped to Amsterdam. Thereafter he returned to Morocco and even served for a while on its diplomatic mission to Spain, but came back to Amsterdam, and accompanied Menasseh ben Israel on his historic mission to Oliver Cromwell in 1655. He remained in London for a decade to officiate as the spiritual leader of the new English community. From 1666 to 1673 he served as rabbi in Hamburg, but subsequently returned to Amsterdam, where, after another episode in Leghorn (1675–80), he functioned as head of the academy, and later as rabbi, to his death in 1698. Sasportas' departure for Leghorn may have been caused by his quarrel with the physician Benjamin b. Emanuel Mussaphia, who died in 1675. This extremely active physician, diplomatic agent, and many-sided businessman, after living for many years in the Hamburg-Glückstadt area, settled in Amsterdam, where one of his scholarly works had previously appeared. For a while he even joined the city's rabbinical council and the communal board (1648). While his rabbinical knowledge could justly be impugned by Sasportas, there was no question about the competence in Hebraic letters of another restless soul, the polyhistor Joseph Solomon Delmedigo (known as Yashar) of Candia, Crete (1591–1655), who in his endless wanderings through European Jewish communities also spent a few years (1626–29) in the Dutch metropolis. Remarkably, he encountered considerable difficulty in connection with his responses to questions on Kabbalah and theology asked by the Lithuanian Karaite Zeraḥ b. Nathan. The Amsterdam elders suspected that his replies were, in part, lacking in orthodoxy.[71]

It is truly amazing how many men of extraordinary intellect and character lived in the relatively small Jewish community of Amsterdam, which averaged little more than 1,000–1,500 souls in the 1630s and 1640s. Among the medical luminaries of the age was Abraham Zacuto Lusitano, possibly a relative of his namesake, the famous astronomer-historian of the period of the Spanish Expulsion. Abraham returned to Judaism in Amsterdam in 1625, at the relatively advanced age of fifty, and died there seventeen years later. His friend, the eminent physician and diplomat Jacob Rosales (originally Manuel Bocarro Francês), left Amsterdam for Hamburg in 1632 and, as we recall, was ultimately raised by Emperor Ferdinand III to the rank of count palatine in 1647. Another physician, Abraham Pharar, compiled for the benefit of his fellow Marranos a detailed Portuguese elucidation of the six hundred and thirteen commandments; it was published in 1627. He may have wished to show thereby his superiority in halakhic learning to the communal elders, who nine years before had disqualified a slaughterer selected by Pharar and had declared all the animals slaughtered by him as banned by ritual law. In the ensuing controversy, Pharar was led into repudiating both the Aggadah and the Kabbalah, and into insisting on the superiority of rationalistic philosophy. In 1647, there died in Amsterdam that fascinating, if erratic, searcher for the truth, Uriel da Costa, whose career fully illustrates the difficulties of Marrano spiritual existence between the two worlds. How little Da Costa understood the fundamentals of Judaism may be seen in the following example. Equating the seven Noahidic commandments with the natural law so extensively debated in Christian scholasticism, familiar to him, he did not see why their observance, according to Jewish law obligatory for all nations, should not suffice for professing Jews as well. Not comprehending that man's struggle for the victory of divinely guided historical forces over those of nature had become an implicit fundamental of the Mosaic religion's opposition to ancient heathenism, he disputed the underlying dichotomy between the Bible and the law of nature, "since God, the creator of nature, cannot act in contradiction to Himself." Going beyond its purely dogmatic aspects, he saw in the elaborate biblical law an obstacle to the unity of mankind. He waxed eloquent about the law of nature:

It is that law which unites all men by love; it is removed from the dissensions which are the cause of all the abominations and all the evils. It is that which teaches honest living, discerning between right and wrong, between beauty and ugliness. The best part of Mosaic law, like that of any other law, is that which is derived from the law of nature. The moment one departs from that norm of nature, one immediately gives rise to disputes and ultimately to dissensions among men; this is the end of peace.

We shall see in another context that such efforts at blurring, rather than comprehending, religious differences, stimulated the existing trends toward religious syncretism or agnosticism, even outright atheism, and mightily contributed to the slowly swelling wave of secularism in the Enlightenment Era.[72]

Best known among the communal rabbis was Menasseh ben Israel, less by virtue of his rabbinic learning than for his public activities and prolific output of scholarly and apologetic works in Spanish. Apart from his numerous extant publications, Menasseh wrote a number of tracts since lost; among them, a sharp attack on Isaac de la Peyrère's "pre-Adamite" theory, despite the latter's advocacy of a restoration of the Jews to Palestine. Menasseh's reputation spread to many countries. His career also was an astonishing example of the close social contacts maintained by distinguished Amsterdam Jews with their Christian colleagues. Grotius was not alone in feeling as he did when he wrote in 1638 from Paris (where he served as Swedish ambassador) to their mutual friend Gerhard Johann Vos (Vossius): "He [Menasseh] is a man of the highest utility both to the state and to the advancement of knowledge." Vos did not need that assurance by Grotius, since five years earlier his son Dionysius had already translated the first part of Menasseh's Conciliador into Latin. (It doubtless was to this work that Grotius himself had alluded when he asked his brother Willem "to buy for me and send me at the first opportunity a map of Judaea, edited by a Jew [Constantin l'Empereur's Latin translation of Benjamin of Tudela's Itinerary?], and the book by another Jew containing the reconciliation of contradictions ['αρτεόφανῶν] of the Old Testament." In his exchange of letters, in particular, with the Polish nobleman Krzysztof Słupecki in 1636–37, Vos agreed that it would be desirable that Jews be converted to Christianity, but he objected to any use of force for this purpose. He insisted that "the Lord alone controls consciences." He seems to have reacted negatively to Słupecki's lengthy complaint about the multitude of Jews living in Poland and to his query about Vos' opinion regarding the recent Blood Accusation in Poland, about which Słupecki himself entertained serious doubts. Yet the Polish leader was puzzled by the earlier acceptance of that accusation by the Church, especially in connection with the much-discussed affair of Trent in 1475.[73]

Interest in Jewish life and letters was not limited to Menasseh's circle of friends. Harking back to the earlier Renaissance appreciation of classical languages and literatures, and stimulated by the deep Protestant concern for all facets of biblical studies, a growing number of Christian Hebraists began intensively cultivating Hebrew letters and institutions in their writings, as well as in their university teaching. Dutch contributors to Hebraic learning, postbiblical as well as biblical, during the seventeenth and eighteenth centuries included an array of distinguished scholars, among them, Joseph Justus Scaliger (1540–1609), Johannes Leusden (1624–99), Willem Surenhuis (Surenhusius, died in 1729) and Campegius Vitringa (the Elder, 1669–1722). To be sure, the first half of the seventeenth century marked in some respects the transition from the essentially secular Renaissance interest in Hebraic studies to a predominantly religious type of scholarship. But even some of the best-informed ecclesiastical writers evinced considerable sympathy for Jews and Judaism, and thus helped to build memorable bridges between the Christian and Jewish worlds. This interest in the Jewish tradition and way of life also communicated itself to the great Dutch artists of that age. The portraits of rabbis, "The Jewish Bride," and other Jewish subjects by Rembrandt Harmenszoon van Rijn aroused much interest among contemporaries and have been widely discussed by modern art historians. Commenting on "The Jewish Bride," one historian has observed: "Its mystery is unfathomable, like that of Mona Lisa or of the Medicean tombs, unfathomable as is the mystery of life itself, which the creators of these works depicted in moments of grace." The unusual facial characteristics and, for Holland, somewhat exotic attire of Jewish scholars, businessmen, and craftsmen often intrigued other Dutch painters; for example, Thomas de Keyser, whose *Joden-Compagnie*, representing typical members of the Jewish upper bourgeoisie, is one of the treasured possessions of the Amsterdam Rijksmuseum.[74]

Not that the Judeo-Christian dialogue was always conducted in a friendly vein. Even Menasseh's *Conciliador* was received by the Theological Faculty of the University of Leiden with considerable reservations, particularly with respect to Menasseh's interpretation of some messianic passages in the Bible. After the Board at the

Leiden school had resolved to September 1633 to take measures against future publications of that kind, the Faculty assigned a Hebraist, Constantin l'Empereur van Oppyck, who had in that very year published a Latin translation of Benjamin of Tudela's *Itinerary,* to teach a course on "the controversial writings among Christians and Jews," a course for which he was to receive an additional salary of 400 guilders a year. The Board also ordered the acquisition, by the University Library, of all pertinent publications. The *controversiarun judaicarum professor* was indeed a hostile innovation; yet it demonstrated that the Jewish apologetical literature was treated with a measure of respect. One of Menasseh's later publications also gave rise to an extensive controversy among Christian theologians. His *De Creatione problemata XXX,* published in 1635 (this volume, originally issued by Menasseh's own firm, was republished by the Christian publisher Jan Jansonius in the following year), was at first hailed by a Christian friend, Casper van Baerle (Barlaeus), professor of philosophy and eloquence at the Amsterdam Athenaeum, with a song of praise. But this accolade, and its underlying tribute to a rabbinic interpretation, were sharply attacked by Nicolaas Videl (Vedelius), professor of theology at Deventer, in a pamphlet entitled *De Deo Synagogae.* Van Baerle's reply, *Vindiciae epigrammatis,* called forth a rejoinder by Videl, *Casparis Barlaei epigramma cum analysi.* This controversy—in which Videl was supported by his Utrecht colleague Martin Schoock, who compared Van Baerle with the heresiarch Vorstius—deeply affected the Amsterdam philosopher-poet, but had no untoward consequences for Menasseh. The University of Utrecht thenceforth became a center of staunchly conservative anti-Jewish polemics. Yet even the ardent debater and maverick theologian Jan Pieterszoon Beelthouwer, while attacking all opposing points of view, especially in his apologetic tract *Schildt der Christenen* (Escutcheon of Christians, against all non-Christians; Amsterdam, 1649), used rather moderate language in his censure of Judaism. After banishment in 1656 from his native Enkhuizen, because of his feud with the local Dutch Reformed clergy, he settled in Amsterdam, where he maintained friendly relations with many prominent Jews, although his conversionary efforts proved utterly futile. In general, such theological controversy merely demonstrated the growing interest in Hebrew culture on the part of Dutch scholars, an interest which, positively even more than negatively, radiated into all other countries, particularly England and her colonies.[75] The outstanding Amsterdam apologist for Judaism was Balthazar (Isaac) Orobio de Castro (*ca.* 1620–87). Escaping from the Spanish Inquisition, he had first settled in Toulouse, where he served as professor of medicine and received from Louis XIV the title of councilor. In 1666 he moved to Amsterdam, where he likewise successfully practiced medicine. He returned to Judaism, adopting the name of Isaac and becoming a leader in the Spanish-Portuguese community. Among his numerous prose and poetic writings were a number of (as yet unpublished) apologetic and exegetical tracts, including his *Prevenciones divinas contra la vana ydolatria de las gentes;* three brief tracts sharply attacking the heterodox views of his former benefactor Juan (Daniel) de Prado; and his searching dialogue with the Dutch pastor Philipp van Limborch, published together with Limborch's reply under the title *De Veritate religionis christianae amica collatio cum erudito Judaeo* (Gouda, 1687).[76]

During this same period, the sensitive leadership of the Portuguese Jewish community felt constrained to counteract what it considered were excesses of free thought, as well as Jewish attacks on Christianity. In 1639 it established, therefore, a sort of Jewish precensorship, which went far beyond that envisaged by the Jewish Council of Ferrara of 1554. With the increasing power of the communal elders, this supervision over Jewish literary output ultimately led to the excommunication of Baruch Spinoza and Juan (Daniel) de Prado, and to other rigid intellectual controls. Even Daniel Levi (Miguel) de Barrios (1625–1701), the former Spanish captain who became a dedicated Jewish poet and historian, to whom modern Jewish scholarship is deeply indebted for much relevant information about Sephardic scholars and writers, was hampered by these controls. Publication of his major poetic work, *Imperio de Dios* (or *La Harmonia del Mundo*), intended to promote world peace through the cooperation of the twelve potentates to whom it was dedicated (some of these personages supplied him with their likenesses and biographical data and promised him financial support), was temporarily delayed because the

Jewish elders had not given their approbation. (It appeared in Brussels, 1670–74.) In an undated autograph letter, extant in the Library of the Academy Ets Haïm in Amsterdam, De Barrios complained that the rabbi and elders of the Portuguese community of Amsterdam had prevented the publication of two of his works, an interference which caused him much financial difficulty. All these complications, both external and internal, were manifestations of the intellectual ferment within the Jewish community, and of Dutch Jewry's close relations with its neighbors.[77]

HOLLAND'S SEABORNE EMPIRE

The Jewish community's rise in Amsterdam and other Dutch cities was also reflected in Jewish participation in the rapid expansion of the Dutch colonial empire in both East and West. As shareholders of the East and West India Companies, the Jews exerted some influence on the management of the colonies, particularly on their trade with the mother country and other European lands, which in essence was the main purpose of their establishment. Sooner or later a number of Jewish individuals found their way to the colonies, laying there the foundations for the subsequent development of regular Jewish settlements overseas.

Apart from general differences in the approach and the relative success of the two companies, there was, with respect to the Jews, a major divergence between the Asian colonies, where native Jewish communities had existed for a long time and where the new Jewish arrivals could expect a more or less friendly reception from local coreligionists, and the American or African colonies, where the Jews settling under Dutch auspices found no persons outwardly professing their religion. There they could expect succor only from occasional New Christian predecessors, some of whom would eventually join them as professing Jews. Such cooperation was doubly important in the trade with Spanish possessions during the eighty years' war between Holland and Spain, when few Dutch citizens ventured to these hostile territories, and Dutch merchants had to use Iberian intermediaries. The most dramatic episodes of this story unfolded in parts of Brazil; but the description of these events must here be relegated to the general history of

Brazilian developments under Portuguese domination, of which the twenty-four-year Dutch rule over the country's northeastern section (1630–54) was merely one important chapter. Concurrently, however, the end of Dutch domination, and Pernambuco's return to Portuguese control, set in motion waves of Jewish refugees escaping Portuguese vengeance, and in many ways marked the true beginnings of the establishment of Jewish communities in many parts of the Western Hemisphere and, to a lesser extent, in Equatorial and southern Africa.[78]

Among the earliest colonies established by the Dutch was Cayenne, where they are recorded first in 1613. However, neither the colony nor any Jewish connections with it became truly significant until after the middle of the century. After 1653, when the West India Company made an effort to develop Cayenne, the Company welcomed representatives of the Brazilian Jewish refugees, especially the enterprising merchant-colonizer David Nassi (also known as Joseph Nuñes de Fonseca or Christovão de Tavora). In the privilege extended to him and his associates in 1659, the Company obligated itself to grant the Jewish settlers freedoms similar to those which the Jews enjoyed in Amsterdam, including the right to have a synagogue of their own as well as a ten-year tax exemption. This privilege attracted Jews from as far as Leghorn. However, owing to constant harassment by the French, and later to the uprising staged by the "bush Negroes" (that is, the fugitive Negro slaves imported from Africa, and their descendants), the Jewish settlement in Cayenne did not prosper. Ultimately, under a French attack of 1664 Jews were forced to leave the settlement and seek refuge in Surinam. It was there and on the island of Curaçao that major centers of Jewish life gradually developed. Both Surinam and Curaçao had regular Jewish synagogue buildings long before 1733, when New York Jewry was able to open the first structure set aside for Jewish worship on the North American continent. Some records refer to Jews in Surinam as early as 1639 and 1643. To be sure, in the crucial early years after 1654, the colony was under English control; hence the Dutch West India Company had little occasion to refer to Jewish arrivals. However, in 1664 the Jewish fugitives from Cayenne were admitted by the English to the colony. Three years later, Surinam reverted to Dutch domination, which made possible the extraordinary development of the Jewish settlement. That story will be told here in its eighteenth-century context.[79]

In Curaçao, on the other hand, the relative continuity of Dutch rule gave rise to some noteworthy early developments in Jewish life. Occupied in 1634 by the West India Company, the island at first did not flourish. The Company actually took under advisement whether it should abandon the colony altogether. True, its intimation to this effect to Peter Stuyvesant, governor of the entire colony of New Netherland (which included Curaçao), was clarified by the headquarters as a merely tentative proposal. Yet the situation was sufficiently unsatisfactory for the Company to welcome Jewish entrepreneurs like Jan (João) de Illan (his Hebrew name was Jeudah or Jeojada) and David Nassi (here also using the alias Joseph Nuñes de Fonseca), who in 1651 and 1652, respectively, offered to help develop Curaçao's agriculture. According to its Directors' privilege of February 22, 1652, the Company granted Nassi and his associates extensive rights, which included the following noteworthy provision:

It is further permitted to Fonseca and partners, in the form of a lease, to select and take possession of all such lands as he, with his colonists, shall be able to cultivate, to obtain every sort of produce, to increase the number of cattle in that country, except only the Salinas [salt pits] and the woods of stock fish hout [logwood], which the company reserves for her own use, the extent of the said lands being calculated to the number of the settlers, viz: for fifty persons two miles [leagues] along the coast; for one hundred persons four miles, and so in the same proportion, with the express condition that they shall be obliged to make a beginning with their cultivation within a year, and that they shall bring within four years the stipulated number of settlers in that country under the penalty of the forfeiture of said lands.

The maintenance of a monopoly over the slave trade by the Company proved to be a serious handicap, however, to the Jewish attempt at agriculture which under the conditions of the time could not be effectively conducted without slave labor. Although the Company finally permitted them to acquire slaves, many Jewish settlers preferred to engage in commerce. Thereupon the Company complained that, instead of developing the agricultural resources of the island, the new Jewish arrivals (12, instead of the promised 50) exported lumber and horses to other Caribbean islands. This business was undoubtedly very lucrative, since horses could not easily survive a trip from Europe, and even their importation from the New England colonies entailed many losses. But the Dutch authorities resented that trade and saw therein a confirmation of earlier suspicions. On March 21, 1651, they had explained to Stuyvesant: "We are willing to make the experiment [of granting the charter to De Illan] and you must therefore . . . accommodate him . . . in conformity with the conditions of the contract." With some resignation they more fully expressed the mental reservation implied by the term "experiment," in a letter to the governor on April 4, 1652. Enclosing a copy of the patent they were issuing to Nassi (Nuñes de Fonseca), they added: "Time must show whether we shall succeed well with this nation; they are a crafty and generally treacherous people in whom therefore not too much confidence must be placed." Stuyvesant was not a friend to Jews, particularly in his main residence in what was then New Amsterdam (now New York): when he learned that the Curaçao Jews had been permitted to import Negro slaves, he complained to the Directors that the Dutch Christians were treated less well than Jews. Despite these initial difficulties, however, Curaçao Jewry gradually established itself on a firm basis in 1659, under the leadership of Isaac da Costa (a nephew of Uriel), who had lived and prospered in Dutch Brazil until the Dutch withdrawal in 1654. The privilege granted to him and his associates on March 31, 1659, specifically provided for the religious freedom of the Jewish settlers. The new community so speedily grew in number and affluence that its synagogue of 1692 had to be replaced by a larger one in 1704. In the eighteenth century it was one of the leading communities in the New World.[80]

The pro-Jewish privileges granted in Surinam and Curaçao were exceeded by those granted "to the People of the Hebrew Nation that are to goe to the Wilde Cust." The area so designated, the authors of that privilege, and its date were long under dispute. While the text was first discovered in a collection of papers relating to English settlements in America in the years 1627–90, the original privilege was issued by the Dutch authorities of Zeeland. One of its major provisions reads: "That all the Hebrews

shall bee admitted for Burgezes as The People of the Province of
Zeeland that shall live in the said Corte and that they shall with
them enjoy, all the Previledges which thei shall enjoy." In addition to economic and religious liberties, Jews were to enjoy an
extraordinary measure of self-government, including even the
right to banish from the Province any misbehaving person "that
should give them anny scandall." Only the find of the original
documentation in The Hague Archive by Samuel Oppenheim
has clarified this privilege. It seems to have been drafted in 1657
by Jews in Holland, who conducted the negotiations with the
Zeeland Committee. It was approved in final form by the Committee on November 12, 1657, although it seems to have been
somewhat amended thereafter. It opened up the area around
Essequibo to Jewish settlement, and accrued to the benefit of both
contracting parties. Indeed, as we are told by an informed local
scholar, N. Darnell Davis, "it would appear that it was to the Jews
that Essequibo owed the introduction of cane cultivation." [81]

In contrast, we know very little about Jews in the Dutch West
African possessions, though there they usually succeeded the Portuguese colonizers, whose population undoubtedly included a
good many New Christians. Even on the Cape of Good Hope,
which was taken over by the Dutch East India Company in 1652
and held by the Dutch until 1795, we have the first reference to
Jews in 1669, in connection with two otherwise unknown individuals, Samuel Jacobson and David Heijlbron, aged twenty and
twenty-two, respectively, who underwent baptism at that time.
Here, too, the real history of the Jewish communities began in the
eighteenth century, to reach its extraordinary climax only in the
late nineteenth and twentieth centuries.[82]

FRESH START

The spectacular growth of the Jewish communities in Holland
marked a new beginning in Jewish history. At first slow, the new
trend gathered momentum, especially after Holland achieved,
through the Peace Treaties of Westphalia, a generally recognized
sovereign status. The constant growth of the Jewish communities
in numbers, affluence, and cultural attainments opened the eyes

not only of their Dutch compatriots but also of their friends or foes abroad to the tremendous economic and intellectual resources dormant among the Jews, particularly among the former Marranos. Holland's unprecedentedly speedy progress in economic, naval, political, and intellectual power was universally admired, envied, or hated; no Western nation could remain indifferent to it. Before very long, keen observers of the European scene began contrasting the marvelous advances of the Netherlands with the accelerating decay of the Iberian kingdoms. To some observers, such as the eighteenth-century economist Élie Luzac, the conclusion readily suggested itself that this difference might be accounted for in part by the contrasting treatment of Jews in these countries. Ever since Luzac's time, students of modern European and Jewish history have often repeated the idea, now almost become a cliché, that Spain's and Portugal's elimination of Jews (and Moriscos) was co-responsible for their sociopolitical decline, whereas the admission to Holland of alert and enterprising Jewish capitalists under favorable conditions greatly contributed to its extraordinary expansion. Werner Sombart was not alone in waxing eloquent on the subject and exclaiming: "Israel passes over Europe like the sun; at its coming new life bursts forth; at its going all falls into decay." These exaggerations have rightly been controverted by numerous scholars from the eighteenth to the twentieth centuries. But one cannot gainsay that they contain a kernel of truth, and that the freer admission of Jews to Holland and other Western lands became a significant factor in the advance of modern capitalism and the growth of modern liberal institutions.[83]

Holland was able to achieve this progress more speedily than its neighbors because it had made a fresh start and was relatively unshackled by legal precedents and ecclesiastical traditions. Emerging from a revolutionary uprising against constituted authority, it could, in the Jewish sphere as in others, view the newly emergent sociopolitical realities from the standpoint of its own long-range interests. Indeed, even in the religious polemics of the time we find important departures from medieval controversies. The fact that there was a new dominant faith, at first Calvinist in nature but soon developing away from Calvin's own teachings, meant that theologically, too, there had been a break with the past. Moreover, the country still embraced, in addition to Jews, a powerful dissident Protestant minority and a considerable number of Catholics. While at times this sectarian heterogeneity persuaded the Dutch Reformed leaders that they had to defend their Church's dominant role by a variety of intolerant measures, it greatly contributed to the growing secularization of politics and the ever-deepening conviction of the political rulers that the country's interests must transcend these sectarian divisions.

Led by statesmen of the rank of William of Orange and his son Maurice, the government early realized that legalization of Jewish settlement in the country would accrue to Holland's great advantage. Although delegating specific regulation to the municipalities, whose policies were often dictated or modified by narrow-minded burghers and churchmen, the legislative and administrative organs of the country at large prepared the ground for a new approach to the Jewish question. Since Holland had largely abandoned the traditional corporate structure of medieval Europe, and was gradually driving toward the formation of a more or less unitarian society—despite the perseverance of some guild and other corporate prerogatives—the newly admitted Jews, too, could no longer be treated exclusively from the traditional standpoint of corporate legislation. No longer were they considered primarily as a corporate body within other corporate bodies, each endowed with a special system of rights and duties. They now were admitted to that growingly uniform society as individuals basically equal to other citizens.

This situation, to be sure, did not prevent either the local or the central authorities from imposing upon the Jews, as upon other religious minorities, certain specific restrictions and disabilities. But they had to grant them all a modicum of equality of rights, minus certain clearly defined exceptions. It was now possible for lesser cities like Alkmaar, Haarlem, and Rotterdam to pioneer, ahead of Amsterdam, with that type of legislation. Grotius' famous *Remonstrantie* of 1616, though somewhat more timid, adhered to that fundamental principle of equality minus specific disabilities. Although not fully adopted by the Amsterdam municipality in its decree of 1619, Grotius' proposals prevailed in essence. Gradually, the disabilities were whittled away, or were simply disregarded in practice, leaving equality less and less impaired, particularly in the economic domain.

It is not surprising, therefore, that after achieving undisputed sovereignty in 1648 the States General proclaimed to the world, on July 13, 1657, that the Dutch Jews were citizens of the Netherlands and in their travels or mercantile dealings abroad must be treated as such, on a par with the country's Christian citizens. This point of view, to be sure, was challenged by Spain, when Holland sought to apply it to Article IV of the Treaty of Münster of 1648, which expressly provided that "the subjects and inhabitants of the lands of the aforesaid lords, kings, and states should be allowed to come and sojourn in one another's domains, and be able to trade and do business there on the sea and other waterways, as well as on land." Spain, supported therein even by the Dutch jurist Van Bymkershoek, argued that, long before the adoption of that article, it had excluded all Jews from its territories. But Holland adhered to its own interpretation and pointed, in particular, to Emperor Caracalla's *lex Antoniana de civitate,* which as early as the year 212 had granted to the Jews of the whole Roman Empire full rights of citizenship. Although evidently unable to budge the Spanish government, the States General further elaborated its proclamation in a resolution adopted on September 21, 1680. Thenceforth the Dutch diplomatic representations in most foreign countries considered it incumbent upon themselves to protect Dutch Jewish interests, which they realized in the ultimate sense ran parallel to their own.[84]

FRENCH AND
ENGLISH AMBIGUITIES

IN CONTRAST to Holland, which was able to start afresh in dealing with the Jewish question, France and England labored under a heavy "burden of heritage"—to use a Karaite religious term—in their treatment of Jewish settlers. Edward I's 1290 decree expelling the Jews from England not only remained on the statute books but was ever present in the minds of legislators and jurists. Despite the absence of professing Jews from the country for several generations, enmity toward Jews and Judaism continued to permeate the thinking of religious leaders and the populace alike. As late as 1608 the influential chief justice of the Common Pleas, Sir Edward Coke, could enunciate the general principle that between the Christians and all infidels, including Jews, "as with the devils whose subjects they be . . . there is a perpetual hostility, and can be no peace!" As late as 1818, this doctrine was still quoted with approval by some English judges. France had even more recent memories of the banishment of Jews. While the final decree of expulsion of 1394 had put an end to the legal settlement of professing Jews in royal France, an additional century passed before the flourishing Jewish communities of Provence and other southern regions were formally uprooted. The arguments that had been advanced in favor of total intolerance must still have been remembered by countless Frenchmen when the turnabout came in the sixteenth century and individual Jews in growing numbers were readmitted to residence in their country.[1]

True, as in the case of other expulsions, probably not all French Jews left the land where their ancestors had lived and died for centuries and to whose culture they had significantly contributed, both materially and intellectually. Many must have gone underground, only exceptionally leaving some traces in the extant records. Very likely, the Jewish physician Raphael mentioned in a

Poitiers document of 1528 belonged to a fairly sizable group of individuals scattered through the country, whose presence or clandestine religious allegiance had escaped official notice. Moreover, these underground survivors were quickly reinforced and outnumbered by the immigrating New Christians, who, outwardly professing Christianity, were not subject to the penalties provided by law against illicit Jewish settlers. Rumors about their secret judaizing were often ignored by royal or municipal officials, who regarded the new arrivals as beneficial to their private interests or to those of their localities and the country at large. Not that the path of the Iberian immigrants was altogether smooth. We recall the numerous vicissitudes suffered even by the relatively safe Marrano arrivals in tolerant Bordeaux and St.-Esprit (Bayonne) during the first half of the sixteenth century. Yet out of that turmoil finally emerged small but vigorous Jewish communities which laid the foundations for a Jewish resettlement in both France and England.[2]

FRENCH TURMOIL

After 1550, small groups of New Christians were allowed to remain in France inconspicuously for a while under Henry II's decree of that year. True, the verbiage of this decree was so broad that, from the outset, certain limits were placed on it by administrative interpretation. If, according to the letter of the law, these newcomers seemed to have been given some procedural advantages over native Frenchmen in disposing of property, the Paris Parlement, in registering the decree on December 22, 1550, added the following restriction: "Provided their heirs and the persons in whose favor they dispose of their goods, are French subjects [regnicolae]." The Accounting Office went further and tried to restrict the registration of families thus privileged to twenty-three, for a fee of 5 gold écus each. Even these restrictions, however, did not restore the traditional rightlessness of strangers, whose estates had long been subject to confiscation under the royal *droit d'aubaine*. In any case, there gradually sprang up small Jewish settlements in Rouen, La Rochelle, Nantes, La Bastide, and Marseilles, although the Jewish identity of the individuals involved can often be deduced only from their names or from occasional references by their enemies. A more or less constant flow of new arrivals from the Iberian Peninsula is attested by contemporary observers. In 1560, as we recall, a French diplomatic agent located at the Spanish frontier reported about the considerable influx of New Christians, "who, under the guise of *Christians,* observe many Mosaic ceremonies and rituals." He expressed the fear that the Spanish persecutions would lead to "a great diminution of commerce" between France and her southern neighbors. On their part, the Iberian Marranos helped promote the emigration of endangered coreligionists. In 1607, they sent a representative to Bordeaux to study the opportunities for settling additional émigrés from Lisbon and Toledo. This migratory movement was sufficiently large to prompt some Spanish authorities to investigate. On October 11, 1608, the Catalan viceroy ordered the bailiffs and consuls along the frontier to ascertain "what manner of people [emigrate] and in what form; also from what places they come and which roads and passes they traverse." There is no evidence, however, that this official curiosity in any way interfered with the exodus, which was stimulated, as we shall see, by the intensified Spanish and Portuguese inquisitorial activities after the "general pardon" of 1604–1605.[3]

Obviously, not all arrivals from the Iberian Peninsula were secret Judaizers or even New Christians. Although in both popular parlance and official documents, the term "Portuguese" in the main connoted New Christian settlers, the émigrés also included numerous merchants of Old Christian descent. Nor do the records clearly indicate how many of each category had come merely as transients on their way to other countries or as temporary visitors. But it appears that the Old Christian group, less afraid of inquisitorial prosecution in the home country, included more travelers of both these categories. A large number of the New Christians, moreover, perhaps the majority, were genuine Christians, who may have resented living in Spain or Portugal under a cloud of suspicion. In time, however, some of their children decided to revert to their ancestral faith or to join the Protestant movement. Many of these sooner or later found it to their advantage, economically as well as religiously, to emigrate to a country like Holland, where they were assured of a brotherly reception by their coreligionists. (Among such émigrés was the D'Espinosa family, whose scion Baruch [Benedict] was to become one of the greatest philosophers of the early modern period.) Hence the nucleus of professing Jews in France was always quite small. Not until the establishment of Jewish communities, whether or not formally recognized by the government, can we be certain of their Jewish membership. These communities very likely embraced only a segment of the Portuguese Judaizers, whose observance of Jewish rites differed greatly from individual to individual and from period to period. By the eighteenth century, moreover, most southern settlements included quite a few Ashkenazic and Avignonese Jews. Down to the French Revolution the total number of Sephardic Jews in France seems never to have exceeded 3,500 souls.[4]

After 1550 the growing ferocity of religious warfare, which then dominated France's domestic and international policies, affected the treatment of New Christians. In a period characterized by events like the Massacre of St. Bartholomew (1572), one could not expect the Marranos—whose unfamiliar ways of life inspired many strange tales among the native population and whose economic successes created many rivalries and jealousies—to escape suspicions of heterodoxy. Apart from being accused of secretly observing Judaism, some of them (not unjustly, it appears) were denounced as sympathizers of the Reformation. In 1574, the relatively tolerant Parlement of Bordeaux assailed on this score some teachers and students of the Collège de Guienne, a few of whom had been appointed by its director, André de Gouvéa (himself of New Christian descent), before his demise in 1548. Such an accusation naturally carried with it strong political implications. Calvinism, especially, forced by circumstances, was gradually developing in France into a major insurrectionary movement, which in the name of God insisted on the believers' right to resist the state's encroachments upon individual conscience.[5]

In the tense atmosphere of religious warfare, judaizing was also viewed as a strongly subversive political factor. Especially violent anti-Marrano sentiments were voiced at the early seventeenth-century trial of a postmaster accused of stealing objects belonging to a group of "Portuguese" who had spent a night at his station on their way from Spain to Bordeaux. Relatives of the accused employed the diversionary tactic of accusing all Bordeaux Portuguese, then numbering from fifty to sixty families, of being Jews. While the prosecutor pleaded that he could discover no misconduct on the part of the Portuguese and that, on the contrary, they were greatly contributing to the city's economy, G. Laroche, the attorney for the defendant, rhetorically exclaimed: "The Jews are worthy of total rejection; as true criminals against all divine and human majesty they deserve to be punished with the most severe tortures. . . . If Jews, known as such, are culpable, how much more are those who, disguising and falsifying their Jewishness, claim to be Christians." [6]

Laroche's plea was included in full in the report submitted by Pierre de Rostéguy de Lancre, a counselor of the Bordeaux Parlement who had been dispatched with a colleague in 1609 to investigate and punish "sorcery," alleged to be widely practiced in southern France. It is truly amazing that a learned and otherwise temperate jurist (incidentally, married to a cousin of the fairly tolerant Michel de Montaigne) could so ardently believe in the presence of witches and sorcerers and use the most Draconian measures to suppress them. Not satisfied with the prosecution of witches, De Lancre also included in his report extensive sections relating to "Jews, apostates, and atheists." Here the jurist rehashed the old accusations against Jews—accusations long standardized in the medieval polemical literature—under the headings (1) blasphemies; (2) impieties and absurdities; and (3) cruelties. He also claimed that the Jews were "great magicians" and that their Talmud had been composed by two demons. However, he inserted only occasional illustrations, as when he told about the alleged desecration of the host by a young New Christian woman in Saint-Jean-de-Luz. This accusation, reported by the rector of the bishop of Bayonne to the archbishop of Tours on March 22, 1619, resulted in the burning of the accused woman by a lynch mob, without a trial.[7]

Popular hostility toward Jews was indeed kept alive by such folkloristic accusations as were symbolized by the annual processions commemorating the Paris *miracle des billettes* of 1290. The story of that affair was retold with great relish by mid-seventeenth-century poets. In 1652, the assassination of a young Paris merchant, Jean Bourgeois, also created an anti-Jewish furor, although no one submitted any proof that Jews or New Christians had had any part in the murder. Perhaps because some "Portuguese" may have engaged in the traditional "Jewish" trade in old clothes, a company of old clothes dealers *(fripiers)* serving in the Paris city guard appeared suspect to unfriendly observers. It availed them little that under Francis I their Paris guild had been the most vocal advocate of demolition of the so-called *Portes de la Juiverie* as unwelcome reminders of the former Jewish quarter. Together with the interested owners of neighboring buildings the guild had secured from the government the removal of these gates, and even helped to defray the costs of demolition. Nonetheless, in 1652 the company of *fripiers,* returning from guard duty, was derisively greeted by a thirty-two-year-old shopkeeper, Jean Bourgeois, with the provocative exclamation: "Here comes the synagogue!" When the company beat up the impudent assailant, it was fined 60 livres, and one of its members was placed behind bars. This punitive action led to a riot and, ultimately, to Bourgeois' assassination. The murder produced a flood of pamphlets and poems which increasingly accused the Jews and even embroidered the story with ingredients of the ritual murder accusation. One pamphlet, for example, bore the telling title "A True and Lamentable Story of a Paris Burgher Cruelly Martyred by the Jews of the Synagogue, on August 26, 1652." Another told of "The Criminal Judgment Rendered against the Synagogue of the Old Clothes Dealers [*Fripiers*] Declaring That Those of Their Number Who Will Be Found To Be Circumcised (Which Is the Mark of Jewry) Be Thoroughly Chased Out So That the Race Be Eliminated from Paris in the Future." As early as September 1, or six days after the assassination, all Paris parishes submitted a joint *Monitoire . . . contre les Juifs de la Synagogue* for having murdered "a notable burgher of the city," and gave it wide circulation in print. In a poem entitled *The Jewish Furor,* addressed to the "Gentlemen of the Synagogue," one Claude Veiras proposed that

> Men of such evil conduct
> Be removed beyond the walls
> Or else by royal order
> Be made to wear a badge

To be marked as non-Christians
And be placed among the dogs.

Yet it appears that, because of the nation's preoccupation with the sanguinary civil war led by the *Fronde,* the Bourgeois affair subsided. It was more important as a symptom of popular credulity about alleged Jewish machinations than in its direct effects upon the position of the struggling New Christian communities in the country.[8]

Despite such popular antagonisms, the Iberian Marranos were able to maintain their foothold in various French communities, with relative impunity. Henry II's tolerant decree of 1550 was never formally abrogated. It was, in fact, confirmed by Henry III in November 1575. In spite of the intervening wave of intolerance under Louis XIII, it was reconfirmed by Louis XIV in December 1656, by Louis XV in June 1723, and by Louis XVI in June 1776. The long arms of the Spanish and Portuguese Inquisitions occasionally tried to reach out into the neighboring land, but there was considerable resistance on the part of the French authorities to such foreign interventions. The tradition of the Gallican Liberties persistently made itself felt, even in the country's relations with Rome. It came to the fore, for example, in the early years of the regency after the death of Louis XIII, when Queen Mother Anne of Austria and Cardinal Jules Mazarin tried to submit a controversial Jansenist tract (Antoine Arnauld's *De la fréquente communion*) to review by the papal Curia. This sign of spiritual dependence on Rome contributed to the uprising of the *Fronde.* As a result of these French crosscurrents, the Spanish Holy Office was informed in 1633 by a Spanish priest who had infiltrated the Jewish community of Rouen that there were 10–12 Jewish families in Paris, 22–23 in Rouen, about 40 in Bordeaux, more than 60 in Bayonne, 10–12 in Dax, more than 40 in Peyrehorade, more than 80 in La Bastide, and 6–7 in Nantes. These data are unreliable, however. It is very unlikely that the numerical strength of the Jewry of Peyrehorade would have equaled that of Bordeaux, or that the community of little-known La Bastide would have exceeded Bordeaux' by 100 percent. Certainly Bordeaux was then, and remained long thereafter, the main center of Jewish life in France. Yet the Spanish report gives us an inkling of the spread and early progress of the Jewish Resettlement in the realm of Louis XIII, the very king in whose name the French government, during the regency of Marie de Médicis, had tried to eliminate all professing Jews from the country.[9]

Needless to say, episcopal surveillance over heresy, and the residua of the domestic inquisitorial courts, could still occasionally play havoc with the incipient, clandestine Jewish communities. However, their fate was decided largely by actions of the secular bureaucracy and by sporadic judgments by the respective Parlements. While the secular authorities could not disregard religious disparity at a time when denominational conflicts dominated the domestic and foreign policies of the country, they also paid considerable attention to the political and economic issues raised by the presence of these newcomers in the provincial centers. Even the French clergy at times proved more moderate than some economically motivated segments of the lay public. When the leading theologians of the Sorbonne were asked in 1633 by Duke Charles of Nevers whether he might continue to tolerate the small Jewish community of Charleville without violating the provisions of canon law, they answered in the affirmative. In their opinion, the scope of which transcended the local issue, they invoked long-established canonical legislation and such leading teachers of the Church as Augustine, Gregory the Great, and Thomas Aquinas, all of whom, as we recall, had advocated the peaceful coexistence of a Jewish minority with the Catholic majority in the Western world. At the same time, the Paris doctors took into consideration such practical aspects as the serious economic disturbances which would accrue to Charleville's Christian population, if, in the face of imminent expulsion, the Jewish moneylenders were to demand immediate repayment of their loans and, if not satisfied, depart with their pledges. Moreover, the existing wartime conditions would expose both the Jewish exiles and their property, including their pawns, to despoliation by highwaymen. For these reasons, the theologians approved the duke's proposed charter for the Jews, subject only to minor modifications, deemed necessary "lest the Jewish infidels through their rituals, divine services, and commandments cause damage to the spiritual and material welfare of Christians." [10]

Needless to say, the Sorbonne theologians would have viewed with disfavor the profession of Judaism by New Christians; together with the majority of canon jurists, they doubtless would have had to declare it tantamount to apostasy. However, this matter rarely had to be acted on by the authorities, except when the issue was specifically raised by some hostile party. In such cases, too, the ultimate decision lay with the secular administration. As a rule, it was even possible for some secret Jews to proselytize among those of their New Christian compatriots who had preferred to adhere to the Christian faith. In four letters addressed in 1611–12 to the learned Dr. Pedro Rodrigues and his wife, Isabella da Fonseca, who had shortly before left Spain and settled in Saint-Jean-de-Luz, the distinguished Jewish physician Elijah Montalto argued ever more strongly for the superiority of Judaism over Christianity and urged his lackadaisical friends to return to their ancestral faith. "If the Lord has drawn you out of Spain by your hair, it was done so that you might discover the true road to salvation and that you should follow the holy Law which He gave on Mount Sinai." Going beyond this private exchange, Montalto circulated several apologetic tracts in defense of Judaism among groups of New Christians in both France and Italy.[11]

INTERNATIONAL RAMIFICATIONS

From time to time the position of the new French communities was affected by the relations between France and its southern neighbors. As in the days of Francis I, most French rulers and their advisers saw in Spain their country's hereditary enemy. Although the Habsburg regimes after Charles V's abdication were divided between the dynasty's Austrian and Spanish branches, as a rule they actively collaborated on the international scene. France, hemmed in between Spain and the Spanish Netherlands on the one hand, and the Habsburg-dominated Holy Roman Empire on the other hand, understandably considered the preservation of Portugal's independence one of its own major political and strategic concerns. Not only did the French authorities differentiate, therefore, between the country's "Portuguese" and "Spanish" residents, but some far-sighted statesmen undoubtedly also felt that at critical moments the strong anti-Spanish sentiment of the powerful Marrano group in Portugal might prove helpful to French national interests. We may thus understand the venturesome scheme of Duarte de Paz, the envoy of the Portuguese New Christians to Rome, who, through his correspondence with Bishop Jean de Bellay of Paris, tried to secure Francis I's intervention with the pope against the establishment of a Portuguese Holy Office in Lisbon.[12]

Under these circumstances, the incorporation of Portugal and her far-flung colonies into Philip II's empire in 1580 was a serious blow to France's European position. To counteract this tremendous gain in Spanish power, France, as well as England, tried to promote the pretensions of Dom Antonio, prior of Crato, to the Portuguese throne. Many Marranos in both countries sided with the Pretender in the expectation that, as the offspring of a New Christian mother, Violante Gómez, from her morganatic marriage with Infante Louis, and thus as the natural grandson of King Emanuel I, he would alleviate their twilight position in the Portuguese homeland. It therefore appeared to be in the best interest of the French king to assist them in their endeavors to resuscitate the independent Portuguese monarchy. Doubtless in connection with these diplomatic moves, the New Christian Alvaro Mendez (or Mendes), at that time residing in the French capital, became *persona grata* at the court of Henry III. A sensation was created in Parisian diplomatic circles when—to cite the September 19, 1581, dispatch of the English ambassador Sir Henry Cobham to the English Foreign Office—"the King dined with a Portugal Alvare Mendez, accompanied by the Dukes of Lorraine and Guise and the minions." Notwithstanding France's excellent intelligence sources in Constantinople, the king probably was unaware that Mendez secretly professed Judaism and that in 1564 he had obtained a letter of recommendation from Sultan Suleiman I to the Venetian Senate asking the Republic to facilitate the journey of Alvaro's father and family to Turkey. In this letter the family was explicit designated as Jewish. In fact, a few years after his dinner with the French king, Alvaro himself settled in Constantinople, publicly reverted to Judaism, and assumed the Hebrew name Solomon ibn Ya'ish. He became a leader of the Jewish community of the Ottoman Empire, and even continued to develop the Jewish settlement in Tiberias initiated by Don Joseph Nasi.[13]

Alvaro's influence on the French Court was doubtless enhanced by his contact with important personalities at the Porte. Ever since the reign of Francis I, French diplomacy had sought to counterbalance the overwhelming might of the Habsburg dynasty through an alliance with the rapidly expanding Ottoman Empire. As is well known, the ensuing Franco-Turkish treaties granted France the right to "protect" the sizable native Catholic population in the Ottoman provinces, a right which gave rise to the system of "capitulations." Before long, the issue of French "protection" of Ottoman residents became important for Middle-Eastern Jews as well. Competing French merchants, to be sure, particularly some Marseilles traders, later secured royal decrees forbidding the French consuls to issue certificates of residence in the Levant or the Barbary States even to Protestants. Yet some Jews evaded the prohibition by using Catholic figureheads for their business enterprises, which in time became so productive of French commercial profits and consular revenues that in the course of the eighteenth century many French officials blandly disregarded the royal prohibition.[14]

On the other hand, we are told by a nearly contemporary historian, Hardouin [de Beaumont] de Péréfixe, that in 1595, and again in 1608, Henry IV (1589–1610) was asked by some "Portuguese" New Christian leaders to extend a general permission for Marranos to enter the country. Henry, who, largely at the instigation of Queen Elizabeth and her New and Old Christian advisers, had sided with Dom Antonio (whom he styled "a king unjustly despoiled of his crown"), might have been inclined to entertain such a suggestion. Yet he had hesitated to grant a similar request while he had been ruler only of Navarre. As king of France he faced even more formidable opposition from a large segment of the Catholic majority, who doubted the genuineness of his recent conversion to Catholicism. Nor could he completely disregard the anti-Jewish orientation of the Counter Reformation popes, particularly his contemporary Clement VIII. Fearing to add fuel to his enemies' charges of infidelity, he refused the New Christians' request by invoking the Franco-Spanish Treaty of Vervins of May

2, 1598. He only added that "if the *Spaniard* should openly infringe it, he should have just cause to receive them into his Protection." (Rather inaccurately the biographer, a bishop of Rodez, connected that application and Henry's refusal in 1608 with the subsequent expulsion from Spain of the Moriscos, who apparently had not been involved in the French negotiations.) Interveningly, in 1602, Henry IV had even promulgated a decree expelling the Jews from Bayonne, which, however, was immediately nullified by the failure of the Bordeaux Parlement to register it. Henry evidently did not press the point, since soon thereafter he was actually engaged in negotiations with some Spanish New Christians for admission to his possessions. Although he had himself complained of "the intolerable arrogance of the Spaniards which was overtaxing French patience," in 1603 he ignored the protests of the municipal authorities of Nantes and took the city's New Christians under his protection—their number reaching, it was said, 500 persons. As a statesman, who generally pursued—in a determined, if often devious fashion—those religious policies which he considered beneficial to France and its monarchy, Henry may not even have deeply resented the public return to Judaism in Amsterdam of his former playmate Manuel Pimentel.[15]

Similar inconsistencies were to plague French Jews throughout the seventeenth century. The story of Marseilles is particularly illuminating. On the one hand, a general permission was issued in March 1669 for foreigners to settle and trade undisturbed, in that old harbor city. After a twelve-year sojourn, they were to be treated as burghers of the city. As a result, a specific privilege, extended on June 16, 1670, to two Jewish brothers-in-law from Leghorn, Joseph Vaïs Villareal and Abraham Atias, allowed them to trade freely in Marseilles. This edict also clearly stipulated that the two merchants "not be molested under the pretext of ordinances issued against the Jews, from the rigors of which we have expressly exempted them." Vaïs Villareal made excellent use of the new privilege. According to a notarial record, in the following nine years he conducted a vast import and export business with the Middle East and North Africa; the goods transported for him on ships alone were insured for 856,400 livres, at a cost of 53,812 livres in premiums. Yet a general return of Jews to Marseilles and the reestablishment there of a Jewish community aroused such strenuous opposition on the part of the local merchants that, as late as May 2, 1682, the leading French statesman Jean Baptiste Colbert, though personally far from antagonistic to Jews, collaborated with Louis XIV in renewing the old prohibition against Jewish settlement and "obliging the Jews who inhabit Marseilles to leave it immediately." However, this intolerant outburst proved to be of short duration.[16]

In many other ways, too, France's foreign relations influenced the position of the emergent Jewish communities. The Marranos' contention that they were Christian Spaniards, which usually served them as an effective cloak for their unfamiliar customs, often affected them adversely during the recurring Franco-Spanish wars, when their foes spread rumors that they were loyal to the Spanish enemies of France. Partly for that reason, it appears, most Marranos preferred to join the "Portuguese" group, though that identification did not always allay suspicions, particularly when Portugal was part of the Spanish empire in 1580–1640. At the approach of the Spanish armies in 1636, the Bordeaux New Christians were forced by the otherwise friendly city jurats, in cooperation with the governor, to leave their dwellings, located close to the city wall, and to move into the center of town. The officials felt that if the Spanish army were to lay siege to the city the wall should be manned by more reliable residents. All this despite the assurances earlier jurats had given the king in June 1625 concerning "the full loyalty and fidelity" of the "Portuguese" residents. At the same time, an attempt was made by hostile burghers to expel the Jews from Nantes and St.-Esprit (Bayonne), because "of their constant relations with the Spaniards." On some occasions, it was Portuguese, rather than Spanish, citizenship which proved more disadvantageous to its holders. During most of the sixteenth century, the merchants of Rouen and the rest of Normandy were in sharp commercial competition with traders living in Portugal, and both parties often resorted to outright piracy. Mutual hatred became so intense that many people predicted imminent war between the two countries. This outward hostility may have contributed to Marrano "clannishness"—reinforced by the wish of the numerous Portuguese settlers to conceal their Jewish practices from their neighbors. Hence came their concentration in a quarter of their own, a tendency interpreted by some neighbors as manifesting an attitude of superiority. A local poet knew of no better comparison to man's arrogant behavior than to say that "he was 'cocky' like a rooster lording it over his hens,/Or like a Portuguese strutting through the Merchants' Exchange." Consequently, during the sixty-year period of the Spanish-Portuguese union, the Portuguese Marranos wishing to settle in Rouen (the first New Christian recorded in that city was Sebastião Vaez in 1587) were even less welcome than their Spanish confreres. Not surprisingly, twenty-two families soliciting naturalization in Rouen in the twenty-year span of 1581–1601, designated themselves as "Spaniards," although some of them gave Flanders or Brabant as their prior residence.[17]

Nationalistic and religious animosities toward the Jewish settlers in France also affected the outlook of many Frenchmen with respect to their grave domestic struggles. The Protestant faction, in particular, used the old argument, frequently repeated during other sectarian conflicts, that the same Catholics who relentlessly persecuted Protestants, and in France murdered them in the Massacre of St. Bartholomew, nevertheless protected the Jewish enemies of Christianity and its founder. Protestant apologists even more sharply blamed the pope, as well as their own French regime, for tolerating Marrano renegades. One of the pamphleteers of the period not only called Sixtus V "the worst and most corrupt (frelaté) monk ever seen under the sun," but also referred to him as "the old rabbi," "the Spanish rabbi," and "the monk-rabbi"— probably because his moderately pro-Jewish legislation had been widely bruited about. In trying to persuade Henry IV, then still a Huguenot, to join the Catholic faith for the peace of the realm, a patriotic Catholic knew of no more forceful demonstration of the evils of religious fragmentation than to point out that "France is already judaizing and the Spanish Marranos hold fairs and markets there." Some agitators actually linked Jews with Spaniards as the chief enemies of France. According to an entry by a contemporary diarist, Pierre de l'Estoile, on August 17, 1590, the anonymous imprecation *Pereat Societas Judaica, cum gente Ibera* (May Jewish society perish together with the Iberian nation) appeared on a Paris wall. Popular feeling ran so high that even Queen Anne of Austria was suspected of conspiring with Spain, forcing Louis XIII in 1618 to remove all Spaniards from her entourage. Nor were these suspicions completely unfounded, since a Catholic apologist publicly advised his coreligionists that they had rather be Catholic Spaniards than Huguenot Frenchmen. On the other hand, before long, Cardinal Richelieu, a prince of the Roman Church, unhesitatingly intervened on the side of the German Protestants in the Thirty Years' War, while Philip IV of Spain was accused of surreptitiously aiding and abetting the French Huguenots in their struggle against their Catholic monarch.[18]

Not surprisingly, the accumulation of such sociopolitical and religious antagonisms persuaded Louis XIII (1610–43), who, despite his recently declared majority, was still dominated by his mother, Marie de Médicis, and was at that time under strong Spanish influence, to issue on April 25, 1615, lettres patentes ordering a general expulsion of secret Jews from France. This decree reflected, in part, the ultramontanist reaction at Court and among the French upper classes, a reaction which had found expression in the sharp debates at the Estates General of 1614. The royal decree was duly registered by the Paris Parlement; but because of the realization by officials that the Jews were useful to the country, it, too, largely remained a dead letter. Disregard of the royal order was facilitated by the ambiguity of both the lettres patentes and the Parlement's registration. The decree spoke of Jews "who under disguise (déguisez) have for several years past spread out through many localities of this Our Kingdom." Perhaps to interpret this phrase the Parlement ordered, on May 18, 1615, the decree's execution "against both the Jews and those who profess and practice Judaism." Even this sweeping formulation did not necessarily affect foreign Marranos, but may have been directed principally against some Frenchmen who secretly professed Judaism, whether or not they represented surviving vestiges of pre-Expulsion French Jewry. Moreover, the lettres patentes certainly did not intend the elimination of all Iberians of Jewish parentage. The French administration was neither equipped nor at all willing to institute careful investigations about the ancestry of each of these aliens along the lines of the Spanish quest for limpieza. For this reason it was easy enough for New Christians to continue living more or less undisturbed in the several French communities.[19]

With its formula the Parlement of Paris may also have aimed at the occasional Old Christians who converted to Judaism. Of course, according to the old statutes, apostasy was a capital crime. In 1621, one convert, Jean Fontanier, was publicly burned in Paris. A native of Montpellier, he had become a Calvinist, later returned to Catholicism and joined a monastic order, and still later served as an attorney at the royal council. Finally, he adopted Judaism and, through his publication the *Trésor inestimable,* tried to persuade other Christians to join him in his new faith. His ultimate retraction saved neither him nor his book from being burned. In 1632 the same fate struck down one Nicholas Antoine in Geneva, which at that time was under the strong influence of the French Huguenots. Antoine had learned Jewish doctrines from friends in Metz, and had been circumcised. Evidently a psychopath, he subsequently ran through the streets of Geneva, shouting blasphemies against Christianity, and refused to retract when given the opportunity. Many other pro-Jewish sympathizers, however, still looked forward to the Jews' ultimate conversion to Christianity, though interveningly they were prepared to recognize the merits of the Jewish faith, and the Jews' right to profess it. One such spokesman of reconciliation was a wealthy citizen of La Rochelle, long a focus of French religious dissent. In the years 1628–38 Paul Yvon Laleu kept bombarding French and foreign kings and statesmen (including Cardinal Richelieu), as well as rabbis, with tracts claiming that he had been called by God to publicize the great jubilee of Scripture (Lev. 25:8–17) and the restoration of all things to their natural state. He announced that the Jews, under the guidance of the king of France, were destined to play a decisive role in that transformation. Perhaps because he was not taken seriously, and because he envisaged that messianic period to be ushered in through the conversion of the Jews, he escaped the fate of Fontanier and Antoine. A similar formula combining admiration for the Jewish people and an expectation that it would ultimately see the light and join the Christian faith, was employed by an anonymous writer in 1657. Describing the victory of the "Church triumphant," he wrote:

The Jews, who since the death of Jesus Christ have become the plaything and object of contempt of all the peoples, will become the masters; they will resume within the Church the rank which their primogeniture safeguards them, and the seat of Christ's empire will be placed in Jerusalem. . . . The Jews will convert themselves to the Catholic faith . . . they will resume their rights of firstborn.[20]

A more significant case of an attempted Judeo-Christian reconciliation was that of Isaac de la Peyrère. Born a Marrano in 1594, Isaac first joined the Calvinist sect, but later returned to Catholicism. In a remarkable book in two parts, which were entitled *Prae-Adamitae* and *Systema theologicum* and were published together in 1655, De la Peyrère developed a comprehensive theory concerning the existence of man prior to Adam, thereby "proving" that Gentiles were of a different stock than the Jews, Adam's genuine descendants. At the same time, he censured the Christians for their anti-Jewish persecutions, and propagated the Jews' return to the Holy Land under the leadership of a French king, but only after their conversion to Christianity. This idea had dominated his thinking ever since 1643, when he published his earlier pamphlet, *Du rappel des Juifs.* De la Peyrère himself had summarized the first two (of five) sections of this remarkable booklet as follows:

My design is to show in this tract that the Jews will be called upon to accept the Gospel, which will consist of what I call their *Spiritual Recall.* In the same way I prove that the *salvation of the Gentiles* is involved in the Recall of the Jews, and that all men on earth will simultaneously be converted to the Christian faith. . . . Secondly, I show that the Recall of the Jews, which I call Spiritual, will also result in their *Temporal Recall,* that the converted Jews will be recalled from all places in the world and be, in a *temporal* fashion, reestablished in the land which had been promised them, namely the Holy Land, and which is their heritage. I show that this Temporal Recall and Reestablishment of the Jews will be achieved by a *Temporal King* who will induce the Jews to cherish the holy zeal to know Jesus Christ, and to serve Him. I make it clear that this Temporal King will be the *Universal King,* foretold by the holy Prophets, and that all other kings on earth will pay him homage. I also show that this king will be the *king of France.*

The author further saw in the restitution of the Jews to the Holy Land, their conversion, and the establishment of a universal monarchy, the most promising means of reuniting the Catholic and Protestant nations. Although the promised continuation of the

Systema was never to appear, De la Peyrère did not give up the idea of the restoration of the Jewish people to Palestine. In his *Deprecatio,* addressed to Pope Alexander VII in 1658, he not only tried to defend his pre-Adamite theory but also urged the pope to take the lead in bringing Jews back to the Holy Land. We have the 1688 testimony of his friend Richard Simon that, while De la Peyrère lived with the Oratorians in Paris during the last years of his life (he died in 1676), his "concentration in his retreat consisted exclusively in the reading of Scripture in order to fortify certain visions which he had concerning the coming of a new Messiah who would reestablish the Jewish nation in Jerusalem." This testimony is the more remarkable as Simon was opposed to De la Peyrère's pre-Adamite theory. In a letter addressed to Isaac in 1671, he roundly declared that he might accept such a theory only as a piece of fiction, similar to the idea, expressed by two French authors, that "Cardinal de Richelieu, Caesar, and some other great men were not descendants of Adam and, because they did not share in the original sin, they were endowed with a genius superior to that of all other men." [21]

Of course, conversions from Judaism to Christianity were far more common than the reverse. A case recorded in a Parisian parish archive referred to the death in 1652 of one Louis de la Garde, said to have been at one time the rabbi of Turin and the only circumciser in the duchies of Montferrat, Piedmont, and vicinity. At his baptismal ceremony King Louis XIII and Queen Anne had served as godparents, and he continued to receive a royal pension under Louis XIV. Another Jew, Pierre Cassin, whose parents lived as professing Jews in Oran, underwent conversion in 1652 under the sponsorship of the marquis de Bussy, whose domestic staff he joined. Similarly, one Louis de Byzance, a Jew of Constantinople (where he had been known as Raphael Levy), had turned Muslim in order to avoid punishment for impersonating a Turkish officer, and at the age of 30 settled in Paris. In 1674, after careful preparation by the local clergy, he adopted Christianity and ultimately became a monk, his annual stipend of 300 livres being defrayed by a friendly patroness. Evidently such conversions affected only professing Jews, not New Christians, all of whom had presumably been baptized in their youth and, hence, according to canon law, were not allowed to undergo the baptismal ceremony for the second time.[22]

CULTURAL INTERRELATIONS

Messianic speculations of this kind were no innovation in French history. Messianic-chiliastic trends had come to the fore in almost all critical periods of medieval French history, including the reign of Charles VIII (1483–98). Savonarola saw Charles as another Cyrus who would usher in a new era of thorough reform of the Church. Others predicted that, after his conquest of Italy, Charles would liberate Jerusalem from Muslim domination. At the same time, Jews interpreted the contemporary turbulent events in their own messianic terms. The impact of the Renaissance and the Reformation deepened both the popular interest in, and the theological interpretations of, such messianic predictions. Inspired by the mystical writings of Guillaume de Postel, and imbued with the new nationalist fervor emergent from the wars of unification, the French kabbalist Guy le Fèvre de la Boderie preached universal harmony among nations. Yet in his *Galliade* (the title of this counterpart to Pierre de Ronsard's *Franciade* was taken from the Hebrew-Aramaic *gelal*, burden) he also taught, "by quoting Josephus, the Zohar, the Talmud, and pseudo-Berossus, that the king of France, a descendent of Frankus son of Hector and of Gomer son of Japheth, was by right of primogeniture the universal temporal monarch" (E. Dermenghem), while assuming the corresponding obligations. Under the influence of the new Renaissance Hebraism and Protestant biblicism, there was a growing interest in, and indebtedness to, Old Testament patterns, in the thinking of some other intellectual leaders of the sixteenth and seventeenth centuries. We recall that, because the Hebraist Lefèvre d'Étaples issued an early, influential French translation of the Bible, a modern scholar has suggested that France ought to be considered the cradle of the modern Reformation. Even the Catholic controversialists of the time, down to Blaise Pascal (1623–62), had to argue in biblical terms if they wished to controvert their Huguenot opponents. Needless to say, not all the writers who made intensive use of the Old Testament were friendly toward

Jews or Judaism. A fervent apologist like Pascal could cite Old Testament passages, even some rabbinic statements—which he knew from a superficial reading of excerpts, both authentic and doctored, presented by Raymond Martini and his imitators—to justify the traditional Catholic doctrine that the miserable condition of the Jewish people was a "great proof" of the Christian religion.[23]

Yet even cursory attempts to gain acquaintance with sources of the Jewish faith, and concern, however superficial, for the destinies of the Jewish people, were slight openings toward ultimate understanding. One outward effect was that Old Testament phrases now colored the French language even more deeply than in the Middle Ages. Because of the growing influence of the French universities on Western civilization, and the considerable influx of foreigners, particularly to the University of Paris, these new attitudes began to affect other nations, through the students returning to their respective homelands. In all this cultural ferment, the contribution of Italian, German, and Spanish converts from Judaism, especially in their capacity as teachers of Hebrew and the Old Testament, exerted a pervasive influence, which can but partially be reconstructed from the extant documents.[24]

Not even the religious controversialists of the period could entirely escape the impact of these new approaches. Many polemists who had never laid eyes on a professing Jew nevertheless debated the Jewish issue because of the reiterated Protestant complaints that Catholicism had long tolerated the Jewish minority but violently suppressed all religious dissent within the Christian faith itself. Catholic apologists as a rule admitted this fact, but they argued that, in contrast to the French Huguenots, a Jewish minority, like the Christian minority in Turkey, could be tolerated without damage to the country, because it was a subject population with no aspirations to political power. In a crude form Jean Bégat (1523–72), head of the Parlement of Dijon, argued:

While living among Christians, Jews are satisfied to be called and designated as such; they thus do not annoy Christians by their presence and [separate] denomination. They admit that their assembly is a synagogue and do not pretend it to be a church. They have their own sacraments of the Mosaic law, which they do not disguise and to which they do not give the names of our *sacraments.* Hence they can be endured. For they do not undertake anything contrary to us, but live, in our Republic, as do dogs in our houses; they are satisfied with bread crumbs falling under the table, without daring to attack the children, for if they dared to do so, we would chase them out after giving them a good thrashing.

Another controversialist, G. Hervet, went so far as to argue that professing Jews might be allowed to return to France. He contended that the main reason for their original expulsion—namely, their excessive usuries—no longer applied, since historic experience had shown that Christian usurers dealt even more harshly with their debtors. Readmission of Jews would actually help to mitigate that evil.[25]

Political realism of this kind found its most effective spokesman in Jean Bodin (1530–96), a famed polyhistor and the most distinguished French political thinker of the century. Whether or not he believed that he was of Jewish descent—that descent itself is still debatable—Bodin immersed himself in the study of medieval, as well as ancient, Hebrew letters, in which he excelled among his Christian contemporaries. In *The Methodus,* offering the major formulation of his philosophy of history, he exclaimed with abandon: "Moses' authority alone ranks so high with me, that I place him far ahead of all the writings and opinions of all the philosophers." It is small wonder, then, that in his remarkable political and philosophic works—particularly his *Republic* and his *Heptaplomeres*—he was able to discuss Judaism and the Jewish question calmly, as part of his general philosophical and political theories. Even when referring to the medieval expulsions of the Jews from France and Spain, he does so without anti-Jewish malice. Ferdinand the Catholic, he puns, "with pitiless piety *(piété impitoyable)* chased them out of his country and enriched himself with their goods." To be sure, unfriendly Grotius somewhat caustically observed that Bodin "was fairly well informed about the Jews' mores and outlook, though not from the inside through familiarity with the Hebrew language, but rather through the friendships he had cultivated with some very learned Jews." But one wonders where in France Bodin would have had the opportunity to associate with erudite rabbis; we have evidence only for his study under Christian professors of Hebrew in Paris, Jean

Cinqarbres (Quinquarboreus) and Jean Mercier (Mercerus). Yet he obviously was able to read Hebrew texts not available in Latin translation and to use them effectively, particularly in his classic debates in the *Heptaplomeres*. As the title indicates, he presented here seven spokesmen for Catholicism, Lutheranism, Zwinglianism, Judaism, Islam, theism, and nonreligious naturalistic philosophy, in friendly exchanges in the house of a Venetian citizen. He was so impartial in his description that, to Christian scholars able to read the manuscript, he appeared to favor agnosticism, Islam, and especially Judaism, over the Christian faith. This book was so revolutionary in outlook that neither Bodin nor his associates dared to publish it, and no less a thinker than Gottfried Wilhelm Leibniz opined in 1669–71 (he was then only in his early twenties and in a generally anti-French mood) that its publication would be to "the great detriment of the public." (Before his death in 1716, however, Leibniz changed his opinion.) In fact, the book did not see the light of day until 1857, long after the Enlightenment had brought forth its devastating critiques of organized religion, critiques which Vladimir Lenin was to hail as "the most effective vehicle of anti-religious propaganda." [26]

Applying his general theories to contemporary political problems, Bodin was convinced that a country was best off when its citizens professed the same religion. He taught that France should strive to achieve full religious homogeneity. But he realistically admitted that few countries could boast of universal conformity. He was convinced, therefore, that if religious minorities must be tolerated, a Jewish minority had a particular claim to toleration because of its antiquity. It was also least likely to disturb the country's unity, because, unlike Christian sects, it evinced neither expansive political ambitions nor strong proselytizing tendencies. That is why, he contended, many kings found it advantageous to tolerate Jews—a possibility which, he clearly intimated, might seriously be considered by the French regime as well. Like other advocates of religious toleration, Bodin pointed emphatically to the Ottoman example:

The king of the Turks who holds a large section of Europe, observes his religion as strictly as the Prince of the world, but he does not force it upon anyone else. On the contrary, he permits everybody to live according to his conscience and, more remarkably, he keeps, close to his Court in Pera, four diverse faiths: those of the Jews, Roman Christians, Greek Christians, and Muslims. He even sends alms to the Christian fathers or monks of Mt. Athos so that they should pray for him. This had been formerly done by Augustus in favor of Jews to whom he extended the usual support.

Not satisfied with pure theory Bodin, in his capacity as deputy (for the Third Estate) to the Estates General of Blois in 1576, defended the principle of liberty of conscience, and by his successful amendment of "without war" to the resolution demanding state action to establish religious conformity, practically nullified the intended forcible suppression of dissent. It is small wonder that this attitude aroused the ire of more conservative Frenchmen, and before very long his memory was intentionally blackened by the epithet "half-Jew." This term and one closely related ("associate" or *gregalis* of the Jews) were apparently first used in 1679 by Pierre Daniel Huet, the polyhistor and bishop of Avranches. In 1651 Huet had visited Amsterdam and had come there under the influence of Menasseh ben Israel. He later referred to Menasseh as to a former close acquaintance, "had he not been a Jew," and one "who was then considered the most expert among them [the Amsterdam Jews], and one most to be consulted about the entire Judaic lore." Yet Huet became increasingly conservative, and was ready to combat the type of freethinking represented by Bodin. We know that for many centuries the designation "half-Jew" or even "Jew" was hurled at nonconforming Christians indebted to Jewish sources. But some of Huet's contemporaries actually attributed to Bodin full Jewish descent through his mother. Even in a society so little obsessed by "purity of blood" like the French, such attribution often sufficed to replace logical arguments in combating an opposing view. [27]

Less demonstrable is the influence of Jewish thought on the flourishing French belles-lettres of that period. Yet in the great transformation from the medieval Passion plays (the performance of which the Parlement of Paris outlawed for a time in 1549) to the sixteenth- and seventeenth-century drama, primarily inspired by the classical Greek tragedy, the presence of "Jews," whether professing or converted, may well have aroused the playwrights' interest and given them some new insights into the biblical stories. It was at this time that Theodore Beza (de Bèze) wrote his *Abraham sacrifiant,* and the trilogy *David combattant, David triomphant, David fugitif.* True, his case was in so far peculiar as his dramatic works were but a side line of his pastoral and reformatory activities. As a distinguished theologian and Calvin's successor in the Geneva pulpit, he wrote his dramatic works from a specific theological viewpoint. Even the choice of biblical heroes for his plays, as he intimated in a letter to a friend on October 1, 1550, was derived from his personal religious experience. He felt a kinship with Abraham, David, and Moses, in that he had been forced to leave his country and settle elsewhere. He was followed in 1572 by Jean de la Taille, whose *Saül furieux* centered around the humanly, as well as theologically, relevant question of why God raised the first Israelitic king out of obscurity to the pinnacle of fortune and power, only to plunge him back into darkness a few years later. In 1580, Robert Garnier—in whose work "French tragedy reached the greatest height in nobility and dignity of style, as well as in exhibition of dramatic passion, to which it attained before Corneille" (A. W. Ward)—based a drama on the story of Zedekiah, the last king of Judah, and his daughters, whose execution the hero had to watch before being blinded. This tragedy, sometimes styled the *Athalie* of the sixteenth century, directly led to the lofty achievements of seventeenth-century French drama in the *Athalie* and *Esther* by Jean Racine. *Esther,* in particular, had very strong contemporary overtones, such as the insistence that Jews were loyal to their rulers, and an implied plea for religious toleration.[28]

In the same period, the Marrano author João Pinto Delgado, a resident of Rouen, wrote biblical poems in Spanish, retelling the stories of Queen Esther, Ruth, the Exodus, the Lamentations of Jeremiah, and others. The poet himself reminisced in his autobiography that in his youth in Portugal he had lived dangerously, "for my progenitors had already planted in my soul the seeds of the Most Sacred Law." This autobiography itself is, in the words of its editor, I. S. Révah, "an outstanding psychological document, introducing us directly into the tormented conscience of a Marrano, forever divided between his spiritual aspiration, which drives him toward choosing his residence in a place where Judaism is publicly practiced, and his worldly interests, which make him linger in a commercial center, where the exercise of crypto-Judaism is never devoid of danger." Nonetheless, Pinto Delgado's allusive poems appeared in Rouen in 1627, with a dedication to the "most illustrious and revered Cardinal De Richelieu." It is not surprising, however, to see the poet use, in addressing himself to a prince of the Church, especially in his *Lamentaciones del Profeta Jeremías,* biblical phrases in the sense given them in the Vulgate, rather than borrowing from available Jewish, or even his own, renditions. On the other hand, he does not hesitate in other poems to allude to aggadic elaborations, and to insist that "even if rebellious and chastised, Zion remains [God's] chosen and beloved" (Aunque rebelde, escogido,/ Querido, aunque castigado).[29]

Rouen became, in fact, an important center of Marrano literary productivity. In the following years, the Marrano playwright and soldier Antonio Enríquez Gómez (1600–1662) published a number of dramatic poems there. He was a son and grandson of two victims of the Spanish Inquisition, although his mother was an Old Christian. His prolific literary output included poems on such biblical themes as *The Tower of Babel* (1649) and *Samson the Nazarene* (1656). The appearance of his *Política angélica* actually created a diplomatic incident. As in some of his earlier writings, Enríquez Gómez in veiled, but unmistakenly sharp, language attacked the Iberian inquisitorial courts. He wrote not in a spirit of general religious toleration, which he knew had few friends in his native land, but rather as a patriot deploring the enormous damage done to his country by the arbitrary proceedings of the Holy Office. He asserted:

Many confiscations impoverish the royal subjects; when the subjects are poor, the kingdom suffers misery. Numerous acts of degradation, affront, and libels tarnish the honor and lustre of the monarchy, when many of its subjects are singled out for infamy. Large numbers are forced into exile which brings about the depopulation of the realm. The country, once deprived of its population, is lost, while the individuals affected live without a fatherland and are completely ruined.[30]

Fearing the impact of this eloquent "subversive" tract, the Portuguese Holy Office persuaded King John IV to protest to Louis

XIV against this attack on, the king claimed, a major governmental institution in a friendly country. Following a strong démarche by the Portuguese ambassador, the Royal Council in Paris decreed on April 8, 1647, that the book, which was "not only pernicious and setting a bad example," but also printed without royal license, be totally suppressed. Yet Rouen's local administration, both secular and ecclesiastical, seems to have sabotaged that order, which the Parlement of Rouen had failed to register. Remarkably, Jean Louis Faucon, the same first president of the Parlement, to whom the decree was addressed, four months later accepted the author's dedication of that volume. Simultaneously, the friar Guillaume de Varr, lecturer in moral theology at a local convent, gave his *imprimatur* in behalf of the Church. Such disagreements between the central and local authorities were not uncommon in French criminal prosecutions of that time, although usually it was the Paris government which overruled the sentences of provincial courts. We shall presently see that this was the case after the trial of the Rouen Marrano community in 1632–33. Another of Enríquez Gómez' well-known writings, *Il Siglo Pitagórico,* not only appeared in Rouen in two editions in 1647 and 1682, but the first edition was also provided with a beautiful sonnet by his coreligionist Augustin Coronel Chacon, subsequently a royalist agent in London. In short, the religious and intellectual ferment stirred up by the Iberian arrivals seems to have helped fructify the great French literary output of that period. These interrelations merit further investigation.[31]

Rouen Jewry's vicissitudes furnish a telling example of the perils arising from the New Christian life between two civilizations. To begin with, each Marrano community was constantly endangered by the presence in its midst of some genuinely professing Catholics, who were ever ready to denounce their "apostate" compatriots. No less menacing were those judaizing members who, when caught by the Inquisition, did not possess enough fortitude to resist the temptation to try to save their own skins by denouncing their fellow "heretics." A major internal conflict of this kind in Rouen in 1632–33 led to a prolonged trial of many Marranos. It began with a semiprivate controversy between the communal leader, Diego Oliveira, and a newly arrived Spanish priest, Diego Cisneros, but it soon drew ever wider circles. Before long, the leadership of the anti-Marrano group was taken over by Juan Bautista de Villadiego, secretary of the Sevillian Inquisition, who had been dispatched to France by the Spanish Holy Office to ferret out the secret Judaizers in the French communities. After three principals and many followers had languished in prison for a time, the trial ended with the acquittal, by the central government, of all accused (June 14, 1633), but not before the Marrano community had offered 250,000 livres for the establishment of a Catholic seminary for poor children and other works of charity as "testimony of their piety, zeal, and perseverance in the Catholic faith." During that turbulent period, many members departed for safer localities, such as Amsterdam and London.[32]

In their constant state of insecurity, the Marranos welcomed any friendly gesture from native Frenchmen. Among the books seized in Rouen in 1633 was a printed address by the visionary Paul Yvon Laleu, provided with handwritten Hebrew and Portuguese letters. The Marranos must have known that Laleu was an unbalanced person; he was, for instance, so sure of his own physical indestructibility—which he compared to that of Isaac, whom Abraham could not sacrifice—that in letters to the various European potentates he challenged his correspondents to slay him, promising them pardon for the crime. Yet he and his expectation of the great messianic role of the Jewish people during the imminent end of days seem to have been taken quite seriously by the New Christians of Rouen. The Marranos' deep attachment to their ancestral faith and to their fellow-sufferers remaining behind on the Iberian Peninsula also made them easy prey for all sorts of charlatans. According to a widely read picaresque story attributed to Estebanillo González, the subject, a Spanish adventurer, reported with great relish that, on his visit to Rouen (about 1630), he had pretended to be the son of a Portuguese Marrano burned at the stake, some of whose ashes he had succeeded in salvaging and which he allegedly always carried close to his heart. "González" also claimed that, during a terrific storm in the Straits of Gibraltar, he had saved the ship by throwing some of these ashes into the sea. In the end, as the story went, he consented to part with a portion of that precious relic, in return for which the Rouen

Marranos provided him with 25 ducats and a letter of recommendation to their coreligionists in Paris, where he resided in a St.-Germain inn belonging to a Spanish refugee named Granados. Behind this "practical joke" loomed the historical reality of the Marranos' interterritorial solidarity and deep loyalty to the memory of their martyrs—attitudes which in many ways compensated them for the physical and financial losses they incurred at the hand of persecutors and prevaricators.[33]

In one case the French government had to make an exception and admit a group of professing Jews. When Queen Marie de Médicis decided to invite the Jewish physician Elijah (Filotheo Eliau) Montalto from Spain (sometime before 1606), he was still acting as a New Christian. Even in this capacity, however, he was able to participate, at Henry IV's request, in a religious disputation, in which he obliquely defended certain Jewish views against some eminent Paris theologians, just as in Spain he had dared to debate the doctrine of selection of the Jewish people with a leading professor of theology in Salamanca. Leaving Paris for Leghorn and Venice, he publicly reverted to Judaism. There he continued, more freely, to debate religious problems with Christian churchmen; for instance, with a Dominican professor of theology in Padua. He also wrote a distinguished commentary in Portuguese on the long-controversial Chapter 53 of Isaiah. Once again recalled to the court of Marie de Médicis in 1614, he felt more secure; he is said to have made it a condition of his acceptance that he and his entourage—which included Saul Levi Morteira, later *hakham* (rabbi) of Amsterdam—be allowed to hold private Jewish services and not be obligated to work on the Sabbath. This is the more remarkable, as he himself had shortly before written, it appears, a Hebrew responsum defending the right of any aged and physically handicapped physician to be driven on the Sabbath to the homes of his patients by a Christian coachman in a carriage and with horses belonging to non-Jews. This was particularly true, he opined, in a large city like Paris, where doctors had to travel great distances from one patient to another, and where he himself had had to appear before royalty in dignified attire, which he could not do after walking through the usually muddy streets of the French capital. That Montalto was also an excellent physician is evidenced by some of his medical publications, as well as by the confidence placed in him by young Louis XIII, whom he accompanied to Tours. During this journey the doctor died suddenly, on February 17, 1616. This Tours episode highlighted the vagaries of the French legislation concerning Jews. Louis himself had continued to enjoy the ministrations of his Jewish physician for several months after he had enacted his sharply intolerant decree of April 23, 1615, ordering all persons practicing Judaism to leave the country, under the sanction of capital punishment and the confiscation of property.[34]

Among Montalto's Paris patients was Léonora Galigaï, the wife of marshal d'Ancre (formerly Concino Concini), and herself suspected of Jewish ancestry. In her entourage were Manuel Mendés, a New Christian perfumer who had served in this capacity at the court of Philip II's daughter Catalina in Spain and Savoy; his nephew by marriage, Francisco Alvarés, who soon became the queen's physician; and the Aragonese Cesare Augustus Garcia, who prepared amulets for Galigaï. We are told by a baptized Jew, Véronne, that Montalto's influence upon the queen and the maréchale d'Ancre stemmed from his assertion to them that enemies might bewitch them merely by looking at them, unless he were present—obviously, a variant of the widespread folkloristic belief in the power of the "evil eye." Only his premature demise kept Montalto from serious complications during the growing attacks upon D'Ancre and his wife for "the crime of Judaism, demonstrated by their bringing Jews into the country." D'Ancre was assassinated on April 24, 1617, while Léonora Galigaï was prosecuted not only for engaging in sorcery but also for having been instructed by Montalto in the tenets of the Jewish faith. She allegedly had left behind at her home a series of Hebrew books, including a *Maḥzor*, or prayerbook for holidays. She and her husband were also said to have sent envoys to Amsterdam to persuade some Jews there to settle in France. More generally, they were indicted for "crimes of irreligion, infidelity, atheism, Judaism, paganism, apostasy, and heresy." As a result, Galigaï was burned alive on July 9, 1617. Many contemporaries, including Richelieu, realized that her trial and sentence were instigated by enemies who wished to lay hands on her enormous fortune (officially estimated at 15,000,000 livres). One of the noteworthy features of her trial was the prosecution's reliance on the chief accuser, Philippe Dacquin (who later became Louis XIV's physician), though he himself had been a Carpentras Jew, named Mordecai Cresque, and had but recently been converted to Christianity.[35]

Another distinguished Jewish physician, Balthazar Orobio (*ca.* 1620–87), settled in Toulouse, after having escaped the tortures of the Seville Inquisition. Although the "Jews' Street" in that ancient center of Jewish life continued to exist under that name to the seventeenth century, it clearly did not harbor a Jewish community. Hence, Orobio's life there must have been sufficiently insecure, for him to emigrate in 1666 to Amsterdam, where he could profess Judaism without hindrance. We recall that, under his fuller Jewish name of Isaac Balthazar Orobio de Castro, he became, through his literary work, one of the leading Jewish apologists of the century. Had he remained in Toulouse, his life might have ended in tragedy in 1685, when the long-smoldering hostility of the local population toward the few remaining Marranos who had found a haven of refuge there finally erupted in an inquisitorial auto-da-fé. As Counselor D'Aguensseau observed:

If it had been a case of their [the accused persons'] simple profession of Judaism, it appears that all that would have happened would have been a royal order for them to leave the realm. But they had done more, for outwardly they had professed the Christian faith, had gone to church, and profaned the sacraments while participating in their performance. It was principally for that sacrilege that they had been denounced. The Parlement decreed their arrest, and sealed off their warehouses, from which, [however,] they had had enough time to remove the most precious objects. . . . These Portuguese had for a long time been established in Toulouse, and some of them became quite wealthy through their trade. It was this success which had drawn upon them the envy and jealousy of the city's other merchants, who were neither as industrious nor as lucky.

The outcome was that seven individuals were condemned to be burned alive and their ashes were to be strewn to the winds, while their families were deprived of all means of subsistence through the confiscation of their property.[36]

Notwithstanding the unabating Franco-Spanish animosities,

some segments of French society began to be affected by Spain's increasing emphasis on "purity of blood." At times, the popular socioreligious aversion to Jews assumed in France, too, the character of outright racial discrimination. The Provençal branch of the Knights of Malta, for example, decided in 1611 not to admit to membership anyone of Jewish ancestry, no matter how far removed. This exclusion persisted until 1778, when at the request of the Provençal nobility, many members of which lived under a cloud of suspicion, a royal edict put an end to it. The French branch of the Carmelite monastic Order likewise adopted, in 1575, 1620, and 1625, a statutory provision barring Jewish offspring in any degree from admission to membership. This racialist ruling speedily affected the entire Order. One wonders whether its leading Carmelite promoters realized that St. Theresa of Ávila, the Order's great reformer, whom they all deeply venerated, herself bore the "blemish" of Jewish descent. Yet, the chances are that, with their irrational hatred of Jews, they would have no more been deterred from their discriminatory practice than were their Jesuit confreres by the realization that Laynez, Polanco, and other influential cofounders of their Order had had Jewish antecedents. Ironically, it was the Theatine Order, founded by the fervently anti-Jewish Gian Pietro Carafa (Pope Paul IV), which declined to subscribe to such racial differentiation in France; as late as 1700, the Theatines specifically exempted France and Germany from that discriminatory provision. More importantly, unlike their Iberian counterparts, the French officials, and to a lesser extent the French lay public at large, steered clear of such racialist excesses, which some of their intellectual leaders in fact exposed to public contumely.[37]

ECONOMIC ADVANTAGES AND DRAWBACKS

So intense was nevertheless the anti-Marrano sentiment that some foreigners thought it the better part of wisdom to claim Moorish, rather than Jewish, descent. This was the case of Alphonse López, who served Richelieu in both diplomatic missions and various phases of domestic planning. Originally a member of the small group of Iberians around Montalto in the queen's and Galigaï's entourage, López pretended to have been a Spanish Morisco, perhaps because by that time the Moriscos appeared more glamorous to certain Spanish and French romantics. The cardinal-statesman who had associated from time to time with the Galigaï coterie, took a liking to López, who became—to cite the standard biography of the cardinal by Gabriel Hanotaux and the Duke de la Forge—Richelieu's "intimate factotum and indispensable agent." Typical of his manifold services as "supplier, spy, diplomat, broker, intermediary," is his letter of October 15, 1640, from Amsterdam. After reporting that he was sending Richelieu some newly purchased Haarlem linen, López added that he had been unable to acquire any of the numerous beautiful objects available for sale from the estate of the recently deceased Peter Paul Rubens, objects which included "paintings in abundance." He also mentioned that Madame de Chevreuse had offered him a string of pearls, *"but I have no money*. There are beautiful tapestries at a good price, *but I have no money*." In fact, López was so short of funds that, at that particular moment, he was in debt bondage in Amsterdam and could not leave Holland for France as planned. Most noteworthy is the cause of that exigency. According to a treaty concluded on August 22, 1639, between France and the widow of the landgrave of Hesse, the lady was to receive 150,000 livres in specified instalments. López had paid her 50,000 livres from his own funds, but had not been reimbursed by the French Treasury for either that advance or the considerable expenses he had incurred in purchasing vessels and powder from Holland for the French armed forces. In short, he served as "a prisoner for the debts of France!" (Henri Baraude). López' posing as a former Morisco did not deceive the sharp-witted French statesman, however, who liked to call López his "seigneur Hebreo." Neither did this New Christian hesitate to advocate, in a memorandum submitted to the cardinal, the opening of the port of Le Havre to foreign merchants, particularly the "Portuguese"—a term which must have appeared to Richelieu, as to most Frenchmen, to be a euphemism for New Christians. Nonetheless, this suggestion seems to have evoked a responsive echo, since the cardinal always evinced great interest in France's commercial prosperity. In his *Testament* he quoted with approval the popular adage "Just as states often augment their territories through war, they usually become rich through commerce in peacetime." [38]

Economic benefits were, indeed, the decisive reason for the toleration of numerous foreigners in any part of early modern France. This was the period of France's large-scale entry into international trade and its adoption of more advanced, capitalist methods of production. While the Middle Ages had offered many opportunities to the merchants of southern France in the trade with North Africa and the Levant, the discovery of America opened up untold opportunities for enterprising individuals and groups settled along the Atlantic coast. These western traders now vigorously participated in the rapidly expanding international commerce with the American and West-African colonies, especially after France herself began occupying vast areas in the Caribbean and on the North-American continent. Nor were the French navigators any more averse to pirating the Spanish silver fleets than were their counterparts from England or Holland, even in periods when France entertained more or less peaceful exchanges with its Iberian neighbors. Domestically, too, the great Commercial Revolution of the sixteenth and seventeenth centuries undermined the exclusive control over the production and distribution of manufactured goods by guilds of artisans and merchants. It enabled many new entrepreneurs to organize ramified home industries, which rapidly increased the production of staples for the market, through a division of labor among numerous workers, including women.[39]

Vested interests of all kinds, to be sure, often obstructed economic progress. But their spokesmen frequently acted as a house divided against itself. In general, the great landowners, usually in positions of political and economic power, were principally interested in promoting the export of their agricultural produce at the highest possible price, and in the acquisition of industrial goods, domestic or imported, as cheaply as possible. Merchants and craftsmen, on the other hand, pursued diametrically opposite aims: they wished to secure cheap raw materials and foodstuffs, but obtain high prices for their wares.[40]

The new economic situation clearly encouraged the immigration of foreigners, including New Christians from the Iberian

Peninsula. In various ways Spain and Portugal had had a head-start over France in the capitalist evolution, and many New Christians had acquired great wealth, as well as new industrial, commercial, and financial skills on the Iberian Peninsula. Forced out of their countries by the Iberian regimes' inveterate hostility and ever threatened by the Inquisition, they were able to place their capital, skills, and international contacts at the disposal of their new countries of settlement. As foreigners, always living under a cloud of suspicion, they were not likely to give up their productive pursuits, even if they prospered commercially or industrially. In contrast, like numerous Old Christian Spaniards and Italians in a similar position, many successful French traders, especially of the second or third generation, used their accumulated wealth to acquire landed property and thereby secure entry into the ranks of the nobility. (Before long, the fees for a patent of nobility became quite exorbitant.) The result was that many leading businessmen withdrew from the market altogether, just when they were at the apogee of their commercial success, and joined the leisure class of nobles; they then sought advancement chiefly through a military or a bureaucratic career or, wherever possible, through service at the royal court.[41]

In the eighteenth century, a few New Christians and even one professing Jew, Moses Eliezer Liefmann Calmer, are known to have followed that example and acquired landed estates with a barony or other noble rank. But for the preceding two centuries no such cases are recorded. Hence commercial wealth could be maintained for several generations with some continuous benefits for the country at large. Even before the era of so-called Colbertism, mercantilist thinking increasingly influenced the policy of many Paris statesmen and provincial governors, who, for this reason, often protected the newcomers against the assaults of conservative upholders of the old order. In the eastern provinces, moreover, the constant wars in which France was engaged—it has been calculated that in the entire seventeenth century there were only twenty-one years without major international conflicts—placed the need of the military above all others in the minds of the commanding generals and provincial administrators. Here the dictates of military logistics made Jewish entrepreneurship in the supply of foodstuffs, clothing, and arms for the soldiers extremely welcome. It is small wonder, then, that despite the frequent legalistic and theological attacks against their very presence in French cities, some New Christian merchants displayed a pride and self-assurance which made them doubly obnoxious to their enemies. Not without reason did the aforementioned Rouen satirist liken an overbearing person to "a Portuguese strutting through the Merchants' Exchange." [42]

Resentment of this kind led to a variety of complaints, not only about the Jews' purported abuses in commerce and banking but also about their alleged socioreligious transgressions. To mention an earlier example: in a memorandum of 1486, the president of the Chambre des Comptes of the Dauphiny complained that the seven Jewish families still remaining in Montelhemart (Montélimar) and the three families in Saint-Paul were deeply corrupting the morals of Christian women. Repeating horror stories current among the population, this official claimed that when such Christian women became pregnant, their Jewish paramours took them into their houses under the pretext of trying to cure them of some severe illness and gave them beverages and medicine causing the death of both the embryos and the women. In the seventeenth century, however, the royal government was less easily misled. It realized that—to cite Jean Baptiste Colbert's instruction to A. M. Morat, intendant of Aix, of November 20, 1681— "commercial jealousies will always induce merchants to favor the banishment of Jews. But you ought to rise above such agitation by special interests and calmly judge whether the commerce which they [the Jews] conduct through their relations with members of their own sect in all parts of the world is likely to accrue to the state's advantage." [43]

As a matter of fact, the Marrano dispersion spread over a large area of western Europe and the New World, and often acting with a solidarity bred from common perils and frequent familial interrelations, served as both a ferment and a cement within the various native economies, then undergoing speedy transformation. Members of the López (Lópes) family, some of whom remained in Lisbon while others settled in Bordeaux and Toulouse, and still others in Antwerp, London, and other cities, often collaborated, at times functioning as an international business combine which wielded greater power than could its individual members working alone in command of relatively modest resources. The family of Luis Fernandes (1542–1602) is another example of such interterritorial cooperation. Of his four sons, apparently only one shared his residence in Antwerp. Another lived in Rouen, and later in Amsterdam or Rotterdam. A third spent several years in London, while a nephew settled in Brazil. They all maintained commercial relations with other members of the family who had remained behind in Lisbon. The evolution described early in the eighteenth century by an enthusiastic correspondent to the London *Spectator* had, indeed, begun unfolding during the preceding two centuries.

They [the Jews] are . . . so disseminated through all the trading Parts of the World, that they are become the Instruments by which the most distant Nations converse with one another and by which mankind are knit together in a general correspondence; they are like the Pegs and Nails in a great Building which, though they are but little valued in themselves, are absolutely necessary to keep the whole Frame together.

It is not surprising that time and again the French authorities viewed with apprehension the departure of wealthy Marranos. In 1692, for instance, one Philippe Mandez or Mandel, then residing in Rouen, had to ask permission to move to Flanders. In a report to the controller-general in Paris, the intendant of Rouen, De la Berchère, claimed that this "Portuguese Jew" had, since his settlement in Rouen, amassed a fortune of 400,000–500,000 livres, which would be lost to France and accrue to the benefit of its Habsburg enemies if Mandez were allowed to transfer his fortune to Flanders. The intendant argued that Mandez should be made "to give at least some money for the benefit of the king." In 1675, a popular riot in Bordeaux, notwithstanding forceful suppression of the mob by government troops, set in motion the hasty departure of a number of "Portuguese" merchants. Thereupon, in several dispatches to Paris, the city aldermen expressed grave alarm that "all trade might cease." [44]

It was the very success of the Marranos which created much envy and helped to stir up opposition to them. When on February 11, 1656, the Council of State ordered the condemnation to galley slavery of all vagrants, discharged soldiers, beggars, Bohemians, and other undesirables, an official suggested in a memoir to the Council that

the Hebrews and Jews traveling through France or sojourning and trading there, be seized, placed on galleys, and their possessions confiscated, unless they possess passports or permits [for such trade]. It is a scandal to see today the said Jews deal, trade, and visit among the French, most of whom do not know them [as Jews] for they have no distinguishing marks. They eat, trade, and dwell together with the French as if they were Christians. One should also note that in the lands of His Holiness [the Pope] and other places where they are allowed to live, they [Jews] are obliged to wear yellow hats in order that they be recognized for what they are. In France, on the contrary, they come unidentified and thereby enjoy greater freedom in doing business, a matter which His Majesty has never wished to allow or tolerate, since they had long ago been banished from the country.

This memorandum had no more effect than similar, earlier petitions. Even the November 20, 1684, order of the Conseil des Dépêches to deport ninety-three "Portuguese" Jewish families established in Bordeaux, Bayonne, Bidache, Dax, and Peyrehorade, evidently failed of execution. Alas, one cannot say the same about the decrees relating to beggars and other vagrants, whose harsh treatment by the secular authorities was but slightly mitigated by the largely ineffectual private and ecclesiastical charities.[45]

RISE OF PERIPHERAL CENTERS

While all the Jewries mentioned in the 1684 order, as well as those of Nantes and Rouen, lived in the ambiguous state between Judaism and Christianity—an ambiguity largely made possible by the incipient secularization of French life—there gradually emerged professing Jewish communities on the French periphery, and these gave new impetus to Jewish Resettlement in the country as a whole. In part, they owed their existence to developments which had taken place before these localities were incorporated into France. This was particularly the case of Alsace, which became part of France through successive annexations, internationally recognized between 1648 and 1681.

In the south, Nice developed a fairly substantial Jewish settlement under the dukes of Savoy. Apart from the frequent depen-

dence of the whole duchy on the French Crown, there were occasional intervals of direct occupation by French troops (especially
in 1600, 1691–96, 1705–1713, and 1744–48), during which the
French administration was forced, from time to time, to deal
directly with a regular Jewish community. In the French heart-
land, to be sure, the nontoleration of Jews remained the guiding
principle of government policy long after the Peace Treaties of
Westphalia. Paris, in particular, which increasingly became the
throbbing center of French life, demographic, political, economic,
cultural, and religious, adamantly excluded Jews from residence,
except for individuals who received a special license from the
king. As late as 1767 the Paris merchants petitioned the Crown
to expel all Jews by renewing the 1615 ordinance. Nevertheless,
Robert Anchel has convincingly argued as we recall, that descendants of some underground survivors among the pre-Expulsion
Jews continued to live a crypto-Jewish life in the French capital,
and that to a large extent they even dwelled in the same old quarters on the banks of the Seine which their ancestors had occupied
ever since Roman times. Among them were members of noble
families holding high positions in seventeenth-century French
society and government. Richard Simon was not wrong in commenting about his discovery of a theretofore unpublished history
of Paris antiquities by Henri Sauval—which among other matters
discussed the status of Jews and their synagogues in the medieval
French capital—that it "could not be pleasant to some Paris families descended from those Jews." It is possible that such descendants of earlier Jewish settlers were later joined by Jewish arrivals
from Alsace, Bordeaux, the Comtat Venaissin, and foreign lands.
In any event, at the outbreak of the French Revolution, a small
Jewish community managed to live, precariously, in the capital.
Although constituting but a tiny minority (500–800 souls, among
more than a million non-Jews), it managed to have its own synagogue and cemetery. While facing frequent police raids, which
tried to ferret out some illegal Jewish residents, the Jewish settlement included in the course of years a variety of individuals.
Among them were Elijah Montalto and his entourage; the Polish-
Jewish expert Zalkind Hurwitz, who served as cataloguer of Hebrew books and manuscripts at the Bibliothéque Nationale; and
such big businessmen as the New Christian Alvaro Mendez and,

possibly, the financier Samuel Bernard (later named De Bernard, or even Chevalier de Bernard), who in 1697, at the age of forty-six, was called "the greatest banker in Europe." At Bernard's demise, millions of francs were owed him by various debtors, including the royal Treasury, which proved largely uncollectible. (Bernard's Jewish antecedents are very dubious, however.) Yet, on the whole, the appearance of such individuals on the Paris scene was for the most part an exception confirming the general rule that, from the time of the medieval expulsions until the mid-eighteenth century, there was no organized Jewish life there or in the majority of the French provinces.[46]

At the same time, however, a new professing Jewish community was speedily arising in Metz, on the northeastern periphery of France; it was soon to develop into one of the greatest centers of Jewish life in the whole realm. As a result of its successful defense by the French troops under Francis, duke of Guise, against Emperor Charles V's siege in 1552–53, Metz and its bishopric lost their independence. Like the rest of Lorraine, the city was still formally under the suzerainty of the Holy Roman Empire, but thenceforth it was governed, to all intents and purposes by French officials. (French sovereignty was not formally recognized until the Treaties of Westphalia of 1648.) The French civil administration was aided by a permanent French garrison stationed in Metz for the defense of its famous fortress, which until 1870 had never surrendered to a besieging army. Soon after the French occupation, the Jews—who had attained a high material and cultural level in the duchy during the Middle Ages, and as late as 1394 had received many refugees from royal France, but had been forced to leave the city in the fifteenth century—gradually began returning to Metz. In 1565, three Jewish individuals were given permission to settle there, under the condition that they would not engage in moneylending, but "would live and conduct themselves like the other burghers." Although that permit was temporary and, after a few months, the local authorities wanted to deport the Jews, the French military governor, Marshal Charles de Scépaux de Veilleville, kept them on, even removing the restriction on their moneylending, an activity which he found useful to both the French garrison and the civilian population. These conditions were formalized in a decree of 1567, in return for a single payment of 200 écus and an annual tax of 200 francs. Eight years later, to be sure, the Jews had to weather a severe storm when the city council, supported by the deputy governor Jean de Tévalle, ordered them to leave the city within two months, because "of the corruption of morals and the scandal which they have introduced into the said city." But King Henry III apparently overruled his own official. In a letter of August 8, 1575, to the president of the city council, Jacques Viart, the king wrote: "A petition has been submitted to me by six Jewish families who had formerly resided in Metz but have since been expelled. They now request permission to reenter the city and engage there in moneylending as they had done before." Henry asked why they had been expelled. Apparently he was dissatisfied with the reasons given, and renewed the privileges of all the Jewish families then resident in Metz.[47]

On the city's protest, in 1582, about the constant increase of both the Jewish population and Jewish usury, Henry III agreed to a gradual reduction in the number of Jewish settlers. The Jews found a particularly strong protector, however, in the new governor of Metz, Jean Louis de Nogaret de la Valette, duke of Épernon, one of the highest officials in the French administration. For years thereafter, D'Épernon not only disregarded the city council's renewed protest of 1583 against "the Jews, Marranos, unknown people, without law and religion, blasphemers of God and His Son, our Lord," but even issued, on January 20, 1603, a new privilege for the Jewish settlers, who by that time had increased to twenty-four families embracing 120 persons and had organized themselves into a regular community under an elected council of three rabbis and three laymen (1595). D'Épernon's decree was soon reinforced (on March 24, 1603) by Henry IV himself after a visit to the city.

We have been duly informed [the king wrote] during Our sojourn there about the faithful deportment of the Jews living in the said city of Metz with the permission of Our predecessors and that they have diligently engaged themselves during the recent troubles to aid, abet, and assist those who were in charge there and were employed in Our service, both in the garrison and otherwise.

The king emphasized that the Jews had fully lived up to the obligations imposed upon them in the earlier ordinances and had often proved helpful to their Christian compatriots. Taking cognizance of the city's complaint, however, he insisted that these present twenty-four Jewish families were all descended from the original eight, and he provided that in the future, too, the Metz Jews should not add to their numbers except through natural growth or by marriage with foreign residents.[48]

Henry IV's favorable decision of 1603 is the more remarkable as but one year earlier he had tried to eliminate all the Iberian settlers from Bayonne (allegedly numbering 800-1,000 families), and as the struggle of the Metz burghers against the dukes of Lorraine was then drawing to a close. It appears that, seeking to pacify the region, as indeed all of France—the struggle against the Huguenots had been mitigated by the Edict of Nantes in 1598—Henry (in his *lettres patentes* of March 28, 1593; March 14, 1603; and October 18, 1605; supplemented by gubernatorial ordinances) was also trying to establish peace between the Jews and their neighbors. The king's hopes were not to come true, however. The Metz burghers continued to fulminate against the constant increase of the Jewish population, as well as against "excessive" Jewish usuries. An ordinance of 1614, made necessary by the increase of the Jewish families from twenty-four to fifty-eight in ten years (such an increase could not easily be explained by early Jewish marriage alone), provided that a register be kept of all Jews and their children by name and surname. At the same time, by confining the Jews to a separate quarter, in the district of Saint-Ferroy, the buildings of which they were allowed to acquire, the authorities hoped to reduce animosities. Thenceforth, indeed, agitation for the banishment of all Jews died down, although there was still constant haggling about the permissible number of Jews and about legal details relating to their business transactions. A quick succession of additional ordinances, in 1619, 1620, 1624, and 1630, failed to settle the controversy. Meanwhile, despite the warlike disturbances and raging plagues of 1623–1625 and 1629, the Jewish population continued to increase. La Valette d'Épernon's decree of 1624 mentions the presence of ninety-six Jewish families, to whom, among other provisions, he granted the right "to judge, decide, and put an end to all the differences arising among them with respect to their religion and the particular supervision over their civil affairs [shall be exercised] exclusively in such a fashion and by such a person as they have been accustomed to follow since their establishment in this city." Characteristically, Louis XIII (who in 1615, at the beginning of his regime, had issued his intolerant decree for all of France), after a personal visit to Metz in 1632, renewed all Jewish privileges, emphasizing especially the important services rendered by Jews to the French garrison. These services must have loomed very large, indeed, in the eyes of a man who, despite frequent illnesses and attacks of nerves, was "all his life a King on horseback, a King commanding his troops" (Tapié).[49]

During the intervening decades, the Jewish interest rates were sporadically reduced from 21⅔ percent to 16 percent (under certain circumstances they went as low as 12, or even 8½, percent), while the duration of outstanding loans, after which lenders were entitled to dispose of their pledges, was lengthened from a year to fifteen months or more. At one point in 1644, the new governor, Marshal Charles de Schomberg, duc d'Halluin or Halluyn, tried to reduce the Jewish population, which had continued to increase despite the severe plague of 1635–36, to the ninety-six families mentioned in the decrees of 1624 and 1632 (in a total population of less than 20,000, in which the Catholics gradually outnumbered the Protestants by 2:1); but his efforts proved unavailing. The Jewish status was given final approval by the new king of France, Louis XIV, who appeared in Metz after the conquest of Montmédy in 1657, and, accompanied by his brother and a large number of dukes and nobles, paid a visit to the synagogue. He expressed his complete satisfaction with the Jews' services during the Thirty Years' War, and ordered the renewal of all their privileges. To be sure, a number of restrictions on Jewish trade were still upheld by a sentence of the Parlement on January 21, 1658, and by subsequent resolutions. Also, such clerics as Jacques Bénigne Bossuet, the famous Catholic apologist, who in the 1650s served as a canon of Metz Cathedral, continued their unrelenting attacks on the Jews, "the laughingstock of all peoples and the object of their aversion." To be sure, in his more closely reasoned *Discours sur l'histoire universelle,* in which the scholar took precedence over the preacher, Bossuet merely voiced the traditional Catholic hope that the Lord will turn toward them [the Jews], and blot out their sins. He will return to them the understanding of the prophecies which they had lost for a long time; this understanding they will successively hand over from generation to generation for all posterity, without forgetting it to the end of the world. . . . In this way the Jews will some day come back, never to go astray again.

Nor could Bossuet deny that his general political theory was deeply indebted to Old Testament doctrines and practices. This debt came clearly to the fore in his *Politique tirée des propres paroles de l'Écriture Sainte,* on which he worked intermittently from 1677 to its publication in 1709. The large majority of the biblical quotations in that treatise stemmed from the Old, rather than the New, Testament. To be sure, he was selective in his choice of passages, citing only those which supported his moderately absolutist political views. It is not surprising to observe the total absence of quotations from the books of Samuel, which vacillate between pro- and antimonarchical orientations. But Bossuet's indebtedness to ancient Israelitic institutions did not necessarily reflect any friendly attitude toward contemporary Jews. Moreover, the majority of the French public listened attentively to his emotional sermons, while his learned tracts were read by only a small intellectual minority. It was in the spirit of unreasoning hostility common among the people that, on January 17, 1670, a Jewish visitor, Raphael Levy, was burned at the stake in Metz for allegedly having committed a ritual murder of a three-year-old Christian child. Curiously, this trial was not brought to Louis XIV's attention by the Jewish elders in Metz until after the defendant had been executed and they themselves had been fined. When the king reproached them for their delay, which had prevented his saving Levy's life, they offered the rather lame excuse that they had not felt entitled to appeal to the Crown in behalf of a stranger to their community. This affair caused an anonymous Jew-baiter to publish an *Abrégé* of the trial, together with the texts of three decisions of the Parlement. On their part, the Jews of Metz republished Richard Simon's earlier *factum* denying the general belief that Jews commit ritual murders as part of their religious observance, and thus demolished the very basis of the prosecution.[50]

On the other hand, all along the Jews enjoyed the cooperation of the military governors, who were more interested in the state of their fortifications and the well-being of their garrison than in the bickerings among traders. There was one instance, however, in which Jewish needs came into conflict with the desires of the military. In 1619, when the Jewish community received permission to establish a cemetery, the logical location, in the vicinity of the new Jewish quarter, was considered undesirable, not only because there was danger of flooding from the Moselle River, but also because the burial ground was likely to encroach upon the city's fortifications. These difficulties were finally resolved in 1690, when the community, seeking expansion of the cemetery, contributed some 35,000 to 50,000 francs toward the rebuilding of a section of the fortifications and toward the erection of an embankment to hold off the floodwaters. The scene was thus set for the remarkable evolution of the Metz community, which in the following century became one of the major centers of Ashkenazic Jewry in western Europe. It also held sway over a number of smaller Jewish settlements then arising in various parts of Lorraine.[51]

On another periphery of France were the Jewish communities of Avignon and the Comtat Venaissin. Until the French Revolution, these communities basically shared the status of their coreligionists in the Papacy's Italian possessions. The changes in this status brought about by the Renaissance popes and their Counter Reformation successors have been mentioned here in earlier volumes. Not surprisingly, for self-protection, the Avignon Jewish elders kept the papal bulls and briefs addressed to them in a special archive, whose custodians were ordered not to allow the documents to be removed for any cause. Yet, because of the area's proximity to, and the linguistic-cultural kinship with, the increasingly powerful French kingdom, there existed certain noteworthy "French" variants in the Comtadine legislation. Reciprocally, the presence of professing Jewish communities in the vicinity of the medieval Jewish settlements in southern France, and the growing immigration of "Avignonese" Jews into the newly arising Spanish-Portuguese Jewish communities there, lent the history of that segment of Church-controlled Jewry certain peculiar aspects, which must be briefly considered in the present context.[52]

More frequently than in Italy the city councils in the Comtat protested against the rights granted the Jews by the papal administration, and demanded their expulsion. True, when Pius V wished to banish the Jews in 1569, the city of Avignon itself asked for an extension of time so that "they [the Jews] should be able to pay their creditors and collect from their debtors what is due them." Such temporary extensions later became permanent, and, despite its renewal by Clement VIII in 1592, the decree of banishment ultimately fell into oblivion. In 1570 it was the turn of the Church Council of Isle-sur-Sorgue to complain of the continued presence of seven Jewish families in that city, but this complaint seems to have caused no interruption in the Jewish settlement there. Even in Carpentras, where Bishop Christophorus Scottus, recently appointed to the episcopal see, had greeted the papal decree with great elation, it was but slightly implemented. The Jewish population of Carpentras increased from 54 families in 1522 to 74 families in 1563. A list prepared in 1571 still showed the presence of 57 Jewish persons, curiously including two "who called themselves slaves." Although this list is doubtless incomplete, it does reflect a temporary decline of the local Jewry, as does another count made in 1629 (this time undoubtedly as the result of a plague). But the number of Jewish families recovered to 83 in 1669. At the same time, the enforced attendance at missionary sermons was limited in Avignon to one sermon annually, without any sanction for nonappearance. Even this minimum requirement constituted a reversal of the decree of 1532 with respect to the Jewries of the Comtat, of which Article xxi specifically provided that "the said Jews may not be forced to go to church, to attend sermons and ceremonies of Christians, or to listen to preachers in their own homes under penalties and censures." Politically, the Jews still remained *cives* and, despite certain legal ambiguities, owned land and houses throughout the period of papal domination. The relative liberality of the Avignon administration, if not of the local churchmen, was also illustrated when the Jewish linguist Abraham Lunel (Caesar Brancassius), shortly after his conversion to Christianity, was appointed by Gregory XIII to the abbacy of the famous monastery of Saint André de Villeneuve-lez-Avignon (1573). Before long, however, the monks, unwilling to serve under a former Jew, began accusing him of secret adherence to Judaism, and forced him to leave the monastery. He died on a journey to Venice in 1578, allegedly after publicly returning to his former faith. In short, perhaps because of the French civil war between Catholics and Huguenots, the Jewries of Avignon and the Comtat were able to pursue their historic careers with less violent interruptions than their Jewish compatriots in the Italian provinces outside Rome and Ancona.[53]

Evidently, the numerical decline of the Jewries of Carpentras and other cities in the Comtat was not owing to any serious decline in the birth rate or increase in mortality, but rather to a moderate rate of emigration. Despite enormous legal difficulties, most émigrés probably found their way into France. Unlike the Iberian New Christians, who formally entered the country as Christians, and unlike their coreligionists of Alsace, who became part of the French population when their home communities were incorporated into France, the Comtadine Jews had to find loopholes in the existing legislation in order to enter France. One of the simplest methods of evasion consisted in their visiting southern French fairs. Even burghers, who were generally reluctant to accept newcomers seen as potential competitors, often welcomed the arrival of strangers at fairs, where they either purchased local or regional products or else offered for sale to merchants (rather than to the general public) goods which were locally in short supply. The Jews of the Comtat had long attended fairs in their own country, especially in Carpentras. Once in France, many of them found ways of staying on after the fairs were over and even trading at retail in "forbidden" goods. So long as they were few in number, they did not arouse much antagonism. But when their immigration increased significantly, they became a problem, not only to the municipal administrations but also to the local Jewish communities. What a Bordeaux intendant reported to the Paris government in 1722 had undoubtedly also been true in the preceding century. He claimed that the twenty-two *Avignonnais* families then living in Bordeaux were "almost all so poor and miserable that I would assume that they are absolutely unable to pay anything in order to obtain permission to remain in this city." Because these new arrivals often became public charges dependent on the Jewish communal chest, they were disliked by their Sephardic coreligionists, although we do hear of some wealthy Iberian settlers who charitably supported their impecunious brethren. More significantly, most "Portuguese" viewed with distaste the "backwardness" of Avignonese manners and ways of life, and sometimes saw in the presence of these "uncouth" aliens a danger to their own tenuous position. This was particularly true since they themselves had secured accommodation with the local burghers by refraining from retail trade and concentrating on larger-scale financial and commercial transactions and industrial production, both domestically and internationally, which accrued to the benefit of the Christian businessmen as well. Nevertheless, in the seventeenth century external antagonism and internal strife did not yet lead to outright decrees of expulsion of the Avignonese settlers, such as were enacted, however ineffectively, in the following decades.[54]

Remarkably, we hear nothing about practicing physicians among the Avignonese Jews in France, although for centuries many Jewish doctors had exercised that profession in the Comtat, in the face of repeated papal decrees forbidding Christian patients to ask for their assistance. This failure to share in that financially and socially rewarding occupation may not have been owing exclusively to the greater difficulty for physicians to scale the existing barriers to immigration, but there may have been greater resistance to their admission on the part of the French doctors. Moreover, the Medical Faculty of Avignon had fallen into bad repute in the sixteenth century because of its utter laxity in granting medical diplomas. One candidate received his doctorate after attending the University for only twelve days (March 6–17, 1532). François Rabelais first obtained a medical license in Avignon on April 3, 1537, and seven weeks later was granted the doctorate. However, Avignon was not the worst offender. In Valence and Orange, the authorities actually sold diplomas to any bidder after a stay of twenty-four hours.[55]

A curious, if short-lived, development took place in Charleville, now in the department of Ardennes. As a result of the existing inheritance laws, the region had come under the domination of Charles, son of Duke Ludovico Gonzaga of Mantua. Charles, bearing the title of duke of Nevers, was later also to serve as duke of Mantua, where he ultimately resided. Like other members of his family, he was interested in founding new cities. In 1606, he established the city of Charleville, and in 1609, wishing to attract new settlers, he invited twenty-four German Jewish families to his new township. Dwelling there on the basis of a typical Italian *condotta,* these Jews erected a number of houses and a synagogue, and lived peacefully with their neighbors. In 1633, however, for no avowed reason, the duke felt sudden compunctions over the toleration of professing Jews in his French possessions. Perhaps the intensification of the religious struggles and the ever more active French participation in the Thirty Years' War, as well as the Mantuan disturbances of 1630–31, raised doubts in his mind on this score. As we recall, Charles approached the leading theologians of the Sorbonne with an inquiry describing the situation in detail and asking for their opinion. He pointed to the toleration of Jews in other parts of Europe (alluding also to French-controlled Metz), and argued that such toleration benefited the Christian faith, since every year some Jews turned Christians, while no Christians adopted the Jewish faith. He also claimed that the withdrawal of toleration at that juncture would endanger Jewish lives, because the War made it impossible for the Charleville residents to return to their original German localities. After an extensive argument, the theologians decided in favor of his continued toleration of Jews, but suggested some modifications of the existing agreement. For example, the reading of Hebrew books was to be restricted to works authorized in Rome and other Italian cities. The Paris doctors also suggested limitation of interest rates and of the Jews' rights to employ Christian servants. Their opinion seems to have sufficiently eased the duke's conscience for the Charleville community to continue its relatively peaceful existence. In 1649–51, even some Amsterdam Jews were planning to settle there. In 1656, Charles II, a grandson of the city's founder, made a new agreement with a Jew named Marco, who obligated himself to attract further Jewish settlers to the city. In this new *condotta,* Jews were expressly allowed to erect a synagogue, establish a cemetery, and repair exclusively to their own judges. They were also allowed to acquire houses and were freed from the billeting of soldiers. But the interest rate was now limited to 12 percent on loans to local residents and 15 percent on those to residents of neighboring Rethel, though there were no legal restrictions on loans to strangers.[56]

However, the Charleville experiment did not confer any lasting benefits upon the Jews, and before long most Jewish residents departed for localities offering them greater economic opportunities. Nonetheless, it helped salvage a number of Jewish families from the German turmoil during the Thirty Years' War. It also set a precedent for toleration of Jews on French soil with both official and theological approval, though not quite with that of the French Crown as such. The impetus it gave to the Sorbonne to go on record in favor of toleration was of equally great significance. During that period of protracted controversies between the Gallican and ultramontanist groups within the Catholic Church, the voice of the Sorbonne was frequently heard; it exerted considerable influence on the dominant groups. We may thus understand the readiness of the French administration, and particularly of Louis XIII and Louis XIV, to extend full protection to the professing Jews of Metz, while pretending that all Marranos living elsewhere in France were real Christians. That fiction could not be permanently upheld; it was to cause many difficulties to both the Jews and the administration in the subsequent decades. But for a time it allowed for the development of several Jewish communities without any hostile interference by state organs.[57]

FRANCE OVERSEAS

Among France's outlying districts were the French colonies in Africa and America. France was relatively late in joining the major colonial powers of Spain, Portugal, Holland, and England, especially as far as Jews were concerned. In the sixteenth century, one can refer only to a few Portuguese New Christians who participated in the early French voyages of exploration—for example, Lopez de Castro of Lyons. Lopez, who had a brother still living in Lisbon, took part in Montluc's 1566 expedition to West Africa, an expedition which failed to reach the Niger River, because of the death of its leader. Only in the seventeenth century did some French Caribbean islands show promising beginnings of Jewish settlement, although many Jewish arrivals, like their Christian counterparts, were but visitors or temporary sojourners. Most of them doubtless claimed to be Dutch, rather than French subjects. Even the French colonists for a long time patronized the Dutch traders (including Jews), who offered them a more dependable assortment of goods at somewhat lower prices than did their own compatriots from the mother country. We have the testimony of Father Jean Baptiste du Tertre, who had spent several years in the Lesser Antilles, that "the Dutch can give better bargains than our Frenchmen, even when offering merchandise they have purchased in France . . . ; they never failed us and always furnished the islands abundantly with everything needed by the inhabitants." Partly for this reason, metropolitan France did not establish a full-fledged West India Company (after abortive experiments in 1626 and 1635) until 1664. In that year, we recall, the French clashed with the Dutch in Cayenne, severely affecting the Jewish settlers there. For the most part, however, the Dutch West India Company was more interested in trade and profits than in political control; and, especially after 1650, the struggle for supremacy in North America was mainly between the English and the French, with Holland and the Iberian powers trying to hold on to their possessions, rather than expand them.[58]

In Martinique, acquired by the French *Compagnie des Îles d'Amérique* in 1635, the French colonizers at first welcomed the cooperation of a Dutch Jewish group of merchants and plantation owners. The number of Jewish settlers rapidly increased after the arrival, in 1654, of refugees from Brazil, variously estimated as ranging from 7 or 8 families to 400 persons. If the latter figure were correct, they would have formed an improbably large segment of the white population of about 5,000, in addition to the vanishing native tribe of Caribs. Their presence made itself sufficiently felt for the Conseil Souverain de la Martinique to forbid them all commercial activities (February 4, 1658), and for public opinion to force abrogation of that decree within six months (August 2). The Company, as well as the government in the mother country, often favored the immigration of Jewish colonists, because of the commercial advantages they offered to both the local population and the developing French Empire. Jean Baptiste Colbert was particularly outspoken on this score. He persuaded Louis XIV to write to the governor of the French colonies in America (on May 23, 1671):

Having heard that Jews settled in Martinique and other islands inhabited by My subjects had incurred considerable expense in cultivating the land, and that they continue to fortify their dwellings so that the public will reap the benefits thereof, I wish to inform you through this letter that it is My intention that you should exert all efforts that they enjoy the same privileges as all other inhabitants of the said islands. You should also grant them full liberty of conscience.

But the king added a restrictive clause, "You will take the necessary precautions that the exercise of their religion should not cause any scandal to Catholics." Thus the Jewish population gradually grew to 21 families (81 persons) in 1680 and to 23 families (92 persons) in 1683. However, the local governors of the family of Dyel Duparquet, who had acquired the island in 1637 (it did not wholly revert to the French Crown until 1674), often sided with the Jesuit and other opponents of Jewish settlement. For a time the anti-Jewish faction was satisfied with curtailing the Jews' trading opportunities, particularly by prohibiting all sales on Sundays and Christian holidays. But after several broader enactments and their revocation, the *Code Noir,* issued in 1685 primarily to regulate the position of the Negro slaves imported onto the island, provided for the expulsion of Jews.[59]

That this part of the ordinance, warmly supported by a large segment of the local white population, did not remain a dead letter, as did similar enactments in many other localities, was demonstrated in 1694, when six Jewish families arriving in Martinique were immediately deported. Since 1685, moreover, Protestants, too, had been barred from the French colonies, even before they were expelled from metropolitan France by the revocation of the Edict of Nantes on October 18 of that year. The "Black Code" was reissued from time to time; for instance, its renewal in March 1724 provided, in Article i, that the authorities "shall banish from the said country all Jews who have established a residence there or may wish to do so." This despite the fact that in those very years a Jewish family, the Gradis of Bordeaux, founded a sort of vertical combine which controlled much of the sugar production and trade in Europe. Members of the family arranged for the cultivation of sugar cane on American plantations, processed it into sugar in their own refineries, and through an effective sales organization reached the final consumers in many lands.[60]

SLOW RETURN TO ENGLAND

Less disparate than conditions in France, though no less ambiguous, was the situation across the English Channel. Practically all our information concerning Jews and New Christians in early modern England before Oliver Cromwell is limited to the community of London and, to a much lesser extent, to those of Bristol, Dover, and York. Of course, Judaism as a religion remained outlawed. Despite the progress of the English Reformation, the antiheretical statutes originally enacted by Richard II in 1381, Henry IV in 1400, and Henry V in 1414 were renewed in 1554 by Parliament under Philip and Mary, "for the xchuing and avoiding of Errours and Heresies whiche of late have rysen, growen, and much encreased within this Realme." These statutes were to be "revived, and be in full force, strengthe and effecte . . . for ever." Clearly, they were not aimed at New Christians, who outwardly appeared to be Spanish or Portuguese Catholics. For a while there even was a church of Spanish Calvinists in London. Founded in 1559 by Cassiodoro de Reina, this congregation enjoyed all the liberties granted by law to foreigners. In 1565, to be sure, De Reina was forced to leave England and the congregation had to be dissolved, but this action did not prevent the constant increase of the New Christian settlement, most members of which at least outwardly professed Catholicism, although some may have been Protestant sympathizers. We may dismiss as obvious exaggeration a seventeenth-century writer's statement, "Store of Jewes we have in England; a few in Court, many i'th Citty, more in the Countrey," and yet concede that a fairly substantial group of Marranos had found its way into Elizabethan England. Some of them achieved considerable success in business, the medical profession, even diplomacy. Lucian Wolf was, indeed, able to identify no less than "eighty or ninety [Marrano] souls living in the England of Queen Bess." [61]

Undoubtedly, it was possible for a number of other overtly or clandestinely professing Jews to escape notice completely; still others may not have been recorded in documents available today. Much of our information is derived from testimonies collected by the Spanish or Portuguese Inquisition, documents which, as is well known, have not yet been fully explored. At his trial in 1556 before the Portuguese Holy Office, Thomas Fernandes of Évora testified against several Marranos in Bristol and London whom he had met during his stay in England. Among them were Fernandes' uncle and aunt, the physician Henrique Nuñes and his wife Beatriz Fernandes. This lady was able effectively to propagate Judaism without ever being denounced to the English authorities. According to her nephew's testimony, she taught many members of the Bristol Marrano community to recite Jewish prayers from memory. Nor did she apparently have any difficulty in securing only ritualistically permitted food and in baking unleavened bread for the Passover holidays. In all these endeavors, the Nuñes family and other secret Jews were greatly inspired by Samuel Usque's *Consolaçam as tribulaçoens de Ysrael* (Consolation for the Tribulations of Israel), which found its way to England within a short time after its 1553 publication in Ferrara. Fernandes testified that that

book was read by confessant once, and he accepted it all and was confirmed in his errors by the teaching of the said book and by what his uncle and aunt told him. And they also read the book, and confessant on going to London returned the said book to Simão Ruiz who had sent it and confessant supposes that he has it still; and it was written in Portuguese, and it was a quarto.

So impressed were some of Usque's Marrano readers in England that, according to Fernandes, one young man decided to copy the entire voluminous *Consolaçam* for his and his friends' private benefit.[62]

During the brief interval of Catholic reaction under Mary Stuart (1553–58), the Bristol community was dispersed, Henrique Nuñes and his wife escaping to France. But the London community weathered the storm and, as we recall, considerably increased in number during the Elizabethan regime. In 1581, it was even possible for a Bohemian Jewish mining engineer, Joachim Ganz or Gaunse, to settle in England and to introduce improvements in copper mining in Cumberland and Wales. Ganz was evidently able to practice his religion freely for seventeen years, until his arrest in Bristol in 1598 because of his excessive frankness in a casual religious disputation. He explained to the judges that, never having been baptized, he was not obliged to believe "any article of our Christian faithe" and apparently was allowed to vanish from sight. Another contemporary, Nathaniel Judah Menda, of unknown origin, lived for some six years as a Jew; in 1577 he was baptized with great solemnity to the accompaniment of a sermon preached by John Foxe. This sermon was immediately published, with the author's dedication to Sir Francis Walsingham, Elisabeth's distinguished secretary of state. Nor were any objections raised, it appears, to the Jewish religious services held, in 1592, at the London residence of Salomon Cormano, Alvaro Mendez' diplomatic representative. Similarly, no court action for heresy ensued when an unrelated civil lawsuit of 1596 revealed that such services had also been held in the private residence of Ferdinand Alvares in London. Although Thomas Wilson, the young servant of the Jewish defendant, described in his testimony the curious Passover services at his employer's home, the Court of Chancery tried to be scrupulously fair toward Alvares. The plaintiff, the widow of Richard May, one of Alvares' several partners, rightfully claimed that the heavy losses incurred by the defendant and his other Jewish partners—one of them, Bernard Leavis, had dared to visit Madrid and had got out of the clutches of the Inquisition only after paying a large sum—as a result of troubles they had had with the Lisbon Inquisition after their ship's arrival in the Portuguese capital, were not legitimate business expenses. Yet, the court "beinge moved with the losses and trobles which the poore Straungers indured persuaded Mrs. May beinge present to deale charitably with Alvares in regarde thereof." Ultimately the suit was settled out of court.[63]

Needless to say, not all the Iberian New Christians in England were secret Jews. As in France and the Netherlands, there were many Catholics, both native and foreign-born, with whom New Christians wishing to adhere to their Catholic faith could readily mingle. There was a difference, however. In England even the native Catholics were an increasingly persecuted minority, whose loyalty to the queen and country were suspect. Did not an English general, Sir William Stanley, after turning Catholic in 1587, betray his queen and surrender the strategic Anglo-Dutch position at Deventer? Together with two-thirds of his troops Stanley went over to the Spanish enemy of both England and Holland. Under the circumstances, many New Christians must have considered it to their advantage to leave the Catholic camp; doubly so, since the Catholics there, rather than closing ranks with other dissident groups, evinced all signs of religious intolerance toward both Jews and Protestants. Rare, indeed, were the Catholics like Robert Parsons (or Persons), who spoke up against the use of force in imposing Catholic conformity. In his defense, in 1580, of the Catholics' refusal to attend Protestant church services, Parsons added the sweeping statement:

Surely, as I am now minded I wold not for ten thowsand worldes, compell a Jewe to sweare that theire weare a blessed Trinity. For albeit the thing be neuer so trew, yet should he be damned for swearinge against his conscience, and I, for compelling him to commit so heynous and greeuous a sinne.

But far more typical of both popular and ecclesiastical opinion was the doctrine summarized in Lawrence Vaux' *Catechism* of 1583, according to which Catholics were to abhor all "who be alienated and utterly separated from the Church of Christ: the Jews and all Infidels, and they that by apostasy forsake their faith. And heretics which, although they be christened, yet obstinately defend error against the Catholic faith." As aliens suspected by Catholics of being heretics and by Protestants of being subversive, many New Christians had every incentive to adhere to their ancestral faith.[64]

International developments likewise had an impact on the status of English Marranos. At first the Elizabethan statesmen viewed with favor the arrival in England of the Portuguese Pretender Dom Antonio, prior of Crato, who, we remember, had left Portugal after his defeat by Philip II in 1580. Hailed by Portuguese Marranos on his arrival in France in that year, he was received with even greater acclaim in England, where the government tried to make use of him in its conflict with Spain in the perilous years before the Spanish Armada. Dr. Rodrigo (Ruy) Lopez (1525–94),

Elizabeth's private physician—who, through his brother's marriage to Alvaro Mendez' sister, was distantly related to Dom Antonio's mother—became the Pretender's host and constant companion in London. It was at Lopez' home that the prior of Crato entertained Queen Elizabeth. Lopez' father-in-law, Dunstan Ames (or Añes), acted as Dom Antonio's chief financial adviser, while two of Ames' sons, William and Jacob, served both England and the prior as intelligence agents in Lisbon and the Azores before Drake's attacks on these islands. However, after the failure of Drake's expedition to Portugal (a venture originally sponsored by Lopez and Ames in 1589) and of the plan, conceived by Lopez in conjunction with Drake and the prince of Béarn in 1591 to capture Brazil in behalf of Dom Antonio, the New Christian leaders quarreled with the Pretender. They thereby antagonized the Essex party, which continued to preach unremitting war against Spain. This shift helped bring about Lopez' downfall and execution at Tyburn on June 7, 1594. Though clearly innocent of the charge that he had conspired to poison Queen Elizabeth, he was definitely involved in some unauthorized negotiations with Spain, which were aimed at securing peace between the two countries, as well as some personal financial gain. This intrigue may have been but a preparatory move toward his projected emigration to Constantinople, where he would have been able to join Don Alvaro as a professing Jew. A belated attempt by Judah Serfatim, Alvaro Mendez' envoy, to obtain postponement of the execution, failed. Writing in French to Lord Burghley on February 7, 1594, Serfatim did not mention Lopez' family relationship with Mendez, but only his being "of the same blood" as his master. Stressing Mendez' long-time devotion to England and its queen, the Jewish envoy asked for postponement of the final act "until my lord [monseigneur] will have the time to communicate in this matter with Her Majesty and Your Excellency, from which fact, one may rest assured, Her Majesty and Your Excellency will derive much satisfaction, as time will show." But Elizabeth, though far from convinced of Lopez' guilt, had to yield to popular clamor and pressure from the Essex party and allow the execution. The large crowd witnessing it jeered at the hapless victim and ridiculed his professions of innocence and love for Christianity by shouting "He is a Jew!" [65]

More circumspect had been similar endeavors several years earlier by another leading New Christian in London, Dr. Hector Nuñes. Combining medical practice with extensive business dealings, Nuñes' services were so highly valued by the Privy Council that once when he found himself in financial difficulties, the Council intervened with his creditors to allow him more time. On several occasions from 1571 to 1574 he was permitted by the Privy Council to carry on his Spanish trade without incurring the penalties provided by a royal ordinance against such traffic. The Council also acted favorably on his claims for compensation for losses he had suffered from the Spanish seizure of his goods. In connection with one such case, Nuñes was described as "a Portugall Doctor of Physicke, having dwelt in England by the space of XXV years" (March 26, 1573). As a result of a lawsuit against the earl of Desmond, he received a grant of land from the earl's possessions in Ireland. Because of his good connections with the English authorities he felt free, in 1585–86, in cooperation with Antonio de Castilio, a former Portuguese ambassador to England, to try to bring about peace between England and Spain. But he worked aboveboard, informally transmitting the British government's proposals to Madrid and receiving replies in return. Such informal exchanges seemed far less binding to the respective parties; they often produced much better results than formal negotiations by ambassadors. Yet the conditions which Sir Francis Walsingham handed to Nuñes in August or September 1585 proved much too harsh for Spain to accept. They included not only the cessation of all hostile actions against the person of Queen Elizabeth, such as had been constantly plotted by the pro-Catholic faction in England with the support of Spanish diplomats, but also demanded greater freedom of religion for the Spanish Netherlands, a demand which Spain was unwilling to grant. Upon the renewal of hostilities, on the other hand, Nuñes was in a position to learn, through his Spanish contacts, about Philip II's preparations for a naval attack on England. He is said to have been the first to warn the English government, so that "it began to take precautions with greater care and earnestness." [66]

Although not an English resident, Alvaro Mendez, whether in Paris or in Istanbul, always sided with England against Spain.

We recall that, like his brother-in-law Rodrigo Lopez in England, Mendez immediately embraced Dom Antonio's cause and effectively espoused it in Paris. The Spanish agent in the French capital, Juan Bautista de Tassis (Taxis), definitely misjudged his discreet activities in behalf of the Pretender, when he advised the Spanish government, on July 8, 1581, that "as a more prudent man, he [Mendez] wishes to sail with the wind." Tassis also suggested that in order for Philip II "to get hold of him the purse is more necessary than words." We do not know whether the agent was authorized to offer a douceur to Mendez, but if he tried, he must have failed miserably. A few years later (on May 23, 1587), Bernardino de Mendoza, the astute Spanish ambassador in Paris, more accurately reported to Philip II:

I have a letter in my hands from Alvaro Mendez who went as a Jew to Constantinople and writes to Don Antonio, signing the letter Solomon. He also writes to the English ambassador and some heretic acquaintances here [Paris] attached to his mistress, saying that your Majesty's truce with the Turk would have been concluded but for him. Your Majesty, he says, demanded the inclusion therein of the Pope, the duke of Florence, and other princes of Italy, and he used influence with Luch Ali to demand, on the part of the Turk, that the queen of England also should be included. Juan Stephano objected to this on the ground that she was at open war with your Majesty, but he, Mendez, had great hopes of being able to induce Luch Ali not to conclude the agreement without her inclusion. He is on very bad terms with the French ambassador (in Turkey) who treats him with contempt, as he knew him here as a professed Christian, whereas now he is a Jew. . . .

Mendez was also the first to announce in Constantinople, early in October 1588, the English victory over Spain's "Invincible Armada," at a time when the Ragusan envoy denied it and when even the English agent and the Turkish Foreign Office seem not yet to have heard about it.[67]

In the following years, Solomon ibn Ya'ish, as he was known in Istanbul, successively sent Salomon Cormano and Judah Serfatim, as messengers to London and even to Madrid to continue various negotiations. Serfatim, especially, while in Spain was described by the Venetian ambassador, Augustino Nani (in his report to the doge and the Senate of March 22, 1596), as "very shrewd; [he] speaks several languages fluently, so no wonder he chatters. He says he has traveled much and has been in England where he has had dealing with Don Antonio of Portugal and with Antonio Perez." Pérez, as we recall, had long been chief adviser of Philip II but, facing prosecution by the Inquisition as a Judaizer, had to leave Spain. Yet he was able to continue his diplomatic parleys in both Paris and London for many years. One of Serfatim's assignments was to arrange for an exchange of prisoners of war between Spain and the Ottoman Empire, a task in which he acquitted himself successfully. While in Madrid in 1596, he also seems to have tried to mitigate the impending expulsion of the Jews from Spanish-controlled Milan, but it was fully carried out in the following year. This despite Mendez' earlier endeavors, known to the English and undoubtedly also to the Spanish intelligence, to deflect the Ottoman armies from their attack on Hungary to an assault on the Spanish possessions, especially Naples. He did not conceal that his various anti-Spanish activities were motivated largely by Spain's persecution of his coreligionists. According to a report submitted by William Waad, clerk of the Privy Council, to Lord William Cecil Burghley on March 19, 1593 [1594], about his dealings with Serfatim, Don Solomon [ibn Ya'ish], "the greate Jew that is at Constantinople," did not mind to admit "the Care he hath, being a Jewe, of his Brethren and Kynsffolkes, whereof he saieth there are more in Germanie [Turkey?] and those ptes. then in Christendome, and he sheweth the reason of Salamon's hate to the K. of Spaine because he dothe burne and prosecute the Jewes." These endeavors failed, and in 1596 Mendez, with the approval of the grand vizier, sent Serfatim to the West "to arrange a universal peace with the House of Austria," evidently referring to both the Spanish and the Austrian branch of the Habsburg dynasty. Soon thereafter, however, Mendez' prestige, for reasons to be discussed in a later context, waned both in Istanbul and in London. With his passing, a few years later, and the impact of the Lopez affair on English society, the influence of Jewish diplomats on England's foreign affairs rapidly declined.[68]

ANTI-JEWISH REACTION

Growing tension in the 1580s, when, for the first time in centuries, the country was threatened by foreign invasion, with the approach of the Spanish "Invincible Armada," caused public opinion to veer sharply against the Jews. Jew-baiting was intensified in the 1590s by the Lopez trial, which fostered the generalization that all Jews were evil. Among the plays containing distinct hints relating to this Elizabethan physician-businessman-diplomat were Christopher Marlowe's *Doctor Faustus*, Thomas Middleton's *Game at Chesse*, Thomas Dekker's *The Whores of Babylon*, and Giles Fletcher's *Women Pleased*. Nor was the anti-Jewish tradition of Passion plays such as the *Croxton Play of the Sacrament* allowed to sink into oblivion, despite the absence of professing Jews from the British Isles for several generations.[69]

Rarely do we find now a sympathetic presentation of a Jewish usurer like that of Gerontus in Robert Wilson's play *The Three Ladies of London* of 1584. Far more representative were Christopher Marlowe's *Jew of Malta* and William Shakespeare's *Merchant of Venice*, written a few years later. In the period after the Lopez trial, especially, London audiences listened with rapt attention to the recital of Jewish wrongdoings, international as well as domestic, presented to them by Barabas, "the Jew of Malta," in a speech to his servant, Ithamore. (Marlowe's drama was first performed on February 26, 1592, and frequently thereafter in England and abroad. Since in the seventeenth century the theater often became an international enterprise—not only plays but actors often traveled to foreign stages—it became quite popular on the Continent as well.) In it the Jew was presented as an incarnation of evil, who gloated:

> Being young, I studied physick, and began
> To practice first upon the Italian;
> There I enrich'd the priests with burials,
> And always kept the sexton's arms in ure [practice]
> With digging graves and ringing dead men's knells:
> And, after that, was I an engineer,
> And in the wars 'twixt France and Germany,
> Under pretence of helping Charles the Fifth,
> Slew friend and enemy with my stratagems:
> Then, after that, I was an usurer,
> And with extorting, cozening, forfeiting,
> And tricks belonging unto brokery,
> I fill'd the gaols with bankrouts [bankrupts] in a year,
> And with young orphans planted hospitals;
> And every moon made some or other mad.

Similarly, the original stage directions of the *Merchant of Venice* prescribed the presentation of Shylock as a typical Jewish usurer with a large hooked nose and a disgusting slovenly appearance—directions which were often disregarded in later generations by the great producers and actors attracted to that drama.[70]

Popular receptivity to Jew-baiting harangues is clearly illustrated by several reports in Philip Henslowe's *Diary* for 1591–96 which show that, even before the execution of the Jewish physician, Marlowe's *Jew of Malta* had attracted greater and more enthusiastic audiences than any of his other plays. In fact, the popularity of Marlowe's *Jew* doubtless influenced Shakespeare to write his *Merchant of Venice*.[71]

It appears, however, that some of the contemporary playwrights, including Shakespeare, were animated even more by antialien feelings than by a spirit of religious intolerance toward Jews. With his deep penetration of the human mind, Shakespeare sought to explain Shylock's ruthlessness as a reaction to the endless acts of oppression to which he and his coreligionists had long been subjected:

He [the debtor] . . . laughed at my losses, mocked at my gains, scorned my nation, thwarted my bargains, cooled my friends, heated mine enemies; and what's his reason? I am a Jew.
If you prick us do we not bleed? If you tickle us, do we not laugh?
If you poison us, do we not die? And if you wrong us, do we not revenge?

Nevertheless, though thus echoing the long-accepted "lachrymose conception of Jewish history," the great poet disliked Jews, not only as men of different faith but as aliens. During Elizabeth's reign, many foreigners had crowded into the English capital, their number had increased from some 3,000 to 10,000. There even existed, as we recall, a Spanish Calvinist church in London in 1559–65, just as there were English exiles at the court of Philip II in Madrid. These strangers displaced certain groups in the native population, creating widespread resentment which grew in intensity in the aftermath of the appearance of the Spanish Armada. The Italian historian-publicist Petruccio Ubaldini, though himself an anti-Spanish Protestant, bitterly commented on the popular state of mind in England: "It is easier to find flocks of white crows than one Englishman (and let him believe what he will about religion) who loves a foreigner." Such xenophobia actually led to antialien riots in 1588, 1593, and 1595. The Iberian residents appeared doubly suspect, whether they were viewed as crypto-Jews or Catholics. Shakespeare's *Merchant* may indeed have proposed a solution for the alien problem in Shylock's ultimate conversion to [Protestant] Christianity and Jessica's marriage to Lorenzo; in other words, in the speedy absorption of alien groups by the native majority. This sentiment may help explain why, as has been noted, both Shakespeare and Marlowe present very attractive Jewesses, a tradition which continued into the nineteenth century and which doubtless reflected the reality of many upper-class Englishmen coming under the spell of beautiful Jewish women.[72]

Economic factors likewise contributed to the diminution of Marrano influence in England at the turn of the century. So long as Holland's new republican regime was engaged in a permanent war with its Spanish overlords, the Jewish and Marrano merchants of Amsterdam often used London as an intermediate trading post in their exchanges with the Iberian Peninsula and the New World. But after the cessation of hostilities, and especially after the proclamation of a truce in 1609, the Amsterdam Jewish colony had direct access to the southern emporia of trade. Simultaneously, the temporary relaxation of anti-Marrano persecution on the Iberian Peninsula after Philip II's death—a détente which ultimately led to the "general pardon" proclaimed by Philip III in 1605—greatly reduced the New Christians' feeling of insecurity. Many potential émigrés now decided to stay home. The sharp religious controversies which had theretofore characterized Anglo-Spanish relations likewise were toned down in the early years of Philip III's regime, although the efforts of the Spanish envoy Juan de Tassis to secure a general decree of toleration for English Catholics proved unsuccessful. At the same time, England's general trade with Spain was declining, so that the formerly privileged status of Spanish importers was no longer justified. Originally, Spanish traders had been favored over most other foreigners, sometimes even over native merchants. The preferential treatment of Spanish importers is well illustrated by the different tariffs for businessmen of various nationalities with respect to customs dues at the beginning of the sixteenth century. For example, in the importation of wax, Spanish as well as English and Hanseatic merchants paid no duty, whereas all other foreign traders had to pay 12d for every hundredweight. For imports of cloth without grain, Spaniards and Englishmen paid 14d (Hanseatic merchants only 12d), while all other aliens were taxed 2s 9d. More remarkably, grain and cloth (dyed scarlet) could be brought in by Spaniards with a duty of 21d, by Hanseatic traders with one of 2s, and by Englishmen with one of 2s 4d; while other strangers had to pay 5s 6d! Such preference continued for a while even during the period of growing hostility between England and Spain, but eventually it had to be abandoned, thus removing one major incentive attracting Iberian New Christian settlers to England. Nor was the English government or public ever seriously dependent on loans from New Christians in England, since English Marranos were principally traders, rather than bankers. There was a generally more liberal attitude toward "usury," such as was formulated by Thomas Wilson in *A Discourse on Usury,* published in 1572. To be sure, Wilson still objected to the former type of "usury," with very high rates of interest. With special reference to Jews, he wrote:

What is the matter that Iewes are so universallye hated wheresoever they come? For soothe, usurie is one of the chief causes, for they robbe all men that deale with them, and undoe them in the ende. And for thys cause they were hated in England, and so banyshed worthelye, wyth whome I woulde wyshe all these Englishemen were sent that lende their money or their goods whatsoever for gayne, for I take them to be no better than Iewes. Nay, shall I saye: they are worse than Iewes.

But Wilson drew a distinction between "usury" as gainful employment and "interest," which is intended to compensate the lender either for outright damages or for the loss of earnings occasioned by the loan. In any case, English merchants could now as a rule secure credit from local Christian bankers at moderate rates in overt transactions.[73]

The diminution of Marrano commerce is well illustrated by the difficulties encountered by Fernando de Mercado, a native of Lisbon but, since 1601 resident, later even burgher, of Amsterdam. Mercado's tangled business affairs led him to England in 1607. Two years later he was denounced by another Portuguese merchant, and his unabashed admission to being a Jew caused a considerable sensation in London. Another affair involving a Jew of Iberian origin assumed even broader international dimensions. From 1608 on, Samuel Pallache served as deputy ambassador and then ambassador of the sultan of Morocco to the Netherlands. In this capacity, we recall, he had been instrumental in arranging for a treaty of alliance between the two countries; the first such treaty between Morocco and a Christian power, which, also because its chief architect was a Jew, attracted widespread attention. As Spain's sworn enemy, Pallache also engaged in extensive privateering on the side, capturing some Spanish silver vessels and bringing them to Rotterdam. One such expedition miscarried, however, and because of a storm in the English Channel, the Jewish diplomat-businessman had to seek refuge in Plymouth. Here, on the accusation of the Spanish ambassador, he was imprisoned in October 1614, and was thoroughly investigated, despite his original English safe-conduct and repeated interventions on his behalf by the Dutch government. Unquestionably, Pallache's Jewish persuasion likewise played a certain role in the English investigation. Ultimately, however, a board of the Privy Council, headed by the lord chief justice, Sir Edward Coke (Cooke), decided in March 20, 1615, that, since Pallache was "the subject of the King of Morruccos (between whom and the King of Spain, as is conceived, there is actual war) and hath from him an especial commission to take the subjects of the said King of Spain," the defendant should be acquitted and the Spanish ambassador be advised to seek redress in a civil suit. Pallache was allowed to return to Amsterdam, where he died a year later.[74]

Privateering was, of course, but a side line in the far-flung business activities of the Pallache family. We know altogether very little about New Christian exploits along these lines. Certainly, if such an enterprise miscarried, secret Judaizers falling into Spanish or Portuguese hands would have been in even more serious jeopardy than their Protestant counterparts, some of whom were tried as heretics by inquisitional tribunals and executed. But in more peaceful international exchanges, the role of Jewish or New Christian merchants seems to have been appreciated even by their Christian rivals. While in medieval England and most other European lands, the merchant and artisan guilds had as a rule been the protagonists of anti-Jewish discrimination and even total exclusion, in Tudor and Stuart England many Christian businessmen found both local and foreign Jews quite helpful in their extensive dealings abroad, particularly in Amsterdam, Hamburg, Gdańsk, Venice, Leghorn, and the eastern Mediterranean. In many of these areas there existed regular English merchant colonies, which were in steady contact with Jewish suppliers, customers, and intermediaries. From a purely commercial viewpoint, they regarded such associates primarily as individuals, rather than as members of a group —an attitude which carried over into the mother country as well.[75]

In the intervening ups and downs in Anglo-Jewish relations, however, the Mercado episode of 1607 seems to have given some impetus to a new outbreak of intolerance. Even in the earlier, more quiescent years, Lord William Cecil Burghley, though a realistic statesman who had had friendly relations with Nuñes and Lopez, once emphatically declared: "That state could never be in safety where there was a toleration of two religions. For there is no enmity so great as that for religion; and therefore they that differ in the service of their God can never agree in the service of their country." Nor were the ruling circles in England prone to forget that many of their Catholic compatriots were prepared to betray their government in its gravest hour, at the approach of the Spanish Armada. Quite a few Catholics were undoubtedly ready to listen to the English expatriate Cardinal William Allen—an important contributor in Rome to the revision of the Vulgate later known as the Sixto-Clementine Bible—who was making strenuous efforts to subvert the regime of his home country. In 1587, he not only praised Sir William Stanley's surrender of Deventer to the Spaniards but urged all other Catholic compatriots to follow that example. In *An Admonition to the Nobility and People of England and Ireland concerning the Present Wars*, Allen also clearly exhorted his readers "at the arrival of His Catholic Majesty's forces . . . to join the said army . . . to help toward the restoration of the Catholic faith and deposing the usurper [Elizabeth]." Not surprisingly, therefore, during the anti-Catholic frenzy after the "Gunpowder Plot" of 1605—whatever may have been its true nature—it was in some respects safer for Mercado and Pallache to admit to being Jews, despite the centuries-old prohibition against Jewish settlement in England. But most Iberian New Christians still formally belonged to the Catholic minority, which the "Act for the Better Discovering and Repressing Popish Remnants" of 1606 had described as ever "ready to entertain and execute any treasonable conspiracies and practices" against the Crown of England.[76]

It is small wonder, then, that the government decided to institute an investigation of the doubly suspect Spanish-Portuguese group and its twilight position between Judaism and Catholicism. Privy Council records for 1609 are unavailable, but other testimony indicates that strong police action was taken against the New Christian community and caused many individuals to leave England precipitously. In 1655, the royalist leader Sir Marmaduke Langdale referred to the events of 1609 in explaining the Jews' support of Cromwell to Sir Edward Nicholas, secretary of state of King Charles II (then living in exile). They "are considerable all the world over [he wrote], and the great masters of money. If his Majesty could either have them or divert them from Cromwell, it were a very good service. . . . But they hate monarchy and are angry for the patent that was granted by King James to my Lord of Suffolk for the discovery of them, which made most of the ablest of them fly out of England." This reminiscence half a century later is confirmed by contemporary dispatches of Italian envoys. The Venetian ambassador Marcantonio Correr reported from London on August 20, 1609:

Many Portuguese merchants in this City have been discovered to be living secretly as Jews. Some have already left and others have had a little grace [commodo] granted to allow them to wind up their business, in spite of the laws, which are very severe on this subject. These men are such scoundrels that, I am told, the better to hide themselves they have not only frequently attended Mass at some one or other of the Embassies, but have actually received the Holy Eucharist.

This behavior ascribed to the London New Christians was clearly but a continuation of the Marrano struggle for survival on the Iberian Peninsula, where secret Judaizers had to camouflage their religious disparity by regularly attending church services. New Christians in Spain certainly could not emulate there the defiance of that Catholic lady in England who (according to Robert Parsons' report of November 17, 1580, to Claude Acquaviva, the general of the Jesuit Order in Rome) "was offered her choice either to stay in prison, or simply to walk through the [Anglican] church without stopping there, or exhibiting any signs of respect; but she declared that she never would." At the most, Marranos residing outside Spain and Portugal could skip certain church services and refrain from appearing regularly at confession where, despite the silence enjoined upon the father confessor, the admission of secret judaizing would place the honest Marrano in serious jeopardy. Clandestine Judaism was facilitated in England by the continued governmental persecution of Catholics, which forced many of them, to quote a 1611 report by Correr, to "declare themselves Protestants with Protestants, and Catholics with Catholics." It also became proverbial that many a person chose "to live as a Protestant, and to die as a Papist." On his part, the Tuscan minister reported home on August 12, 1609, that the reason for the 1609 crisis was a falling out among the New Christians themselves so that some of them accused others of clandestine observance of Jewish rituals. They "have, therefore, been ordered to leave the Kingdom with much despatch, for the pertinent law makes them subject to the death penalty." This anti-Jewish climate of opinion also accounts for the aforementioned sharp assertion of 1608 by Sir Edward Coke, then chief justice of the Common Pleas, that between Christians and all infidels, including Jews, "there is a perpetual hostility, and can be no peace." Coke took the occasion of including in his *Institutes* extracts from Edward I's *Statutum de Judaismo,* to make other harsh comments about Jews, and concluded by urging the reader to peruse that statute carefully "to the end it may be a precedent and pattern in like cases to apply the like Remedy." As "perpetual enemies" Jews were, in Coke's opinion, to be totally disqualified from appearing as witnesses at English courts. The "raucous tone" of Coke's harangues against Catholics and Protestant dissenters, as well as against Jews, a tone which was carried into his judgeship from his days as prosecutor, may have displeased other judges, but it did reflect the prevailing temper of England's ruling circles.[77]

Yet even during the period of anti-Jewish reaction from 1594 to 1609, some segments of English opinion continued to evince considerable sympathy toward Jews and Judaism. For example, in contrast to Marlowe and Shakespeare, Joseph Wybarne of Cambridge University (where Marlowe, too, had studied in 1580–87) wrote a Latin drama entitled *Machiavellus,* which was performed at Cambridge in 1597. The Jewish character presented here is "a shrewd, intriguing fellow, of considerable humour, who, to obtain possession of a girl, puts a number of tricks on the Machiavel of the piece, and generally outwits him." By choosing that name for the Jew's opponent, Wybarne may have consciously protested against Marlowe's attempt to blacken the Jewish character by making his Barabas a "sound Machiavel." In his Prologue, Marlowe had announced: "We pursue the story of a rich and famous Jew who liv'd in Malta: you shall find him still, in all his projects, a sound Machiavel; and that's his character." That liberal thought sometimes prevailed even in the life of this period, is indicated by the case of the physician Dr. Jacob Domingo. In 1605, he succeeded in proving his qualifications before the College of Physicians and subsequently passed the required examination under the Board of Censors, whereupon he was admitted in 1606 to the practice of medicine, although he probably was a New Christian.[78]

UPSURGE OF BIBLICISM AND DISSENT

On the whole, the Jews' position was much more deeply affected by the rise of diverse religious movements than by secular literary outpourings. Many dissenting groups, particularly the Puritans, attached ever-increasing significance to the scriptural word. At first, the ruling circles of state and Church were fearful of the impact English versions of the Bible would have on the masses, as were the medieval Spaniards and other Continental leaders. Not without cause did William Tyndale, the distinguished pioneer in rendition of the Bible into English, complain in 1530 that "malicious and wily hypocrites" contend

that it is impossible to translate the Scripture into English: some, that it is not lawful for the lay people to have it in their mother tongue; some, that it would make them all heretics; . . . and some, or rather everyone, say that it would make them rise against the King, whom they themselves (unto their damnation) never yet obeyed.

Yet, growing public interest, abetted by the vigorous Protestant appeal to the exclusive authority of the Bible, overcame all these obstacles. The ever-recurrent endeavors to make the word of God available to all interested English-speaking laymen culminated in the classic achievement of the Authorized Version, completed in 1611 under King James I's personal sponsorship. As observed by G. M. Trevelyan, "While other literary movements, however noble in quality, affected only a few, the study of the Bible was becoming the national education. . . . The Bible cultivated here, more than in any other land, the growth of individual thought and practice." Ultimately, we remember, even the Amsterdam Jewish printer Joseph Athias could boast of having exported a million volumes of the English Bible to England and Scotland. Although this return to biblical lore aroused interest primarily in the ancient Israelites, it also drew considerable attention to contemporary Jews.[79]

As on the Continent, the awakening of interest in Hebrew studies in England led to many personal contacts between Christian scholars and Jews, as well as learned Jewish converts. True, the position of even devout converts was not always secure. John Immanuel Tremellius, who taught Hebrew at Cambridge in 1549–53, had good reason to fear the Catholic reaction upon the accession of Queen Mary, since he had originally left Judaism for Catholicism but had subsequently changed over to Protestantism. He escaped to Germany. But on his return visit to England in 1565 he enjoyed the hospitality, at the Lambeth Palace, of Archbishop Matthew Parker, whose son Matthew had been Tremellius' godson. Another convert, Philippus Ferdinandus, during his stay as instructor of Hebrew at Cambridge University, published a treatise on the commandments observed by contemporary Jews. A native of Poland, Ferdinandus likewise left Cambridge for the Continent, where he taught Hebrew at the yet more celebrated center of Christian Hebraism, the University of Leiden. Queen Elizabeth herself had mastered the language sufficiently to correspond in it, we are told, with Hugh Broughton of Amsterdam. Nor may we overlook in this connection her successor's personality, his often devious methods, or his general religious ideology. The son of Mary Stewart, and born a Catholic, James I (king of Scotland, 1567–1625; king of England, 1603–1625) became a Protestant before ascending the English throne. He was a classical scholar and a political writer of some competence, and he pursued also in the Bible translation sponsored by him his major political aims of strengthening the power of the state over the Churches (against the so-called Hildebrandism of the Catholic hierarchy) and of achieving, as far as possible, domestic religious peace through a modicum of mutual toleration. Hence the outburst of intolerance against the Jews in 1609 was more a temporary expedient than a basic characteristic of his regime. It was, in fact, a combination of scholarly curiosity and restraint toward the Jewish religion which induced him to welcome information about Jewish rituals supplied by the pertinent work by Leon da Modena.[80]

The study of Jewish mysticism likewise attracted more and more Christian devotees. They saw therein less need to justify their conversionist ideas (there were too few Jews around) than to draw lessons for a deeper penetration of the mysteries of the Christian religion. Other facets of postbiblical Judaism, and its rabbinic elements also aroused considerable interest of English intellectuals; among them John Selden (1584–1654), John Lightfoot (1602–1675), Edward Pococke (1604–1691), and the great poet-stateman John Milton (1608–1674), whose immortal poetry and influential political views were permeated with Hebraic elements. Milton's translation of some Psalms, his Christian theology as formulated in De Doctrina Christiana, and above all his Paradise Lost testified to his effective use and understanding of many Hebraic sources available to him in the original, as well as in translation. Among his successors was Sir Thomas Bodley (1545–1613), who left a living memorial in the great Hebraic collection assembled at the Oxford Library bearing his name. Soon there emerged a number of other bibliophiles, whose specialty was to collect rare manuscripts of Hebrew Bibles and other works; for instance, the famous Kennicott Bible, originally copied and illuminated in fourteenth-century Spain. These few examples of the multifarious Hebraic contributions by English scholars and writers will become clearer in the context of the respective disciplines in our analysis of the Jewish intellectual history of the period. Here we need concern ourselves only with the rapprochement between Christian and Jewish scholars, including converts, and the influence it exerted toward a more balanced appreciation, among Christian leaders, of the values of the Jewish heritage.[81]

Finally, the rising spirit of capitalism also brought some English thinkers closer to Jewish modes of thought. Reference has already been made to the new emphasis on "calling," of which, for instance, William Perkins became an outspoken protagonist. It is not surprising, therefore, that Parliament in 1647 appropriated £500 for the purchase, from a London bookseller, George Thomason, of "a Library or Collection of Books, in the Eastern Languages, of a very great Value, late brought out of *Italy,* and having been the Library of a learned *Rabbi* there, according to the printed Catalogue thereof: And that the said Library or Collection of Books be bestowed upon the Publick Library in the University of *Cambridge.*" No lesser scholars than John Selden and John Lightfoot took care of that collection consisting principally of Hebraica. The new respectability attained by the Hebrew book, and the growing demand for it by scholars and libraries, also helped New Christian printers to maintain small Hebrew presses, initially designed to provide Hebrew Bibles and prayerbooks for the worship of the Marrano community.[82]

From here was but a step to the more sympathetic consideration of contemporary Jews. Even some Catholics, now in the minority, effectively invoked the old canonical prohibition against forcing Jews to become Christians. We recall Robert Parsons' objection (in 1580) to forcing a Jew "to swear that there was a Blessed Trinity." A similar plea against the use of force was voiced in 1613 by the London humanist Isaac Casaubon, when his former Jewish assistant, Jacob Barnett or Bernard, had left Oxford before his scheduled baptism. That at the end Barnett was banished from England was doubtless owing as much to his sudden disappearance as to his admitted profession of a religion which was still formally outlawed. More radically, some Millenarians began assigning to the Jewish people an outstanding role in the final drama of Christian redemption; of course, only after its ultimate conversion. Some of these dissidents also argued that Jews ought to be tolerated in England and thus be given the opportunity to listen to the Word of God as preached by His "true" spokemen. An outstanding early seventeenth-century theologian, Thomas Draxe, published in 1608 *The Worlde's Resurrection, or the Generall Calling of the Iewes,* a commentary upon the eleventh chapter of St. Paul's Epistle to the Romans. Draxe claimed that God's wisdom, power, and providence had manifested itself "in the mystery and matter of predestination, in the illumination and blinding, saluation and condemnation both of Iewes and Gentiles; it is most deepe, yea and past man's founding." He also emphasized the historic achievement of dispersed Jewry in having, despite all persecutions and wanderings, preserved the authentic Hebrew Bible for posterity, and declared, "We must not roightly either contemne, much less condemne the Jews, nor expell them out of our coasts and countries, but hope well of them, pray for them, and labour to win them by our Holy zeal and Christian example." Six years later, a distinguished Baptist, Leonard Busher, drew the logical conclusion of Draxe's ideas when he presented to James I the memorandum *Religious Peace; or, a Plea for Liberty of Conscience,* in which such religious liberty was expressly recommended for Jews, too. Combining the standard mercantilistic argument that the Jews would contribute to the English economy with the reasoning that new opportunities would be offered for their ultimate conversion to Christianity, Busher insisted that after their admission to England they would

inhabit and dwell under his majesty's dominion to the great profit of his realms, and to their furtherance in the faith; the which we are bound to seek in all love and peace, as well as others, to our utmost endeavours, for Christ hath commanded to teach all nations.

He also pointed out that, in contrast to conversion by persuasion, one secured by force was usually inefficacious, as may be seen from the example of Marranos generations after the event. First published in 1614, Busher's memorandum was reprinted in 1646 and enjoyed a considerable vogue, especially among the religious dissenters.[83]

Some thinkers went even further. Sir Henry Finch (1558–1625), a distinguished lawyer and the author of a number of theological tracts, published in 1621 his famous treatise *The World's Great Restauration; or, the Calling of the Ievves, and (With Them) of All the Nations and Kingdomes of the Earth, to the Faith of Christ.*

Going beyond his predecessors (including Francis Kett, Andrew Willet, and the more influential Thomas Brightman and Giles Fletcher), Finch envisaged that the messianic era would be ushered in through the restoration of the Jews to the Holy Land, of course after their adoption of Christianity.

Then shall be established [he wrote] that most glorious kingdom of Jerusalem, under which all the tribes shall be united. So ample shall be their dominion that not only the Egyptians, Assyrians, and the most extensive countries of the East, converted by their example, but even the rest, the Christians, shall of their own accord *submit* themselves and acknowledge their primacy.

To be sure, England's ruling circles were not yet ready for a calm consideration of such advanced ideas, and both Finch and his publisher Goudge were arrested. Because of his great distinction as a jurist, he was speedily released; but he was sharply censured by speakers in Parliament, including William Laud (who was later, as archbishop of Canterbury, to play an historic role during the trial and execution of Charles I) and John Prideaux, Regius Professor of Theology at Oxford University. Nonetheless, similar sentiments were to be sounded shortly thereafter by Isaac de la Peyrère in Holland and by Paul Yvon Laleu and the anonymous author of *L'Ancienne Nouveauté de l'Écriture Sainte* (1657) in France.[84]

In this connection we need but briefly refer to James Harrington's utopia, *The Commonwealth of Oceana*, first published in 1656, which advocated the colonization of Jews in otherwise troublesome Ireland, against an annual rental of £4,000,000. Ireland may have been chosen because it had very few Jewish settlers but had manifold legendary associations with some biblical heroes. Harrington probably did not suspect that Dunstan Ames' brother, Francis, who had distinguished himself as burgomaster and commandant of the English garrison in Yonghal (1583–85), and Dunstan's son, William (depicted by the Spanish ambassador Bernardino de Mendoza as "a young fellow of twenty, well built, with a fair and handsome face and a small fair beard"), were secret Judaizers. However, Harrington's proposal reflected the new situation created by the contemporary debates on the readmission of the Jews to England, for which the pre-Cromwellian episodes were important overtures. In the very introduction to his renowned utopia, Harrington argued that the repopulation of the devastated island might best be accomplished by replacing the former Irish settlers with persons of "a new Race." He added:

[It] might have been best done by planting it with Jewes, allowing them their own Rites and Lawes, for that would have brought them suddenly from all parts of the World, and in sufficient numbers, and though the Jewes be now altogether for Merchandise, yet in the land of *Canaan* (since their exile from whence they have not been Landlords), they were altogether for agricultur; and there is no cause why a man should doubt, but having a fruitfull Country, and good Ports too, they would be good at both.[85]

More directly related to the status of the Jews in England were the writings of a Christian Hebraist, John Weemes (or Weemse). In 1623, he published a more technical book of biblical scholarship, *The Christian Synagogue,* in which, among other matters, he recommended to "studious young divines" that they read "the holy Scriptures in their owne proper language, the *Hebrew* and the *Greek*; so that they speake not to you by an interpreter; and that the proverbe in the *Talmud* may not be applied to you, *Ben Zoma semper foris est: this man is never within.*" Weemes' book enjoyed sufficient popularity to reappear in three further editions within a dozen years. In 1636, Weemes turned his attention to the contemporary treatment in England of "the four degenerate sons." Once more using biblical legislation as a model, he discussed in detail what laws should govern the position of these four groups: atheists, magicians, idolaters, and Jews. With respect to Jews, he drew the distinction between those lacking "affection" for the country and hating "Christ and the Christian religion," who were not to be tolerated at all, and those embracing the dominant faith, who were to "enjoy all the privileges, which the Christians enjoy." In between were those Jews who, though generally loyal to their country, insisted upon maintaining their old religion. Abhorring forcible conversion, Weemes suggested that such Jews ought to be "suffered" and allowed to perform circumcision and erect synagogues. But they should be subject to certain disabilities, such as the prohibition against employing Christian servants. Characteristically, he was not opposed to a Jewish couple continuing to live together after one mate was converted to Christianity, provided only that the children would be raised in the Christian faith. In general he felt that such a modicum of toleration of Jews would well serve the major goal of their ultimate conversion to Christianity.[86]

Some sectarians went further still and began adopting certain Jewish rituals, such as observing the Sabbath on Saturday. Needless to say, the majority of the people and particularly the government and the Church of England looked askance at these manifestations of religious "extremism." Among the messianic dreamers, Francis Kett paid with his life for his predictions. In 1612, two "Arians" were executed because they denied the divinity of Christ. In 1618–20, many followers of the Puritan John Traske were prosecuted for judaizing. The lengths to which Traske and his associate Hamlet Jackson were prepared to go, and the confusion arising from their radical teachings, are well illustrated by an anonymous letter to Mrs. Traske, which read in part:

Hamlet Jackson draweth Mr. Trask to points of Judaism, as to the observation of Laws touching Meat, Drink, Apparel, Resting, Working, Building and many other matters. And thus, if there be a Law for doing of such and such things, we are, said he, to leave our own thoughts and other men's opinions, and follow that Law for the doing thereof. Upon which Tenet came in the observacion of legal Ceremonies, and one Law after another as occasion did minister itself; yea and much distraction was bred, so that it was not safe to eat, drink, to come into a house, to sit down, nor buy anything in a Market, nor to walk in the streets, for fear of touching others that observed not those Laws, and so were unclean. . . .

The understandable reaction of the official circles of both Church and state was expressed by Bishop Lancelot Andrewes at the Star Chamber trial of Traske: "It is a good work to make a Jew a Christian: but to make Christian men Jewes hath ever been holden a foul act, and severely to be punished. . . . He [Traske] is a very Christened Jew, a Maran, the worst Jew that is. . . ." In 1621, in connection with the debate in the House of Commons concerning a new bill regulating Sabbath Day observance, the archbishop of Canterbury suggested omitting the word "Sabbath" altogether, because of "the aptness of divers to enclyne to Judaism as the newe sect of the Thraskites." All these persecutions did not suppress judaizing, however. Traskites, including Jackson and Christopher Sands, moved to Amsterdam, where they could freely practice Judaism in full or in part. Jackson apparently became a full-fledged Jew and was known under the name Abraham the Ger (Proselyte), while Sands and others lived in an intermediate position as "Noachists," observing only the six or seven "Noahidic commandments." [87]

Despite the rejection of these "extremes" by the majority of the population, and occasional repression by the government, such pro-Jewish sentiments time and again broke through the official wall of hostility. Although still permeated with conversionist-messianic ideology, they cropped up with renewed vigor during the turbulent 1640s, when the long-smoldering Puritan revolt led to sanguinary civil war, the execution of Charles I, and Oliver Cromwell's rise to power. In those years the toleration of all religious dissenters, including Jews, became an issue of paramount importance. Among its leading advocates were Hugh Peters, Samuel Richardson, and Roger Williams. Serving as chaplain in Cromwell's revolutionary army, Peters suggested in 1647 that "strangers, even Jews, [be] admitted to trade and live with us." Arguing in the same year for *The Necessity of Toleration in Matters of Religion,* Richardson attributed many of England's troubles to God's retribution for the country's general religious intolerance. Alluding darkly to the original expulsion of the Jews, he exclaimed: "Who knows but this is come upon us for troubling, undoing, despising, and banishing the people of God into so many wildernesses." In a similar vein, Roger Williams, in *The Bloudy Tenent of Persecution for Cause of Conscience. Discussed in a Conference between Truth and Peace,* written during his stay in England in 1643–44 and published there in 1644, demanded that Jews be given the opportunity of proving that they could be good and faithful citizens. He felt that the discrimination theretofore practiced was unjust, and in a pamphlet of 1652 he contended that for their "hard measure, I fear, the nations and England hath yet a score to pay." Williams' preachment of religious toleration was the more persuasive as it came not from a statesman who was religiously indifferent or lukewarm, but from one who "was the most passionately religious of men" (Perry Miller). The pro-Jewish theme was the keynote also of Edward Nicholas' (possibly Jewish-inspired)

Apology for the Honourable Nation of the Jews, and All the Sons of Israel, of 1648. Nicholas, who likewise attributed the numerous trials and tribulations of the English nation to its unjust treatment of Jews, concluded his peroration with an appeal

> that the same Authority that proceeded against them formerly, that now the same power and authority will repeal those severe Laws made against them. That our receiving them again, and giving them all possible satisfaction, and restoring them to commerce in this kingdom, may be exemplary to other Nations that have done them, and continue to do them wrong; till which time (God putting their tears into his bottle) God will charge their sufferings upon us, and will avenge them on their persecuters.[88]

Needless to say, these views did not necessarily represent the majority opinion even among the Puritan rebels. Yet they reflected, in part, the growing realization in business and governmental circles that England's economy needed immigrants, Jews as well as Protestants. Arguments were now advanced against certain monopolistic practices of the Merchants Adventurers, John Lilburne pointing to the example of "the Dutchman [who] always goeth to the cheapest, though from a Christian to a Jew." On the other hand, in 1642, when Parliament enacted a 5 percent tax on all goods exported from England, some London merchants "afraid of making known their wealth . . . adopted the expedient of bringing over some Jews from Amsterdam to provide the money and carry away the goods in instalments" (Gerolamo Agostini). It was therefore now possible for Antonio Fernandez (Abraham Israel) Carvajal to make an astonishingly fast career. It is still uncertain whether this new Londoner was a Portuguese New Christian or an Old Christian from the Canary Islands who adopted Judaism on his own. After settling in London in 1630, Carvajal petitioned the House of Lords in 1643 for the release of 300 barrels of gunpowder. According to Lucien Wolf, his average annual imports of bullion to Britain amounted to £100,000. Carvajal was joined in London by a number of New Christian refugees from Rouen after their disastrous experiences of 1633; they included some of his own relatives. This small group, while outwardly professing Catholicism, held Jewish divine services in Carvajal's residence. More remarkably, in 1645, when Carvajal was denounced under the Act of Conformity, even his competitors joined in petitioning Parliament in his behalf, and the House of Lords quashed the proceedings. Out of this reversal of the previous policy of intolerance finally sprang, in 1649, a petition to the new revolutionary regime, overtly pleading for the readmission of Jews to England; it was presented, from their residence in Amsterdam, by Joanna and Ebenezer Cartwright. In many ways this petition marks the beginning of an active movement for the formal recognition of the resettlement of Jews in the British Isles.[89]

IN NASCENT EMPIRE

In Britain's European possessions outside England proper, only a few Jewish individuals appear in the records before 1650. Even in Ireland, where small Jewish settlements had existed in the Middle Ages, the records become silent after the thirteenth century. Only occasional references—such as those to the aforementioned Irish land grant to Hector Nuñes; to several members of the Ames (Añes) family, William, Francis, and his nephew William, who served as mayors and soldiers in Yonghal in 1555–85; or to Paul Jacob, who was living in Londonderry before his conversion and departure to England in 1623—give us an inkling that some Jews did appear on the scene in the early modern period. We know little more about Paul Jacob than what he himself communicated to King James I in an undated letter, probably written after his arrival in England. This epistle, a typical letter of solicitation, reveals an effrontery and a biblical sophistication which might not have been expected from an Iberian crypto-Jew who had lived precariously in Ireland until his conversion. He argued:

It is a wonder, if not a miracle, to see a son of Abraham, a child of that great King, owne Your Majesty to be his natural sovereigne. To confess that the scepter is departed from Judah, the most obstinate of my brethren are compelled to doe, but that it is rightly devolved into your hands, is their stumbling-block, but my faith. For if only true believers be the genuine children of Abraham, and you onely are that King of the true believers, it is a consequence undeniable, that you onely are the true King of the Jews, true successor and heir, in a mistery of that King whose faith you defend, who was—though crucified—the sonne of David, the heir of Abraham.

He felt entitled, therefore, to ask the king for a stipend for himself and his family. Most of the population doubtless shared the aversion to both Protestants and Jews which was typified by the remark of a Dublin priest in the mid-sixteenth century. Upon listening to a sermon against the mass delivered by his patron, Edward Staples, bishop of Meath, the priest burst into tears and exclaimed: "Before ye went last to Dublin ye were the best beloved man in your diocese that ever came in it, now ye are the worst beloved . . . Ye have preached against the sacrament of the altar and the saints, and will make us worse than Jews." After 1656 the progress of Jewish settlement was still very slow, although Jews encountered few legal obstacles, even in acquiring land. One of the newcomers, David Sollom, "a quondam Jewish merchant," purchased in 1678 the estates of Syddan and Woodstown in the county of Meath. But his wife was a Christian, as was his daughter, Esther, married to Thomas Emlyn, reputedly the first Unitarian minister in England. It was only in 1660 that the first modern Jewish community was established by Jacome Faro and the brothers Manuel and Francisco Pereira, three Portuguese New Christians mentioned in the Spanish inquisitorial records from the Canary Islands. In Scotland, on the other hand, we know of practically no Jews until the nineteenth century. Nor were there any organized Jewish communities in such other British possessions in Europe, as Gibraltar or Malta, until the eighteenth century, though from time to time the presence of individual Jewish captives and others engaged the attention of contemporary Jewish leaders in other lands.[90]

Similarly, in England's North American colonies, professing Jews begin to be recorded sporadically only after the English takeover of some of the Caribbean Islands. There the new colonizers often found small groups of New Christians who could more freely observe their Jewish rituals under the fairly liberal English administration. In Barbados, for example, which was occupied by the English in 1625, we hear three years later of one Abraham Jacob complaining to the earl of Carlisle, proprietor of the island, that business had proved utterly unprofitable to him. Not until 1656, however, was a formal decree issued, granting Jews the enjoyment of the "privilege of Laws and Statutes of ye Commonwealth of England and of this Island, relating to foreigners and strangers." On the other hand, the island of Jamaica, where before very long Kingston was to embrace one of the largest and most affluent Jewish communities in the New World, was not taken over by the English until 1655. (Even then Kingston achieved importance only after one of the recurrent earthquakes in the region had destroyed the capital of Port Royal in 1692.) The tiny New Christian settlement of the island under Spanish domination, which at the time of the British occupation counted altogether 3,000 whites and their black slaves, was suddenly reinforced by the influx of Jewish refugees from Recife, Brazil, after its reoccupation by the Portuguese in 1654. This movement of Brazilian exiles, as we shall see, was destined to furnish a number of founding fathers to several Jewish communities in North America; among them, New York.[91]

Before that time only Mexico had offered a haven of refuge for some Jews on the North American Continent. If in 1621 we hear of one Isaac Legardo in the colony of Virginia, we are not even certain that he was of Jewish descent. The first known Jew to appear in that leading British colony, Moses Nehemias, seems to have come there in 1658 to take part in a litigation, rather than for purposes of settlement. However, the Pilgrim Fathers, and their successors in Massachusetts and in the other English colonies, were deeply affected by the Hebraic spirit of the Bible. As refugees from English persecution, they often compared themselves to the ancient Israelites who had left Egypt. Typical of the high esteem in which the Hebrew language was held by many of the new settlers was the following comment of William Bradford (1590–1657), one of the arrivals on the *Mayflower* and later governor of Plymouth Colony:

Though I am growne aged, yet I have had a longing desire to see with my own eyes, something of that most ancient language, and holy tongue, in which the Law and oracles of God were write, and in which God and angels spake to the holy patriarch of old time; and what names were given to things from the creation. And though I cannot attain to much herein, yet I am refreshed, to have seen some glimpse hereof; (as Moyses saw the land of Canaan afarr of) my aime and desire is, to see how the words and phrases lye in the holy texte; and to discerne somewhat of the same for my own contente.

In the Preface to his *History of "Plimouth Plantation,"* from which these lines are taken, Bradford was able to include a few Hebrew letters. Similar Hebrew insertions had appeared even earlier in the *Bay Psalm Book,* which was published in 1640, the first book ever printed in the English colonies.[92]

More significantly, the builders of the nascent American civilization were imbued with a high sense of mission. Unlike the Spanish colonizers, some of whose idealistic leaders saw in their work of exploration of new lands a sign of God's will that they spread the Christian gospel among the heathens, the Puritan settlers were themselves refugees from religious persecution. They viewed their main task in terms of erecting a new Zion dedicated to moral self-improvement and setting an example of righteous living for humanity at large. In 1630, Puritan settlers still on their way across the Atlantic listened to this exhortation by Governor John Winthrop:

Wee must Consider that wee shall be as a Citty vpon a Hill, the eies of all people are vpon vs; soe that if wee shall deale falsely with our god in this worke wee have vndertaken and soe cause Him to withdrawe His present help from vs, wee shall be made a story and a by-word through the world.

They also felt that, like the ancient Israelites, they had made a covenant with the Lord, with all the privileges and obligations appertaining thereto—obligations even more than privileges. This idea had constantly been repeated to them, especially by John Hooper. That is why many of their leaders envisaged the nascent commonwealth as an area to be governed by biblical law. The application of Pentateuchal patterns was strongly advocated by Rev. John Cotton in his *Moses, His Judicials,* which appeared in London in 1641, under the more descriptive title *An Abstract of the Lawes of New England, As They are Now Established.* While these political ideas had little immediate bearing on contemporary Jews, they contributed to a new openmindedness among the colonists toward association with the physical descendants of Abraham, Isaac, and Jacob—an attitude which was to help lay the foundations for the memorable evolution of Jewish life in the United States and Canada.[93]

If in the western Atlantic the English explorers and colonizers followed in the footsteps of the Iberians, the Dutch, and to some extent even the French, they were relatively late arrivals on the African and Asian continents as well. Of course, before very long they outstripped all their rivals, and ultimately they ruled from the Cape of Good Hope to Cairo, Calcutta, and Sydney, over the greatest empire in history. But their initial steps in the period here under review had little bearing on Jewish history in those areas. We obtain only occasional glimpses of Jewish individuals in contact with British merchants and explorers in those vast lands and teeming populations. For example, a Moroccan Jewish linguist is recorded to have participated in 1601 in the earliest expedition of the English East Indian Company (it had received its first charter from Queen Elizabeth on December 31, 1600) to the Indian subcontinent. He even helped the English to negotiate a favorable treaty with the sultan of Achim. Much later (1682–92) another Jew, Abraham Navarro, likewise served the Company in the double capacity of interpreter and diplomatic negotiator. By that time there already existed a small Western Jewish community in Madras. But those were mere beginnings of Western Jewish settlements, living side by side with the much larger and old-established native Asian Jewish communities.[94]

UNSPOKEN ACCEPTANCE

Basically, the same contrast between unlimited future potentialities and rather slight beginnings characterized Jewish life in England and in France. Both kingdoms were entering at that time their period of greatest expansion, and were destined to play leading roles in the unprecedented historical drama unfolding in the modern world. But unlike Holland, which could build a new order after its liberation from the shackles of Spanish overlordship (in contrast to the once-flourishing, but now retarded, southern provinces), both of the large monarchies were hampered by their age-old traditions; in the Jewish question even more than in other areas. Yet the marvelous progress made by Holland economically, politically, and culturally, despite her meager natural resources— her very food supply often depended on land wrested from the sea by human ingenuity and untiring labor—served as an ever-present challenge and an invitation to constructive emulation.

It was well within the framework of English constitutional developments to let the New Christian community, including its professing Jewish segment, grow organically into English society without the government clearly formulating its attitude by parliamentary legislation. From time to time the authorities may have taken some direct action, as in their intolerant moves of 1609, but generally matters were allowed to follow their own course, without official interference, until the issue was raised on a major scale during the revolutionary 1650s. More remarkably, France, too, preferred for the most part to ignore the issues raised by the presence of the new, semiclandestine Jewish communities, rather than articulate any clear-cut policy, which would have been consonant with the French national temper and constitutional history. Yet even when Henry II issued in 1550 his sweepingly tolerant decree and, when, in sharp contrast thereto, Louis XIII proclaimed in 1615 the total suppression of Marranism as a governmental objective, actual practice diverged greatly from either legal theory. The differences, moreover, between one French region and another were enormous: it is hard to find a greater contrast in French constitutional law than that between the acceptance of the increasingly flourishing and internally diversified Jewish community of Bordeaux and the persistent rejection of any organized form of Jewish life in the otherwise pace-setting capital.

Such legal inconsistencies merely mirrored the inner contradictions in the evolution of these two great powers. Religious intolerance, a major factor in the ultimate exclusion of Jews from settlement in the Late Middle Ages, was somewhat mitigated by the intellectual individualism and laicization characteristic of the Renaissance era. Although greatly exacerbated in both lands by the Reformation and Counter Reformation, the quest for religious conformity now aimed principally at eliminating the Huguenot minority in France and the Catholics and Dissenters in England. The Jewish issue appeared definitely secondary. If anything, the English and Huguenot struggle against Catholicism and, particularly, the growing resentment of the Spanish Inquisition's harsh persecution of Protestants created an atmosphere of comparative friendliness toward that Inquisition's New Christian victims. The impact of the so-called Black Legend about Spanish atrocities could only result in an humanitarian acceptance by the English of some Spanish and Portuguese refugees from the Iberian Holy Offices. In France, on the other hand, Gallican traditions generated considerable resistance to the Counter Reformation, principally espoused and militarily defended by Spain, considered by most French and English leaders to be the national enemy of their countries. That is why the French hierarchy and public were rather slow in their implementation of the resolutions of the Council of Trent, although the French delegation had played a prominent role in some of the Council's decisive sessions. Neither were the Jesuits at first as popular in French society as they were in the Mediterranean countries, Poland, or the Catholic sections of Germany. Moreover, the deadlock created by the Wars of Religion, though superficially glossed over by the Edict of Nantes proclaimed by Henry IV in 1598, left a strong Protestant minority in the country, at least until the revocation of that Edict in 1685.[95]

Nor was national intolerance now so clearly defined as in the earlier periods of the struggle for territorial unification in France and for politicocultural fusion of the Norman and Anglo-Saxon populations in England. By now both countries were sufficiently integrated and homogeneous to be more hospitable to the numerous strangers settling in them, including some secret and even professing Jews—provided only that the new individuals would not form conspicuously divergent enclaves. More, the same patriotic fervor which led to the ascendancy of both France and England to the position of world powers also set them on a course of expansion resulting in the establishment of large colonial empires. While the colonies did not usually become integral parts of the home countries, they injected into the bodies politic new heterogeneous elements, racial, cultural, and religious, which somewhat mitigated the adverse effects of the National State upon the status of the Jewish minority.[96]

Even more significant were the dichotomies in the economic sphere. While the traditional, vested interests in France and England still resented the arrival of potential competitors, and in both countries (as well as in Holland) largely succeeded in barring Jews from the retail trade and from guild-controlled crafts and professions (of interest primarily to the petty bourgeoisie), the new capitalist methods of production and international trade favored the admission of foreigners. Iberian New Christians were doubly welcome because they were endowed with capital resources, commercial and industrial skills, and manifold international contacts and experiences. The increasingly dominant mercantilist theory of economics—through its emphasis upon the increase of the national wealth in the form of precious bullion, either directly by the importation of capital or indirectly by an increase in production and a favorable balance of trade—likewise encouraged the benevolent treatment of strangers.

At the same time, the methods of agricultural production lagged behind the speedy changes in industry and commerce generated by the Commercial Revolution. As a result, there was a tremendous increase in social mobility domestically, too. "Although there was a hard core that remained fairly wedded to their native parishes," observes Julian Cornwall, "most men changed their residence once in their lives, at least temporarily in some cases." The population of the English cities now consisted of a great many immigrants from the countryside, as well as from foreign lands, and the presence of a New Christian group, particularly in the cosmopolitan setting of London, appeared far less exceptional. Social mobility also accounted for the entry of many wealthy merchants into the landowning class, and the increase of intermarriage between the upper bourgeoisie and the old aristocracy, a process which also facilitated the intermingling of aristocratic (including ducal) and Jewish families. Out of this welter of conflicting interests and attitudes arose the zigzag course of governmental policies and the sudden shifts in public opinion which characterized both the French and the English relations with the Marrano communities in the sixteenth and early seventeenth centuries.[97]

Not surprisingly, both the pro- and anti-Jewish factions fell back upon history to support their positions. Curiously, the main English argument ran along legalistic lines, with constant referral to the decree of expulsion of 1290, which had never been abrogated. Although centuries had passed since its enactment, leading jurists like Sir Edward Coke and William Prynne regarded the statute enacted by Edward I as inviolate. Compared with these lay jurists, English churchmen were much more flexible. In France, on the other hand, the historic argument based on the decrees of expulsion promulgated in various parts of France during the fourteenth and fifteenth centuries lost much of its force because of the vagaries of the original French legislation concerning Jews and the contradictory nature of the pertinent legal enactments and judicial decisions of more recent vintage. Hence France was more likely to fall back on the old religious antagonism toward the "infidel" people, and the other traditional elements of medieval anti-Jewish propaganda, including the alleged enmity of Jews toward all Christians and Christianity, as exemplified by the Blood Accusation, and charges of the poisoning of wells and the desecration of the host. Nor were Jewish economic exploitation through usury and other elements of an alleged Jewish drive toward world domination overlooked. Most French historians of the sixteenth and seventeenth centuries uncritically repeated the accusations they found in their medieval sources—particularly the Great Chronicle of St. Denis, which they often merely paraphrased. These accusations and denunciations of Jewish behavior served them to justify the recurrent expulsions of Jews from royal France, but they remained largely silent on the readmissions of Jews and their causes. Nor did they tell much about the flourishing Jewish culture, particularly in Champagne or Provence, or about the toleration extended to Jews by many French princes. Implied, rather than fully spelled out in these narratives, was a justification of the general intolerance toward professing Jews (which was assumed to prevail in contemporary France), while there was a nearly total silence about the incipient Jewish Resettlement in the French South. Even François de Belleforest, who in *Les Grandes Annales* (1579) condemned some of the atrocities committed on Jews in the course of ages and intimated that force was not effective in bringing about their conversion, failed to draw from his description the lesson that Jews ought to be tolerated in sixteenth-century France.[98]

Yet this chorus of accusations was greatly weakened by the polarity of medieval Catholicism's combination of a modicum of toleration with discrimination and segregation. The "opinion" rendered by the theologians of the Sorbonne in the Charleville case in 1638 clearly illustrated how much leeway this polarity gave to individual churchmen in deciding specific cases. At the same time, the nationalistic historiography of the period was no longer quite so hostile to Jews and Judaism. The progressive secularization of historiography tended to diminish the sharply anti-Jewish biases in the treatment of the Jewish past, which ultimately affected the appreciation of contemporary Jews. Under the impact of these new historical approaches it became possible for a French Huguenot like Jacques Basnage, sieur de Beauval (1653–1723), to embark, later in the seventeenth century, upon the first modern endeavor at a comprehensive and on the whole sympathetic history of the Jewish people since the days of Josephus. Although himself a theologian and religious controversialist, Basnage, as the official Dutch historiographer in The Hague, later wrote a predominantly secular history, *Annales des Provinces-Unis,* an approach which, like that of his Jewish history, adumbrated many of the intellectual trends underlying the nineteenth-century *Wissenschaft des Judentums.*[99]

While the old historic experiences had largely conveyed anti-Jewish lessons, the new historic realities of the nascent capitalist order, the standing armies, the international power struggle, and the overseas expansion, combined with the new approaches in religion and science, all favored the admission of Jews to the Western lands. In short, while the historical record of the preceding centuries had operated against the Jews, history in the making paved the way for their resettlement and, ultimately, for their emancipation and integration into Western society.

IBERIAN DOWNGRADE

WHILE THE GROWING Marrano and Jewish communities in Holland, France, and England were thus paving the way for the Jewish Resettlement in western Europe, the old habitats on the Iberian Peninsula were not completely abandoned. The northern Marranos continued to maintain close relations with their coreligionists left behind in Spain and Portugal. At times, some members of the same family stayed in Lisbon carrying on their old businesses, while others helped to expand these commercial enterprises into new territories.

Combined with the shared secret observance of Jewish rites, such international mercantile cooperation often involved the New Christians in a dangerous game against inquisitorial spies. But the financial success of their numerous ventures during the rising prosperity of the northern lands made these hazards economically quite rewarding. Many Marranos also found that in the bitter sectarian struggles of the Wars of Religion, they could best avoid involvement on either side by tacitly or, wherever possible, publicly adhering to Judaism. Having long since learned to live dangerously, they doubtless considered the risks sufficiently worth-while to keep their New Christian mask for decades, even generations.

PHILIP II'S INTRANSIGENCE

At times, foreign Marranos, particularly those settled in Holland, tried to help their Iberian coreligionists to cultivate certain Jewish practices in secret. Unwittingly, Menasseh ben Israel, in the presence of another Dutch Jew, betrayed an aspect of such religious assistance to an informer. According to the deposition given in 1639 by one Feliciano Dourado, a native of Paraíba, Brazil, before the Lisbon Inquisition, Menasseh had four years earlier complained of the oppression of his Spanish brethren and had added, with much feeling and passion, that whatever they might do in Spain they would not prevent them [the Marranos] from being Jews, because all the New Christians in Spain were Christians by violence, and that every year there went certain Jews from Holland to the capital of Madrid and to many other parts of the realm of Spain to circumcise the New Christians. Hereat the other Jew caught hold of his hand, intimating to him that he did ill to reveal this before the deponent, because he would return to Spain and recount it, and might do harm to the persons of his Nation. After this warning, the said Menasseh treated the matter jokingly, saying that he had not meant it seriously.

In 1673 an inquisitorial spy wrote from Madrid to the inquisitor-general about the numerous Marranos of Bayonne and Peyrehorade who traveled to Spain under assumed names, either for commercial purposes or "in order to introduce Judaism to our New Christians who are unfamiliar with it, as well as to seduce them to leave for France or the northern countries. Some of them may go to Castile, from where they might proceed to the infested countries."[1]

The Inquisition was also kept informed of these underground activities by its own agents stationed in the northern cities, as well as by Marrano repatriates who, either in self-defense or for conscientious reasons, turned against their brethren. A few testified that, during their sojourn abroad, they had witnessed Jewish rituals performed by such and such Marrano acquaintances. Thereupon the denounced persons, if in reach of the Inquisition, were arrested and, under torture, made to confess. All foreign New Christians were considered fit targets for blackmail. When the prominent London businessman Bernard Leavis, who together with partners was engaged in large-scale trade with Portugal (the cargo of one of his ships alone was valued at £25,000), arrived in Lisbon sometime before 1596, he was threatened with denunciation by two New Christians, Anthony de Veiga and John Ferdinandes. He was ultimately arrested, and only after the expenditure of large funds was he released and given permission to return to England. Nevertheless, the occasional messengers dispatched from Amsterdam and other cities helped to strengthen the backbone of the Marranos still living on the Peninsula. At the same time, rumors circulating about such disguised visitors, rumors doubtless magnified in the popular mind, must have inflamed the passions of the Spanish and Portuguese peoples, further irked by the general identification of their citizens abroad with secret Judaism. A widely believed story had it that when the influential Spanish ambassador to England, Don Diego de Sarmiento de Acuña, count of Gondomar, an intimate of King James I, wished Sir Francis Bacon a "Happy Easter," he received the reply "A Happy Passover to you." This allusion must have been most galling to the haughty diplomat, who, although he received the title count only late in life, was descended from Castilian nobles on both his father's and his mother's side and was a sworn enemy of all heretics.[2]

Spain's unpopularity grew in proportion to its meddling in the affairs of other countries and the arrogance of its diplomats and soldiers abroad. This change in attitude was particularly noticeable in Germany during the long reign of Philip II (1556–98). In Charles V's lifetime the combination of Germany's imperial power with that of Spain and its far-flung possessions flattered those Germans who could not forget the great world-wide claims for supremacy of their early medieval emperors. In the person of Charles some romantics saw Frederick Barbarossa redivivus, the twelfth-century emperor glorified in German legend and poetry. Nor did Philip II altogether give up his imperial dreams. After his father's abdication, to be sure, the imperial crown of Germany, almost pledged to him in 1551, eluded his grasp, and his uncle Ferdinand I was elected instead. Yet he never relinquished the hope of acting as the head of both Houses of Habsburg. In 1562, when the Council of Trent reconvened for its third assembly and called for a representation of the Catholic powers, Philip suggested to Ferdinand that they be represented by a joint ambassador, a suggestion which Ferdinand was the less able to accept as he was trying to use the conciliar deliberations to bring the German Protestants back to the Catholic fold and thus restore denominational peace to the strife-ridden Empire. Subsequently, some of Philip's counselors advised him to assume the title "Emperor of the Indies." But even if he had followed that suggestion, he would not have been the "Holy Roman Emperor," claiming succession from the ancient Roman rulers as far back as Augustus and Constantine. At the same time, the appearance of Spanish troops in and around Germany from the Schmalkaldic War on, and the usual misbehavior of an unruly soldiery toward the civilian population, called forth increasingly unfavorable comments from German intellectuals, particularly those favoring Protestantism. Many Germans loudly denounced Spanish attempts at world domination. The poet Fischart, for example, rejoiced over the defeat of the Spanish Armada, because it was a blow to "the king's monarchical world drive/ and his subjects' world greed." Nor were the "bloody sentences" of the Spanish Inquisition or the government's "Machiavellian" policies readily overlooked. The occasional Spanish inquisitorial investigations of Marrano personnel employed by foreign embassies contributed to the anti-Spanish feeling among diplomats; it called forth, in 1526, a protest even from Jan Dantyszek (Dantiscus), the envoy of distant Poland. Ultimately, the spread of the "Black Legend" in England and on the Continent created an image of the "ugly Spaniard"—to paraphrase a modern parallel—which was but slightly mitigated by the much admired literary and artistic glories of Spain's Golden Age.[3]

Some of these accusations, particularly among Protestants, had a distinct religious bias. Philip II increasingly considered himself the champion of Catholicism and the Catholic Restoration in all lands. He was ready to support all anti-Protestant forces and even to promote the Spanish concept of racial *limpieza* among reluctant populations. For political reasons he may have made temporary concessions to professing Jews in the duchy of Milan; he may also have tried to secure some backing for his imperial policies from the Neapolitan Jewish exiles in Rome, as his father had done. But neither on the Iberian Peninsula nor in the Spanish Netherlands did he tolerate the slightest religious deviation.

Even Pius V, one of the least tolerant of the sixteenth-century popes, was amazed by the king's intransigence. When, in 1570, he suggested to Philip the appointment of his favorite, Francisco de Reinoso, as archdeacon of the Cathedral of Toledo, the king refused because of Reinoso's *converso* ancestry. The pope could not understand why a man of outstanding virtue and learning should be disqualified merely because of his Jewish origin. Pius finally prevailed upon the king to appoint Reinoso to the bishopric of Cordova. The pope also doubtless disregarded Philip's wishes when he conferred the rank of cardinal on a Spanish New Christian Jesuit, Francisco de Toledo, equally distinguished as scholar and diplomat—with a residence in Rome, of course, rather than in Spain. He also paid little attention to Philip's demand that he establish in Rome a special tribunal for the adjudication of litigations arising from the statutes of *limpieza,* litigations which, in the king's opinion, were inadequately handled by the papal *Rota.* It was this type of resistance to what Pius considered infringements of canon law, as well as the pope's insistence that Philip pay him "obedience" (despite the king's argument that he had already paid homage to the Papacy twice, as king of Naples and as king of Spain), and that Archbishop Carranza be removed from the Spanish inquisitorial prison to one in Rome, which led the Spanish envoy to Rome, Don Luis de Requésens, in his early dispatch of April 26, 1566, to advise Philip to pay formal obedience to the newly elected pontiff. In discussing Pius' weaknesses, Requésens described the new pope as "a bit choleric, suspicious, and little flexible in diplomatic negotiations, for all his life he had dealt only with religious affairs." Pius' "inflexibility" with respect to Spain's treatment of New Christians must have shocked Philip, in view of Pius' previously harsh record as Rome's inquisitor-general and his continued active participation in the proceedings of the Roman Inquisition to the end of his reign. Understandably, it took many years of negotiations before Philip succeeded in persuading the more moderate Sixtus V to promise him, in 1588, not to appoint New Christians to bishoprics in Spain and Portugal—a promise which, according to Philip's complaint, was broken in Portuguese Brazil, then under Spanish domination, when high ecclesiastical offices were entrusted to deserving New Christians. Sixtus, who personally disliked Philip, drew from the king's acts the conclusion that "while the preservation of the Catholic faith is a primary concern of the pope, it is but a pretext for His Majesty [Philip], whose chief objectives are the security and aggrandizement of his dominions" (1589). Spanish diplomats found it easier to persuade the less tolerant Clement VIII to agree, in 1600, not to entrust pastoral duties to priests of Jewish or Moorish descent down to the seventh generation.[4]

Philip's relations with the Papacy would doubtless have been even more strained, were it not for the dependence of the Spanish Treasury on its fiscal revenue from the Church, one of the wealth-

iest segments of Spanish society, Without adopting the extreme
ideological position of French Gallicanism, the Spanish hierarchy
of the Golden Age was perfectly willing to follow the leadership of
an increasingly absolutist and nationalist monarchy. We shall presently see how independent of papal direction the Spanish Inquisition was in compiling its own lists of prohibited books. The
Spanish prelates attending the Council of Trent also consistently
pursued a nationally oriented policy, and after the Council's conclusion Philip hesitated for more than a year before he allowed its
canons, as promulgated by Pope Pius IV, to be published and
circulated in his country (1565). At the same time only a papal
proclamation could procure for the deficit-ridden royal Treasury
the much-needed income from a *cruzada,* the special tax to help
finance a crusade against the Turks. It has been estimated that this
impost alone yielded some 4,000,000 reals in 1566, and double that
amount in 1598. Other significant revenues were derived from the
royal tithes and the so-called *subsidios* of the clergy, which proved
particularly helpful in the years preceding and following the battle
of Lepanto. In 1563–74, the Spanish clergy annually contributed
substantial sums—from a high of 187,025,263 maravedis in 1564
to a low of 114,516,767 in 1566—toward the upbuilding of the
navy for the decisive struggle with the Eastern enemy. The total
for the whole twelve-year period was over 1,640,791,000 maravedis;
that is, an average of some 136,732,500 maravedis per year. It is
small wonder, then, in the light of this religiopolitical interdependence of Spain and the Papacy, that Pius V could not gainsay
Requésens' assertion that, without the full support of the Inquisition, his king could not effectively protect Catholic interests in
his realm.[5]

Philip's increasingly implacable adherence to the principle of
limpieza in his Spanish provinces is the more remarkable as he
had, as crown prince, refused to cooperate with his former tutor,
Archbishop Juan Martínez Silíceo, in enforcing the Toledan statute
of 1547. By 1561, however, the plea of some leading citizens of
Tudela, including priests, that he allow the local New Christians to
occupy public offices, fell upon deaf ears. In vain did the burghers
eloquently argue: The *conversos'* "fathers and grandfathers have
converted to Christianity more than sixty-two years ago. They

themselves are competent and modest and have good mores and customs, and neither they nor their fathers have been guilty of any crime which would justify their exclusion from the enjoyment of general rights." On the other hand, the king did not himself hesitate to employ New Christians when their services were in his own, or the state's, interest. Just as his grandfather and father had used the medical ministrations of Francisco López de Villalobos, so Philip entrusted his and his family's health to the care of the eminent New Christian physician Luis de Mercador of Valladolid, who continued to serve, after Philip II's demise, as court physician to Philip III, until his own death. Similarly, the rise and fall of Antonio Pérez, Philip II's outstanding royal counselor, was little influenced by the king's suspicion of his Jewish antecedents. Most remarkably, Philip's inward Catholic piety responded so deeply to the teachings of St. Theresa de Jesús, whose so-called Theresian Reform was one of the profoundest and most enduring aspects of the Spanish Counter Reformation, that he was prone to forget her Jewish ancestry. (Theresa herself was the king's great admirer.)— All this despite the king's unfounded generalization, echoing similar assertions by his father and his former tutor, Silíceo, that "all the heresies which have sprouted in Germany and France, have owed their origin to descendants of Jews, as was also seen and still is seen daily in Spain." [6]

During the four decades of Philip's reign the Spanish Inquisition celebrated one victory after another, particularly over the hapless Marranos. If the Holy Office was daring enough to depose the primate of Spain, Archbishop Bartolomé de Carranza, and to keep him in prison for eighteen years (it failed to burn him at the stake only because of direct papal intervention and his removal to a Roman prison), there was no one in the country who could feel entirely secure. Among other matters, the archbishop may have annoyed the inquisitors with a sermon he delivered on August 21, 1558, which contained an eloquent plea for mercy in the treatment of heretics. In its attempt at total thought control the Inquisition—especially under the leadership of Inquisitor-General Fernando de Valdés, a typical ecclesiastical bureaucrat and Philip II's confidant—issued independent Indexes of forbidden books, disregarding the wishes of both the Papacy and the Council of

Trent. Valdés' Index of 1559 spoke in its introduction of the co-operation of Paul IV, but it failed to pay any attention to the Index issued by that pontiff in the same year. Not that Paul's Index was particularly lenient. On the contrary almost immediately after issuing it, the pope himself, partially at the prompting of Diego Laynez, the New Christian general of the Jesuit Order, prepared a *moderatio* of his Index, though this modification was not formally promulgated until 1561 by his successor Pius IV. It was this extremism of Paul's index which caused the Council of Trent, at the very beginning of its third assembly in January 1562, to entrust the preparation of a new Index to a commission of its own. However, even Paul's strictness did not quite satisfy Valdés and his associates. The difference between the Spanish and papal Indexes is well illustrated by their provisions with respect to Hebrew books. While Paul IV included in his compilation the outlawry of only "the Hebrew Talmud and all its glosses, annotations, interpretations, and expositions," the Valdés catalogue prohibited "all Hebrew books, or those written in any other language, relating to Jewish ceremonies," as well as those "belonging to the Old Law." Similarly, all the work done by the Index Commission of the Council of Trent and its final product, the Index published by Pius IV in 1564, were almost completely disregarded by the Spanish ecclesiastics. They glossed over particularly the Tridentine Index's modifying clause that the Talmud could be tolerated if it were published "without the title 'Talmud' and without insults and calumnies against the Christian religion." Spanish Indexes issued long after the Council's close, continued to repeat the Valdés formulation without any modification.[7]

Strict supervision over the printed word was further extended by the requirement of a royal license for the printing and sale of any book. Nor did such a license necessarily protect the author or bookseller from inquisitorial prosecution. Hence some authors preferred to publish their works abroad, particularly in Paris; if need be, anonymously or under a pseudonym. Even such confirmed Catholics as the sons of the last Castilian chief rabbi, Abraham Seneor, known under their new family name as Luis and Antonio Coronel, sought a measure of security in the foreign publication of their thoroughly orthodox theological tracts. To safeguard himself against malicious denunciations, Luis also made it a practice to deliver his sermons from manuscripts carefully prepared in advance. This happened years before his death in 1530; that is, during the initial, hesitant steps toward the exclusivist laws regarding *limpieza*. One may imagine the state of mind of a preacher when he had to replace the spontaneous fervor of religioethical exhortation with a deliberate scrutiny of every word or phrase in his sermon lest he incur the displeasure of some unknown inquisitorial informer in the audience.[8]

Otherwise, however, the Indexes as such and the related regulations had little practical effect on the Spanish Marranos. They would not have been able to own talmudic texts, however expurgated, without arousing suspicions of heterodoxy; the ensuing inquisitorial trials would have entailed serious consequences for them even if they were ultimately acquitted. True, the provision in the Valdés Index outlawing "any Bible translated into Castilian or any other vernacular language" was aimed principally at Old Christians. It appealed to the deep-seated popular suspicions of the use of such Bibles in support of heretical teachings, suspicions which, as far back as 1234, we recall, had induced James I of Aragon and the Church Council of Tarragona to try to suppress all Bibles in "Romancio." Yet this prohibition must have affected the *conversos* more deeply than the Old Christians. Since few individuals, other than clerics, could interpret the Latin Vulgate, the *conversos'* main source of information about Judaism came from whatever traditional Old Testament interpretation they had learned from their parents and teachers or from what they themselves were able to deduce from the biblical text in a Spanish or Portuguese translation. The Book of Esther, in particular, describing the vicissitudes of a secret Jewess, and her divinely inspired victory over the anti-Jewish agitator Haman, frequently served as a source of hope and comfort to the clandestine Iberian Judaizers in their darkest moments. But, largely shut off from the rejuvenating influence of direct contact with the Scriptures, the Marranos would have had to rely exclusively on secretly circulated books of Jewish customs, prayers, and the like, the mere possession of which would have served as *prima facie* evidence of judaizing.[9]

Remarkably, despite the contagious spread of exclusivist policies toward the descendants of former converts, both the Church and the state continued to pursue their missionary activities among the few practicing Jews within their reach. While professing Jews were threatened with speedy execution the moment they set foot on Spanish soil, converts to Christianity in other lands, including Marranos returning to the fold, were welcome as residents in Spain. The conversion of an occasional Jewish visitor from North Africa was often performed with great solemnity, although everyone must have realized that such newcomers would merely swell the ranks of unwanted New Christians.[10]

NEVER-ENDING SUSPICIONS

Before long, developments in Spain directly affected neighboring Portugal. Yet, just as the Holy Office had considerable difficulty in establishing itself in that country and could not start large-scale operations until 1547, so did the doctrine of *limpieza* make slow progress even in the Portuguese Church. Only after the Inquisition of Coimbra sentenced three New Christian canons and one professor of canon law for judaizing did an anti-*converso* reaction set in. At first the exclusion of men of Jewish ancestry from civil and ecclesiastical offices was limited to officials of the Inquisition itself, an exclusion repeated by an ordinance of 1570. Only gradually did appointments to all ecclesiastical benefices come under the ban. Ultimately, the archbishop of Évora decreed that descendants of Jews on the paternal side should forever be excluded, while those on the maternal side should be disqualified only to the seventh generation. These provisions for "purity of blood" were repeated in 1596 in Évora, and in 1625 in Oporto and Coimbra. At the same time the bishopric of Elvas excluded New Christians only to the fourth degree; that of Braga, to the second degree.[11]

However, these developments might not have occurred if Portugal had not been annexed by Philip II in 1580. Although the country retained its complete autonomy and independent administrative structure, including separate inquisitorial tribunals, the impact of royal intolerance unavoidably made itself felt in the Portuguese provinces as well. At the outset some New Christians in Portugal and abroad tried to forestall the annexation of Portugal by the Spanish monarch. They followed therein the example of their Navarrese coreligionists, who in 1512, after the occupation of their country by Ferdinand the Catholic, had sided with Prince Henry of Viana, the French-supported pretender to the throne, against the Spanish king. However, the local pro-Viana party had been quickly overwhelmed and many Marranos had been forced to flee the country. In 1580 the Portuguese New Christians had additional reasons to oppose Spanish domination and, hence, to side with the native pretender to the throne, Dom Antonio, prior of Crato. They were afraid, to cite the English agent in Portugal, Edward Wotton, "of being subject to the cruelty of the Spanish Inquisition which is much more severe than the Portuguese." Another reason suggested by the envoy was that Dom Antonio "has bastards by base women, most of them by 'New Christians,' " and many nobles feared that these children might be advanced by the new king at their own expense. It escaped the Englishman's attention that Dom Antonio himself was of partial Jewish descent and certainly would not have met the stringent Spanish criteria for *limpieza*. After overcoming the "Pretender's" weak resistance, Philip took sharp reprisals against Portugal's entire Marrano population. No sooner did he occupy the country than he speedily closed the gates to New Christian emigration. In 1583 he abrogated John III's specific enactment of 1537, and demanded that the Marranos wear headgear of yellow color, under the severe sanction of a fine of 100 cruzados and public flogging. The Portuguese Inquisition now likewise intensified its efforts. In the first two decades of Spanish rule (1580–1600), no fewer than fifty autos-da-fé were staged. While the records of five are lost, the other forty-five involved 162 burnings in person, 59 in effigy, and 2,979 "reconciliations." Understandably, many New Christians now felt safer in Spain proper. The more populous and heterogeneous country, where by that time secret judaizing had been largely suppressed, offered greater anonymity and, to some, better economic opportunities. As stressed at the trial of Felipe de Nájera, a Portuguese New Christian physician, many of his compatriots shared the hope of quickly earning 8,000–10,000 ducats and then proceeding to a place abroad where they might live an orthodox Jewish life. But the more numerous and prosperous these "Portuguese" settlers became, the more their presence in Spanish society led to redoubled vigilance on the part of the Spanish Holy Office.[12]

Long before the occupation of Portugal, however, the Spanish regime and public suspected the New Christians of lack of patriotism. The provocation was indeed enormous. A keen modern student of the early operation of the doctrine of *limpieza* rightly noted its adverse psychological effect on many well-educated and socially prominent New Christians. He wrote:

Men used to make a cult of honor, ready to seize the sword to avenge the slightest insult, find themselves completely powerless to alter the asphyxiating atmosphere which surrounds them. It is difficult to imagine today the kind of life lived by a village nobleman with an obscure blemish in his genealogy.

Daily observations of this sort induced the Venetian ambassador Lorenzo Priuli to report home in 1575 that exclusion from public office, in particular, was creating widespread discontent among the *conversos*. Casting aside his usual diplomatic restraint, he opined that, were it not for the entrenched royal power and its rigorous law enforcement, New Christians would stage a major uprising. Similar apprehensions, doubtless reinforced by exaggerated memories of the New Christian role in the *comunero* movement, inspired the ever anti-Marrano Castilian Cortes to insist, in a resolution of 1563, that all the higher local officials *(alcaldes y corregidores)* on the frontiers and in maritime centers, as well as all captains of galleys, be of Old Christian stock. These were, of course, the points most exposed to attack by enemies and corsairs, often considered Ottoman allies. Nor was departure from the Iberian Peninsula easy, in view of the government controls over emigration. It certainly came as no surprise to Philip II when he learned of the anti-Spanish activities of Don Joseph Nasi at the Porte. So irked was the king by the Jewish duke's hostile moves that, as we recall, he was prepared to do all in his power to lay hands on the Jewish statesman, dead or alive. Even Don Joseph's rival at the Sultan's court, however, Don Solomon Ashkenazi, was blamed for having, after the battle of Lepanto, mediated the separate peace between Venice and the Ottoman Empire and for thus making the great Republic sever its ties with the League. Philip undoubtedly realized that it was only Dom Antonio's ineptitude and unreliability which eventually discouraged Alvaro Mendez and his New Christian friends from continuing the struggle in the Pretender's behalf.[13]

Under Philip's reign the Portuguese Inquisition began to share with its Spanish counterpart the vices of an uncontrolled bureaucracy which considered itself accountable only to God— that is, to its own conscience. Such nearly absolute power made it increasingly irresponsible and corrupt. These deficiencies, need- less to say, existed to some extent even before the Spanish annexa- tion. As early as 1561, when the Portuguese Holy Office had been in full operation for only fourteen years, its abuses had already begun to approach those of its older sister institution across the border. Ordered to institute an investigation, the papal nuncio in Portugal, Bishop Prospero (Publicola) de Santa-Croce of Chis- samos, found that the local inquisitors, among them Gerónymo da Azambuja (better known as Hieronymus ab Oleastro), had per- formed their duties with excessive cruelty. He claimed that many persons convicted for judaizing were pious Christians and that countless other defendants were allowed to rot in dungeons for years without trial. The nuncio questioned whether such extreme measures were not driving the population to the point of despera- tion and whether one could not devise better means of securing the genuine conversion of doubtful Christians. But even the moderate Pope Pius IV was unable to remedy the situation, and Portugal's unification with Spain only reinforced the underlying degenerative factors.[14]

By virtue of the Holy Office's rapid expansion and the favoritism prevailing in ecclesiastical and governmental circles, the inquisi- torial personnel in both Spain and Portugal not only proliferated in number (in the seventeenth century the Portuguese Inquisition alone had fully thirty branch offices) but declined in its intellectual and moral qualifications. Some leaders tried to overcome these shortcomings through frequent inspections by *visitadores*. But the latter's reports, however damning, rarely led to the dismissal of guilty officials. When, in 1544, Dr. Alonso Pérez reported that all but two members of the Barcelona Holy Office had had improper relations with women, that all of them accepted bribes and made illegal charges, and that, for the most part, they quarreled with one another, the Suprema admitted the validity of these accusations but, except for verbal reprimands and warnings for the future, failed to punish the offenders. In 1579, and again in 1583, the Cortes of Castile bitterly complained that any individual quarreling with an inquisitor ran the risk of being arrested and immured in a secret prison for years without trial, a procedure which, even in the case of his ultimate acquittal, inflicted permanent disgrace on his family. Philip II promised to investigate these abuses, but apparently did nothing to stem them. In 1600, finally, the inquisitor-general, Cardinal Ferdinand Nino de Guevara, submitted to Philip III a memorandum emphasizing that many inquisitors were completely unfit for their tasks. Rather than discharge these officials, however, the king merely suggested that they be transferred to other positions, for their public exposure, he feared, would discredit the Holy Office.[15]

Not surprisingly, the Inquisition became one of the most hated institutions. Its activities greatly contributed to the creation of the "Black Legend" in England and on the Continent. Nonetheless, the institution maintained its hold on the Iberian population, through its terrorist methods, the dependence of royal power on its support, and the apparent absence of any alternative to combat what was considered the even greater menace of overt or underground heresy, with its disruptive effect on the unity of the realm. Certainly, the Inquisition could count on the public's unflinching support for its measures against alleged Judaizers, who were considered the most dangerous divisive factor. Its sharp anti-Marrano bias came clearly to the fore in a discussion at its Council, when it was suggested that the inquisitors be ordered not to conclude trials against circumcized Judaizers, in contrast to other offenders, without first consulting the Council. "For in such cases one has to see whether it might be appropriate to impose upon them some extraordinary penalty. It is held to be more frequently indicated that they should not be admitted to reconciliation without conclusive proof of penitence and without their giving signs of genuine conversion which would rectify the damage caused by their infidelity." [16]

Practically no one was safe from the Inquisition's grasp, however. Because the University of Salamanca had become a major center of theological and biblical study, as well as the chief power-house for the political rationales of the existing order, "whose most genuine offshoot was Philip II, the most Spanish among our kings" (L. Pereña Vicente), its professors were doubly exposed to prosecution for alleged deviations. Those teachers who happened to have Jewish (or Moorish) blood in their veins were automatically suspect. Among these individuals and their colleagues at other universities were, as we recall, men of the standing of Luis de León, Cristóbal de Grajal, Alonso Gudiel, and Martín Martínez de Cantalapiedra. Clearly, the essential conflict of principle between the conservatives in the Holy Office and the Renaissance Hebraists who had learned to study biblical texts in accordance with the more exacting demands of grammar and comparative philology, sufficed for the former to condemn all such new approaches as outright heresies. The mere acceptance by these scholars of some of the more literal interpretations by Jewish Bible commentators, in contrast with the metaphorical and hermeneutic expositions regnant in the Catholic tradition, was evidence enough to brand them as confirmed deviationists.[17]

It is small wonder, then, that the Iberian authorities viewed with suspicion the distribution of Hebrew Bibles, even among Old Christians. On one occasion in June 1562 the Portuguese ambassador in London sharply protested to the queen against English interference with Portugal's economic preserve in Morocco. One of his objections was that, instead of aiding the Portuguese efforts to christianize the Moroccans, the English and French merchants supplied the "infidels" with arms and metals for the manufacture of ships. He cited as an example a ship bound for Larache in September 1561, which "was freighted openly with oars, lances, tin, and other metals, and secretly with certain armours and weapons defensive, and with 120 great coffers laden with bibles and other books in Hebrew for the Jews dwelling in those countries." In its reply of June 15, 1562, the English government expressed surprise that the shippers were able to pick up so many Hebrew Bibles in England, which suffered from a shortage of these books, and also contended that it saw no reason why Scriptures "should not be sold to Jews, Saracens, and all other nations seeing they contain God's true law." To which the Portuguese diplomat irately retorted, on June 19, that he had not come "to dispute whether it is right for Christians to sell Bibles to Jews," but that it was a fact that "twenty-six chests of bibles and books were brought from Flanders" and he felt that the king of Portugal was correct in prohibiting foreigners from doing "the same thing that he forbids his own subjects." According to the ambassador, those volumes had originated not from England but from Flanders, undoubtedly from the famous Plantin press, founded but seven years before in Antwerp. This press was said to have "made its most substantial profits from the sales of Roman Catholic devotional books"; and a competitor, Paulus Manutius, was later to complain that the Plantin firm shipped copies of the new Tridentine *Breviary* to Spain and Portugal in contravention of an earlier agreement. Nonetheless, Philip II himself soon became one of its best customers.[18]

FROM PRUDENCE TO CRONYISM

Philip II's death in 1598 brought no abrupt change in Spanish anti-Marrano policies. Rumor current among some New Christians had it that the king's painful and disgusting disease (his body had been covered with odorous boils during the fifty-three days of his last illness at the Escorial) had been predicted by a clergyman of Jewish descent as a punishment for his mistreatment of suspected Judaizers. But the Iberian New Christians could expect at best the replacement of a strong reign by a weak one subject to all sorts of outside influences which at times might mitigate the pressure on them. Philip II is said to have complained that "God who had entrusted me with so many kingdoms, has denied me a son capable to govern them." However, much of his son's weakness was caused by the father's rigidity and implacability in the face of changing constellations. As Edward Grierson observed with reference to the successful Dutch rebellion, "by 1590 Spain had become a nation of bewildered and self-questioning zealots. Doubts about her well-being which could have been faced in the days when she was outward-looking, festered once she had turned in upon herself." Philip III (1598-1621), characterized by a recent Spanish historian as a "good-natured, bigoted, lazy . . . gourmand," certainly was not the man to stem the forces of decay in his far-flung empire. As early as 1596, Francisco Sorranzo, the Venetian envoy, drew an interesting comparison between father and son in which he contrasted Philip II's greater experience, defiance of the grandees, and considerable independence of the Church, with his son's leaning on his counselors, and reluctance to antagonize either the aristocracy or the hierarchy. From the outset, Philip III delegated responsibility for the management of his vast empire to a favorite, Don Francisco de Sandoval, Marquis de Denia, Count de Lerma. For some twenty years the count, with a small clique of his own protégés, ran the country's affairs, always with an eye toward self-aggrandizement and luxurious living. According to a contemporary estimate, the count's annual income amounted to some 600,000 ducats. Because of his intensive involvement in financial affairs, Lerma fully appreciated the commercial importance of the Portuguese for the country. In a letter dated September 16, 1605, he wrote: "It is well known that the Portuguese merchants are most responsible for maintaining the trade and commerce of Europe, since they reside in all major business centers, the principal among them being Lisbon and its residents." [19]

Other royal cronies were even more mercenary than Lerma. One of them was Don Pedro Franquesa, Count de Villalonga, the secretary of state, whose venality during his tenure of office from 1600 to 1606 is well attested, though the statement that his dealings with Jews had accrued for him some 1,000,000 ducats is clearly exaggerated. This allegation did not appear at all among the 374 charges presented by the prosecutor at his trial in 1607 and after. But other charges were well substantiated, and the count ultimately landed in prison. More importantly, the finances of the Treasury fell into increasing disarray. Some people claimed, with obvious overstatement, that Philip III spent in one year what his fathers had saved in seventy. More realistically, Henry IV of France, in a letter to Nicholas de Neufville de Villeroy of May 16, 1601, commented that he did not fear continued war with Spain, because Philip III "is no better provided with money than the others." In his desperate need of funds, Philip III resorted to questionable methods of securing appropriations from the provincial organs. As early as 1599, he committed "shameless duplicity" in first promising to remedy the Catalan complaints against inquisitorial abuses and then secretly countermanding his pertinent requests from the Holy See. In utter confusion the Spanish Treasury began issuing more and more "vellon" in a blend of copper and silver of varying purity, which understandably led to growing inflation and was one of the causes of Spain's rapid decline.[20]

Fiscal stringency, as well as the personal greed of royal advisers, paved the way for negotiations with the Portuguese New Christians about a relaxation of anti-Marrano persecution. Such negotiations had behind them a time-honored tradition. During the very struggle for the establishment of the Inquisition in Portugal, both King Emanuel and King John III had shown themselves amenable to compromise (1533, 1535, 1548). Even the pious Crusader King Sebastian was induced in 1577 to accept a negotiated settlement with New Christians in return for their financial assistance (variously estimated as amounting to 225,000 ducats or 250,000 cruzados) toward his ill-fated North-African Crusade. Remarkably, Philip II himself, who had censured Sebastian's action, seems toward the end of his life to have contemplated, with the aid of a commission headed by Inquisitor-General Pedro Domínguez de Portocarrero, some major modifications in the existing statutes of the "purity of blood." While no official documentary evidence is available, credible rumors were circulated then, and persisted long after, that he was planning to limit the discrimination against descendants of Jews and Moors to either the fourth generation or a century after the ancestor's original conversion. This project was abandoned, however, after Philip's death in 1598, and Portocarrero's retirement and demise in 1599–1600.[21]

On the international level, too, some important changes appeared to be under review. A noteworthy anonymous report by a writer of the first decade of the seventeenth century refers to an unsigned memorandum submitted to Cristóbal de Moura which suggested to Philip II that in his struggle with the Ottoman Empire he enlist the cooperation of influential New Christians.

Here it was proposed that the King entrust the conquest of the Kingdom of Jerusalem to that nation, by naming a king of that caste and helping this enterprise with a major portion of his troops. With these forces and those they could gather in the whole world they could easily become masters [of the Holy Land] and thereby relieve Spain [of the New Christian population].

Such a scheme for the conquest of Palestine by the Spaniards in cooperation with the Jewish people may not have been quite so venturesome as it appears. True, messianic dreams did not require much realism, particularly in periods of great stress. In despair the New Christians were ready to embrace even the millenarian trends emanating from their Old Christian neighbors, like that represented by Gonçalo Annes Bandarra earlier in the century (especially 1530–40). Nor should we forget the Reubeni episode, in which both the Papacy and the Portuguese monarchy had given serious consideration to the Oriental "messenger's" proposal of a Western alliance with the alleged Jewish kingdom in the East, against the Ottoman Empire. In the 1590s the international constellation appeared quite favorable for the renewal of such an undertaking. Both Don Joseph Nasi and Don Solomon ibn Ya'ish (Alvaro Mendez), dukes of Naxos and Mytilene, respectively, had been engaged, with the sultan's approval, in successively building up a Jewish colony around Tiberias, with the view of establishing there a semi-independent center of Jewish life. There is no way of telling whether the proposal here discussed emanated independently from the Iberian New Christians or, what appears less likely, if they acted with the tacit approval of some Jewish leaders in Constantinople. We know that Ibn Ya'ish, at first an ardent supporter of Dom Antonio, subsequently broke off relations with the unreliable Pretender. After the defeat of the Spanish Armada in 1588 and the progressive relaxation of Spanish-English tensions —a détente which finally led to the peace treaty of 1604—the Jewish leader, too, may have made peace with Philip II. Yet, whatever merits the proposal for a Spanish Jewish proto-Zionist enterprise may have possessed in the eyes of some royal counselors in Madrid, it also aroused much opposition. The very writer of the memorandum to which we owe our knowledge of the proposal, seems to have voiced the prevailing feeling that the plan would run counter to the intent of Scripture and that Spain could rid herself of that unwelcome segment of the population by a simple decree of expulsion. While Bishop Piñero (Antonio Pineiro?)

allegedly supported the project, it was opposed by the Spanish viceroy in Portugal, Don Cristóbal de Moura, and was ultimately rejected by the king. Philip reportedly instructed his ambassador in Rome to prevent the Papacy from making any such concessions to the New Christians.[22]

Be this as it may, during the transition of rule from Philip II to Philip III a few influential individuals suggested a liberalization of the stringent policies vis-à-vis the *conversos*. About 1600 an unnamed writer submitted to Philip III a memorandum in which he praised the 1492 expulsion of the Jews by the Catholic monarchs, but criticized the continued discrimination against *conversos* more than a century later. He pointed out that the Lord himself chastised sons for the sins of their forefathers only to the fourth generation, and demanded that the king follow that example. More important was the public appeal of the popular Dominican preacher Fray Agustín Salucio, whose sermons had attracted multitudes, overtaxing the capacity of the largest Madrid churches. Even Philip II was said to have been so impressed by the preacher's oratory and sincerity that he observed to Don Diego de Cordoba, "Verily, this is a friar and preacher of truths; I ought always to listen to him with much benefit." Two or three years before his demise in 1601, Salucio published his *Discurso . . . acerca de la justicia y buē gobierno de España, en los estatutos de limpieza de sangre: y si conviene, o no, alguna limitación en ellos,* claiming that, weighed down with years and close to his death, he felt it to be a matter of conscience for him to state his views on a subject "most important to the service of God and the welfare of the realm." Among the arguments he presented for a limitation of the statutes of *limpieza,* perhaps the most interesting are those relating to the disequilibrium created by them within Spain's class structure and to their impact on foreign nations. Domestically, Salucio insisted, the laws had become seriously prejudicial to the nobility, whose genealogical records were fairly intact, "whereas among the lower classes the memory of infidel ancestors rarely goes back fifty years." As a result, the country had been torn apart into two warring camps and lived in a state akin to civil war. Abroad Spain's reputation had suffered severely. "The statutes have caused foreigners indiscriminately to call us Marranos. Nor can we escape being considered disreputable or insane.

The ill fame is justified, since Spain finds it necessary to disqualify such a multitude of persons; we are regarded as insane, for we defame ourselves unnecessarily." While not spelling out in detail which measures were to be taken, Salucio advocated a distinct revision of the existing laws, without in any way interfering with inquisitorial trials of persons suspected of heretical beliefs or practices.[23]

No one could deny the persuasiveness of Salucio's complaint about the equation of Spaniards and Portuguese with Marranos, particularly in France and Italy, which was extremely galling to the proud Iberians. The following comment by Gonzalo Fernández de Oviedo is typical of the reaction of the Spanish intellectuals to what they considered an insulting generalization: "In France, as well as in Germany and Italy, for purposes of vituperation they indiscriminately call all Spaniards Marranos without understanding what a Marrano is. They do it only because they want to exasperate all Spaniards by calling them Jews, just as in various lands they call any German a Lutheran, which means neither more nor less than that he is a heretic. All of which causes much pain and infamy [to many persons] and accrues to greater injury than one can express or contemplate." Nevertheless Salucio's general plea for modification of the statutes relating to the "purity of blood" evoked little favorable response among the generally cowed opponents of the inquisitorial system, and it was quietly repudiated by the conservative forces as well as by the populace at large. According to Henry Charles Lea, Philip III immediately outlawed the circulation of the *Discurso,* but he was unable to prevent its long-range impact, as demonstrated by the numerous pamphlets favorably or unfavorably commenting on some of the major issues raised by the Dominican preacher. Though rarely dated, most of these tracts seem to have been written in the early years of Philip IV's reign, when the issue of the statutes and their administration once again came under review.[24]

COSTLY PARDON

Unexpectedly, Salucio's arguments actually strengthened the hand of Philip III's administration in its negotiations for a general amnesty for Marranos. Discussions began within a few months after Philip's accession to the throne. On December 28, 1598, the papal nuncio, Cardinal Enrico Caëtani, reported to the secretary of state, Cardinal Pietro Aldobrandini (the pope's nephew), that the New Christians were offering the king funds "in return for favors." By 1601 the new papal nuncio, Domenico Ginnasi (Gymnasius), could be more specific. In his report to Aldobrandini of June 22, he spoke of the New Christians' wish to secure a general pardon from the pope. Negotiations conducted to this effect in Rome were confirmed by Aldobrandini in his reply of July 13, 1601. In the following months the secretary and the nuncio frequently referred to such negotiations in both Madrid and Rome. They also mentioned the opposition of the Portuguese bishops, some of whom were ready to travel to Rome to intervene with the pope against the contemplated amnesty. Also confronted with the objections of the Spanish viceroy in Lisbon, Philip III and Lerma had to proceed very cautiously. In 1601 they only issued an ordinance removing the obstacles to Marrano emigration and another which generally prohibited insulting New Christians. For this concession the Treasury received the substantial payment of 170,000 cruzados. But this was merely a first step. Eager to secure the more than tenfold payment offered by the New Christians, the government rode roughshod over the opposition of the three Portuguese archbishops and of large segments of the public, represented by the numerous student rioters at the University of Coimbra and elsewhere. The continued negotiations with the papal see ultimately resulted in a brief issued by Clement VIII on August 23, 1604, granting a general pardon to the Portuguese New Christians. This papal ordinance was officially announced in Lisbon on January 16, 1605, and was soon extended to the Latin American colonies. In return the Treasury received a pledge of 1,860,000 cruzados (according to one estimate) from the New Christian community. Lerma secured an additional 50,000 cruzados for himself, while other officials of both the Inquisition and the government divided further spoils of 100,000 cruzados. These were very substantial sums, considering that some eighteen years later, despite progressive inflation, the royal revenue from all of Spain's and Portugal's far-flung possessions totaled no more than 26,000,000 ducats.[25]

Even the earlier, more limited decree of 1601 had resulted in some immediate, if not long-range, benefits to the Treasury. Although its main provision allowed the Marranos to emigrate and take along their property, not all their possessions could be readily removed. To be sure, there is no way of telling how many New Christians made use of the newly granted freedom to emigrate in the period 1601–1610. According to the confirmed Jew-baiter Fray Francisco de Torrejoncillo, who wrote a quarter century later (1634), no fewer than 2,000 Marranos had emigrated to the Low Countries alone. This is an obvious exaggeration by an antagonist who did not fail to emphasize that the "purity of blood" statutes were rightly designed to apply to New Christians forever, since inquisitors had found that some *conversos* of as late as the twenty-first generation (!) had reverted to Judaism. We recall that even in 1616, when the city of Amsterdam for the first time seriously considered the presence of Jews in its midst, the Jewish community was still very small; it was not to reach the figure of 2,000 souls until some thirty years later. Nonetheless, the Crown stood to gain much from both the confiscation of property belonging to suspected heretics remaining in the country and the appropriation of real estate left behind by émigrés. That the Inquisition's sequestrations and confiscations involved large sums may be noted from the records of the Granada Holy Office, which in the two and a half years from May 1, 1599, to November 15, 1601, had collected from this source 23,678,987 maravedis. In dire financial straits, the Treasury welcomed such accessions to its resources, by whatever means.[26]

At the same time, the Inquisition continued with its work of suppressing heresy. Unwilling to let the persons then under investigation go scot-free, the Lisbon Inquisition staged another auto-da-fé on January 16, 1605, at which 155 persons appeared in their sanbenitos. But, after confessing and promising to repent, they were all discharged. Similarly, a major auto originally scheduled in Seville for November 14, 1604, was canceled at the last moment by a special royal order transmitted by a courier who had traversed the distance from Valladolid to Seville in the amazingly short time of three days. But this suppression of a grand spectacle, which had attracted thousands of visitors to the southern emporium, caused a bitter outcry, not only among the inquisitors and their allies but also among the populace at large. Under pressure the king was forced to revoke his cancellation, and the auto was staged as originally planned at a later date, although apparently no victims were burned at the stake. Moreover, the king reassured the archbishops of Lisbon, Évora, and Braga that, though he had helped to secure the pardon from the pope, he had no intention of opening public offices and dignities to the New Christians. Nevertheless, popular discontent continued at a high pitch. A contemporary Portuguese poet, Pero Rioz Soares, writing in a mixture of Portuguese and Castilian, doubtless reflected public opinion when he prayed, "May God hold His hand and pardon these pardons." Not surprisingly, in 1610, when the New Christian payments began lagging, the king changed his mind and revoked the general pardon, including the license for the emigration of Marranos, under the vague excuse "that they had badly abused it and because of other inconveniences." As later pointed out by a contemporary, Martín González de Cellorigo, this revocation of a bilateral contract paid for by the other party, was enacted without any public discussion.[27]

It is unclear to what extent the revocation was connected with the new attitude taken by the government toward the Spanish Moriscos, whose position was then reaching its ultimate crisis. Although technically they, too, belonged to the general category of New Christians and indeed revealed many similarities to those of Jewish ancestry, most Moriscos were of the same ethnic descent as the Old Christians and, being a predominantly rural and impoverished population, appeared less interesting to the inquisitorial agents and publicists outside Granada. Nevertheless, the Spanish government long conducted an implacable campaign to uproot their old folkways. Philip II issued, in 1568, a harsh decree which, among other matters, forced many Morisco parents to place their children in Old Christian homes for a fully Christian education, a measure reminiscent of a similar Visigothic enactment with respect to children of Jewish converts. The increasingly oppressive inquisitorial prosecutions, which led to the condemnation of a fourteen-year-old girl for exclaiming "Mohammed," and of another "culprit" for stating that God would reward the good deeds of Muslims and Jews; the cruel treatment of Morisco prisoners, as described by Bartolomé de Lescano in 1557; as well as numerous arbitrary acts of discrimination by officials and landlords, led in 1500–1570 to a chain of uprisings, the so-called *rebelión al-pujarreña* (named after the inhabitants of Alpujarra, a mountainous district in Andalusia), which was suppressed with much difficulty. Thereupon many Moriscos were dispersed throughout Spain. But the embers of revolt still smoldered for years, and a small-scale guerrilla war was carried on by some Morisco mountaineers in the vicinity of Granada. For a while Christian burghers were even afraid to appear on the streets of distant Seville. This and other uprisings highlighted the dangers to Spain of the presence of an "Ottoman fifth column," abetted by North-African princes. According to information supplied to the French government in December 1569 by three wealthy Jewish merchants of Constantinople, who had come to Paris to discuss the liquidation of debts owed by the French king to Don Joseph Nasi, a Turkish armada was due to attack the coast of Spain sometime in 1570. According to other dispatches, the kings of Morocco, Fez, and other Barbary states, urged the Turks to take the offensive in a sort of pan-Islamic movement to "lend color and support to the Spanish Moors."[28]

This danger to Spain was averted by the allied victory at Lepanto. But secret profession of Islam continued, even in the more remote bishoprics of Cuenca and Sigüenza. In 1576 Gregory XIII appointed Miguel Tomás bishop of Segorbe, because of "the particular affection the said doctor had shown for the conversion of Muslims and New Christians in Spain," and some eleven years before had written a conversionist tract for this purpose. After the uprising of 1568–70, the Inquisition of Granada complained that the rebels went about boasting of the number of Old Christians they had killed, and that none of them appeared at confession. No fewer than 780 Moriscos, in a total of 998 persons sentenced, appeared in the 12 autos staged in Granada between 1550 and 1580; 14 of them were burned alive, and 65 in effigy. Some New Christians of Jewish descent were said to have evinced considerable sympathy for their Morisco compatriots. In his trial under Philip III, for example, Felipe de Nájera was accused of having, among other misdeeds, glorified Turks and Moors. Moreover, many

Spaniards were particularly concerned about what they considered a disproportionate rate of population growth among both the Marranos and the Moriscos. In his *Discurso* (1598/99), Agustín Salucio referred to widespread apprehension that, because of their early marriages and restricted emigration to the Indies and other lands, the Moriscos multiplied "like rabbits" and, few as they were at the time, in some centuries they might outnumber the Old Christian Spaniards. In a similar vein, when asked by the prosecutor why the mass emigration of New Christians from Portugal had not reduced that segment of the population, Nájera is said to have replied that it was "because neither New Christian males nor females become monks or nuns, but on coming of age even cousins married one another and procreated like mice." He also declared that one served God much better through matrimony than through celibacy—a tenet sharply condemned by the Inquisition. Under those circumstances, many Old Christian Spaniards felt that their people faced the alternative of either successfully assimilating both minorities or else banishing them from the country.[29]

Expulsion seemed, at least superficially, an easier solution in the case of the Moriscos than in that of the Marranos. The New Christians of Jewish origin were too closely woven into the fabric of both Spanish and Portuguese society, they had penetrated too deeply into the ruling groups of the population, and had become economically too indispensable, for the government seriously to consider the repeated suggestions that they be banished. In fact, however, Philip III's edict expelling all Moriscos on September 22, 1609, was carried out only after the application of utterly ruthless methods, over a period of six years. Contrary to expectations, the impact on the domestic economy, too, was quite severe. To be sure, the number of Moriscos affected by the decree has been subject to extended debate in recent years. Accepting the more reasonable estimates, ranging from 310,000 to 340,000 (in part going back to the figures supplied in 1618 by Jaime Bleda, whose anti-Morisco bias had long been nurtured by his personal experiences with them in a Valencia parish)—these figures contrast sharply with the inflated totals of some 2,000,000 Jews and 3,000,000 Moriscos given by another contemporary chronicler, Pedro Fernández Navarette, in 1626—Henri Lepeyre and Pierre Chaunu have shown how greatly the Muslim population of Granada had declined since that province's conquest by the Catholic monarchs a little more than a century before. The expulsion now affected altogether 2,026 Moriscos residing in the region of their old kingdom, as against 117,464 in the kingdom of Valencia alone. Yet, it can hardly be denied that the loss of more than 300,000 industrious persons from Spain necessarily left a void, one which an upsurging economy might have been able to fill but which the declining and increasingly disorganized imperial regime could ill afford. For the Marranos this act entailed not only diminution of economic opportunities but also the loss of whatever comfort the presence of another minority group might have been to them, as well as greater concentration on them by the inquisitorial prosecutors.[30]

Needless to say, there also were other destructive biological and economic forces which adversely affected both the majority and the minorities. In the first half of the seventeenth century the Iberian Peninsula suffered gravely from a series of pestilences which were quite costly in human lives and greatly impeded population growth. It is estimated that the plague of 1596–1602 alone caused the death of some 500,000 persons, led to the flight of untold multitudes from one infected area after another, and played havoc with the municipal services in many cities. As in other periods of great tension, the New Christian minority was affected not only by the plagues themselves but also by the increasing hostility and suspicions of the majority. In addition, the New Christians must have sustained greater losses in life, limb, and property from the ensuing unsettled conditions, the growing crime wave, and the general insecurity on the streets of the major cities. Whatever protection was offered individual citizens by the special concern for law and order of the various "holy brotherhoods"— one of these fraternities, the Brotherhood of Talavera, in 1746 invoked the example of Moses' and Jethro's behavior in emergencies —doubtless benefited Catholics more than it did suspected infidels or heretics.[31]

Although the seventeenth-century plagues compared neither in virulence nor in geographic extension with those of the fourteenth century, and did not leave behind many ghost towns and depopulated countrysides, their impact on the Iberian population must have been quite marked. Regrettably, we cannot tell to what extent they specifically affected the New Christian segment. We need not take at face value contemporary assertions about the relatively large increase of the Marrano and Morisco ratios in the population, though the abovementioned rationales for this discrepancy sound quite plausible. In any case, because of the very secrecy of their profession of Judaism, it is unknown how many real Judaizers were found among the New Christians in the country, whose general number itself, despite all the researchers of *limpieza* by the inquisitorial offices, is shrouded in obscurity. Nor can we tell to what extent the New Christians employed slaves in their households or businesses. The French traveler Antoine de Brunel observed in 1655 that almost all the domestic servants in Seville were slaves, Negro or Moorish, who had not been freed even after their adoption of Christianity. Another traveler compared the physiognomy of Seville with a chessboard, where black figures alternated with white ones. Yet we rarely hear of Negro slaves in the households of secret Judaizers. The inquisitorial records frequently offer the testimony of servants from the defendants' households, but these witnesses evidently were for the most part free Spanish or Portuguese proletarians. Nor did the great Marrano international traders appear to have played an independent role in the growing slave trade, of which both Lisbon and Seville were major centers. Occasional references like that to the purchase of a boatload of slaves by Manuel Rodriguez Lamego (a brother of the Rouen Jewish leader) are too rare to be typical. Perhaps the ever-present danger of denunciation to the Inquisition by disgruntled slaves served as a major deterrent.[32]

GROWING MALAISE

Internal difficulties in the New Christian camp further aggravated its critical situation. From the outset some New Christians, considering themselves pious Catholics, did not see any reason why they should pay for a pardon which, they claimed, was none of their concern. To be sure, after close examination of the records of Oporto, Tomar, and Beja for the years 1536–1616, I. S. Révah came to the conclusion that in the early seventeenth century the majority of New Christian inhabitants of these cities were secret Judaizers. Some of them, including members of the clergy, later became pillars of the Synagogue in Amsterdam and other more tolerant localities. But many residents of Lisbon and other major Portuguese cities, and particularly those who since 1580 had settled in Spain, felt sufficiently secure not to wish to participate in the heavy contributions (totaling about 2,000,000 cruzados). Quite a few actually protested to the king that Alfonso Gómes, the chief negotiator of the pardon, was not entitled to represent them. At the same time the fiscal organs were interested in spreading the payments over as many individuals as possible, so as to ensure their ultimate collection. That is why they supported Gómes and the other New Christian leaders in making all likely taxpayers of this category share the burden. Not surprisingly, however, as time went on, the number of evaders increased, and payments to the Treasury began lagging far behind schedule.[33]

Occasionally, maladjusted refugees returned home from abroad and, at least formally, rejoined the Catholic community. Whenever the Inquisition got hold of such repatriates, it tried to secure from them information about other former Marranos, now overtly professing Judaism, with whom they had been in contact in the foreign countries. Such information not only was used to detect one or another of these "apostates" who dared to visit Spain or Portugal on business or for family reasons but also often served to incriminate their Iberian relatives. At the very least it helped the Holy Office to reconstruct genealogical data which would deny the "purity" of descent to some New Christian families at home. An outstanding example of such a witness was Hector Mendes Bravo. Born about 1591 in Lagos, southern Portugal, he was taken to Italy at the age of fifteen by his widowed New Christian mother, who had been frightened by the arrest of one of her friends. After spending more than a decade in the rapidly growing Jewish communities of Venice, Hamburg, and Amsterdam, where he got into difficulties with the local authorities, he returned to Lisbon. On December 11, 1617, he suddenly appeared on his own initiative before the Lisbon inquisitor, confessed his sins, and in the course of repeated hearings, furnished him with full lists of names of Marranos whom he had met in the three cities. He thus obtained for himself full "reconciliation" with the Holy Office, and his testimony proved very helpful to the inquisitorial agents abroad, as well as at home.[34]

Internal disunity was exacerbated by the general ambiguity of the Marrano position. Its psychological impact is well illustrated by the reminiscences of the sensitive poet João Pinto Delgado. Describing the impression originally made upon him by the beautiful landscape of his native Algarve, the Portuguese district bordering on Spanish Andalusia, the poet declared that, after he reached the age of discernment, his environment began to appear to him as both dismal [humilde] and dangerous.

Dismal, because of the few opportunities it offers for the proper employment of hours to be spent in the study of science; dangerous, for my ancestors had implanted in my soul saplings of the Most Holy Law, the fruits of which I could not touch for sustenance during my 'orlah [uncircumcision]. This anxious concern has inclined my mind to make everything appear different from what it was. I have timidly dissimulated the truth with deceitful appearances so as to deflect any suspicion which might give rise to an investigation resulting in the loss of the three supreme values in the world: honor, life, and property.

For better camouflage Pinto Delgado wrote a laudatory poem on an anti-Jewish tract by João Baptista de Este, a newcomer from Venice who had undergone baptism there, the Portuguese ambassador serving as his godfather. As late as 1616, the youthful poet collaborated with one Luís de Tovar in the writing of an enthusiastic poetic biography of Saint Anthony of Padua. Such precautions seemed doubly necessary, since in 1613–14 the Portuguese authorities had conducted a census of all New Christians absent from their original habitats, and the Pinto Delgado family was listed as having moved from Vila Nova to Lisbon. Only after the family had circumvented the prohibition of emigrating abroad, reenacted in 1610, and had found a relatively peaceful resting place in Rouen, could young João reveal his innermost feelings and exhort his fellow Marranos to "fear and adore exclusively/ the King of Kings/ Who was, will be and is/ [and] to proclaim:/ One God, one People, one Law." The last two verses are clear echoes of

the Jewish liturgical praise of the eternity of God (in *Adon 'olam*
[Lord of the Universe] and other prayers), and of the well-known
rabbinic apothegm that "God, Israel and the Torah are one." It
is also possible, as suggested by I. S. Révah, that the poet (or one of
his New Christian predecessors) thus wished to underscore the
difference between the Jewish profession of faith and the oft-
cited call to arms by the Spanish poet Hernando de Acuña: "One
Monarch, one Empire, one Sword!" [35]

Nor was the debate on the merits of the doctrine of *limpieza*
and its application in the treatment of the peninsular New Christians completely silenced. As early as May 12, 1603, the deputy
Juan Serrano argued at the Castilian Cortes that economic reforms
were necessary to stimulate the people's working habits and reduce
their penchant for luxury. In the face of the progressive economic
deterioration, Gabriel Cimbrón of Ávila submitted in February
1618 a memorandum to the Cortes, analyzing the effects of the
existing statutes and stressing the difficulties which they had
created by opening the gates to a flood of unfounded denunciations, born of malice or envy, against many perfectly honorable
persons of "pure" blood. Only individuals of obscure and lowly
lineage, whose ancestry was nowhere recorded, had no difficulty
in being baptized as old Christians. Cimbrón assured the Cortes
that he had no intention of seeing "the statutes abrogated *in toto*
or in any substantial part, for they are most holy, just, good, and
necessary in the present state of our Commonwealth." But he
wished that they would "be applied with the least offense to God
and with as little damage to one's neighbor as possible." He
proposed, therefore, that a committee of learned men be appointed
to reexamine the statutes, that a time limit be set for their operation, particularly with respect to descendants of "impure" persons
on the distaff side, and that no unsigned denunciation of any person be accepted. Cimbrón's proposition was debated in the parliamentary session of March 12, 1618, at which another member,
Don Juan del Collado of Cuenca, delivered an enthusiastic oration
in praise of the statutes. Yet he stated:

Our country has, through its bravery, prudence, and valor, conquered
the world, and has thereby made itself the mistress and superior of the
most noble nations; it has gained and amplified its nobility through

the force of arms and letters. It is therefore undignified for the nation to defame itself by badly applying those statutes. Rather it is appropriate that the country should mirror its reputation by emphasizing its noble aspects and discontinuing the difficulties created by certain aspects of *limpieza.*

However, there was no majority for any specific proposal, and the Cortes merely recommended to the king the appointment of a committee to review and suggest remedies for the existing shortcomings.[36]

More resolutely antagonistic to New Christians was the intervention of the Council of Portugal, the country's supreme governmental organ under the king. Spurred on by the Portuguese Inquisition, it submitted a memorandum *(consulta)* to Philip III on January 17, 1619. The inquisitor-general had previously argued for the total elimination of New Christians. Referring to an auto-da-fé of November 1618 in Coimbra and similar events in Oporto, he claimed "that without any question all of Portugal was contaminated in the matter of Judaism and that it is necessary to apply remedies speedily that these kingdoms of your Majesty should not suffer the penalties which such heresies deserve." The threat of divine vengeance for the passive acceptance of religious deviations had often been used by clerical spokesmen of religious intolerance. It may have carried extra weight with a king as superstitious as Philip III. Not wholly subscribing to the Inquisition's extreme demand, the Council wrote:

Since the principal obligation of your Majesty consists in cleansing his Kingdoms of every kind of heresy and infidelity and since it has been demonstrated by experience over a long period of time that Jewish infidelity has caused great evils to the Kingdoms of Portugal and that it is one of the two principal causes why God has inflicted such grave chastisements on them, it appears that your Majesty has the obligation by divine and natural law to order the deportation from his Kingdoms and Dominions of all those who have been declared heretics or, as suspects in matters of faith, have been obliged to abjure *de vehementi.*

In other words, rather than blame the country's political and economic reverses on the government's misguided policies, including its unbounded racialism and religious extremism, the Council attributed Portugal's deterioration to God's ire over the minor relaxation in the maltreatment of the minorities. Yet the Council suggested merely a partial expulsion, allowing the majority of New Christians who had not been condemned by the Inquisition to remain in the country.[37]

On the other hand, a most effective plea in favor of the New Christians was submitted by Martín González de Cellorigo, who in 1619, after serving for twenty-eight years as an inquisitorial advocate, held the position of judge over all property confiscated by the Holy Office. Though designated to plead for the accused, most inquisitorial advocates had a very bad reputation among the defendants. Since their main task consisted in trying to persuade the accused to confess their infidelity, the majority of defendants considered them its worst enemies. González de Cellorigo seems to have been an exception, however. From the outset he was an enlightened student of Iberian society and perceived that many socioeconomic evils were generated by the prevailing religious intolerance. In 1597 he wrote a memorandum in favor of the Moriscos, while in other memoranda of 1600 he argued for important economic reforms.

By 1619 he was ready to lend a sympathetic ear to some endangered New Christians and to submit to the king an extensive memorandum in their behalf. On the basis of his rich experience, he argued for many procedural alleviations in the inquisitorial prosecutions, stressing in particular the need for defendants to be told the names of their accusers. As a jurist he pleaded that law must conform with reason, and pointed out that, because of their irrationality, the statutes of *limpieza* affected innocent good Christians along with secret Judaizers. In fact, he observed, the word "Jew" was used as a term of opprobrium for three diverse categories—namely, real Jews, who obstinately adhered to their "vain creed"; Christian neophytes, who might legitimately be excluded from religious orders; and Christian-born descendants of Jews, whose inclusion under this designation was "contrary to charity and the just consideration needed in this case." Probing more deeply into the existing conditions, González de Cellorigo pointed out that, because of its misplaced and exaggerated emphasis on "honor," Iberian society generally shunned work in agriculture and commerce. He argued that the New Christians had been saving the country by their trade with the East Indies and Brazil, which annually averaged 600,000 and 800,000 ducats, respectively; by their major share in the slave trade, amounting to some 800,000 ducats a year; and by their large share in the customs duties, which in the case of their silk imports alone annually yielded 200,000 ducats.

It is they [the writer insisted] who maintain and support this kingdom by their industry and work because none of the others enter the aforementioned occupations. Seizing all public offices and honors, those among them [the Old Christians] who consider themselves the most honorable, shun that type of work, while the others, that is the artisans, have not applied themselves to commerce and are incapable of it today because they have neither the capital nor the business experience and [foreign] correspondents, nor any of the other qualifications naturally found among the said nation.

In the light of these realities, González de Cellorigo suggested, the king ought to reverse the government's policies. He pointed out that a more tolerant attitude would actually bring back some of the New Christian exiles from other countries, which would help to repopulate such declining Castilian cities as Toledo, Valladolid, Burgos, and Medina del Campo; that the departure of New Christians from the Low Countries would undermine the strength of the Dutch rebels against Spain; that, domestically, New Christian enterprise would prevent the exploitation of the country by foreigners; and, finally, that it would give the New Christians a feeling that Iberia was their real fatherland.[38]

Subjected to such conflicting pressures, Philip III adopted what he may have considered to be a middle course. Replying to the Council of Portugal, he approved only the confiscation of the property of those convicted to abjuration *de vehementi*, and asked the Council to submit to him a list of all Portuguese New Christians residing in Castile. On March 13, 1619, he formally abrogated the remaining vestiges of the pardon of 1605, but he refrained from the extreme of expelling all New Christians as he had banished all Moriscos ten years before. He thus left to his successor much unfinished business, which was to plague Philip IV's administration through most of his reign.

ACCELERATED RETROGRESSION

Almost immediately after his accession to the throne at the age of sixteen, Philip IV (1621–65) had to deal seriously with the New Christian question. Although styled by a seventeenth-century writer "the ubiquitous Catholic, perpetual and invincible defender of Christ's Bride, the Church," he was nonetheless open to persuasion, because of his great need of funds. He has been aptly characterized by a modern historian thus: "An excellent horseman, fine sharpshooter, dancer and hunter, a man of great personal dignity and majestic appearance, an admirer of fine arts and beautiful women, a friend of the theater and patron of artists, from time to time even himself a writer, he only lacked the taste for the elusive tasks of government." Evidently, such a king was not equal to the epithet "the Great," as he was sometimes called by admirers among his contemporaries and early successors. He preferred to delegate not just unpleasant routine jobs but the whole range of planning, directing, and supervising the complicated governmental machinery of his vast empire, to trusted favorites. Philip's most influential adviser, Gaspar de Guzmán, conde (later duque) de Olivares, who for twenty-two years until his fall in 1643 was the actual ruler of Spain, was rather friendly to the Marranos, perhaps because of his opposition to the inquisitorial excesses. He was also a staunch upholder of Spanish royal prerogatives against the Papacy and the domestic hierarchy. Ultimately, he was himself in danger of falling victim to the Inquisition, in connection with the publication of an apology for his regime entitled *Nicandro* (meaning "antidote"), published during the short span between his disgrace and death in 1645. He had allegedly cited there a number of biblical verses in an unorthodox vein. But apart from destroying all readily available copies of the work, the Holy Office refrained from any action against the former royal favorite.[39]

Olivares shared with the king a keen awareness of the country's economic depression and the Treasury's financial difficulties. At the very beginning of Philip IV's regime, a member of the Cortes, Mateo de Lisón y Biedma, graphically described the sufferings of the peasants who "had abandoned their lands and were now wandering on the roads, living on herbs and roots." Enormous funds were being expended, both on the administration of the vast, disorganized empire and on the prosecution of the Thirty Years' War, from which Spain was to emerge greatly impoverished and weakened. From the outset, the king and his favorite entertained, therefore, grandiose notions of reform, which usually miscarried, however. They started by infusing new life into the theretofore inactive *Junta de Reformación,* established at the end of Philip III's regime. Now, the commission undertook to review the shortcomings of the various branches of the royal administration, including the Holy Office. In its report, submitted on October 28, 1622, to the Spanish cities represented at the Cortes, it echoed the views expressed in 1618 by Gabriel Cimbrón concerning the inadequacies of the proceedings of the inquisitorial courts. It asserted:

On occasions when a person had to meet the requirement of the purity of blood and nobility for [admission to] military orders [*hábitos*], colleges, holy offices, and churches, much room was left for malice and fraud, which perverted the sacred institution of the Statutes and nullified the good effects experienced therefrom while they had been employed in good faith. From this practice the country has sustained much damage, for the persons affected have very frequently lost life, honor, and property through no fault of their own or that of the tribunals.[40]

As a result the *Capítulos de reformación,* adopted on February 10, 1623, included the long-sought safeguards against anonymous denunciations. The pertinent *Pragmatica,* subsequently elaborated on March 22, 1638, and made more permanent by inclusion in the two great codes of law, the *Nueva* and *Novísima Recopilación de leyes,* also called for the elimination of the practice of investigating a candidate time and again before each new appointment, promotion, or transfer to another locality. It ruled that no more than three successive proceedings *(tres actos positivos)* were needed and that thereafter the final clearance should be considered a *res judicata (cosa juzgada).* Realizing the great damage done to the ruling élite by the circulation of genealogical works which (like the Aragonese *Libro verde de Aragón* and the Castilian *Tizón de la nobleza),* traced the "impure" (Jewish or Moorish) ancestry of certain more or less distinguished families, the *Pragmatica* outlawed the possession of such compilations, under the sanction of a fine of 500 ducats and a two-year exile from one's permanent residence. This provision proved to be a mere palliative, however. Although as a result of the decree some of these incriminating books were publicly burned, which accounts for their survival in but a few original copies, they were too greatly cherished by the public, and particularly by would-be informers, to disappear totally from circulation. Nor did the edict produce major changes in the substantive law which excluded descendants of Jews and Moors from many offices and dignities without any time limitation. Neither the *Junta* nor the king in any way mentioned the idea, originally entertained by Philip II and Agustín Salucio, that such "blemishes" of descent be disregarded a century after the original ancestor's conversion.[41]

Remarkably, a few Marranos themselves conceded a need for some discrimination. In an interesting Spanish memorandum which the wealthy merchant Duarte Gómes Solis submitted to Philip IV in 1622, after having approached the Duke of Lerma with a briefer Portuguese letter on the same subject, Gómes proposed the following compromise: New Christians should not be given any honors, in order not to exacerbate popular animosity. Similarly, the true *hidalgo* families should not intermarry with New Christians, though those nobles who already had Jewish blood in their veins should be allowed to do so. In any case, children of such intermarriages should be admitted to "all charges and offices." Gómes, who had apparently amassed considerable wealth while living in the Indies, made many other proposals, aiming, in particular, to improve Spain's international trade and shipbuilding—all of which, together with greater religious toleration, he contended, would make the country more competitive with the Dutch and the English. He pointed out that "those [Iberian] ships which travel from Lisbon to the Indies do so to the injury of the Kingdom, the merchants, and the navigators," as had often been demonstrated by the Dutch or the English who, after capturing Portuguese ships, made no use of them. There is no record of an official reply to Gómes' memorandum, and very likely none was given. Needless to say, it occasioned no change in either the religious or the maritime policies of the government.[42]

Before long, however, the king and his minister were once more considering an offer of a substantial, though at first unspecified, payment in exchange for a new pardon for the Marranos' past transgressions and their freedom to emigrate. In these negotiations, which began in 1621 and extended over more than a decade, the Marranos were apparently prepared to pay 1,000,000 ducats or more, for these two concessions. However, this time the leading churchmen, especially the inquisitors-general (Luis de Aliaga, 1619–21; and Andrés Pacheco, 1622–26) and the papal nuncio, objected strenuously. In a brief undated memorandum, the king's father confessor, Antonio de Sotomayor, who served as the main intermediary in these negotiations, reported to Philip the nuncio's argument that the earlier pardons, granted by Clement VII, Paul III, and Clement VIII, had failed to turn the Marranos into good Christians, and had merely facilitated the expansion of the Jewish sect, whose perfidy was notorious.

In any case, he [the nuncio] asks your Majesty that, if at some time the question of a pardon should come into consideration, the entire negotiation be submitted to the Holy Father, as was always done by your Majesty's glorious predecessors. In this way the Holy See, which has the sole legitimate authority in these matters, may with its usual maturity of judgment and determination adopt a resolution most appropriate for the service of God and Religion. Essentially, this is also your Majesty's objective.

An unnamed writer likewise advanced historical and economic reasons why the project was neither laudable nor advantageous. He cited the adverse opinion of the eminent Jesuit theologian Francisco Suárez, who generally espoused the doctrine of the supremacy of Church over state; hence, ecclesiastical interests must enjoy priority. Suárez had contended that, while the state derived its authority from the people and thus was a purely human organ, the Church was not *of* this world but *in* this world, a divine creation, supreme in all spiritual matters. Consequently, the theologian opposed any new general pardon for Marranos, whose pernicious influence on Portugal he claimed to have had frequent occasions to observe during the twenty years (1597–1617) of his stay at the

University of Coimbra. Another revered authority cited by the memorialist was Philip II, who had tried to dissuade King Sebastian of Portugal from accepting much-needed money for his religiously inspired African campaign. The writer finally cautioned the government that the contemporary Jews had become too poor to fulfill any major financial obligations they might assume.[43]

Among the New Christians who took the initiative in trying to secure some amelioration of their condition under the new regime were Manuel Ruiz d'Elvas and Duarte Fernandez, in an address directed to the king, and Melchior Gómez and Ruiz Diaz, in an appeal to the Council of Portugal. The king submitted both petitions to Sotomayor on March 20, and October 14, 1622, respectively. Sotomayor (who in 1632, at the age of seventy-seven, was to be appointed inquisitor-general, a post he held until 1643), was a rather moderate member of the Holy Office, and the king felt that he could trust his judgment concerning these applications. There is no way of telling whether two other, unsigned documents, likewise preserved in the Lisbon archives, stemmed from the same New Christian group. But the arguments presented in them undoubtedly reflected the views of the endangered New Christian community. One of the petitions pointed out that, because a desecration of the host had taken place at the church of Santa Engracia in Lisbon, a number of New Christians had been arrested without further proof, and the public indiscriminately blamed all New Christians for the sacrilege. As a result, there had been riots in the streets, leading to the death and wounding of some totally uninvolved persons, attacks by the students of the University of Coimbra on their New Christian colleagues, and various other acts of violence. This rumormongering caused a panic in New Christian circles, which was aggravated by the earlier curtailment of their freedom to emigrate. The other petition emphasized the damage done to the Portuguese economy by the new persecution of *hombres de negocio* (lit., businessmen; a term often used as a veiled synonym for New Christian traders). Because of the stagnation of commerce caused by that state of insecurity, the revenues of the kingdom had greatly diminished; it lost much of the 100 percent duty it formerly collected on imports from the Indies. Moreover, by being forced to insure their shipments in foreign localities, the traders unwittingly revealed the movements of Portuguese ships to hostile navies and rendered them subject to attack and seizure on the open seas. While agreeing that anyone guilty of a real crime should be convicted and severely punished, the New Christian petitioners emphasized that all others should be effectively protected against rumormongering, insults, and physical assaults. They suggested the appointment of a commission to scrutinize the existing conditions and to recommend the necessary remedies to the king. In recompense they offered money, at first an unspecified amount. On December 26, 1622, Philip IV ordered his counselor to propose instead a loan of 150,000 ducats, though he reserved any final agreement to his own discretion. Out of these and other deliberations emerged the *Pragmatica* of 1623 as a sort of compromise between the conflicting approaches.[44]

The matter did not come to rest with this halfway measure. In the following years the idea of a pardon and freedom of emigration combined with a permit to take funds out of the country, reappeared time and again in discussions of the governmental agencies. At the same time, the government also weighed the opposite idea of a general expulsion of Marranos. The example of the elimination of the more densely concentrated Moriscos was still fresh in everyone's mind. Some officials suggested selective banishment and confiscation of the property of only specific Marrano suspects or those condemned by the Inquisition. Total expulsion had, in theory, the support of the inquisitor-general (very likely Cardinal Antonio de Zapata) who, in an extended memorandum written about 1630, submitted the following major arguments in its favor: (1) It is always advisable to separate the guilty from those whom they might infect with their corruption, (2) The Church had consistently segregated apostates and heretics from the faithful; and the Sixth Council of Toledo had actually demanded that no prince be allowed to ascend the throne without pledging the elimination of non-Catholics from his country, (3) The Roman emperors and all states which had adopted common law had followed that procedure. Since the number of Judaizers and apostates among the New Christians was extremely large, all New Christians should be counted in that category. Hence only total elimination would stem the frequent sacrileges committed by them, (4) Experience had taught that pardons had never induced New Christians to mend their ways; not sweetness but rigorous treatment might bring them back. Therefore, they deserved to be condemned for the crime of *lèse-majesté* and executed.

True [the inquisitor added], some learned men insist that this reasoning applies only to heretics and apostates who persevere in their unbelief, but that the New Christians, even if they had apostasized, might nevertheless repent, confess their errors, and be reconciled to the Church. This argument is incorrect, however, because, first, convicted Jews always remain heretics and apostates at heart; they claim to be converted only in order to escape death and fire. . . . Secondly, many of those who go into exile declare themselves Jews in other countries and, if a few of them remain in Portugal, it is only because of their family ties and property, as well as because they are afraid of the fate awaiting them in exile.

However, as a first step the inquisitor-general would have been satisfied with the immediate expulsion of only those Marranos who had been condemned for serious transgressions *(de vehementi)* and who, he argued, should be forced to leave, notwithstanding all practical objections. On the other hand, the Council of the Portuguese Inquisition had on September 5, 1622, gone on record against the expulsion even of all those who had been "reconciled." It maintained that removing this class of conspirators to other lands would merely increase the latter's infestation with Jewish doctrines and deprive its own prosecutors of valuable witnesses against other culprits. It also claimed that indiscriminate exile might be welcomed by the Judaizers themselves. "If persons of that nation promise a quantity of gold to secure a general pardon, they would pay double that amount for the free departure of reconciled persons," who would thus be definitely withdrawn from inquisitorial supervision.[45]

Curiously, a slightly more tolerant policy was advocated by the Portuguese clergy assembled in a synod in the city of Tomar in 1628. Its main resolutions and arguments were summarized for the king by a special commission *(junta)* in a comprehensive memorandum and were forwarded by him to Sotomayor on March 25, 1632. This is not the place to reproduce all the arguments pro and con advanced by the Portuguese churchmen and the observations thereon by the commission. Suffice it to mention the following few

novel points: The *junta* repudiated the suggestion that, in order
to prevent the further expansion of Judaism by intermarriage with
Old Christians, the king should forbid Marranos to give their
daughters dowries of more than 2,000 cruzados, any excess to be
divided between the Treasury and the informer. It also rejected
the proposition that Old Christians married to Marranos be barred
from all public offices and other honors. It argued that freedom
to marry was a basic right and that any governmental interference
would merely hinder the propagation of the human kind, the very
purpose of marriage. On the other hand, the memorandists agreed
that New Christians of Jewish parentage even of the tenth degree
should be barred from all ecclesiastical offices and benefices; but,
in their opinion, this could be achieved by a simple refusal to
ordain such persons. Appointments to secular offices, on the contrary, should be open to New Christians, since the ancient Romans
had shown that attracting vanquished peoples to public service
was the best way of instilling in them loyalty to the state. Moreover, any discrimination of this kind would merely help to con-
serve Judaism. At the end, however, although the king himself, on
March 25, 1632, strongly supported some accommodation with
the Marranos for the sake of religion, justice, and the good of the
state, nothing tangible emerged from these official exchanges.[46]

REPETITIOUS MONOLOGUE

Expulsion of the Marranos was also discussed outside official
circles. At least one writer, João Pinto Ribeiro, wrote a book denying the utility and justice of such a move. Perhaps for this reason
his book was not allowed to appear, while pronouncedly anti-
Jewish writings circulated freely. The Braga archdeacon, Fernão
Ximenes de Aragão, combined sharp attacks on Judaism with a
defense of Christianity. Even more vituperative was Vicente da
Costa de Mattos (or Matos), who assembled all sorts of rumors and
insinuations relating to the Jews and their faith. There was little
originality in any of these publications. Some of them merely
repeated the vulgar commonplaces long known from Alphonso de
Spina's *Fortalitium fidei*. Only a few of these seventeenth-century
writers discussed the differences between Judaism and Christianity

on the more dignified plane of the apologetic works by Luis Vives and Alphonso de Zamora.[47]

Understandably, in the increasingly chaotic condition of the Spain of Philip IV, attacks on Olivares combined references to his mismanagement of public affairs with those attributing to him excessive favoritism toward Jews. Francisco Gómez de Quevedo y Villegas, once an ardent admirer, turned into an implacable enemy of the "count-duke." He alluded to the latter's "impurity of blood" because Olivares' grandmother Francesca Niño was the daughter of Lope de Conchillos, an Aragonese *converso* who was an influential adviser of Ferdinand the Catholic. In two satires—one written by Quevedo; the other falsely attributed to Quevedo—the minister was accused of having a special fondness for Jews. In explaining the verses aimed at Olivares in *La Cueva de Meliso* (The Grotto of Meliso), the pseudo-Quevedo wrote:

He [Olivares] defended the Talmud and frequently communicated with Jews whom he had brought from Salonica. He proposed that they should be assigned a street in Madrid where they could live their separate life. His proposal was repudiated, however, by the Councils of State and Inquisition. At that time placards appeared in Madrid reading: "Long Live the Law of Moses and may that of Christ Die!" Cardinal Cesare Monti, the papal nuncio, spoke vigorously to the king against that project of the count [Olivares] so that the count could not raise his head.

In *Isla de los Monopantos,* written by Quevedo in 1639, the poet likewise depicted Olivares as attending an international Jewish meeting in Salonica to discuss means of seizing the power and riches of Spain. Allusion to the Spanish statesman's "impurity" was clear to initiated readers in the name Prágas Chincollos (an anagram of Gasper and Conchillos; that is, of Olivares' first name and the family name of his great-grandfather), which Quevedo gave to the prince of the Monopantos, "a republican people inhabiting certain islands in the Black Sea." Among the participants at the meeting was a Rabbi David ben Nachman, representing "the disguised Jews who masquerade as Christians." The keynote speech delivered by another rabbi, Saadías, included such confessions as "of the law of Moses we retain only the name, giving it instead to the exceptions with which the Talmudists have forced us to belie the Scripture . . . and have turned our atheistic inclinations into seditious politics for the convenience of civil life. They have thus transformed us from the sons of Israel to sons of Mammon." Perhaps stimulated by the more recent banishment of the Moriscos, the then more than a century-old problem of the expulsion of the Jews from Spain in 1492 was still frequently discussed in the literature of the seventeenth century. Remarkably, it is almost impossible to find a Spanish or Portuguese writer who failed to extol this act of Ferdinand and Isabella. For one example, Fray Benito de Peñalosa y Mandragón spoke glowingly of the Catholic monarchs, who no sooner had become "masters of all of Spain (except for Portugal and Navarre) than they considered it a good occasion to cleanse their realm of that canaille." [48]

A number of anti-*converso* writers continued to take issue with Agustín Salucio's memorandum of 1598–99, which had culminated in the alleviations of the *Pragmatica* of 1623. Among the outstanding opponents of such liberalization was the Llerena inquisitor, Juan Escobar del Corro, who assumed an extreme racialist stance in his *Tractatus bipartitus de puritate et nobilitate probanda* (written about 1633, although not published until 1637). He strongly believed in the hereditary transmission of ethical traits. Hence he needed only to prove the Jews' general immorality to claim that their descendants for many generations would unavoidably reveal the same penchant for all kinds of misdeeds, to the detriment of Spanish society. Of course, by implication he had to argue against the old biblical evolution toward personal responsibility, and against the ultimate rejection by the Old Testament prophets of the doctrine that the sins of fathers be visited upon their children. But this difficulty did not deter him from repudiating especially the provision of the 1623 *Pragmatica* relating to the *tres actos positivos* which relieved any candidate for office or promotion from further investigation. According to Escobar, if for any reason a candidate's *limpieza* appeared dubious, the results of the three previous investigations should not be considered an impediment to a fourth, fifth, or more reexaminations. In short, no one would be safe from double, even quadruple or quintuple, jeopardy. This position was indeed assumed by many military orders, colleges, and churches, in total disregard of the royal ordinance of 1623, which was never formally abrogated. Moreover, Escobar insisted that the burden of proof rested with the candidate, rather than with the body considering his admission or appointment; and, in his opinion, that body did not have to give any reason for its refusal to accept the evidence submitted by him.[49]

It is small wonder, then, that Escobar del Corro also upheld the long-controversial secrecy of testimony affecting inquisitorial defendants or candidates for office. To be sure, the old Jewish argument (voiced in 1354 by the rabbinical synod of Barcelona), that informers had little to fear from defenseless Jews, no longer held true, because the New Christian "culprits" often were in positions of trust and confidence, which might indeed have enabled them, their relatives, or their friends to inflict bloody vengeance on their accusers or on hostile witnesses. This danger actually increased in proportion to the distress suffered not only by the persons under investigation but also by their relatives, however distant, whose own legal and social status might have been jeopardized by proofs submitted against the *limpieza* of the investigated individuals. Yet, that such fears were exaggerated, and that the invalidation of testimony by accusers spontaneously named by the defendants as their enemies often was sheer pretense, can be seen, for example, in the trial of so important a citizen as Manuel Fernandes Villareal. Though this influential diplomat was immediately able to identify his unrevealed accuser as an old foe, this revelation did not deter the Inquisition from pursuing its investigation, which ultimately resulted in the execution of the defendant. Nor did identification of a hostile informer have any untoward consequences for him or his relatives, despite certain obvious falsehoods in his testimony.[50]

Another case of opposition to the *Pragmatica* is more problematic. Superficially, the Hieronymite friar Jerónimo de la Cruz' *Defensa de los estatutos y noblezas españolas*, likewise published in 1637, appears as a polemic against Agustín Salucio's *Discurso*, De la Cruz actually trying to deny the eminent preacher's authorship of that tract. He insists that that "apocryphon" had vastly exaggerated the number of Spaniards "infected" with Jewish or Moorish blood, in however minute a dose. He vigorously repeats arguments, voiced by apologists of *limpieza* for generations, as to why the pertinent Statutes must be observed without any limitations. With all his sound and fury, however, De la Cruz leaves the main purpose of Salucio's treatise unimpaired. The Seville Dominican, as we recall, had aimed his shafts not at the principle of *limpieza* as such but rather at the imperfections in its implementation by the inquisitorial tribunals, and at the long duration of the Statutes' validity, which jeopardized the position of almost all Old Christians as well as New. In the Introduction to his work, De la Cruz announces his own intentions in terms almost identical with the Dominican's intrinsic aims, and writes: "We differ only in method; he begins by dishonoring all [Spaniards]. I pay tribute to them all, without injury to anyone. He speaks against the Statutes, I against their misuse. But we agree on the main purpose of trying to declare all [Spaniards] pure and honorable and of seeking to terminate the rigors of their exclusion." Nevertheless, superficial readers regarded De la Cruz' book as an effective plea for the undisputed authority of inquisitorial courts to scrutinize any person's ancestry as often as they wished. As a matter of fact, public opinion backed both the principle and the application of the Statutes to such an extent that by the mid-seventeenth century many secular institutions, including universities, city councils, and military orders, undertook investigations of their own without awaiting the results of the longer, but somewhat more orderly, inquisitorial proceedings.[51]

Apart from appealing to the public at large, some defenders of the Statutes and the methods of their implementation addressed themselves in private memoranda to influential statesmen. For example, Inquisitor Juan Adam de la Parra in 1630 submitted a memorandum to Infante Fernando, the king's brother and primate of Spain, sharply attacking all attempts to weaken their enforcement. Emphasizing the fear that the door might thus be opened for the entry of "Jews" into honorable positions, he went so far as to argue that "although it is certain that nothing can limit the supreme authority of the monarch, . . . [the king] ought to submit to the regulations of the Church enacted for the preservation of religion and its cult." Another staunch defender of the established order was Bartolomé Ximénez Patón in his *Discurso en favor del santo y loable estatuto de la limpieza,* published in Granada in

1638. Although he was a humanistically trained lay notary of the Holy Office, Ximénez Patón resorted to true sophistry when he stated that the New Christians had wrongly invoked the *Pragmatica* of 1623 to secure a mitigation of the investigations against them. He argued that the *Pragmatica* had gone into oblivion because it had not been applied in the intervening years, and because it lacked specific pontifical confirmation, which would have abrogated the earlier provisions of various pontifical bulls. As Antonio Domínguez Ortiz rightly pointed out, however, these bulls had left the methods of securing evidence of *limpieza* entirely to the discretion of local courts and governmental organs. Certainly the *Pragmatica* did not lose its validity merely because some inquisitorial courts had failed to apply it or because the accused, often terrified and helpless, had refrained from invoking it.[52]

In the 1630s the anti-*converso* polemics had thus become ever more heated. They were almost entirely one-sided for we shall look in vain in the literature of the Golden Age for any outright defenders of secret Judaizers. Despite the general richness and diversity of approaches among the numerous talented writers and artists of the period, there was almost complete unanimity in blaming Jews for the numerous shortcomings of Spain's "Establishment."

Nor were the determined Jew-baiters interested in consistency. For example, most Spaniards had for many generations considered a long nose a sign of discretion and ingenuity. Yet in the case of Jews, the same physical trait was regarded as a blemish. Not only a full-fledged antagonist like Quevedo but even more moderate individuals like Tirso de Molina and Félix Lope de Vega Carpio played up that "defect" in the Jewish physiognomy. In his well-known *Vida de Buscón*, Quevedo refers to the multitude of Jews in Alcalá de Henares "with long noses that cannot even suffer the odour of bacon," while in a discussion in *El Árbol del mejor fruto*, Tirso de Molina presents a soldier distinguishing between the long noses of Jews and those which he calls *romas y hidalgas* (aquiline and aristocratic). A character in a drama by Lope de Vega rejoices over the fact that "in the entire Court there is no one who can cover up a certain defect. . . : the large nose, which, thank God, no barber, apothecary, or surgeon can make appear smaller." More fundamentally, the old accusation of Jewish deicide was repeated *ad infinitum*. It was often combined with some variation of a sale of some object for 30 shekels—a clear allusion to Judas' betrayal—as well as derision of the Jews' messianic expectations. In a comedy by Luis Vélez de Guevara, a courtier impatient about the slow fulfillment of royal promises declaims: "As to waiting, I have little of the Jew, and pretensions for the coming of a messiah I leave to others." Some classical writers of the period even refer to ideas bordering on Zionism among contemporary Jews.[53]

Jewish rituals, understandably, came under the most frequent, hostile scrutiny; the Jews' abstention from pork products being a preferred target. Jewish business practices and the purported "avarice" of all Jews likewise offered much ammunition for Jew-baiting. Nor is it at all surprising to witness the revival of the old medieval accusations of Jewish ritual murders, doctors killing Christian patients, and the like. To a polemicist like Fray Francisco de Torrejoncillo, rightly observes Miguel Herrero García, "Jews are and have always been lying, treacherous, presumptuous, restless, vainglorious, seditious, and ungrateful people, as well as avowed mortal enemies of Christianity." As an example of utter *converso* duplicity, Torrejoncillo adduces the father-confessor's report of a little boy who, asked for his name, replied: "At home it is Abraham, outside Francisquito." (This story illustrates, of course, the dangers confronting Marrano parents wishing to bring up their children with a minimal adherence to Judaism much more than their penchant for lying.) Torrejoncillo was seconded in his vituperations by several writers, including Diego Gobían Vela and J. A. de la Peña.[54]

Most remarkably, the anti-Jewish atmosphere affected the great masters of the Spanish Golden Age, which coincided with the onset of the political and economic decline of the country. One may detect a Jew-baiting animus even in some of the great paintings of Diego Rodríguez de Silva y Velázquez and his associates. For example, in a famous New Testament scene (now at the Prado Museum) depicted by Velázquez' slave, the hated Jewish publican is shown with a costume and traits clearly resembling those of contemporary Spanish Marranos. This is the more remarkable since, according to some modern scholars, Velázquez himself was not completely free of a tinge of Jewish blood and, for this reason, had actually found it difficult to become a member of the military Order of Santiago. This is not surprising. Though born in Seville, he was the son of immigrants from Portugal, where the name Da Silva was frequent among the Marranos. Similarly, the *limpieza* of Miguel de Cervantes Saavedra was not beyond reproach, although his contemporaries may not have been fully aware of it. Yet, in his *Don Quixote*, which deals but tangentially with political problems, Sancho Panza invokes some honorable acts of his as proof that he must be wellborn [*bien nacido*] or at least an Old Christian. On another occasion Sancho explains that he is a good Christian "and a mortal enemy of the Jews" and that, hence, he deserves mercy from historians. In still another episode Cervantes presents a Jewish slave trader who sells a beautiful Christian girl. All these instances are relatively trivial, compared with other contemporary tirades, but they show that even moderate observers of the existing conditions could not entirely escape the impact of the prevailing anti-Marrano bias. On the other hand, Cervantes, with his generally perceptive and skeptical mind, could not completely disregard the damage done to Spanish society by its obsession with *limpieza*. With subtle irony he depicted, in *El Retablo de las maravillas*, the terror which seized the population of a village tricked by the ruse of a roving band of actors. In advance of the performance, the players announced that their presentation would be visible only to truly *limpio* onlookers, whereas all "contaminated" persons would see only an empty stage. Of course, the stage remained empty, while the members of the audience tried to outdo each other in enthusiastically applauding the invisible mimics, lest they be suspected by their neighbors of being of Jewish or Moorish descent.[55]

We also recall the anti-Jewish references in the writings of the two greatest Spanish dramatists, Lope de Vega and Calderón de la Barca. Their *Autos sacramentales*, especially, like other poems of that genre, were strongly imbued with the spirit of the Counter Reformation and the ensuing insistence on undeviating religious conformity. Both masters of Spanish dramaturgy were, in fact, obsessed with the figure of Satan. While there is no direct evidence that they followed their medieval predecessors in trying to convey the demonic qualities often attributed to contemporary Jews and

Marranos, this nexus may have easily arisen in the minds of the audiences. In no less than nine comedies written by Lope de Vega in the years 1594–1614, the figure of the lord of the underworld plays a major role, although as a rule he is eventually outsmarted by the good and honest persons in the various plays. Such a character was represented even more frequently in Lope's *autos sacramentales*. In his *El Pastor Ingrato* of 1628, for example, the demon actually plays the main part. In all, twenty-two *autos* of 1585 to 1635 include such figures, who, possibly with reference to contemporary New Christians, often act as creditors. When we bear in mind the great popularity of theatrical performances, both sacred and secular, among the inhabitants of Madrid and other Spanish cities, we can easily gauge the impact of these representations upon the public at large. This is particularly true in the case of the *autos sacramentales* by Calderón and other poets. Whatever difficulties these authors may have encountered in staging the plays in large public squares, their performance must have impressed a multitude of onlookers, recruited not only from among Madrid's theatergoing upper classes but also from among the local laborers and the numerous illiterate peasants who came to the city expressly to view them. Thus even the masses of farmers and workers, who could not read the anti-Jewish literature of the age, were infected by the anti-Marrano virus of such public spectacles, among which the autos-da-fé were by far the most gruesome and, for that very reason, most impressive.[56]

Clearly, the attitude of these great writers toward Jews and Judaism was colored by religious piety, whether genuine or intended merely for public display. Referring to Cervantes, for example, Américo Castro asserts that "he is a clever hypocrite, and he must be read and interpreted with extreme reserve in evaluating his relation to religion and official morals." This view, first expressed by José Ortega y Gasset, and supported by the fine Cervantes expert Paul Hazard, is, to be sure, controverted by another prominent student of Spanish literature, Luis Astrana Marín. However, in contrast to Lope and, to a lesser extent, Calderón, who openly extolled the Inquisition and the doctrine of *limpieza,* Cervantes studiously avoided any direct reference to them, except in a few veiled, rather ironical, allusions, such as the aforementioned statements of Sancho Panza. This restraint is doubly suspect, as he generally did not hesitate to criticize the Spanish social life of the period; indeed he often was as outspoken as the more radical publicists of his generation. Cervantes' lack of orthodoxy is ironically illustrated by the great frequency with which he quoted biblical passages in *Don Quixote* and other works, although he did not try to display a knowledge of Hebrew phrases, as occasionally did the two great playwrights in their *autos*. Since he was a rather mediocre Latinist, he hardly could have acquired close familiarity with the Bible by studying the Vulgate. Moreover, as Abraham Cardoso intimated in his autobiographical reminiscences, to read even the Latin Bible, at least for a boy of twelve, entailed "great danger throughout Spain." At the same time, we recall, vernacular Bibles had long been viewed with grave disapproval by the Spanish Church and were largely outlawed in Cervantes' lifetime by both the Spanish censors and the Council of Trent. From the data assembled by Juan Antonio Monroy it appears that the famous author may have derived most of his biblical knowledge from studying the Ferrara Bible, with which he had become acquainted during his prolonged visits to Italy. He hardly would have been discouraged from using it had he known that that Bible had been produced by Marranos in two editions, one addressed to Jews and the other to Christians. If Monroy's assumption can be confirmed by a closer examination of all the scriptural citations in *Don Quixote* and Cervantes' other works, it may lend support to suggestions made by various scholars that Cervantes himself had some Jewish ancestors.[57]

It is not surprising that many great writers of the period were deeply impressed with biblical themes, often giving them christological interpretations. Lope de Vega, for instance, interpreted the biblical Esther as a prefiguration of Mary (while the Marranos saw in her the prototype of the clandestine Jewess who served the divine purpose of saving her people at a critical moment). Similarly, the theme of the patriarch Jacob's love for Rachel—long treated by Spanish and Portuguese poets, under the influence of Luís de Camoëns, as a prototype of great and enduring love—is reinterpreted by Lope as a symbolic representation of love for otherworldliness (Rachel) as opposed to this-worldliness (Leah). In contrast, Daniel Levi (Miguel) de Barrios emphasized Rachel's early death as a lesson in the transient nature of all earthly concerns, including a great and devoted love for a woman. This is, of course, but one more illustration of the long chain of conflicting interpretations of the Bible in support of individual or group biases. That Lope was a confirmed Jew- and *converso*-baiter all his life is manifest to any reader of his works. He apparently could never forget his services as a familiar of the Inquisition, a position he proudly announced on the title page of his *La Jerusalem conquistada. Epopeya trágica,* which he dedicated to Philip III and published in 1609. The functions of these part-time assistants of the Holy Office were aptly described by a sixteenth-century visitor from the Low Countries: "They are thus designated, for they circulate among the people in a familiar fashion, listening to and spying on everything that seems to controvert our holy Roman Catholic faith. They are obliged to report these matters to the inquisitors immediately and in great secrecy. They are paid and salaried for it from the goods seized and confiscated from those condemned by the Holy Office." Not surprisingly, these services did not shield the poet himself from being cited before the Inquisition, which found in his comedy *De la conversión de San Augustin* certain arguments "indecent for presentation in public." [58]

With typical inconsistency, the seventeenth-century Spanish and Portuguese writers, churchmen, and politicians did not hesitate to bestow a unique dignity upon a woman of partial Jewish descent. Four years after St. Theresa d'Ávila's canonization in 1622, the Spanish Cortes decided to proclaim her the country's patron saint, in lieu of St. James. This decision was confirmed, in part, by Pope Urban VIII, in a brief dated July 21, 1627, with the proviso that the action should be without prejudice to St. James' continued patronage. A literary battle royal on the issue was fought by Francisco Quevedo, the defender of St. James, and Morovelli de Puebla, who espoused the cause of St. Theresa. It stands to reason that the advocates of the great mystic's canonization and elevation to the patronage of Spain did not know of her Jewish antecedents. But the Inquisition, before which Theresa had once appeared as a defendant, must have accumulated sufficient genealogical evidence to cast at least some doubt on the appropriateness of this proposal, had it wished to do so. We also recall that all three of Philip IV's predecessors had disregarded the "blemish" of Jewish ancestry in the case of a few special favorites, whom they treated, so to say, as honorary *limpios*. [59]

Such inconsistencies were far from infrequent. The Old Christian wife of Dr. Francisco López de Villalobos, the eminent physician-in-ordinary to Ferdinand the Catholic and Charles V, seems to have loved and admired her husband. Yet she spoke about another New Christian court physician, Francisco de Almazán, as a man not to be trusted, and generalized: "Neither is any man who was a *converso*." Utterances of this kind must have greatly irked the proud López de Villalobos, styled by a modern Spanish historian "physician to kings and prince of writers." In a poem addressed to the duke of Nájera, one of Spain's grandees, the doctor compared the high standing of a physician like himself—whose father, grandfather, and earlier ancestors had served as physicians —with the dignity of an heir to a long line of nobles, and exclaimed: "If any good comes out of your family, it is all owing to us who are the 'chosen people and the kingdom of priests.'" According to another tale, Villalobos was once assailed by a lady, while he attended church service, for having killed her husband through his medical ministrations. At the same time he was implored by a young man to come to the aid of his very ill father. The eminent physician asked the youth whether he did not fear for his father's life after hearing the lady's denunciation. Pointing to a picture of the Virgin, the doctor added: "And she, too, weeps, saying that I have slain her son!" [60]

What Villalobos could do in the first half of the sixteenth century, could not be repeated by his successors a century later, however. Now the Marranos could not venture to defend the Jewish faith or rituals, since such an apologia would immediately serve the Inquisition as indisputable evidence of heretical tendencies. They could not even reply to specific accusations, except perhaps in memoranda addressed to the king, in which they often complained of the unjust treatment they had received from officials, ecclesiastical and lay, or from the public at large. Only Marranos living under conditions of relative safety in France, Italy, or Holland dared to take up the cudgels for their religion. In a tract published in Rouen in 1547, Antonio Enríquez Gómez sharply attacked the Inquisition. More broadly, two distinguished apologists, Balthazar (Isaac) Orobio de Castro and Isaac (Fernando) Cardoso, were soon to publish memorable works in defense of Judaism. But, though they were born in Portugal in the first half of the seventeenth century, their literary activity belongs to the period after the Thirty Years' War.[61]

However, the Peninsular Marranos and their Old Christian sympathizers did not remain completely silent. If they could not defend Judaism as such, they could at least seek to exonerate their Jewish ancestors from the charge of Christ-killing and could claim for them an antiquity which conferred distinction on both the Jews and the country. To achieve this aim, they resorted to the then quite customary falsification of history. Without employing obvious forgeries (as had their enemies with the aforementioned spurious letter of the Jews of Spain to their coreligionists in Constantinople), they indulged in a far more innocuous "reconstruction" of ancient history. Here they met the ingrained gullibility of medieval and early modern man and his proneness to believe any legend likely to enhance the stature of his ancestors or fatherland.

One of the widely believed legends had it that Jews had emigrated from Palestine to Spain in the days of Nebukadrezzar, and that among them were descendants of disciples of Elisha, Elijah, and even Enoch. Other sagas, now lovingly fostered by the New Christians, contended, as we recall, that the mother of the Maccabees was a Spaniard, as were fifty-two of the seventy Greek translators of the Septuagint, and that Eleazar, archisynagogus of Toledo and chief of all Spanish Jews, had believed in Christ's miracles and had written to his Spanish coreligionists urging them to accept baptism. These and other legends, included in the "chronicles" of Liudprand (Luitprandus) and Julian Petri, found widespread acceptance. In his tract on moral theology, published in 1652, Fray Antonio Quintanadueñas argued that at least the descendants of those Jews who had originally refused to deny Jesus Christ should be allowed to join the military Orders, for "their [the Jews'] blood and ancestry as such were the most noble of all, . . . their only blemish being that the Hebrews took part in the death of the Lord Christ." Naturally, those who had opposed the crucifixion were free of that blemish. The author claimed that he had heard of some New Christian nobles in Toledo and Zamora who, for this reason, had been admitted to the Order of Santiago. This, despite the fact that some skeptics, like the Jesuit Antonio Mendo, pertinently asked how, after more than sixteen centuries, one could prove such descent, and whether descendants of any Jews converted to Christianity in the days of Jesus had not long ago been treated as Old Christians. From another angle, a tract variously attributed to the Dominican Sarmiento or the Jesuit Juan de Mariana but probably stemming from some associate of Agustín Salucio, claimed that Spain consisted of only three classes: the nobility which had been in charge of the *Reconquista;* the New Christians; and all the remaining Old Christians, including the peasantry, many of whom were obviously descendants of Moors. This tract defended the cause of the class of northern *hidalgos,* whose claim to distinction because of noble descent was often overshadowed in the popular mind by that of persons displaying certificates of *limpieza.* Although it could easily be proved that it was precisely the nobility that had been deeply infiltrated by New Christians, the author of this tract maintained that the nobles were the only racially pure class in Spain.[62]

NATIONAL ECONOMY VERSUS *LIMPIEZA*

More importantly, officials responsible for governmental and military operations could not help but welcome the presence of Marrano bankers and contractors *(asentistas)* in Spain as an extremely useful element for both the economy and the Treasury. Under Philip IV's regime the country's economic conditions steadily deteriorated. Sometimes prices gyrated wildly. In the year and a half between March 1641 and August 1642, wholesale prices in Seville rose by 93 percent. But in a few days following the deflationary decree of September 15, 1642, they dropped about 87 percent, or much more than they had risen. (To form an impression of this phenomenon, one need but compare the Great Depression in the United States from September 1929 to February 1933, when wholesale commodity prices fell only 37.86 percent.) At the same time, the old evils of unwillingness to work, contempt for manual labor, widespread beggary and vagabondage, primogeniture, excessive display of luxuries, and so forth, became an ever-increasing burden on the productivity of both agriculture and industry. The upper classes, in particular, felt that, in the words of a contemporary adage, "not to live on rents, is not to live nobly." The Church, which had been in the vanguard of anti-Marrano discrimination, contributed its share to the decline of production. The growing number of ecclesiastics, the indiscriminate distribution of alms, and a growing mortmain of ecclesiastical estates shifted the burden of taxation increasingly to fewer and fewer real producers. Vagrancy, augmented by the presence in the country of fairly numerous gypsies without permanent residence or occupation; the replacement of industrious by unwilling farm laborers and, in part, by imported Negro slaves; bureaucratic corruption; and deteriorating moral standards—all further aggravated the economic decline. In 1624 Fray Angel Manrique complained that there was no town in Spain in which the number of convents had not trebled in the preceding fifty years. The monetary manipulations of the government resulted in oppressive taxation. The dependence of the state on foreign bankers, particularly Italian, French, and German, often drained profits to foreign lands, while the military campaigns, especially during the Thirty Years' War, consumed whatever revenue the silver fleets brought from the American colonies. As a result, Philip IV's regime had to declare bankruptcy four times (1626, 1647, 1652, 1662), although what it really meant was that short-term borrowings from bankers were converted into long-term loans payable in small instalments with lower rates of interest.[63]

Under the circumstances, Philip IV and his minister were very happy that they found an alternate source for loans in the Portuguese New Christians, now residing mainly in Madrid and Seville. In the very year of the first insolvency (1626), which had ruined a number of Genoese merchants, Manual Rodríguez de Elvas, Nuño Díaz, Mendez de Brito, Duarte Fernández, Manuel de Paz, Simón Suárez and Juan Núñez Saravía, all of whom (with the possible exception of De Paz) were New Christians, were able to offer a loan of 400,000 escudos (valued at 430 maravedis each, since Philip III's decree of 1612) for the operation in Flanders. Although they demanded a number of concessions which the Supreme Economic Council (*Consejo de Hacienda*) considered too onerous, the hard-pressed king and his minister accepted them. The bankers also knew that the Council had long been prejudiced against them. In a report submitted on July 24, 1622, it had spoken of

the ill repute in which those of that Nation who deal in rents and commodities are held because in these transactions they remove much gold and silver from our lands without a license. They ship them to others of their Nation who, having fled from the Inquisition, reside in La Rochelle and other parts of France, or in other countries and states, and with whom they correspond. In the same fashion they smuggle [into Spain] a large quantity of vellon coined in La Rochelle, Holland, Germany, England, and other parts.

There is no evidence that the Council had endeavored to ascertain the justification for that "ill repute" or whether any of these suspects had ever been tried and convicted. In any case, the king and Olivares could not act on so general an accusation, and in 1627 they must have rejoiced when the same group of New Christians (save for Rodríguez de Elvas, who was replaced by Simon and Lorenzo Pereira) offered to serve as contractors. They undertook to provide for the whole estimated royal budget of the following year, amounting to the huge sum of 1,852,000 ducats (with interest and gratuities: 2,159,438 ducats). Like other financiers, they hoped that revenue from the American colonies and domestic taxation would more than cover their prepayment. (In some years such contracts were drawn even in advance of any votes taken by the respective Cortes providing for the internal revenue.) Everybody knew that this was a risky business, and at least formally the rates of interest did not appear to be high; but in view of the frequent depreciation through the circulation of poorer varieties of vellon, the real rates could readily be camouflaged. According to Antonio Domínguez Ortiz, despite the limitations decreed in 1623, such loans could command a premium of 50 percent, in addition to another sizable gain at the ultimate repayment. On the other hand, apart from the immediate risks, the contractors had to consider the long range instability of their fortunes. Even an indisputable Old Christian, the Genoese Carlos Strata, a leading officer in the Order of Santiago, was not sure that he could safely bequeath his fortune, estimated at some 2,000,000 ducats, to his heirs. According to the contemporary diarist José de Pellicer (in his entry dated May 31, 1639) Strata piously provided in his testament for 75,000 masses in church, yet the king ordered the immediate sequestration of his entire property until a review and possible renegotiation of all his past government contracts were completed.[64]

The Thirty Years' War, particularly after the entry of France in 1635, facilitated the rise of the Portuguese bankers and contractors. Olivares needed more and more funds to maintain the Spanish armies in fighting condition and to rebuild the navy, which had never recovered from the English blow in 1588. With tremendous effort he actually succeeded in restoring Spain's preeminence in naval warfare, all of which required considerable borrowing of funds and securing of adequate supplies. This task could be carried out only with the help of *asentistas* ready to advance ever-increasing sums to the needy Treasury. According to Alvaro Castillo's preliminary study, the total amount of *asientos* rose from less than 1,000,000 ducats in 1626 to a peak of 61,833,000 ducats before the whole system was eclipsed by the crisis of 1647. During the two crucial intervening decades the New Christian merchants proved doubly helpful, perhaps because, unlike the Castilian individualists and most foreign traders, they were able and willing to pool their resources and form temporary partnerships for major enterprises. The war also helped to eliminate many foreign merchants, particularly Frenchmen, as enemy aliens, and thus reduced competition. In 1625, when Philip IV issued an order for the confiscation of all French property and many French traders were imprisoned by the Inquisition, Cardinal Richelieu declared that "very frequently they are placed behind bars not for the good of religion but as a pretext for many other things." Of course, France retaliated with a similar move against Spanish and Portuguese merchants, a move which to some extent affected the Rouen Marranos.[65]

Among the New Christian bankers was Manuel Cortizos de Villasante who, despite his Jewish origin, succeeded in entering the highest echelons of Spanish society. He is said to have purchased the office of *receptor* of Spain's Economic Council for 30,000 ducats. Later, he added the high-sounding offices of *contador mayor de rentas* and *escribano mayor del Reyno* (chief controller of rents and chancellor of the realm). Although competitors found a way of denouncing him to the Inquisition, before which he was eventually summoned, the behind-the-scenes intervention of his powerful protectors secured his release. This discharge was the more remarkable as Olivares, whose wife had in 1637 acted as hostess at one of Cortizos' lavish parties, had simultaneously welcomed the investigation of his contractor's alleged misdeeds. All of this did not prevent Cortizos from taking an active part, along with such foreign bankers as Carlos Strata, in the social whirl around the royal court, including a ten-day party attended by the king and queen in 1637. He actually became a member of the military Order of Calatrava; his brother Sebastián, admitted to the Order of Santiago, became Spanish ambassador to Genoa; his cousin, Sebastián Ferro or Hierro de Castro, assumed one of the highest offices in Spanish-dominated Naples; and so forth. In return for these rewards, Manuel equipped two companies of cavalry at his own expense to fight the Catalan rebels in 1642, in a struggle of decisive importance in the war with France. On this occasion, we are told, he was robbed by the rebels of a vast amount of capital, variously reported by contemporaries as amounting to 70,000 reals of silver or to 40,000 ducats.[66]

Manuel Cortizos also astutely played his political game. While generally an associate of Olivares, he did not mind securing the good will of Queen Isabel of Bourbon, who later turned out to be the person most responsible for Olivares' downfall. Once when the queen was refused a loan of 800,000 escudos unless she pledged all her jewels, Cortizos stepped in and advanced her the desired amount without any security and without interest. It is small wonder then that he died in peace in 1649. To be sure, rumors spread in Madrid that, shortly before his demise, Cortizos had quietly planned to move to Amsterdam in order to profess Judaism publicly. It was also said that, apart from his very elaborate Catholic funeral, some women were paid for reciting Jewish prayers for his soul. Shortly thereafter, his wife and other female members of the family were subjected to a close inquisitorial investigation, although they seem to have been speedily acquitted. All of these complications did not prevent Cortizos' son, called Manuel José, from assuming in 1668 the title of Viscount de Valdefuentes. He and his family continued to play a considerable role in both banking and diplomacy for several decades. There is no way of telling to what extent they still secretly observed Jewish rituals, however. Yet in 1712, during the confusion created by the War of the Spanish Succession, a cousin of Manuel José, likewise called José Cortizos, left for London, where he publicly returned to Judaism, arranged for the circumcision of his son, and served as a pillar of the London synagogue until his death in 1742; ironically, a century after his father, Sebastian Cortizos had been admitted to the Order of Santiago.[67]

Less fortunate was his compeer, Juan Núñez Saravía (in Portuguese, João Nunes Saraiva). Born in Troncoso, a district in northern Portugal which gave birth to many distinguished New Christians (among them Isaac [Fernando] Cardoso), Núñez Saravía worked his way up in the business world. Later testimony seems to indicate that he accumulated considerable wealth through methods which were not always within the law. However, except for a civil suit which he fended off with apparent ease, he had no difficulty in joining the consortium of asentistas which, beginning in 1626, was negotiating contracts with the government. In this way he, as well as his brother Enrique, who resided for the most part in Bayonne or Bordeaux, ultimately commanded fortunes of 300,000 and 500,000 ducats, respectively. In 1631, however, he was cited before the Inquisition as a secret Judaizer and, primarily on the testimony of servants, was imprisoned and subjected to a lengthy trial. The accusation was later supported by reports which the aforementioned emissary of the Inquisition in France, Juan Bautista de Villadiego, sent back from Rouen. In addition, Núñez Saravía was indicted for allegedly having helped Morisco refugees to salvage some of their property after their expulsion in 1609–1614. He and others supposedly removed such property—including gold and silver, the export of which was strictly prohibited—to France, for the relatively small commission of 10 percent. It appears that neither Olivares nor the king was able or willing to shield Juan and Enrique from prosecution by the Holy Office. Perhaps irked by some difficulty they had had in getting Juan Núñez Saravía to fulfill a part of his contract in 1630, the king and his minister succeeded only, if they interceded at all, in securing a milder type of torture, during which Juan staunchly denied all guilt. More lenient treatment was in any case called for by the defendant's illnesses (he suffered from both gout and a hernia) and his generally weakened physical condition. Ultimately, after languishing in prison for six years, the brothers were convicted and had to appear at an auto-da-fé on December 13, 1637, abjuring their sins *de vehementi*. They emerged from their tribulations totally impoverished—their fortunes had been sequestered by the Inquisition at the beginning of the investigation—and, with few friends. In a similar fashion the prosperous career of another international New Christian merchant, Fernão Martins, was cut short by an inquisitorial prosecution in 1651–56.[68]

Most remarkably, in 1625 Philip and Olivares brought a professing Jew, Jacob b. Ḥayyim Cansino (or Cancino), from Oran in North Africa to Madrid, although he had stipulated in advance that he must be allowed to profess Judaism publicly. This permission was evidently granted, notwithstanding the 1492 degree of expulsion, which called for the death penalty to any Jew setting foot on Spanish soil, and which had never been abrogated. The prohibition and the penalty had been officially restated in 1599; the only exceptions were to be for North-African envoys and for immigrants who, before their entry into the country, would declare before a notary and witnesses that they wished to be baptized. Cansino's great-grandfather and namesake, probably a native of Seville or its environs, had been appointed in 1556 by Charles V to be the first "vassal of his Catholic Majesty and his interpreter of languages in the locality of Oran" (this high-sounding title, used by Jacob Cansino in 1638, had apparently been held by his grandfather Isaac, father Ḥayyim, and brother Aaron till 1633). Jacob himself survived an unfortunate incident in 1646. Probably at the instigation of Manuel Cortizos' private enemies and business rivals, possibly with Olivares' connivance, Cansino was accused of having helped to prevent some unfavorable testimony against the banker from being submitted to the Inquisition. Although with rare

unanimity public opinion and the contemporary writers extolled
the banishment of the Jews in 1492 (as well as that of the Moriscos
in 1609–14), the death penalty seems not to have been invoked in
Cansino's case, even after his temporary imprisonment in 1646. He
stayed on in Madrid until the 1650s, when he returned to Oran.
Subsequently, he often acted as a spokesman for that North-African
Jewish community, which in 1656 extended a large loan of 800,000
ducats to the Spanish monarchy. He died in 1666, without sus-
pecting that two years later (August 22, 1668) the community
would be banished by royal decree. At any rate, the presence of an
unconverted Jew living an avowed Jewish life in the Spanish capital before and after the Count-Duke's downfall, must have scan-
dalized many Catholic conservatives; it doubtless also enhanced
the credibility of the repeated rumors concerning Olivares' alleged
negotiations with Salonican Jews for the establishment of a regular Jewish congregation in Madrid.[69]

The intriguing personality of Jacob Cansino or Cancino, who
lived for a quarter of a century in Madrid, for the most part in a
very desirable residential quarter, and apparently walked through
the streets of the Spanish capital in the typical garb of a North-
African Jew, is known to us chiefly from the later testimony of a
compatriot, Luis de Acosta. Born in Fez the son of one Aaron
Cohen, Luis seems to have been animated by an intense wander-
lust: he spent some time in Lisbon, where he changed his name
to Acosta; resided for many more years in the Low Countries; and
finally settled in Madrid. He had first met Cansino in 1625, but
became friendly with him only in 1637. With his knowledge of
the Low Countries, he helped Cansino prepare a memorandum
for Olivares about trade conditions in that area. Of course, his
1651 testimony about Cansino is not entirely reliable. But it furnishes some insights into the career of this extraordinary "vassal"
and "interpreter," who further endeared himself to Olivares by
publishing in 1638 in Latin characters the *Extremos y grandezas
de Constantinopla* of the well-known Salonican rabbi Mose ben
Baruch Almosnino (1510–80), a descendant of two Aragonese
martyrs of the Inquisition. The Spanish statesman, to whom the
work was dedicated and whose picture adorns the volume, may
have viewed the transliteration as a means of promoting trade
with the Levant and other countries.[70]

Nor should one completely dismiss the rumors about negotiations between Olivares and Salonican or other foreign Jews. We recall the comparative ease with which the professing Jews of Amsterdam and London could communicate with their secret coreligionists on the Iberian Peninsula through special messengers dispatched to their former homeland from time to time. From inquisitorial records we also learn about the occasional arrival of qualified circumcisers, who apparently were able to visit Spanish and Portuguese localities and clandestinely perform their task without being apprehended. As late as 1707, we are told, a secret synagogue was discovered in Madrid. It probably was attended for the most part by the local Marranos, but we should not rule out the possibility that foreign visitors gave them instruction and guidance in performing their long-forgotten divine services.

For this reason the following statement of an eyewitness, Francisco Vilches (in his letter of August 16, 1634, to Rafael Pereyra), may indeed contain a grain of truth: "The favorite [Olivares] is planning to admit Jews to Spain. It is certain that they are coming and going, negotiating with the king and submitting memoranda to him. Today I have seen one wearing a white turban at the gate of the royal quarters; it caused me pain." Another account, by the chronicler Matéo de Novoa, certainly has a basis in fact, despite its hearsay character and the writer's general enmity to Philip IV. In the midst of his antigovernmental harangue, Novoa reports (under the date of 1638):

I have heard it said that the Jews of Oran and those who inhabit the interior of Africa have found here sponsors for their admission to the environs of Madrid. It is proposed that these [the African Jews] be given land on which they might live in freedom according to their Law; the same should be done for many more [of their coreligionists] who might wish to live with them. For this concession they would pay many millions. Who would doubt that in this case none [of the secret Judaizers] would remain in the kingdom of Portugal or in any other parts [of the realm] without trying to settle here? Woe unto the noble families of Castile! Many of them were endangered before when they had them [Jews] here. What will they do now under the present exigencies?

Characteristically, similar proposals emanated from some ecclesiastical circles. An unnamed churchman, perhaps a Jesuit, submitted a memorandum to Philip IV arguing for the readmission of professing Jews to Spain. While praising Ferdinand and Isabella for the banishment of Jews in 1492, the writer pointed to the example of other countries, including the Papal States, which had greatly benefited from their new Jewish settlers. He insisted that "Jews not only had caused no damage but had proved rather useful" to the very Church, because their presence had helped to confirm the truths of the Christian faith and had furnished a number of new converts to it. Yet none of these alleged projects were brought to fruition. That of 1638 failed, we are told by Adolfo de Castro, as a result of direct intervention by the papal nuncio, who spoke up against it in strong terms in a public audience with the king. Nonetheless, the subject was to reemerge time and again in Spain's ruling circles during the following generations. According to unsubstantiated rumors, both Charles II (1661–1700) and Charles III (1759–88) seriously entertained proposals for the readmission of professing Jews. There is no question that Don Pedro Varela, the high-ranking secretary of the Despacho Universal de España e Indias, submitted to Charles IV (1788–1808) a memorandum suggesting that Jews be readmitted to Spain because they possessed "the major riches in Europe" and might substantially help the country during its war with England. However, this proposal was rejected, and a new royal decree of 1800 specifically forbade the issuance of passports to foreign Jews for travel in Spain. This decree was included in the *Novísima Recopilación* of 1802 and was repeated on August 16, 1816.[71]

Among the numerous strange episodes during Philip IV's regime, one may cite the extraordinary case of Tommaso Pignero de Veiga (Pinheiro de Veiga). Although apparently a New Christian (Ludwig von Pastor calls him "ein ehemaliger Jude" or "a convert Jew"), he seems to have encountered no difficulty in securing the post of royal procurator in Lisbon. In 1636 a serious dispute arose between him and the local churchmen concerning the so-called *capillas*, legacies left by testators under certain conditions such as that masses be said for them or their relatives on specified dates. In the great fiscal stringency facing the Treasury, Pignero laid hands on these funds. The controversy reached its climax in 1638, when the papal collector Alessandro Castracani protested against such expropriation, whereupon the procurator threatened both Castracani and his Jesuit supporters with expulsion from Portugal. Castracani retaliated by warning that he would impose ecclesiastical censures on the royal agent and his associates. Ultimately, Pignero banished Castracani from the country and, assisted by the police, escorted him to the frontier. Thereupon the papal collector excommunicated all officials involved in the proceedings, and even placed Lisbon under an interdict. It took some time before an agreement between the pope and the Spanish ambassador in Rome established peace between the conflicting parties. Yet, there is no evidence that Pignero became the object of an inquisitorial investigation on this score.[72]

Regrettably, not enough information is available about the details of the business transactions and intellectual activities of the leading New Christian merchants, physicians, and scholars in Madrid and Seville. The main interest of modern investigators in these individuals has been aroused by the availability of records from the various branches of the Holy Office, which prosecuted some of them and collected much information concerning their private lives. Understandably, the principal objective of the prosecutors was to ascertain the extent to which the accused practiced Jewish rituals or otherwise betrayed heretical leanings. While the size and location of the defendants' properties were not completely neglected, because these were subject to immediate sequestration and possible confiscation, the details of the owners' earlier business transactions were of secondary interest to the Inquisitors and occupy, therefore, relatively little space in the testimony of witnesses or of the accused themselves. Even these data have not been examined with the necessary attention to detail—as have been, for example, the records of the Economic Council and local archives relating to the far-flung business activities of such leading merchants as the Ruiz family (carefully reviewed by Henri Lapeyre) and several other plutocrats of the prosperous era of Philip II.[73]

Nor should we lose sight of the fact that, next to the leading New Christian merchants, there lived a host of business associates, employees, craftsmen, petty traders, and moneylenders, who attracted far less attention from the Holy Office and whose very existence is not even mentioned in the extant records. When we hear, for example, that no fewer than 2,000 Portuguese New Christians lived in Seville alone, clearly a large majority of these consisted of members of the lower middle class or workers eking out a meager sustenance under the harsh conditions of the age. Very likely most of the insecure New Christians did not share the general contempt for hard work of their Old Christian compatriots, in whose behalf the Sevillian municipality protested against Philip IV's ordinance of 1637 requiring the expropriation of all slaves in private employ to replace the depleted manpower on the royal galleys. Pointing out that these slaves were already Christianized, and were born and bred in Spain, the city fathers maintained: "They work to provide for their masters, consisting, for the most part, of impoverished persons and widows, as well as of honorable citizens who have no other means of earning a livelihood except through their [the slaves'] effort. This situation is quite common hereabouts." It stands to reason, however, as mentioned above, that Judaizers largely refrained from employing Negro Christian slaves, who were no less a menace to them than were free Christian domestics. That is perhaps why we so rarely find records of prosecution by the Inquisition of Negro proselytes to Judaism. Even less is known about Marrano holdings of Moorish and Turkish slaves, usually recruited from prisoners of war. Although tacitly permitted to persevere in the Muslim faith, they were as a rule not very docile, and could hardly be relied on not to divulge their masters' secret observance of Jewish rituals.[74]

INQUISITORIAL RIGIDITY

On the other hand, the intellectual eminence and high social standing of some New Christians were additional incentives for personal enemies and inquisitorial officials to question their *limpieza* and, with it, their orthodoxy. In fact, "matters have reached such an extreme," observed Juan de Mal Lara, "that inability to sign one's own name has become the mark of noble lineage." For this reason, Rodrigo Méndez Silva, though anything but a dedicated Judaizer, and an official enjoying royal protection, did not escape unscathed. Serving as royal *cronista general* (royal historiographer, a post earlier sought in vain by Lope de Vega), and as a high official of the supreme Council of Castile, Méndez Silva seems to have felt secure behind the protective façade of a number of patriotic works he wrote—among them one relating to Spain's population which he dedicated to Manuel Cortizos. Some of his writings made a great impression, and were praised by Lope de Vega, Calderón de la Barca, Tirso de Molina, and others. Nevertheless, he was accused in 1659 not only of judaizing but of participating in a ritual murder. He was subjected to severe torture and condemned to perpetual imprisonment, and the confiscation of all his property. His wife, too, was tried and condemned. However, undoubtedly owing to the intervention of high-placed personages, he managed to emigrate to Venice in 1663, where he embarked on a new career and established a new family. (Because of the age difference between the husband of sixty and his new wife of eighteen, some local wags punned on his title, changing it from *cronista* to *cornista*—a horned man). Ironically, one cannot even say that Méndez Silva suffered all these tribulations for the sake of deep religious convictions; while living in relative freedom in Italy, he often betrayed free-thinking proclivities which probably made him rather unwelcome to the more staunchly orthodox members of the Venetian community.[75]

Similarly enlightening is the story of Felipe Godínez, born in Seville about 1585, who became a popular preacher at a local church and attracted wide audiences. He also wrote a number of distinguished plays, which ultimately placed him in the front rank of the dramatists of the Golden Age. One of his dramas, *O el fraile ha de ser ladrón, o el ladrón ha de ser fraile,* was issued by an unscrupulous publishing firm under the name of Calderón de la Barca, without arousing any suspicion about its authorship. Nonetheless, Godínez was denounced to the Inquisition, imprisoned, and after a trial condemned to seclusion in a monastery for a year, loss of his clerical office, and exile from Seville. He marched at the auto-da-fé of November 30, 1624, at which the following noteworthy justification of his sentence was read:

Father Godínez, priest, preacher, and confessor residing in Seville, thirty-nine years of age, is a descendant of Jewish New Christians. A faithful adherent of the Law of Moses, he performed its rites and ceremonies, convinced that it was the true religion and that in it alone he would find salvation. This fact is proved by the numerous heretical propositions advanced in his sermons and his other erroneous and audacious blasphemies. From an early age he observed the fast days of the said Law of Moses; he abstained from eating or drinking anything during the day until nightfall and the appearance of stars. At that time he took only fish or fruit, never meat. Desirous to observe that law with even greater fidelity than the other members of his family, at the age of nine or ten he used to inquire whether after the fast he was to continue fasting. . . . He was such a devotee of the Law of Moses that he composed many poetic works drawn from Old Testament history, such as the two comedies *Queen Esther* and *The Harp of David,* in which were noted some such strange propositions as that the angel Gabriel had appeared to Queen Esther, announcing that out of the people of Israel would arise the Son of God whose mother would bear him free of the original sin. He has also contended that he comprehended a passage in Holy Scriptures misunderstood by Saint Jerome in his commentary. . . . In his sermons he preached doctrines favoring the Jewish nation, such as that the Lord had given it His word in the person of Jacob that He would not abandon the people of Israel without redeeming it. He [Godínez] intimated that, since that promise had not been fulfilled, God had thereby deprived Himself of His freedom of action for He cannot abandon it [Israel] until the promise is fulfilled— clearly an heretical proposition.

Godínez had the good fortune, however, of being rehabilitated by the Inquisition after but two years, the Holy Office probably yielding to the pressure of public opinion and the intervention of powerful friends. After moving to Madrid, he was able to resume his career as a writer and lecturer, in which capacity he delivered, for instance, one of the several funerary orations on the death of Lope de Vega—a fine piece of rhetoric subsequently included in Juan Pérez de Montalván's (or Montalbán's) collection entitled *Fama posthuma . . . del . . . Lope Félix de Vega.* This oration was delivered with great fervor and sincerity, although Gódinez may have heard of Lope's snide comment on one of his comedies, popularly known as *La Godína:* "They tell me that it treats of a Jewess, rather than of one of the Goths." While continuing to produce dramas on biblical themes, including some borrowed from the New Testament, Godínez seems to have taken sufficient precautions to avoid another investigation for heresy, doubly dangerous in the case of second offenders. It is even possible that he learned his lesson and became a pious Catholic to the end of his life.[76]

More typical of the average defendant helplessly facing the elaborate machinery of the Holy Office was Bartolomé Febos or Febo, undistinguished in the world of letters, commerce, or public affairs. Son of Antonio Rodríguez Lamego, whom we have encountered as a leader of the Marrano community in Rouen, Febos had lived for many years with an aunt in Lisbon and had grown up as a pious Catholic under Jesuit guidance. Later he spent three or four years with his father in Rouen, where he imbibed many Judaic lessons and began observing Jewish rituals. Upon his settlement in Madrid in 1627, at the age of nineteen, he lived peacefully for five years until his name came up in connection with the aforementioned reports of the Inquisition's emissary to France. Ultimately he was accused of judaizing, of entertaining crypto-Jews, and of irreverence toward Christianity. Febos succeeded in enlisting the help of the highly regarded Fernando Cardoso who, unbeknown to the inquisitors, was himself a secret Judaizer. Cardoso testified that he had known the defendant for four years, and had treated him medically, entering his home at odd hours. On none of these occasions had he noticed any suspicious strangers, though he had seen Febos entertain at meals "honorable people, including musicians, poets, and ladies of fine conduct." Nonetheless, Febos was convicted. Perhaps because of such friendly testimony, however, he got off with a moderate fine and "reconciliation." [77]

In general, the Holy Office was left free to prosecute heretics and infidels, regardless of their services to the country. With typical inconsistency Philip IV and Olivares were either unwilling or unable to save some of their protégés from the inquisitorial prosecutors. Moreover, from time to time the king, the queen, and other dignitaries attended a major auto-da-fé, such as that staged in Madrid in 1632, thus adding to the solemnity of the occasion. So important was the royal presence deemed for that auto that the spectacle was transferred by the Toledan Inquisition to Madrid to accommodate the queen, who was convalescing after giving birth to Prince Baltasar Carlos and was to be spared an arduous journey. Because of this last-minute change of location, the preparations for this "act of faith," the largest ever performed in Madrid, had to be completed in nine days (June 25–July 4)—an undertaking which, despite the municipality's plea that it had no funds, involved the expenditure of considerable sums for day and night labor. This haste also gave rise to the contractors' complaint that some of their equipment had been stolen during the work at night. Royal support of the Inquisition was one of the mainstays of the popular acceptance of Philip IV's long regime, widely disparaged by contemporaneous and later historians. A character in *El Caballero de Gracia* by Antonio Mira de Amescua (or Mescua) voiced a belief cherished by many of the king's subjects when he declaimed: "I am the Faith of Spain/ Animated by the Inquisition/ To which Don Philip the Fourth/ Lends so much support/ That for me it alone portrays/the palace in which he resides." Lope de Vega, to whom this work was sometimes attributed, frequently extolled the Holy Office in his authentic writings. For instance, in his dramatization of the Blood Accusation of La Guardia, he had the following praise for the Catholic monarchs: "You have done well, O Kings, amen/That you have placed the Holy/Tribunal in such a state./For you have not conferred on Spain/Any benefit equal to that/of the Holy Office." [78]

Even more enthusiastic was the approval of the inquisitorial proceedings by the masses of the population. As mentioned before, the spectacular ceremonies associated with autos-da-fé attracted greater audiences than the most widely publicized *autos sacramentales* or bullfights. We are told by contemporaries that the Sevillian autos of 1570 and 1660 attracted 100,000 onlookers each. They seem to have been surpassed in splendor and attractiveness by the "act of faith" performed in the capital on June 30, 1680. As described by an official of the Inquisition, José Vicente del Olmo, an eyewitness of the events, the inhabitants of Madrid were invited by public announcement to the spectacle; they were promised that "all those who shall in any way contribute towards the promotion of, or be present at, the said auto, will be made partakers of the spiritual grace granted by the Roman pontiff." Fifty master builders and their workmen had ceaselessly and enthusiastically labored on the erection of the amphitheater. On the day before the execution, the persons to be relaxed were visited by an inquisitorial deacon, who informed each of them: "Brother, your process has been examined by persons of great learning and knowledge, and your crimes are so great and of such a nature that it has been deemed proper to pronounce a sentence of death, in order to punish you. Tomorrow you die. Prepare yourself as you ought; for this purpose I leave with you two monks." On the following morning, the auto began with a colorful procession at 7 A.M., followed by the reading of the individual verdicts and sermons until 4 P.M., whereupon those to be burned were handed over by the secretary of the Holy Office to the secular judge, with the stereotyped request that he deal "mercifully and kindly with them." When some of the condemned threw themselves into the flames, the public was informed that this was not a sign of valor, but rather a culpable act of despair. On that occasion the execution lasted through the night until after 9 A.M. the next morning. In fact, even the incipient dawn of the Enlightenment Era in the eighteenth century did not completely end these sanguinary pageants.[79]

As before, defendants of various kinds appeared among the condemned at such ceremonies, but the main targets remained suspected Judaizers. For example, in the auto celebrated on July 4, 1632, in Madrid, four persons were sentenced for blasphemy, four for witchcraft, and four for bigamy. But in the archival record each verdict is provided with the remark: "All four have abjured de levi," which was a relatively mild punishment. Of another group of nine accused of miscellaneous transgressions, seven individuals were likewise sentenced to abjuration de levi; one was exiled from the locality, and another was condemned to prison. At the same time, five Portuguese Judaizers were condemned to perpetual imprisonment; seven were relaxed; and four were burned in effigy. Remarkably, after declining somewhat during the regimes of Philip III and Philip IV, the number of Judaizers sentenced by the Inquisition began increasing again in the second half of the seventeenth century. Of the 399 persons then appearing in public autos in Cordova, 324 defendants were condemned for judaizing. In Toledo, 556 Judaizers were recorded among the 855 accused. Of the 85 defendants prosecuted in Valladolid in 1699, 78 were Judaizers. Spain's intense hatred, official and popular, of secret Jews came to the fore even in the Treaty of Utrecht of July 1713. Forced to cede Gibraltar (which back in 1473 had been proposed as a place of refuge for the Marranos) to Great Britain, the Spanish government formally stipulated in Article x "that no leave shall be given, under any pretext whatsoever, to Jews or Moors to reside, or have their dwellings, in the said town of Gibraltar." Although this provision quickly sank into oblivion and Jews soon played an important role in the life of that British outpost, it could be invoked against them by the unfriendly governor Sir Richard Gardiner, as late as the 1840s. Independently, the Inquisition of Valencia on June 8, 1815, sentenced Ysrael Benoria, a native of Gibraltar, aged twenty-one, to "spontaneous abjuration of the errors of Judaism and reconciliation with our Catholic religion." [80]

Confiscation of property usually accompanied any severe sentence and served as a major inducement to both prosecution and condemnation. In 1659, for example, the Cordova Inquisition was able to collect from twelve Portuguese Judaizers of moderate means the very large sum of 690,875 reals, or 5,550,625 maravedis. The largest amount ever yielded by inquisitorial confiscation came after the condemnation of numerous Majorcan Chuetas in 1678. This affair created a great sensation, not only on the Balearic Islands but also in countries outside the Iberian Peninsula. It started with an auto-da-fé in 1675, at which a seventeen-year-old Jew, Alonso López, was burned at the stake. Along with other Jewish refugees from Oran, from which the Jews were banished in 1669, López and other Jews had been taken off their ship when it stopped at Palma, Majorca, on its way to Leghorn. Investigation had shown that only López was a former New Christian, born and baptized in Madrid, who had been taken by his father to North Africa, after a brief stay in Malaga. Apparently inspired by the messianic prophecies of Shabbetai Zevi, the young man now resisted all efforts at persuasion and chose to suffer martyrdom rather than to abjure his Jewish faith. Thereupon the Inquisition became interested in the local Chuetas, and by October 13, 1667, no fewer than 237 New Christians were arrested. After a lengthy investigation, all the defendants were "reconciled" as first offenders. But they lost most of their property, at least in so far as they had been unable to secrete it with Old Christian friends. This was by no means the end of suffering for the community. Later, numerous defendants were accused of relapsing to their "evil" ways; 88 of them were sentenced on March 7, 1691, to temporary or perpetual imprisonment, galley slavery, or the payment of a variety of fines. Another group of 21 "hardened offenders" of both sexes were burned at the stake in an auto-da-fé on May 1, 1691.[81]

As a result of these Majorcan trials, the confiscation yielded an enormous sum to the Holy Office. Estimates of the yield by contemporaries and modern scholars vary in detail, but they all range close to 1,500,000 pesos, which, according to Henry Kamen, was the equivalent of some 2,500,000 ducats. Most remarkably, although the royal Treasury was supposed to share such revenue to the extent of one-third or more, the Holy Office stubbornly resisted submitting any figures relating to these confiscations. Ultimately, it appears, the Treasury had to be satisfied with the minute share of 4.66 percent. The losses to the Chueta community were three or four times the size of the Inquisition's gain, for quite apart from the generally low yields of forced property sales, the inquisitors' friends were often allowed to acquire valuable items at a fraction of the price which might have been obtained at a regular auction. In one case the chief inquisitor simply made a gift of a precious string of pearls to the beautiful wife of the lay secretary of the Holy Office. In general, inquisitorial bureaucrats found it difficult to resist the temptation to get "rich quick," while they persuaded themselves that they were performing holy deeds in the service of the Church. The impact of this lopsided system on the Spanish economy and society was tremendous. Henry Charles Lea did not exaggerate when he asserted:

To it also is greatly attributable the stagnation of Spanish commerce and industry, for trade could not flourish when credit was impaired, and confidence could not exist when merchants and manufacturers of the highest standing might, at any moment, fall into the hands of the tribunal and all their assets be impounded.

In the Majorcan case the memory of these trials and their effects on the Majorcan population proved unusually enduring. Deep into the twentieth century the Chuetas formed a segregated community on the island. The inmates of the *calle* ("Jew Street"; it really consisted of a number of streets) long continued to be called *judíos* or *hebréos* by their neighbors, and married only within their own small circle, under a partially imposed and partially voluntary endogamous system.[82]

PORTUGUESE REACTIONS

While in Spain under Philip III and Philip IV the pressure on Marranos was slightly eased and at least governmental hostility toward New Christian subjects (whose ranks were greatly increased by Portuguese immigrants) abated, in Portugal itself the intergroup tensions affected wider and wider circles. This contrast became doubly significant as during the sixty years of the three Philips' reign over Portugal the country still enjoyed autonomy in most internal affairs. Even its Inquisition was not united with the Spanish Holy Office, despite efforts by Philip II to obtain a papal decree combining the two headquarters, a decree which Gregory XIII roundly refused to issue. As a result, there was no mutual extradition of "culprits" between the two parts of the realm. Portuguese public opinion, too, nurtured by memories of the glorious days of Henry the Navigator and Emanuel I, for the most part followed an independent path.[83]

However, both parts of the realm apparently were united in their hatred of the New Christians. Although the principle of *limpieza* had a less persistent history in Portugal than in the Spanish provinces, the Portuguese were no less ardent practitioners of the art of trying to preserve the "purity" of their race. But they found the task much more difficult, on account of the higher percentage of persons of Jewish descent in their country. If our aforementioned estimate of the number of forced converts in 1497 is at all correct, their New Christian descendants in the sixteenth and seventeenth centuries may well have exceeded 10 percent of the population, after discounting their higher rate of emigration to Portugal's American colonies, Western Europe, Italy, and the Muslim lands. The country's economic decline, accelerated by its participation in the Empire's foreign adventures and currency manipulations, in some respects surpassed that of its larger neighbor, adding fuel to the existing animosities. Paradoxically, even the unprecedented prosperity of the sixteenth century was condemned by some moralists because of its undesirable psychological side effects. Juan Adam de la Parra, a Spanish poet and writer officiating as an inquisitor, resorted to many specious arguments in pleading with Philip IV in 1630 against the removal of Jewish disabilities. He attributed to the New Christian group, for example, the sole responsibility for Portugal's expansionist policies toward both the East and the West Indies. He claimed that the *conversos* had thus underhandedly helped to corrupt the morals of the Portuguese nation with its suddenly acquired wealth and luxurious mode of living; in this fashion they had "succeeded in eliminating the heroes and destroying the heroic spirit which had rendered Portugal so formidable." Still more sharply did the native Portuguese Vicente da Costa de Mattos (or de Matos), in a crudely written volume of 1622, blame all Jews and their descendants for the world crisis. He insisted that many Christian heretics were themselves either Judaizers or descendants of Judaizers, and ascribed the ensuing decline of the Spanish realm to their all-pervasive influence. Using biblical terms, he taught that, while in ancient times God had punished the Jews' enemies for ill treatment of the chosen people, since the rise of Christianity the situation had been reversed and now God punished those nations which tolerated Jews. Hence, he argued in his concluding chapters, the only solution was a total elimination of New Christians from both Spain and Portugal.[84]

Opposition to the New Christians was not only the result of the intensified racialism accompanying their growing integration into Portuguese society without complete absorption. It was also a phase of the general religious revival stimulated by the Counter Reformation. As in Spain, though to a somewhat lesser extent, the impact of Erasmian and other humanistic teachings, so powerful in the first half of the sixteenth century, gave way to increasing religious conformity in both thought and practice.

The manifold manifestations of a return to the medieval type of religious orthodoxy were but slightly modified by the new mysticism and the reformatory ideas espoused in Spain by Juan de Ávila and St. Theresa. Last but not least, we must bear in mind the ever-sharpening tensions generated by the economic expansion of the sixteenth century, and the subsequent depression and shrinking opportunities of the seventeenth.[85]

So long as Spain remained the leading power in the Western

world, and its armies celebrated victory after victory, Portuguese national feeling had to remain subdued. Like other subject peoples in despair, the Portuguese found an outlet in messianic dreams. Disregarding the historic fact that their last independent king, Sebastian, had fallen in the battle of Alcazarquivir (Al-Kasr al-Kabir) in 1578, the masses cherished the belief that the king had been miraculously saved and that he was due to reappear and claim his throne. This belief had sunk so deeply into the Portuguese psyche that the expectation was not dimmed by the appearance of several pseudo-messiahs, each claiming to be the surviving King Sebastian and each in turn apprehended by the Spanish authorities and condemned to either death, life imprisonment, or galley servitude. Nor did the hope completely fade with the passage of time. Even two centuries later, many persons still yearned for the return of the celebrated king-crusader. Some New Christians, too, were seized by that semimessianic frenzy. So level-headed a man as Jacob Rosales (of the widely dispersed Bocarro-Francês family), who later resided in Hamburg as a leading Jewish businessman and diplomat, while still living in Portugal composed in 1620 a poem in strictly Sebastianist terms. He dedicated it to Duke Theodosio, of the formerly regnant dynasty of Braganza, whom he hailed as the restorer of the kingdom. The Spanish censor quickly suppressed the work, although he was not always very strict with respect to Sebastianist publications.[86]

In general, the Spanish authorities considered the Sebastianist "dreams" to be politically innocuous manifestations of popular messianic yearnings, like those in vogue in the first half of the sixteenth century. One such movement, inspired by the Trancoso shoemaker-prophet Gonçalo Annes Bandarra, harked back to biblical predictions, particularly to the "four kingdoms" of the Book of Daniel. Like Camoëns, Bandarra identified these successive monarchies as the Assyrian, Persian, Greek, and Roman Empires (including the Holy Roman Empire), which were now to be followed by the fifth universal monarchy led by Portugal. Although J. Lucio d'Azevedo and other scholars have denied that Bandarra had any New Christian ancestors, the fact that he lived in the small town of Trancoso with its strong and intellectually creative New Christian population, and that he combined his occupational activities as a cobbler with intensive study of the Bible —a combination frequently found among the Portuguese New Christians—makes the denial somewhat dubious. In any case, the popular folk prophet must have been exposed to strong influences from his New Christian neighbors.[87]

Going far beyond mere verbal exchanges, the Portuguese government enacted ever-new discriminatory laws. On November 10, 1621, and February 23, 1623, it issued decrees forbidding the appointment of New Christians to chairs at universities. This was an abrupt departure from previous practices, since the University of Coimbra and other Portuguese universities, though outposts of the Counter Reformation movement, had long insisted on keeping their gates open to New Christian teachers and students. The Coimbra statute of 1559 had called for a permanent chair in the Hebrew language, a chair which probably had often to be entrusted to a New Christian professor. Although his salary of 50,000 reals did not compare favorably with those of the six professors of Latin, which ranged from 70,000 to 100,000 reals, it was comparable with those of the professors of Greek, mathematics, and others. In fact, Julio Caro Baroja calls Coimbra "a notorious shelter for New Christians." The impetus to the discriminatory legislation of the 1620s may have been given by the António Hómem affair. Born of a good New Christian family in Coimbra in 1564, Hómem made a remarkable career in theology, ultimately becoming professor of canon law and dean at the University of Coimbra. He enjoyed a national, in some respects even international, reputation as an authority on canon law. He was consulted on this score by jurists, government officials, and churchmen from various localities, and apparently had a considerable following among the Coimbra faculty and students. But his excessive self-assurance aroused enmities, as well as competitive appetites, among some colleagues and acquaintances and ultimately caused his downfall. In 1616 he was first accused of misconduct in his office at the University. It was claimed that he had "served as a suborner in appointments to university chairs, it being said that he received money from candidates and students for distribution [among his colleagues] and that for this purpose his doors were always open at night." Soon the accusations took on more danger-

ous hues and extended to charges of sodomy; that is, of homosexuality. Most importantly, he was also sentenced for judaizing.
"Since the last general pardon [of 1605]," the sentence read, "he
lived apart from our holy Catholic faith and became a believer in
the Law of Moses, considering it beautiful and truthful and seeking his salvation in it. When he had occasion to speak about us
Christians and matters of [the Christian] faith, he laughed and
joked while discussing these matters with persons of his Nation,
apostates from the faith, to whom he declared himself to be a
Jew." It was proved that he and a number of others attended
Jewish services in a secret synagogue located in an isolated house
behind a potter's workshop. After several years of grueling investigation, he was burned at the stake in Lisbon on May 5, 1624; his
house was razed and later replaced by a Capuchin chapel.[88]

Hómem's investigation drew into the inquisitorial net a number
of other distinguished New Christians; among them, the leading
jurist Tomé Vaz (or Velasco), born in Coimbra in 1553, who was
distantly related to Hómem. He, too, was convicted for "separating himself from our holy Catholic faith and adopting the Law of
Moses." His life, however, was spared; and, apart from a relatively
brief imprisonment and being forced to wear a sanbenito at an
early auto-da-fé of November 25, 1618, he was allowed to abjure
his errors and resume a normal life. Still another victim was the
mathematician André de Avelar (or Avelhar). His prosecution,
begun in 1620, resulted in his condemnation at an auto-da-fé on
June 18, 1623. His lengthy sentence included the following revealing passage:

During the fast day of the month of September the accused joined
many persons of his Nation [at a service] at which all appeared bare-
foot, with their bodies and beards clean, and their heads uncovered. A
certain person [Hómem], whom the accused and the others of his group
considered their high priest and respected as the chief rabbi of the Law
of Moses, repeated certain passages from the Old Testament and certain Psalms, without the *Gloria Patri,* giving them interpretations in
Latin, translated into Portuguese by the accused.

Avelar was condemned to perpetual imprisonment.[89]

These and other trials created a great sensation in Coimbra and
Lisbon, and touched to the quick numerous admirers of these

scholars, especially those of Hómem. Some New Christian partisans were said to have planned to establish a "Confraternity of Saint Antonio," in his memory; but the Inquisition detected the hidden motives behind that move and prevented its realization. This idea was not new, an example having been set by the sequel to an auto of August 3, 1603, at which a young friar Diogo de Assumpção was burned. During the investigation, lasting four years, this defendant had claimed that "among his brother friars he had found only lies, falsehoods, and cheating." After escaping from the monastery, he had lived with a New Christian merchant, Gaspar Bocarra, who, however, refused to help him flee via France to Flanders, where he wished to become a full-fledged Jew. Betrayed by another acquaintance, De Assumpção was arrested, but he resisted all efforts by Christian theologians to persuade him that Christianity alone was the true religion. When pressed to give the name of God, he insisted that the Lord Himself had declared that He was "the God of Abraham, the God of Isaac, and the God of Jacob . . . This is My name for ever, and this is My memorial unto all generations" (Exod. 3:15). After Diogo's fiery death, which was mourned by coreligionists in far-off Amsterdam and lamented by poets like David Jesurun, some of his friends apparently succeeded in perpetuating his memory by founding a "Brotherhood of St. Diogo." [90]

Of all these victims it was Hómem whose execution made the deepest impression on Portuguese society. The declaration of the Dominican friar António de Sousa at the auto of 1624, that the group around the *preceptor infelix* (unfortunate teacher)—as Hómem was widely called—was "offensive in conduct, deficient in honor, and a menace to the faith," and that anyone associating with that group became a Jew, was shared by most of his compatriots. So was Sousa's contention that all New Christians, especially those residing in Beja, Évora, Tomar, Coimbra, and Oporto, were secret Judaizers. Even more outspokenly racialist was the sermon delivered on July 14, 1624, by the renowned Franciscan preacher João de Ceita. Addressing the large crowd assembled to witness the auto held on that day in Évora, the friar took as his scriptural motif the Psalmist's exclamation: "They return at evening, they howl like a dog, and go round about the city" (59:7). Applying to

Jews and Judaizers what the ancient poet had said about the un-
believing Gentile nations, De Ceita delivered a venomous attack
on New Christians in general. This sermon, combining "fanatical
racism [with] biting sarcasm and a total lack of Christian charity,"
was immediately published in Portuguese, and within five years
appeared in a Spanish translation. Most disheartening to the Portuguese public was the number of priests convicted for judaizing.
As Miguel de Castro, emissary of the Portuguese Inquisition to
Madrid, emphasized in a memorandum submitted to the king
on February 27, 1627, the 231 defendants condemned for "infidelity" by the Portuguese Holy Office in the preceding eight
years included 15 priests, 44 nuns, 15 theologians (2 of them professors), 11 bachelors (licentiates), 20 advocates, and 20 physicians.[91]

Denunciations of New Christians, rather than being toned down
with the passage of time, were now voiced with increasing frequency and venom. They included such odd folkloristic accusations as that the Jews need the blood of Christian children as a
remedy against a menses-like flow affecting Jewish males. More
widely repeated was the old tale that Jewish doctors kill Christian
patients. Miguel Pais de Almanza, physician of Queen Marianna
of Austria, not only reiterated the time-worn misconception that
the Talmud orders Jews to murder Christians but also reported
the alleged confession of a Portuguese doctor that, in his lifetime,
he had killed 4,600 Christian patients by injecting vipers' venom
into their bloodstream. From another angle, the New Christians
were accused of disloyalty to Crown and country. Many were allegedly engaged in spying for, and conspiring with, foreign enemies, be they Turks, North-African Muslims, or Dutch heretics.
According to a rumor widely believed in 1634, a Dutch naval force
of 18 ships, under the command of the Jew David Peixotto and
destined for Pernambuco, would have been diverted to an attack
on Coimbra if the commander had had his way. Said to be most
unreliable were the New Christians residing in Portugal's conquered territories in America, Africa, and Asia. Individual incidents of other kinds also contributed to the intergroup animosities.
A theft of sacred objects, including the host, from the church of
Santa Engracia in Lisbon on January 15, 1630, was widely attributed by the public to New Christians, without any proof, of

course. (A similar incident had occurred in Oporto sixteen years earlier.) This rumor created a panic among the Marranos, many of whom fled to Spain and other countries. While Francisco Manuel de Melo's estimate that 2,000 New Christians, in possession of much capital, had left one Lisbon parish, was definitely exaggerated, a major migratory movement undoubtedly took place. Among the Lisbon refugees was the wealthy Simão Dias Solis, who succeeded in reaching Amsterdam, where he publicly professed Judaism under the name Eleazar de Solis and became a friend of Menasseh ben Israel.[92]

Anti-Marrano forces were most concerned about the rapid increase in the number of New Christians—a fear undoubtedly attributable in part to the hostility of neighbors who suspected secret judaizing even where none existed. The widening net of the Inquisition, as well as the growing emphasis on *limpieza,* which was carried over from neighboring Spain into Portugal's public opinion, if not quite to the same extent into its statutory law, likewise magnified the judaizing menace out of all proportion. At the same time, the considerable natural increase of the New Christian population which, as we recall, the accused Marrano physician Felipe de Nájera had tried to explain with respect to Spain in 1609, occurred in Portugal, too. In the "Tractate about the People of the Hebrew Nation of the Kingdom of Portugal" the country's leading theologians, assembled in Tomar in 1629, advanced the following reasons for the large increase in the number of Judaizers: (1) the force of imitation among the Marranos and their emulation of one another's ways; (2) the great natural proliferation of the race, like "the sands of the sea"; (3) the example set by persons of high social standing; (4) the tradition circulating among the New Christians that God bestows many temporal goods on all adherents of the Laws of Moses. With these assumptions went exaggerations in the number of New Christians who had left Portugal for Spain. In a memorandum to the king in 1624 the corrector-general of books, Francisco Murcia de la Llana, claimed that since the expulsion of the Moriscos from Spain in 1609–1614 it was "believed to be certain" that no less than 70,000 New Christians of Jewish descent had entered Castile, 40,000 of them settling in Madrid. Of course, the memorandist added, none of them had joined agricultural or mechanical pursuits; they were engaged largely in profiteering from currency manipulations and selling at a high price goods they imported from Portugal to Castile. Living in many strategic ports and maintaining close contacts with their coreligionists in France, England, and Holland, they allegedly also constituted a security risk for the country. And yet they remained in Spain, where they felt relatively safe under the protective hand of Olivares.[93]

PORTUGAL RESTAURADO

Restoration of Portugal's independence and the return to power of the House of Braganza in 1640 did not bring about any substantial change in the status of New Christians. Curiously, despite their exposure to the rigid, often arbitrary, Spanish regime, some Marranos actually favored the *status quo*. They must have been discouraged by the vigorous propaganda among the Portuguese patriots, who promised to free the masses from alleged Marrano exploitation and infidelity, both of which were said to have been abetted by the Spanish regime. Moreover, many New Christians had a strong commercial interest in maintaining the political unity of the Iberian Peninsula. They feared that Portugal's secession from the Spanish Crown would weaken the economies of both countries and strike a particularly hard blow to their own international commerce. They had good reason, moreover, not to trust the local Portuguese administration, which was open to negotiation so long as it was controlled by the relatively friendly Olivares. Their apprehensions proved justified; when Olivares fell in 1643, his departure indeed entailed many untoward consequences for the New Christians.

Yet, notwithstanding this lack of confidence, aggravated by the behavior of certain members of the Braganza family itself who, like Dom Duarte, supported the Spaniards, most Marrano leaders in Portugal seem to have remained on the sidelines. Similarly, there is no evidence that any of them were involved in the Catalan uprising of 1640, which had given so great an impetus to the outbreak of the Portuguese War of Liberation. The only New Christian merchant who is known to have participated in the conspiracy to assassinate the new Portuguese king, John IV (1640–56) was Pedro de Baeza of Lisbon. The passive stance of the Marranos is the more remarkable as one of the leaders of the conspiracy, Dom Sebastião de Matos de Noronha, archbishop of Braga, had held out to the New Christians the promise that, if the Spanish regime were restored, it would grant the New Christians freedom of worship and perhaps would even totally suppress the Holy Office. Many writers of the period, nevertheless, kept accusing the Marranos of siding with Spain (which did not recognize Portuguese independence until 1668). One such author, Father António Carvalho de Parada, in "The Justification of the Portuguese," published in 1643, devoted fully two chapters to an attempt to prove that the Spanish regime had tried to reintroduce formal Judaism into the Peninsula. On its part, the delegation sent by the new Portuguese government to Rome issued a manifesto denying King John's alleged plan to attract Jews, a plan which, it insisted, was rather a Castilian scheme.[94]

The author of that manifesto, published in 1643 but really presented early in 1641, that is, within a few weeks after the coronation of John IV, seems to have been none other than Pantaleão Rodrigues Pacheco. He had accompanied Dom Miguel of Braganza, King John's nephew and bishop of Lamego, to Rome to present his credentials to the pope, but Dom Miguel was not received by Urban VIII because of sharp Spanish objections. Dom Miguel finally prevailed upon the papal advisers to grant him an audience as a bishop paying obedience to the Holy Father. Despite efforts by the French ambassador in support of Dom Miguel's mission, it was not given any official standing in Rome. In fact, the Spanish ambassador and the bishop had a bloody encounter on a Roman street: three men were killed, but the perpetrators of the brawl disappeared before the arrival of the police. This futile attempt to assassinate the Portuguese representative created a great sensation and enlisted much sympathy for the cause of Portugal's independence in many parts of Europe. When Dom Miguel left the papal capital, Pacheco remained behind to continue the diplomatic negotiations, which from the outset had enjoyed the unstinted support of the French embassy. This policy was in line with the 1636 report of a French agent dispatched by Richelieu to Lisbon: "All Portugal cries aloud: 'When will the king of France deliver us from the Spanish Pharaoh?' " It doubtless was abetted by such New Christian Portuguese in Paris as Manuel Fernandes Villareal (see below). On the other hand, other Marranos, allied with the Habsburgs in foreign countries, tried to help Philip IV and Olivares to suppress the revolt. Jacob Rosales, as we recall, actually supported Ferdinand III and the Spaniards in the hiring of mercenaries for their battles against the Franco-Dutch-Portuguese alliance.[95]

At home, the Portuguese public was overwhelmingly opposed to the New Christians; it frequently attributed the prosperity of the leading Marrano bankers and contractors in Madrid, Seville, and Lisbon to Olivares' favoritism. Now the Portuguese Côrtes, assembled on January 28, 1641, included in their resolutions several articles aimed at the local Marranos. The three Estates were united in demanding the outlawry of intermarriage between New and Old Christians. Should any couples defy that prohibition, their children were to be forbidden to hold public office. Neither should any New Christians be allowed to serve as apothecaries, while all doctors and surgeons were to be obliged to write prescriptions in Portuguese, rather than in Latin, so as to prevent malpractice among Old Christian patients. Neither were they to wear uniforms of the military orders, or be called to serve in the local administrations of cities or villages. In fact, all were to be discharged from public office, gradually and quietly so as not to create financial panic. Finally, declared offenders against the Christian faith, and their children, were not to be allowed to ride on horseback, nor were their wives to be driven in coaches. The Estate of nobility added some postulates of its own, including the prohibition (once suggested by the Assembly at Tomar) banning Marranos from giving their daughters "excessive" dowries, which it considered the main cause of the latter's intermarriage with the Portuguese *fidalgos*.[96]

On his part King John, who had reluctantly abandoned a soft and pleasurable life on his vast estates to assume the Crown, long vacillated between the intolerant demands of the public and the leading inquisitors (headed by Inquisitor-General Francisco de Castro, bishop of Guarda, who had languished in prison for several months because of his part in the conspiracy against the new king) and the political and economic exigencies of the state. But he soon came under the influence of a Jesuit father, António Vieira, who had lived in Bahia, Brazil, since 1614, but had hurried to Lisbon in 1641. "All in all," writes the judicious historian of Brazil Charles Ralph Boxer, "Vieira ranks as a great historical as well as a great literary figure, and he was certainly the most remarkable man in the seventeenth-century Luso-Brazilian world." Equally distinguished as an orator and a statesman, Vieira became John IV's most intimate friend and adviser. With his extraordinary combination of practical realism and visionary dreaming about the future, he saw in John the ultimate creator of a universal empire ushering in the messianic era. His tremendous energy enabled Vieira to make the perilous journey across the Atlantic seven times, and to engage in difficult diplomatic missions to France, Holland, England, and Italy; he ultimately became a most effective missionary among the Brazilian natives. Ironically, all these activities in behalf of the Church and his country did not save him from falling into the clutches of the Inquisition, which, however, was unable to condemn him.[97]

Reorientation in the treatment of New Christians became an integral part of Vieira's new political program. As early as 1641, he formulated for royal consideration his "Reasons in favor of the New Christians so that they be excused from the confiscation of their goods entering the commerce of the Realm." Two years later he gave the king "A proposal representing the miserable condition of the Kingdom and the consequent necessity to admit to it Jewish merchants who travel through various parts of Europe." In various other memoranda submitted to the king in the following years, as well as in a famous public sermon delivered at the Church of St. Roch in 1644, Vieira suggested the foundation of two Portuguese mercantile companies for Brazil and India, modeled after the West and East India Companies in Holland. He believed that, with proper encouragement, New Christian capitalists might be attracted to participate in the new companies with both their funds and their commercial expertise. In 1646–47 Vieira was sent to France and Holland to negotiate with the governments and the New Christian or Jewish communities there. Despite much opposition at home, later even from Portugal's supreme Economic Council, a charter for a single company to embrace both the eastern and western possessions was issued on February 6, 1649. Although one of the charter's major safeguards was directed against the confiscation of goods belonging to foreign "heretical" merchants, the preamble asserted that the charter was issued principally for the defense of the country and for the purity and preservation of the "Catholic faith of the inhabitants" of Portugal and her colonies. Because the new company would help to strengthen the Portuguese economy, the king implied, it would best serve to counteract the machinations of the "northern heretics" (the Dutch and the English). Many New Christians joined the venture with alacrity. Among the major subscribers were such Lisbon merchant families as the Carvalhos, who contributed 60,000 cruzados; the Botelhos and Serrões, who subscribed for 40,000 each; and the Silveiras, who paid in 20,000 cruzados.[98]

Vieira's parallel proposal for the establishment of a Bank of Portugal (similar to the Bank of Amsterdam) was not implemented, however. For this and other reasons, the new company made but very slow progress. It was greatly hampered by the change in the international situation after the Treaties of Westphalia, which included formal recognition of Holland's independence. Thenceforth, the intermittent eighty years' war between Holland and Spain was ended, but the clashes between the Dutch and the Portuguese colonists in Brazil and West Africa continued unabated. The domestic opposition, too, brought about some international complications. Because he needed funds and wished to placate the New Christians, the king in 1649 reduced the Inquisition's authority to confiscate the property of accused heretics. Thereby touching the most sensitive area of inquisitorial operations, he brought down upon his head not only the wrath of the Portuguese Holy Office, which claimed that no secular power had the right to intervene in its operations relating to religious conformity, but, at its appeal, also a condemnation by Pope Innocent X. Even Vieira now had to recommend to the king that he use his royal prerogative and forbid the publication of the pertinent papal brief in the country. But the conflict smoldered on; and ultimately the Inquisition issued a ban on all those who participated in this drastic curtailment of its funds. Although the ban named no one, everybody understood that the king was included. Nor could the tension be allayed by the mediation of the Portuguese episcopate. Because the Papacy had joined Spain in refusing to recognize the independence of Portugal, even after 1648, no new bishops were appointed for years. By 1649 the leadership of the Portuguese Church was greatly depleted and had lost much of its influence on the public affairs of the country. Finally, John's death in November 1656, while not completely terminating the controversy between the monarchy and the Inquisition, removed the main supporter of the company, the activities of which were sharply curtailed in the following year.[99]

All along, needless to say, Vieira remained a devout Catholic, an ardent member of the Society of Jesus, and a confirmed missionary. During his journeys abroad, when he had occasion to meet professing Jews, he often debated with them the respective merits of the two faiths, hoping to convert his interlocutors to his point of view. In Amsterdam he went to synagogue and heard a lengthy sermon by Menasseh ben Israel. Later he met the rabbi and engaged with him in several disputations concerning the Jewish and Christian messianic doctrines. He found less eager debaters in Menasseh's colleagues Saul Morteira and Isaac da Fonseca Aboab. Yet, he apparently was more impressed by Aboab's simplistic adherence to rabbinic doctrines than by Menasseh's elaborate apologetic discourses. He was supposed to have observed: "Menasseh says what he knows, Aboab knows what he says." As usual, these exchanges ended in stalemates. Vieira seems to have been more successful in debating with recent Judaizers, whose knowledge of their faith and culture was extremely superficial. At least in his later hearing before the Holy Office he pleaded in his own defense that

while in Holland he had conversed with, and convinced, an educated Jew, who was said to have been a Castilian of that [New Christian] Nation and had served as a friar of a certain order. He [that ex-friar] had declared concerning persons he did not name that *in order to convince Jews, one must never absolutely deny that they might some day be restored to their Fatherland.* One must first prove to them, with the aid of Scripture, that such restitution, if it is to take place at all, must serve the good of the Faith. This means that it cannot come through the messiah they are awaiting, but rather through the genuine Messiah,

Jesus Christ, who already came once before. The said Jew was completely converted to the faith of that Christ whom he now holds as the true God and promised Messiah.

Evidently, even this statement, inserted for the purpose of exonerating his frequent communication with Amsterdam Jews, reveals but minor missionary success, especially when compared with his subsequent effective proselytizing among the Brazilian Indians.[100]

RETURN TO "NORMALCY"

Failure of the great experiment initiated by Vieira had immediate adverse effects on Jewish life. The unusual alliance between the New Christians and the Jesuits, according to the best-informed historians, saved both Brazil and national independence for Portugal. But when the third naval expedition sent out by the Brazil Company from Portugal to Pernambuco in December 1653 forced the small Dutch garrison to surrender, it also put the remaining Jews to flight in various directions. Thereby was ended for some two centuries the settlement of overtly professing Jews in the largest Latin American country. Domestically, too, the breach between the Jesuits and the Holy Office caused no permanent deceleration of inquisitorial operations. True, at a crucial moment King John IV had ignored the protests of the inquisitor-general, Dom Francisco de Castro, against Vieira's project, and between two appointments with Castro (on January 13, and February 6, 1649) he issued the charter to the new Company. But he piously continued to attend autos-da-fé staged by the Inquisition, and in no way directly impeded its prosecutions.

Nonetheless, the king's acceptance of Vieira's thesis that the sequestrations and confiscations of the property of defendants convicted or merely under investigation by the Holy Office, were playing havoc with both the lives of New Christian families and the economy at large, temporarily undermined the financial strength of the Holy Office. The support extended to the Jesuits by an array of distinguished theologians and jurists and such exclamations as one attributed to Vieira, that "the Inquisitors live off the Faith, the Jesuits die for it," doubtless impressed a great many opponents of the inquisitors' tyrannical procedures. But they had no permanent results. A major factor in the ultimate victory of the Holy Office was the Jesuits' inability to secure a relaxation of the inquisitorial procedures through appeals to the Papacy. Both Urban VIII and his successor, Innocent X, had been under constant pressure from the Spanish government not to recognize the "rebellious" Portuguese regime; hence Portugal had no official representation in Rome. (In fact, most foreign powers, including even Spain's foes France, England, and Holland, were far from persuaded of the durability of Portugal's independence. While Portugal had appointed seven ambassadors and a number of other envoys to foreign countries, no foreign embassy had as yet been established in Lisbon.) Moreover, the general of the Jesuit Order in Rome was not altogether on Vieira's side. Especially after 1647, when the general's new Portuguese assistant, Nuno da Cunha, happened to be one of Vieira's enemies because of a difference of opinion regarding the Order's internal organization, the New Christians were unable to influence the Papacy to issue the required ordinance. We also recall that Innocent X's brief on the issue was so hostile to the reformist point of view that John IV had to prohibit its circulation in Portugal. On their part, the Évora inquisitors, later joined even by a few original supporters of the royal decree of 1649, insisted that technical and substantive flaws had from the outset invalidated its provisions. In short, nothing had really changed to impede the trials by the Holy Office, which in 1663–67 brought about the temporary imprisonment and prolonged investigation of Vieira himself.[101]

In some respects, indeed, the condition of the Portuguese New Christians now took a turn for the worse. Once the country's independence was reestablished, freedom of movement between Portugal and neighboring Castile was greatly circumscribed. This factor explains, in part, the further diminution, in both frequency and intensity, of inquisitorial trials on the Spanish mainland, since in the second part of the seventeenth century, these trials still affected Marrano immigrants from Portugal, almost exclusively. For instance, the eighty-one Judaizers who appeared at the Seville auto-da-fé of 1660, seven of whom died in the flames, were virtually all of Portuguese birth. Those who had settled in smaller Spanish localities seem to have better managed to escape detection. At the same time, in Portugal the inquisitorial agents continued ferreting out all manifestations of Marranism, and held many trials which, even if they did not result in tragic burnings, usually followed long pretrial imprisonment and torture, and often culminated in sentences to galley slavery and the confiscation of the victim's property. Typical of these trials was that ending in the Lisbon auto-da-fé of 1647. Among the 69 persons involved, 34 had been accused of judaizing. Most of the other 33, sentenced for various crimes, including Protestant heresy, witchcraft, and bigamy, got off with lesser penalties; only 2 Old Christians were burned, for sodomy and religious visions. Of the 34 Judaizers, 4 were burned in the flesh and 4 more in effigy. Even the death of a defendant in an inquisitorial prison during the protracted investigation did not appease the vengeful (often also greedy) prosecutors. Francisco Fernandes, a tax farmer, had been arrested in Lisbon on September 15, 1638, at the age of seventy. A year later he died in prison, leaving behind three children, aged 9 to 14, from a second marriage. Yet in 1645–46, in now independent Portugal, the investigation of Fernandes was resumed, and ultimately his bones were exhumed and burned at the stake. Of course, his property was confiscated. The same treatment was meted out to a Dominican nun, Marianna de Macedo, whose mother was a New Christian. Even her brother, Miguel, a high dignitary at court and the governor of Macao, could not save her from death in prison in 1642, or prevent her subsequent exhumation and burning in 1647. The most eminent martyr of that auto, attended by the king, the queen, and the infantes, as well as by the English and French envoys, was the talented twenty-one-year-old Jewish poet, Isaac de Castro Tartas (so named from his alleged birthplace in the department of Landes), who had been instructed in Judaism when he was eight years old, by a Levantine Jew visiting Tartas. Living in Bahia, Brazil, under the assumed name of Joseph de Liz, Isaac was brought to trial in Lisbon. In the Lisbon prison he staunchly tried to observe the Jewish rituals, and for some two years he prepared himself for his ultimate martyrdom. Although there was some doubt about the competence of the inquisitorial tribunal to judge him, for it could not be proved that he had ever been baptized (unbaptized Jews were not subject to inquisitorial prosecution for heresy or apostasy), he was finally condemned to burn.[102]

Another noteworthy victim of the Portuguese Inquisition was Manuel Fernandes Villareal. Born in Lisbon in 1608 into the family of a well-to-do New Christian tax farmer, he served for two and a half years in the Spanish garrison in Tangier, apparently rising to the rank of captain. After several years back home, where he lived in Lisbon, Seville, Madrid, and Malaga, he settled in France in 1638. Before long, he got in touch with Cardinal Richelieu, who was anxious to learn from him about conditions in Portugal, where, ever since 1636, the French statesman had been trying to foster the uprising against Spanish overlordship which was finally to lead to Portugal's independence in 1640. Early in 1641, Villareal published in Portuguese a tract glorifying the personality and activities of the French cardinal which speedily appeared in France in two editions under different titles. Best known under that of the second edition, *El Politico Christianissimo,* this tract was personally presented to Richelieu by the Portuguese ambassador, and was widely read. It soon appeared in a French translation dedicated to Cardinal Mazarin, as well as in an Italian and a German version. Among other matters, Villareal argued here for a reform of the inquisitorial proceedings in his homeland, especially as they affected the New Christians. Opposing their extreme harshness, he maintained:

The wish to bring back one's subjects to the true faith through violence or strictness does not produce in them any change of heart, however much one vanquishes and humiliates them. One may execute them, but the memory of their error does not perish thereby. One ought not to take up arms against one's subjects in order to destroy, but rather to bring them back to the line of duty. Penalties should be employed to induce them to mend their ways, rather than to satisfy one's hatred.

The author also severely criticized the Holy Office's confiscations of property belonging to the culprits' wives and children who were completely innocent. "This is to covet their riches rather than to correct their conduct." It is not surprising that this tract was subjected to strict censorship in Lisbon. The censor suggested that many passages be expurgated before the tract might be allowed to find its way into Portuguese libraries, and added the note that "the author deserves to be investigated and interrogated so that he will be obliged to state explicitly what he seems to wish to teach obliquely." Doubtless for this reason, Dom Miguel of Portugal, bishop of Lamego, warned Count de Vidigueira (better known under his later title, marquês de Niza), the Portuguese ambassador in Paris, on June 14, and again on August 10, 1642, to be wary of Villareal and many others of that group.[103]

In 1649 the Portuguese Inquisition finally apprehended Villareal. In the intervening years, to be sure, he had served as Portuguese consul in France. His official duties had forced him to live in Paris; but, as was later revealed, he had placed his wife and children in Rouen, where they could live a fuller Jewish life, in the midst of the Marrano community there. He frequently visited them, particularly during the Passover holidays. He also collaborated with António Vieira during the latter's French missions, and helped him develop the aforementioned plans for a reform of the status of New Christians and for the establishment of the General Mercantile Company. It was in this connection that Villareal, casting all caution aside, paid a visit to Lisbon; he probably relied upon the king's protection. Indeed John IV not only reconfirmed Villareal's appointment to the consular post but planned to extend his activities in France; he was to supervise the hiring of mercenaries and the purchase of munitions and foodstuffs for Portugal, as well as the collection of funds owed by France for certain Portuguese exports. However, neither the king nor the New Christian diplomat had reckoned with the alertness of the Holy Office personnel. Soon after his arrival in the Portuguese capital, Villareal was summoned before the Inquisition to defend his liberal views and to explain his possession of seventeen prohibited works among the five hundred books he had brought with him from France. One of the incriminated works was Menasseh ben Israel's *Thesaurus of Laws Which the People of Israel Is Obliged to Observe,* published in five parts in Amsterdam in 1645–47. Villareal explained that he had received this work as a curiosity from a friend in Rome; but a hostile witness falsely testified that Villareal had purchased it on his own initiative in Amsterdam. Further testimony brought out Villareal's secret observance of Jewish rituals and his contacts with numerous Marranos in France and Holland. While in prison, according to spies planted by the Inquisition, he continued to abstain from food on Jewish fast days and, what was least pardonable, he had detected one of the inquisitorial devices used to overhear private conversations between prisoners. He was steadfast enough, even under torture, not to incriminate any New Christians living in Portugal. All the names he mentioned were of persons living abroad, outside the reach of the Portuguese Holy Office. His vigorous defense did not save him from condemnation, however. After an investigation lasting thirty-nine months, he was finally burned in an auto-da-fé on December 1, 1652, the twelfth anniversary of the Portuguese revolution, in the presence of the king, the queen, the crown prince, and a large crowd of onlookers.[104]

Some of the eminent secret Jews were more fortunate. How difficult it often was to ascertain the Jewish parentage of distinguished writers is well illustrated by the case of the poet Miguel da Silveira (or Silveyra). A native of Celorico de Beira, Silveira lived in Madrid for twenty years and lectured at the royal court before he wrote his major epic poem, *El Macabeo,* which, however, circulated for several years in manuscript only. He himself cautiously described the origin of that epic:

Out of love for my fatherland I decided to write the *Macabeo.* Yet I was still afraid to come out with it in public. To be sure, I should have had some confidence in my uninterrupted forty years of study at the Universities of Coimbra and Salamanca, where I have applied myself to learning about philosophy, jurisprudence, medicine, and mathematics from their sources. More, for twenty years I have delivered lectures at the court of his Catholic Majesty about various scientific disciplines and, particularly, about poetry.

El Macabeo, covering some 540 printed pages, was widely hailed as a great work of art, Silveira's fellow-Marrano Antonio Enríquez Gómez placing it among the great epics of world literature, alongside Homer's *Odyssey,* Virgil's *Aeneid,* Tasso's *Jerusalem,* and Camoëns' *Lusiads.* Lope de Vega, who knew Silveira well (together with Cervantes, Quevedo, and other luminaries, both men had belonged for many years to the same socioliterary club, founded in 1608 under the picturesque name "Brotherhood of Slaves of the Most Holy Sacrament"), likewise had only words of praise for Silveira's "considerable and rich [poetic] vein." He knew that Silveira had many enemies, but neither he nor even Quevedo, with his sharp eye for every sign of New Christian descent, betrayed any suspicion that Silveira was a secret Judaizer. In fact, so sure of himself was Silveira that, like Isaac Cardoso, he dared to appear as a character witness for the accused at Bartolomé Febos' trial (March 30, 1634). However, it appears that the Inquisition became suspicious of the poet's orthodoxy and started an investigation. Possibly aided by influential friends, Silveira eluded the inquisitorial net and moved to Naples, where he published *El Macabeo* and two other lengthy poems. If it were not for later Jewish writers, like Miguel de Barrios and Thomas (Isaac) de Pinedo, who was born in 1614 in the same Portuguese province of Beira and claimed to be related to him, Silveira's Jewish ancestry might have remained unknown even to modern scholars.[105]

In contrast, the ultimate fate of Antonio Enríquez Gómez, another member of that Madrid literary circle and a later émigré, was more tragic. The poet, whose high evaluation of Silveira's *El Macabeo* appeared in his own biblical epic *Sansón Nazareno,* referred to that ancient hero as an illustration of "the glorious triumph of the people of God." Although he married an Old Christian woman, and his son-in-law was serving as a fiscal of the Inquisition, he moved, as we recall, to Rouen and later to Amsterdam, where he publicly professed Judaism. Nevertheless, his plays continued to enjoy a considerable vogue in Spain, probably because they had appeared under a pseudonym. In time, however, his identity became known, and he was tried by the Inquisition *in absentia.* Some time later Enríquez Gómez returned to Spain, assumed the name Fernando de Zárate, and settled in Seville. Possibly he had been a "maladjusted refugee" in Amsterdam, somewhat similar to Uriel da Costa. His deep love for his native land may also have beclouded his judgment and made him hope that, under his new name, he could escape detection. For a time this stratagem worked and he was able to publish a number of comedies under that name. But eventually his true identity was discovered; and, although we do not have the full record of a new trial and condemnation, he seems to have died in an inquisitorial prison before his apparently scheduled appearance at the auto-da-fé of 1660.[106]

DEBILITATING CONSERVATISM

Few other instances are known in modern history of such a rapid rise and decline of leading empires like those of Spain and Portugal in the century from the abdication of Charles V in 1556 to the death of John IV in 1656. Naturally, as in most historic phenomena, a multiplicity of causes and events brought about that sharp reversal. However, there is little question that unswerving adherence to the racialist persecution of the New Christian and Morisco minorities was a major contributory cause. Notwithstanding the great diversity of opinion among the leading thinkers of the age or the occasional pleadings of ecclesiastics from Salucio to Vieira, the treatment of the New Christian minority under the doctrine of *limpieza* and the practice of autos-da-fé staged by the Inquisition prevented any permanent alteration in the course pursued by the regimes of the three Philips in Spain and Portugal and by Sebastian and John IV in Portugal alone during the periods of its sovereignty. In vain did Vieira call attention to the fact that Portugal had prospered under Emanuel I and John III, both of whom had treated the New Christians mildly, but had lost its independence after Sebastian broke his promise to grant them a general pardon. Similarly, warnings that the persecution of New Christians greatly contributed to the deterioration of the country's economic and military strength were no more effective coming from Vieira than they were when sounded by political thinkers with respect to the currency manipulations or the generally detrimental import and export policies pursued by the successive administrations. Regardless of the persuasiveness of such warnings, the Holy Office was allowed untrammeled sway in maintaining religious conformity in both Spain and Portugal.

All these phenomena bore out the contention of a Spanish Franciscan monk (probably Francisco de Uceda) that

one is not held in Spain in such infamy and disgrace for being a blasphemer, thief, highway robber, adulterer, a person guilty of sacrilege, or infected with whatever other vice, as for being a descendant of Jews, even if his ancestors had been converted to our holy Christian faith two or three hundred years ago. From this discrimination follows the other intolerable manifestation of ignorance that, when two men compete for an ecclesiastical dignity, benefice, or other office or prelacy . . . and one of them is learned and virtuous but is a descendant on one side of most ancient *conversos* of the Jewish race, and the other is without learning and without virtue but an Old Christian, the latter will definitely be preferred.

The author of that anonymous tract tried to reinforce his arguments by contending that God had from the outset decided to build His Church from elements of the Jewish and Gentile peoples in order to establish peace among them. Yet his tract did not even receive the hearing given to printed publications and has remained unpublished to the present day. On the contrary, the endless chain of prosecutions continued unbroken into the eighteenth century and beyond. A comprehensive manuscript in six volumes, compiled by an eighteenth-century Portuguese author from primary sources, presents a list of 598 inquisitorial processes in Portugal alone.[107]

The extent to which judaizing superseded almost all other concerns of the inquisitors is well illustrated by the Lisbon auto-da-fé of April 3, 1669. As described by an English eyewitness, Francis Perry (secretary to the English ambassador Robert Southwell), of the 80 condemned marchers in the procession, only one Old Christian, a priest, was sentenced, for sodomy. All the other condemned persons were Judaizers. Some of these defendants were acquitted for lack of evidence of heresy and were discharged after paying the costs of the trial. Most others had to wear sanbenitos for specified periods, and lost all their property. But one, likewise a Catholic priest, was burned at the stake, because "he had confessed that he believed a man might be saved by either [Jewish or Christian] Law, and that he therefore sometimes observed one, sometimes the other." So deeply rooted was the hostility to Jews that Spain, in ceding the island of Minorca to the British in 1762, stipulated, as in the aforementioned case in Gibraltar, that no infidels be admitted to residence there. Allegedly because the British did not live up to that stipulation and allowed Jews, Moors, and Greeks to settle in Minorca, Spain decided to reconquer it and, with the aid of France, succeeded in reoccupying the island in 1782, though not yet in a final way.[108]

Obviously, Spain paid a very high price for its religious intolerance and its obsession with *limpieza*. Even from a purely sectarian
point of view, the momentary gains in religious conformity were
more than canceled out by the need for greater and greater
rigidity in its enforcement and by the consequent withering of the
creative élan which had characterized the penetrating religious
thought of Loyola and Vitoria, St. Theresa and Suárez. What
Tarsicio Herrero del Collado said, with special reference to the
trial of the *converso* Archbishop Hernando de Talavera of Granada, may generally be applied to the entire historical career of
the Holy Office. "We venture to assert," Herrero declared, "that
the inquisitorial Tribunal of the mixed character functioning in
Spain was created for the noble purpose of upholding religion.
But it was converted instead into an instrument of evil against the
very faith which it pretended to uphold." The relative petrification
of Spanish religious thought affected the nation's secular creativity
to an even greater degree. The modern European intellectual
evolution largely bypassed Spain. Having abandoned Erasmian
and humanistic influences, the country's Golden Age from 1550
to 1650 was in many ways but a glorious sunset of the medieval
heritage. Thereafter Spain participated very little in the Age of
Reason, in the democratic and capitalistic upsurge of the Western
societies, or in the extraordinary development of modern science
and technology. In all these areas Spain and Portugal were more
recipients than contributors. True, as some apologists of the Inquisition contend, the Iberian Peninsula was thereby spared many
of the upheavals which shook the modern Western world. But this
was a peace of stagnation, rather than a quiet sharing in the progress of humanity.[109]

On the Jewish side the unrelenting persecution of New Christians perpetuated the stream of Marrano emigration, which included an élite often distinguished by economic and cultural
achievements, and which, by its numbers, gave impetus to the
emergence of new Jewish communities in both East and West. On
the Iberian Peninsula itself the severe repression in time produced
a reaction in a certain strengthening of the backbone of the persecuted minority. Rather than causing the Marranos to vanish
totally from the Peninsula, as the state and the Church may have

hoped at the beginning, the persistent reminders of the "impurity" of their blood almost forced them to try to preserve at least a minimal heritage of Judaism, as part of their unique identity. It is small wonder, then, that in 1706 and 1720, more than two centuries after the original "expulsions," regular synagogues were found in Lisbon and Madrid, respectively; their elders were in communication with their coreligionists in Leghorn and other areas. Outwardly, to be sure, the Jewish question lost much of its importance in the course of the eighteenth century. But it did not completely fade from the national consciousness of the Spaniards and the Portuguese, nor did the few remaining Marranos completely forget it. It was only during the great transformations of the twentieth century that new overtly Jewish settlements sprang up in the major cities and that the Jewish question now assumed the more customary modern coloring, with all its lights and shadows.

IBERIA'S COLONIAL EMPIRES

NTÓNIO VIEIRA's Mercantile Company highlighted the novel international role played by New Christians in world trade and imperial conflicts. Scholars are fairly unanimous in considering the armaments and funds supplied by the new Company and its Marrano shareholders a decisive factor in saving most of Brazil for Portugal. By helping the Portuguese navy to recapture Angola, then a major source of manpower for Brazilian agriculture and mining, the Company enabled South America's Portuguese colonists to supply their homeland with important raw materials and precious metals. Notwithstanding some rather indirect French military aid, without these Brazilian supplies the Portuguese could not have held their own against the Spanish army in their War of Independence, which lasted twenty-eight years (1640–68).

At the same time, however, the Dutch New Christians and professing Jews significantly promoted the overseas expansion of the Netherlands, Portugal's main adversary in America, Africa, and Asia, though its ally in the struggle against Spain. By their influence on Europe's major money markets and emporia in Antwerp, Amsterdam, Hamburg, London, Leghorn, and Venice, Jews and Marranos were in a strategic position to help shape certain international developments favorable to themselves, really or putatively. They thus opened up ever-new opportunities for their own participation in the mainstream of European politics and economics. Nor should we underestimate the importance of their interrelations with the masses of Sephardic coreligionists who had found safe abodes in the countries of Islam. It was particularly the Ottoman Empire which, even in its incipient decline at the end of the sixteenth century, still was a major force in the power politics of the age.

Simultaneously, tragic episodes like that of Isaac de Castro Tartas, who was transferred from Bahia, Brazil, to a Lisbon inquisitorial prison and his ultimate martyrdom in 1647, underscored the intimate interrelations between the Old World and the New in the all-pervasive realm of religion. The burning of the young poet, and the ensuing mourning for him among the Dutch and other Jewries, greatly contributed to the internal solidarity of the dispersed communities in their struggle against the outstretched tentacles of the Iberian Holy Offices.

All along, the discovery of new lands in the Western and Southern Hemispheres opened fresh outlets for the Marranos' tireless energy and enterprise and secured for them havens of refuge in their recurrent emergencies. To be sure, their paths were strewn not only with the staggering difficulties confronting all colonial pioneers but also with the never-ending suspicions of personal enemies who might at any moment denounce them to the omnipresent inquisitorial bureaucracy. With the organization of inquisitorial headquarters in Lima (1569), Mexico (1570), and Cartagena de las Indias (1610), no place in the vast expanses of the Spanish Empire could be considered safe. Similarly, the establishment of a branch of the Portuguese Inquisition in Goa in 1560 undermined whatever feeling of security might have animated the New Christian refugees in Asia. The growing mobility of the Marrano dissenters found its counterpart in the ubiquity of the inquisitorial agents and in the presence of spies planted by the Holy Office in the midst of struggling groups of new immigrants in the most unexpected places. In the long run, the unrelenting persecution of the Marrano remnant by the heavy hand of their fanatical enemies merely stiffened the resistance of that significant minority of potential martyrs. Defying all dangers, the Marranos continued to cultivate their ancestral faith in the secrecy of their homes and frequently produced ever-new witnesses ready to sacrifice their lives in the "name of their Lord." Like their ancestors, they thus carried the perennial struggle between "history" and "nature" to an at least partially successful conclusion.

EUROPEAN POSSESSIONS

Little need be said about Spain's South-Italian dominions. After the expulsion of the Jews in 1541 only a few New Christians seem to have remained behind, and the Inquisition had infrequent opportunities to investigate suspected Judaizers. Moreover, without effective statutes of *limpieza,* enthusiastically supported by the public, the ancestry of individuals was far less accurately traceable. Hence it was much easier for descendants of earlier converts to escape the vigilant eye of inquisitorial officials. Nor did the Inquisition itself enjoy here the nearly unanimous public backing which it had on the Iberian Peninsula. In fact, the Neapolitans long resisted the establishment of a Spanish-type tribunal. When in 1509 Ferdinand the Catholic finally prevailed and founded a formal Holy Office in the Kingdom of Naples, it had to be modeled after the Roman institution, closer at hand. Thenceforth, the ultimate jurisdiction did not rest with the Suprema in Madrid, but rather with the papal Inquisition in Rome, to which some culprits had to be brought for final sentencing and execution. Despite its other numerous shortcomings, the Roman institution evinced less anti-Jewish ardor, and also expected far less revenue from confiscations, than did its Spanish counterpart. Consequently, our knowledge of prosecutions of Marranos in the Neapolitan kingdom is quite limited. Many religious deviations doubtless went unrecorded because of the failure either of informers to denounce "culprits" or of zealous officials to pursue the leads thus given with vigor and devotion.[1]

Several of the cases identified by scholars as relating to Jewish "infidelity" were reported by a few bigoted Theatine friars. In 1569, for example, they claimed to have found in both Naples and the provinces numerous families of Jewish origin who had remained in the country notwithstanding the various decrees of expulsion. According to one report, some of these suspects were condemned to public abjuration, others to similar declarations in private. In any case, the details of these proceedings were confided to only a small circle of officials in the archbishop's entourage. In 1571, however, twelve(?) Catalan women were brought to public trial for judaizing and, after confessing their "crime" under torture, were transported to Rome and executed. More sensational was the discovery in 1582 that no less a personality than Don Alonzio Sancies, doctor of law, former Neapolitan ambassador to Venice and general treasurer of the kingdom, had, together with his family, observed Jewish rituals. At the time of the disclosure, however, he had already been dead for several years. The Inquisition could do no more than exhume his body and remove it together with his large mausoleum to a "more suitable location." Of great interest also is an extant record of the 1584–85 trial of the physician Joseph Perrotta. The protracted hearings, of which we possess rather good summaries, yielded only the information that Joseph had studied Hebrew with a Jew and had Hebrew books in his possession. A list of works found in his library included, next to several Hebrew grammars, a book on Hebrew accents and orthography, and other innocuous writings, as well as a slightly more objectionable work briefly described as relating to the "messiah of Christians and Jews in Hebrew and Latin," and a Hebrew grammatical handbook by the Protestant Sebastian Münster. The hearings further revealed that the three main witnesses for the prosecution were all inspired by professional jealousy toward the accused, and that Perrotta had quickly guessed their identity. Under the circumstances, the inquisitors, sitting in the archbishop's presence, could only impose upon the doctor a fine of 45 ounces of gold and a promise that for six months he would offer medical services without charge to all patients of the Monastery of the Blessed Mary.[2]

Many other denunciations undoubtedly also were the result of private grudges. For example, in 1657, Don Odoardo Váez, count of Mola, refused to allow two of his cousins to marry a servant girl and a barber, respectively, whereupon the scorned fiancés accused him of judaizing. This denunciation sufficed for the Inquisition to arrest the count; transfer him to a Roman dungeon, where he languished for fourteen years; and have him publicly abjure, garbed in a sanbenito (in Naples called a *habitello*). A few other "culprits" appear only with their name and the general description of "judaizing," in lengthy lists of persons condemned by the Holy Office for a variety of transgressions. As in Rome, the main victims were Protestants and their sympathizers, as well as Catholics accused of witchcraft, blasphemy, or various sexual offenses. A remarkable instance of the last sort was the protracted trial of the Neapolitan Sister Giulia, who perpetrated individual and group sexual orgies under the guise of deep religious devotion. All along, moreover, the Neapolitan Inquisition had its hands full with Waldensians, sheltered in the mountain recesses of Calabria, who continued to adhere to their sectarian faith for several centuries.[3]

The usual inconsistency in the treatment of Jews was glaringly illustrated by the practice in the city of Lanciano. While the rest of the Neapolitan kingdom formally tolerated no Jews even on a temporary basis, Lanciano uninterruptedly extended its hospitality to them during the local fairs. Jews are also recorded in the city on other occasions; in the years 1532–1664 they are mentioned in 98 extant notarial documents, principally in connection with business transactions of various kinds. In 1533, and again in 1561 and 1564, some Jews were allowed to visit the city in connection with a mission to ransom captives taken by the Turks. Individual Jewish bankers are also referred to in the records. The number of such strangers seems to have grown sufficiently for the authorities to issue, on July 17, 1572, an ordinance requiring them to wear a distinctive yellow badge on their headgear, under the severe sanction of five years of galley slavery. This segregationist provision was sharpened by a resolution of the diocesan synod meeting on December 9, 1572, under the chairmanship of the Neapolitan archbishop, Antonio Rodriguez. It provided "that Christians should not receive Jews in their homes, nor eat meals with them, nor serve such to them. The said Jews should not enter the Church of Santa Maria del Ponte except during the delivery of sermons." Another characteristic incident occurred on July 20, 1613, when the vicar and some priests entered a "synagogue" during services, imprisoned all worshipers in the archiepiscopal palace, and seized all Hebrew books. Jews protested that, having the right to attend fairs, they were entitled to hold divine services in private. The prisoners seem to have been speedily released, perhaps after the payment of fines. In any case, Jews continued to visit Lanciano in the following generations. Even the sharply intolerant edict, issued by Charles III on September 18, 1746, did not put an end to Jewish visits, as is attested by a letter written some four years later by the president of the province. All in all, however, the presence of the few professing Jewish visitors or even of occasional secret Judaizers among the residents of various parts of the kingdom merely confirmed the rule that Judaism was outlawed in the entire country after 1541 and that no Jewish communities were re-established in the area until the nineteenth century. As we recall, the same situation prevailed in Spain's other European possessions, especially the duchy of Milan, and the southern Netherlands after the emergence of an independent Holland.[4]

CANARY AND CARIBBEAN ISLANDS

Under the reigns of the three Philips, inquisitorial prosecution of heretics, and particularly of Judaizers, continued in the Canary Islands, though with somewhat reduced intensity, probably because few Marranos dared to settle in the islands. The frequent absenteeism of higher ecclesiastics from the islands, which evoked a special royal prohibition on February 16, 1612, doubtless also interfered with the efficacy of inquisitorial prosecutions. Yet vestiges of the earlier controversies continued to undermine the feeling of security of many individuals for decades thereafter. As late as 1570 the possible heterodoxy of the then long-deceased Ruy Lopes Merlo of the island of Gomera came under review, merely because in 1526, or nearly half a century before the investigation, he had allegedly stated that the Jewish faith was not totally replaced by the Christian religion. In support, he had quoted Jesus' saying, "Think not that I am come to destroy the law or the prophets; I am not come to destroy, but to fulfill." Some enemies of Merlo's family now demanded that because of his imprudent, if accurate, remark, he be retroactively declared a Judaizer and his bones be exhumed and burned. Undoubtedly the main purpose of the charge was to deny Merlo's children, lacking *limpieza,* the right to wear silk and velvet garments or to display jewelry and gold ornaments, as well as to question his grandson's freedom to travel to the Indies and Flanders. More serious was the investigation directed against García Osorio in 1574. Osorio, then holding the important office of *regidor* (alderman) of Grand Canary Island, was accused of having made false statements about his ancestry before assuming office. Some witnesses claimed that his earlier application for the office of *alguacil* (constable) had been rejected because he was of *converso* descent. We do not know the outcome of this denunciation, but it appears that Osorio had sufficiently influential friends to quash the investigation. During the last quarter of the sixteenth century there were several other accusations against individuals who allegedly performed such suspicious acts as removing the sinews from certain parts of animals before eating them, cooking their food with oil rather than lard, and betraying other symptoms of Jewish "infidelity." Less routine was the case of a centenarian Negro, Pedro Álvarez, who was reported to have insisted that God had commanded all men to be circumcised. There was no trial, because Álvarez died in prison.[5]

For peculiar local reasons the Peace Treaty of 1604 between England and Spain proved a serious obstacle to further inquisitorial prosecutions. The Canary Islands generally depended greatly on their export of wine and sugar, particularly to England and her American colonies. Any sustained prosecution of Protestant or judaizing merchants might have seriously interfered with that trade by stirring up deep antagonisms among the producers and exporters of these commodities. That is why even an evident "heretic" like the Englishman Thomas Nichols was able to spend much time on the Canary Islands without being gravely molested. Since the Inquisition itself derived considerable revenue from its own vineyards, it was financially interested in maintaining wine exports on the highest possible level. Nonetheless, some investigations were resumed in the 1630s. Among those denounced to the Holy Office were members of two prominent Jewish families, the De Fonsecas (many of them also known under the name of De Pina) and the Pintos. In 1631 a witness testified that some eight or nine years before, he had seen Antonio de Fonseca and his wife wearing a sanbenito in Oporto because both had been sentenced by the Portuguese Inquisition. (In 1625–26, indeed, twelve members of the De Pina family had been condemned by the Coimbra Holy Office, three of them to burning, while one, Pablo de Pina, had fled to Amsterdam and, under the name of Reüel [Rohel] Jesurun, had become a prominent leader of the Amsterdam community.) Antonio de Fonseca escaped, however, before his arrest. In this connection we learn from the inquisitorial records that he had five brothers, two of whom lived on the Canary Islands and one each in Pernambuco, Lisbon, and France, while an uncle and a cousin had moved to Holland. The Fonsecas-Pinas thus offer another illustration of the frequent interterritorial dispersal of New Christian families, a factor which often aided them in developing international trade.[6]

How far-fetched some denunciations were could be seen in the case of Ana Pérez of Las Palmas. In 1625, under the impact of a newly proclaimed Edict of Faith, Ana felt impelled to report to the Holy Office that about five years previously Catalina Domínguez, mother-in-law of a sailor named Francisco Rodríguez, had advised a woman friend then on her deathbed to call upon "King Gideon." The designation "king" for Gideon (the Bible places him among the ancient "judges") is less surprising—we need but recall the name Abimelech (meaning "my father, the king") of his son and would-be successor—than the magic role apparently attributed to him in some Marrano circles. Possibly the miracles performed for him at God's behest, as described in the book of Judges (6:11 ff.), inspired some Judaizers in distress to expect his name to work wonders for them, too. Another accusation was aimed at an eighty-year-old Jewish prisoner, Mardoqueo. Styled "a very learned man who knew many things," Mardoqueo had allegedly taught a fellow-prisoner to recite a certain prayer in order to be relieved of an affliction, as well as to use some papers to secure great wealth. Nor were witnesses lacking to testify that heretical handbills circulating in Spain and reading "Long live the Law of Moses, and death to that of Christ, for all laws except the former are false" were imported into the islands. Among the defendants also was a licentiate, Diego de Artiaga, accused of breaking the seal of confession, averting his eyes from the host while carrying it in the procession, and expressing heretical views on the dogma of Transubstantiation. Aroused by a quarrel with another cleric, he had allegedly exclaimed "If I cannot repay live Jews, I shall pay painted ones," and thereupon, to the scandal of many onlookers, had struck a painting of Jesus. However, in so far as one can judge from the extant records, none of these investigations led to the burning of the accused. But discrimination against New Christian defendants and their progeny in appointments to public office or to ecclesiastical posts was extensive, and public opinion continued to be greatly influenced by the doctrine of *limpieza*.[7]

In general, because of the great mobility of the Spanish colonists, the unreliability of witnesses in regard to the identity of particular defendants or to the types of transgressions of which they
were accused, was even greater in the colonial possessions than on
the mainland. For example, in 1603 one Matheos Pinero was
troubled by an Edict of Faith which exhorted listeners to report
to the Holy Office all persons who practiced Jewish rituals. He
appeared before the Inquisition and informed it that, some thirty-
two years before, he had seen a Hieronymite friar cut out the
sinews from a joint of meat. Since the friar claimed that the meat
would roast better that way, he had himself followed that example
once or twice in his life, not knowing that he was thereby performing a Jewish custom. Pinero added that, being an Old Christian on both his parents' sides, he would rather see his hand cut
off than do a thing like that. Very likely the Canariote Inquisition
was also hampered by the general failure of the Holy Office in the
mother country to divulge to it the data accumulated in Iberian
files concerning certain suspected New Christian individuals and
families. We recall that even Philip II could not elicit from the
Spanish Holy Office an answer to the simple question of whether
a particular individual was held in an inquisitorial prison. In 1678
the Spanish Suprema went so far as to threaten inquisitors who
divulged the presence of any prisoner in an inquisitorial dungeon,
with severe excommunication, from which they could be absolved
only by the pope. Since most of the later Marrano settlers on the
Canary Islands must have come from Portugal, the difficulty of
ascertaining their family backgrounds, or any earlier religious deviations by them in their native country must have been staggering.[8]

Even less is known about New Christians residing in Spain's
Caribbean colonies. Although some of the New Christian sailors
who had joined Columbus' expeditions, including Luis de Torres,
settled on one or another of these islands, we know very little
about their activities there. We are not even sure how many of
them lived on the main island, Hispaniola (comprising the present-
day Dominican Republic and Haiti), which for a time served as
the headquarters of the Spanish colonial administration. Perhaps
Alonso de la Calle, who died there on May 23, 1503, was a *converso,* as is sometimes asserted, because his name may have been

derived from the designation often given to the Jewish street. Torres, hospitably received by the natives of Cuba, was the first European to settle and die there. He even received a royal annuity of 8,645 maravedis. Undoubtedly many other New Christians established themselves in the West Indies in the course of the sixteenth century. However, the information given to Philip II, in behalf of a witness named Tomé Rodríguez, by Juan Quesada de Figueroa, and transmitted by the king to authorities in Santo Domingo on August 21, 1596, is certainly overstated. According to that witness, many secret Judaizers lived on all the West Indian islands; they were well informed about the secret proceedings of the Holy Office and, when arrested, were treated leniently by the local clergy. Similar inaccuracy also underlay the vastly exaggerated report submitted by Governor Pedro de Valdéz of Cuba to King Philip III on December 15, 1605. He claimed that the "Portuguese" on the island "have shops and sell openly, and in Seville they have correspondents of their same nation. All the money is in their hands, gold and silver which they send from here." More dependable data come from occasional references to New Christian settlers at inquisitorial hearings against defendants on the mainland. For example, at the 1642–45 trial of a thirteen-year-old New Christian boy, Gabriel de Granada, the young defendant mentioned an aunt "Doña Margarita de Rivera engaged to be married to a cousin of hers called Miguel Nuñez, said to be in Havana." More directly, in 1613 one Francisco Gómez de León of Havana confessed that he was a secret Jew; thereupon, he was executed, and his property, valued at 149,000 pesos, was confiscated. Fourteen years later Antonio Mendez, Luis Rodrigues, and several others were arrested, while in 1636 Blas de Paz Pinto, Juan Rodrigues Mésa, and Francisco Rodríguez de Solis were seized on the same charge and had to pay 150,000 pesos each. A few other such cases are mentioned by scholars, all of which seem to indicate that the Havana New Christians were among the wealthiest citizens of the island. It is, of course, possible that the inquisitors' appetites were particularly sharpened by the wealth accumulated by these "culprits," whereas other, less prosperous New Christians were left alone because their prosecution seemed financially unrewarding. However, the major evolution of Jewish settlements in the Caribbean occurred mainly after the annexation of some of them by the Dutch, English, and French, especially when they received a substantial influx of Jewish refugees from Recife, after its recapture by the Portuguese in 1654.[9]

NEW WORLD PECULIARITIES

A decisive turn for the worse in the status of New Christians occurred throughout the Spanish possessions in America after the establishment of branches of the Spanish Holy Office in Lima in 1569, in Mexico in 1570–71 (both these cities had been archiepiscopal sees since 1546), and in Cartagena de las Indias in 1610. Even after the addition of the Cartagena office the authority of the Mexican headquarters extended not only over the area of the present-day Mexican Republic and most of Central America but also over the adjacent territories in what is now the southern United States and even as far west as the Philippines. Naturally the vast area to be covered and the relative paucity of inhabitants per square mile made the prosecution of heretics very difficult. Even with respect to book censorship the inquisitors had to concede, in 1585, that their supervision left much to be desired, because the country was "very large and sparsely populated." Nonetheless, the specialized Holy Office was much more efficient than the preceding episcopal Inquisition, which, in the days of so unbending a prosecutor of infidelity as Bishop Juan de Zumárraga, had lacked the force of consistency and single-mindedness.[10]

Because of its great emphasis on religious conformity and the thoroughness of its preliminary investigations, the Inquisition accumulated an enormous number of personal records, which have no parallel in history. As Seymour B. Liebman rightly points out, the sheer quantity of the material preserved in the Archivo General de la Nación in Mexico City alone—1,621 large volumes of documents; the Indexes thereto aggregate almost 3,300 pages—makes any research in this field extremely arduous. Moreover, thousands of additional documents are scattered in other libraries, whether listed in a general way, as in the various Conway collections, or still largely uncatalogued, as are those of the Huntington Library in Pasadena, California. The quality of that material is also unique. As the perceptive French scholar Pierre Chaunu has observed, the insights offered by this vast documentation into the thought processes of both prosecutors and victims, on the conscious and subconscious levels, furnish students unparalleled opportunities for understanding the working of their minds. "It is far from certain that our own period will leave behind for posterity documentation of equal value for a study in depth of behavioral patterns and for a global psychoanalysis of society." The only regrettable aspect of our source material relating to New Christians is that, except for some writings left behind by Luis Carvajal the Younger, we possess few data from the pen of an Iberian Jew in North America from the period before 1650. Nor did the European Jews concern themselves sufficiently with their coreligionists in these remote overseas areas to record their experiences in any detail. As we shall see, only the Dutch Jews maintained more direct relations, at least with the ephemeral Jewish community of Brazil.[11]

Considering the enormous difficulties of travel across the Atlantic Ocean, as well as within the American colonies themselves at that time, the immigration of numerous New Christians to the Latin American territories, and their mobility therein, are truly amazing. To be sure, like their Catholic compatriots and numerous other Europeans, many were animated by the great sense of adventure stimulated by the epochal discovery of new lands; some were looking to the untold opportunities of the New World for the ultimate realization of their utopian dreams. It was principally, indeed, the discovery of America which had inspired the great utopian literature of the Renaissance, from Thomas More to Tommaso Campanella, which reciprocally influenced similar writings in America. However, the perils of the journey were doubtless magnified in the case of New Christians. During the weeks or months it took to reach their ultimate destination, they could unwittingly betray their innermost beliefs to their fellow-passengers, particularly in moments of great stress, as when they faced raging storms or piratical attacks. Any imprudent utterance or unusual behavior doubtless aroused the suspicions of fellow-voyagers and crews alike, some of whom took instantaneous hostile action or else, upon arrival at an American port, denounced the suspects to agents of the Holy Office. Even sympathetic Catholics may have been terrified into submitting such information by listening, on arrival or later, to the proclamation of an Edict of Faith. At the same time, the secret Judaizers often had an overwhelmingly powerful motivation to leave the inhospitable Iberian shores, especially if they felt threatened by inquisitorial prosecution.[12]

In general, the treatment of New Christians in the colonies depended, to a large extent, on the central Spanish administration in Madrid, which issued the laws, and the *Casa de la Contratación* in Seville, which supervised their execution in detail. On the whole, Spanish law, as it had developed on the Peninsula since Visigothic times, retained much of its validity in the Spanish colonies. Yet there were certain fundamental differences between the status of New Christians in the home country and their position in the New World. To begin with, according to the legislation initiated by Ferdinand the Catholic, neither New Christians nor persons condemned by the Inquisition nor their offspring were to be allowed to emigrate to the New World. Curiously, for those who succeeded in circumventing these legal obstacles by various means, the prohibition often turned out to be a blessing in disguise. Since they had to camouflage their New Christian origin by assuming new names, usually of Old Christian families, their detection in the new country of their settlement was greatly impeded. Nor do we have any records of actual deportation of such culprits merely because they had secured illegal entry. Only if they were haled before an inquisitorial tribunal for other reasons, did their illegal methods of immigration count against them.[13]

More importantly, the New Christians belonged to the small white minority, which constantly needed strengthening by the influx of new settlers. Even if we accept Juan Friede's estimate that the extant catalogues of Spanish immigrants to the American possessions represent only about 15 percent of the total number, the lack of Spanish manpower made itself felt in many areas of economic and political life. The public at large was less hostile, therefore, to the New Christian arrivals than its counterpart on the Iberian Peninsula. Moreover, since the majority of the population consisted of Indians—who ranged from the highly cultured Aztecs and Incas to the extremely primitive, even cannibalistic, inhabitants of some of the islands and the mountain recesses of both North and South America—the position of the New Christians, as members of the small ruling group, was considerably enhanced. State and Church alike considered Indians too primitive to be punished for their nonadherence to Christian principles, and hence left them largely to the supervision of bishops and monasteries, rather than the Holy Office. The ensuing jurisdictional conflicts between the episcopate and the Inquisition likewise helped to weaken the inquisitors' monolithic authority. Under these circumstances, the steady growth of the New Christian population in several major Spanish colonies proved irresistible.[14]

It was even possible for secret Judaizers to impress some of their teachings and practices on one or another Indian group. To be sure, we have no record of any direct New Christian missionary activity, but quite a few Marrano settlers undoubtedly shared the romantic notions brought back to Europe by Christian missionaries that the Indians were descendants of the Lost Ten Tribes of ancient Israel. (Even twentieth-century travelers have been intrigued by the presence in Mexico of an Indian tribe which displayed many signs of possible judaization several generations before.) Quite independently, moreover, several primitive Indian groups exhibited certain patterns of individual and collective behavior which reminded many Europeans of the biblical descriptions of early Israelitic life in ancient Palestine. Noticing these apparent ancient Israelitic vestiges among the Indians, a few early arrivals like Francisco Roldán Jiménez rushed to the conclusion that these Amerindians were descendants of exiles from Northern Israel after the destruction of Samaria in 721 B.C.E. They were encouraged in the identification by the apocalyptic passage in IV Esdras:

These are the ten tribes which were led away captive out of their own land in the days of Josiah [more correctly: Hosea] the king, which (tribes) Salmanassar the king of the Assyrians led away captive; he carried them across the River, and (thus) they were transported into another land. But they took this counsel among themselves, that they would leave the multitude of the heathen, and go forth into a land further distant, where the human race had never dwelt, there at least to keep their statutes which they had not kept in their own land. And they entered by the narrow passages of the river Euphrates. For the

Most High then wrought wonders for them, and stayed the springs of the River until they were passed over. And through that country there was a great way to go, (a journey) of a year and a half; and that region was called Arzareth.

This theme was taken up by Gregorio García in a book on the origins of the New World Indians published in 1607.[15]

As we shall see in another connection, the theory that the American Indians were descendants of the Lost Ten Tribes was further elaborated by English colonizers after their confrontation with North America's native tribes. The hypothesis gained wide circulation after the publication of Thomas Thorowgood's tract on this subject in 1650. Thorowgood was able to produce further supporting evidence from the testimony interveningly submitted to the Amsterdam rabbinate by a Jewish visitor to America, Antonio Montezinos (Aaron Levi), in 1644. Montezinos had reported meeting on his journey Indians who spoke to him about the harsh treatment of the "holy people" by the Spaniards and who were able to recite the *Shema‘* (Deut. 6:4-9) in Hebrew. Ultimately the identification of Indians with the Lost Ten Tribes was to play a certain role even in Menasseh ben Israel's negotiations with Oliver Cromwell for the readmission of Jews to England.[16]

Writings of this kind were merely literary curiosities without any practical effect in Latin America. If some Catholic theologians and missionaries, like Francisco de Vitoria and Bartholomé de las Casas, consistently preached humane treatment of the aboriginal population, a position which was advocated, at least in theory, by the Spanish government as well, the individual colonists paid little attention to these "doctrinaire" demands, which interfered with the pursuit of their own interests. But the postulates did help to bridle the excesses of the inquisitorial prosecutors. Moreover, the Spanish-American Church as a whole was much more subject to governmental controls than its counterpart in the mother country. The influence of the Papacy, especially, was greatly circumscribed. New dioceses were established in the colonies without prior consultation with Rome, and communications sent out by the popes to the New World bishops were not transmitted to them without viceroyal consent. To that extent the Spanish autocracy reversed the medieval trend toward papal supremacy in all spiritual and many temporal matters which had emerged from the centuries-long struggle between the Papacy and the Empire. This was not the result of ideological differences or the regime's religious indifference. On the contrary, the government itself evinced a strong missionary bias (we recall that Columbus' second journey was professedly undertaken mainly for the purpose of Christianizing the New World), and it indeed bent every effort to prevent heterodox, Judaic, or Muslim teachings from interfering with the desired religious conformity of the population. Yet its application of these principles was of necessity less consistent and uniform than on the Iberian Peninsula. Moreover, the Indian problem was further complicated by the presence of numerous mestizos, as well as a growing Negro population imported by slave traders from Africa to meet the manpower shortages in the new territories. In short, history repeated itself and, as elsewhere when Jews were not the sole, nor the most important, minority in an otherwise growingly homogeneous society, they were on the whole treated less severely here than in the developing national states.[17]

Not surprisingly, because of their general tendency to arrogate to themselves more authority than was granted to them by public law, the inquisitorial officials often disregarded the exclusion of Indians from their jurisdiction. Such encroachments understandably led to considerable confusion, particularly when efforts were made to draw a line between a "pure Indian" and one who lacked his own kind of *limpieza*. Mestizos especially, often became playthings in the conflicts between bishops and inquisitors. Nor could they expect much protection from the secular authorities, since in contrast to the Indians, their numbers constantly increased, both by natural causes and by the accretion from ever-new racial mixtures. The alarm sounded by Viceroy Luis de Velasco as early as 1554 was echoed by many white colonials in later years. "The mestizos," the viceroy wrote to Philip II on February 7, 1554, "multiply very rapidly. They all show so many bad traits and are so capable of all sorts of shameful acts, that they and the Negroes must be feared." [18]

From the economic standpoint, the New Christian immigrants were an important asset. The Spanish colonists brought with them from their home countries a conviction that Jews were astute in both business and the professions. Some of them may have remembered the old Spanish proverb that one could find "neither a stupid Jew nor a lazy hare." The colonists had also brought with them from their Iberian homeland a distaste for manual labor, as was exemplified by Hernando Cortés when he refused a large tract of land from the Crown. He stated that he had come to the New World to accumulate gold, not to work the land like a peasant. While the clandestine Jews, too, were concentrated in urban occupations, some of them owned landed property which they, like their Catholic compatriots, cultivated with the aid of Indian or Negro labor. Regrettably, we do not have enough information about the Jewish economic structure in colonial Mexico. But, according to Seymour B. Liebman, in a random survey of 300 Marrano males in Mexico over a period of three hundred years, there were 20 priests and monks, 5 doctors, 6 soldiers, 2 carpenters, 3 tailors, 5 silver- and goldsmiths, 3 shoemakers, 1 dueling master, 21 merchants, 16 brokers (including slave traders), 24 shopkeepers, 17 government officials, and so forth. This occupational distribution, taken from different periods, does not seem to have differed radically from that of the rest of the white population. Moreover, the impact of the big businessmen at home —who, as we recall, included in the seventeenth century a growing percentage of New Christians—likewise made itself strongly felt in the mercantilistic policies of the colonial administration.[19]

Demographically, too, the frightful decline of the Indian population, particularly in the sixteenth century, made a more or less indiscriminate immigration from the Old World welcome to the local colonizers. According to the detailed estimates of Sherbourne F. Cook and Woodrow Borah, the Indian population of Central Mexico numbered 16,871,408 in 1532. Within thirty-six years it declined to 2,649,573; to fall further, to 1,063,255, in 1608. This sharp diminution was even greater in the lowlands, which were reached by the European colonists at an earlier date and in greater numbers. Here the estimates given are: 5,645,072 in 1532, 418,397 in 1568, and 217,011 in 1608. In so far as New Christians were concerned, it is very likely, though it can hardly be proved by the existing documentary evidence, that the immigration of Marrano women may have kept pace with that of men, to a much greater extent than among the Old Christians. The dangers threatening the Marranos in the home country, which were partially responsible for their emigration to the New World, doubtless induced numerous heads of families either to take their wives and children along with them or to have them follow a short time thereafter. For this reason, it appears, New Christian women were frequently among the defendants in inquisitorial trials; when asked about their marital status, they usually answered: *feliz casada* (happily married). Of course, there also were numerous bachelors who sought their fortune in the new environment. Characteristically, bigamy rarely appears among the inquisitorial accusations hurled at New Christians, in contrast to its frequency among the Old Christian defendants.[20]

Nor was the cultural contribution of the New Christian settlers of minor importance. Coming as many of them did from well-educated Marrano circles in Spain and Portugal, they must have contributed more than their share to the development of the new culture in Mexico and elsewhere. True, probably few of them were such convinced Christians that they joined the constant stream of missionaries who, often under untold hardships, settled in the remotest villages of the new continent in order to spread the gospel among the native population. But, as in the homeland, many of them must have sought in the clerical profession the modicum of protection it offered against inquisitorial prosecution. That is why, notwithstanding the general proliferation of ecclesiastical personnel, the 7 percent ratio in the aforementioned sample of 300 Marrano males doubtless was somewhat larger than the ratio in the overall white population. The 20 New Christian priests and monks included in that sample are known to us almost exclusively from the records of the Holy Office; that is, they were under inquisitorial investigation. Probably many more members of the clerical profession escaped prosecution entirely. This may be particularly true of the Jesuit Order (in the New World as elsewhere a "prime mover in the field of education"), which, well into the seventeenth century, was relatively liberal in admitting New Christian members outside the Iberian Peninsula. Notwithstanding the increasing racialist tendencies which manifested themselves within the European branches of the Order in the course of that century, the spiritual heritage of the numerous original New Christian members may well have colored some of the Order's religiopolitical activities.[21]

MEXICAN INQUISITION

Nonetheless, the new era of inquisitorial trials, begun in 1571, made itself increasingly felt. No sooner was the new Mexican inquisitor, Pedro Moya de Contreras (former inquisitor of Saragossa and Murcia, and later archbishop of Mexico and viceroy), installed on November 4, 1571, than he speedily issued his first Edict of Faith (November 10) and set in motion preparations for the first auto-da-fé, which was celebrated with great pomp on February 28, 1574. Prosecutions for judaizing received a new impetus from that edict, which included the following threats against those who failed to fulfill their obligation:

Upon those who disobey this edict shall come the plagues and maledictions which came and descended upon the king Pharaoh and his associates because they resisted the divine commands. They shall be afflicted with the destruction which befell Sodom and Gomorrah when they were burned down and which struck Korah, Dathan and Abiram whom the earth swallowed alive for their insubordination. They shall be forever hardened in their sin, the devil shall be at their right hand, and their speech shall always be counted as a sin in the eyes of the Lord. Their days shall be few, their name and memory shall be lost on the earth, and they shall be cast out of their habitations into the hands of their enemies. In their final judgment they shall be condemned by the divine tribunal together with Lucifer and the traitor Judas. Their children shall become orphans and beggars, without finding anyone to befriend them. They shall in addition sustain the other penalties and censures established by law against such persons who fail to obey the Holy Office and the apostolic commands. They shall also incur the penalty of major excommunication.

These maledictions, so heavily indebted to the Old Testament, remind one of the oath of abjuration demanded by some Eastern churches from new Jewish converts to Christianity. The population responded enthusiastically, and there followed a quarter century of unmitigated terror, directed to a very large extent against alleged Judaizers.[22]

It has been calculated that, between the years 1574 and 1600, 879 cases were tried by the Mexican Inquisition. Although somewhat handicapped by the bishops' attempts to preserve a modicum of their earlier jurisdictional authority, the Holy Office functioned smoothly and efficiently, aided by a renewed royal order of 1585 insisting on its inquisitorial monopoly. Among the accused, Judaizers were a major group, although the inquisitors apparently needed more time for investigation of that form of heresy than for prosecuting other transgressions. As a result, no Judaizers appeared at the three autos staged by the new Inquisition in quick succession on February 28, 1574; March 6, 1575; and February 19, 1576; and only two New Christians suffered death by burning before 1579. In contrast, in the years 1577–96 the Holy Office tried 63 Judaizers, of whom only one was acquitted; 15 were burned in effigy, while 10 were executed. The high percentage of Judaizers is further illustrated by a rather fortuitous collection of 307 cases tried by the Mexican Inquisition between 1572 and 1800 and recorded in a David Fergusson manuscript. Here this offense occurs in 71 cases, second only to "bigamy," which was very widespread, since many colonists left their wives in the old country and married again in the New World. The distances were so great, and communication between the different centers of New Spain was so limited, that many a man who, for one reason or another, left one area could easily establish another family in his new residence. A more detailed examination of available records has persuaded Seymour B. Liebman that fully 1,500 defendants accused of judaizing faced the Inquisition during the three centuries from 1500 to 1800. If only 100 of these individuals were burned at the stake, no fewer than 200 more died in prison while awaiting trial. An additional 100, condemned to galley slavery for up to ten years, rarely survived that ordeal.[23]

Regrettably, it is still extremely difficult to estimate what percentage of the white population consisted of New Christians and how many of them escaped prosecution. One defendant's confession (around 1550) that "among the Spaniards in the Colony there are many more Jews than Catholics" doubtless is a gross exaggeration. Even Liebman's far more moderate estimate that, at the height of inquisitorial prosecutions in the middle of the seventeenth century, some 2,000–3,000 Judaizers lived in New Spain, within a total white population of about 20,000 in addition to ecclesiastical personnel, may be a bit too high. Their ratio may actually have been higher in the second half of the sixteenth century, when the terrors of the Portuguese Inquisition at home had forced many Marranos to seek refuge in safer areas, among which Mexico must have loomed large. Next to the Judaizers, there were numerous Protestants, including for a time Englishmen and Dutchmen who had suffered shipwreck and found refuge in Mexico or some other Spanish possession.[24]

Nor were execution or many years of galley slavery the only severe penalties. Imprisonment for life of the survivors of several years' pretrial incarceration, combined with the loss of all property and other rights, was often an equally horrible punishment, particularly in view of the extremely unsanitary conditions in most colonial, as well as Iberian, jails. A lucky escape to another country, out of reach of the Inquisition, as a rule helped only the individual concerned, not his family. Suffice it to cite here part of the sentence pronounced on March 22, 1609, on the absentee Jorge de Almeida, who was condemned to be burned in effigy:

And as the said Jorge de Almeida has not been arrested, we have also commanded the statue, or effigy representing his person, which has been brought before us, to be dressed with a *sanbenito* and armed with a *corona* [rosary] and clothed with all the other garments and insignia of convicted and condemned criminals, and also that a card bearing the name of Jorge de Almeida and a statement of the present sentence be attached or affixed or pasted on the said statue, which shall then be delivered to the secular authority, namely, the Mayor of the city, in order that the said authority may cause the said effigy to be publicly burned and reduced to ashes. And we do further command that the whole property of Jorge de Almeida be confiscated and appropriated to the Crown, the said confiscation and appropriation to take effect from the date on which the said Jorge de Almeida first committed the crimes of which he has been convicted. And the sons and daughters, if any, of the said Jorge de Almeida are hereby disqualified from serving in any public office, or occupying any public position of honor or trust, whether in the secular or ecclesiastical branches of the government; and they are also forbidden to wear about their persons any ornament or jewel of gold or silver, or precious stones, or coral, or to dress in silk or fine cloth, or any other fine material of any kind.

Not even minors were immune from prosecution. According to a contemporary, Ludovico à Paramo, one of the condemned members of the Carvajal family was a girl of seventeen, who astonished the inquisitors with her ability to recite from memory, even backwards, the Psalms of David and other prayers derived from the Bible. In the 1640s an entire trial was conducted around the testimony of a thirteen-year-old boy, Gabriel de Granada. In fact, the inquisitors consistently tried to encourage domestic spying by children and servants.[25]

THE CARVAJALS

Among the New Christians who faced inquisitorial trials were several members of the distinguished Carvajal family, into which Jorge de Almeida had married. The most prominent victim was the Portuguese-born Luis de Carvajal y de la Cueva, el Conquistador (1539–90). Although of partially New Christian descent, Carvajal had been sent at the age of eight to a relative then serving as abbot of a monastery in Sahagún. There he received a thoroughly Christian education and believed, perhaps sincerely, that he had a noble parentage. At an early age he moved to Mexico, where, after defeating an English naval detachment off the coast of New Spain, he received in 1508 the title of admiral, without salary, from the king. Later, as mayor of the city of Tampico, he equipped a squad of twenty men which forced the surrender of eighty-eight hungry and desolate survivors of Sir John Hawkins' pirate vessel. Many English captives subsequently appeared at the first Mexican auto-da-fé, in 1574. Carvajal was also allowed to bring with him to America one hundred persons, without having to ascertain, as was usually required, that they were of Old Christian descent. From 1579 on (according to a contract probably drawn up for Philip II by his influential secretary Antonio Pérez), he served as governor and captain-general of the "new kingdom of León," covering an area of some 280,000 square miles, or more than one-third of the present Mexican land surface (including parts of Texas), which he opened to Spanish colonization.[26]

Since the boundaries of the area under Carvajal's administration were ill-defined and impinged on the rights of other conquerors in four provinces, he antagonized the viceroy Lorenzo Suárez de Mendoza, who seems to have secured a sharp royal censure of the governor's conduct. In his rescript of August 8, 1587, Philip II referred to reports which had reached him about the governor's cruelties toward the native population. Possibly because of Pérez' intervening demotion and flight abroad, the king appeared to be completely oblivious of the fact that in his 1579 contract with Carvajal he had himself demanded that the governor take stringent measures against the Indians, who had rebelled, during the preceding five years, against the established authority, had given up their Christian faith, and destroyed many churches and other property. "The Viceroy," the contract had added, "has sent captains and soldiers to subdue them. These captains have tried hard but have been unable to pacify the region. You are, therefore, obligated to bring these Indians to peace and Christianity within eight years from this date [May 31, 1579]." Now after the expiration of that eight-year term, Philip felt free to reprimand Carvajal, who according to his accusers, had recklessly undertaken to conquer and pacify the vast territory of New León at his own expense, without adequate resources, and hence had had difficulties in hiring soldiers for his campaigns. He had had to promise the mercenaries that, after "pacifying" the rebellious Indians, he would assign them as slaves for ten to fourteen years to the conquerors. As a result, Indians who peaceably welcomed the new arrivals and expressed readiness to revert to Christianity, were condemned to servitude for various alleged transgressions and were handed over to Carvajal's soldiers, who subsequently sold them to others. Although summoned before the royal audiencia in Mexico, the governor was allegedly able by various delays to avoid setting the prisoners free. The royal cedula now enjoined the administration to execute the original order and to punish the guilty. Perhaps because the viceroy was unable to enforce the new ordinance immediately, or even to prove Carvajal's guilt, the latter's enemies resorted to an attack on his New Christian ancestry and handed his case over to the Inquisition. There he was accused not of himself having secretly judaized but only of having failed to denounce his Marrano niece Isabel, who had "dogmatized [proselytized] for the Law of Moses." The inquisitorial fiscal, Lobo Guerrero, suggested that Carvajal "be transferred to one of the Inquisition's prisons, both as a punishment and as an inducement for him to reveal all he knows about the said niece." With relative dispatch he was tried. Although it became clear from the testimony that he was a confirmed Catholic—on the one occasion when his niece had denied Jesus, he had slapped her face so hard that she fell to the ground—he was found guilty and sentenced to march in an auto and be reconciled with an abjuration *de vehementi*. All his property was confiscated, and he was banished from New Spain for six years. Before he was able to depart, however, he was transferred to the secular prison under another criminal charge trumped up by the administration, and died there at the age of fifty-one. Thus ended the career of this talented and versatile entrepreneur, military commander, and administrator. Ruthless as he was in his public life, and far from interested in sacrificing anything for his ancestral faith, he had retained enough family loyalty not to denounce his sister-in-law or her children, whom he had helped to emigrate from Spain to Mexico.[27]

Even more dramatic was the trial of his nephew Luis de Carvajal el Mozo (the Younger), who was, unlike the uncle, a devoted Jew. He called himself Joseph Lumbroso (the Illumined or Enlightened), in remembrance of his illumination when he saw the light of Judaism. After a first trial in 1589–90, he was reconciled, but condemned to life imprisonment. Later granted freedom of movement, he was again accused of judaizing and was arrested in February 1595. In a moving letter to his sisters Leonora and Isabel (who was later condemned as a "dogmatizer)" soon after his incarceration, he wrote:

I am in irons, but neither these nor live coals shall take my soul away from the sweet Lord, who has unveiled before me, here, many of His mercies. . . . I was in a dark cell for three weeks. My meals were brought to me by candlelight, but my blessed God took me out of there, blessed be His name, and brought me to a prison in this yard. It has a window through which I watch the sky, day and night. What more can I say about His divine grace? That for eight days I had a honeycomb full of sweetest nectar from the mouth of the Lord, during which time I perceived great mysteries over the heavens and [saw] the joys that await us. . . . I beg God to grant me my wish of seeing you;

but if not, I am comforted by the thought that we shall see each other before death, and afterward for an eternity in the land of glory, among the beautiful angels and saints.

In another letter he tried to comfort his sister Catalina by referring to Joseph, who "was in prison for thirteen years, only to rule afterwards," and to God's miraculous saving of Daniel, Hananiah, Mishael, and Azariah. In his last will and testament he fervently prayed to God that he be given the strength to resist temptation and die as a martyr.[28]

Extremely high-strung, Luis was dumfounded at the mere sight of the inquisitor Alonso de Peralta, whom the admiring narrator of the auto-da-fé of 1596 described as apparently "created by God to be an inquisitor because of his perspicacity." In a critical moment, Luis yielded to torture and listed about a hundred and twenty names of Judaizers, a confession he later partially retracted. His attempted suicide on February 16, 1596, made his frail body still weaker; and at the last moment while marching in the final procession, he apparently mumbled the prescribed phrases to escape being burned alive. Otherwise, he was never contrite, but defiantly professed his ancestral faith. Ultimately condemned as "a judaizing heretic, an apostate from our holy Catholic faith, and an accomplice and concealer of judaizing heretics, a false and simulating proselytizer, impenitent, relapsed, a pertinacious dogmatist," he was garroted and burned at the stake on December 8, 1596. During his trial he had revealed some familiarity with Jewish religious thought, and in many ways was a forerunner of the kabbalistically inspired Marranos who played such a great role in the religious movements of the seventeenth century. True, having no access to any of the kabbalistic classics, his mystical utterances were of a rather naive, folkloristic kind. Nor was he made of the heroic stuff of martyrs. But humanly and spiritually he was indubitably the most fascinating personality of the sixteenth-century Mexican Marranos. Despite his failings in his life and death, he bore memorable testimony to his ancestral faith as he understood it. The impression he made, even upon so devout a Catholic as Fray Alonso de Contreras, who wrote an eyewitness report of Carvajal's last hours, is well documented by the following comment in that report:

He was always such a good Jew and he reconciled his understanding, which was very profound and sensitive, with his highly inspired Divine determination to defend the Law of God—the Mosaic—and to fight for it. I have no doubt that if he had lived before the Incarnation of our Redeemer, he would have been a heroic Hebrew and his name would have been as famous in the Bible as are the names of those who died in defense of their law when it was necessary.[29]

Despite the vast amount of study which has been devoted to Luis' tragic career, many problems are still unsolved. We do not know, for example, whether the name Joseph was chosen by Carvajal himself because he saw the ancient patriarch as the prototype of a prisoner who was ultimately released and embarked upon a glorious career, or whether it was the Hebrew name given him by his judaizing father, as was often the case in Marrano circles. That Luis' Jewish learning was very limited and was largely derived from his often naive interpretation of the Old Testament and some Apocrypha is evident from all his writings and oral testimony. In addition he knew a few Hebrew prayers brought to Mexico by New Christian immigrants. Curiously, the main post-biblical source of information concerning Jewish beliefs, the Thirteen Articles of Faith formulated by Maimonides, "unknown and unheard of in the lands of captivity," came to Carvajal's notice from a biblical commentary by the Portuguese theologian Gerónimo Oleastro, who, as we recall, had represented Portugal at the Council of Trent and was anything but a friend of Jews. How deficient Luis' early initiation into Judaism was may also be noted from his ignorance of the Jewish ritual of circumcision. He discovered it by reading the story of Abraham in Genesis, and was particularly impressed by the biblical statement that any descendant of Abraham who failed to undergo that ritual would "be cut off from his people; he hath broken My covenant" (Gen. 17:14). Thereupon Carvajal hastened to perform that painful operation on himself with old scissors. Subsequently he reminisced that "from the very day I received this sacred seal and sacrament on my flesh, it served as my armor against lust and as a help for my chastity. As a weak sinner on many previous occasions I now merited the fatal wound that saved me from the same sin my father committed—that of marrying the daughter of a Gentile father." [30]

That reference to his mother reflected Luis' overzealous nature, for she had become an ardently professing Jewess and ultimately shared his martyrdom, being executed with him, along with three of her five daughters. Like him they had been reconciled in 1590 and were now treated as relapsed converts. As usual, all members of their family, including children and grandchildren, were to be disqualified from holding any position of trust and dignity and forbidden to wear jewelry or costly garments. Only Luis' brother Gaspar was exonerated by the Inquisition, because the unanimous testimony of witnesses had confirmed that he lived an exemplary Catholic life as a monk dedicated to his work for the Church. He was not even charged with having failed to denounce his mother and siblings to the Holy Office. Two other brothers, Baltasar and Miguel, later apparently known as David and Jacob Lumbrozo, had returned to Spain, and from there had moved to Italy and Turkey, respectively, and had thus escaped the clutches of the Inquisition. Less lucky were a number of other contemporaries. Among them we need but mention Clara Enríquez, whose trial is described by a well-informed modern historian as "one of the most interesting of that generation of Jews." Connected with the prosecution of Clara was that of Catalina Enríquez and her husband, Manuel Lucena. Apart from shedding much additional light on the curious ritualistic observances in Marrano circles which had long lost contact with the mainstream of Judaism, the testimony here presented, though far from reliable, showed that a couple like the Lucenas could meet, marry, and live together for some time before each spouse accidentally discovered that the other was of Jewish descent and a secret practitioner of Jewish rites.[31]

Nor did most of the persons once listed by Carvajal as secret Judaizers suffer serious consequences, because he was prone to include in his list persons who, only on flimsy impressions, appeared to him to have been clandestine Jews. This was the case, for example, of his identification of a devoutly Catholic hermit, Don Gregorio López, as a "Jew observing the Law of Moses with greater perfection than he himself." In his religious enthusiasm Carvajal evidently misunderstood what he read in López' distinguished *Exposición al Apocalypsis*. Because of that author's unusual familiarity with the Old Testament, Luis concluded that he must have been a Judaizer. Other "evidence" he adduced included López' quotations from the Esdras Apocalypse, his praying and meditating for several hours while standing upright *without* covering his head, his frequent fasts, his being a native of Toledo, where many descendants of Jews lived, and his wearing a long beard. These arguments, some of which did not even relate correctly to Orthodox Jewish observances, did not sound plausible to the inquisitorial prosecutors, who had once before acquitted López of the charge of heresy. He was to die a natural death in 1596, five months before the Carvajal auto-da-fé. His life as a hermit, his great benefactions to neighboring Indians, and his remarkable theological and scientific publications earned him great reverence among many disciples and followers; including his original inquisitorial prosecutor, Francisco Losa, who became his admiring first biographer. Ultimately, it was Philip IV himself who, in 1626, but thirty years after López' death, recommended his canonization to the pope, and the Church of Rome consented at least to his beatification. Nonetheless, López all along had evinced considerable sympathy for the suffering New Christians, whom he recognized as his ethnic brethren, and he had refused to join their persecutors. We cannot even tell whether in his conversations with Carvajal and others he had made any effort to deepen their Christian allegiance.[32]

With the execution of several members of the Carvajal family ended a remarkable episode in Mexican Jewish history. Although in more recent generations certain Mexican residents claimed descent from the Carvajals, and some Indians maintained that their ancestors had been converted to Judaism by members of the governor's family, the last traces of the Carvajal clan disappear after 1706. Thus was cut short the career of a family which might have played a great role in the subsequent development of Mexico and its neighboring territories. But the place of the Carvajals was taken by other New Christians, the prosecution of whom became a major preoccupation of the Inquisition during the following decades. Nor was the spiritual message of the younger Carvajal, "the first Spanish-American Jewish poet and mystic," completely lost on the Mexican public. It undoubtedly stimulated the Dominican friar Hernando de Ojéa to publish in 1602, a few years after Carvajal's execution, an apologetic tract addressed to Marranos and Christians alike. His impact on the surviving Mexican New Christians seems to have been too slight, however, to justify the designation "apostle to Jews," given him by a modern historian.[33]

The seventeenth century began dramatically with a spectacular auto-da-fé in Mexico City held on March 25, 1601, attended by the viceroy and 700 Catholic priests, as well as a multitude of onlookers of all classes and races. The 135 persons sentenced included 45–47 defendants accused of judaizing. But only two of these were garroted and burned, Thomas de Fonseca Castellanos and Doña Mariana Núñez de Carvajal, an unmarried sister of Luis de Carvajal the Younger. Spared in 1596 because of insanity, she was now executed for relapsing to Judaism. Another defendant, Francisco Rodríguez de Ledesma, was allowed a new hearing. But after his death in prison his body was consigned to the flames at the next major auto, in 1603, at which only one living victim, Juan Núñez de León, was garroted and burned. However, many Judaizers were executed in effigy, or else their bodies were exhumed from the grave and burned at the stake. Their ashes were usually thrown into a canal, lest any trace of their physical existence remain for idealization by like-minded persons or descendants. That Rodríguez was one of a multitude of defendants who died in prison is easily explainable by the length of the investigations (which often extended over many years), the utterly unsanitary conditions in the inquisitorial cells, the physical maltreatment by guards, and their own mental anguish. Some of them tried to allay their guilt feelings—whether occasioned by "heretical" deviations or by regrets at having to deny their true Jewish allegiance—with fasting and self-castigation. Quite a few were driven to commit suicide, though they may have known that Judaism was opposed to taking one's own life. Even if unsuccessful, as was the case with Luis de Carvajal the Younger, suicide attempts must have further undermined the defendants' resistance to disease and starvation. But no regular statistics of such victims are available. Of course, here, as in many other cases, persons supposedly condemned for other crimes may well have included Judaizers. The summaries preserved in Mexican archives often listed persons under the crimes with which they were first charged, even if in the course of the investigation it became known that they had been circumcised or otherwise practiced Jewish rites, and they were thereupon charged with the more serious "crime" of judaizing.[34]

RESPITE AND INTENSIFICATION

"Judaizing heretics" in the Americas obtained a respite when their fellow Marranos in Spain had secured from Pope Clement VIII and King Philip III the "General Pardon" in 1604–1605. Only one such defendant happened to be in a Mexican prison at the time when the news reached the colony, and he was speedily released. But the impact of that royal amnesty was felt for many years, even after the revocation of the edict in the home country. With a single exception, no large-scale burnings for judaizing were staged until 1646. Mexico, in particular, now offered an even more persistent lure to European New Christians, among them Matéo Alemán, who immigrated to the colony with his wife and children in 1607, and died there completely disillusioned and embittered, although apparently a sincerely professing Christian. Not only residents of the Iberian Peninsula, who felt somewhat more protected there from the Inquisition, but also individuals who had spent years in safer European countries, could not resist the spirit of adventure and the appeal of the New World's great economic opportunities. For example, Simón Montero, born in 1600 in the town of Castello Branco (located in one of the two areas in Portugal from which many Marranos were constantly leaving for various lands), lived in France and Italy and even studied there to become a rabbi. Yet he left Europe and ventured to Mexico. Before long, he was denounced for having asked a Mexican abbess to sell him a "virgin" tomb for a deceased lady friend—evidently because he wished to see her buried in an unconsecrated plot of land. However, he resisted torture and was acquitted in 1635. Another defendant under a similar indictment, Duarte de León Jamarillo, was also subjected to torture, "which was administered to him with some moderation because of his infirmity." He was ultimately condemned to abjuration *de vehementi*. But, as we shall see, both men were less fortunate fourteen years later.[35]

Not that the Mexican Inquisition was completely idle during the period of the pardon; it was occupied with prosecutions for sorcery, for sexual solicitations at the confessional, and the like. In 1625, 1626, 1628, and 1635, many Judaizers were reconciled, mostly with severe penalties of lashes, several years in prison, and total loss of property, while a number were burned in effigy. For example, the auto celebrated on April 2, 1635, involved no fewer than 18 Judaizers; one of them, Simón Paredes, being burned alive, and 6 in effigy. In contrast, a sixty-three-year-old chaplain of the Convent Regina Coeli, who was convicted of having seduced, during his tenure of office as father-confessor for six or seven years, fourteen nuns, "his spiritual daughters," and of having maintained with them long-lasting affairs, was sentenced in a private session to a mere abjuration *de levi,* was forbidden to serve as confessor to women, and exiled from Mexico for a period of four years. Moreover, the Iberian offices of the Inquisition were quite busy prosecuting Marranos and taking down their and the witnesses' depositions. The Madrid and Lisbon headquarters kept in constant communication with their respective branches (though not as fully with one another), transmitting to them whatever incriminating evidence was assembled concerning residents of New Spain. Similar materials were submitted by the Lima inquisitors to their colleagues in Mexico City, and vice versa. These blacklists were kept for future use, and proved quite helpful during the investigations of the 1640s. Furthermore, condemnation to lesser penalties could likewise have serious consequences, not only for the culprits themselves but also for their families. As we recall, when Jorge de Almeida disappeared before his trial, the Mexican Holy Office, after a prolonged investigation, sentenced him in 1609 to be burned in effigy because he had "forsaken Our Holy Catholic Faith and relapsed into the observance of the dead Law of Moses, awaiting the coming of the Messiah promised by the said Law and keeping and observing all the rites and ceremonies of the same." Personally, Almeida could shrug off that symbolic execution, so long as he did not fall into the inquisitors' hands. But he and his family automatically lost whatever property he left behind in his headlong flight. In addition, his children were disqualified from wearing fine clothes and jewelry and were barred from all public office, ecclesiastical or secular.[36]

Potential confiscations of this type whetted the appetites of greedy inquisitors. During the quiescent first decades of the seventeenth century, the numerical and financial strength of the Marrano community had constantly grown, and its relative wealth became in the 1640s a major incentive for the resumption of large-scale inquisitorial trials. True, some economic historians consider the period of 1620–80 one of a general slowdown in Mexico's economic expansion. Yet enough opportunities remained open for venturesome New Christians to accumulate considerable fortunes. A renewed drive for confiscations was also dictated by the growing financial stringency of both the Spanish Treasury and the Mexican Inquisition. In fact, conflicts between the two institutions on this score preoccupied many administrators on both sides of the Atlantic Ocean for many decades. From a recent archival study of the related activities of the Inquisition in Lima (about which more will be said below), we learn how close-mouthed the American branches of the Inquisition (as well as the Suprema in Madrid) were, and how staunchly they refused to give the secular government the required accounting of either their revenues from confiscations and fines or their expenditures. At the same time, they insisted upon the continuation of governmental subsidies of about 10,000 pesos a year for the salaries of their highest officials (2 inquisitors, 1 fiscal, and 1 secretary) and for other expenses. Engaged in a hopeless struggle against deficits, arising particularly from Spain's involvement in the Thirty and Eighty Years' Wars, the royal Treasury repeatedly demanded its share of the inquisitorial revenue, but all its efforts were sabotaged by delays and other circumventions on the part of the inquisitors. During the prolonged intermission (1605–1635) in its intensive prosecutions, the income of the Mexican Inquisition had indeed fallen below the minimum maintenance level. In 1625 its budget had a deficit of 4,000 pesos. Two years later, the visiting inspector Martín Carrillo y Alderete threatened: "If no speedy remedy is applied, one may have to close this tribunal within a few days." With this powerful incentive the inquisitors gladly resumed their trials, with the view that even if the majority of transgressors were "reconciled," their property would still be confiscated. As a result, the revenue accruing to the Inquisition from the trials of the 1640s not only restored the solvency of the Holy Office but yielded tremendous surpluses. In 1646, it has been estimated, the confiscations yielded 38,732 pesos; in 1647, 148,562 pesos, though far less than the alleged revenue of 3,000,000 pesos in Lima in 1649. Thenceforth, by investing its surpluses in landed estates and other revenue-producing ventures, the Inquisition became quite prosperous, while all appeals of the Treasury and the viceroys for revenue sharing were either ignored or rebuffed. In essence, such mutual distrust characterized also the financial exchanges between the Mexican Holy Office and the central authorities in Madrid and Seville.[37]

Regrettably, we are as yet unable to estimate, even by way of rough approximation, the wealth of the New Christians as a group or even the assets of some of its leading members. But the opportunities for amassing large fortunes were well demonstrated by the famous controversy between Bishop Juan de Palafox y Mendoza of Puebla de los Angeles (Tlaxcala) and the Mexican Jesuits in 1641–49. Among his numerous attempted reforms, the bishop wished to abolish the exemption from tithes long enjoyed by the Society of Jesus. In this connection Palafox cited valuations of various properties controlled by the Order, the taxing of which would immediately have helped to relieve the fiscal insufficiency of the Church. For one example, he pointed out that the Jesuits alone owned six sugar refineries (which on the average were then valued at 700,000 pesos each), yielding annually a profit of 300,000 pesos for the Order, whereas the whole secular priesthood and the other monastic orders together had between them only three refineries. The Jesuits also controlled many landed estates, including cattle and sheep ranches, mines, and so forth. Since the death of Luis Carvajal the Governor, to be sure, no New Christian capitalist seems to have penetrated the upper ranks of the Mexican bureaucracy or landowning plutocracy. Yet the prospect of taking over the property of wealthy merchants like Simón Váez (Báez) Sevilla, must have been an almost irresistible temptation to the local inquisitors.[38]

International developments likewise gave new zeal to the inquisitorial prosecutions in the New World. When Portugal became independent in 1640 and joined the anti-Spanish alliance, all Por-

tuguese settlers in New Spain became, so to say, "enemy aliens."
In the case of the numerous New Christians among them, political
disloyalty appeared to be compounded with religious deviation.
Hence, on July 13, 1642, started a new series of large-scale inquisitorial prosecutions, which led to a number of autos-da-fé between
1646 and 1649. Among the prisoners was an unusual twenty-three-
year-old Marrano named Juan Pacheco de León (in Hebrew: Solomon Macharro), who had arrived in Mexico but three years before.
His final indictment quite prominently stressed his supposed disloyalty to the Spanish Crown. Of the one hundred and four counts presented by the inquisitorial fiscal Juan Saenz de Mañozca—one of
the longest indictments ever entered against a Mexican Judaizer
—the seventy-third count asserted that the defendant, "although
being a Portuguese and a descendant of such [the fiscal must have
known that Pacheco-Macharro was born in either Antequera,
Spain, or Leghorn, Italy, although his father may have emigrated
from Portugal together with others who left after 1580], did many
things against the Crown of Castile and the king our lord, and
rose against the kingdom, as they have done in Portugal, killing
Castilians, and destroying the Holy Office of the Inquisition. They
also burned its buildings and gravely maltreated inquisitorial
officials." This was a patent falsehood, since the defendant had
lived in Italy or Turkey, at least from the age of two on and probably had never set foot in Portugal.[39]

Other features of this trial are also noteworthy. To begin with,
Pacheco-Macharro had been brought up by his father, David Macharro, in Leghorn, and had there been raised as a professing Jew,
sent to Hebrew schools, and even dispatched to Turkey, particularly to Smyrna, for a more intensive Jewish education. Shortly
before his arrival in Mexico, at the age of twenty, he had lost his
father on the journey to America. He was hospitably received by
the local Marrano community, which had long been inured to
mutual self-help. Much better-informed about Jewish law and
practices than the local Marranos, who had never seen a Hebrew
book and had always practiced Jewish rites in the manner of their
equally ill-informed parents, he instantly became the spiritual
leader of the community. Theretofore, Doña Blanca Enríquez had
been the communal "expert," but she now graciously submitted

to the superior learning of the young newcomer. For example, she had taught her neighbors that when the Day of Atonement fell on a Saturday they ought to fast on the preceding Friday. But she now accepted Macharro's decision—which was correct according to Jewish law—that unlike other fasts that of the "Sabbath of Sabbaths" (Lev. 16:31) overrides the prohibition against fasting on Saturday and that hence its usual observance is to take place according to the calendar. It is even possible that, as intimated by Mañozca, the defendant had been sent by the Leghorn Jews or a Turkish community to the New World to impart some of the rudiments of Jewish learning and customs to the cut-off remnant of Israel there. We recall that such emissaries had been sent by Dutch and English Jews to their Iberian coreligionists for underground instruction and morale building. The final count in the indictment actually accused Pacheco-Macharro of having "concealed the accomplices of his transgression with whom he had negotiated and communicated in Florence and Leghorn, Italy; in Spain, Turkey, and the Barbary States; and particularly in Seville, Cadiz, the harbor and city of new Vera Cruz, Puebla de los Angeles, and this city of Mexico and town of Queretaro." For this reason, the fiscal added, the defendant had "proved himself unworthy of the mercy which this Holy Office customarily applies to good and true penitents." [40]

Of interest also is Pacheco-Macharro's contact with the mysterious personality Guillermo Lombardo de Guzmán or Guillen Lamport, while they both languished in prison. Among other matters, Lombardo expressed the "opinion" which, as in his numerous other writings in prison, he doubtless backed up by exact source quotations from memory, that the Inquisition had no right to demand from any defendant proof that he had been baptized, and that his mere assertion to this effect should suffice. This "opinion" underscored the dilemma in which Pacecho-Macharro and other Marranos in a similar situation had found themselves. If they claimed that they had never been baptized and that, hence, as legitimately professing Jews, they were not subject to the jurisdiction of the Holy Office, they could be executed on the basis of the original Spanish decree of expulsion of 1492, which had forbidden Jews to set foot on Spanish soil, under penalty of death.

If they admitted to having been baptized, however, they were not entitled to practice any Jewish rituals without becoming heretics, and were then subject to burning. Pacheco-Macharro may have hoped to persuade the inquisitors at one point that, because he had been baptized in Antequera, he was not barred from reentering any of the Spanish possessions, but that because he had been raised as a Jew since the age of two, he could not be classified a Christian heretic. This argument, of course, made little impression upon the inquisitors. Incidentally, we do not know whether Pacheco-Macharro became in any way involved in Lombardo's venturesome claim to being an illegitimate son of Philip III and an Irish woman. With the aid of forged papers, Lombardo had even proclaimed himself "king of the Americas and emperor of the Mexicans." His scheme has often been viewed as an early adumbration of Mexico's nineteenth-century liberation movement.[41]

As elsewhere, much of the "evidence" used in the trials conducted by the Mexican Holy Office was either extracted from the defendants through torture or collected from such untrustworthy witnesses as Gabriel de Granada, then a boy of thirteen, and José Sánchez, a mestizo. Sánchez had been raised from early childhood by his Old Christian half-sister María de Zárate but, for some unknown reasons, he passionately hated María and her Marrano husband, Francisco Botello. Some more reliable data were assembled by agents provocateurs placed in inquisitorial prisons as supposed codefendants. These agents were often able to overhear conversations among the other prisoners, who, however guarded their talk, frequently betrayed the identity of other Judaizers. One such informer, Gaspar de Alfar, regularly reported to the inquisitors the substance of the frequent confidential exchanges between Pacheco-Macharro and Francisco Botello, held in a neighboring cell. For example, on one occasion Pacheco-Macharro told Botello about his special fasts, which he could best observe at the home of Simón Váez Sevilla, the richest and most powerful Marrano merchant in town. (Simón Váez' home was later described by an inquisitorial reporter as the center of attraction for "all the Judaizers arriving from Spain, Peru, or the Philippines, and the various parts of these realms.") The young prisoner was said to have added, somewhat recklessly:

At the home of Simón Váez Sevilla conditions were most favorable
for offering a *súchil* [fast]; I swear to you that all joined together,
mother and daughters, sons-in-law and grandchildren, and all the members of the families of Simón Váez and his wife; and we all celebrated
with the greatest secrecy and prudence; we all got together in the large
room for lunch with a great deal of pretense; in case someone should
enter, he would see nothing untoward; we all made ourselves understood through signals, and so we were certain we would never be found
out. Were it not for the Blancas [the family of Blanca Enríquez,
Simón's mother-in-law] they would not now be prisoners.

Naturally Simón and all his family were arrested and subjected to
close scrutiny. His brother Antonio had already been reconciled
in 1625 and hence had little chance for survival at the new in-
quest. Simón himself, however, was sentenced merely at that time
to wearing the sanbenito, expulsion from Mexico, and the confiscation of all his property. He heard that sentence publicly proclaimed at the grand auto-da-fé of April 11, 1649, at which
Pacheco-Macharro, Doña Ana de León Carvajal, Montero, Jaramillo, and several others were executed.[42]

Remarkably, Francisco Botello, later classified by the official
reporter as "the most hardened Jew in many centuries chastised
by the Holy Office," escaped execution in 1649, although, together
with Simón Váez, he suffered martyrdom at the next grand spectacle, on November 19, 1659. Possibly he was temporarily spared
because he was married to María de Zárate, who, by an historical
irony, was distantly related to the family of Archbishop Juan
Martínez Silíceo, the initiator of the intense Spanish obsession
with *limpieza*. As far as we can tell from the incompletely preserved documentation, she herself was arrested but not severely
punished. All the autos were, of course, conducted with great
pomp. "The great *auto general* of April 11, 1649," writes Henry
Charles Lea, "marks the apogee of the Mexican Inquisition. . . . A
month in advance, the solemn proclamation announcing it was
made in Mexico . . . with a gorgeous procession to the sound of
trumpet and drum. . . . A fortnight in advance of the appointed
day, crowds began to pour in, some of them from a distance of one
hundred or two hundred leagues, till, as we are told, it looked as
though the country had been depopulated." Apart from 135 "reconciled" Judaizers, 67 defendants were burned in effigy and 14
were burned in the flesh, 13 of them after previous garroting.[43]

The one defendant burned alive was the distinguished citizen, Tomás Treviño de Sobremonte. A native of Spain, he was the son of an Old Christian nobleman and a New Christian mother, who taught him some Jewish religious doctrines and rituals. He had first come under suspicion in Mexico in 1624, in connection with the trial of his mother and brother Jerónimo in Valladolid, Spain, but he was reconciled in 1625. His prison experience actually deepened his devotion to Judaism, and it was then, we are told, that he was circumcised by a companion, Antonio Váez, another future victim of the auto of 1649. After his release, at which he was deprived of all his property and the right to wear costly garments, Treviño somehow managed to amass a new fortune and became an influential businessman. In 1631–33 he secured from the grand-inquisitor, Antonio Zapata of Spain, an exemption from the general prohibition forbidding wearers of sanbenitos to ride on horseback or to appear in public in luxurious attire. Before long, however, he was again denounced to the Inquisition. In 1644 he was seized on his way to Acapulco, from where he planned to sail for the Philippines. After a lengthy and dramatic investigation, he was burned in 1649. To the very end, he staunchly defended his faith in the one and only God of Israel, and even tried to persuade the priests who spent his last twenty-four hours with him trying to convert him to Christianity, that, if they cared for the salvation of their souls, they had better embrace Judaism. To the crowd of some 30,000 viewers, however, his intrepid acceptance of the painful death by burning appeared as a confirmation of his being a "depraved and astute grand Jew," or an "indomitable and rebellious Jew," to quote some of the numerous epithets used by the inquisitors during the trial. Until about 1910 the house in which he had lived in Mexico City was called in popular parlance "the house of the Jew." Spain's inquisitor-general, Arce y Reynoso, did not exaggerate when, in his congratulatory letter to Philip IV of October 15, 1649, he declared that the Mexican auto-da-fé had been a source of joy and consolation to the masses and had been greeted with universal applause. The king expressed his own gratification and instructed the inquisitor-general to convey his royal thanks to the officials of the Mexican Holy Office. Clearly, such encouragement from the mother country could merely intensify the zeal of the Mexican officials. In 1659, as we recall, they staged another grand auto, officially presided over by the viceroy, in the absence of the ailing archbishop. Among the victims was Diego Díaz, who, in contrast to his wife, Ana Gómez, burned alive in the 1649 auto, had then been let off with a mere abjuration and sentence of exile. However, he was rearrested in 1652 and executed, together with Botello, who unwaveringly professed his Jewish faith and was apparently burned alive. Díaz to the end denied all guilt but he refused to kiss the cross; hence he was only half garroted before being placed on the pyre.[44]

Treviño de Sobremonte's first arrest, ordered in 1624 by the Holy Office of Mexico, occurred in the village of Antequera in the valley of Oaxaca. Sooner or later most provincial suspects were brought for trial and eventual sentence to Mexico City. Inquisitorial records reveal the presence of Jews in many other provincial localities in the vast area under the control of the Mexican Inquisition.

In the middle of the seventeenth century [asserts Seymour B. Liebman], there were about fifteen [Jewish] congregations in Mexico City and environs, at least three in Puebla, at least two in Guadalajara and Veracruz, and one each in Zacatecas and Campeche. It is probable that there was at least one each in Mérida, Monterey, Guatemala, Nicaragua, and Honduras.

There doubtless were secret Judaizers in many other towns and villages as well; but if, for some reason, they escaped the attention of the inquisitorial agents, or managed, through bribery or otherwise, to elude arrest and prosecution, their names were not included in any inqiusitorial record, our foremost source of information concerning New Christians in colonial Spanish America. Happy were those men and women who, according to an old adage, "had no history." Only occasionally is that veil of obscurity pierced by flashes of light emanating from persistent oral traditions, unreliable as such family transmissions frequently are. A case in point is the Yucatán Peninsula. Because of its numerous coves and inlets, Yucatán attracted many settlers, both temporary and permanent, who did not choose to land in open ports. It is also possible that, because of the importance of slaves to the Mexican economy, the government and the Church closed their eyes to the presence in Yucatán of Protestant and judaizing importers of that human merchandise. That is probably why, despite the residence there today of some families widely considered to be of Jewish descent, only one, unfinished case of an inquisitional investigation was recorded in Yucatán in more than two centuries. However, intensive research in inquisitorial and other local archives may yet reveal the presence at one time or another of some hitherto unknown New Christian groups, especially in the Central-American republics.[45]

SOUTH AMERICA

Treviño de Sobremonte had his South American counterpart in a Chilean New Christian, Francisco Maldonado de Silva, executed ten years earlier. Nonetheless, compared with their Mexican brethren, the Marranos living under the jurisdiction of the other great center of the Latin-American Inquisition—that of Lima, Peru—suffered relatively little. Not that there was an absence of zealous inquisitors. In fact, the Holy Office in Lima was established in 1569, but thirty-four years after the city's foundation; it actually was fully operative a year before its sister institution in Mexico City. Whether or not the number of New Christians seeking shelter in South America was smaller, the main reason for this discrepancy doubtless derived from the vast expanse of land under the authority of the Lima Inquisition. Until the establishment, in 1610, of a new Holy Office in Cartagena de las Indias to supervise the faith and morals of the Spanish inhabitants of New Granada (which embraced the Caribbean Islands, parts of Central America, and important northern segments of the South American continent), the Lima Inquisition's jurisdiction extended over this entire area, in addition to the rest of South America, with the exception of the Portuguese possessions in Brazil. The distances were so enormous that the sheer expense of transporting defendants 1,500–2,000 miles from a provincial city to the inquisitorial headquarters made prosecutions financially unrewarding, particularly if the accused person was not very wealthy and the confiscation of his property held little promise of compensating the Holy Office for its outlay. Even guarding the prisoners en route, through the many winding roads and thinly populated settlements, taxed the resources of the inquisitorial police; many, indeed, were the prisoners who vanished and settled in some distant locality under assumed names. These fiscal and administrative considerations were weighty enough to prevent the authorities in Madrid from establishing additional inquisitorial offices (other than in Cartagena), as was frequently urged by local officials.[46]

As a result, few southern Judaizers suffered prosecution in the sixteenth century. True, a general decree of 1543 ordered the expulsion of descendants of New Christians from the entire area. But, as elsewhere, it was honored in its breach. No sooner was the Inquisition established, however, than a licentiate, Juan Álvarez, and his wife were accused of judaizing, but were apparently acquitted. Less fortunate were two other Judaizers reconciled in 1581, and another two in 1592. The first "relaxations" did not occur until December 17, 1595, when four persons were executed (including Jorge Núñez, a thirty-year-old Portuguese) and five were reconciled. On December 10, 1600, two Judaizers, Baltasar Lucena and Duarte Núñez de Cea, were burned alive, and twelve "culprits" were reconciled. After this bloody performance, the inquisitor Antonio Ordóñez y Flores, gleefully reported that "the auto was performed with much peace and quiet. The viceroy and the people were greatly edified by the righteousness of the sentences and the mercy shown the defendants."[47]

All along, the inquisitors complained that there were a great number of Judaizers in the area under the Lima Office's jurisdiction. As early as February 1570, Eusebio de Arrieta, secretary of the Holy Office, reported to Spain's inquisitor-general: "In view of the small number of Spaniards in these parts, there are twice as many New Christians here as in Spain." Four months later, another inquisitor claimed that the Holy Office found it difficult to recruit sufficient literate personnel among the Old Christians. With greater justification these complaints became louder after 1580. The annexation of Portugal by Philip II opened the gates to a large-scale immigration of Portuguese New Christians into Spain's overseas possessions, particularly the colonies adjoining Portuguese-controlled Brazil. In 1597, shortly before his death in disgrace, the Lima inquisitor Antonio Gutiérrez de Ulloa contended that Buenos Aires and the provinces of Paraguay and Tucumán were overrun by Portuguese illegally exporting much gold and silver, and added: "Their majority are *confesos* [New Christians], and I believe that one may say, Jews following their Law." Five years later, Philip III ordered, in fact, the expulsion from that area of all Portuguese and foreigners who had entered it without a license. In 1604 the king decreed, even more explicitly:

We command and ordain that no one recently converted to Our holy faith, be he Moor or Jew, or the offspring of these, should settle in Our Indies without Our distinct permission. Furthermore, we forbid most emphatically the immigration into New Spain of anyone newly reconciled with the Church; of the child or grandchild of those who had ever publicly worn the sanbenito; of the child or grandchild, through either male or female descent, of any person who was either burnt as a heretic or otherwise punished for the crime of heresy. Should anyone [falling under these categories] presume to violate this law, his goods will be confiscated in behalf of the royal Treasury, and upon him shall fall the full measure of Our displeasure, so that under any circumstances and for all times he shall be banished from Our Indies. Whosoever does not possess personal effects, however, shall atone for his transgression by the public infliction of one hundred lashes.

These royal enactments doubtless had some immediate effects. Together with the royal Pardon of 1605, which encouraged many Iberian Jews to remain in Europe, they may have been responsible for the small number of trials of Judaizers in the first quarter of the seventeenth century.[48]

After a short time, however, both the amnesty and the restrictive immigration laws lost their effectiveness, and the number of Portuguese New Christian residents, as well as inquisitorial defendants, increased considerably. Astute businessmen, strengthened by their inner solidarity and stimulated by their need of money to help stave off overinquisitive local officials, some of these South American settlers achieved great wealth, and at times virtually controlled the economy of their cities and regions. They were aided in their endeavors by the unwillingness of many of their Old Christian compatriots to engage in gainful employment outside landownership and public office. An old adage had it that no sooner did a Spaniard arrive in one of the colonies than he was ready to don a wig and a sword. The New Christians, on the other hand, often had to take a circuitous route to reach their American dreamland. They went to Guinea or Angola and, under the guise of bringing along slaves, found entry into Buenos Aires and vicinity. Others took service with Old Christian masters, whom they "accompanied" to the New World, subsequently to move on to Lima or another desired locality.

It was relatively easy to make a career in the Peruvian capital, grandiloquently called the "city of kings." Its Spanish population in 1630 was estimated at only 6,000 residents and 19,000 transients, in addition to a multitude of Indians, mestizos, Negroes, and Mulattoes. Many of the "pure-blooded" Christians, moreover, came from the uneducated classes and were hardly fit to engage in more advanced mercantile or administrative work. Complaining in 1580 of his inability to recruit adequate personnel for the Holy Office, Inquisitor Antonio Gutiérrez de Ulloa wrote: "In view of the few Old Christians, both learned and unlearned, who pass through these areas, we suspect that he who does not ask for such things, is not suitable for them." Cervantes once devastatingly called the Latin American colonies "a refuge and shelter of Spain's desperadoes, an asylum for fraudulent bankrupts, a safe-conduct for murderers, a cover-up for gamblers . . . a lure for loose women, a common deceit for many, and a special remedy for few." True, the great writer himself once applied for permission to travel to Latin America, and cited in his favor his former military service and loss of an arm at the battle of Lepanto. But that application seems to have been an impulsive reaction in a moment of despair, perhaps aggravated by the author's apprehensions concerning his own lack of *limpieza*. Though Cervantes did not carry out these plans, other émigrés, whose New Christian descent was more widely known (among them Matéo Alemán), did take that decisive step. On April 26, 1619, the representative of the Inquisition in Buenos Aires, Francisco de Trejo, informed his superiors in Lima of the arrival of eight ships carrying Judaizers. He suggested that drastic action was required to counteract "the facility with which the Jews enter and leave this harbor, which cannot be prevented, since, all of them being Portuguese, they cover up for one another." Four years later the Lima Holy Office complained to the Suprema in Madrid about the increasing number of "Portuguese" spreading in the provinces. These complaints, and similar reports to the king himself in 1635, went unheeded, although some officials like Captain Manuel de Frías, procurator-general of the provinces of Rio de la Plata and Paraguay, emphasized, in a lengthy memorandum of February 3, 1619, the ensuing dangers to Spanish security. De Frías pointed out that the Spanish forces in the area were not sufficiently large to resist the inroads of corsairs and other enemies, and claimed that the assailants were aided by many disloyal New Christians. Perhaps even more telling was De Frías' argument that "these Portuguese New Christians of Jewish descent, entering and leaving the provinces of Peru, belong to the rich and influential merchants, who are highly expert in all kinds of merchandise and Negro slaves," and that they were able to maintain extensive relations with their coreligionists in other parts of the New and Old Worlds. According to another official report, of 1636, the New Christians controlled the entire merchant marine, and a *limpio* Castilian had no chance of competing with them.[49]

In contrast, we hear very little about Marranos holding important positions in the two most respected occupations in Spanish America: officialdom (civil, military, and ecclesiastical) and landholding. While relatively well represented among the lower clergy, most of them probably sought to avoid the limelight connected with any high office, especially if they wished to cultivate Jewish rites in the secrecy of their homes. To be sure, according to the *Obandina* (see below), the upper echelons of the Peruvian, and indeed of all the Latin American, aristocracy and bureaucracy included many members of Jewish descent. But our detailed and relatively reliable information about non-*limpio* Spaniards is largely derived from inquisitorial records, which refer as a rule only to those accused of secret judaizing. Marranos also had every reason to shun ownership of the latifundia, considered a most desirable form of investment by their Old Christian compeers. Apart from the general legal difficulties of acquiring any real estate encountered by non-*limpio* persons, they found that the royal decree of July 23, 1559, specifically tried to perpetuate the ownership of encomiendas in the hands of the ruling Old Christian families by the exclusive system of primogeniture. More, an accusation that a particular individual was seen observing a Jewish festival or abstaining from ritualistically forbidden food often sufficed for the Holy Office to order the arrest of the "culprit" and the immediate sequestration of his property. Such a defendant still had some chance, with the aid of friends, to conceal his movable possessions or temporarily transfer them to an outsider, but landed property would almost invariably be a target for early confiscation. Nor are we likely to encounter among the inquisitorial defendants many small New Christian property owners scattered through villages like Antequera, where Trebiño de Sobremonte was arrested. Rarely did such "obscure" individuals, often living at a great distance from an inquisitorial office, come to the attention of prosecutors, or, if they did, they were probably not considered worth the expenditure of energy and money required for a lengthy investigation.[50]

Many of the New Christians of the area were neither prominent nor wealthy. Studying the Lima inquisitorial records, Günter Friedländer was able to compile the following breakdown: The 132 defendants whose occupations were mentioned in the documents, included 66 who were engaged in some form of business (including 22 traveling salesmen and peddlers, 17 shopkeepers, and 5 employees), 15 were monks and other members of the clergy, 7 physicians, 3 writers, 2 scribes, 1 lawyer, 12 artisans, 4 officials, 6 miners, 4 slave traders, 4 transport workers, 2 mariners, 2 soldiers, and 2 professional gamblers. Another occupational distribution of Marranos is reported for Buenos Aires in the early seventeenth century. Of the 96 gainfully employed persons listed, there were 34 small farmers, 25 artisans, 14 members of the merchant marine, 3 day laborers, 2 soldiers, 2 doctors, but only 4 merchants, 6 living "from their intelligence" (agents or clerics), 1 beggar, and 5 of undetermined employment. About the same time (1606), Governor Sancho de Alquiza reported home that Venezuela had only 46 foreign residents, including 41 Portuguese. Of the 36 "Portuguese" (as elsewhere, most of them doubtless were New Christians) with known occupations, 6 owned encomiendas (landed estates), and 9 others were farmers. The rest consisted mainly of artisans (4 silversmiths, 1 sword maker, 1 barber, 3 cobblers, 2 tailors, 1 cartwright, 1 carpenter, and 1 mason) and a few traders (2 grocers, 1 slave factor, 1 street vendor), in addition to 2 teachers and 1 doctor. These may not have been representative samples. Yet they offer a picture of well-diversified socioeconomic groups. Many Marranos also lived in rural districts. The mining center clustered around the great silver mountain of Potosí, which bestowed of its bounty on the whole Spanish Empire, likewise attracted New Christians, miners as well as traders, only a small fraction of whom ever came under inquisitorial purview.[51]

"GREAT CONSPIRACY"

In Lima, as on the Iberian Peninsula, it was the great wealth of the leading Marrano merchants that aroused the inquisitors' cupidity. In 1610, appetites in Buenos Aires, the southernmost outpost of the Inquisition, were sufficiently whetted for the governor and other officials to suggest to the higher authorities in Seville and Madrid the establishment of a full-fledged tribunal in the Argentinian city. Although they cogently argued that the great distance from Lima made effective prosecution of offenders extremely difficult, their suggestion for a new tribunal was rejected by the royal government for reasons of economy. This was, indeed, a financially difficult period for both the Lima Holy Office and the home government. Set up on a modest scale in 1569, with an annual royal subvention of 10,000 pesos, the Lima headquarters got along during its first decade with a budget of which that subvention constituted fully 83.85 percent. The Inquisition's total income was rounded out by the yield of fines (10.55 percent), confiscations (2.64 percent) and miscellaneous other items. Because of the expansion of its personnel (a notable example of "Parkinson's law"), the same royal subsidy dropped in 1579–85 to 51.78 percent of the total budget, while the ratio of fines and confiscations increased to 14.4 percent and nearly 20 percent, respectively. Subsequently, the broadening of the scope of inquisitorial activities, without a corresponding increase in revenue, caused a tightening of the budget. Now the Lima inquisitors had to make repeated appeals (December 30, 1594, and July 30, 1596) both to the government and private donors. Beset with grave fiscal commitments in Europe, even Philip II paid no heed to these urgent requests. Private donors were somewhat more responsive, and in

1595–1600 their gifts covered 15.15 percent of the budget. Matters were further complicated by the royal "Pardon" of 1605. Although the royal decree and the implementing order by the Suprema did not reach the Lima office until February 13, 1606, thirteen months after their promulgation in Madrid, the Peruvian authorities not only had to suspend further trials of alleged Judaizers but also were told to restitute fines and confiscated property collected (or expected to be collected) from sentences during the two years following the enactment of that decree. An even more serious situation was created by the suspension of the royal subvention in 1611 and, again, in 1629. However, neither Philip III nor Philip IV could withdraw the royal bounty for long. They soon yielded to the vigorous protests and appeals from Lima, resumed the annual subsidies, and even paid up the intervening arrears. In the meantime the Holy Office was saved by rents from earlier investments of occasional surpluses in its revenues during the last quarter of the sixteenth century. In the period 1611–18, 78.38 percent of its income outside the royal subvention was derived from rents, while confiscations brought in only 10.37 percent, and fines (principally for gaming) yielded but 8.39 percent. This disproportion became even more marked in the years 1619–25, when the Inquisition's total budget of nearly 96,000 pesos was covered mainly by the royal subsidy and rents (together with the return of capital), which contributed over 47,000 pesos each. At that time fines amounted to only 909 pesos, and donations to about 306 pesos, while there was no yield at all from confiscations.[52]

It is small wonder, then, that the Inquisition now intensified its activities, particularly in ferreting out suspected Judaizers. In an auto-da-fé staged on December 21, 1625, two Marranos perished at the stake; two others, who had committed suicide in prison, were burned in effigy; and ten more were reconciled. But this auto and a few others in the following years were mere adumbrations of the climactic performance of 1639, which resulted from the so-called *complicidad grande* (great conspiracy). At the beginning, the prosecution emphasized the political as well as religious features of that "conspiracy." The New Christians of Lima were accused of conspiring with the Dutch in both Holland and the parts of Brazil occupied by Dutch troops. They were said to have attempted not only to promote Dutch trade but also to distribute subversive Protestant books in Peru and generally prepare for the ultimate take-over of much of the Spanish colonial empire by the Dutch. To be sure, evidence of that political "conspiracy" was hard to come by, and the inquisitors concentrated on the far easier task of proving that certain defendants observed Jewish ceremonies and maintained trade relations with Jews abroad. Among other matters, they accused the defendants of sending money to a charitable Jewish society in Amsterdam for the redemption of captives taken by pirates. These disjointed bits of evidence sufficed for the inquisitors to postulate the existence of a major cabal.

As often happens, the affair was precipitated by a minor incident. A Marrano agent, Antonio Cordero, refused to make a sale on a Saturday, which led to his arrest in May 1635 and his confession, under severe torture, that he was a secret Judaizer. In this connection he implicated a number of other Marranos. But the real incentive for the mass prosecution was the presence in Lima of a growing Marrano community, which commanded great wealth. According to the official report submitted on May 18, 1636, to the Suprema in Madrid by the three inquisitors of the Lima Holy Office, Juan de Mañozca, Andrès Juan Gaytan, and Antonio de Castro y del Castillo,

for the last six to eight years a great number of Portuguese have entered this Kingdom of Peru (where even before there were many) through Buenos Aires, Brazil, New Spain, the New Kingdom [of Granada], and Puerto Bello. This city has been their goal, some arriving married, many more single. Having made themselves the masters of commerce, they almost wholly took over the so-called Street of Merchants; the [neighboring] alley became entirely theirs, as did to an even greater extent the stalls on the Plaza. They also traverse the streets with their satchels selling goods in the way the linen merchants display theirs. In this fashion they control the entire trade from brocades to sackcloth and from diamonds to cumin seed [a contemporary variant reads: from the cheapest Negro slave from Guinea to the most precious pearl], all of which goes through their hands. A Castilian who fails to enter a partnership with a Portuguese firm appears to have no prospect of success. They have cornered an entire mercantile fleet through credit they extend to one another without possessing substantial capital; they also distribute merchandise through agents of their own people throughout the kingdom.

After obtaining Cordero's confession, the inquisitors arrested his employer and two others on May 11, 1634, and seventeen more suspects three months later. On May 18, 1636, they reported to the Suprema that they had already incarcerated eighty-one persons, while eighty others under suspicion could not be accommodated in their prison, even though it had been substantially enlarged.[53]

As a result of this investigation—which, the inquisitors emphasized, enjoyed the eager, unflinching support of the viceroy, Luis Gerónimo Fernández de Cabrera, conde de Chinchón—not only the Marrano community but the whole city was seized by panic. The general feeling of insecurity was aggravated by the insolvency of the only banking house in the city, the firm of Juan de la Cueva. According to the Inquisition's report to Madrid on January 29, 1636, the bankruptcy of that bank with liabilities totaling about 1,050,000 pesos, had been brought about by the arrest of the Judaizers Diego López de Fonseca and Antonio de Acuña, each of whom admitted to holding deposits of 60,000 pesos in the bank (a similar amount had been held by Garci Mendez de Duenas, a victim condemned in the auto of 1625), on which "depended the entire operation" of Lima's economy. As usual, after the arrest of the two suspects, the Holy Office immediately sequestered their property, and no payments could be made by them to their creditors. Economic life in the city thus came almost to a standstill. The psychological impact was no less pronounced. In their own report the inquisitors emphasized that they had discovered so great a mass of Jews scattered over all sections of the kingdom "that we are led to believe that they are equal to all other nations." They added: "All the people walk around despondent; they do not trust one another," since some of the defendants had been betrayed by their best friends.[54]

Of great interest in this connection is a remarkable contemporary description of Peru—particularly of Lima, with its Calle de Mercaderes—written by a Portuguese Jew at the beginning of the seventeenth century. This anonymous writer addressed his description of the population (the mores of which he severely criticized) and of the economic and political conditions, to the authorities in Holland, where he evidently lived at that time. Apparently with a view toward a possible invasion of the country by the Dutch, he also stressed the military weakness of Lima, which had neither walls nor fortifications and only a few militiamen, permeated with little fighting spirit. Aside from the more than 9,000 Spaniards, the inhabitants included Frenchmen, Italians, Englishmen, Germans, Flemings, Greeks, Ragusans, Corsicans, and even Moriscos and some East-Indians and Chinese. He especially pointed out the presence in the city and its environs of some 40,000 Negro slaves, whose hatred of their Spanish masters could readily lead to an uprising, were it not for the ordinance forbidding them to bear arms and the inner divisions among them. That fear of attack, especially by fugitive slaves, was quite widespread, is also borne out by other contemporary records.[55]

After several more years of investigation, the Holy Office staged an auto-da-fé with great pomp on January 23, 1639. Apart from 1 bigamist, 2 persons who had broken the Inquisition's rules, and 5 witches, the condemned consisted exclusively of Judaizers, of whom 7 were acquitted, 44 were reconciled with varied punishments, and 7 were released after an abjuration *de vehementi,* while 11 were burned at the stake, 7 of them alive. One prisoner who had taken his own life, was burned in effigy. (This was the most sanguinary performance of the Peruvian Inquisition, which is said to have cremated alive a total of but 40 persons in the entire two and a half centuries of its operation.) In almost all these cases the sequestered possessions were confiscated, although the revenue resulting from the liquidation in the early years allegedly disappointed its beneficiaries. In their report of May 26, 1638, the inquisitors expostulated to the Suprema that the confiscated amounts were far less than was generally believed, because the accused had, before their arrest, secreted most of their possessions. In addition, all sorts of claimants had initiated a host of civil lawsuits against the arrested businessmen, so that the Inquisition had to appoint a special *defensor* to represent the accused, or rather its own interests. At times the inquisitors compromised with the plaintiffs and paid out certain amounts from the confiscated possessions. These settlements brought down upon them, in 1635, the wrath of the Suprema, which resented any disbursements of what it considered its legitimate spoils. In its own defense the Lima office asserted that the prisoners' liabilities had totaled some 800,000 pesos, a sum equal to the city's entire capital resources; and that failure to meet some of the claims might prove ruinous to the whole community. Despite these excuses, however, the yield of the seized properties to the income of the Holy Office was, in fact, very substantial. In the years 1626–29 the revenue from confiscations had already amounted to 52,922.31 pesos, for the first time exceeding the royal subsidy, which totaled 50,833.31 pesos. Savings from these sums, profitably invested, helped the Inquisition weather the financial storm resulting from the deficit financing of the royal Treasury during the costly final stages of the Thirty Years' War. Complaining that the three branches of the Holy Office in America cost the Treasury some 32,000 pesos a year, Philip IV after lengthy negotiations obtained the papal brief of March 10, 1627, confirmed by royal decrees in 1629–30, which obliged all Spanish-American bishoprics to give up one canonicate and turn the yield over to the Inquisition. Although this revenue was to replace the governmental subvention, the king promised in 1634 that any deficiency would be made up by the royal Treasury. Not surprisingly, therefore, the Holy Office in Lima became even more than usually reluctant to divulge to its own Suprema the value of the property confiscated during the suppression of the "great conspiracy." Modern scholars have estimated that the confiscated property yielded for the Inquisition an immediate revenue well in excess of 100,000 pesos. Even before the complete liquidation of that property, the accounts for 1631–42 showed that the "rents" had increased to 90,505.35 pesos, as against the total of 110,922.58 pesos collected from the royal subsidies and canonicates combined. Moreover, by grossly understating the revenue from confiscations, the Inquisition was able to invest its large surplus profitably. The greatest amount was collected after the auto of 1649, which yielded, according to some estimates, as we recall, the enormous sum of 3,000,000 pesos. Even if we consider this amount vastly exaggerated, there is no question that thenceforth the Inquisition was able to run its operations on a much sounder financial basis.[56]

At the same time the Lima inquisitors evidently enjoyed the full cooperation of the non-Marrano community, many members of which had long resented the prosperity of the "Portuguese" newcomers which, as usual, was magnified beyond all true proportion in the popular imagination. There doubtless also were some devout Catholics whose conscience was deeply troubled if they did not denounce suspected heretics. One Edict of Faith, addressed to all burghers and residents of the royal city, began by stating: "Inasmuch as you ought to know that, for the greater glory of the faith, it is necessary to separate the bad from the good seed and to avoid any disservice to our Lord, we order you all, collectively and severally, to declare and report to us, whenever you learn, see, or hear said about any person, alive, absent or deceased, that he or she had spoken or expressed heretical words or opinions which are suspect, erroneous, wanton, indiscreet, scandalous, or blasphemous." Incidentally, we must not entirely disregard the role played by the doctrine of *limpieza,* a rather astonishing facet of a civilization so racially mixed as that of the Latin-American countries. It cropped up even in unexpected places like the testimony taken in connection with the unrelated affairs of one Don Jacinto de Laríz, who for nearly seven years (1646–53) had served as governor of Rio de la Plata.[57]

Remarkably, the number of women sentenced in that great trial was disproportionately small. Apart from five or six "witches," none of Jewish descent, there appeared on the list only Doña Mayor de Luna, born in Seville of Portuguese parents and married to Antonio Moron, and her daughter Doña Isabel Antonia. Both ladies were reconciled, though condemned to perpetual imprisonment, deportation from the Indies, confiscation of their property, and the obligation to wear a sanbenito at each public appearance. In contrast, Isabel's husband, Rodrigo Váez Pereira, was burned alive. This female ratio was far below even the low percentage of single women who had left the Iberian Peninsula for the Americas in the sixteenth century. [58]

Among the most noteworthy victims of the Inquisition in 1639 was the so-called *capitán grande* (a designation often associated with the office of governor), Manuel Bautista Pérez, the leading Lima merchant, with a fortune estimated at half a million pesos. At the subsequent sale of his possessions, Pérez' carriage alone fetched 30,400 reals, while his palatial dwelling was known for generations as the *Casa de Pilatos.* Born in 1593 in Seville, he had come to Lima about 1620. Proud and self-assertive as he was, he refused, because he was a Spaniard by birth, to pay the "composition" which the authorities extracted from Portuguese settlers in return for a residence permit. After a struggle with the authorities lasting three years (1622–25), he won his case and went on to ever-greater business ventures. Regrettably, we have little information about the details of his far-ranging commercial undertakings, which included agriculture, mining and probably shipping. Like his confreres of other faiths, he may have been quite ruthless in his mercantile dealings. If we are to believe another victim, Francisco de Vergara, Pérez had persuaded him to advance 12,000 pesos to Don Juan de Navarrete before the latter's bankruptcy, while Pérez himself was salvaging his own investment. However, this charge, which served as an excuse for Vergara's imprudent transaction, need not be taken at face value. Manuel Bautista was at the same time known as a man of culture and some intellectual attainment. According to inquisitorial reports, "he possessed many spiritual books and often discussed theological subjects with learned churchmen of Portuguese descent." As a patron of learning, he also subsidized many worthwhile educational projects. The famous University of San Marcos inscribed literary works to him with "dedicatory lines full of adulation and encomia, assigning to him first rank [among its patrons]." It is small wonder, then, that the Marrano community considered him its leader, in the spiritual as well as the material sense. According to rumor, he maintained a synagogue, on a street named after a Christian miracle (*del Milagro*), where he conducted services and encouraged his co-religionists to hold steadfastly to their faith. The very inquisitors paid him unwitting tribute in their aforementioned report to the Suprema of 1636 (midway between his arrest and his final execution), when they wrote:

Manuel Bautista Pérez, merchant, a native of Ansan, of the district of Coimbra in the kingdom of Portugal, aged forty-six [he was, in fact, born in Seville and was then aged forty-three], is married to his relative whom he brought over from Seville and has children. He is a man enjoying considerable esteem on all sides and is held as an oracle by the Hebrew Nation, it being understood that he is foremost in the observance of the Law of Moses. He is in charge of a large mercantile enterprise worth over 130,000 pesos so far as it is known today. He is being accused by a large number of witnesses, but he remains a *negativo*.[59]

Naturally, Pérez' activities were misinterpreted by hostile neighbors, who in the course of the protracted investigation testified that he had allowed his companions to commit sacrilegious acts against the Christian faith. Others accused him of dealing with Spain's Dutch enemies in Brazil and betraying important state secrets to them. All this was pure hearsay, though not necessarily untrue. While in prison, through years of great mental anguish and physical suffering, Pérez behaved with unbending dignity. Even during repeated severe tortures he did not divulge the names of any secret Judaizers. Down to the very end he also refused to repent for his alleged sins. preferring to die as a *negativo* by being burned alive at the stake.

In some respects even more remarkable, was another martyr of the same auto-da-fé, Francisco Maldonado de Silva, a surgeon at the royal hospital of La Concepción in Chile. Born of New Christian parents in Peru, Francisco grew up as a pious Catholic. At the age of eighteen he read the apologetic classic *Scrutinium scripturarum* by Bishop Paul de Santa Maria of Burgos. Although written by a converted former rabbi for the purpose of combating Judaism, this tract had a contrary effect upon Maldonado's receptive mind, and rather set him to thinking about the essence of the Jewish faith. After further reflection and some Jewish teachings communicated to him by his theretofore very secretive father—who had been previously investigated by the Inquisition and formally "reconciled" (1601–1605)—Francisco became deeply engrossed in the study of Jewish religious thought. He was arrested in 1627, after denunciation by his two sisters, Isabella and Felipa (a nun), and was subjected to a succession of fifteen theological debates with prominent Jesuits and other Christian theologians. But he staunchly defended his newly acquired understanding of Judaism, frequently with the aid of biblical passages which he quoted in Latin from memory. At the very first hearing, he shocked the inquisitor by refusing to take the required oath according to the usual Christian formula, unless he could take it in the name of "the living God who created heaven and earth and who is the God of Israel." From time to time he submitted to the Holy Office memoranda elaborating certain theological minutiae. Deprived of pen and paper, he ingeniously contrived a method of writing on maize husks with ink made of coal dust, and a pen fashioned from a chicken leg. With these materials he also composed in prison two lengthy tracts of one hundred leaves each, which were so cleverly bound together that they had the appearance of printed pamphlets. Maldonado even succeeded in fashioning some husks into a strong rope which enabled him to escape through a window. But rather than flee for his life, he merely sought out other New Christians in the neighboring cells and tried to instill in them greater fortitude in resisting conversion. He was caught by the guards and, after an incarceration of twelve years (mainly because the Holy Office held back his execution until it could stage the major auto of 1639), he perished at the stake. He died courageously, tenaciously invoking the name of his God. Although he had become familiar with the tenets of his ancestral faith rather late in life and mainly through his own interpretation of Old Testament passages taken from the Vulgate, he was, by word and example, in life and in death, a truly "great preacher" of Judaism—as he was called not long after his death by Isaac Cardoso.[60]

INTERNATIONAL REPERCUSSIONS

The "grand auto-da-fé" of 1639, celebrated with much fanfare in Lima and widely publicized throughout the Spanish possessions, must have made a profound impression upon the Marranos of other lands. It doubtless focused attention on South America, especially because of its connection, however remote, with the struggle between Holland and Portugal over the possession of Recife. Nor could the West-European Jews overlook the further prosecutions of their secret coreligionists by the Lima Inquisition in the 1640s which, though for the most part ending in acquittals and reconciliations, greatly increased the insecurity of the surviving Marranos on the vast continent. Understandably, the example of the Dutch, occupying an important area of Brazil, liberating the Marranos there from inquisitional prosecutions, and making possible the establishment of the first professing Jewish community on the South-American continent, must have opened the eyes of some of the imperiled Peruvian New Christians to the changing constellation of power in Europe concomitant with the Thirty Years' War. We need but recall the arguments presented in the anonymous Jewish memorandum cited above. Going beyond empty dreams about the downfall of the oppressive Spanish regime, some Lima Marranos may have actually been in touch with the Jews in Recife. There may even have been a kernel of truth in the testimony of those witnesses who accused the *capitán grande* of conspiratorial contacts. It has been suggested that Manuel Bautista Pérez himself at one time devised a plan for blowing up the Spanish arsenal of San Guadelupe.[61]

Spain's growing military and financial weakness and its diminishing grip on its far-flung empire, may also have prompted a former Marrano, Simon de Cáceres, one of Oliver Cromwell's Jewish intelligencers, to conceive a scheme for an English conquest of Chile. In 1655 he submitted a memorandum to the lord protector proposing a number of military and naval moves which would lead to both the occupation of a large strip of land along the Pacific coast of South America and greater efficiency in attacking the Spanish silver fleets, which transported precious metals from the New World to the Old. In view of the relative weakness of the Spanish garrisons, De Cáceres thought that these objectives could be attained if "his highnes would prepare foure friggats or shippes of warre, together with foure victualling shippes ladden with provisions of food and ammunition, and about 1000 souldiers to bee imbarqued in them." Reciting various other preparations necessary for a successful expedition, Simon enumerated a number of benefits which would accrue to England:

1. The countrey of Chili is unquestionably stored with gold beyond Peru, or any countrey in the world, there being few parts of it but yeeld it. . . .

2. That countrey hath in it a wholsome and well-temper'd ayre, abounding in fruites, corn, cattle, fish and fowle for the life of man.

3. There is in this people an irreconcilable hatred against the Spanyards for theire former cruelties, and will side with any people for the rooting of them out; and are the most warlick of all the Indians.

4. Besides these things, the fregatts will serve to scowre the whole south sea, upon the West-Indie coast, and to take the Spanish treasure (as hath bene formerly advised) from Chili to Arica, and thence to Panama, by Lima, and Guavaquil.

5. They will serve to seize the two ships, which use yeerly to come from the Philippinas unto Acapulco, laden with the riches of the East-Indies of incredible value.

6. Thereby the Spaniard being assaulted on both sides and seas at once, will be utterly dismaied and broken, and that by farre sooner, then by falling on him only by the north sea-side.

To implement this proposal De Cáceres suggested that he would be prepared to "engage some young men of my owne nation, and promise to conduct them in my owne person, by the Lord's permission." Undoubtedly, this native Portuguese, who had spent many years in Hamburg and London engaged in a successful business career, envisaged the collaboration of Dutch and English Jews in carrying out his scheme.[62]

Why did De Cáceres select Chile as the preferred target? His immediate incentive may have come from information received about the growing unrest among the Araucanians and other Chilean Indians (to whom he alluded as "most warlick") in that country, unrest which, in February 1655, led to their memorable insurrection against the Spanish regime. Though not comparable to the Aztecs and the Incas in their cultural evolution, Chile's Indian tribes, particularly in the southern sector, fiercely defended their independence and engaged in an intermittent guerrilla war, which was facilitated by the high mountains and extensive forests of the area. But the northern tribes were quickly enslaved by the conquistadores and were treated very harshly by the white settlers thereafter. Certainly, the early admonitions of Bartolomé de las Casas (1474–1566), the famous Dominican "Apostle of the Indies," who demanded humane treatment of the native population throughout Spanish America, had few enduring effects. His eloquent pleas for social justice may well have been stimulated by his consciousness of his Jewish heritage. Américo Castro has convincingly and repeatedly argued that Las Casas was of Jewish descent—a fact which in Castro's opinion explains not only Las Casas' mentality and behavioral characteristics (sensitively perceived especially by Marcel Bataillon) but also his abiding interest in science and history. These interests were, indeed, shared by such distinguished New Christian contemporaries as Gonzalo Fernández de Oviedo, Alonso de Santa Cruz, José de Acosta, Andréa Laguna, the Portuguese García de Orta, and many others who had fewer connections with the Iberian empires. We shall presently see that they found worthy successors in the León Pinelo brothers. Las Casas' pleas in behalf of the Indian population made a strong impression on Spain's ruling circles, despite the contrary arguments advanced by his leading opponent, Juan Ginés de Sepúlveda. The ideas of Las Casas contributed greatly to humanizing some of the early enactments of Charles V and Philip II in favor of the Indian majority. These decrees proved quite ineffective in the centers of Spanish administration in Mexico City and Lima, however; and they were totally disregarded by the colonists in the more distant provinces. The resulting harsh treatment of the Indian slaves in Chile—at times they were deliberately maimed by their masters in order to prevent their escape (this cruel measure was facilitated by the antinative decrees issued in 1608 and 1625)— played into the hands of the insurrectionary leaders.[63]

At the same time the strategic weakness of the colony was demonstrated by the successful operation over the preceding decades of the piratical *Hermandad de la Bandera Negra* (Brotherhood of the Black Banner), headed by a New Christian, Subatol Deul, in collaboration with Henry Drake, son of the famous "sea dog" Sir Francis Drake. This Brotherhood frequently attacked Spanish shipping. Ultimately defeated by a Spanish expeditionary force in 1640, Subatol disappeared among the native Indian tribes, married the daughter of an Indian chief, and probably continued to agitate among his new allies against the hated Spanish rule. (In 1926 a treasure-trove of the Brotherhood was discovered which contained, among other things, documents written in a mixture of Hebrew and other characters.) In the end, however, De Cáceres' plan was not followed up by Cromwell and his advisers, probably because they learned that the Spaniards had entered into negotiations with the rebellious Araucanians and had temporarily pacified them by promising to adhere to the noteworthy Pact of Quillen of 1640 (which left the land south of the Bio-bio River in Indian hands). And, in general, by 1655, England was more interested in fighting its powerful rival, the Netherlands, than in plotting against the rapidly declining might of Spain.[64]

UNUSUAL PHENOMENA

Of course, not all South American New Christians were secret Judaizers. Among the sincere Christians were members of the distinguished *converso* family whose most illustrious scion was Antonio Rodríguez de León Pinelo. In the words of the Argentinian historian Bartolomé Mitre, this "jurist, historian and writer had no equal in the Americas. He was the most notable man of letters of his period and, like Justinian, he gave his name to the largest monument of early American legislation." After his grandfather Juan López had been burned as a Judaizer at a Lisbon auto in 1595, his father, Diego López of Lisbon, emigrated to Buenos Aires in 1604 and, after a successful business career, became an influential churchman. Beginning in 1628 he even served as chaplain and major-domo to Archbishop Fernando Arias de Ugarte, whom he followed to Lima two years later. After Arias' death, Diego published an epitome of the prelate's life. In 1630 he was appointed *regidor* of the important city of Cuzco. Yet it was only the archbishop's protective hand that saved him from the Inquisition, which on May 15, 1637, transmitted to the Suprema in Madrid a dossier containing extensive testimonies "from the province of Tucumán, the port of Buenos Aires, and the city of Potosí, where he [López] had resided a long time and accumulated much capital in business. He was always held to be a New Christian." Diego's son Antonio, with the surname De León Pinelo, successfully combined profound, multifaceted learning with practical acumen and amazing industry. Probably born in either Lisbon or Valladolid in 1590–91, he attended schools in Buenos Aires and Cordoba (Tucumán), as well as the University of San Marcos in Lima, where he secured the degree of licentiate in law (1619) and later served as a substitute lecturer. While still in Lima he prepared his voluminous *Epítome de la Bibliografía oriental y occidental náutica y geográfica*, first published in Madrid in 1629, an astounding monument of erudition, which attested the high level of culture attained by Peruvian intellectuals at the beginning of the seventeenth century. Even the Preface, dedicated to the king, was a learned piece, provided with thirty-eight scholarly notes. To be sure, León Pinelo accepted many current notions rather uncritically. In a discussion of languages, for instance, he naively referred to the Hebrew idiom as "the mother of all languages, spoken, according to many scholars, by our father, Adam. It remained the only language in the world until the building of the Tower of Babel." In this work, León Pinelo laid the foundations for all subsequent bibliographical studies relating to the Americas. It was compiled largely on the basis of books and manuscripts Antonio had assembled in his own noteworthy private library, which he later bequeathed to the Council of the Indies. When in 1623 he returned to Spain, he embarked on an even more important work, his recodification of the laws concerning Spain's American colonies—the first compilation of which, promulgated in 1543, had become outdated. By 1635, Antonio and several associates completed the first draft of the gigantic restatement of the "Laws of the Indies" in nine books containing some ten thousand laws. He continued to work on this *magnum opus* to the end of his life, in 1660. It was principally on the basis of his additional materials that the *Recopilación de Leyes de los Reynos de las Indias* was finally promulgated by Charles II in 1681. Among his other works, we need but mention *El Paraíso en el Nuevo Mundo,* published in two volumes in Seville in 1656 and *Anales de Madrid, Reinado de Felipe III, años 1598 a 1621.* Probably a sincere Catholic, Antonio may have been prompted by his family history to assert time and again that he intended to "adjust all his propositions to the letter of Scripture." At the same time, he did not fail to emphasize the unique quality of the Holy Land, with which he wrote, no country "can be compared, for God Himself has chosen it, called it the best, and always designated it as His." His Madrid friends included Lope de Vega, to whom he undoubtedly furnished many details and insights for the dramas dealing with Latin American topics. Antonio's brother Diego de León Pinelo (died in 1671), the third son of Diego López of Lisbon, studied in Salamanca in 1627–32, after which he became professor of canon law and rector of the University of San Marcos, official "protector of Indians of the Kingdom of Peru," and a close collaborator of the distinguished viceroy, P. F. de Castro, Count de Lemos. He wrote a number of juridical works, and was later styled by Father Antonio Larrouy "the prime literary glory of his country."[65]

It is small wonder, then, that even before the great trials of the 1630s, the wealth and intellectual distinction of some New Christians aroused the envy and cupidity not only of the Inquisition and other enemies but also of would-be blackmailers. Literary extortion was facilitated by the frequently partisan and slipshod historical literature of the time, which abounded in writings based upon partially or fully fabricated documents, used to defend a variety of claims. We recall that the Jesuit Jerónimo Román de la Higüera's inventions about Spanish Jewry's ancient origin and its readiness to accept Christianity were used as an argument against the racialist statutes spreading in seventeenth-century Spain. It was even easier to establish, through genuine or spurious genealogies, the Jewish, Moorish, or heretical ancestry of some prominent citizens either to discredit them or in order to undermine the general acceptance of the principle of *limpieza*.

Opportunity thus beckoned to a local writer, Pedro Mexía de Obando (or Ovando), an adventurer who had traveled through many countries, as well as through most provinces of Latin America, and had developed, on the side, a certain expertise in genealogical research. He could utilize his data, authentic or falsified, to enhance or lower the dignity of prominent Peruvian families. Unlike the authors of the concise *Libro verde de Aragón* and Castilian *Tizón de la nobleza,* Mexía de Obando produced a large volume in which he discussed the antecedents of many families with feigned "impartiality," but in a way which cast aspersion on some of their living members. For example, being resentful of the then Peruvian viceroy, Francisco de Borja y Aragón, prince of Esquilache, a man equally distinguished as an administrator and a poet, Mexía de Obando devoted a long chapter to "the genealogy and descent of the most noble and ancient house of Borja, which touches on many ancient matters." In this chapter, more by indirection, the author was able to allude to the alleged Jewish ancestry of Popes Calixtus III and Alexander VI of the House of Borja (Borgia). Simultaneously, we are informed by a fiscal of the Inquisition, Licentiate Gaspar de Valdespina, Mexía de Obando collected from certain individuals fees of 50 pesos or more for the inclusion, and probably also for the suppression, of data bearing on their own racial purity. Not surprisingly, the publication of the book in Lima in 1621, under the provocative title *Obandina, donde se trata la naturaleza y origen de la nobleza política y de muchas y nobilisimas casas, con los que an pasado de ellos a estos Reynos y al de Nueva Espana,* "created a great scandal in the whole place and many readers came to us [the Holy Office] to denounce it." The result was that, after further investigation, the Inquisition condemned the book, destroying all the available texts. Only a single copy survived, which the distinguished Spanish historian Manuel Serrano y Sanz republished with a lengthy introduction in 1915. The action by the Inquisition evidently prevented Mexía de Obando from publishing other works, including a continuation of the *Obandina* under the equivalent English title "A Chronicle of the Civil Nobility." [66]

In the 1630s there also was an upsurge of prosecutions by the newly established Inquisition of Cartagena. On the whole, however, this center of cosmopolitan trade, with ships of various countries frequenting its harbors, meted out rather moderate sentences to its defendants. Perhaps the New Christian population of the city and its environs was distinguished by neither numbers nor wealth to attract much attention. In 1615, for instance, there were only two prisoners in the local inquisitorial jail, and only one of them, the Portuguese Francisco Gómez de León, was accused of judaizing. He was reconciled in 1617–18. According to some estimates, the Spanish population of Cartagena at the beginning of the seventeenth century did not exceed 500 souls. Hence the "Portuguese" residents may have often been mere transients. Their wide-ranging migrations are well illustrated by the career of one of the accused, Baltasar de Araujo of Bayona, Spanish Galicia. At the age of ten, Baltasar had joined his parents and eight siblings in trying to get to Salonica via Flanders and Venice. During a sojourn of four months in Venice, the boy was circumcised and sent to a Jewish school, where he studied the Bible and the Mishnah. Upon reaching Salonica, he traveled with an elder brother to Alexandria and later, after a risky visit to Spain, went to Constantinople. It was in Turkey rather than in his home country that he was taught by a friend the principles of Christianity and was persuaded to go to the New World in quest of riches. But there he reverted to secret Judaism. Another New Christian, Luis Franco Rodríguez, a native of Lisbon, embarked in Seville for America, under the pretense of serving as a page to a legitimate traveler. Otherwise he could not have emigrated to the Indies, particularly since his mother, two brothers, and a sister-in-law had been arrested in Seville, while his father and three other siblings had escaped to

Flanders. In Zaragoza de las Indias Franco Rodríguez established himself as a successful businessman. Before long, he was denounced by other New Christian defendants (1624) but he was reconciled, losing only one-third of his property, and being exiled from Cartagena and Zaragoza. Remarkably, Franco Rodríguez knew some Hebrew, a rather rare phenomenon among the New World Marranos. Another Cartegena defendant of special interest was Luis Gómez Barreto, who was arrested in 1636, at the age of sixty-five. He had come to Cartagena via West Africa and Brazil and, after acquiring some money, had purchased the post of *depositario general de Cartagena*. Perhaps because of his official connection, he was acquitted by the local Inquisition, but he was rearrested in 1648 on orders of the Suprema, because of a damning report by a visiting inspector, Pedro de Medina Rico. Ultimately Gómez Barreto was again discharged from prison, this time at the age of eighty-two.[67]

Gómez Barreto's vicissitudes demonstrated the general instability of living under the permanent threat of even so relatively mild a tribunal as that of Cartagena. At his original investigation, in 1636–38, he was but one of a considerable number of Judaizers being tried by the Holy Office. Nine of the defendants, an unusually high proportion, were completely absolved, and their sequestered goods were returned. Eight others were reconciled, with penalties rarely spelled out in detail; but no one was executed. Even more than in Lima, the inquisitorial officials were busy fighting among themselves and with the secular authorities, rather than trying to ferret out heretics. On November 9, 1645, the Junta de Guerra de Indias had to intervene by urging the Suprema to instruct the Cartagena tribunal not to excommunicate the governor and the captain-general, because such moves might undermine the authority of the entire government. It also appears that, despite the proximity of northern Brazil, with its growing Jewish population, relatively few Judaizers chose to settle in the northern parts of Spanish South America or the adjoining islands, and thus offered fewer targets for the inquisitorial prosecution.[68]

Basically the same conditions prevailed also in the other South American colonies, except Paraguay, whose socialist theocracy, established by the Jesuit missions, was unfavorable to the private enterprise system under which alone the Marrano merchants were able to function more freely. True, some New Christians, like the León Pinelos, held public office, which often could be acquired by purchase, a system openly encouraged by the central administration. But such employment was highy precarious, because anyone desiring to replace them often needed but a denunciation to the Inquisition, which might readily prove their lack of *limpieza* and thus disqualify them from office, or worse. Moreover, many offices were preempted in Paraguay by Jesuits, who in the seventeenth century, as we recall, increasingly followed a racialist trend in the admission of new members. Curiously, it was precisely there that the biblical legislation played a greater constitutional role and more deeply affected the daily life of the people than anywhere else in the Western Hemisphere, except perhaps in the English colonies of North America. It was this impact of ancient Israelitic law which made François René de Chateaubriand sing the praises of that "evangelical republic" which had been formed out of the "wandering tribes of Paraguayan savages." This early nineteenth-century spokesman for the Catholic revival further claimed that "while Europe had as yet but barbarian constitutions, formed by time and chance, the Christian religion revived in the New World all the wonders of the ancient systems of legislation." Chateaubriand wrote this encomium at a time when the glaring shortcomings of the Jesuit administration—the "socialism" of which had by no means prevented harsh discrimination against the Indians, discrimination which provoked native uprisings in 1660 and later—had led to Paraguay's almost total ruination.[69]

BRAZIL'S INDIVIDUALITY

An entirely different development took place in Brazil. Here the Portuguese performed one of the greatest colonial experiments in racial mixture called "lusotropical" by one of the foremost Brazilian anthropologists Gilberto Freyre. His major, somewhat overapologetic, thesis that, as a result of this moderately successful blending, there emerged in Brazil "a *mestizo* society, sociologically Christian in the decisive aspects of its behavior and in the dominant traits of its culture," has often been criticized, but one cannot deny the Brazilian society's distinctive melting-pot qualities. It appears that this process was facilitated during the formative sixteenth and seventeenth centuries by the absence of a full-fledged local Inquisition along Mexican or Peruvian lines.[70]

For a time even many Jesuits, including their outstanding leader, António Vieira, were opposed to that institution. Not that religious martyrs were lacking among the New Christians. From time immemorial bishops had exercised surveillance over heterodox groups and individuals everywhere in the Catholic world. On February 12, 1579, Cardinal Henry, who had long served as inquisitor-general of Portugal, specifically recommended to Bishop António Barreiros of Salvador-Bahia that he investigate the behavior of the New Christians in the province. He also suggested that Barreiros might benefit from the cooperation of some Jesuits, particularly Fray Luis da Grã. But partly because defendants had to be sent to Lisbon for trial, their number was not very large. Only after the appearance of a visiting inspector *(visitador)* from the Lisbon office and his proclamation of an Edict of Faith—as happened for the first time in 1591 when Licentiate Heitor Furtado de Mendoça came to Bahia and, after spending two years there, continued his visitation in Recife in 1593–95—did prosecutions increase in number and intensity. However, before the Inquisition could strike deep roots in the country, its operations against the New Christians, the major class of defendants, were suspended by the "General Pardon" promulgated by Pope Clement VIII on August 23, 1604, and King Philip III on January 16, 1605. Brazil's Marrano community was assessed the amount of 18 coutos reis, estimated at some 45,000 cruzados, as their contribution to the huge total ransom of some 2,000,000 cruzados (according to the varying computations discussed in the last chapter). Under the circumstances, the likelihood of condemnation for heresy appeared sufficiently remote not to deter numerous Marranos from settling in the country. Moreover, Portugal used Brazil as a penal colony for "criminals" of all kinds and forcibly settled there a number of New Christians sentenced by the Inquisition in the mother country. It thus indirectly fostered the establishment of foci of clandestine Judaism in Bahia and other parts of the colony. It is not surprising, therefore, that among the relatively few white settlers in Brazil, estimated in 1612 at no more than some 44,150 (after an increase from some 17,200 in 1570) by a contemporary writer (probably Diogo de Campos Moreno), the ratio of New Christians may have been as high as 10-20 percent of the population in the main cities such as Bahia, Olinda, Rio de Janeiro, and Recife, all of which "were mere villages in comparison with Mexico City, Lima, and Potosí" (Boxer). The percentage of "criminals, degraded persons and fugitives" was also very high. According to a report sent to the Madrid Suprema in 1629, they totaled some 10,000 persons.[71]

More importantly, before long the Dutch cast covetous eyes on the promising land. While they greatly feared the prowess of the Spanish army, they generally held the Portuguese troops in low esteem. They were emboldened by the aforementioned description of the weakness of the Peruvian defenses submitted to their authorities by a Portuguese Jew. Not by mere chance, the foundation of the Dutch West India Company, in 1621, after two decades of desultory talks, coincided with the expiration of the twelve-year truce between the Netherlands and Spain. Although that truce had been limited to Europe, the new Company now felt freer to attack the Spanish-Portuguese silver fleets, bringing home much booty. The acceleration of these attacks is evident in the increase of Portuguese ships captured by the Dutch, from 28 in 1616 to 70 in 1623 and a total of 477 more in the following fourteen years. In 1628 alone, the loot captured by Admiral Piet Pieterszoon Heyn and his associates was valued at 11,500,000 to 15,000,000 florins. As observed by Charles Ralph Boxer, "the humiliating nature of the catastrophe, and the fact that it had not cost a drop of Dutch blood, was even harder to bear than the loss of the treasure itself." [72]

However, the directors of the Company and the Dutch government realized that these windfalls could not last forever. Hence they slowly prepared for the occupation of parts of the Brazilian mainland, whose sparse and scattered settlements under a weak and diffuse administration were particularly tempting. In a surprise attack in 1624 the Dutch occupied Bahia, the capital and main harbor of the vast colony. According to rumors widespread then and later further exaggerated by both the populace and historians, the Brazilian Marranos had incited the Dutch to invade Brazil. Some local New Christians, as well as many Old Christians, may indeed have helped the arriving Dutch, at least after returning to the city, from which they had fled before the occupation. According to a report *(relatorio)* submitted by Vicar Manoel Themudo of the Cathedral of Bahia in 1632, his investigation of the events in the city in 1624–25 had produced seventeen witnesses who incriminated twenty-two persons or groups. Among the names he gave, only six can be identified as New Christian. Other Marranos coming from Holland joined the new administration of the conquered colony. In 1641 the inquisitors of Évora claimed that their Office possessed transcripts of trials which had proved that some Marranos had intervened to bring about the fall of Bahia and, later, Pernambuco. These testimonies were, of course, but an attempt to whitewash the local Portuguese commanders, who had failed to prepare these major Brazilian cities for the expected attack. In its report of June 23, 1623, to King Philip IV, the Council of Portugal emphasized the natural weakness of a coast "extending over more than 800 leagues" and suggested that at least Bahia and Recife be strongly fortified. Nowhere, however, did the Council voice any apprehension about an alleged presence of a New Christian "fifth column." Nor should we overlook the deep cleavages between the attitudes of the Portuguese colonists and their Spanish overlords before 1640. While for strategy-oriented Spain considerations like those suggested by the Council of Brazil carried considerable weight, for the Portuguese, many of whom hated their Spanish rulers, Brazil was of mainly economic, rather than political, interest. On the other hand, after the city's occupation by the Dutch forces, their proclamation of general liberty of conscience caused the return to Bahia of a considerable number of refugees, including many New Christians. These "traitors" naturally had every reason to encourage the Dutch to resist the return of the Portuguese. If we are to believe the notation of a Portuguese soldier of April 12, 1625, a Dutch prisoner claimed that the Dutch forces were very strong "and that many Jews and Jewesses, who had come with them from Holland and were now inside Bahia, encouraged them to defend themselves, and supported them with large sums of money." [73]

This short-lived venture, to be sure, ended in disaster when the Portuguese recaptured the city within less than a year. But it gave the Dutch valuable experience and much information about conditions in the country, and enabled them to establish numerous contacts with disaffected segments of the local population, including some New Christians. After six years they made another, more sustained effort to seize the territory of Pernambuco in the northeast section of Brazil which, because of its relative proximity to Portugal, Angola, and the West-Indian islands appeared particularly propitious to international trade. Some Portuguese New Christians had long been settled in the area and, as appeared in the testimony presented to Furtado de Mendoça in 1593–95, had even maintained a secret synagogue in the town of Camaragibe. From Pernambuco the Dutch West India Company hoped to fan out into the interior and ultimately take over the entire colony. Allegedly, some sanguine New Christians, as we recall, hoped that the élan of the Dutch expansion would bring the Dutch forces into Peru and other Spanish possessions in South America; while Simon de Cáceres was soon to propose to Cromwell that the English take over Chile. Such expectations were greatly encouraged when, in 1630, the Dutch established their own regime in Recife which, especially under the brilliant administration of Count Johan Maurits (John Maurice) of Nassau-Siegen (1637–44), embraced several captaincies. Well-garrisoned, the Dutch colony was rapidly advancing economically, as well as politically.[74]

From the outset both the local Portuguese officials and Spain's central authorities tried to lay the blame on the New Christian minority for having first incited the West India Company to invade and then collaborated with the occupying forces and subsequent administration. Apart from the usual search for a scapegoat, on whom they could blame the surrender of Bahia in 1624 almost without the firing of a shot, the Portuguese rulers had too guilty a conscience not to expect the oppressed Marranos to view favorably their liberation by the more tolerant Dutch. On the Dutch side, too, the expectation of such Marrano collaboration may have been nurtured by the Amsterdam Jews, who were in frequent contact with the secret Judaizers in South America. However, even without such encouragement, many Dutch businessmen and

politicians were convinced that all of Portugal's American possessions were ripe for foreign conquest because of the Portuguese
settlers' general dislike of the Spanish regime after 1580, as well as
the discontent brewing among the Negro slaves. In fact, in his
Toortse der Zeevaart (Torch of Navigation), published in 1623,
Dierick Ruiters sweepingly predicted that the crypto-Jews—who,
he contended, formed the majority of inhabitants in the cities
between the Amazon and the Rio de la Plata—"would rather see
two Orange flags than one inquisitor." To be sure, Willem Usselinx, the main promoter of the idea of a West India Company, was
less sanguine. As a young man he had lived in the Azores and there
imbibed many anti-Jewish prejudices. He now condemned the
Portuguese New Christians as "a faithless and pusillanimous race,
enemies to all the world and especially to all Christians, caring
not whose house burns, so long as they warm themselves at the
ashes," and added that they "would rather see 100,000 Christians
perish than suffer the loss of 100 crowns." [75]

In truth, however, the New Christian communities were as
divided on this issue as on many others. To begin with, a number
of members were genuinely professing Catholics, and as such
abhorred the Dutch heretics. Others must have anticipated with
trepidation the prospect of pillage by an invading army. That
these fears were far from unfounded could be seen from the well-
attested chagrin of the mercenaries under Dutch command at
finding the occupied Bahia houses devoid of precious jewels, garments, or furnishings. Moreover, many New Christians doubtless
felt less insecure under a Portuguese administration (albeit dependent on the Spanish monarchy after 1580) than under direct
Spanish rule, since the principle of *limpieza* had fewer adherents
in the Portuguese colonies, and there was no effective Inquisition
to enforce it on the spot. This was particularly true of the
southern parts of the country, around Rio de Janeiro and São
Paulo, which did not even have to cope with *visitadores* from the
Lisbon Holy Office. As a result, these regions had few Marrano
victims. Referring to São Paulo, the present Brazilian metropolis,
Paulo Prado writes: "The fact is that no other populated locality
in our colonial territory gave the immigrant Jew a better reception." Furthermore, the enormous economic impact of sugar

production and distribution, in which the New Christians had a vital role, blunted the edge of inquisitorial prosecutions throughout the country. "There is evidence to the fact," observed Gilberto Freyre, "that he [the Jew] was one of the most active agents in the winning of a market for the sugar producers of Brazil. . . . He would appear to have been the most efficient of those technicians responsible for the setting up of the first sugar mills. The history of patriarchal society in Brazil is, for this reason, inseparable from the history of the Jew in America." That is also why the New Christian descendants of Jews later suffered from relatively little discrimination, even if they did not altogether succeed in concealing their Jewish ancestry. Until 1624, therefore, most of them seem to have been patriotic Portuguese, as were the majority of their Old Christian countrymen, although in general, religious, regional, or local loyalties exceeded attachment to king and country. Even among many secret Judaizers, the prospect of financial losses as a result of war may well have counterbalanced the expectation of greater religious toleration under the Dutch conquerors. Once the Dutch occupation was accomplished, however, the majority of them probably heaved a sigh of relief and ultimately found it to their advantage to collaborate with their new rulers.[76]

Of course, New Christians and professing Jews residing in Holland had every reason to support their country in its military and maritime ventures. This phenomenon lent itself to easy exaggeration. In a memorandum submitted to the Suprema in Madrid on April 23, 1634, Captain Esteban de Ares Fonseca blamed the success of the Dutch expeditions on the Amsterdam Jews, as well as the Brazilian New Christians. His tale, though provided with the names of specific persons and locations, has long been discounted as in part pure fabrication and in part vast exaggeration. He stated:

The Jews of Amsterdam were responsible for the capture of Pernambuco & the principal one was one Antonio Vaez Henriques alias Mosen Coen, who went with the said Hollanders & instructed them & gave them plans showing how to take the said place, for he had spent many days in the said Pernambuco & was well acquainted with the entrances & the exits. The said Hollanders did this by his secret counsel & he lived with them in the said Pernambuco for more than a year. He is now a merchant in Seville & is nothing but a spy to learn when the fleet comes & goes and when an assault can be made, so as to give information as he did at the capture of the fleet by Piter Hens [Piet Heyn], in whose company was this said Antonio Vaez. Last year this spy came to Amsterdam & said he wanted to submit a plan for the capture of Habana & the Hollanders tried to go with a great armada. . . .

The capture of the island of Fernando de Noroña was by order of a Jew of Amsterdam named Francisco de Campos, who had been hidden there & who is now captain of the said island. This captain has moreover as his lieutenant in the said island a brother named Manuel de Campos alias Isaac de Campos and many others whom they called to populate the said island, which I am informed can easily be retaken, as they have only 32 soldiers & the population is very small & he has only four pieces of cannon. Their only hope is based on the fact that the entrance is very narrow. The fathers of these Jews are in the said Amsterdam & the States make much account of them. . . .

The West India Company, which is a Brazilian company and composed of pirates, is governed entirely by Jews of Amsterdam, for all the rich ones give their money for the said company.

We have seen in another context that the last statement was completely untrue and that the share of Jews in the early stages of the West India Company was quite small. Similarly, the Dutch could rely on information given them by two Dutch mariners who had been imprisoned in Bahia for some time and were subsequently released. In 1630, too, it was Antonio Dias Paparrobalos, a former resident of Pernambuco but now a Dutch Jew, who helped guide the Dutch forces through the unknown territory. Even the reference to Fernando de Noronha Island has an ironical twist, since the island was originally discovered by, and named after, an early New Christian explorer in behalf of the Portuguese regime.[77]

Inquisitorial witnesses, moreover, were prone to accuse even New Christians residing in the Spanish possessions of collaborating with the Dutch conquerors in parts of Brazil. In fact, despite numerous obstacles placed in their way by Spanish law and administrative chicaneries, Pernambucan and other Brazilian businessmen had long cultivated fairly extensive trade relations with the neighboring Spanish colonies, especially to the south. During the Lima Inquisition's lengthy interrogations related to the "great conspiracy" in 1635–39, a witness testified that one of the defendants, Simon Ossorio (or Rodríguez), a twenty-eight-year-old Flemish New Christian residing in Quito, had maintained close relations with the Dutch in Recife. Simon had allegedly boasted that he and his brother had invested "8,000 ducats in the squadron dispatched by the Dutch Company to parts of Brazil against his Majesty [the king of Spain]." For these and other offenses, Simon was condemned to abjuration *de vehementi,* 100 lashes, six years of galley slavery, and lifelong exile from the Indies.[78]

In Spain, too, the sudden loss of Bahia caused consternation in government circles and among the public. Three months after the event it was the subject of an anxious debate in the Madrid Council of State. Even after the recapture of Bahia by the Portuguese in 1625, Lope de Vega wrote the play *El Brasil restituido,* in which a New Christian, Bernardo, was presented as boasting that his "nation" had invited the Dutch to come and free them from another dreaded visitation by an inspector of the Lisbon Inquisition. The actual record of the Dutch takeover, however, shows that Jewish collaboration was very minor. We recall that as late as 1632, seven years after Bahia's reconquest in 1625, Manoel Themudo's investigation of all Portuguese subjects who had remained in the city or had otherwise been in contact with the Dutch occupying forces, identified only 6 New Christians in a total of 22 such alleged traitors. On the other hand, there also were some New Christian fighters on the Portuguese side; among them Mateus Lopes Franco, a native of Oporto or Lisbon and owner of a sugar mill, and the landowner Diogo Lopes Ulhoa. Mateus' patriotic services did not spare him from being arrested as a Judaizer, transported to Lisbon for trial, and sentenced to death. But, perhaps in consideration of his services to the country, he was ultimately released.[79]

After Johan Maurits' return to Holland in 1644, however, a successful rebellion of the local Portuguese, led by João Fernandes Vieira and aided by the Portuguese Crown, placed Recife under a prolonged siege and finally led to the expulsion of the Dutch in 1654. The West India Company, as a corporation bent on quick profits, had only halfheartedly supported the actual colonization of Pernambuco and had not been prepared to make the necessary long-term sacrifices in blood and money to maintain that outpost.

It has been estimated that in the years 1623–36 the Company spent 45,000,000 florins on the conquest and administration of its Brazilian acquisition. At the same time its revenues from the area, including 547 Iberian ships and other booty captured, yielded no more than 37,000,000 florins. Nor was the deficit made up by a favorable balance of trade. For the Dutch government, too, the Brazilian undertaking was but a side issue in its major imperial schemes, and as such, was subject to sudden changes of policy under different imperial constellations. After 1640 Portugal's separation from Spain, and her growing rapprochement with England, offered a much greater threat to Holland's economic and political security than did the various schemes (like the aforementioned plan for a sort of continental blockade) propounded by Spain's Philip IV. Before long, the weakness of the Dutch in Brazil was compounded by Holland's war with England, as well as by the great difficulties, both political and financial, which the Company was facing at home. An opposition party, led by the influential Bicker brothers, after their successful manipulation of the Company's shares in its early stages, now agitated for its complete liquidation. Since the directors were unable to distribute regular dividends to shareholders, the anti-management group gained more and more adherents in business and government circles in Amsterdam. By 1644, at the time of Johan Maurits' resignation, there was talk of merging the Company with the more prosperous East India Company. Although this danger to its identity was averted, its income rapidly declined and it could offer but limited assistance to its officials in Brazil. Ultimately, despite the huge compensation of 8,000,000 florins which Portugal paid the Company in 1661 as an indemnity for its Brazilian possessions, it had to be totally reorganized in 1674.[80]

AUSPICIOUS TURNING POINT

The Dutch conquest opened a new chapter in Jewish history in the New World. For the first time Jews as a group could publicly profess Judaism. There was no absence of opposition, to be sure. The Portuguese Christian settlers resented the favors extended by the government to their formerly deprecated Marrano compatriots, as well as to the numerous professing Jews arriving from Europe. Most of the latter had a command of both Dutch and Portuguese and could be used to good advantage as official interpreters. They also brought with them extensive contacts and considerable experience in international trade. The major articles of export from Brazil, sugar and brazilwood—the former was called by the seventeeth-century author of the *Diálogos das Grandezas do Brasil* (probably the New Christian Ambrósio Fernándes Brandão) "the principal nerve and substance of the country's wealth"—were to a large extent handled by New Christians, on both sides of the ocean. A fairly typical success story was that of Moses Navarro, who had come to Brazil as a naval cadet in the expeditionary force of 1630 but soon thereafter left the service and joined a group of "free civilians." His business enterprises proved so remunerative that, within eight years, he became the country's leading tax farmer. In 1638, it appears, the government disposed of a part of its fiscal revenue to agents for a total of 280,000 florins. Among the successful bidders, Navarro figured prominently with the 203,000 florins he offered for the farming of sugar taxes in Pernambuco and Paraíba. Examples like this dispose of J. Lucio d'Azevedo's objection to the general assumption that Jews played an important role in the development of the Brazilian sugar industry, because, he argued, arriving as penniless refugees, they did not have enough funds to start producing sugar cane and refining it in their own mills. Even the relatively young Jewish communities of Antwerp, Hamburg, and Amsterdam actively participated in that remunerative business. At the outset, Jews were also allowed to acquire some of the sugar mills abandoned by the fleeing Portuguese and auctioned off by the Dutch for the substantial sum of 2,000,000 guilders.[81]

Moreover, the New Christians had every reason to expect that a Dutch regime would bring with it liberty of conscience and some civil rights for religious dissenters—a system prevailing in the home country and also applied during the short-lived Dutch occupation of Bahia in 1624–25. They also must have heard of the instruction prepared by the Dutch government on October 13, 1629, ahead of the invasion of Pernambuco, which in part pledged that "the Spaniards, Portuguese, and natives of the land, be they Roman Catholics or Jews, shall be maintained in their liberties, without being disturbed or investigated in matters of conscience or in their homes. Nor shall anyone dare to annoy or molest them or place obstacles in their paths," under severe penalties. This promise was largely kept after the conquest. Contrasting the freedom they thus enjoyed under Dutch domination with the persecutions they had suffered under Spanish-Portuguese rule, the Brazilian Jews became staunch supporters of the new regime, which in turn considered them the most reliable element in the population. Because of their deeply ingrained fear of inquisitorial reprisals, they were even more dependable than the relatively few Dutch Calvinists settled in the new land.[82]

Before long, however, an increasing number of Calvinist merchants began viewing the Jews as their principal competitors, who had the advantage of greater familiarity with the local terrain and the Spanish-Portuguese idiom. On their part, some Dutch Reformed churchmen complained that the Jews displayed anti-Christian behavior, including purported blasphemies against Jesus. Less dubious was their displeasure over the Jews working and sending their children to school on Sundays. The mere fact that the Jews were able to establish two congregations was a thorn in the flesh of the conservative Calvinist clergy. The Brazilian Council of the Dutch Reformed Church time and again joined the growing Dutch merchant class in Recife in protesting to Amsterdam against the Jews' allegedly unfair business practices, and it kept objecting to the frequent concubinage and intermarriage between Christian women and Jewish men. The latter complaint seems to have been partially justified. Outwardly living as professing Christians during the preceding years, the Brazilian Jews naturally maintained close social contacts with the Old Christian population. As an unorganized minority, they were in no position to prevent their members from having sexual relations, or even intermarrying, with Christian women of Indian-Mestizo, Negro-Mulatto, or Iberian stock. Lucien Wolf's rather exaggerated observation concerning the European situation was more likely to be true in the case of the scattered Marrano settlements in the New World:

Despite the watchfulness and persecution of the Inquisition they had not only preserved their Judaism in secret, but they had in a sense conquered the Portuguese themselves, and to a great extent also the Spaniards, by the facility and impunity with which they had taken to themselves Old Christian wives and husbands. These intermarriages had, indeed, been carried out on so large a scale in Portugal that at this period throughout Europe the Portuguese were all looked upon as Jews. The contamination, however, had been mutual, and it is not often realized, even by Jewish historians and anthropologists, how little of the old racial Jew survived in the seventeenth century Marrano.

However, Brazil's white colonial society displayed sufficient signs of both xenophobia and nascent Portuguese-Brazilian nationalism (unwittingly promoted by some New Christian writers) to counteract the forces of total absorption of the Jewish element.[83]

On the whole, neither the Dutch West India Company nor the States General paid much heed to the anti-Jewish accusations. Partly influenced by the Company's Jewish shareholders, who were soon to control, as we recall, an average of 4 to 10 percent of its entire stock and partly guided by international considerations, the directors and the government insisted upon the equitable treatment of Jews. In the charter, issued on January 9, 1634, and repeated in 1636 during the administration of Johan Maurits, the protective article of the Instruction of 1629 was publicly pronounced. It was not substantially weakened by the following qualification: "provided that the aforementioned Roman Catholics or Jews shall refrain from committing public scandals and from bringing dishonor to the holy name of God, our Saviour." Most outspoken were the directives issued by the States General on December 7, 1645, to the Supreme Council in Brazil. Reacting to a petition from the Amsterdam Jewish communal elders, the government took the "Hebrew nation in Brazil" under its special protection.

The said Supreme Government [it wrote] that now is or hereafter shall be in Brazil, shall favor and be of service to the aforenamed Jewish nation on all occasions according to, and as their loyalty and valor deserved, and also in all cases let them enjoy the result thereof without in any manner making or observing, or causing to be made or observed, any greater or lesser distinction or division between them and those of our other nationals, not doubting that the said Jewish nation will thereby be more and more animated and encouraged to further the service in this state and that of the puissant West-India Company, they being also assured that we and the said Supreme Government will look out for their good with fatherly care.

This reiteration of a long-established policy had apparently become necessary a year after Johan Maurits' resignation, when the future of the Dutch regime in Brazil began to appear increasingly dubious.[84]

Not that the distinguished governor was altogether friendly to Jews. Himself a pious Calvinist, he promoted the Dutch Reformed Church with all means at his disposal. He sought to convert not only Indians but also Catholics and Jews. According to the contemporary chronicler Kaspar van Baerle (Barlaeus), he considered it necessary to "undermine the inveterate Jewish opinion concerning the eternal validity of the law of Moses and the ultimate restoration of the kingdom of Jerusalem. The Jews ought to be guided to revere and have faith in Jesus Christ, the son of Mary, as the promised Messiah who has already been born." Baerle also claimed that the count had imposed upon Jews and "Abramites" the following restrictions:

They were not to erect any new synagogues. They were not to be allowed to marry Christian women or keep Christian concubines. Nor were they to convert anyone from the Christian to the Mosaic faith, from evangelical liberty to the burdens of the Law, from light to darkness, nor to blaspheme against the sacrosanct name of Christ. In any census of the [white] population [*proxenetarum*] they were not to exceed the ratio of one-third. They were to cheat no one in business. Children born to a Jewish and a Christian parent were, after the parents' death, to be handed over to the Christian parent's relatives for education; if these were destitute, impecunious children were to be put into orphanages, while wealthy ones were to be placed under the care of the senators of the Secret Council.

True, Baerle must have realized that his last statement contradicted the prohibition of mixed marriages. He must also have known that there existed more than one synagogue in the Dutch colony, each evidently established *after* the Dutch occupation. In his general review of Johan Maurits' legislation, he admitted that much of it was in the form of advice given to the people, rather than in legally enforceable ordinances, and that some of it certainly did not enjoy the full backing of Amsterdam. In an effort, particularly, to persuade the parsimonious directors of the Company to increase its allotments for the colony's defense, Maurits pointed to the growing dissatisfaction among the Portuguese settlers. Doubtless on his orders, his emissary, Secretary Tollner, argued before the Board of the Company that the Portuguese "detest our impositions and laws and the liberty of religious conscience which the Jews possess." The count found it particularly objectionable that Jews were allowed to observe their Sabbath publicly, whereas the Portuguese were restricted in their practice of Catholic rituals. Despite these convictions, however, Johan Maurits resisted the manifold pressures exerted on him by both the clergy and the local merchants, Dutch as well as Portuguese, sharply to curtail Jewish rights. At the assembly of representatives of the residents of the Pernambuco, Itamaracá, and Paraíba captaincies—"the first Parliament to convene in South America then and long after," which met from August to September 1640—the Paraíba deputies demanded that all Jews be expelled. The Dutch administration replied that only delinquent Jews would be duly punished. When the count's term of office expired, Jews, perhaps under the governor's subtle prompting, offered him an annuity of 3,000 florins if he agreed to stay. In their letter of May 1, 1642, the Jewish leaders pleaded with abandon that "if His Excellency could be paid to stay in this land by the purchase of anything in the world, they would find no price too great to pay, even if it were their own blood, if only they might retain him." At any rate, the vast economic opportunities offered by his orderly administration enhanced the attraction of the original sweeping pronouncements in favor of basic Jewish equality, which were decidedly uncommon in the seventeenth century.[85]

FIRST JEWISH COMMUNITY

Looking forward to these unprecedented freedoms, both religious and economic, Jews began arriving in entire boatloads in the new Dutch possession. In 1638, and again in 1641, we are told, no fewer than 200 Jews disembarked at Recife. The transport of 1641 included Isaac b. David Aboab da Fonseca, one of four functioning ministers of the Spanish-Portuguese Congregation in

Amsterdam, who assumed the post of spiritual leader of the Jews in the colony. It was a testimony to the interveningly acquired wealth of its members that the community could offer the new rabbi the handsome salary of 1,600 florins annually. It also engaged a second Amsterdam rabbi, Moses Raphael de Aguilar, together with other officials, adopted a noteworthy constitution, and settled down to a more permanent form of Jewish life. According to the hostile petition submitted on January 10, 1641, by 66 Christian merchants, the Jewish community embraced settlers not only from Spain, Italy, Turkey, and the Barbary States, but also from Germany and Poland. In other words, some Ashkenazim now began joining their Sephardic brethren in the New World. The romance of the new land, with its liberty of conscience and many other freedoms, as well as the riches which one could amass there quickly, overcame whatever hesitations Jewish émigrés may have felt about settling in a completely unfamiliar region, with an uncertain future under the Dutch regime. Even Menasseh ben Israel was anxious to secure the rabbinical post in Recife. For this purpose he hurriedly wrote the second part of his *Conciliador,* which he dedicated to "the most noble, and most prudent and most fortunate Gentlemen of the Council of the West Indies." He explained that, just as kings often send ambassadors ahead, he was sending this volume to them, as a token of his capabilities and studies to serve as a sort of ambassador announcing his willingness to come. Although he had secured excellent introductions, and both Gerhard Johann Vos (Vossius) and Hugo Grotius were already deploring the loss of their departing friend, the Recife congregation preferred to invite Aboab and Aguilar.[86]

In 1644, upon Johan Maurits' departure, the congregation was prepared to offer 600,000 florins for his palatial residence, which it intended to convert into its main synagogue. It is estimated that, by 1645, the total number of Jews reached about 1,450 souls, or about one-half of the entire white civilian population in the colony, but that it declined to 720 souls three years later. These figures, suggested by Arnold Wiznitzer, are necessarily conjectural. A Jewish ratio of fully 50 percent in 1645 may not even have existed in the town of Recife; it probably was much less in the provincial cities of Mauricia, Itamacá, Paraíba, and Rio Grande.

The vast interior of the country still was practically devoid of white settlers, who, but a short time before, had been censured by the author of the *Dialogues about the Greatness of Brazil* for staying within a narrow strip some ten leagues wide along the coast and neglecting all but the production of sugar. Similarly, the figure of 720 Jews in 1648 does not quite square with Wiznitzer's assumption that the ratio of adult males to women and children was only 2:1:1. This assumption would justify the multiplication of the number of the approximately 180 congregational members by only two and would result in a total of barely 360 Jews. It is quite possible indeed that, as in later periods of Jewish migrations, many more Jewish émigrés took their families along with them than did the Dutch or other white immigrants. Likewise, those members of the congregation who had originally been living as New Christians in Recife or elsewhere in South America and who now reverted to Judaism in public, very likely had their families with them. It is, of course, also possible that the mortality of Jewish women was somewhat below the average, despite the contrary assertion of the physician Willem Piso, who had come to Brazil with Johan Maurits. Piso claimed that, because of their frequent ritualistic ablutions, Jewish women often skipped their menstrual periods—a fact which they tried to conceal, but which helped to undermine their health. This assumption is not borne out by the better-known vital statistics of modern Jewish communities elsewhere. In view of these uncertainties, it might be safer merely to assume in a general way that the Jewish population had been rapidly increasing until 1645, but that it subsequently declined. However, if we accept the figure given for the Jewish exiles of 1654 as being in excess of 600 persons (see below), the decline was neither so large nor so consistent as is often taken for granted. Certainly, Jews had fewer choices of migrating to other countries, except for Holland, than did their Christian compatriots.[87]

Small in numbers though it was, Brazilian Jewry (like its New Christian predecessors) included distinguished professionals, such as an engineer and bridge builder, a doctor, and a lawyer. The lawyer's admission to the bar, however, was secured only by the direct intervention of his Amsterdam coreligionists. Apparently less difficult was the Jews' entry into the medical profession. According to Gilberto Freyre, "as early as the seventeenth century, there were already Jewish converts [in Bahia] skilled in the treatment of the sick and who prescribed pork so that no informer might throw suspicion on them. . . . [Jacob de Andrade] Velozino, one of the greatest Jewish physicians of the seventeenth century, was from Recife." He was, indeed, the son of the communal cantor Joshua Velozino. Born in 1639, he had to leave Brazil at the return of the Portuguese, and became a distingiushed anti-Spinozist philosopher, as well as a physician, in Amsterdam. Of course, not all the major ventures of the Jewish professionals proved to be a financial success. The bridge builder, Balthasar de Fonseca, for instance, made a serious miscalculation when he contracted with the regime to build a bridge across the Berberibe River, which separated the newly established suburb of Mauricia (Mauritsstad) from Recife. Although he had had previous experience in bridge building, he seems to have underestimated the powerful currents in the river, which made the completion of the bridge with the projected stone pillars impossible. Hence the final span had to be ingeniously constructed with wooden beams of special shape placed at carefully calculated angles (1641–44).[88]

The cultural contributions of the Marrano and Jewish groups likewise were of considerable significance. The "father of Brazilian poetry," Bento Teixeira, a native of Oporto, a great center of Portuguese Marranism, betrayed in his poem *Prosopopeia* a certain indebtedness to traditional Jewish and Marrano ideas. Although dedicated to Governor Jorge de Albuquerque of Pernambuco, the poem did not save its author from inquisitorial investigation during the *visitador*'s inspection of the region in 1593–95. He was arrested in 1595, brought to trial in Lisbon, and sentenced, in the auto of January 31, 1599, to abjuration *de vehementi* and life imprisonment. Having contracted tuberculosis in prison, he died in July 1600. More fortunate was Ambrósio Fernándes Brandão, almost undoubtedly the author of the encyclopedic *Diálogos das Grandezas do Brasil,* a most noteworthy collection of facts and insights concerning the natural and socioeconomic conditions in the country at the beginning of the seventeenth century. This work quite pointedly refers to Old—not New—Testament episodes; among them Solomon's famous expedition to

Ophir. The author believes that that port could be identified with the Brazilian city of São Jorge, and that the Brazilian Indians were really descendants of the ancient Israelites. He is at pains to explain the decline in their culture by attributing it to the Indians' forgetfulness of their old heritage because of the great distance separating them from their ancient homeland. But he believes that one could still detect among them certain vestiges of the old civilization, such as "many words and proper names pronounced according to the Hebrew language and, in the same manner, certain customs, such as taking their nieces in genuine wedlock," which they still maintained. The *Diálogos* thus contributed to the spreading myths of the Amerindians' Israelitic ancestry. It appears that even before the anonymous publication of this work, Brandão's Judaic proclivities aroused some suspicion among his neighbors. Because he was serving as administrator of a Camaragibe sugar mill belonging to a fellow New Christian, he was denounced in 1591 as a Judaizer who attended the local synagogue and made his slaves work on Sundays. Apparently the denunciation was not taken seriously, and although a similar charge was repeated to the inquisitorial agents by a Mulatto slave in 1606, nothing untoward seems to have happened to the distinguished author, whose work has served modern scholars as an inexhaustible mine of information concerning Brazil's early evolution.[89]

Of more direct Jewish interest were the intellectual activities of professing Jews after the Dutch conquest. The first Hebrew author in the New World was Isaac b. David Aboab da Fonseca, the congregational rabbi. In 1646, after less than five years' stay in Recife, he published a Hebrew poem, *Zekher 'asiti le-nifleot El* (I Have Made a Memorial for God's Wonders), in which he described the "miraculous" events which had led to the establishment of the oldest Jewish congregation in the Americas. In 1655 he continued this tale by showing how that congregation had been dissolved after the reconquest of Recife by the Portuguese in the preceding year. In the meantime he also composed a Hebrew grammar, *Melekhet ha-diqduq* (The Art of Grammar), undoubtedly for use in his Hebrew school. Another scholarly functionary of the Recife Congregation Zur Israel (Rock of Israel) was Moses Raphael de Aguilar, Aboab's colleague in the ministry of the Spanish-Portuguese Congregation in Amsterdam, both before and after their sojourn in Recife. Aguilar seems to have left for Amsterdam as early as 1648, perhaps because the membership and financial resources of the community had so greatly diminished after Maurits' departure. In Holland he engaged in fruitful literary activity, although only two of his books appeared in print, in 1660 and 1681.[90]

Even more remarkable was the life and death of the young martyr Isaac de Castro Tartas. Born in Portugal in 1625, he was educated by his parents and other relatives in southern France (where he added the name of the small town of Tartas to his family name) and Amsterdam. Subsequently, he proceeded on his own to Recife and from there to Bahia, where he was arrested as a Judaizer in 1644. He tried to contend before the Inquisition that he had been born in France and had never been baptized and that, hence, he was not subject to the jurisdiction of the Holy Office. When this assertion was disproved, he endeavored to explain his early departures from Amsterdam and Recife by an alleged homicide in which he had been involved and his ensuing quest to escape the reach of the Dutch authorities. This story, too, seems to have been fabricated, for homicide was apparently more excusable in the inquisitors' eyes than trying to instruct New Christians in the tenets of Judaism. But this latter activity seems to have been Tartas' real motive. He may have been chosen, because of his excellent familiarity with several languages, his high intelligence, and his devotion to Judaism, to serve as an emissary to explain Jewish tenets to the ill-informed New Christians in the parts of Brazil still under Portuguese domination. When this mission, too, was divulged by witnesses in successive interrogations, he declared himself a Jew, believing that salvation could be attained only by adherence to the Law of Moses. To the very end, he bore witness to his ancestral faith, and in the great Lisbon auto of 1647 he was burned alive, while invoking *Ely Adonai Ṣebaot* (My God, the Lord of Hosts). He appears to have been the only one among the 400 Brazilian Jews tried by the Lisbon Inquisition to have suffered that form of execution. Seventeen others were burned after being garroted. The spectacular death of this young man made a great impression upon Jews and non-Jews alike. The

French chargé d'affaires in Lisbon, Lanier, in his report to Cardinal Mazarin, urged the French government to be more watchful in the area of Tartas, "swarming with the pest of Judaism, as also are the environs of Bayonne, and the cities of Bordeaux, Rouen, and Nantes." But he could not quite suppress his admiration for the twenty-two-year-old martyr, who "unwaveringly persisted in his unfortunate creed and with his last breath loudly proclaimed *Ely, Adonay, Sabahot!* One has never seen such determination and constancy." Isaac's death was especially mourned in Amsterdam, where the leading rabbi *(ḥakham)* Saul Levi Morteira delivered a eulogy, and poets composed dirges in Hebrew and Spanish in memory of the youthful martyr who had "sanctified the Name of the Lord." [91]

Obviously, the commercial and industrial opportunities for all settlers in the young colony were much greater. Under the tolerant and vigorous administration of Johan Maurits, particularly, the rapid Jewish economic advances aroused much envy, particularly among competitors. Complaining in 1637 that Jewish immigrants were flooding the country, the Chamber of Olinda advanced the usual religious and socioeconomic arguments. "As a nation so hated by all nations of the world and as enemies of Christ our Saviour, they [the Jews] do not deserve any courtesy." Undoubtedly generalizing from a few scattered incidents, the Chamber also accused the Jews of being ever-inclined to cheating and to fraudulent bankruptcies. Three years later, the so-called Cortes assembled in Recife demanded the outright expulsion of all Jews. Even during the turbulent period of the Portuguese uprising, when the Jewish population declined considerably in both numbers and affluence, Martim Moreno Soares, in a letter of September 30, 1645, to King John IV, complained that the Jews were behaving like "masters lording it over the majority and controlling the best commissions which our captaincies possess." [92]

PORTUGUESE RECONQUEST

Dutch animosity came to the fore even in the face of common danger. Unable to stem the advances of the Portuguese "rebels," the Dutch authorities in Recife in 1653 sent three envoys—two

Dutchmen and the Jew Abraham d'Açevedo—to Holland to plead with the Dutch government and the West India Company for reinforcements in men and money. Should Holland be unable to spare any manpower or funds because of its difficult war with England, the emissaries were to ask that negotiations be conducted with the Portuguese government about the inevitable surrender in order to secure the conquerors' guarantee for the personal safety of both the Dutch and the Jews. In the midst of these delicate conversations in The Hague and Amsterdam, the two Dutch emissaries tried, behind D'Açevedo's back, to obtain some limitation of the rights of the Pernambuco Jews. This intrigue proved unsuccessful only because the Jewish delegate learned about it in time and, with the aid of the Amsterdam Jewish leaders, managed to counteract it. It was also speedily disavowed by the Recife authorities, who declared that the two envoys had acted without even notifying their superiors.[93]

In his petition to the authorities in Holland, "in the name of the Jewish nation of Amsterdam and Brazil," D'Açevedo stressed above all the loyalty of Brazilian Jewry to the Dutch regime. He contended that "the said Jewish nation have always been willing and vigilant in keeping guard by day and by night, like the other inhabitants there. As a result, several of them were shot dead by the enemy." From the beginning of Dutch rule there, Jews were, indeed, obliged to serve in the local militia, although they were usually exempted from guard duty on Saturdays in return for the payment of a fee. During critical periods such exemptions caused much resentment, however, and the privilege was withdrawn in June 1645, when the colony's military position had begun to deteriorate. During the increasingly numerous armed clashes from 1646 on, Jewish soldiers served in the regular army and occasionally even formed their own detachments under Jewish officers. On a contemporary map of Recife and neighboring Olinda we read of *excubiae judaeorum,* probably a designation for small forts manned by Jews. On one occasion a company of forty Jews set out in a boat in the northerly direction to fight the enemy guerrillas at their bases. Eight months later, however, because of a change in the strategic situation, they were ordered back to Recife. It was, therefore, a clearly anti-Jewish bias which induced a seventeenth-century Portuguese officer-writer to assert that the ultimate surrender of the Dutch was brought on by faint-hearted Jews, who had implored them to capitulate. Remarkably, the Jewish part in the defense of Dutch Brazil was destined to play a role in connection with the rights which the Recife exiles were seeking to obtain in New Amsterdam, now New York. Supporting them in this struggle, the Amsterdam Jews, in their petition to the West India Company of 1655, emphasized, among other matters, that "it is well known to your Honors that the Jewish nation in Brazil have at all times been faithful and have striven to guard and maintain that place, risking for that purpose their possessions and their blood." [94]

With the changing fortunes of war, however, the Jews' security was totally undermined. They knew that their protection depended mainly on the Company's remote headquarters and the States General in the Netherlands, a protection maintained even after Portugal's separation from Spain in 1640. Although Holland now was Portugal's ally, Dutch naval forces tried to expand the Dutch colonies in both America and Africa before the truce took effect. Nevertheless, many Dutchmen, Jews and Christians alike, began leaving Brazil. As early as August 1646, rumors reached Europe about the enormous difficulties confronting the Dutch garrison in Recife. According to a report published in the *Augsburger Zeitung*, only the timely arrival of a Dutch ship prevented widespread starvation in the city, which allegedly had but a six-day supply of food on hand. That not all émigrés reached their European destinations, goes without saying. In 1646 a boat carrying numerous Jewish passengers suffered shipwreck near the Isle of Wight, with the loss of 120 lives from among 148 passengers and crewmen. Characteristically, the New Christians who had remained in Bahia and elsewhere in Portuguese Brazil loyally defended their country against Dutch attacks and later helped to finance the spreading revolt in the Northeast. In 1644 fully 17 percent of the financial contributions locally raised in support of the "rebels," came from the pro-Portuguese New Christians in Bahia. The Dutch position became almost untenable after 1652, when the Netherlands became involved in a protracted war with Oliver Cromwell's England and had to marshal all its naval and military resources for that purpose, leaving Pernambuco practically undefended two years later.[95]

A real turning point in that war of attrition against the beleaguered Dutch minority had come with the foundation in 1649 of the Brazil Company (Companha Geral do Comércio do Brasil), initiated by the Brazilian Jesuit António Vieira. We recall that this outstanding Brazilian preacher and missionary had become King John IV's influential adviser in Lisbon, and that he often cooperated with New Christian friends, especially the Lisbon banker Duarte da Silva, a native of Bahia. It was as early as 1646, in fact, that Da Silva had established in the Portuguese capital a central warehouse for the importation of sugar and tobacco from Brazil, produce which, as a rule, he reexported to cities with a sizable settlement of Sephardic merchants. At that time the Treasury owed him the substantial sum of 44,000 cruzados. In 1647 Da Silva helped equip a Portuguese armada, for which his ungrateful country allowed him in the following year to be arrested by the Inquisition. The king and Vieira realized, however, that they could not possibly raise the funds needed for the new Company without granting the New Christian shareholders immunity from the seizure of their property by the Holy Office. The Portuguese inquisitor general, Dom Francisco de Castro, strenuously objected and claimed that such immunity would merely encourage secret judaizing. Contending that the Marranos feared loss of property even more than that of life, he exclaimed with abandon: "And if with such a heavy penalty, Judaism has continued to flourish recently because of our sins, what will happen when it sees itself free and immune therefrom?" The inquisitor also insisted that, without the revenue from confiscations, the Holy Office could not continue to function, and he enlisted the aid of the Papacy in resisting the projected immunity.[96]

Yet facing the possibility of losing not only his Brazilian but also his African possessions and seeing no other way of building up the Portuguese navy and merchant marine, John IV paid no heed to the ensuing papal brief and consented in his decree of February 7 [6], 1649, to the establishment of the Brazil Company with the aid of New Christian capital. On his part, António Vieira, with typical "Jesuit" casuistry, argued that the 1649 decree pledging immunity from property seizure to Marrano investors in the new Company did not run counter to canon law. Although the latter provided that conviction for heresy should lead to confiscation of the culprit's property, Vieira contended that, according to that law, the property was to be turned over to the government Treasury. Hence the king was entitled to sign a contract in advance, promising, in return for the immediate payment of certain sums, to restore such property to its owners. Subscriptions for shares at 20 cruzados each were open to everybody, including foreign citizens (the organizers doubtless had Amsterdam Jews principally in mind). All were guaranteed against government seizure of their funds, even if their country should happen to find itself in a state of war with Portugal. But most of the capital of 1,255,000 cruzados was subscribed by Portuguese New Christian shareholders, who, understandably, also exerted great influence on the board of directors. The Company soon built and chartered a number of large, well-equipped vessels which were able to convoy Portuguese ships successfully in both directions. Ultimately, its navy was even able to blockade Recife, and thus helped to bring about the Dutch garrison's final surrender, formalized in an agreement signed at Taborda on January 26, 1654. Charles Ralph Boxer is indeed right in asserting that "the Portuguese colonial empire had been saved from collapse by the money raised from his New Christian friends by Padre António Vieira—a singular if patriotic combination of Jews and Jesuits." [97]

Forward-looking as Vieira was in his public activities, he was by no means a preacher of religious toleration as such. He was impressed by the life of Dutch Jewry during his visits to The Hague and Amsterdam, and actually considered advocating sufficient permissiveness for Jews to have synagogues on Portuguese soil. But his ultimate concern was to see the New Christians and even professing Jews join the Catholic majority. This, despite the fact that, quoting St. Paul's Epistle to the Romans, he maintained that "faith, religion, and sanctity came naturally to the Jews, but [were] against nature to Gentiles," a contention which brought down on him the wrath of the Holy Office. It was, indeed, to form a major article of the inquisitorial accusation against him. Vieira was also firmly convinced, as he assured King Affonso VI, that

Portugal "has for its particular and special goal the propagation and extension of the Catholic faith in heathen lands, for which purpose God raised and founded it. And the more that Portugal acts in keeping with this goal, the more assured and certain is its preservation; and the more that it diverges therefrom, the more doubtful and dangerous is its future." In his messianic dreams about the "Future," Vieira assigned to Brazil, and especially its most backward part, the district of Maranhão, to which intensive preaching of the Gospel had come only in 1615, an outstanding role in mankind's final redemption. To this end he interpreted as relating to Maranhão the ever-puzzling prophecy of Isaiah (18:2): "Go, ye swift messengers,/ To a nation tall and of glossy skin,/ To a people terrible from their beginning onward;/ A nation that is sturdy and treadeth down,/ Whose land the rivers divide!" Vieira's messianic yearnings were greatly inspired during his stay in Portugal and Holland by the current eschatological trends in New Christian and Jewish circles. Memories of the preachment of Bandarra, itself influenced by early sixteenth-century Marrano expectations, were now revived by the publication in Nantes of the cobbler-messiah's *Trovas,* at the expense of the marquês de Niza, one of Vieira's frequent correspondents. In Holland, the Brazilian preacher must have heard Menasseh ben Israel expatiate on Jewish messianic doctrines. It probably was more than a mere coincidence that Vieira's *História do Futuro* was first written (though thereafter constantly revised) in 1647, shortly before the publication in 1650 of Menasseh's *Esperança de Israel.* Vieira was doubtless also influenced by Isaac de la Peyrère's *Du rappel des Juifs.* He envisaged not only the restoration of the Jews to the Holy Land—of course, combined with their adoption of the Christian faith—but also a "concordat" between the Jewish people and the Christian nations for the world's ultimate redemption. But while medieval messianists had looked to the country of Prester John or to the Middle or Far East as the locale of the incipient cosmic transformation, Vieira, like the Peruvian Diego Andrés Rocha and the Spanish Hebraists of Jewish descent Benito Arías Montano and Luis de León, among others, had moved the scene of that expectation to the Western Hemisphere. To Vieira Isaiah's obscure allusions pointed specifically to his native Brazil.[98]

More realistically, the Portuguese were also able to capitalize on the fundamental mistake of the Dutch West India Company in not enlisting the full cooperation of the underprivileged masses of Indians, mestizos, Negroes, and mulattoes. At first the Dutch conquerors had been greeted with much relief, especially by the downtrodden workers on the sugar plantations and in the refineries. But it soon became manifest that the slaves and peons were treated no better by the new employers. More, while the principle of humane treatment of the Indians and Negroes was always preached by the central administration in Lisbon (although it was thoroughly sabotaged by the local colonists), the Dutch West India Company, in the main a commercial enterprise, shared with its local bureaucracy and colonial entrepreneurs an overriding concern for profit. The new Portuguese regime of John IV, on the other hand, now made special efforts to enforce its humanitarian theories, at least partially, and to extend some immediate benefits to the Indians.

Jews and Calvinists, however, felt deeply threatened by the mass appeal of these royal promises and the ensuing popular uprising led by the effective guerrilla fighter João Fernandes Vieira. On their part, the Dutch negotiators, even in their defeat and capitulation, tried to protect the rights of Jews. In 1646, the Dutch government had already intervened in behalf of eight Jewish prisoners of war taken by the rebels from the Rio São Francisco area. The Supreme Council in Recife was instructed to see to it "that the detained Jews be freed in the same manner as our Christian subjects and residents." The Portuguese side basically accepted this premise, making an exception only in the case of convicted Marranos. It insisted that such "renegades" were subject to legitimate inquisitorial prosecution, with which no secular authority ought to interfere. If the investigation were to prove that a prisoner had been born a Jew, he would be immediately discharged. As a matter of record, even most of the Marrano defendants who ultimately appeared at the auto-da-fé got off with prison terms. The large majority of both Calvinists and Jews succeeded in leaving the country before the final surrender of the Dutch forces in 1654. After the departure of the Jewish community, which had then still numbered some 600 souls, there was no further need for the communal institutions it had established with much sacrifice and over much opposition from the Dutch Reformed Classic. Under the pressure of the Calvinist clergy, Jews had been allowed to perform their divine services only very quietly, so as not to cause any offense to the ears of pious Christians. In 1657 Francisco Barreto de Menezes, commander-in-chief of the Portuguese army which reconquered Recife, presented the synagogue building, which had also accommodated the Jewish school and served as the center of all communal activities, to João Fernandes Vieira. In this way he satisfied but a small part of the exorbitant demands for royal compensation which this leading freedom fighter untiringly claimed as due him for his courageous leadership of the anti-Dutch revolt. It was an historical irony that the house of worship, from which eleven years earlier its officiating rabbi, Isaac Aboab, had offered a deprecatory characterization of the "cruel Mulatto," should have been handed over to that ruthless enemy. The Jewish cemetery—located at some distances from the city and accessible only by ferry until the bridge over the Berberibe River, separating Mauricia from Recife, was completed in 1644—was given to Henrique Dias, black commander of the Negro troops participating in the uprising. If any secret Judaizers remained in the country, they went underground and, for generations thereafter, they but sporadically appeared in the records of the Holy Office.[99]

However, the inquisitorial prosecutions primarily affected New Christians residing in Bahia and other parts of Brazil which had remained in Portuguese hands during the period of 1630–54. The immediate sequel of the Dutch capitulation in 1654 was mitigated by the terms of the aforementioned Taborda agreement. To the surprise of some of the Jews themselves, the Portuguese conquerors indeed treated them in accordance with this agreement. At least, the Amsterdam rabbi, Saul Levi Morteira, writing some years before his death in 1660, observed in his hitherto unpublished work, *Provvidencia de Dios con Ysrael:*

Almighty God in His infinite power protected His people and saved it from all imminent dangers by influencing the heart of Governor Barreto. The latter prohibited any person of the Hebrew nation from being touched or molested, and provided severe penalties against those acting contrary to this prohibition. And not only this, he also agreed to let the Jews sell their merchandise and he permitted them to embark for Holland, the more than six hundred persons of our people who were present there. Since Dutch ships were not available in sufficient numbers, Barreto placed Portuguese vessels at their disposal, so that they embarked on sixteen ships. By divine grace and providence, all of them saved themselves and escaped many tortures and other misfortunes. One of these ships was captured by the Spaniards, who wanted to surrender the poor Jews to the Inquisition. However, before they were able to carry out their evil intentions, the Lord caused a French ship to appear on the scene, which freed the Jews from the Spaniards and took them to safety in Florida, or the New Netherlands, whence they arrived peacefully in Holland.

According to the terms of the treaty, moreover, the West India Company was to collect indemnities for the émigrés' possessions, which now fell to the Portuguese administration. These included houses, sugar mills, and other properties left behind by Jews, who subsequently claimed their share of the 8,000,000 florins for which the indemnity was ultimately settled in 1661. The Company's officials were still busy in 1663 reviewing the validity of individual claims. Most importantly, however, while the majority of Jewish refugees reached Holland, where they contributed to the phenomenal rise of the Dutch Jewish communities, a considerable number came to the West Indian islands and the North American New Netherlands. The Brazilian dispersion thus was instrumental in laying the foundations for many new Jewish communities, including that of the future United States.[100]

PORTUGAL'S AFRICAN COLONIES

Dutch-Portuguese confrontation was not limited to the Western Hemisphere. It extended, in fact, over the entire area of the vast Portuguese Empire, the rapid expansion of which in the early sixteenth century had also secured for Portugal a near-monopoly over Europe's trade with central and southern Africa and the countries bordering on the Indian Ocean. This extraordinary growth overtaxed, however, the manpower and other resources of the small mother country, with its population of little more than one million. It was followed in the seventeenth century by slow disintegration. Nonetheless, despite the blows received from its more powerful antagonists, Holland, England, and France, parts of the Portuguese Empire have survived until the present day. Ironically, while in recent decades the great British, French, Dutch, and Belgian colonial possessions have fallen away from their mother countries, Portugal has thus far succeeded in holding on to her African possessions, which it claims are not colonies but integral parts of the mother country. In contrast, Spain—which through the occupation of Portugal in 1580–1640 had dragged its smaller neighbor into its own misguided imperial ventures and contributed greatly to the weakening of Portugal's international position—had lost most of its colonies, including the Philippines, even before the general collapse of colonialism after the Second World War.[101]

West Africa was geographically closest and most intimately connected with the economic and military developments in Brazil. Ships crisscrossed the Atlantic Ocean in both directions with relative frequency. Brazil's agricultural and industrial production increasingly depended on the importation of African slaves, most readily supplied by traders who acquired them from local African chieftains and slave hunters. For this purpose the Portuguese needed to occupy only thin strips along the coast leaving the interior under the control of local rulers. As in the New World, the colonizers often mouthed the pious expectation that the subject populations would ultimately adopt Christianity. But they rarely made the necessary effort to penetrate the often mountainous, jungle-covered interior of their colonies. In Angola, for example, the boundaries of which extended further than those of the present Portuguese colony (set by the conference of Berlin in 1885–86), the first Portuguese governor, Paulo Dias de Nováis, was reproached by Jesuit missionaries for his laxity in occupying the countryside, where there is no "better sermon than the sword and the iron rod [*espada e vara de ferro*]." After receiving in 1571 a royal charter to exploit a coastal area of some 125 miles and its hinterland as a semiprivate concession, this grandson of Bartholomeu Dias (the first European to circumnavigate Africa, in 1486) learned from experience that war and conquest often resulted merely in the flight of the natives deeper into the jungles and the drying-up of the vital reservoir of manpower. Trade in human merchandise, pursued even by some Dominican friars, was indeed a very lucrative occupation. A slave purchased in Africa for a few squares of palm-cloth could be sold in Peru for 4–6 pesos. Yet it was decidedly cheaper to obtain the 10,000–15,000 slaves who in the 1570s and 1580s represented the annual average of exports (in the seventeenth century this average is said to have declined to 10,000, and in 1700–1730 to but 6,000) from the Angolan king, who sold prisoners, as he claimed, "in order not to execute them." In East Africa, on the other hand, the Portuguese, though trying to reduce Arab competition in trade and shipping, relied largely on the long-established Arab slave hunters and merchants to supply the much sought-after commodity.[102]

Portuguese interest in Angola and most other African colonies thus differed fundamentally from that in the American and Asiatic possessions. Apart from securing for the conquerors, and ultimately helping them to dominate, the "Spice routes" to the East Indies, Africa offered few opportunities for the exploitation of its natural resources under the conditions of the time. Except for the relatively small gold mines in São Jorge da Mina (Elmina, Gold Coast), and a few places in East Africa, where the colonists had to depend entirely on native transportation, the quest for precious metals proved disappointing. The main objective in the occupation of African lands, therefore, was the supply of slaves for both the home country and the American colonies. Slave trade had been carried on throughout the African continent from time immemorial. East Africa, in particular, had long been a major source of supply of unfree manpower for the Arab countries, and through Arab traders, for India and other Asiatic lands. This trade was greatly facilitated by the general submissiveness of the population to its rulers, noted as early as the fourteenth century by the famous traveler and keen observer Ibn Baṭṭuṭa. The assertion of the Angolan king that he sold only persons who would otherwise be executed, refers to the fact that the numerous prisoners taken in the interminable tribal wars were liable to execution when no opportunity for gainful disposal of them was offered by traders. The deification of rulers by some African tribes contributed its share to the lack of resistance even to their own chieftains, who sold them into slavery out of sheer greed. That is why this, to us, objectionable trade in human beings was as much the fault of the tribal leadership itself as it was of the predominantly Arab slave hunters and the Western traders. One may also understand why even such a humane moralist as António Vieira saw nothing reprehensible in the slavery system.[103]

Unlike Brazil, Angola and the other Portuguese possessions in both West and East Africa had some precolonial Jewish antecedents. By the very nature of the extant documentation, to be sure, Jewish influences south of the Sahara are shrouded in obscurity. Yet it appears that even before the rise of Islam, some Jewish traders and refugees from persecution found their way not only into East-African localities south of Ethiopia—in which country a sizable remnant of ancient Jews, the Falashas, has survived to the present day—but also into the Central and West-African lands. Starting out from the Carthaginian and Roman possessions in North Africa, some enterprising Jews seem to have ventured south in ancient and early medieval times. Following the expansion of Islam throughout North Africa, in particular, some Arabic-speaking Jews joined their Muslim compatriots in establishing trading posts among the Negro tribes on both coasts. We recall the stories told by Eldad the Danite in ninth-century Kairuwan, and their partially realistic historical background. Persistent oral traditions ascribed the presence of Jews among the Berber and Negro tribes of Northwest Africa to Jewish exiles from Khaibar in northern Arabia after they had been ousted by Mohammed. Time and again more-or-less substantiated rumors about Jewish or judaizing tribes were reported by travelers, geographers, and chroniclers. Such tribes had played a particularly important role in the early Berber resistance to the Arab expansion, as exemplified by the Jewish prophetess Dahya al-Kahina. The famous twelfth-century geographer Al-Idrisi (Edrisi) reported that many of the inhabitants of Qamnūrīye in southern Mauritania and many members of the tribe of Lamlan, living south of Ghana, were professing Jews. To be sure, being by tradition a nonproselytizing people, these Jews could not permanently resist the inroads of Islam. Supported by the overwhelming economic and military power of the neighboring Arab states, the Muslim traders effectively spread Muslim teachings and practices among various pagan tribes, although the

Islamization of many such converts often proved to be both superficial and temporary.[104]

A new impetus to seek shelter in the unexplored "Dark Continent" was given to Jewish refugees from the Iberian persecutions after 1391. In the area around Tendirma (some 60 miles southwest of Timbuktu), founded in 1496, Jews had allegedly lived for generations under seven kings, each of whom had an army of 12,000 knights. Other reports describe various groups of Jews who, by digging wells and introducing a number of metallurgical crafts, pioneered in local agriculture and industry. Most of these reports relate to Jews or Judaizers living in Muslim lands or on their periphery. They will be discussed somewhat more fully in connection with the story of Jewish life under late medieval and early modern Islam. Here we are concerned only with the few stray—and for the most part rather questionable—data relating to Jews in Afro-Asian areas conquered by the Portuguese during their great sixteenth-century expansion.[105]

It has been suggested by no less an authority than Friedrich Ratzel that the island of São Tomé (St. Thomas), discovered by the Portguese in 1471 and subsequently used as a place of deportation for Jews unwilling to adopt baptism (we recall the forcible removal of Portuguese Jewish children to that locality in 1497), may have been instrumental in the settlement of many Jews in the neighboring West-African lands. It is quite possible that Jewish children and adults were chosen to serve as part of an experiment of how the Portuguese could adjust to life in the tropics. Reference has frequently been made especially to an African tribe of Mavûmbu in the Bay of Loango, whose customs, according to some nineteenth-century travelers, bore the unmistakable imprint of biblical Judaism. Some of these natives may indeed have in part been converted to Judaism by Jewish visitors or settlers at some earlier period. Judaic rites often survived the strong efforts made by Portuguese missionaries to uproot all vestiges of Judaism and replace them with Christian observances. Anthropological and linguistic researches in various other parts of Africa have likewise produced a number of attractive, if still rather uncertain, hypotheses about Jewish influences on local tribal traditions during the precolonial age, as well as after the Portuguese explorations.

These tenuous lines of investigation have been pursued mainly by anthropologists who have looked for patterns of thought and behavior reminiscent of those known among Jews and found among various African tribes and their descendants transplanted to the New World. Representative of that school of thought is Joseph J. Williams, whose work on "Hebrewisms" in West Africa still is a major source of information, both substantive and speculative. Beginning with the study of Ashanti descendants living in Jamaica, Williams writes:

In the first place, many Hebrewisms were discovered in the Ashanti tribal customs. Then, several Ashanti words were found to have a striking resemblance to those of equivalent Hebrew meaning. Finally, the Supreme Being of the Ashanti gave strong indication of being the Yahweh of the Old Testament. The question naturally rose, how to explain these parallels of cultural traits? Should they be ascribed to mere coincidence—to independent development? Or, have we here a remarkable instance of diffusion across the entire breadth of Africa?

Of course, since these descendants of the Ashanti tribesmen lived alongside of, sometimes in the very households of, Jamaican Jews, the origin of such contacts in the Ashantis' original African habitat can no longer be ascertained.[106] Portuguese New Christians seem to have been less hampered here than in either Brazil or Goa. Whatever Inquisition existed in Portuguese Africa was even more dependent on the Lisbon headquarters than were the Brazilian branches of the Holy Office. From the outset the number of Marrano colonists outside São Tomé was extremely small. In his original charter of 1571, King Sebastian imposed upon Dias de Nováis the obligation to raise a force of 400 armed men for the area of his administration. Although this force was to include one physician and one barber, the king stipulated that no New Christian be admitted. Probably on Dias' prompting, the king relented and, on January 24, 1574, allowed the governor to open the gates of São Tomé and Angola to six New Christian persons for a period of three years. Evidently the number of New Christians, Protestants, or other heretics was not sufficiently large to require more than perfunctory attention on the part of the ecclesiastical authorities. The occasional presence of older Christian groups, belonging to the various Eastern denominations, must also have proved discouraging to the Western Catholic missionaries. It has been estimated that there were no fewer than two hundred Church movements in East Africa which, whether aligned with the Greek-Orthodox Church or pursuing independent lines of thought and ritual, had long successfully resisted the impact of Islam and were now prepared to fight for the preservation of their identity in the face of the Catholic missions. Moreover, the entire Portuguese population clustered around certain seaports, like Luanda, venturing but rarely into the interior. Since the hot and humid climate, with manifold tropical diseases as yet uncontrolled by medical science, caused a high mortality among the European residents, many Western settlers sooner or later looked for more hospitable surroundings. The missionaries who traveled there with high hopes of converting masses of infidels were often disappointed by the lukewarm support they received from the governmental authorities. Most decisively, the majority of Portuguese arrivals, including the New Christians, were but transients, who came to Angola and the other colonies for specified periods, with the view of either returning home or else proceeding to more promising parts in the East or West Indies. We indeed have records of Marranos who spent some time in São Tomé or Angola before proceeding to Brazil, where they ultimately fell into the hands of the Inquisition.[107]

ASIA'S OLD CULTURAL MILIEUS

Quite different was the situation in Portugal's Asiatic possessions. In the Middle East, in particular, the Portuguese encountered long-established, predominantly Arabic-speaking, Jewish communities, intertwined with their Arab neighbors through centuries of common commercial and cultural life. To be sure, even after Francisco de Almeida's victory over an Egyptian fleet at Diu (February 1509), the Portuguese colonialists did not dare to penetrate any of the Muslim heartlands from Egypt to Persia. They never achieved control over the Red Sea, and therefore their contacts with the Ethiopian Falashas and the Yemenite Jews were rather sporadic. Elsewhere on the Indian Ocean and in its vicinity they usually tried to destroy the Arab-Turkish merchant marine, and implacably persecuted the Arab traders. The early seventeenth-century Spanish envoy to Persia, García de Silva y Figueroa, reported home:

Some years after the Portuguese began their annual voyages to India, with the inborn hatred that their soldiers and seamen had for all Muslims, they not only sacked, burnt, and destroyed those settlements, but barbarously put all the inhabitants to the sword, without distinction of age or sex. Even nowadays, these islanders, who are half-breed Kaffirs and Arabs, preserve the memory of the great terror caused by the wounds which the Portuguese gave with their swords.

It was rather on the fringes of the Ottoman and Persian provinces that the Portuguese permanently occupied certain outposts, such as the island of Ormuz (Hormuz) in the Persian Gulf, which became a pivotal point in their Indian commerce. Ormuz, which had a cosmopolitan population of Persians, Arabs, Armenians, Turks, Indians, and Jews, became so important that the inhabitants considered it the "navel of the earth." Here, too, the Jewish community had a long socioeconomic and cultural history of its own, and the conquerors had to take cognizance of its traditions along with those of the other racial, religious, and ethnic groups. In most of these areas we have both Jewish and non-Jewish sources recording the medieval history of these communities, which of course continued to develop independently outside the few scattered Portuguese military and commercial strongholds.[108]

Ormuz was occupied in 1515 by the Portuguese explorer Affonso de Albuquerque, assisted by a newly converted Jew, Alexander d'Atayde, also called Hucefe of Castile, and other Jewish residents. (Alexander, who remained in Albuquerque's service in India and later tried to exonerate his master before King Emanuel in Lisbon from the accusations of enemies, ultimately returned to Judaism and settled in Cairo.) The relations between the Portuguese administration and the Jewish community of Ormuz were from the outset quite friendly. Dependent as we are on the one-sided missionary reports, we are led to believe that even the strong missionizing efforts by Jesuits did not antagonize the Jews—which does not seem likely. It may be assumed that men of such outstanding intellectual capacity and character as St. Francis (Francisco de)

Xavier and Gaspar Francisco Barzaeus (Berze) made a great impression upon the leaders of the numerous groups living in that major emporium. The appearance of learned Catholic theologians among the Middle-Eastern Jews, who had shared with their Arab neighbors the relative intellectual stagnation since the thirteenth century, must have presented Christianity in an entirely different light from that familiar to them through their old-fashioned Christian neighbors, divided as these were among various, often quarreling, Eastern sects. According to Barzaeus—from whose reports to the Jesuit headquarters in Europe we learn much about conditions in Ormuz during the two and a half years he stayed in the city (1549–51)—the Jewish population of Ormuz included immigrants from Baghdad and vicinity who were descendants of the ancient Babylonian exiles, as well as from Europe. The fugitives from Portugal and Castile embraced many *conversos,* but also "others who more stubbornly adhered to their errors." The Jesuit claimed that he had established a close friendship with the two rabbis of the community, Solomon and Joseph; had been entertained at Solomon's home; and had even been allowed to preach in the synagogue. On two such occasions he had allegedly engaged in public disputations with the rabbis, while some private debates had been continued at their homes "until late at night." Understandably, the Jesuit leader, then in his mid-thirties, was sanguine enough to expect that the rabbis themselves might be converted to Christianity. But he was disappointed. Except for converting a few Jews and Muslims and some "Gentiles," particularly among the Yogis, he had little to show for his ardent missionary efforts. Barzaeus complained to the home office in Coimbra that lack of personnel prevented him from securing more converts among the Russians, Poles, Hungarians, Janissaries, Greeks, and so forth.[109]

In general, the sixteenth-century missions to the Middle and Far East radically differed from earlier Christian efforts. During the Middle Ages the main emphasis was laid upon the conversion of entire nations and tribes. In the early modern period, on the other hand, not even the more backward African tribes underwent wholesale conversion, only individuals and small groups joined the Christian faith from time to time, and quite a few of these converts later relapsed to their former beliefs. There also were numerous renegades from Christianity to Islam. One of Barzaeus' major activities, therefore, consisted in trying to persuade such apostates to return to the fold, as well as to prevent Jewish or Muslim masters from converting their pagan slaves to their own faith. Yet, generally speaking, intergroup relations, even in family and sexual domains, were rather friendly, and mutual toleration was the order of the day. Such conditions naturally offered little incentive for inquisitorial prosecutions.

Obviously Barzaeus and his colleagues were better prepared than their Jewish interlocutors for debating religious issues. Coming from western Europe, which had a long tradition of religious disputations with Jews, they undoubtedly had at their disposal books and notes reproducing arguments presented by their predecessors over many centuries. If Barzaeus' library was at all comparable to that of St. Francis Xavier, he undoubtedly owned a considerable number of theological and controversial tracts which furnished him both rationales for the Christian point of view and standard replies to Jewish strictures. If he had in his possession, for instance, Nicholas de Lyra's *Postilla* or Paul of Burgos' *Scrutinium scripturarum,* he could even quote to his Jewish listeners not only ancient Greek and Aramaic versions of the Bible, with which they were completely unfamiliar, but also certain rabbinic authorities (interpreted from Christian angles) whom they highly revered. Moreover, Barzaeus' reputation as a learned and honest man was so great (according to a later follower, he was regarded as a "holy prophet" by his Muslim and Jewish contemporaries) that even if he misspelled some rabbinic names they did not dare to controvert him on this score (probably not all the misspellings in the extant texts are due to ignorant copyists). Most Jesuit and other missionaries, moreover, had undergone special training before leaving their home countries, and were astute propagandists. In contrast, the Middle-Eastern Jews had long ago abandoned any efforts at converting infidels, were not interested in the few Hebrew controversial tracts written in the West—we learn only about an Ormuz Jew bringing 48 Hebrew Bibles from Venice for sale among his coreligionists—and were generally ill-prepared for religious debates, from which they could gain little but lose a great deal. This is clearly illustrated in Barzaeus' two polemical discourses of December 10, 1549, and November 24, 1550, which are preserved in an abbreviated form. They dealt with the two major areas of contention between the two faiths: the Trinitarian dogma and the Christian belief that the messiah had already come. To justify the former doctrine, Barzaeus resorted to the oft-reiterated Christian argument that the Old Testament itself was purposely ambiguous about this aspect of the Godhead, as when, in the very first verse of Genesis, it used the singular predicate *bara* (created) for the plural subject *Elohim* (God). Similar scriptural "proofs" have been adduced by Christian apologists for centuries. More philosophically, the Jesuit father argued that a single entity may well appear in three different manifestations without in any way losing its unity. As a popular example he adduced "fire," which remains the same single entity despite its appearance as a flame, as an object shedding light, and as one having a particular color and causing heat. With respect to the advent of the messiah, the Jesuit preacher likewise needed but to resort to the ancient "testimonies," collected by Christian theologians and missionaries in the early centuries of the common era. It is small wonder, then, that the rabbis facing Barzaeus often admitted to being "confused," and that the Jesuit polemist optimistically predicted a mass conversion of the Jews to be forthcoming.[110]

In time, Barzaeus, conceding failure, explained it to his European headquarters as due to the self-interest especially of the Jewish moneylenders, who feared that, upon conversion, they would have to cease charging interest to Christian borrowers. All Jews, moreover, were convinced that, even after conversion, they would still face Portuguese discrimination, at least until the fourth generation. The Jewish community, in fact, continued to flourish in Ormuz after Barzaeus' departure. The Yemenite poet-traveler Zechariah b. Saadiah ad-Dāhri (az-Zahiri) spent six months there later in the sixteenth century. More directly, the Spanish New Christian Pedro Teixeira, who lived in Ormuz in 1593–97, estimated that the island's population then embraced some 150 Jewish families, a figure reduced in 1617 by García de Silva y Figueroa to 100 families in a total population of 2,500–3,000 families. Together with the number of other inhabitants, the size of the Jewish community began declining in 1622, however, when the Persian

Shah Abbas I established Bender Abbas on the mainland as a rival center of trade.[111]

All along Ormuz seems to have attracted but few Portuguese New Christians, doubtless because the ruling Portuguese circles could not give up their racial prejudices, imported from their homeland. This was, indeed, the experience of a New Christian who arrived in Ormuz in 1550 and admittedly was a man of extraordinary learning and character. Yet because of his Jewish ancestry he was refused admission to the Franciscan Order and the Society of Jesus. Francis Xavier himself had insisted that the Society should avoid admitting persons of Hebrew lineage, despite the fact that he must have known that Loyola's closest collaborators, including his successor, Diego Laynez, and his secretary, Joannes Alphonso Polanco, were New Christians. The Ormuz incident occurred a mere three years after the enactment of the statute of *limpieza* in Toledo which had served as a clarion call for anti-Marrano racism in Spain and elsewhere. All of which did not prevent some energetic New Christians from gaining economic power and influence in the East Indies as well. According to Balthasar Dias, vice provost of the Indian province, two New Christians who had recently arrived from Portugal had the province's "entire trade in their hands, and they say that, through their gifts [to dignitaries] they are already beginning to rule and govern that land." [112]

It was this ambiguity of socioeconomic power and socioreligious discrimination which led to the establishment of a formal Inquisition in the East Indies in 1560. The headquarters of the Holy Office were in Goa, the capital and one of the three pillars (together with Ormuz and Malacca) of Portugal's Asian empire and commerce. Although for a time very successful, both commercially and culturally, the Portuguese never endeavored to colonize their Asian possessions in the way they colonized Brazil. The area was too densely populated by peoples of old, established cultures, who rarely yielded to their missionary suasion. True, many natives learned the Portuguese language, which for a time even served as a lingua franca among the various tribes and ethnic groups. As has been pointed out, the century of Portuguese hegemony over the Indian Ocean left behind many more permanent vestiges in the local cultures than did the Dutch predominance of the seventeenth century. Yet demographically, economically, and politically, the Portuguese had remained but a tiny upper stratum of society, which was wiped out by the Dutch, and later by the English, conquerors even more speedily than it had been established.[113]

Remarkably, the New Christian element played a relatively minor role in that phase of Portuguese colonization. To be sure, the opportunities for getting rich quick must have appealed also to enterprising young Marranos. However, the difficulties were much greater here than in Brazil. Most of the trade in the Afro-Asian possessions was controlled by the government through a bureaucracy recruited largely from the noble families and supported by a powerful ecclesiastical hierarchy. Many officials, even among the clergy, were personally engaged in trade on the side, and they viewed New Christian merchants as undesirable competitors, rather than as a welcome accession to the mercantile resources of the colonies. Hindu competition was also very keen, as was that of the Arab, Armenian, and other local traders, although the Portuguese made special efforts to undercut the long-dominant Muslim merchant marine. More importantly, neither the climate nor other environmental conditions appeared attractive to the Portuguese in general. The so-called *soldatos* had no choice but to follow orders and go where they were sent. Unless they deserted, theirs was a lifelong occupation; they had the sole alternative of getting married and leaving the army. At the same time, there were few European women available, since the Afro-Asian areas, unlike Brazil, had a very slight female immigration from the Iberian Peninsula. Although, as we shall presently see, this factor may have played but a minor role in the case of New Christians, it nevertheless served as an additional deterrent to their immigration, and helped to enforce the 1568 Portuguese outlawry of their entry.

Even men were reluctant to proceed to the Far East. True, the great appeal of missionary ideals in that religiously enthusiastic age induced many Jesuits and others to follow the example of St. Francis Xavier and try to convert the Indians, Japanese, and other Asiatics to Christianity. The ability of some officials, after but a few years of service in the East, to return home with a sizable fortune of more than 5,000 cruzados and a collection of precious gems, must also have served as a powerful lure. In fact, despite the numerous legal restrictions and general suspicions, a few New Christians and professing Jews played a considerable role in the commercial and even diplomatic service of the Portuguese colonial administration. Together with Old Christian officials and merchants, some of them also supplied important information to the Dutch during the latter's rapid expansion in southeast Asia in the seventeenth century. As a countermeasure the aforementioned action undertaken in 1649 by António Vieira and Duarte da Silva to organize the Brazil Company not only accrued to the benefit of Brazil and Angola but also helped to save Portugal's Asiatic empire from early dissolution. However, as we recall, this undertaking proved to be short-lived, at least as far as the Marrano community was concerned. Hence a new proposal for an accommodation with the Portuguese New Christians was made about a quarter of a century later. According to that project, not unlike the earlier arrangement, the New Christians were to hire and equip 5,000 men for India and dispatch them there at the rate of 1,200 a month. From 1674 on, they also were to pay 20,000 cruzados annually; assist the work of missionaries; share the expenses in securing the installation of Indian bishops; and help to organize a special company devoted to these tasks.[114]

Nonetheless, it is estimated that the total Portuguese population in the Asiatic lands at no time exceeded 7,000 persons. The very dangers connected with the long journey must have discouraged all but the most daring individuals. Nonstop travel from Lisbon to Goa, the so-called *correia da India,* required six to seven months, under unpredictable weather conditions, in contrast to a duration of but three months for the crossing to Brazilian destinations over the better-charted route of the Atlantic. Plagued by sudden climatic changes and subject to a variety of tropical diseases, often up to half the passengers embarking for the East Indies died during the journey. With only a 50–60 percent chance of survival on the voyage, even the threat of inquisitorial prosecution must have loomed as less risky. On the other hand, some of the Marranos who had defied all dangers to make the journey may have decided, upon arrival, that they would do well to mingle with the local Jewish population, wherever such existed, and altogether disappear from the purview of the Portuguese Inquisition. Such professing Jews became members of the local Jewish communities and shared with them their destiny, which will be analyzed here in a later chapter. Many Old Christians, too, preferred to settle in areas distant from the main Portuguese-controlled harbors, marry or live in concubinage with native women, and gradually be absorbed by the local majorities.[115]

GOA INQUISITION

Nevertheless, some New Christian names appear in the Goa inquisitorial records. For example, in the auto-da-fé of October 25, 1569, performed with great pomp in the presence of Archbishop Jorge Themudo and Inquisitor Alexius Dias Falcão, the eighteen defendants included one man and one woman condemned to burn at the stake. The woman was none other than Catharina de Orta, sister of the distinguished scientist Garcia de Orta, whose bones were later exhumed and burned (1580). Another Jewess suffered martyrdom on October 12, 1572. The disproportionate share of women among the New Christian martyrs may have been owing to the anxiety of many Marranos to avoid exogamy, a concern which caused them to travel in family groups, or to have their wives follow them in larger numbers than was the case among their Old Christian compatriots.[116]

Both the hierarchy and the government officials, moreover, retained their Old World prejudices. A resolution adopted by the provincial Council of Goa in 1567, sharply outlawed the settlement in the Portuguese colonies of any descendants of Jews or Muslims. This resolution was followed by a similar ordinance issued by Viceroy Antão de Noronha. However, efforts to deport New Christians already established in the Far East, proved futile in the face of economic realities. These racial prejudices received an unusual twist in a memorandum submitted on June 1, 1575, to Everard Mercurian, general of the Jesuit Order, by Francisco de Porres, who for over a decade had served as the representative of the Society of Jesus at the court of Philip II in Madrid. The main point he was trying to convey was that no Spanish Jesuits should

be sent into Portuguese territories. Among his ten, mainly xeno-
phobic, arguments was that "Castilians are held in ill repute
among the Portuguese because Castile had once accommodated
numerous Jews, many of whom ultimately came to live in Portugal." Porres evidently overlooked the fact that in 1575, and still
more after 1580, many more Portuguese New Christians settled in
Spain than vice versa. In any case, even after the union of the two
countries under Philip II's regime, an agreement was made that,
to avoid friction, citizens of one country should not settle in the
colonies of the other. However, this agreement was not strictly
enforced. Just as many Portuguese and Brazilian New Christians
settled in Peru and other Spanish possessions in South America, so
did some Spanish officials and missionaries serve in Portugal's
Asiatic colonies, bringing with them the far more rigid adherence
to *limpieza* of their home country. After 1580, in particular, the
colonial administrators appointed by the three Spanish Philips
were prone to apply their racialist approaches even against the
background of the multiracial local societies. On November 20,
1598, a royal decree specifically forbade fortress commanders and
other officials in the East Indies to employ New Christians in any
office, "under severe penalties." On the following day, the king
ordered the viceroy, among other matters, to continue paying
"punctually" the salaries of the Goa inquisitors. The Franciscans,
for instance, looked askance on the relative liberality with which
many Jesuits viewed the admission of New Christians to their
Society. Some of the Jesuit leaders actually voiced displeasure over
the distinction between Old and New Christians. Irksome as it
was in Spain, the doctrine of *limpieza* made little sense to them
in the midst of an overwhelming majority of peoples of other
races; they doubtless also saw in it a serious handicap to their
conversionist drives.[117]

It is not surprising that the Italian Alessandro Valignano (or
Valignani), who served as a *visitador* in India in 1574, was keenly
aware of the evil effects of that doctrine. Generally a rather severe
disciplinarian, who was said to have driven some subordinates to
the brink of suicide, he was quite outspoken in this respect. In his
remarkable dispatch of January 13, 1574, to the headquarters of
the Jesuit Order, he dolefully reminisced on the historic record

of the mass conversions of Spanish and Portuguese Jews by Ferdinand the Catholic and Emanuel of Portugal some 70–80 years before. He exclaimed: "May God our Lord forgive them both, as well as the counselors who advised them in this matter!" He contended that many of the New Christians had thus been enabled to amass great wealth and intermarry with the nobility, while many others had continued to live a secret Jewish life and had frequently been forced to appear before the Inquisition. What was even worse, because of prevailing suspicions, many of them were still being excluded from public office, colleges, and various other corporate groups. In contrast, it may be noted that, in reply to a request from Rector Melchior Nunes Barreto, Diego Laynez, the New Christian general of the society of Jesus, took time out from his arduous labors as a papal "theologian" at the Council of Trent to suggest to the Portuguese branch of the Society that it secure from the king a prohibition forbidding "white Jews" from Turkey and Persia to enter India. This was five years before the resolutions of the Goa Council of 1567. Ecclesiastical intransigence came to the fore also in the Goa hierarchy's negative reply of April 9, 1579, to the query as to whether some local pagan rituals were to be tolerated. Its arguments were supported by rather forced reasoning from certain provisions of canon law, the example of Julian the Apostate's relations to ancient Jewry, and the expulsion of the Jews from Spain.[118]

It is small wonder, then, that the attitude of many Jesuit leaders toward the Goan Inquisition was rather ambivalent. At first, they were actually the driving force in the establishment of that Holy Office. As early as 1543—when, as we recall, the Inquisition in Lisbon and Coimbra had only begun to function—the prominent Jesuit missionary Miguel Váez, suggested that such a tribunal was necessary for the Asiatic colonies. Three years later, he was seconded by no less an authority than St. Francis Xavier, who now argued that too many persons "live according to the Mosaic Law or the Moorish sect without any fear of God and to the shame of the world." King John III at first paid no heed to these suggestions. He was probably guided by the same considerations as were later voiced by the Portuguese ambassador to Rome, Lourenço Pires. In 1557 Pires expressed his apprehension that such a move would accrue to the disadvantage of God and the realm, for it would merely bring to Basra and Cairo many refugees who would assist the enemy both in finance and war. Yet after the death of the hesitant John in the same year, the much weaker Regency gradually yielded to the pressure of the Jesuits and other missionaries. Also in 1557, Gundisalvus de Silveira described to Cardinal Henry, the Portuguese inquisitor-general since 1539, the conditions in India, and emphasized the strong opposition encountered by the Christian missions. Among other opponents he particularly mentioned the "great and most perverse Jewry," which was sharply antagonistic to Christian conversion. He insisted that the only remedy against both Jews and bad Christians would be the establishment of an Inquisition. Under the pressure of these and other intercessions, royal papers approving the general idea were brought to India by another Jesuit, Sebastian Pinheiro, in 1554–55, although it was not until 1560 that the tribunal was fully set up.[119]

No sooner was the Holy Office established, however, than the attitude of the Jesuit spokesman on the spot began changing. Perhaps a minor irritant was the fact that Jesuits in general were given less prominent positions at the new court than Dominicans or, to a lesser extent, Franciscans, who had traditionally administered the Holy Office in almost all countries. Ultimately, in their correspondence with the headquarters of the Society of Jesus in Rome, they assumed a sufficiently critical position for General Everard Mercurian to issue an order to all members of the Society in the Far East not to participate in the actual prosecutions and trials but only to assist in such functions as hearing confessions from imprisoned heretics and being present at autos-da-fé. Yet, in practice, members of the Society of Jesus could not well avoid direct involvement. It is estimated that in the years 1500–1788 no less than 25 percent of the recorded 100 deputies in inquisitorial proceedings were recruited from the Jesuit Order. It was now left only to outright opponents, like the enlightened Frenchman Claude de Dellon, who had himself spent five years in an inquisitorial prison, sharply to condemn these proceedings. Typical of Dellon's observations, in a volume published in 1688, was the following statement: "The cruel Inquisition, so holy in name but so terrible in its conduct, which is established in all the places under the domination of the king of Portugal, has greatly contributed to the alienation of idolaters from baptism and to causing those who had already received it to apostasize. One will see the reasons thereof when I discuss the maxims of that redoubtable tribunal." He also emphasized, in particular, the injustices committed by the Inquisition against accused Judaizers.[120]

Of course, with their world-wide view, the Jesuits, most of whom had come to the Far East to spread the Gospel among pagans, Muslims, and Jews, were far less interested in prosecuting secret Judaizers than in persuading professing Jews to become Christians. They must have realized that the anti-Jewish and anti-Muslim resolutions of the first Church Council of Goa of 1567, the pertinent ordinance by Viceroy Antão de Noronha in the same year, the rumors about the harshness of inquisitorial prosecutions, and the suspicion that many arrests were motivated by greed rather than by religious zeal, could only discourage Jews from joining the Christian faith. The Jesuit leaders were most interested, therefore, in preparing special catechisms aimed at persuading the polytheistic populations of the superiority of Christianity over Islam and Judaism.

At the same time, the Portuguese authorities tried to forestall the spread of apologetic and polemical tracts emanating from Muslims and Jews, as well as the importation of Protestant writings from Europe. For this purpose they introduced a strict censorship, taking as their guide the catalogue of prohibited books published by Cardinal Henry in 1551. Censorship became so strict that even the inquisitor Gundisalvus da Silveira had to ask the cardinal for a license to read books by Moors, Gentiles, and Jews in their own languages so as to be able to find the proper answers for use in his conversionist efforts. Silveira apparently read Greek, but he probably used interpreters to translate Hebrew, Arabic, and other theological works for him. In the mother country Geronimo Nadal worked out in the summer of 1561 a special statute for the censors in the Orient. The administration also tried to prevent Jewish and Muslim masters from converting their pagan slaves to Judaism or Islam. The Jesuits established in Goa a house of catechumens, in which they tried to teach pros-

pective converts the principles of the Christian faith. They rejoiced, of course, if a Jew, like Joseph d'Atayde, formerly of Ben-
gal, joined their faith. With equal jubilation, the Spanish Jesuit
Francisco Pérez, described in 1548 the conversion of a Jewish
woman together with her two daughters and a son—the Jesuit
father did not fail to mention in this connection that they were
all wealthy: "I think that each of them commands a fortune of
1,500 ducats"—as well as that of a Roman Jew who had frequently visited his church and discussed religious teachings with
him. This Jew "was very well known," Pérez added while describing the convert's baptism performed with great pomp. On
the whole, however, the few Jewish individuals recorded in the
sources as adopting Christianity contrasted with hundreds of
"Gentiles," whose group baptism was often turned into a spectacular pageant—a pageant which in no way prevented many later
relapses.[121]

In Malabar the Portuguese ran upon a further difficulty. There
they encountered a large sect of Eastern Christians going under
the name of Disciples of St. Thomas. According to Gregorius de
Castro's 1574 report to Antonio Possevino, secretary-general of the
Society of Jesus in Rome, these sectarians, numbering some 70,000
souls, had been originally influenced by Chaldean and Armenian
priests and they staunchly resisted the efforts of the Western missionaries by adhering to their "errors." They also preserved many
Judaic elements in their theology and rituals. A later report by
the Spaniard Manuel de Faria y Sousa mentioned that they recited prayers in Chaldaic (Syriac) at three daily services, observed
the rituals of circumcision and fasting, denied the virginity of
Mary, refused to worship images, and rejected confession. At the
same time, they played a highly significant commercial role because they enjoyed, according to old royal privileges, a monopoly
in the Malabar pepper trade. They remind one of other cohesive
sectarian minorities, like the Quakers and the Mormons in the
United States, whose solidarity, partially in response to outside
pressures, helped them to achieve remarkable successes in business. In his generally laudatory description of the Disciples of St.
Thomas in 1579 another leading Jesuit emphasized that among
their other traits they were well-mannered and valiant warriors,

but added: "In their majority [they] live from trade, buying local produce and ivory and even entering into illicit contracts. They are more persuasive [*pláticos*] in trading and generally richer than the Malabar Jews and Muslims." Castro, too, had emphasized that, apart from "thousands upon thousands of pagans, one finds here also some Moors and Jews," attracted to the region by its wealth and large traffic. This region included the old, racially mixed Jewish community in Cochin, which appears quite frequently in the Jesuit reports of the period.[122]

On their eastward march the Portuguese made even slower progress. According to another Jesuit report of 1579, in the whole area east of the Ganges there were only some 70 Portuguese families, 200 single soldiers, and 4,000 native Christians. This figure doubtless included Eastern Christians settled in the Far East before the arrival of the Portuguese, who now also encountered Spaniards coming from the Pacific Ocean. The Philippines, the most remote colony of the Spanish Empire, seem to have attracted but few New Christians. To be sure, after the establishment of the Mexican Inquisition in 1570, the islands were subject to its authority. Despite the great distances separating the two colonies, and the paucity of shipping from Acapulco to Manila, we hear of occasional Marranos sent for trial from the Philippines to Mexico City. Two such Judaizers, Jorje and Domingo Rodríguez, appeared in a Mexican auto of March 28, 1593. But they escaped with a mere reconciliation, although they undoubtedly lost their property and may have had to start afresh upon their return to Manila. A third New Christian, Diego Hernández, who had attained the important position of *regidor* of Vitoria, was imprisoned, and his property was sequestered, solely on his cook's testimony that she had been ordered to slaughter chickens by cutting their throats rather than by strangling them. While the Inquisition was still searching for further data from his earlier residence in Oporto, he died in prison. Another incident is recorded in 1663. Upon arrival in Manila, the new inquisitorial commissioner José de Paternina Samaniego, an Augustinian friar, brought with him the reputation of having led a disorderly life in both Spain and Mexico. He was formally denounced by his fellow-Augustinian Fray Cristóbal de León, who cited a previous reprimand of Paternina by the prior-general of the Augustinian Order for immoral behavior during his visitation to various convents in Old Castile. Paternina reciprocated by denouncing Cristóbal to the Augustinian provincial as a Jew and usurer, whereupon Cristóbal was arrested and so harshly treated that he never left prison alive. But these few incidents, in the main culled by the indefatigable José Toribio Medina from inquisitorial archives, doubtless are mere exceptions proving the rule that few New Christians sought shelter in these distant islands. We know even less about professing Jews living there before or after the Spanish occupation. Regular Jewish communities were established on the Philippine islands only after the Spanish-American War.[123]

WORLD-WIDE EXPANSION

Coinciding with the vast European expansion begun late in the fifteenth century, the growing Marrano dispersion opened new outlets for the energies of the most persecuted segment of the Jewish people. Increasing numbers of Marranos found shelter in the Spanish and Portuguese possessions of the New World, some daring souls penetrating even the Iberian possessions in Africa and Asia. The Marrano Diaspora thus formed nuclei for future Jewish settlements in areas theretofore unknown to Europeans. It required only the occupation of these Spanish-Portuguese territories by more friendly nations like the French, the English, and particularly the Dutch, for the early settlers to cast off their Christian masks and to become professing Jews.

The most spectacular example was offered by Brazil. The Dutch occupation of its northeastern region, though lasting only twenty-four years (1630–1654), gave rise to the first professing Jewish community in the New World, fully organized along traditional lines. While the return of the Portuguese to Pernambuco forced most of these Jewish settlers to leave the country (undoubtedly but a small number went underground and remained in Brazil), a substantial residuum of Jews lived on in the Guianas, especially Surinam, which in the eighteenth century embraced one of the largest and most affluent Jewish communities in the Americas. At the same time, Brazilian Jewish refugees reinforced the small groups of Jews already residing in the Caribbean Islands and laid the foundations for new settlements, including those in the North-American English colonies. Nor did the crypto-Jews totally vanish from Mexico, Peru, or the rest of Spanish America.

Of course, numerically all these scattered settlements added up to a small fraction of the Jewish people. The masses of Sephardic Jewry who had found accommodation in the Ottoman Empire or North Africa did not join the procession of their brethren who were belatedly leaving the shrinking remnants of their communities on the Iberian Peninsula or in its West-European dependencies. Even less did this great historic evolution affect the growing Ashkenazic population in Poland-Lithuania and Germany. It was only during the Thirty Years' War that many German Jews began seeking asylum in Holland and other West-European lands. But few ventured across the Atlantic Ocean. Polish Jewry began its large-scale westward migrations only after the Cossack massacres of 1648–49 and the following decade of disturbances in their home country. However, even then it sent out very few pioneers on the trans-Atlantic trek.

Religious restraints doubtless contributed to the discouraging complexities of living in a totally new environment, from most of which they were barred by the law of the land. To Marranos migrating into West-European and American areas the new opportunities for secretly observing their Jewish laws seemed quite inviting. Even in Spanish-dominated Latin America, with its rigid religious controls by the Holy Office, most secret Judaizers undoubtedly escaped prosecution. Where an effective Inquisition was missing, as in Brazil or the French colonies, not to speak of the territories dominated by the Protestant powers of Holland and England, the security of an individual who practiced Jewish rites in the secrecy of his home must have appeared to be a great blessing compared with the ever-present threat to Peninsular Marranos caught in the observance of some Jewish ritual. To the Ashkenazim, on the other hand, life in the New World appeared then and long after to be a serious menace to the perpetuation of their traditional way of life. Even during the mass migration of East-European Jewry at the turn of the twentieth century, many rabbis in Eastern Europe and the United States expressed deep apprehension about the inroads made in the observance of Jewish law by the assimilatory pressures of the new environment, though the Jewish immigrants were perfectly free to pursue their own religious mode of living. In the earlier periods, when the existing tiny communities were able to supply only minimal religious facilities and had few persons able to offer religious guidance to old and young, complete disappearance loomed as a distinct possibility. Intermarriage, too, was considered a major menace to Jewish survival. It took, therefore, much time before the overwhelming local and regional pressures, demographic, economic, and political, forced substantial masses of Jews to change their residence from one continent to another.

However, even in its burgeoning phase, Europe's overseas expansion opened vast new opportunities to persecuted groups, including persons publicly or secretly professing Judaism. It thus marked an epochal turn in the destinies of the Jewish people. Just at the time when their fortunes seemed at the lowest ebb, the expanding horizons of the European man opened unexpected new outlets for the survivalist energies of the most desperate branch of world Jewry.

NOTES

ABBREVIATIONS

AHR	American Historical Review
AHSI	Archivum historicum Societatis Iesu
AJA	American Jewish Archives
AJHQ	American Jewish Historical Quarterly, continuation of *PAJHS*
AKKR	Archiv für katholisches Kirchenrecht
Américo Castro Jub. Vol.	Collected Studies in Honour of Américo Castro's Eightieth Year, ed. by M. P. Hornik. London, 1965.
Annales ESC	Annales Economies, Sociétés, Civilisations
ARG	Archiv für Reformationsgeschichte
b.	ben or bar (son)
BAE	Biblioteca de autores españoles
BAH	Boletín de la Real Academia de la Historia, Madrid
BEC	Bibliothèque de l'École des Chartes
BEP	Bulletin des études portugaises
BGN	Bijdragen voor de Geschiedenis der Nederlanden
BH	Bulletin hispanique
BHR	Bibliothèque d'Humanisme et Renaissance
BHS	Bulletin of Hispanic Studies
BIHR	Bulletin of the Institute of Historical Research of the University of London
BJRL	Bulletin of the John Rylands Library
BMGJW	Bijdragen en Mededeelingen of the Genootschap voor de Joodsche Wetenschap in Nederland
BSOAS	Bulletin of the School of Oriental and African Studies, University of London
BVG	Bijdragen voor vaterlandsche Geschiedenis
CH	Church History
CHE	Cuadernos de historia de España
CODOIN	Colección de documentos inéditos of the Academia de la Historia in Madrid
EcHR	Economic History Review
EHR	English Historical Review
Festschrift Simon Dubnow	Festschrift zu Simon Dubnows siebzigsten Geburtstag. Berlin, 1930.
HAHR	Hispanic American Historical Review
HJ	Historia Judaica
HTR	Harvard Theological Review

HUCA	Hebrew Union College Annual
HZ	Historische Zeitschrift
JC	Salo W. Baron, *The Jewish Community.* 3 vols. Philadelphia, 1942.
JFF	Jüdische Familien-Forschung
JGJCR	Jahrbuch der Gesellschaft für Geschichte der Juden in der Čechoslowakischen Republik
JGLA	Jahrbuch für Geschichte von Staat, Wirtschaft und Gesellschaft Lateinamerikas
JHSE	Jewish Historical Society of England
JJGL	Jahrbuch für jüdische Geschichte und Literatur
JJLG	Jahrbuch der Jüdisch-Literarischen Gesellschaft, Frankfurt a.M.
JJS	Journal of Jewish Studies
JMH	Journal of Modern History
JNOS	Jahrbücher für Nationalökonomie und Statistik
JQR	Jewish Quarterly Review (new series, unless otherwise stated)
JSS	Jewish Social Studies
KS	Kirjath Sepher, Quarterly Bibliographical Review
MCV	Mélanges de la Casa de Velázquez
MGWJ	Monatsschrift für Geschichte und Wissenschaft des Judentums
PAAJR	Proceedings of the American Academy for Jewish Research
PAJHS	Publications of the American Jewish Historical Society
PL	Patrologiae cursus completus, series Latina, ed. by J. P. Migne
PMLA	Publications of the Modern Language Association
RABM	Revista de Archivos, Bibliotecas y Museos
RBPH	Revue belge de philologie et d'histoire
REJ	Revue des études juives
RH	Revue historique
RHPR	Revue d'histoire et de philosophie religieuses
RMI	Rassegna mensile di Israel
SR	Studia Rosenthaliana
TG	Tijdschrift voor Geschiedenis
TJHSE	Transactions of the Jewish Historical Society of England
TRHS	Transactions of the Royal Historical Society
VSW	Vierteljahrsschrift für Sozial- und Wirtschaftsgeschichte
ZHB	Zeitschrift für hebräische Bibliographie
ZRGG	Zeitschrift für Religions- und Geistesgeschichte

NOTES

CHAPTER LXIII: DUTCH JERUSALEM

1. C. Rahlenbeek, "Les Juifs à Anvers," *Revue de Belgique*, VIII, 137–46, esp. p. 140; J. Toussaert, *Le Sentiment religieux en Flandre à la fin du moyen âge*, with a Preface by M. Molat, p. 216. See also R. Doehaerd's general observations in her "Commerce et morale à Anvers au XVIe siècle (à propos d'un manuscrit de la Bibliothèque de Leyde)," *RH*, CCIV, 226–33 (with special reference to a manuscript written in Antwerp in 1576); H. van der Wee, "Das Phänomen des Wachstums und der Stagnation im Lichte der Antwerpener und südniederländischen Wirtschaft des XVI. Jahrhunderts," *VSW*, LIV, 203–249, esp. p. 246; and other monographs reviewed by H. Lapeyre—with particular attention to Antwerp's commerce with the Netherlands, France, Italy, Spain, and Portugal; its monetary market; and its prevailing prices and salaries—in his "Anvers au XVIe siècle d'après des travaux récents," *Revue d'histoire moderne et contemporaine*, XI, 191–202. On Antwerp's earlier history, see E. Schremmer's "Antwerpen als Warenhandelsplatz im 15. und 16. Jahrhundert und seine wirtschaftliche Beziehungen zu Mitteleuropa," *JNOS*, CLXXVIII, 270–84; such more detailed monographs as W. Brulez's *De Firma della Faille en de internationale Handel* (The Della Faille Firm and the International Trade of Flemish Firms in the Sixteenth Century), with a Foreword by C. Verlinden; and E. Coornaërt's comments thereon in his "À Anvers au XVIe siècle: la firma Della Faille," *Annales ESC*, XVI, 127–35 (also instructive for the business practices of the New Christian firms); and other data mentioned *supra*, Vol. XIII, pp. 119 ff., 368 ff. nn. 62–70.

2. This document, preserved in the Brabant Archive, is cited here from a copy prepared by the late Izaak Prins, which is now in the possession of the Jewish Historical General Archive in Jerusalem, No. P87/15. I am indebted to the administration of the Jerusalem Archive for their permission to inspect and use some of the documents left behind by that indefatigable student of the history of Dutch Jewry.

3. Philip II's complaint reproduced in L. P. Gachard's ed. of *Correspondance de Philippe II sur les affaires des Pays-Bas (1558–1577), publiée d'après les originaux conservés dans les archives royales de Simancas*, I, 327 No. xxv; Fray Lorenzo de Villaviçencio's letters to Margaret of Parma, summarized by A. Cauchie and L. van der Essen in their *Inventaire des Archives Farnesiennes de Naples au point de vue de l'histoire des Pays-Bas Catholiques*, p. 81 Fasc. 1317/1; M. Dierickx, *Documents inédits sur l'érection des nouveaux diocèses aux Pays-Bas (1521–1570)*, III, 55 ff. No. 488, 263 ff. No. 608, 297 f. No. 629, 302 No. 631; Provost Maximilien Morillon's letter to Cardinal Granvella, dated Louvain, September 29, 1566, in E. Poullet, ed., *Correspondance du Cardinal de Granvelle (1565–1588)*, I, 501. On Margaret's personal attitude, see F. Rachfahl's biography, *Margarete von Parma, Statthalterin der Niederlande*. While Morillon and other officials tried to attribute the success of Protestant

propaganda to Portuguese Marranos, I. S. Révah has rightly observed that the two leading New Christian Calvinists, Marcus Pérez and Fernando Bernuy, were of Spanish, rather than Portuguese, extraction (*REJ*, CXXII, 128; see *infra*, nn. 4 and 22). See also P. J. Hauben, "Marcus Pérez and Marrano Calvinism in the Dutch Revolt and the Reformation," *BHR*, XXIX, 121–32. This fact is also borne out by the lists of Protestant heretics submitted by the government's intelligence agents in 1566–67: among others, Pérez is specifically mentioned as "a Spaniard, Jew by race"; only a few Portuguese names are recorded in these lists.

Of interest for the history of the Hebrew book are the names of two suspects: Carl van Bomberghe, son of Daniel, the famous publisher of the Talmud, the rabbinic Bible, and other rabbinic works in Venice; and Christophe Plantin, the printer of the Antwerp Polyglot. See L. van der Essen, "Episodes de l'histoire religieuse et commerciale d'Anvers dans la seconde moitié du XVIe siècle. Rapport secret du Gerónimo de Curiel, facteur du roi d'Espagne à Anvers, sur les marchands hérétiques ou suspects de cette ville, 1566," *Bulletins* of the Commission royale de l'histoire of the Belgian Academy of Science, LXXX, 321–62; idem, "Le Progrès du luthéranisme et du calvinisme dans le monde commercial d'Anvers et l'espionnage politique du marchand Philippe Dauxy, agent secret de Marguerite de Parme, en 1566–1567," *VSW*, XII, 152–234, esp. pp. 209 f., 212 No. 20, 220, 223; and *infra*, n. 21. See also P. Goemaere, "Comment Plantin échappa au bûcher," *Revue générale belge*, 2d century (1965), I, No. 4, pp. 47–52 (because of the publication by his Leiden press of a pamphlet strongly supporting Dom Antonio's claim to the throne of Portugal, Plantin found it extremely difficult to prove his personal noninvolvement); and P. Theunissen, "Arias Montano et la Polyglotte d'Anvers," *Lettres romanes*, XIX, 231–46; and *supra*, Vol. XIII, pp. 391 n. 4. Of interest also is P. T. van Beuningen's comprehensive biographical study of Willem Damaaszoon van der Lindt, who served as inquisitor in the crucial years 1560–69. See his *Wilhelmus Lindanus als inquisiteur en bisschop* (W. L. as Inquisitor and Bishop: a Contribution to His Biography, 1525–1576).

4. I. S. Révah, "Pour l'histoire des Marranes à Anvers; recensements de la 'Nation Portugaise' de 1571 à 1666," *REJ*, CXXII, 123–47, esp. pp. 132 ff. Docs. A–D. See J. Denucé, "A Secret Synagogue in Antwerp in the XVIth Century" (Dutch), *Antwerpsch Archievenblad*, 2d ser. IV, 151–54 (also conceding the possibility that other secret synagogues existed in the city in 1579–83 and in 1594). See M. Dierickx, "La Politique religieuse de Philippe II dans les anciens Pays-Bas," *Hispania* (Madrid), XVI, 130–46 (p. 146 English summary), esp. pp. 134 f.

5. See É. Scholliers, "Un Indice du loyer; les loyers anversois de 1500 à 1873," *Studi in onore di Amintore Fanfani*, V, 593–617; R. Boumans, "Le Dépeuplement d'Anvers, dans le dernier quart du XVIe siècle," *Revue du Nord*, XXIX, 181–94; W. Brulez, "Anvers de 1585 à 1650," *VSW*, LIV, 75–99; V. Vázquez de Prada, *Lettres marchandes d'Anvers*, I, 140 f., 144 ff., 157 ff. See also the slightly different figures cited *supra*, Vol. XIII, p. 119. Antwerp's commercial and financial difficulties, as well as the noteworthy tenacity of its mercantile class, are well illustrated by the data supplied by H. Pohl in "Die Zuckereinfuhr nach Antwerpen durch portugiesische Kaufleute während des 80-jährigen Krieges," *JGLA*, IV, 348–73, esp. pp. 352 and 359 ff.; R. B. Outhwaite, "The Trials of Foreign Borrowing: the English Crown and the Antwerp Money Market in the Mid-Sixteenth Century," *EcHR*, 2d ser. XIX, 289–305; W.

Brulez's interesting survey "Le Commerce international des Pays-Bas au XVIᵉ siècle, essai d'appréciation quantitative," *RBPH*, XLVI, 1205–1222 (showing, among other aspects, that fully one-quarter of the industrial production was intended for export); his "The Balance of Trade of the Netherlands in the Middle of the XVIth Century," *Acta historica neerlandica*, IV, 20–48; H. Lonchay's article cited *infra*, n. 7; and other studies listed *supra*, Vol. XIII, pp. 371 f. n. 67. On the Jewish situation, see S. Ullmann, *Studien zur Geschichte der Juden in Belgien bis zum XVIII. Jahrhundert*; E. Schmidt, *Geschiedenis van de Joden in Antwerpen* (A History of the Jews in Antwerp), with an Intro. by N. Gunzburg (mainly analyzing the more recent periods). The voluminous work by F. Prims, *Histoire d'Anvers*, however, contributes little to our knowledge of the Jewish status.

6. See M. Dierickx, "La Politique religieuse," *Hispania* (Madrid), XVI, 134 f.; J. Lefèvre, ed., *La Correspondance de Philippe II sur les affaires des Pays-Bas*, Part II: Recueil destiné à faire suite aux travaux de L. P. Gachard, esp. pp. 517 ff. Nos. 1092–93; and *infra*, n. 20.

7. C. Demeuré, "Les Juifs en Belgique," *Revue de droit international*, XX, 246–59, 464–75; E. Ouverleaux, "Notes et documents sur les Juifs de Belgique sous l'ancien Régime," *REJ*, VII, 117–38, 252–71; VIII, 206–234; IX, 264–89, esp. VII, 257 and the sources cited there; H. Lonchay, "Étude sur les emprunts des souverains belges au XVIᵉ et XVIIᵉ siècle," *Bulletin* of the Académie r. de Belgique. Classe des Lettres. 1907, pp. 923–1013, esp. pp. 962 ff. On the contemporary contradictions in the Spanish homeland, see *infra*, Chap. LXV, nn. 27 ff. We shall presently see that the same issue arose after 1648 through the inclusion in the Treaty of Münster of a more permanent provision relating to the reciprocal treatment of Dutch and Belgian subjects. See *infra*, n. 12. In general, the application to Jews of the principle of reciprocity among states agitated the minds of many statesmen and was subjected to varying interpretations as late as the nineteenth and early twentieth centuries.

8. H. Lonchay, J. Cuvelier, and J. Lefèvre, eds., *Correspondance de la Cour d'Espagne sur les affaires des Pays-Bas au XVIIᵉ siècle*, I, 434 No. 1051, 472 No. 1184 (see also *ibid.*, VI, 50 ff., relating to the original 1601 Portuguese New Christians' offer of 1,000,000 ducats in exchange for a general pardon; according to Archduke Albert's Madrid agent Canon Juan Carillo, the money was to be used by Spain for its war against the Dutch rebels; see *infra*, Chap. LXV, nn. 25 ff.). In all these negotiations the attitude of the archducal pair seems to have played a more decisive role than the vacillating policies of the central government in Madrid, since, according to C. H. Carter, the couple had much greater independent authority than is usually attributed to them. See his "Belgian 'Autonomy' under the Archdukes, 1598–1621," *JMH*, XXXVI, 245–59; and, more generally, his *The Secret Diplomacy of the Habsburgs, 1598–1625*. But in regard to the admission of Jews there seems to have been little disagreement between the Belgian rulers and Philip III's Madrid counselors.

9. H. J. Elias, "L'Église et l'État: théories et controverses dans les Pays-Bas catholiques au début du XVIIᵉ siècle," *RBPH*, V, 453–69, 905–932; A. Cauchie and R. Maere, eds., *Recueil des instructions générales aux nonces de Flandre (1596–1635)*, Nos. iv, pp. 36 ff. and 44; v, pp. 57 ff., 65; vi, 75 ff., 80; J. Lefèvre, ed., *Documents relatifs à la jurisdiction des nonces et internonces des Pays-Bas pendant le régime*

espagnol (1596–1706). See also A. Pasture, "Le Placard d'hérésie du 31. décembre 1609, sa portée juridique et son application pendant le règne des archiducs Albert et Isabelle (1609–1633)," *Mélanges d'histoire offerts à Charles Moeller*, II, 301–310. In Brussels, too, the Flemish Council of State, which was recruited from the high local aristocracy and still retained considerable influence on domestic affairs, shared the rulers' anti-Jewish prejudice but slightly tempered by considerations in the interests of the state. Its attitude is well illustrated by the Council's report of June 19, 1607, on a proposal submitted by a New Christian Benedictine monk, Martin, who had enabled many Jews to move from Spain to France. If the proposal (here not detailed) were to prove acceptable, the Council opined, Martin's brother, arrested and condemned to death for illegal importation of copper vellon, should be released and provided with a pension, so that he could settle somewhere "far from the Inquisition, of which he lives in terror." See Lonchay *et al.*, eds. *Correspondance de la Cour d'Espagne*, I, 255 f. No. 582.

10. S. Ullmann, *Histoire des Juifs en Belgique jusqu'au 18ᵉ siècle (notes et documents)*, p. 70; I. S. Révah, "Pour l'histoire," *REJ*, CXXII, 141 ff. Docs. E–F; *infra*, n. 48. See also J. A. Goris, *Étude sur les colonies marchandes méridionales (Portugais, Espagnols, Italiens) à Anvers de 1488 à 1567*, pp. 54, 614 ff.; and other literature listed *supra*, Vol. XIII, pp. 369 ff. nn. 64 ff. While generally approving a proposed treaty with Duke Frederick of Holstein, Philip IV demanded from Isabella, since Albert's death in 1621 sole sovereign of Flanders, certain stipulations which would exclude the Portuguese residing in Holland from the reciprocal benefits of that treaty. See his letter to Isabella of April 24, 1626, with the editor's note thereon, in H. Lonchay *et al.*, eds., *Correspondance de la Cour d'Espagne*, II, 277 No. 890.

11. R. Mols, "Bilan d'ensemble des recherches de démographie historique en Belgique depuis une vingtaine d'années," and H. Van Werveke, "La Mortalité catastrophique en Flandre au XVIIᵉ siècle," both in *Actes du Colloque international de Démographie historique*, held in Liège, April 18–20, 1963, pp. 121–53, 457–64; J. Charlier, *La Peste à Bruxelles de 1667 à 1669 et ses conséquences démographiques* (with some corrections by C. Bruneel in his review thereof in *RBPH*, XLVIII, 515–19; H. Lonchay *et al.*, eds., *Correspondance de la Cour d'Espagne*, III, 524 No. 1629, 584 No. 1798, 619 No. 1903. The family name of the first-mentioned Jewish prisoner was erroneously given by the governor as Bruno in the 1645 dispatch, but it was subsequently corrected to Bueno in that of 1647. There were several families called Bueno (with various spellings) and, of course, others named Cohen, in Amsterdam. See, for instance, the Index to H. I. Bloom's *The Economic Activities of the Jews of Amsterdam*, pp. 268 ff. On the expiration of the truce in 1621, Spain's attempt in 1626 to force Holland to its knees by a sort of Continental blockade, and the dismal failure of this undertaking, see R. Ródenas Vilar, "Un Gran proyecto anti-holandés en tiempo de Felipe IV: La destrucción del comercio rebelde en Europa," *Hispania* (Madrid), XXII, 542–58; and *infra*, Chap. LXV, n. 63.

12. H. Lonchay *et al.*, eds., *Correspondance*, VI, 659 No. 618 (in a reply of July 9, 1650, to a dispatch of the Spanish ambassador in The Hague, Antoine Brun). The opinion of the Commission appointed by Archduke Leopold William on December 11, 1653, is reproduced in the Spanish original, with a French translation, by É. Ouverleaux in his "Notes et documents," *REJ*, VII, 260 ff. Other aspects are treated

in R. Boumans, "Le Dépeuplement d'Anvers, dans le dernier quart du XVIe siècle," *Revue du Nord*, XXIX, 181–94; F. Prims, "Jews in Antwerp in 1682–1694" (Dutch), *BGN*, XV, 166–74 (includes documents of interest for the earlier period); E. Schmidt, *Geschiedenis van de Joden in Antwerpen;* and, more generally, S. Ullmann, *Studien zur Geschichte der Juden in Belgien bis zum XVIII. Jahrhundert;* and some documents included in his *Histoire des Juifs en Belgique*, esp. pp. 70 ff. See also C. H. Carter, "Belgian 'Autonomy' under the Archdukes," *JMH*, XXXVI, 249; as well as some other studies listed by A. van Laar in his *Bibliographie van de Geschiedenis van de Stad Antwerpen* (Bibliography for the History of the City of Antwerp); and by H. Lapeyre in his aforementioned review article, *supra*, n. 1.

Innocent X's sharp intervention against any relaxation of the ban on Jewish settlement, with which Philip IV concurred (*REJ*, VII, 267 ff.), may be attributed in part to some general considerations. As we recall, only a short time before, the pope had lodged a protest against the Treaties of Westphalia, which had provided for mutual toleration of Catholic and Protestant minorities in the belligerent countries. He and his advisers doubtless considered it inconsistent with this policy to allow the Spanish regime, theretofore the staunchest supporter of the Counter Reformation, to comply with the treaty provisions to the extent of tolerating a Jewish congregation, holding public services, in a land from which Jews had been barred for several centuries. See also P. Voltes's general observations on "Iglesia y estado en el epílogo de la dominación española en Flandes," *Hispania sacra*, X, 91–118 (emphasizing the interrelations between the weakening ecclesiastical controls and the decline of the political regime). On its part, the Dutch government insisted that "all Jews, whether or not born in Spain, shall be given all liberties and rights for persons and property, as stipulated in the Treaty." See the *Resolutiën van de Staten van Holland* of July 27, 1649, and March 23, 1651, cited by M. Wolff in "The First Settlement of the Jews in Amsterdam: Their Political and Economic Status" (Dutch), *BVG*, 4th ser. IX, 365–400; X, 134–82, 354–69; 5th ser. I, 88–101, 350–76, esp. IX, 385; *supra*, n. 7; and *infra*, nn. 17 and 84.

13. H. Lonchay *et al.*, eds., *Correspondance*, V, 8 No. 17; VI, 686 No. 1578.

14. I. S. Révah, "Pour l'histoire," *REJ*, CXXII, 145 ff. Doc. G; K. Liberman, "La Découverte d'une synagogue secrète à Anvers à la fin du dix-septième siècle," *REJ*, C, 36–48. Don Garcia de Yllan is indeed called by C. J. R. Burenstam "the very rich Portuguese Israelite" whom the queen caused to be appointed by the king of Spain as his resident in Antwerp at the beginning of 1654. See his *La Reine Christine de Suède à Anvers et Bruxelles 1654–1655*, p. 8 (citing a Simancas archival document). The strictures against this identification which are advanced by J. Denucé in his "Queen Christina of Sweden in Antwerp, 1654, and Don Garcia de Yllan" (Dutch), *Antwerpsch Archievenblad*, 2d ser. II, 31–36, are inconclusive. See *supra*, Vol. XIII, pp. 127 f., 374 n. 72.

For that matter, even Old Christians were not necessarily immune from judaizing. Later in the century, Doña Isabel de Correa, a native Spaniard, married a Colonel Nicolás de Olliver y Fullana, who was converted to Judaism under the name of Daniel Juda. Both of them emigrated to Antwerp, where, among other writings, in 1693 the lady translated into Spanish Giovanni Battista Guarini's very popular *Pastor Fido;* through a drama by Moses Ḥayyim Luzzatto, Guarini's work influenced even

384   LXIII: DUTCH JERUSALEM

modern Hebrew literature. See C. Cabezas Alguacil, "Doña Isabel de Correa, traductora y poetisa sefardí," *Miscelánea de estudios árabes y hebráicos*, X, 111–29.

15. John Keymor, *Observation Made Upon the Dutch Fishing, about the Year 1601;* J. E. Barker, *The Rise and Decline of the Netherlands*, pp. 249 ff.; Jan Pieterszoon Coen, *Bescheiden omtrent zijn Bedrijf in Indie* (Documents Relating to His Service in India), ed. by H. T. Colenbrander, supplemented by W. P. Coolhaas's ed. of additional *Bescheiden*, Vols. I–II [VII, 1–2]; R. Ródenas Vilar, "Un Gran proyecto anti-holandés en tiempo de Felipe IV," *Hispania* (Madrid), XXII, 542–58. Although not himself a Jew, Coen and his successors opened up many opportunities in Far-Eastern trade for Dutch Jewish businessmen. See *infra*, nn. 78 ff., 82.

16. See the pertinent remarks by P. de Jong in "Can Political Factors Account for the Fact that Calvinism rather than Anabaptism Came to Dominate the Dutch Reformation?" *CH*, XXXIII, 392–417; G. Griffith in "Democratic Ideas in the Revolt of the Netherlands," *Archiv für Reformationsgeschichte*, L, 50–63 (illustrating his thesis with four documentary excerpts; pp. 56 ff.); and G. Güldner, *Das Toleranz-Problem in den Niederlanden im Ausgang des 16. Jahrhunderts*.

17. H. D. J. Van Schevichaven, *Penschetsen uit Nijmegen's verleden* (Sketches from Nijmegen's Past, Part 2: Something about the Jews); J. J. F. W. Van Agt, "The Jewish Community of Nijmegen and the Eighteenth-Century Synagogue in the Nonnenstraat" (Dutch), *SR*, III, 168–92 (with an English summary), which includes a brief sketch of the earlier history of that community; *Succincta enarratio miraculorum quae gloriose operatus est Dominus per venerabile Sacramentum in sacello sacri loci in Amstelredam*, Amsterdam, 1346 (photo offset ed.; includes official reports by bailiff and city council); R. R. Post, "The Sacrament of the Miracle in Amsterdam" (Dutch), *Studia Catholica*, XXX, 241–61; *Groot Gelders Placaat Boek* (Great Broadside Book of Geldern), I, 16, 59: *Groot Placaat Boek . . . Utrecht* (Great Broadside Book Containing All the Broadsides, Ordinances, and Edicts of the Province and City of Utrecht to 1728), ed. by Johan van de Water, I, 411 ff. (reproducing five decrees of 1545–1713); also cited by S. Ullmann in his "Geschichte der spanisch-portugiesischen Juden in Amsterdam im XVII. Jahrhundert," *JJLG*, V, 1–74, esp. pp. 7 f. On the "miracle of Sainte-Gudule" in Brussels, see *supra*, Vol. XI, pp. 169 f., 368 f., and the literature listed there, to which add P. Lefèvre's more recent, broader study, "La Representation du mystère eucharistique à Bruxelles au XVIe siècle," *Cahiers Bruxellois*, XIII, 10–26. See also M. Wolff's aforementioned Dutch essay, "The First Settlement of Jews in Amsterdam," *BVG*, 4th ser. IX-X; 5th ser. I; and, more generally, J. Stengers, *Les Juifs dans les Pays-Bas au Moyen Âge*, pp. 30 ff., 152 ff.; and *supra*, Vol. X, pp. 16 ff., 306 ff. nn. 15–20. On the purported Jewish quarter and cemetery in Nijmegen in 1540, see *supra*, Vol. XIII, p. 120.

18. Desiderius Erasmus of Rotterdam, *Querela pacis* in his *Opera Omnia*, ed. by J. Clericus, IV, 633E; idem, *Opuscula*: a Supplement to the *Opera omnia*, ed. with introductions and notes by W. K. Ferguson, pp. 104, 316 f., 323 f. (the statements referring to Aleandro and Pfefferkorn are taken from the *Acta Academiae Lovaniensis contra Lutherum*, which were most probably written by Erasmus); idem, *Opus epistolarum*, ed. by P. S. Allen *et al.*, II, 500 ff. No. 549; III, 116 ff. No. 694, 122 ff. Nos. 697 and 700–701, 143 No. 713, etc. See the numerous other entries listed by B.

Flower in her Index, *ibid.*, Vol. XIII, p. 117; R. H. Bainton, "Erasmus and the Perse-cuted" in *Scrinium Erasmianum Mélanges historiques* on the 500th Anniversary of Erasmus' Birth, ed. by J. Coppens, II, 197–202 (referring to a few personal interven-tions for Reuchlin and others); other essays in that collection; and *supra*, Vol. XIII, pp. 188 f., 391 f. n. 4, 408 f. n. 22. To the literature listed there, add G. Kisch's recent study, *Erasmus' Stellung zu Juden und Judentum*. Public opinion, especially its Church-oriented segment, remained antagonistic to Jews at least until the end of the sixteenth century, and only gradually took on a more sympathetic hue. See Stenger's *Les Juifs*, pp. 52 ff.; H. Bovenkerk, "The Jews as Seen by Medieval and Sixteenth-Century Writers" (Dutch), in H. Brugmans and A. Frank, eds., *Geschiedenis der Joden in Nederland* (A History of the Jews in the Netherlands), Vol. I, pp. 105–156; and H. Brugmans, "The Attitude of State and Church in Respect to Jews" (Dutch), *ibid.*, pp. 617–42. This volume includes valuable essays on the history of the Jews in Holland until about 1795. Regrettably, Volume II, which contained additional studies for the later period, was printed on the eve of the Nazi invasion of Holland and was completely destroyed in Wageningen at the inception of hostilities.

19. C. Wilson, *The Dutch Republic and the Civilization of the Seventeenth Cen-tury*, p. 81; R. van Uytven and W. Blockmans, "Constitutions and Their Application in the Netherlands during the Middle Ages," *RBPH*, XLVII, 309–424. We remember how effectively the Antwerp municipal council had invoked the city's "liberties" to protect its Marrano settlement even against Emperor Charles V, who, as a native and frequent resident of the Low Countries, was much more popular there than his son Philip. See *supra*, Vol. XIII, pp. 119 ff., 368 ff. nn. 36 ff.

20. See M. Dierickx's aforementioned "La Politique religieuse de Philippe II dans les anciens Pays-Bas," *Hispania* (Madrid), XVI, 130–46 (distinguishing four chrono-logical phases, of which the second, 1567–73, under the oppressive regime of the duke of Alba acting on the king's express orders, led to the outbreak of the revolt); and *supra*, nn. 3, 6, and 12.

21. See N. Japikse, ed., *Resolutiën der Staten-Generaal van 1576 tot 1609* (Resolu-tions of the States General from 1576 to 1609), I, 579 No. 732; D. S. van Zuiden, "On the Relations of Prince William of Orange and His Brothers with Jews" (Dutch), *BMGJW*, V, 211–24; and, particularly, I. (J. H.) Prins's careful Hebrew study, "Prince William of Orange and the Jews," *Zion*, XV, 93–105. See also J. Hansen, "Der Niederländische Pacificationsvertrag zu Köln im Jahre 1579," *Westdeutsche Zeit-schrift für Geschichte*, XIII, 227–72, esp. pp. 257 ff.; T. Wittman's analyses of "La Première decennie de la révolution des Pays-Bas," *Acta historica*, VII, 3–55; and "La Victoire de la révolution aux Pays-Bas du Nord (1585–1609)," *ibid.*, 189–99; and *supra*, Vol. XIV, pp. 77 ff., 102 ff., 335 n. 6, 343 f. n. 33. On Joseph zum Goldenen Schwan and on the Marranos in Cologne and other German cities, see the data and sources supplied *supra*, Vol. XIV, pp. 191, 205, 376 f. n. 48, 380 f. n. 59; and, more generally, R. van Roesbroeck, *Emigranten* (Emigrants: Dutch Refugees in Germany, 1550–1600). Needless to say, such emigration was not limited to the war years. Analyzing specifically the "Problèmes concernant l'émigration protestante belge aux XVIe et XVIIe siècles," *Annales* of the Société d'histoire du protestantisme belge, IV, 351–56, E. M. Braekman discerns five major phases in that movement—namely,

1535–40, 1550–51, 1567–73, 1584–90, 1620–40—the first two of which preceded the uprising. Many of the Protestant émigrés were doubtless recruited from among the New Christians.

William's instruction to the Antwerp burghers is the more remarkable as his status as leader of the Dutch rebellion was constitutionally quite uncertain, and as the various forces favoring the uprising, both in the North and in the South, revealed many internal cleavages. See H. Lademacher, *Die Stellung des Prinzen von Oranien als Statthalter in den Niederlanden von 1572 bis 1584. Ein Beitrag zur Verfassungsgeschichte der Niederlande (= Rheinisches Archiv,* LII); the observations in the review thereof by B. A. Vermaseren in *BGN,* XV, 68–72; F. Rachfahl's more comprehensive study, *Wilhelm von Oranien und der niederländische Aufstand;* and the Marxist interpretations by A. N. Tsiitozvonov in his *Niderlandskaya burzhuaznaya revolutsiia XVI vieka* (The Dutch Bourgeois Revolution of the XVI Century), with the very negative review thereof by Z. R. Dittrich in *BGN,* XIV, 57–67; as well as the survey by B. Töpfer in "Die Bürgerliche Revolution in den Niederlanden," *Zeitschrift für Geschichtswissenschaft,* XIII, Sonderheft, pp. 51–70; and *infra,* Chap. LXV, nn. 3, 19, etc.

22. E. M. Koen, "Duarte Fernandes, Merchant of the Portuguese Nation in Amsterdam" (Dutch), *SR,* II, 178–93 (with an English summary), esp. pp. 182 f. (describing the activities of one of the Jewish pioneers, who, at the age of about 57, settled in Amsterdam in 1598, lived there till 1620, and then moved to Hamburg, where he died in 1625 or 1626); A. A. van Schelven, "The Petition Offering Three Million Gold Guilders (October, 1566)" (Dutch), *BVG,* 6th ser. IX, 1–42; S. Ullmann, "Geschichte der spanisch-portugiesischen Juden in Amsterdam," *JJLG,* V, 1–74; J. Zwartz, "The First Rabbis and Synagogues of Amsterdam According to Archival Sources" (Dutch), *BMGJW,* IV, 147–271, esp. pp. 158 f., 249 App. iii; R. Feenstra, "A quelle époque les Provinces-Unies sont-elles devenues indépendantes en droit à l'égard du Saint-Empire?" *Tijdschrift voor Rechtsgeschiedenis (Revue d'histoire du droit),* XX, 30–63, 182–218, 479–80 (claiming that this was a gradual development culminating in the Treaty of 1648); and *infra,* n. 32. "The Union of Utrecht, 1579–1929: Its Consequences for the Jews in the Netherlands," is analyzed by J. S. da Silva Rosa in his Dutch essay under this title in *Vrijdagavond,* V, Part 2, pp. 267–69.

The general involvement of Marranos in the Reform movements in the Low Countries has not yet been investigated in detail. Some data have become available, however, from inquisitorial records, as well as from reports by Spanish spies. See esp. P. Fredericq, *Corpus documentorum inquisitionis haereticae pravitatis neerlandicae;* L. van den Essen, "Le Progrès du luthéranisme et du calvinisme dans le monde commercial d'Anvers," *VSW,* XII, 160 ff.; P. Kalkoff's older, but still useful, summary, *Die Anfänge der Gegenreformation in den Niederlanden;* and *supra,* n. 3.

23. H. Noordkerk, ed., *Handvesten ofte privilegien ande Octroyen . . . der stad Amstelredam* (Handbook of Privileges and Ordinances of the City of Amsterdam), [II], 471 f. (Sept. 30, 1656); IV, 19 f. (Feb. 27, 1747); Daniel Levi (Miguel) de Barrios' censure cited from *Nederlandsche Stemmen,* V, 81 n. 5, by S. Ullmann in his "Geschichte," *JJLG,* V, 30 f. Some Marranos actually collaborated with the Spaniards during the Thirty Years' War. We recall Jacob Rosales' (Manuel Bocarro Francês') boast that he had advanced 15,000 ducats of his own, to hire mercenaries for the Spanish forces. And he was at that time officially a member of the Jewish community

of Hamburg, although by decree of Emperor Ferdinand III he had been cleansed of "the blemish of Jewish ancestry." See *supra*, Vol. XIV, pp. 282 f., 408 f. n. 59.

24. J. A. Goris, *Étude sur les colonies marchandes méridionales . . . à Anvers*, pp. 599 ff.; the data referred to in connection with the negotiations of 1653–54 for readmission of Jews to Belgium on the basis of the Peace Treaties of Westphalia, analyzed *supra*, n. 12; *REJ*, VII, 258 ff. On the importance of "The Diaspora of the Antwerp Merchants at the End of the Sixteenth Century," see the informative Dutch article by W. Brulez in *BGN*, XV, 279–306.

25. Andrew Marvell's poem, *The Character of Holland*, London, 1672 ed., p. 4; in his *Poems and Letters*, ed. by H. M. Margoliouth, p. 97 nn. 71 ff.: J. Romein's brief sketch of "The Miracle of Amsterdam" in his *Carillon der Tijden* (Melody of Times: Studies and Addresses on Aspects of Cultural History), pp. 275–89; as well as the comprehensive *Geschiedenis van Amsterdam* (History of Amsterdam from the Beginning to the Present) by Hajo Brugmans.

26. Uri Phoebus b. Aaron ha-Levi, *Narração da vinda dos Judeos espanhões a Amsterdam*, reed. with an Intro. by J. S. da Silva Rosa; Daniel Levi (Miguel) de Barrios, *Triumpho del govierno popular en la Casa de Jacob* (see W. Chr. Pieterse's analysis of *Daniel Levi de Barrios als geschiedschrijver* [D. L. de B. as Historian of the Portuguese-Jewish Community in Amsterdam in his "Triumpho del govierno popular"] in her Amsterdam dissertation under this title and her judicious summary of "The Historical Value of D. L. de B.'s Work," pp. 133 ff.); and *infra*, n. 77; David Franco Mendes, *Memorias do estabelecimento e progresso dos Judeus Portugueses e Espanhoes nessa famosa Cidade de Amsterdam no anno 1769* (analyzed by J. Mendes dos Remedios in *Os Judeus portugueses en Amsterdam*, pp. 88 ff.). On the author, see J. Melkman's Amsterdam dissertation, *David Franco Mendes: a Hebrew Poet*. The relationships between these three sources, and their frequent mutual contradictions, have already been briefly analyzed by H. Graetz in his *Geschichte der Juden*, 4th ed., IX, 559 ff. Note 11. See also *infra*, n. 27. Scattered earlier data on New Christians who made an appearance in that region have been assembled by I. Prins in *De Vestiging der Marranen in Noord-Nederland in de zestiende Eeuw* (The Settlement of Marranos in the Northern Netherlands in the Sixteenth Century), esp. pp. 41 ff., 71 ff., 119 ff.; M. Grunwald's *Portugiesengräber auf deutscher Erde*, pp. 145 f. (from Menaḥem b. Solomon ha-Levi's Yiddish *She'erit Yisrael* [The Remnant of Israel], fol. 58b; also available in a Dutch trans. by L. Goudsmit with notes by G. I. Polak); A. Cassuto, "Ueber portugiesische Juden in Emden," *JFF*, V, 173–75; *supra*, Vol. XIII, pp. 280, 408 n. 56; J. M. Hillesum, *Uri Ha-Levi, der eerste Mohel, Chazzan en Predikant der Portugeesche Joden te Amsterdam* (Uri ha-Levi, the First Circumciser, Reader, and Preacher of the Portuguese Jews in Amsterdam in 1593); C. Gebhardt's ed. of *Die Schriften des Uriel da Costa*; J. Zwarts, "The First Rabbis and Synagogues of Amsterdam" (Dutch), *BMGJW*, IV, esp. pp. 251 f. Apps. vi-vii (also identifying Moses Uri with the Philip Joosten of a notarial document of 1621).

27. The very complicated problems of these and other early sources, the date and authorship of which are not always easily ascertainable, have been largely clarified in S. Seeligmann's letter to Max Grunwald of November 2–5, 1902, with the Postscript thereto of July 17, 1905; published by the latter under the title "Ueber die erste

jüdische Ansiedelung in Amsterdam. Eine Ergänzung zu Grunwald, Portugiesen-gräber auf deutscher Erde" in *Mitteilungen für jüdische Volkskunde*, n.s. II, No. 17, pp. 1–13. See also, more generally, M. Wolff's aforementioned "The First Settlement," *BVG*, 4th ser. IX-X; 5th ser. I; J. S. da Silva Rosa, *Geschiedenis der Portugeesche Joden te Amsterdam, 1593–1925* (A History of the Portuguese Jews in Amsterdam, 1593–1925); H. I. Bloom, *The Economic Activities of the Jews of Amsterdam;* J. G. van Dillen, "Foreigners in Amsterdam in the First Half of the Seventeenth Century, I: Portuguese Jews" (Dutch), *TG*, L, 4–35 (with interesting documentary data on the Jews' trade with Brazil and the Barbary States; pp. 33 ff. Apps. 6–9); E. M. Koen's more recent review of "The Earliest Sources Relating to the Portuguese Jews in the Municipal Archives of Amsterdam up to 1620," *SR*, IV, 25–42.

The general history of the Jews in Holland has also been treated in the older, but still valuable, study by H. J. Koenen, *Geschiedenis der Joden in Nederland* (A History of the Jews in the Netherlands), with some additions and corrections in his "The Jews' Adventure, particularly in the Netherlands" (Dutch), *BVG*, VI, 75; A. de São Payo, "Subsídios" and "Novos subsídios para a história dos Judeus Portugueses nos Países Baixos," *Arquivo histórico de Portugal*, II, 445–65; III, 257–62 (mainly concerned with the genealogy of the intriguing Diego Teixeira de Sampayo, discussed *supra*, Vol. XIV, pp. 283 f., 409 n. 60; according to H. Kellenbenz in "Das Testament von Manuel Teixeira," *SR*, III, 53–61, Manuel's son Diego, on his conversion in 1647, assumed the Hebrew name Abraham Senior, because he claimed direct descent from the last Castilian "chief rabbi" and 1492 renegade); S. Ullman, "Geschichte," *JJLG*, V, 1–74; S. Seeligmann, *Bibliographie en historie* (Bibliography and History: a Contribution to the History of the First Sephardim in Amsterdam); and particularly the well-documented work by J. Zwarts, *Hoofdstukken uit de Geschiedenis der Joden in Nederland* (Chapters from the History of the Jews in the Netherlands), with an Intro. by H. Brugmans (includes the study "A Marrano Countess in the Netherlands," describing Doña Mencia de Mendoza and her wedding; pp. 74–87); and various essays ed. by Brugmans and A. Frank in their *Geschiedenis der Joden in Nederland*, I. Of interest also are the more popular sketches included in J. Meijer's *Zij lieten hun Sporen achter* (They Left Their Traces Behind: Jewish Contributions to Dutch Civilization). See also *supra*, Vols. XIII, pp. 119 ff.; XIV, pp. 215 ff., 271 ff.

28. E. M. Koen *et al.*, comps., "Notarial Records in Amsterdam Relating to the Portuguese Jews in that Town up to 1639," *SR*, I, Part 1, pp. 109–115; Part 2, pp. 110–22; II, 111–26, 257–72; III, 113–25, 234–54; IV, 115–26, 243–61; V, 106–124, 219–45; VI, 107–23 (to be continued; it is remarkable, however, that this noteworthy collection of regesta—the title of which was changed, in the second instalment, to: "Amsterdam Notarial Deeds Pertaining to the Portuguese Jews in Amsterdam up to 1639" and later to "Notarial Records Relating to the Portuguese Jews in Amsterdam up to 1639"—fails to mention H. I. Bloom's pioneering work in this field; see *infra*, n. 29); A. M. Vaz Dias, "The Founders of Beth Yaacob" (Dutch), *Vrijdagavond*, VIII, 195–97, 222–24, 238–40, 247–49; Menasseh ben Israel, *The Humble Addresses to his Highnesse the Lord Protector of the Commonwealth of England, Scotland and Ireland*, p. 8, reproduced in L. Wolf's ed. of *Menasseh ben Israel's Mission to Oliver Cromwell*, p. 88. The data in the Amsterdam marriage registry are not wholly dependable, however. It appears that, in order to confuse the spies of the Spanish Inquisition who lived among the Jews of Amsterdam and elsewhere, many former New Christians and their children often entered false birthplaces on their marriage registrations, so

that the identification of relatives who had remained behind would be more difficult. This may have been the reason why Menasseh ben Israel, at his wedding in 1623 (at the age of nineteen), gave La Rochelle, France, rather than the Portuguese colony of Madeira, as his birthplace. The Ben Israel family had lived in La Rochelle only a short time. But as a Huguenot stronghold and the locale of a sizable New Christian community, it doubtless offered fewer opportunities for Spanish undercover agents to pursue their nefarious investigations. On Menasseh's birthdate, see the debate between J. M. Hillesum and L. Cardozo de Béthencourt, mentioned by C. Roth in *A Life of Menasseh ben Israel*, p. 29. See also, from another angle, Saul Levi Morteira's resp. quoted *infra*, Chap. LXV, n. 96.

29. Johan de Witt, or rather Pieter de la Court, *Interest van Holland ofte Gronden van Hollands-Welvaren*, Amsterdam, 1662, I, Chaps. v and xviii; in the English trans. entitled, *The True Interest and Political Maxims of the Republick of Holland and West-Friesland*, London, 1702 ed., pp. 26, 81; the Holland resolution of March 17, 1615; Abraham b. Joseph ha-Levi, '*Ein mishpaṭ* (Fountain of Law; responsa), with a Foreword by J. Kubo and D. Pisano, IV, No. xlv, reproduced in a German trans. by H. J. Zimmels in *Die Marranen in der rabbinischen Literatur*, pp. 155 ff. (on this responsum and its author, see L. Grünhut's "[Bibliographische Notiz über] Abraham Halevi's Responsen," *ZHB*, IX, 97–98); D. Henriques de Castro, *Keur van Grafsteenen op de Nederlandsche-Portugeesche-Israëlietische Begraafplaats te Ouderkerk a/d Amstel* (Auswahl von Grabsteinen auf dem Nieder.-Portug.-Israel. Begräbnisplatze zu Ouderkerk an den Amstel nebst Beschreibung und biographischen Skizzen), I (Dutch and German; no more appeared), Intro.; S. Ullmann, "Geschichte," *JJLG*, V, 25 ff. (also stressing that two other loan banks were soon attached to the two younger congregations, until 1639 when both the congregations and the banks merged into single institutions); and other sources listed by J. S. da Silva Rosa in his *Geschiedenis*, pp. 8 ff.; and H. I. Bloom in *The Economic Activities*, pp. 5 ff. Many important details have recently become available through W. C. Pieterse's publication of the *Livro de Bet Haim do Kahal Kados de Bet Yahacob*, Original Text, ed. with an Intro., Notes, and Index. This record of the first burials goes far beyond enumeration of the individuals concerned, and offers many insights into the social life of the period.

Regrettably, much of our information about the early Jews of Amsterdam is highly complicated by the various aliases under which they appear in the records, and is derived largely from their business transactions as certified by Amsterdam notaries. While the notarial archives have been preserved in great quantity and are an extremely valuable source of information (which to a large extent, made possible Herbert I. Bloom's vivid reconstruction of the various facets of Jewish economic endeavor in the Dutch metropolis) they have thus far been but partially explored. See E. M. Koen et al., "Notarial Records," *SR*, I, Part 1, pp. 109 ff. and *passim*. Quite apart from the incomplete preservation of the records, one must note that notarial confirmation of deeds was sought by only a fraction of the businessmen engaged in major transactions. For example, the numerous unlicensed Jewish brokers, the so-called interlopers, had good reason to avoid recording their deals before the notaries. See E. M. Koen, "The Earliest Sources," *SR*, IV, 28 ff. Most important, business records of this type are liable to furnish a one-sided picture because they deal primarily with commercial data and exclude most other facets of life. We get from them only faint glimpses into the multifarious religious, intellectual, and communal pursuits of that agglomeration of strong individuals with diverse interests and outlooks who shaped the rapidly evolving communal morphology of Amsterdam Jewry. See also I. S. Emmanuel, "New Data on the Portuguese Community of Amsterdam" (Hebrew), *Oṣar Yehude Sefarad* (Tesoro de Judíos Sefardíes), VI, 160–82; VII, 122–30; VIII, 139–49; IX, 111–24; X, 92–104 (includes lists of the early Sephardic elders).

30. Hugo de Groot (Grotius), *Remonstrantie nopende de ordre dije in de Landen van Hollandt ende Westvrieslandt dijent gestelt op de Joden* (Memorandum concerning the Order to Be Established for the Jews in the Lands of Holland and West Friesland), ed. by J. Meijer. Meijer had at his disposal the MS preserved in the Ets Haïm Academy in Amsterdam, which was probably written by Grotius' brother and secretary, and contained a few marginal notes in Grotius' own hand. See also W. J. M. van Eysinga's brief analysis, against the background of the famous jurist's general legal teachings, "Grotius' Jew Law" (Dutch), *Mededeelingen* of the K. Nederlandse Akademie van Wetenschappen, n.s. XIII, Part 1, pp. 1–8 (also controverting Meijer's attempted identification of Van Pauw's memorandum; p. 2 n. 2).

31. See J. Meijer, "Hugo Grotius' Knowledge of Hebrew," *HJ*, XIV, 133–44. Meijer goes too far, however, in concluding that "rabbinic literature was a *terra incognita* for Grotius" and that his "knowledge of Hebrew sources derived from secondary translations and not from Hebrew originals." The great jurist-theologian may not have been able independently to navigate in the "sea of the Talmud," but he was able, when necessary, with the aid of available dictionaries, to check a quotation against the original sources. His knowledge of biblical Hebrew, moreover, was much better. Like many Christian Hebraists of the period, he did not hesitate to consult Jewish Bible commentators, often doubtless also at second hand. This, too, was a prevailing practice among the humanists. Yet it was a considerable advance over the frequent medieval practice of totally ignoring the Jewish point of view. Also pertinent are E. Slijper's unpublished Dutch lecture "The *Annotationes* [*in Vetus Testamentum*] by Hugo Grotius" as summarized in his Dutch note in *BMGJW*, VII, 112; the older study by A. Kuenen, "Hugo Grotius as Old Testament Exegete" (Dutch), *Mededeelingen* of the K. Nederlandse Akademie van Wetenschappen, Section Letters, n.s. XII; and, more generally, W. J. M. van Eysinga, *Hugo Grotius, eine biographische Skizze;* and *infra,* nn. 32–34.

32. Hugh Broughton issued his conversionist tract in several versions during the same year. One had the Hebrew title *Parshegen ha-nishtevan ish ʿibri*, borrowed from Ezra 7:11, and was accompanied by a Greek and a Latin translation; another, reading *yehudi* instead of *ʿibri*, had the additional Latin title *Responsum ad epistolam Judei;* still another had the Hebrew text alone, but included a Hebrew epistle of Abraham b. Reuben, who in 1596 had replied from Constantinople to some of Broughton's strictures. See also Broughton's *Works of the Great Albionean Divine,* with a biographical Preface by John Lightfoot, London, 1662, pp. 929 ff., 949 f.; A. E. Cowley, *A Concise Catalogue of the Hebrew Printed Books in the Bodleian Library,* p. 128; and the debate between H. F. Wijnman and L. Hirschel in Wijnman's "Jan Theunisz, alias Joannes Antonides (1569–1639), Bookseller and Owner of the Music-House D'Os in de Bruyloft in Amsterdam, with a Bibliography of His Editions and Writings" (Dutch), *Jaarboek* of the Genootschap Amstelodamum, XXV, 29–123, esp. p. 56; L. Hirschel's "Jodocus Hondius and Hugh Broughton: a Contribution to the Knowledge of the First Hebrew Publications in Amsterdam" (Dutch)

Het Boek, XVII, 198–208; and Wijnman's reply, "Should Jodocus Hondius or Jan Theunisz Be Regarded as the First Printer of Hebrew Books in Amsterdam?" (Dutch), *ibid.*, pp. 301–313. See also Wijnman's more recent essay, "The Hebraist Jan Theunisz Barbarossius alias Johannes Antonides as Lecturer in Arabic at the University of Leiden (1612–13)" (Dutch), *SR*, II, 1–29, 149–77. On the antagonistic stance of the Middelburg churchmen toward Jews and Judaism, see J. H. van't Hoff, "The Erstwhile Portuguese Jewish Community and the Church Council of the Reformed Community in Middelburg" (Dutch), *Archief* of the Zeeuwsch Genootschap der Wetenschappen (Zeeland Association for Sciences), 1922, pp. 14–18; *supra* n. 22; and *infra*, n. 49.

Among the books in Grotius' private library was Broughton's *Commentarius in Danielem* (originally published in London, 1596, in English under the title *Daniel: His Chaldic Visions and Ebrew. Both Translated after the Original and Expounded*) in the Latin trans. by Broughton's fellow-pastor of Middelburg, Joannes Boreel. This copy, as well as two grammatical works by Elijah Levita in Sebastian Münster's Latin translation, were heavily underlined and occasionally annotated in Grotius' hand. Through Queen Christina's acquisition, these copies reached Sweden and are now found in the libraries of the Lycée in Västerås and the University of Lund. See F. Dovring, "Nouvelles recherches sur la bibliothèque de Grotius en Suède et en Italie," in *Mededeelingen* of the K. Nederlandse Akademie van Wetenschappen, n.s. XIV, Part 10, pp. 6 No. 5, 7 No. 9.

33. Hugo Grotius' Letter to Isaac Vos (Vossius) of July 28, 1640, in his *Epistolae quotquot reperiri potuerunt*, Amsterdam, 1687 ed., p. 636 (expressing hope that his numerous annotations to the Old Testament would help shed some light on the Law and the Prophets): not yet included in his *Briefwisseling* (Correspondence), ed. by P. C. Molhuysen and B. L. Meulenbroek; idem, *De veritate religionis christianae*, i.1 and 14, v.1 ff., in J. Clarke's English trans., *The Truth of the Christian Religion*, corrected and illustrated with Notes by Mr. [Jean] le Clerc, pp. 2, 22 f., 208 ff.; and K. Repgen, "Grotius 'papizans,' " *Reformanda reformata. Festgabe für Hubert Jedin*, II, 370–400, esp. p. 390, citing a remark by Petavius, then professor of "positive theology" in Paris, that on the basis of his numerous conversations with Grotius, he considered the latter "in his heart a Catholic." Although a clear overstatement, this observation accurately reflects Grotius' considerable sympathy for medieval scholasticism. See also, more generally, J. Schlütter, *Die Theologie des Hugo Grotius*, esp. pp. 3 ff.; and A. Löwenstamm, "Hugo Grotius' Stellung zum Judentum," *Festschrift . . . des Jüdisch-Theologischen Seminars Fraenckelscher Stiftung*, Breslau, II, 295–302. .

34. See J. Meijer, "Hugo Grotius' *Remonstrantie*," JSS, XVII, 91–104, esp. pp. 95 ff.; M. Balaban, "Hugo Grotius und die Ritualmordprozesse in Lublin (1636)," *Festschrift Simon Dubnow*, pp. 87–112 (reproducing Grotius' correspondence with his Polish Protestant follower Jerzy [Georgius] Słupecki; pp. 110 ff.); *supra*, n. 31; Vol. XI, pp. 146 ff.; and *infra*, Chap. LXVII. See also B. L. Meulenbroek's notes on Grotius' letter to Słupecki of December 12, 1636, in his ed. of Grotius' *Briefwisseling*, VII, 576 ff. No. 2884. That Jews were needed to help Christian scholars improve their knowledge of Hebrew and understanding of the Old Testament had been stressed by Christian Hebraists (for instance, Johannes Reuchlin) quite frequently during the Renaissance. This argument had actually induced the intolerant city council of Nuremberg to grant exceptional visiting rights to a Schnaittach Jewish teacher so that he should be available to the reformer Andreas Osiander for consultation in

Hebrew studies. See *supra*, Vol. XIII, pp. 184, 232, 407 n. 27, 431 f. n. 31. One suspects, however, that only persons who generally advocated toleration of Jews would
have employed this argument—which, by stressing the self-interest of the Christian
peoples, reduced the risk that its authors would be considered promoters of the
Jewish interest.

The entire tenor of Grotius' presentation gives the impression that he was employing an effective forensic strategy in first conceding some points to the Jew-baiters'
contentions, in order that he might then the more effectively demolish them. See also
the incidental observations scattered through Grotius' extensive correspondence,
collected in the *Epistolae* and in the more complete *Briefwisseling* (Correspondence),
several volumes of which are yet to be published. For example, in his letter of April
5, 1630, to his brother, Willem, he wrote, with evident elation: "It is reported from
Germany that there is great hope of converting many Jews who are despairing [*fessos*]
of the expectation of the Messiah's temporal reign, and are turning their attention to
the spiritual interpretation of the pertinent prophecies. However, though they abhor
the Roman superstitions, they are made uncertain about such counsel by the Protestant strictures [*seissurae*]." *Ibid.*, IV, 177 f. No. 1489. The *Briefwisseling* also includes
numerous scholarly observations on Hebrew terms, ancient Jewish history, and so
forth; see, for instance, IV, 199, 492 ff.

35. Hugo Grotius' Letter of March 23, 1633, to Gerhard J. Vos (Vossius) in his
Epistolae, p. 111; *Briefwisseling*, V, 109 No. 1826; idem, *Remonstrantie*, ed. by J.
Meijer, *passim;* Meijer's analysis thereof in *JSS*, XVII, 91–104; and some of Grotius'
other writings, listed in J. ter Meulen's and J. J. Biermanse's *Bibliographie des écrits
imprimés de Hugo Grotius.* On Grotius' correspondent and close friend Vossius—a
polyhistor and distinguished classical, but not Hebrew, scholar—see C. S. M. Rade-
maker's Dutch dissertation at the Catholic University in Nijmegen, *Gerardus Joannes
Vossius (1577-1649)*, esp. pp. 212 f., 217 ff. (summarized in his English article,
"Gerardus Joannes Vossius (1577-1649)," *Acta Historiae neerlandica*, IV, 217–33). The
question of intermarriage and free sexual relations between Jews and the "daughters
of the land" seems to have agitated many minds. Perhaps for this reason, Grotius
found it necessary to expatiate on this problem. Van Pauw, Grotius' fellow-member
on the committee of two appointed to resolve the Jewish question, doubtless was
even more outspoken. In fact, in 1619, on the initiative of the elder Van Pauw, the
authorities expressly forbade any such interfaith relationships and even ordered the
Jewish representatives to take an oath that their constituents would strictly observe
that prohibition. See *Resolutiën van Holland* of July 8, 1619: and H. Noordkerk's
Handvesten, I, 471 f. of Sept. 30, 1656, cited by S. Ullmann in his "Geschichte," *JJLG*,
V, 28. Connected with the fear of interfaith sexual relations was the old prohibition
forbidding Jews to employ Christian domestics. See also I. Prins, "Contributions to
the Knowledge of Servant Problems among Jews of Amsterdam (1616)" (Dutch),
Ha'Ischa, I, No. 12, pp. 5–7; II, No. 1, pp. 13–15 (with reference to the pertinent
resolutions of the Council of the Dutch Reformed Church in 1614 and 1620, and
describing in some detail an unfortunate affair between the apothecary Abraham
Israël and his Christian maid).

36. A. K. Kuhn, "Hugo Grotius and the Emancipation of the Jews in Holland,"
PAJHS, XXXI, 173–80. See also the charming biographical sketch of "Hugo Grotius,
the Oracle of Delft," included together with those of "William of Orange, the Liber-

ator," "Ian Pieterszoon Coen, Cost What May," "Benedictus Spinoza, the Godless Godseeker," and others in J. and A. Romein's *Erflaters van onze Beschaving* (Ancestors of Our Civilization: Dutch Personalities of Six Centuries), esp. I, 134–69; II, 36–69, 70–107, 290–323; and in the selections from these essays trans. into German by U. Huber-Noodt, under the title *Ahnherren der holländischen Kultur*, pp. 43–76, 114–48, 206–245.

37. *Handvesten . . . der stad Amstelredam*, cited *supra*, nn. 23, 35; C. Bake's "Jewish Oath" (Dutch), *De Navorscher*, LXXI, 52–53, in the English trans. by H. I. Bloom in *The Economic Activities of the Jews of Amsterdam*, p. 20 n. 93, also citing the related oath of *Doleantie*, pertaining to property valuation, reproduced in the *Groot Placaatboek* (The Great Broadside Book of Enactments, Ordinances, etc., of the States of Holland and Zeeland, 1576–1785), ed. by C. Cau *et al.*, V, 98. Other variants in the formulas used in Amsterdam and Rotterdam are cited by J. Meijer in his "Hugo Grotius' *Remonstrantie*," *JSS*, XVII, 98 f. n. 20. Even less objectionable than the oath quoted here was the one administered, in 1720, to Jacob Hiskia Machado, an official of the Utrecht Company, as reproduced in J. Zwarts's *Hoofdstukken*, App. pp. 11 f.

38. See J. Zwarts, "The First Rabbis" (Dutch), *BMGJW*, IV, 258 App. xv, 265 ff. Apps. xx ff.; idem, "Jewish Archival Fragments" (Dutch), *Vrijdagavond*, IV, 46–47, 169–70, 283–84, 349–51, 395–97, 461–63, 520–21, 616–17, 698–700, 765–66, 828–29; V, Part 1, pp. 11–12, 110–11, 118, 396–97, 411–12; Part 2, pp. 108–110, 156-58, 248–52, 302–303; VIII, Part 1, pp. 61–64 (this series of excerpts in chronological order was to be continued in the subsequent volumes of that periodical), esp. V, Part 1, pp. 411 f.; the *Resolutiën van Holland* of December 13, 1619; *Kerkeraad der Gereformeerde Gemeente van Amsterdam, Nieuwerzijds Kapel*, Eighth Session, fols. 47 f., cited by A. M. Vaz Dias in "An Attempt to Segregate the Jewish Inhabitants of Amsterdam in a Ghetto" (Dutch), *Nieuw Israëlietisch Weekblad*, LXXIII, Nos. 18 p. 13; 21 p. 6; H. I. Bloom, *The Economic Activities*, pp. 27 f. n. 120; J. S. da Silva Rosa, *Geschiedenis*, pp. 10 ff.; Hugo Grotius, *Remonstrantie*, Arts. xvi, xxi–xxii, xxvi ff., ed. by J. Meijer, pp. 117 ff.; the aforementioned responsum by Abraham b. Joseph ha-Levi, *supra*, nn. 29 and 35; and *infra*, n. 65.

39. See *supra*, n. 29; *Gratulaçao de Menasseh ben Israël em nome de sua Naçao, ao celsissimo Principe de Orange Frederique Henrique, na sua vinda a nossa Synagoga de T. T. [Talmud Torah] Em companhia da Serenissima Raynha Henrica Maria dignissima consorte do Augustissimo Carlos Rey da grande Brittania, França e Hibernia;* and C. Roth, *A Life of Menasseh ben Israel*, p. 66, also reproducing the title page of the Latin edition of that address.

40. Cornelius Callidius Loos, *Ecclesiae venatus sive altera eius functio, circa fidei ministerium, in reducendis deviis*, cited by H. Heidenheimer, "Zur Geschichte und Beurteilung der Juden vom XV. bis XIX. Jahrhundert," *MGWJ*, LIII, 148 ff. On the forcible baptism of minors, in the discussion of which Loos referred to the mass conversion of Jewish children in Portugal and its condemnation by a contemporary, Bishop Osorio, sees *supra*, Vols. IX, pp. 15 ff., 247 f. nn. 14 f.; XI, pp. 247 f., 408 f. n. 71; XIII, pp. 197 f., 251 f., 413 n. 43, 442 n. 52. Needless to say, all Dutch churchmen welcomed voluntary conversions or reconversions of Jews and Marranos. An interesting controversy arose in connection with the then customary controls over charitable

and educational foundations by the donors' families. A New Christian who, as a professing Jew, had contributed a fund to the Santa Companha de dotar orphas y donzellas, died, leaving behind two younger sons who had become Jews and his eldest son, who had remained a conforming Christian. The latter's son later reverted to Judaism, however. The subsequent controversy over who should help to administer the fund was decided by the local rabbi, Jacob b. Aaron Sasportas, in favor of a younger son and his heirs. See Sasportas' *Ohel Ya'aqob* (Tent of Jacob; responsa), ed. by his son Abraham Sasportas, Amsterdam, 1737, No. 59.

41. See J. Zwarts, "The First Rabbis" (Dutch), *BMGJW*, IV, 147 ff. and *passim,* esp. the numerous documents excerpted in the Appendices, pp. 248 ff. Nos. i, iv-v (Tirado or Tyrado, or Emanuel Rodrigues Vega, an identification rejected by most other scholars), vi-vii (Uri ha-Levi or Philip Joosten), xxiv ff. (David Pardo and Isḥaq Uziel); A. M. Vaz Dias, "Miscellaneous Contributions to the History of the Jews in Amsterdam, VI–VII" (Dutch), *Vrijdagavond,* VI–VIII; numerous other essays listed by L. Hirschel, comp., in the "Bibliography of Writings by A. M. Vaz Dias" (Dutch), *BMGJW,* VI, 182–87; *supra,* n. 28; S. Ullmann, "Geschichte," *JJLG,* V, 34 ff.; and I. S. Emmanuel, "New Data on the Portuguese Community of Amsterdam" (Hebrew), *Oṣar Yehude Sefarad,* VI–X, (*supra,* n. 29). See also J. S. da Silva Rosa's aforementioned ed. of Uri Phoebus b. Aaron ha-Levi's *Narração da vinda dos Judeos espanhões a Amsterdam* (*supra,* n. 26).

42. See E. M. Koen, "Notarial Records," *SR,* V, 222 No. 436; and the literature quoted *supra,* n. 41. Interesting illustrations of communal and religious activities of the early Portuguese settlers in Amsterdam are offered by S. Seeligmann in his careful review of the extant publications from that period. See his *Bibliographie en Historie* (Bibliography and History: a Contribution to the History of the First Sephardim in Amsterdam). On the local synagogue, see the recent discussion by H. J. Zantkuil in his "Reconstruction of an Early Seventeenth-Century Synagogue" (Dutch), *Jaarboek . . . Amstelodamum,* LVII, 199–207; and E. M. Koen in her "Where and for Whom Was the Synagogue of 1612 Erected?" *ibid.,* pp. 209–212. These and other aspects of Dutch Jewish communal life will be more fully treated in later chapters.

43. D. M. Sluys, *De Oudste Synagogen der Hoogduitsch-Joodsche Gemeente te Amsterdam* (The Oldest Synagogues of the High-German Jewish Community of Amsterdam 1635–1671); idem, "The Protocols of the High-German Jewish Community in Amsterdam 1635–1671" (Dutch), *BMGJW,* IV, 110–29; idem, *De Ambtsdata van de oudste Opperrabbijnen van de Hoogduitsche Joodsche Gemeente te Amsterdam* (Official Data about the First Chief Rabbis of the High-German Jewish Community of Amsterdam); and A. M. Vaz Dias, "New Contributions to the History of the Amsterdam High-German Jewish Community" (Dutch), *BMGJW,* VI, 153–81 (includes the statistical data of the marriages registered in 1635–70, mentioned in the text, and a study of the Ashkenazic cemetery at Muideberg; pp. 165 ff.). See also the brief sketch of the early period in J. Meijer's *"Moeder in Israël": een Geschiedenis van het Amsterdamse Asjkenazische Jodendom* ("Mother in Israel": A History of Amsterdam's Ashkenazic Jewry), pp. 9 ff.; and the literature listed *infra,* n. 44.

44. D. M. Sluys, "A Contribution to the History of the Polish Jewish Congregation in Amsterdam" (Dutch), *BMGJW,* III, 137–58; the De Pinto letter cited by T. Malve-

zin in his *Histoire des Juifs à Bordeaux*, pp. 213 f. See the even sharper separatist declaration in the *Letters of Certain Jews to Monsieur Voltaire, containing an Apology for Their Own People and for the Old Testament*, English trans. from the French, Paris, Kentucky, 1845, pp. 37 f., as cited in my *JC*, II, 365. See also A. Hertzberg, *The French Enlightenment and the Jews*, pp. 268 f.; and, more generally, H. J. Zimmels, *Ashkenazim and Sephardim*, esp. pp. 164 ff., 233 ff., 251 ff. On the less rigid separation between the two groups in Leghorn and Venice, despite the high status of the Sephardim there, see *supra*, Vol. XIV, pp. 91 ff., 107 f., 340 f. nn. 21–22, 345 f. n. 37.

45. I. Kracauer, *Geschichte der Juden in Frankfurt a.M.*, II, 45 f.; E. Boekman, "Amsterdam's Population in 1795" (Dutch), *TG*, XLV, 278–92; H. I. Bloom, *The Economic Activities*, pp. 31 f.; and the sources cited by J. A. Faber in "The Decline of the Baltic Grain Trade in the Second Half of the 17th Century," *Acta historiae neerlandica*, I, 129 f. (admitting that studies in the history of Holland's population still are in their infancy). Of interest also are such monographic articles as I. Maarsen's "The *Maḥzor* (Manuscript) of the Ashkenazic Community in Amsterdam" (Hebrew), *BMGJW*, III (= L. Wagenaar Jub. Vol.), 28–57 (this holiday prayerbook is neither dated nor of identifiable authorship); and the more general comparison, by S. Hart and J. Polišensky, "Prague and Amsterdam in the Seventeenth and Eighteenth Centuries: Demographic Changes and the Economic Development of the Two Cities" (Czech), *Československý Časopis Historický*, XV, 827–46 (with an English summary). Although the Hart-Polišensky essay stresses the sojourn in Amsterdam of the famous Czech thinker Jan Amos Comenius (1656–70), it also discusses, among other matters, the so-called Pardon Tax, the records of which reveal that during the second half of the seventeenth century quite a few Prague Jews were attracted to the Dutch metropolis by the economic opportunities it opened to newcomers from other lands (pp. 841 ff.).

46. S. Seeligmann, "Die Juden in Holland," *Festskrift . . . David Simonsen*, pp. 253–57. The impression made on Grotius by the decrees issued earlier by other Dutch cities became evident from the context of the early manuscript of his *Remonstrantie* when it was acquired by the Ets Haïm Library of Amsterdam in 1899 (see *supra*, n. 30). This manuscript had first been offered for sale in 1864 at a Nijhoff auction which included, among other papers, a manuscript of the Haarlem decree of 1605 (see *infra*, n. 47). Clearly, these materials formed a single unit which had originally been in Grotius' possession. See J. Meijer, "Hugo Grotius' *Remonstrantie*," *JSS*, XVII, 91 ff.

47. M. Wolff, *De Geschiedenis der Joden te Haarlem, 1600–1815* (A History of the Jews in Haarlem, 1600–1815), pp. 57 ff. App. i, reproducing the text of the 1605 ordinance; J. S. da Silva Rosa, "A Projected Settlement of Spanish and Portuguese Jews in Haarlem in the Year 1605" (Dutch), *Nieuw-Israel* (an Amsterdam weekly, 1915; also reprint); Joseph Justus Scaliger, *Scaligeriana*, [anonymously ed. by Isaac Vos], The Hague, 1666, pp. 183, 185; and J. Bernays's older study, *Joseph Justus Scaliger*, esp. pp. 35 f., 122 ff. (pointing out the deficiencies of Scaliger's autodidactic efforts to learn Hebrew). On this distinguished Orientalist, see also E. J. Lefroy's brief sketch, "Joseph Justus Scaliger, 1540–1609," *Proceedings* of the Huguenot Society of London, XX, 485–98. Scaliger's special interest in talmudic texts was evidenced in 1599, when he persuaded Philippus Ferdinandus Polonus, a converted Polish Jew who had taught Semitic languages at Oxford and Cambridge, to take over the chair of Arabic

at Leiden, at the relatively high salary of 25 florins a month. Scaliger was interested in this teacher principally because his "talmudic knowledge was amazing, though his grammar was weak." Unfortunately, Philippus Ferdinandus, who arrived in Leiden in August 1599, died there four months later. See S. Stern, "Philippus Ferdinandus Polonus, a Sixteenth-Century Hebraist in England," *Essays in Honour of . . . J. H. Hertz*, pp. 397–412; *supra*, Vol. XIII, pp. 166 f., 396 f. n. 9; H. F. Wijnman, "Philippus Ferdinandus, Professor of Arabic at the University of Leiden, the First East-European Jew in the Netherlands" (Dutch), *Jaarbericht* of the Vooraziatisch-Egyptisch Genootschap *Ex Oriente Lux*, VI, 558–80. Scaliger's impact on Hebrew studies in Holland is well illustrated by two Hebrew letters addressed to him in 1605 by Johannes Drusius, Jr., then seventeen years old. Apart from their rather fulsome praise of the master, combined with the writer's self-deprecation, these letters reflect the great respect in which Scaliger was held in scholarly circles, particularly among the Christian Hebraists. See L. Fuks's edition "The Collection of Hebrew Letters by Johannes Drusius, Jr.: Hebrew and Hebraists in the Netherlands around 1600" (Dutch, with an English summary), *SR*, III, 1–52, esp. pp. 18 f. Nos. vii–viii. Probably only his death at the age of twenty-one prevented Drusius from carrying out his plan of studying under Scaliger.

On the admission of the Jews to Haarlem, see also the earlier resolution of the city council, dated April 18, 1605, and summarized by Wolff, pp. 7 f.; J. Zwarts, "The First Rabbis," *BMGJW*, IV, 191 ff. (also contending that the biting remark attributed to Scaliger about one R. Asher of Amsterdam—"for a Jew [he] is an honest man"—occurring in a letter of January 21, 1609, is probably spurious; p. 192*); and S. Seeligmann, "The Marrano Problem from the Economic Standpoint" (Dutch), *ibid.*, III, 112, and 134 f. n. 21. It should be noted that Haarlem had long pursued an independent course of action in many other matters, too. See, for instance, H. P. H. Camp's "The Municipal Statute of Haarlem: a New View" (Dutch), *Miscellanea Mediaevalia* in memory of Jan Frederik Niermeyer, pp. 293–304. On the intercity competition in attracting New Christians and Jews, see *supra*, Vol. XIV, pp. 203 ff., 272 ff., 278 ff., and the notes thereon.

48. See J. H. Scheffer, "A Privilege Granted the Jews of Rotterdam in 1610" (Dutch), *Algemeene Nederlandsche Familieblad*, I, No. 26 (Rotterdam, August 30, 1883); E. Italie, "The History of the Jewish Community of Rotterdam" (Dutch) in *Rotterdam in den loop der eeuwen* (Rotterdam in the Course of Centuries), II, Part 6, pp. 120–95; S. Seeligmann, "The Marrano Problem," *BMGJW*, III, 110 ff.; J. Zwarts, "The First Rabbis," *ibid.*, IV, 204 ff.

49. C. W. Bruinvis, *Israëlieten te Alkmaar*, pp. 3 ff.; J. Zwarts, "The First Rabbis," *BMGJW*, IV, 186 ff.; idem, *De Joodsche Gemeente van Amersfoort, Gedenkschrift* (The Jewish Community of Amersfoort: a Memorial Volume); A. van Bemmel, *Beschryving der Stad Amersfoort* (Description of the City of Amersfoort), I, 178; J. Zwarts, *Portugeesche Joden te Maarssen en Maarsseveen in de 17e eeuw* (The Portuguese Jews in Maarssen and the Maars District in the 17th Century); J. H. van't Hoff, "The Erstwhile Portuguese Jewish Community and the Church Council of the Reformed Community in Middelburg" (Dutch), *Archief* of the Zeeuwsch Genootschap der Wetenschappen, 1922, pp. 14–18; W. Smit, "Jews in Middelburg" (Dutch), *Zeeuws Tijdschrift*, XVIII, 8–18; *supra*, n. 32; H. Poppers, *De Joden in Overijsel van hunne vestiging tot 1814* (The Jews in Overijsel from Their Settlement to 1814); H.

M. Corwin, "The *Pinkas* or Minute Book of the Jewish Community of Oldenzaal" (Dutch), *Verslaagen en Mededelingen* of the Vereeniging tot beoefening van Overijselsch Regt em Geschiedenis (Association of the Study of Overijsel Law and History), LXXXV, 69–96; D. E. Cohen, "The So-Called Portuguese Community of Nijkerk" (Dutch), *BMGJW*, III (= L. Wagenaar Jub. Vol.), 20–27; S. H. Hertweld, "Contributions to the History of the Jews in Gelderland" (Dutch), in *Geldensche oudheden* (Geldern Antiquities), ed. by G. van Hasfelt, I, Part 9, pp. 515–54; and J. Zwarts, *De Oudest geschiedenis der Joden te Utrecht* (The Earliest History of the Jews in Utrecht; reprinted from *Oud-Utrecht*, 1929). On Nijmegen, see *supra*, n. 17.

The numerous variations in the attitudes of these Dutch cities were in part owing to the considerable diversity in the social stratification of their inhabitants; despite the dynamic social changes in the two main commercial and maritime provinces, Holland and Zeeland, during the early modern period, the other, mainly agricultural, districts still bore the earmarks of the medieval heritage. See J. A. van Hutte's succinct observations in his "Gesellschaftliche Schichten in den Städten der Niederlande," *Untersuchungen zur gesellschaftlichen Struktur der mittelalterlichen Städte in Europa*, pp. 259–76; and H. Klopmaker, "Les Villes néerlandaises au XVIIe siècle: Institutions économiques et sociales," *Recueils* of the Société Jean Bodin, VII, Part 2, 577–601.

50. J. G. Nanninga, *Bronnen tot de Geschiedenis van den Levantschen Handel* (Sources for the History of the Levant Trade); H. I. Bloom, *The Economic Activities, passim*; H. Wätjen, "Das Judentum und die Anfänge der modernen Kolonisation," *VSW*, XI, 338–68, 565–606 (also reprint); A. M. Vaz Dias, "The Participation of Marranos in the Founding Capital of the East India Company" (Dutch), *Jaarboek* of the Genootschap Amstelodamum, XXXIII, 43–58 (noting that Elisabeth Pinto, who with her 3,000 florins investment was one of the first two Jewish shareholders, did not appear in the list of Portuguese residents of Amsterdam in 1602—another indication of the incompleteness of our source materials in this area; p. 58 App. iii); J. G. van Dillen, ed., *Het Oudste Aandeelshoudersregister van de Kamer Amsterdam der Oost-Indische Compagnie* (The Oldest Register of Shareholders of the Amsterdam Chamber of the East India Company), esp. pp. 49 ff.; H. Kellenbenz, *Sephardim*, pp. 112 f., 452 ff. See also, more generally, D. W. Davies, *A Primer of Dutch Seventeenth-Century Overseas Trade*, esp. pp. 23 ff., 46 ff.

51. Philip III's letter to Viceroy Martin Affonso de Castro of January 18, 1607, and the decree of March 15 (with a postil of March 20), 1568, in R. A. de Bulhão Pato's ed. of *Documentos remettidos da India* (covering the years 1605–1619), I, 100 ff., 106, 316; II, 215 ff.; III, 510 ff., cited by M. Kayserling in his *Christopher Columbus*, English trans., pp. 129 ff.; Esteban de Ares Fonseca's highly prejudiced 1634 complaint to the Inquisitorial Suprema, cited by H. C. Lea in *A History of the Inquisition of Spain*, III, 279 (see *infra*, n. 52); and other sources quoted by H. I. Bloom in *The Economic Activities*, pp. 115 ff. The general role played by Marranos and professing Jews in undermining the Iberian near-monopoly of Western Europe's trade with the Far East, and in the shift of the center of international commerce to the northern lands, will become clearer in our discussion of the major economic trends of the period in a later chapter. See also the *Generale Missiven van gouverneurs-general en Raaden* (General Messages of the Governors-General and Councilors to the Commission of Seventeen of the United East India Company), ed. by W. P. Coolhaas, esp. II,

332 ff., 353 f. No. viii, 770 ff., and 881 No. iv; and I. Prins's affirmative answer to his query, "Did the Dutch Find Jews upon Their Entry into Java?" (Dutch), *Nieuw Israëlietisch Weekblad*, LXV, No. 4 (of June 7, 1929), p. 13, briefly summarized in *BMGJW*, V, 68–69; and, more generally, T. I. Poonen (Punan), *A Survey of the Rise of Dutch Power in Malabar, 1603–1678;* K. W. Goowardena, *The Foundations of the Dutch Power in Ceylon, 1638–1658;* and *infra*, Chap. LXVI, nn. 113 ff., 122.

Of some Jewish interest also is M. Vermeulen-Forrier's study "The Organization of Commercial Activities by the United East India Company in Persia (1623–38)" (Dutch), *TG*, LXXX, 472–85, emphasizing—mainly on the basis of the materials assembled in H. Dunlop's *Bronnen tot de Geschiedenis der Oostindische Compagnie in Perzië* (Sources for the History of the East India Company in Persia), I, 1611–1638, esp. pp. 147 f. No. 74, 351 ff. and 357 No. 197, 665 ff. and 669 No. 325—that the area around the Persian Gulf was the Company's most profitable source of revenue. Vermeulen-Forrier expects to expatiate on this aspect in another study. As in other parts of Asia, the Dutch followed here in the footsteps of the Portuguese, whose exploits in that area, and the Jewish aspects thereof, particularly in Ormuz, are discussed *infra*, Chap. LXVI, nn. 109 ff. Of course, fuller light on these problems is to be shed in the analysis of the historical evolution of the Jewish communities amidst the Asian peoples, hopefully to be presented in Vol. XVII.

52. S. Oppenheim, "The Early History of the Jews in New York, 1654 to 1664," *PAJHS*, XVIII, 1–91, esp. pp. 14 ff.; C. Adler, "A Contemporary Memorial Relating to Damages to Spanish Interests in America Done by Jews of Holland (1634)," *ibid.*, XVII, 45–51, esp. p. 50, with reference to H. C. Lea, *A History of the Inquisition of Spain*, III, 279 (see *infra*, Chap. LXVI, n. 77); C. R. Boxer, *The Dutch in Brazil, 1624–1654*, p. 121; Menasseh ben Israel, *The Humble Addresses to his Highnesse the Lord Protector*, reprinted in L. Wolf's ed. of *Menasseh ben Israel's Mission to Oliver Cromwell*, pp. 88 f.; E. M. Koen, "Notarial Records," *SR*, V, 219 f. No. 425 n. 34; and other sources cited by H. I. Bloom in *The Economic Activities*, pp. 124 ff.

At times Jews were on the less enviable receiving end of the Company's policies. For instance, a group of 152 Leghorn Jews, who had settled in Cayenne in 1660, after a perilous journey across the Atlantic Ocean, were forced to leave the city four years later when the Company ceded it to France. See L. Cardozo de Béthencourt, "Notes on the Spanish and Portuguese Jews in the United States, Guiana, and the Dutch and British West Indies during the Seventeenth and Eighteenth Centuries," *PAJHS*, XXIX, 7–38, esp. pp. 19 f.; the scattered data presented in H. D. Benjamin and J. F. Snelleman, eds., *Encyclopaedie van Nederlandsch West-Indië*, 2d ed.; and *infra*, Chap. LXVI, nn. 8 f. See also the more recent discussion between W. J. van Hoboken and J. G. van Dillen in the former's "The Dutch West India Company: the Political Background of Its Rise and Decline," in *Britain and the Netherlands . . . Oxford-Netherlands Historical Conference, 1959*, ed. by J. S. Bromley and E. H. Kossmann, pp. 41–61; Van Dillen's "The West-India Company: Calvinism and Politics" (Dutch), *TG*, LXXIV, 145–71; continued in Hoboken's "A Reply concerning the West India Company" and Van Dillen's "Postscript" (both in Dutch), *ibid.*, LXXV, 49–53 and 53–56.

53. A. M. Vaz Dias, "On the Wealth of Amsterdam Jews in the Seventeenth and Eighteenth Centuries" (Dutch), *TG*, LI, 165–76 (also in *Vrijdagavond*, VIII, 182–83, 218–19, 242–44, 262–63); R. Doehaerd, "Commerce et morale à Anvers au XVIe siècle

(à propos d'un manuscrit de la Bibliothèque de Leyde)," *RH*, CCIV, 226–33, esp. pp. 231, 233 (also quoting an anonymous tract, probably written by a Catholic theologian, trying to justify the 12 percent interest rate); J. G. van Dillen, "Foreigners in Amsterdam" (Dutch), *TG*, L, 4–35; I. Maarsen, "The Council of Four Lands and the Amsterdam Congregations in the Seventeenth Century" (Hebrew), *Ha-Zofeh*, VIII, 289–300; S. Seeligmann, "Ein Originalbrief der Vierländersynode nach Amsterdam aus 1677," *Livre d'hommage à . . . Samuel Poznanski*, pp. 147–52; S. H. Lieben, "Briefe von 1744–1748 über die Austreibung der Juden aus Prag," *JGJCR*, IV, 353–479, esp. pp. 391 ff. No. 17, 394 f. No. 20, 408 No. 26, 409 No. 28, 415 ff. No. 33, 447 f. No. 62; H. I. Bloom, *The Economic Activities*, pp. 70 f., 102 ff. See also A. Castillo, "Dans la monarchie espagnole de XVIIᵉ siècle. Les banquiers portugais et le circuit d'Amsterdam," *Annales ESC*, II, 311–16; G. Guitton, "En marge de l'histoire du prêt à intérêt. Lyon jaloux d'Anvers et d'Amsterdam (1654–1678)," *Nouvelle Revue théologique*, LXXV, 59–69; and, on the far-flung enterprises of Jewish bankers in Antwerp, *supra*, Vol. XIII, pp. 119 ff., 369 ff. nn. 63 ff.

54. See J. G. van Dillen, "Foreigners," *TG*, L, 14; idem, *Bronnen tot de Geschiedenis der Wisselbanken* (Sources for the History of Exchange Banks; Amsterdam, Middelburg, Delft, Rotterdam), particularly informative for the period after 1580 (see, for instance, I, 260 No. 318 item 7); idem, "The Establishment and Function of the Amsterdam Exchange Bank in the Seventeenth Century, 1609-1686" (Dutch), reprinted from *De Economist*, 1928, in his *Mensen en Achtergronden* (Men and Backgrounds). Studies Published on the Occasion of the Author's Eightieth Birthday), pp. 336–84; idem, *Geschichte der wirtschaftlichen Entwicklung der Niederlande und die Amsterdamer Wechselbank, 1609–1820;* idem, "The Bank of Amsterdam" in his ed. of *History of the Principal Public Banks*, pp. 79–123; idem, "Postscript," *TG*, LXXV, 54; idem, "Amsterdam, marché mondial des métaux précieux au XVIIᵉ et XVIIIᵉ siècle," *RH*, CLII, 194–201; and other sources cited by H. I. Bloom in *The Economic Activities*, pp. 172 ff. In "The Earliest Sources," *SR*, IV, 27, E. M. Koen raises the number of Jewish clients of the Exhange Bank to 21 in 1609, and to 114 in 1620. But this is mainly owing to her fuller indentification of the Bank's clients as Jews; *ibid.*, n. 9. On the rivalry of the Dutch guilds and the Jews, see S. Seeligmann, "The Guilds and the Jews" (Dutch), *Vrijdagavond*, V, Part 1, pp. 135–37.

55. R. Ehrenberg, *Das Zeitalter der Fugger, Geldkapital und Creditverkehr im 16. Jahrhundert*, II, 333 (citing De Koopman), 336.

56. J. Grossman, *Die Amsterdamer Börse vor zwei hundert Jahren: Ein Beitrag zur Geschichte der Politik und des Börsenwesens im mittleren Europa (1672–1673). Nach den Akten des Wiener Staats-Archives;* J. G. van Dillen, "Foreigners," *TG*, L, 4–35; R. Doehaerd, "Commerce et morale à Anvers," *RH*, CCIV, 230; H. I. Bloom, *The Economic Activities*, pp. 178 ff. (with a floor plan of the Amsterdam Stock Exchange).

57. The somewhat dubious 1618 report of the French diplomat was first reproduced by L. Vignols in "Le Commerce hollandais et les associations juives à la fin du XVIIᵉ siècle," *RH*, XLIV, 327–30. See also, more generally, M. F. J. Smith, *Tijdaffaires in Effecten aan de Amsterdamsche Beurs* (Futures Trade in Stocks at the

Amsterdam Stock Exchange); L. Samuel, *Die Effektenspekulation im 17. und 18. Jahrhundert, ein Beitrag zur Börsengeschichte.*

58. Joseph Penso de la Vega, *Confusión de Confusiones, diálogos curiosos entre un philosopho acudo, un mercader discreto y un accionista erudito, discriviendo el negocio de las acciones, su origen, su etimología, su realidad, su juego y su enredo;* idem, *Die Verwirrung der Verwirrugen. Vier Dialogue über die Börse in Amsterdam,* German trans. with an Intro. by O. Pringsheim. A new edition of the *Confusión de Confusiones* with a Dutch translation by J. Geers was issued with an Introduction and Notes by M. F. J. Smith; while its *Portions Descriptive of the Amsterdam Stock Exchange. Selected and Translated* were published in English by H. Kellenbenz. See also M. Bataillon's succinct, but meaningful, review of a 1958 photooffset reprint of De la Vega's original 1688 edition in *BH*, LXII, 343–53; and M. B. Amzalak's analysis, *Trois précurseurs portugais; Santarém, et les assurances; Freitas, et la liberté des mers; Vega, et les operations de Bourse.* This and other important works by De la Vega will be more fully analyzed in later chapters.

59. H. de Castries, *Les Sources inédites de l'histoire du Maroc,* 1st ser. Dynastie saadienne. Archives et Bibliothèques des Pays-Bas, I, xv ff.; II, 50 ff., 163 ff., 402 ff., 570 ff., 621 ff.; III, 326 f.; and the scores of other references to Samuel Pallache and his relatives, listed in the Index to the 1st series, Vol. VI, pp. 682–85; and in the 2d series, Archives et Bibliothèques d'Angleterre in the Index to Vol. III, p. 684; J. Zwarts, "The First Rabbis," *BMGJW,* IV, 199 ff.; D. Henriques de Castro, *Keur* (Auswahl), pp. 91 ff. No. 15 (Samuel Pallache's epitaph); K. Heeringa, *Bronnen tot de Geschiedenis van den Levantschen Handel* (Sources for the History of the Levant Trade), Vol. I: 1590–1660, esp. p. 375 No. 179 (in this report to the States General of February 21, 1633, Cornelis Haga, Dutch envoy in Constantinople, describes his visit to Jerusalem, where he was approached by the Greek-Orthodox patriarch with the request that the Greek religious group be taken under Dutch protection against the severe persecution it was suffering from the Roman Catholics —a telling example of how Middle-Eastern trade was intertwined with religion and politics), 1106 ff. (on the Pallache family); idem, "A Treaty between the Netherlands and Morocco" (Dutch), *Onze Eeuw,* VII, Part 3, pp. 81–119; H. I. Bloom's biographical sketch of Samuel Pallache in "A Jewish Diplomat," *Jewish Institute Quarterly,* IV, Part 1, pp. 24–26; and the additional data offered by E. M. Koen in her "Notarial Records," *SR,* V, 111 f. No. 368, 224 No. 442. See also *infra,* Chap. LXIV, n. 74. On the Dutch negotiations with Morocco in 1609, and the 1615 complaints by Spain about Joseph Pallache's piratical activity (*infra,* n. 60), see also the official correspondence between Johan van Oldenbarnevelt and Dutch envoys in S. P. Haak and A. J. Veenendaat's ed. of his *Bescheiden* (Reports concerning His Diplomatic Activity and His Family), II, 374 f. No. 269; III, 82 f. No. 70, 156 f. No. 157; and, more generally, J. Caillé, "Ambassades et missions marocaines aux Pays-Bas à l'époque des sultans saâdiens," *Hespéris-Tamuda,* IV, 5–67, esp. p. 30, dealing with the Pallache family, in part on the basis of G. Chavis's 1955 thesis at Rabat University, *Samuel Pallache, agent diplomatique des sultans saâdiens* (typescript).

60. See H. Kellenbenz, *Sephardim an der unteren Elbe,* pp. 148 f. (includes a reference to similar negotiations with Glückstadt in 1653); S. Seeligmann, *Biblio-*

graphie en Historie, p. 43; and other sources cited by H. I. Bloom in *The Economic Activities*, pp. 79 ff. Incidentally, the almost hereditary succession to diplomatic posts by members of the same Jewish or Marrano families was not unique to the representatives of the more liberal Muslim rulers. For example, much material on the careers of "Manuel (ca. 1640–1704), Marcus (1667–1743), and Philip (1702–1777) de Fonseca (Deffonseca): three generations of high Belgian public servants of Jewish descent" has been assembled and briefly described in an unpublished Dutch essay by Izak Prins (in his large collection deposited at the Jewish Historical General Archive in Jerusalem).

61. See the rich documentation assembled by J. G. van Dillen in his compilation of *Bronnen tot de Geschiedenis van het Bedrijfsleven en het Gildewezen van Amsterdam* (Sources for the History of Industry and Guilds of Amsterdam), I, 622 Nos. 1054–55 (1604), 632 No. 1066 (1605), 784 No. 1353 (1604, all relating to silk); II, 6 No. 16 (1612, brokerage); 121 f. No. 219 and 348 No. 582 (1615, 1619, both relating to diamond cutting); 245 No. 393 and 327 No. 542 (1617, 1619, both on Jewish slaughtering for meat consumption); 752 No. 1329 (1631, Menasseh ben Israel's printing contract; see *infra*, nn. 66–67), contrasted with pp. 690 f. No. 1245 (1629, prohibiting Jews from serving as tobacconists), etc.; N. W. Goldstein, "Die Juden in der Amsterdamer Diamanten-Industrie," *Zeitschrift für Demographie und Statistik der Juden*, III, 178–84 (referring also to an unsuccesful effort made in 1748 to organize a guild of diamond workers in order to shut the Jews out of that flourishing trade, which they had helped to introduce); E. E. Danekamp, *Die Amsterdamer Diamanten-industrie*, p. 19. Diamond cutting had become so desirable a craft that fathers often paid heavily for the apprenticeship of their sons with skilled professionals. See the 1611 contract summarized in E. M. Koen's "Amsterdam Notarial Deeds," *SR*, V, 227 No. 460. See also, from the linguistic and historical point of view, I. Löw, "Der Diamant. Ein Kapitel aus meinen Mineralien der Juden," *Jubilee Volume in Honour of Berndt (Bernhard) Heller*, pp. 230–38, esp. p. 237.

62. J. J. Reesse, *De Suikerhandel van Amsterdam* (The Sugar Trade of Amsterdam from the Beginning of the Seventeenth Century to 1813: a Contribution to the Commercial History of the Fatherland, mainly on the Basis of Archival Data), pp. 30 ff., 187 ff., cxxvii ff. App. G; E. M. Koen, "Amsterdam Notarial Deeds," *SR*, II, 263 No. 58; V, 225 No. 449 (incidentally, this collection of excerpts also reveals how risky the sugar trade could be to unwary traders in view of the varying qualities of sugar and the not infrequent substitutions of inferior for high-quality merchandise by unscrupulous suppliers; see, for instance, IV, 251 No. 300; V, 116 No. 388, 118 No. 396); H. Kellenbenz, *Unternehmerkräfte im Hamburger Portugal- und Spanienhandel, 1590–1625*, pp. 52 ff.; E. Baasch, *Hamburgs Schiffahrt und Waarenhandel vom Ende des 16. bis zur Mitte des 17. Jahrhunderts* (reprinted from *Zeitschrift des Vereines für hamburgische Geschichte*), p. 31; and other data supplied by J. G. van Dillen in his *Bronnen . . . Bedrijfsleven*, esp. pp. 622 f. Nos. 1054–55, 632 No. 1066, 658 No. 1115 (1608); his *Geschichte der wirstschaftlichen Entwicklung der Niederlande und die Amsterdamer Wechselbank;* H. I. Bloom, "A Study of Brazilian Jewish History, 1623–1654, Based Chiefly upon the Findings of the Late Samuel Oppenheim," *PAJHS*, XXXIII, 43–125; idem, *The Economic Activities*, pp. 33 ff.; J. S. da Silva Rosa, *Geschiedenis der Portugeesche Joden te Amsterdam*, pp. 32 ff. Much material on the production, refining, and trade of

cane sugar has been assembled by I. Löw in *Die Flora der Juden*, I, 747 ff.; IV, 579 ff. and *passim* (see Indexes, IV, 682, 730). See also, more generally, F. Baasch, *Holländische Wirtschaftsgeschichte*. On the role of Jews in the Brazilian sugar industry, see *supra*, Vol. XIII, pp. 141 f., 383 n. 84; and *infra*, Chap. LXVI, n. 71. In an interesting entry in the minute book of the Hamburg Spanish-Portuguese congregation, dated Iyar 22, 5414 (May 17, 1654), we are told that a son of Isaac Nunes who had arrived from Holland had been refused admission to the community. But as soon as the elders learned that he was a tobacco worker, he was allowed to stay for a month, possibly to teach that trade to some Hamburg Jews. See J. C[assuto], "Aus dem ältesten Protokollbuch der Portugiesisch-Jüdischen Gemeinde in Hamburg," *JJLG*, VI 40. The Isaac in question here evidently was not identical with either the Isaac Nunes or the Nunes Henriques mentioned in other Hamburg sources. See H. Kellenbenz, *Sephardim an der unteren Elbe*, pp. 170 f., 306.

63. P. J. Blok, ed., *Relazioni veneziane. Venetianische Berichten over de Vereenigde Nederlanden* (Venetian Reports about the United Netherlands from 1600 to 1795), assembled and ed., p. 201 No. xl; M. Hume, *The Court of Philip IV. Spain in Decadence*, new ed. pp. 129 ff.; H. J. Koenen, *Geschiedenis der Joden in Nederland*, pp. 142, 206 ff.; Glückel von Hameln, *Zichroines* (Memoiren, 1645–1719), ed. by D. Kaufmann, pp. 144 ff.; in the somewhat condensed English trans. by M. Lowenthal, entitled *The Memoirs of Glückel of Hameln*, with Intro. and Notes, pp. 95 ff.; and other sources quoted by W. Sombart in *Die Juden und das Wirtschaftsleben*, p. 463 n. 413. On the reversal in the attitudes toward luxury, see Charles Wilson, *The Dutch Republic*, pp. 34 f.

64. A. M. Vaz Dias, "On the Wealth of Amsterdam Jews in the Seventeenth and Eighteenth Centuries" (Dutch), *TG*, LI, 165–76 (*Vrijdagavond*, VIII); J. S. da Silva Rosa, *Geschiedenis der Portugeesche Joden te Amsterdam*, pp. 182 f.; H. I. Bloom, *The Economic Activities*, pp. 203 ff.; S. H. in *The Asmonean*, I, No. 1 (October 26, 1849), p. 2, cited in my *Steeled by Adversity: Essays and Addresses on American Jewish Life*, ed. by J. M. Baron, p. 140; C. Bruneel, "Un Épisode de la lutte contre la mendicité et le vagabondage. La maison de correction *(tuchthuys)* de Bruxelles," *Cahiers bruxellois*, XI, 29–72. According to the French diplomat Jean [Hérauld] de Gourvilles, on the approach of the French armies in 1672, the Amsterdam Jewish community offered Louis XIV, through him (probably through the mediation of an Amsterdam Jew, Mendez Flores), a contribution of 2,000,000 florins to spare the Jewish quarter. This may be pure legend. In any case, the French did not occupy Amsterdam at that juncture. See L. Lecestre, ed., *Mémoires de Jean [Hérauld] de Gourvilles (1670–1702)*, I, 240 n. 3; II, 57.

65. Hugo Grotius' reply (dated Feb. 2, 1640), to Gerhard Johann Vos' (Vossius') communication of Jan. 1640, in his *Epistolae*, p. 596; C. Roth, *A Life of Menasseh ben Israel, Rabbi, Printer, and Diplomat*, pp. 49 ff., 315 n. 2; E. M. Koen, "Notarial Records," *SR*, V, 123 No. 416 and n. 30; W. C. Pieterse, *Daniel Levi de Barrios*, pp. 153 f. No. 12, 168 ff. Nos. 17–19; W. F. H. Oldeweit, "Two Centuries of Amsterdam Business Failures and the Course of a Business Cycle (1636 to 1838)" (Dutch), *TG*, LXXV, 421–35, esp. the tables pp. 432 ff. These tables show that the annual number of failures, ranging from 55 to 63 in the years 1636–39, declined in the early 1640s, but rose sharply, to from 58 to 90, in the period 1644–50. See also, more

generally, A. E. Sayous, "Die Grossen Händler und Kapitalisten in Amsterdam gegen Ende des sechzehnten und während des siebzehnten Jahrhunderts," *Weltwirtschaftliches Archiv*, XLVI, 685–711; XLVII, 115–44, esp. XLVI, 687, 702; XLVII, 122 f., 127, 134, 137 n. 2; and V. Barbour, *Capitalism in Amsterdam in the Seventeenth Century*. With respect to the perennial question about the interplay of economic and intellectual forces, I. Schöffer has given an affirmative answer to his query, "Did Holland's Golden Age Coincide with a Period of Crisis?" *Acta historiae neerlandica*, I, 82–107, except that he considers the seventeenth century more a period of consolidation than one of crisis. The discrepancy between economic decline and intellectual flowering is, of course, even more obvious in the case of Spain's *siglo d'oro*.

66. See such monographs as L. and R. Fuks, "The Hebrew Production of the Plantin-Raphelengius Presses in Leyden, 1585–1615," *SR*, IV, 1–24 (also reprint); I. S. Révah, "Fragments retrouvés de quelques éditions Amstelodamoises de la version espagnole du rituel juif," *ibid.*, II, 108–110 (with good facsimiles of two fragments); J. M. Hillesum, "Hebrew Printing in the Netherlands" (Dutch), *Catalogus der Tentoonstelling van der Ontwikkeling der Boekdrukkunst* (Catalogue of the Exhibition of the Development of Bookprinting in the Netherlands), November 1923, pp. 177–83; J. Zwarts, "The Two Oldest Editions of the Hebrew Bible in Amsterdam" (Dutch), *Het Boek*, XV, 99–108; various entries in J. S. da Silva Rosa's compilation of the new *Catalogus der Tentoonstelling in het Portugeesch-Israëlietisch Seminarium* (Catalogue of the Exhibition in the Portuguese-Jewish Seminary "Ets Haïm" on the Three-Hundredth Anniversary of the First Hebrew Book Printed in Amsterdam by Menasseh ben Israel), 1927; his list of "Die Spanischen und Portugiesischen gedruckten Judaica in der Bibliothek des Jüd. Portug. Seminars 'Ets Haïm' in Amsterdam. Eine Ergänzung zu Kayserlings 'Biblioteca Española-Portugueza-Judaica,'" *BMGJW*, V, 177–210 (previously supplemented by Kayserling himself in his additional "Notes sur la littérature des Juifs hispano-portugais," *REJ*, XXII, 119–24); the numerous bibliographies of the publications by Menasseh ben Israel as both author and printer, including the study by L. Fuks, "What Has Menasseh ben Israel Written and What of It Has Been Printed; in Memory of the Three-Hundredth Anniversary of Menasseh ben Israel's Death (November 20, 1657)" (Dutch), *Het Boek*, XXXII, 330–35.

Much can also be learned from the background materials offered by N. de Roever in his "Amsterdam Printers and Booksellers of the Sixteenth Century" (Dutch), *Bijdragen tot de Geschiedenis van den Nederlandschen Boekhandel*, V, 189–262; and by P. Burger in "The Dutch Book in the Seventeenth Century" (Dutch) in the aforementioned 1923 *Catalogus der Tentoonstelling*, esp. pp. 15 and 19. Additional information about the businesses of a number of Jewish printing firms is supplied by M. M. Kleerkooper and W. P. van Stockum in *De Boekhandel te Amsterdam* (The Book Trade in Amsterdam, especially in the Seventeenth Century), esp. I, 10 ff. (Joseph Athias), 33 f. (Emanuel Benveniste), 363 ff. (Philips Levy), 410 ff. (Menasseh ben Israel); II, 1633 ff.; and by H. I. Bloom, *The Economic Activities*, pp. 44 f. Of some interest also are the works by E. Cockx-Indestege and G. Glorieux, *Belgica typographica, 1541–1600*, and by I. H. van Beghen, *De Amsterdamse Boekhandel* (The Amsterdam Book Trade, 1618–1725).

67. See J. S. da Silva Rosa, "Joseph Athias (1635–1700). Ein berühmter jüdischer Drucker," *Soncino Blätter*, III, Parts 2–4 (Festschrift für Heinrich Brody), 107–111

[183–88]; I. H. van Eeghen, "A Public Auction of Athias' Books in 1688" (Dutch), *SR*, II, 30–41 (with an English summary); and the literature listed *supra*, n. 66. On the eminent Utrecht scholar mentioned in Athias' advertisment, see the bio-bibliographical sketch of "Johannes Leusden as Hebraist" (Dutch) by M. L. Hirschel, a Nazi victim—posthumously published, revised, and amplified by A. K. Offenberg in *SR*, I, Part 1, pp. 23–50. Before long, Amsterdam also became a center of Yiddish printing, the products including a Yiddish Bible translation and the semiweekly *Kurant* (1687–88), after the *Gazeta de Amsterdam* (1678) the earliest Jewish periodical in the world. See L. Fuks *et al.*, *Joodse Pers in de Nederlanden en in Duitsland* (Jüdische Presse in den Niederlanden und in Deutschland, 1647–1940); I. Prins, "The Old Dutch Freedom of the Printing Press from the Standpoint of the Jewish Book" (Dutch), *BMGJW*, V, 147–76; L. Fuks, "The Two Yiddish Bible Translations Simultaneously Published in Amsterdam in the Seventeenth Century" (Dutch), *Het Boek*, XXXII, 146–65 (with reference to those issued in 1676–79 by Uri Phoebus ha-Levi and Joseph Athias, respectively, of which only the latter had secured a genuine endorsement from the Polish Council for Four Lands); J. L. Voorzanger and J. E. Polak, Jz., comps., *Het Joodsch in̊ Nederland* (Yiddish in the Netherlands: on Loanwords and Idioms Borrowed from Hebrew and Other Languages), esp. pp. 16 ff., 25 ff.; H. Beem's more recent compilations, *Jerȯsche* (The Heritage: Yiddish Proverbs and Idioms in the Dutch Language Area), esp. pp. 11 ff.; and *She'erit Resten van een Taal* (Surviving Remnants of a Language: a Dictionary of Netherland Yiddish); A. R. Hulst, "Bible Translating into Dutch," *Babel International Journal of Translation*, IX, 79–82. The dramatic story of Dutch Jewish printing, as it unfolded particularly in the latter part of the seventeenth century, will be told in greater detail in a later context.

68. E. N. Adler, "A Letter of Menasseh ben Israel," *TJHSE*, V, 179 f. (Spanish). 183 (English, with minor variations); idem, "The Jews of Amsterdam in 1655," *ibid.*, IV, 224–29; C. Gebhardt, ed., *Die Schriften des Uriel da Costa, mit Einleitung, Übertragung, und Regesten*, with the editor's valuable texts and comments; K. Müller's Berne dissertation, *Das "Exemplar humanae vitae" des Uriel da Costa*; A. M. Vaz Dias, *Uriel da Costa: Nieuwe Bijdrage* (a New Contribution to His Biography); I. S. Révah, "La Religion d'Uriel da Costa, Marrane de Porto (d'aprés des documents inédits)," *Revue d'histoire des religions*, CLXI, 45–76 (includes interesting data on Uriel's ancestry); *supra*, Vol. XIV, pp. 282 f., 408 n. 59; the totally unhistorical painting of Uriel da Costa holding Spinoza on his lap (inspired by Karl Ferdinand Gutzkow's play *Uriel Acosta*) accompanying J. Zwarts's "Jewish Archival Fragments, XXV: Uriel da Costa in a Utrecht Ban (1627)" (Dutch), *Vrijdagavond*, VIII, Part 1, pp. 61–64; A. M. Vaz Dias in cooperation with W. G. van der Tak, *Spinoza Mercator et Autodidactus*, *Oorkonden* (Spinoza, Merchant and Autodidact: Documents and other Authentic Sources relating to the Philosopher's Youth and His Relatives), esp. pp. 47 ff., 55; Van der Tak's further data relating to Baruch de Spinoza and his family, in his Dutch report for *Het Spinozahuis*, XXXVIII (1935); idem, *De Firma Bento y Gabriel de Spinoza*. In his *Spinoza et le Dr. Juan de Prado*, I. S. Révah rightly questions the epithet of autodidact given the philosopher by the otherwise well-informed Vaz Dias. While no conclusive documentary evidence has thus far been discovered for any formal schooling enjoyed by young Baruch, there is a strong likelihood that he received a thorough rabbinic and secular education. The scholarly friends who edited his

Opera posthuma of 1677, published only a few months after his death, undoubtedly had reliable data to support their contention that "from an early age he was nurtured on literary works and in his adolescence he intensively studied [*exercuit*] for many years." See their Preface to that edition. Many other biographical facts and hypotheses have been adduced over the generations in the enormous bibliography relating to Spinoza's life and works. See A. S. Oko's comprehensive *The Spinoza Bibliography* (a name index, particularly of authors, would greatly facilitate the use of the 20,000 or more cards here photographically reproduced); supplemented by J. Wetlesen's *A Spinoza Bibliography, particularly of the Period 1940–1967* (mimeographed).

69. Jacques Richard's 1655 report to the French ambassador in The Hague (Antoine Brun), published by V. Brants in "Une Page de Sémitisme diplomatique et commercial. Incidents de la vie d'Amsterdam au XVIIᵉ siècle d'après des pièces inédites," *Bulletin* of the Académie Royale de Belgique, Classe des Lettres, 1905, pp. 573–96, esp. p. 581. (Brants also cites from a Brussels archival document a warning, addressed to the king of Spain as early as December 1, 1614, not to trust two Jews who were performing some services for him; p. 576 n. 2.) The multiplicity of names among the Portuguese Jews of Amsterdam and other cities was dictated not only by fear of the Inquisition but also by the fact that the Hebrew names used in and outside the synagogue were only gradually uncovered from family traditions passed down through the generations in Marrano circles. See *supra*, Vol. XIV, pp. 273 f., 405 n. 49.

70. M. Wolff's essay on "The First Settlement" in *BVG*, 4th ser. IX–X, and 5th ser. I; D. Henriques de Castro, *Keur van Grafsteenen*, pp. 53 ff., etc.; J. A. van Prag, "El Diálogo dos Montes de Rehuel Jessurun," *Mélanges de philologie offerts à Salverda de Grave*, pp. 242–55; J. Rubio, "Antonio Enríquez Gómez, el poeta judaizante," *Miscelánea de estudios árabes y hebráicos* (supplement to the *Boletín* of the University of Granada, IV); M. Kayserling, *Sephardim. Romanische Poesien der Juden in Spanien*, esp. pp. 175 ff., 216 ff., etc.; idem, *Biblioteca española-portugueza-judaica and Other Studies in Ibero-Jewish Bibliography*, selected with a Prolegomenon by Y. H. Yerushalmi, *passim*; C. Roth, *Marranos*, pp. 245 ff.; H. I. Bloom, *The Economic Activities*, esp. pp. 31 f. On Enríquez Gómez' earlier and later activities, particularly in Rouen, see *infra*, Chaps. LXIV, n. 30; LXV, nn. 61 and 106.

71. See Abraham Sasportas' Intro. to the ed. of his father Jacob b. Aaron's Responsa, *Ohel Ya'aqob* (The Tent of Jacob); M. Kayserling, *Biblioteca española-portugueza-judaica*, p. 98; H. Kellenbenz, *Sephardim an der unteren Elbe*, pp. 331 ff. (on Mussaphia) and *passim*; B. Brilling, "Die Frühesten Beziehungen der Juden Hamburgs zu Palästina," *JJLG*, XXI, 36 f.; A. Geiger, "Josef Salomo del Medigo" in his *Nachgelassene Schriften*, ed. by L. Geiger, III, 1–33, esp. pp. 17, 32; I. Heilbronn, *Die Mathematischen und naturwissenschaftlichen Anschauungen des Josef Salomo Medigo, dargestellt nach seinem Sefer Elim* (Diss. Erlangen); J. d'Ancona, "Delmedigo, Menasseh ben Israel and Spinoza" (Dutch), *BMGJW*, VI, 105–152; idem, "The Arrival of Marranos in the Northern Netherlands" (Dutch) in H. K. Brugmans and A. Frank, eds., *Geschiedenis der Joden in Nederland*, I, esp. pp. 257 ff., 275 f., 281 f. On some of the businessmen who shuttled back and forth between Hamburg, Glückstadt, and Amsterdam to meet exigencies created by the

Thirty Years' War or mercantile constellations, see *supra*, Vol. XIV, pp. 272 ff. See also the respective entries in the *Encyclopaedia Sephardica neerlandica*, Vols. I–III. Needless to say, the names of many of the personalities mentioned in this section will often recur in our later chapters, especially those dealing with the intellectual evolution of early modern Jewry.

72. M. de [Oliveira] Lemos, *Zacuto Lusitano;* H. Kellenbenz, "Dr. Jakob Rosales," *Zeitschrift für Religions- und Geistesgeschichte*, VIII, 345–54; *supra*, Vol. XIV, pp. 282 f., 408 f. n. 59; M. Kayserling, *Sephardim*, pp. 209 ff., 216 ff., 310; M. B. Amzalak's bibliographical sketch *Abraham Pharar (Farrar), Judeu do destêrro de Portugal;* Uriel da Costa, *Exemplar humanae vitae;* and C. Gebhardt's intro. and notes thereto in his ed. of *Die Schriften des Uriel da Costa*, pp. 103 ff., 259 ff.

73. See the literature listed *supra*, n. 63; Hugo Grotius' *Epistolae*, p. 564 and Nos. 286, 390, 423, 439, 452, 454, 467, 470, 476, 564; idem, *Briefwisseling*, VI, 165 f. No. 2237; *Gerhardi Johannis Vossii Epistolae et clarorum virorum ad eum*, comp. by P. Colomesius, Augsburg, 1691 ed., I, 229 No. 185, 330 f. No. 308, 351 f. No. 324; and other sources cited by C. Roth in *A Life of Menasseh ben Israel, Rabbi, Printer, and Diplomat*. Vos' correspondence with K. Słupecki (*Epistolae*, I, 320 f. No. 295; II, 183 f. No. 252) had been partially reproduced in his *Opera*, Amsterdam, 1695 ff., IV, *Epistolae selectiores*, p. 212 No. 392. On the remarkable personality of Isaac de la Peyrère, his pre-Adamite theories, and his peculiar proto-Zionism, see *infra*, Chap. LXIV, n. 21.

Menasseh's far-flung correspondence at times became an unexpected source of trouble to the recipients. In the case of Manuel Fernandes Villareal, Portuguese consul-general in Paris, a lengthy letter to him from Menasseh in 1648, answering in detail a number of questions relating to biblical chronology, was used by the Portuguese Inquisition as partial evidence of the diplomat's heretical leanings, in a trial which led to his execution in 1653. See J. Ramos-Coelho, *Manuel Fernandes Villa Real e seu processo na Inquisição de Lisbôa;* I. S. Révah, "Manuel Fernandes Villareal, adversaire et victime de l'Inquisition Portugaise," *Iberida Revista de filologia*, I, 33–54, 181–207; C. Roth, *A Life of Menasseh*, pp. 136 ff., 325 n. 25; and *infra*, Chaps. LXIV, n. 31; LXV, nn. 103–104. Menasseh's historic role in the return of the Jews to England will be discussed in a later volume. So will his rabbinic functions, as well as those of his colleagues, some of whom were much superior to him in rabbinic learning. See, for the time being, S. Seeligmann, *Bibliographie en Historie;* and J. Zwarts's aforementioned archival study of the first Amsterdam rabbis in *BMGJW*, IV.

74. See F. Landsberger, *Rembrandt, the Jews, and the Bible;* and such monographs as H. M. Rottermund, *Rembrandt's Handzeichnungen und Radierungen zur Bibel;* the comment made on "The Jewish Bride" by W. R. Valentiner, cited by J. Zwarts in "The Married Couple in 'The Jewish Bride' by Rembrandt" (Dutch), *Onze Kunst*, XLVI, 11–42 (also discussing other Jewish personalities in contact with Rembrandt); idem, *The Significance of Rembrandt's The Jewish Bride;* Valentiner's new study "Noch einmal, 'Die Judenbraut,'" *Festschrift für Kurt Bauch*, pp. 227–37; Zwarts's "A Portrait of Ḥakham Jacob Sasportas by Nicholaas Maes" (Dutch), *Oude Kunst*, 1930, pp. 215–21; idem, "Haham Saul Levy Morteyra and His Portrait by Rembrandt" (Dutch), *Oud Holland*, XLIII, 1–17; idem, "Rem-

brandt's Phoenix and the Old Insignia of the Portuguese Jewish Community of Amsterdam" (Dutch), *ibid.*, 61–72; R. van de Waal, "Rembrandt and the Feast of Purim," *ibid.*, LXXXIV, 199–223; R. H. Fuks, "The So-Called *Jewish Bride* and the Problem of 'Presentation' in Rembrandt's Work" (Dutch), *TG*, LXXXII, 482–93 (with an extensive bibliography); I. Prins, "Thomas de Keyser's 'Joden-Compagnie' in the Amsterdam Rijksmuseum" (Dutch), *BMGJW*, I, 45–51 (with reproductions of two fragments and a bibliography). See also F. Szper, "An Art-Loving Family of the Seventeenth Century" (Dutch), *Vrijdagavond*, I, 99–103 (on the Duarte family). Regrettably, painters other than Rembrandt, some of whom were likewise attracted by Jewish physiognomies, have thus far received but scant attention. Studies on such artists—one is being prepared by a young art historian now—should offer interesting insights, not only into art history but also into the social life of Amsterdam Jewry and aspects of Judeo-Christian relations. For this reason, it is also to be deplored that the dramatic story of Christian Hebraism in Holland has not yet been told in full detail.

75. See C. Roth, *A Life of Menasseh ben Israel*, esp. pp. 87 ff., 152 ff.; L. Hirschel, "Jan Pieterszoon Beelthouwer and the Rabbis: a Contribution to the History of the Jews in Amsterdam" (Dutch), *Vrijdagavond*, VI, 210–11, 227–28; S. B. J. Zilverberg, "Jan Pieterszoon Beelthouwer (1603–1669) and the Jews" (Dutch), *SR*, III, 156–67 (with an English summary); I. Prins "The Old Dutch Freedom of the Printing Press," *BMGJW*, V, 147–76, and the extensive literature cited in the notes thereto. Menasseh also had many Christian friends and admirers abroad; among them, the distinguished French polyhistor Pierre Daniel Huet. See *infra*, Chap. LXIV, n. 27.

76. See H. Graetz, "Don Balthasar Isaak Orobio de Castro. Eine biographische Skizze," *MGWJ*, XVI, 321–30; M. Kayserling, *Biblioteca española-portugueza-judaica*, pp. 81 ff.; and H. J. Schoeps, "Isaak Orobio Castros Religionsdisputation mit Philipp van Limborch," *Judaica*, II, 89–105; I. S. Révah, *Spinoza et le Dr. Juan de Prado*, pp. 23 f., 84 ff. App. v (publishes from a Paris MS De Castro's three tracts directed against De Prado, in full or in large excerpts). See also *infra*, Chaps. LXIV, n. 36; LXV, n. 61.

77. See I. Prins's "The Old Dutch Freedom of the Printing Press," *BMGJW*, V, 147–76; Daniel Levi (Miguel) de Barrios, *Relación de los poetas y escritores españoles de la Nacion judayca Amstelodama*; and *Hez Jaim arbol de la vida*, both ed. by M. Kayserling in "Une Histoire de la littérature juive de Daniel Lévi de Barrios," *REJ*, XVIII, 276–89; XXXII, 88–101; I. S. Révah, *Spinoza et le Dr. Juan de Prado*, pp. 70 ff. App. iv (republishes, from the collections of De Barrios' poems, four texts especially referring to De Prado); idem, "Les Écrivains Manuel de Pina et Miguel de Barrios et la censure de la communauté judéo-portugaise d'Amsterdam," *Oṣar Yehude Sefarad* (Tesoro de los Judíos sefardíes), VIII, pp. lxxiv-xci (the elders objected not only to religiously or politically suspect passages but also to some erotic verse which they considered inappropriate for an orthodox Jew); W. C. Pieterse's aforementioned dissertation (*supra*, n. 26); and, more generally, M. Kayserling's *Sephardim, Romanische Poesien der Juden in Spanien*, pp. 256 ff.; and his *Biblioteca*, reed. by Y. H. Yerushalmi, esp. pp. 16 ff., 189 ff. It is possible that, because of the often negative attitude of the Jewish elders, De Barrios published

many of his writings in Brussels. See the excursuses in the recent ed. of J. Peeters-Fontainas, with the collaboration of A. M. Fréderic, comps., *Bibliographie des impressions espagnoles des Pay-Bas méridionaux*, II, 717 ff. App. 1, Nos. 1398–1413. De Barrios' complaint about his mistreatment by Jewish communal censors (in the undated letter preserved in the *Ets Haïm* manuscript 48 A 5 No. 6) bears a later annotation that on Tebet 10, 5439 (December 25, 1678) the community gave him the magnificent subsidy of a little over 6 guilders. In this connection perhaps, De Barrios dedicated, on February 7, 1674, his sixteen-page collection of poems entitled *Metros nobles* "to the most illustrious Gentlemen Parnassim and Gabay of the Holy Kahal of the distinguished City of Amsterdam," whom he named. Some time later this small collection was published in Antwerp. Much new light on the poet's ambiguous position as both a cavalry captain in the Spanish army (until his resignation in 1674) and an intellectual leader of the Amsterdam Jewish community, with which he was often at odds, has been shed by K. R. Scholberg's observations on his selection of *La Poesia religiosa de Miguel de Barrios*, with E. M. Wilson's comments on this anthology in his "Miguel de Barrios and Spanish Religious Poetry," *Bulletin of Hispanic Studies*, XL, 176–80; Scholberg's "Miguel de Barrios and the Amsterdam Sephardic Community," *JQR*, LIII, 120–59; and E. Glaser's, "Two Notes on the Hispano-Jewish Poet Don Miguel de Barrios," *REJ*, CXXIV, 201–211. De Barrios' artistic and historiographic contributions to Jewish culture will be analyzed here in their respective spheres in later volumes.

78. See *infra*, Chap. LXVI, n. 100. In Africa and Asia the Dutch followed in the footsteps of the Portuguese, and gradually displaced Portuguese rule with their own. Reference has already been made to the collaboration of Cochin Jewry with the Dutch along the coast of Malabar and elsewhere. It was only natural that this extraordinary Jewish community fell under direct Dutch control in 1663 and continued in this fashion until 1795. Similarly, the question of whether the Jews had been in Java before the Dutch conquests of what was to become modern Indonesia has been briefly alluded to. See *supra*, n. 51. However, this story, as well as the further Portuguese expansion to Formosa and continental China, will have to be treated more fully here in a later volume.

79. *Essai historique sur la colonie de Surinam: Sa fondation, ses révolutions, ses progrès . . . avec l'histoire de la nation juive portugaise et allemande y établie*, Paramaribo, 1788 (published by "Régens et Représentans" of the local Jews Moses Pas de Leon *et al.;* also in a Dutch trans., 1791), esp. pp. 11 ff.; S. Oppenheim, "An Early Jewish Colony in Western Guiana, 1658–1666 and Its Relation to the Jews in Surinam, Cayenne and Tobago," *PAJHS*, XVI, 95–186; with "Supplemental Data," *ibid.*, XVII, 53–70; F. O. Dentz, *De Kolonisatie van de Portugeesche Joodsche Natie in Suriname* (The Colonization of the Portuguese Jewish Nation in Surinam and the History of the Jewish Savanna), esp. the documentary appendix, pp. 40 ff. and chronological list, pp. 51 ff.; P. A. Samson, "Privileges Granted the Jews of Surinam" (Dutch), *Indische Gids*, 1949: and other sources quoted by H. I. Bloom in *The Economic Activities*, pp. 152 ff. See also the pertinent entries in the two Dutch encyclopedias *Encyclopaedie van Nederlandsch West-Indië*, ed. by H. D. Benjamin and J. F. Snelleman, esp. pp. 340, 392 f.; and *Encyclopedie van de Nederlandse Antillen*, ed. by H. Hoetink *et al.* (esp. I. S. Emmanuel's brief survey, "The Jewish Communities" [Dutch], pp. 313–18). T. J. Condon, *New York*

Beginnings: the Commercial Origins of New Netherlands, though dealing principally with the New York area, sheds considerable light on the other Dutch possessions in North America as well. It must be noted that, beginning with its founder, Willem Usselinx, the Dutch West India Company was much more deeply influenced by its Calvinist background than its East India counterpart. An outstanding example of its narrower orientation was offered by the well-known administration of Peter Stuyvesant as governor of the New Netherlands, which included most Dutch colonies in the Caribbean. See also J. G. van Dillen, "The West India Company: Calvinism and Politics" (Dutch), *TG,* LXXIV, 145–71; *supra,* n. 52; and, particularly, the comprehensive works by I. S. Emmanuel, cited *infra.* n. 80.

We must also bear in mind that a charter from the West India Company did not necessarily guarantee free and unmolested settlement. At times local officials, bent on personal advantage, effectively sabotaged orders from the Company headquarters. David Nassi—the chief Jewish colonizer in the West Indies for the period—and his associates time and again had to fight such staunch resistance. According to depositions made by them on May 11, 1660, before the well-known Amsterdam notary Pieter Padthuisen, and attested by the skipper of a Dutch ship which had landed in Guiana in January of that year, Jews and others had arrived on two ships in order to develop a colony there. The skipper testified that, although the Jews had secured the necessary permission from the West India Company, the local governor, Jan Claszoon Langendijk refused them permission to settle. He claimed that the island belonged to him and his friends. Although little of the colony was under cultivation, he finally assigned marshy and unsuitable land to the newcomers. A summary of this unpublished document was graciously communicated to me by Mr. Seymour B. Liebman.

80. J. M. Corcos, *A Synopsis of the History of the Jews of Curaçao from the Day of Their Settlement to the Present Time;* A. M. Chumaceiro, *Toespraak ter gelegenheid van den 50 jarigen hereeniging van Curaçao met Nederland* (Address on Isaiah 65:22, on the Occasion of the Fiftieth Anniversary of the Union of Curaçao with the Netherlands): G. H. Cone, "The Jews in Curaçao. According to Documents from the Archives of the State of New York," *PAJHS,* X, 141–57, esp. pp. 147 ff. Art. 5; S. Oppenheim's essay cited *supra,* n. 79; I. J. Cardozo, *Three Centuries of the Jews in Curaçao: Oldest Synogogue in the New World;* and other sources cited by H. I. Bloom in *The Economic Activities,* pp. 144 ff. It is remarkable that, contrary to their usual complaints about the Jews' trade in horses, the Dutch administration did not mind when Abraham Ysaac Pereyra shipped a number of horses from Aruba (where until 1730 only occasional Jewish visitors were recorded) to Curaçao. On this occasion 21 horses died during the journey, Pereyra blaming it on the skipper of the vessel "d'Oud Vader Abraham." Through his Amsterdam representative David Saraya Coronel, Pereyra complained that, in order to sell sugar in various Caribbean islands, the skipper had made unnecessary stops; he had thus greatly delayed the arrival of the horses at their destination, and was responsible for the premature death of a considerable number. See the summary of a notarial document, *ibid.,* p. 146; and on Pereyra's relationship to the Hamburg Pereiras, see H. Kellenbenz, *Sephardim,* p. 134 n. 83. See also I. S. Emmanuel's "Jewish Education in Curaçao (1692–1802)," *PAJHS,* XLIV, 215–36; his comprehensive *Precious Stones of the Jews of Curaçao; Curaçaon Jewry, 1658–1957,* with

its informative Intro., esp. pp. 102, 104; and his and S. A. Emmanuel's detailed and extensively documented *History of the Jews of the Netherland Antilles;* and, more generally, H. Wätjen, "Das Judentum und die Anfänge der modernen Kolonisation," *VSW,* XI, 338–68, 565–606; idem, *Das Holländische Kolonialreich in Brasilien. Ein Kapitel aus der Kolonialgeschichte des 17. Jahrhunderts;* C. R. Boxer, *The Dutch Seaborne Empire, 1600–1800;* D. W. Davies, *A Primer of Dutch Seventeenth-Century Overseas Trade,* esp. pp. 112 ff.; and other studies analyzed by W. P. Coolhaas in *A Critical Survey of Studies on Dutch Colonial History,* esp. pp. 130 ff.

81. See M. J. Kohler, "Some Early American Zionist Projects," *PAJHS,* VIII, 75–118, esp. pp. 77 f., 91 ff.; and S. Oppenheim, "An Early Jewish Colony," *ibid.,* XVI, 102 ff., 108 ff., 176 ff., both reprinting the text of the "Priveleges Granted To the People of the Hebrew Nation That Are to Goe to the Wilde Cust," found in an English translation in an Egerton MS in the British Museum, and previously published and analyzed by L. Wolf in his "American Elements in the Re-Settlement," *TJHSE,* III, 76–100, esp. pp. 82 ff. Kohler and Oppenheim were right in arguing from the outset, against Wolf, that the original decree must have dealt with a Dutch colony, even though in the form presented in the Egerton MS it was written in English. Aided by the findings in the 1858 *Report of the U. S. Commission on the Venezuela-British Guiana Boundary* (also published as Senate Document No. 91, 55th Congress), the controversy was finally settled by Oppenheim's discovery of the original documents in The Hague Rijksarchief. By his researches in the Dutch archives, Oppenheim was also able to shed much light on early Jewish colonization in the other Dutch possessions in the area as well.

If Jews did pioneer in cane cultivation in Essequibo, it is further testimony to their enterprising spirit, since they must have paid dearly for the necessary manpower. According to an Amsterdam notarial document of August 26, 1658 (likewise communicated to me by Mr. S. B. Liebman), one Abraham Rodrigues had to pay the Company, which enforced its monopoly in the slave trade, 450 Flemish pounds for one male and one female slave, whereas, according to another notarial record, dated November 10, 1659, the Company directors promised to deliver to the colony of Guiana up to 1,000 slaves at the price of but 150 guilders each.

82. See L. Herrman, *A History of the Jews in South Africa from Earliest Times to 1895,* South African ed., pp. 49 ff.; G. Saron and L. Hotz, *The Jews in South Africa: a History,* p. 2. On the whole, the Dutch expansion along the African coast actually preceded their penetration of the Western Hemisphere. See the pertinent entries in H. D. Benjamin and J. F. Snellemen, eds., *Encyclopaedie van Nederlandsch West-Indië,* 2d ed.; C. R. Boxer, *The Dutch Seaborne Empire;* and other sources discussed *supra,* nn. 50 f.; *infra,* Chap. LXVI, nn. 101 ff.; and the forthcoming Vol. XVII.

83. E. Luzac, *La Richesse de la Hollande,* London, 1778 (in 2- and 5-volume editions); also in a Dutch trans. entitled *Hollands Rijkdom of Tafereel van Neerlandsch Koophandel en Zeevaart* (Holland's Wealth, or a Picture of Its Trade and Seafaring), 2d ed., esp. I, 340 ff.; III, 359 f.; W. Sombart, *Die Juden und das Wirtschaftsleben,* p. 15; idem, *The Jews and Modern Capitalism,* English trans.

with Notes by M. Epstein, p. 13. See also, more generally, such opinions voiced by foreign travelers as are reviewed in J. Bientjes's Groningen dissertation, *Holland und die Holländer im Urteil deutscher Reisender, 1400–1800;* and *supra,* Vols. XII, pp. 235 ff.; XIII, p. 158.

84. The proclamation of the States General of July 13, 1657, and their resolution of September 21, 1690, are both cited by H. J. Koenen in his *Geschiedenis der Joden in Nederland,* pp. 151 ff. The divergent interpretations of "reciprocity" in international obligations and practices became a particularly burning issue in the Emancipation era, when Holland, as well as France, England, and the United States, sought to secure for their emancipated Jews equal treatment with their own Christian citizens in countries of nonemancipation. These problems, often aired by statesmen, jurists, and publicists in the nineteenth and early twentieth centuries, will be analyzed here in their modern contexts.

CHAPTER LXIV: FRENCH AND ENGLISH AMBIGUITIES

1. Sir Edward Coke's report on the judgment of the Exchequer Chamber (VII, 17ab), cited by H. S. Q. Henriques in *The Jews and the English Law*, pp. 186 f. See *infra*, nn. 77 and 98; and *supra*, Vols. X, Chap. XLIII, *passim;* XIII, 115 ff.

2. See S. Ben Sidoun, "Les Juifs en France au XVIe siècle," *Trait d'Union*, III, 36–41; and other data cited *supra*, Vols. X, pp. 91, 343 f. n. 44; XIII, pp. 117 f., 367 n. 60.

3. J. Bacquet, *Les Oeuvers*, I, 1 and 11, Paris, 1664 ed., I, 2 ff., 33 ff.; I. S. Révah in "Les Marranes," *REJ*, CXVIII, 63 f.; the French agent's report of 1560, cited from a somewhat damaged MS by F. Michel in his *Histoire du commerce et de la navigation à Bordeaux*, II, 416 f.; R. Anchel, *Les Juifs de France*, pp. 125 ff., 132 f.; *supra*, Vol. XIII, pp. 116 f., 366 ff. nn. 59–61; J. M. Millás Vallicrosa, "Emigración masiva de conversos por la frontera catalano-francesa en el año 1608," *Sefarad*, XIX, 140-44. Millás connects the increased emigration of 1608 with the preparations for the expulsion of the Moriscos from Spain in 1609 and the following years, events which must have deepened the Marranos' feeling of insecurity. But it seems that this feeling was engendered far more by their disappointment over the results of the "pardon" which they had obtained from the Spanish-Portuguese Crown at a very high price in 1604–1605. See *infra*, Chap. LXV, nn. 25 ff.

4. See Z. Szajkowski, "Notes on the Demography of the Sephardim in France," *HUCA*, XXX, 217–32; idem, "Population Problems of Marranos and Sephardim in France, from the 16th to the 20th Centuries," *PAAJR*, XXVII, 83–105. After carefully reviewing much of the vast documentation available in the French archives, Szajkowski reached the tentative conclusion that "the majority of the first Marranos who came to France at the end of the 15th century, during the entire 16th century, and some even of those who came at the beginning of the 17th century, remained Christians. Very few of them came back to Jewish life. The Sephardic Jewish population of Bordeaux, St.-Esprit, Peyrehorade, Bidache and a few smaller communities in the 18th century was composed of new Marranos, who had come from Spain and Portugal in the 17th century and, to a large extent, during the 18th century" (*ibid.*, p. 91). The uncertainties connected with any such conclusion are doubly ·evident when one considers that, in the earlier period of the prosperous Spanish-Portuguese economy, many Old Christian merchants from Lisbon and other Iberian cities had come to France and had established important business firms there. See L. de Matos, *Les Portugais en France au XVIe siècle. Études et documents;* and J. Mathorez' comprehensive work, *Les Étrangers en France sous l'Ancien Régime. Histoire de la formation de la population française.*

The usual onomastic criteria are extremely unrealiable in this case, for such family names as Mendes and Lopes, as well as biblical first names, were quite common among the Portuguese both of Jewish and of non-Jewish extraction. Weighty objections to Szajkowski's theory were raised by I. S. Révah on the basis of the numerous Portuguese records he had studied in Rouen. Révah showed that from among the families who maintained a clandestine Jewish community in Rouen for about a hunderd years, at the most four or five became Catholic Frenchmen. See Révah's "Les Marranes," *REJ*, CXVIII, 65 f.; and, more fully, his publications relating to Rouen and esp. to the poet João Pinto Delgado, quoted *infra*, nn. 9, 17, and 29. Révah's objections have not been completely invalidated by Szajkowski's reply in "The Marranos and Sephardim in France," *Abraham Weiss Jubilee Volume*, pp. 106–127 (all three essays by Szajkowski are reprinted in his *Jews and the French Revolutions, 1789, 1830 and 1848*, pp. 1–23, 24–44, and 135–50). See also, more generally, idem, "Jewish Emigration from Bordeaux during the Eighteenth and Nineteenth Centuries," *JSS*, XVIII, 118–24; and the brief observations by A. Hertzberg in *The French Enlightenment and the Jews*, esp. pp. 12 ff. Although most of the dependable data now available are from the eighteenth and nineteenth centuries, much can be deduced from them, substantively as well as methodologically, about the conditions prevailing in the preceding two centuries.

5. See T. Malvezin, *Histoire des Juifs à Bordeaux*, pp. 111 f.; E. Gaullieur, *Histoire du Collège de Guyenne, d'après un grand nombre de documents inédits*, esp. Chaps. xiv and xxi; and, more generally, R. M. Kingdon, "The Political Resistance of the Calvinists in France and the Low Countries," *CH*, XXVII, 220–33; and L. Arénilla, "Le Calvinisme et le droit de résistance à l'État," *Annales ESC*, XXII, 350–69. See also L. E. Halkin's brief communication, "La Vie religieuse dans les pays de langue française à la fin du XVIe siècle," *Rapports* to the XII International Congress of Historical Sciences, Vienna, 1965, III, 153–58. On the Collège de Guyenne and its outstanding director, André de Gouvéa, see *supra*, Vol. XIII, pp. 118 f., 367 f. n. 61; and J. Verissimo Serrão, *António de Gouveia e o seu tempo (1510–1566)*.

6. G. Laroche's address, extensively reproduced, from Pierre de Rosteguy de Lancre's work, by T. Malvezin in his *Histoire des Juifs à Bordeaux*, pp. 119 ff. See the next note. See also L. Cardozo de Béthencourt's interesting genealogical studies in "Le Trésor des Juifs Sephardim; Notes sur les familles française israélites du rit portugais," *REJ*, XX, 287–300; XXV, 97–110, 235–45; XXVI, 240–56, with special emphasis on the descendants of the early families.

7. Pierre du Rosteguy de Lancre, *L'Incrédulité et miscréance du sortilège pleinement convaincues*, extensively cited by T. Malvezin in his *Histoire des Juifs à Bordeaux*, pp.116 ff. See also De Lancre's comprehensive *Tableau de l'inconstance des mauvais anges et démons, ou il est amplement traicté des sorciers et de la sorcellerie. Livre très utile et nécessaire, non seulement au juges, mais à tous ceux qui vivent soubs les loix chrestiennes*, new ed. rev. and augumented "de plusiers nouvelles observations, arrests, et autres choses notables." See also L. Lamothe, "Pierre de Lancre et la sorcellerie en Gascogne," *Revue de Bordeaux*, 1854, pp. 105–106; Israel Lévi, "Le Traité sur les Juifs de Pierre de l'Ancre," *REJ*, XIX, 235–45; and Z. Szajkowski, *Franco-Judaica*, p. 117 No. 1393. Another instance of an otherwise prudent and humane seventeenth-century French jurist (Henri Boguet) who acted with extreme cruelty in all cases involving alleged witchcraft was cited *supra*,

Vol. XI, pp. 176, 372 n. 71. On the accusation of host desecration at Saint-Jean-de-Luz see H. Léon, *Histoire des Juifs de Bayonne*, pp. 26 ff.; H. P. [Pierre Haguenauer], "Un Autodafé à Saint-Jean-de-Luz," *Annuaire des Archives Israélites*, XIX, 37–52; and W. Webster, "Hebraizantes portugueses de San Juan de Luz en 1619," *BAH*, XV 347–60; with Isidore Loeb's remarks thereon in his "Notes sur l'histoire des Juifs en Espagne," *REJ*, XXII, 104–111, esp. pp. 107 ff. See also *infra*, n. 27; some additional passages revealing De Lancre's strongly anti-Jewish sentiments, cited by F. Secret in his "Notes sur les Hebraïsants chrétiens et les Juifs en France," *REJ*, CXXX, 231 ff.; and, more generally, R. Mandrou, *Magistrats et sorciers en France au XVIIᵉ siècle. Une analyse de psychologie historique*.

8. See the various 1652 publications included in the so-called *Mazarinades* and listed by L. Kahn in *Les Juifs à Paris depuis le VIᵉ siècle*, with a Foreword by Zadoc Kahn, pp. 42 f. n. 4; and by Z. Szajkowski in his analytical bibliography *Franco-Judaica*, pp. 117 f. Nos. 1395–1413. See also Israel Lévi's analysis in "L'Affaire Bourgeois (1652)," *REJ*, XXVII, 180–206; and Szajkowski's "Mazarinades of Jewish Interest," *Studies in Bibliography and Booklore*, VI, 29–37 (includes "A List of Mazarinades in the Affaire Bourgeois," 22 items; pp. 33 ff.). The role of the old-clothes dealers in the demolition of the "Jewry Gates" is described by H. Sauval in his *Histoire et recherches des antiquités de la ville de Paris* (see *infra*, n. 46); and, more generally, by R. Anchel in *Les Juifs de France*, pp. 128 f. On the *miracle des billettes* and its persistent effect on the Paris public, see *supra*, Vol. XI, pp. 167 ff., 368 nn. 58–59. It should be noted that in the popular mind the *fripiers* were identified with Jews not only because of the large share of Jews in that craft in other areas but also because the Paris street in which most of these artisans lived and plied their trade happened to be located—perhaps not quite coincidentally—in the former Jewish quarter. The equation in Paris of *friperie* with *Juiverie* appears, indeed, in a contemporary pamphlet attacking Molière. But the prosecution of the Bourgeois murderers rightly insisted that all parties concerned were Christians. See L. Lazard, "L'Antisémitisme sous Louis XIV," *Annuaire des Archives israélites*, 5650 (1889–1890), 63; Israel Lévi in *REJ*, XXVII, 191, 204 ff.

9. F. A. Isambert *et al.*, eds., *Recueil général des anciennes lois françaises depuis l'an 420 jusqu'à la Révolution de 1789*, XIII, 173 ff. No. 133 (August 1550); O. A. Ranum, "Paris and the Fronde," *Colloquium*, 4, pp. 1–11; and, more generally, idem, *Paris in the Age of Absolutism: an Essay*; I. S. Révah, "Les Marranes," *REJ*, CXVIII, 66 f.; idem, "Le Premier établissement des Marranes portugais à Rouen (1603–1607)," *Annuaire* of the Institut de philologie et d'histoire orientales et slaves in Brussels, XIII (*Mélanges Isidore Lévy*), pp. 539–52; and *infra*, nn. 29 and 32. On the small community of La Bastide, see G. Nahon's "Notes inédites de V. Montiton sur les Juifs portugais à Labastide-Clairence," *REJ*, CXXIII, 175–89. Victor Blaise Montiton, who served in 1898–1901 as that township's secretary, assembled numerous notes of local historical interest, including some pertaining to La Bastide Jewry. They offer valuable information only for the period after 1650, however. Of interest also is a 1684 responsum by Jacob Sasportas referring to a ban issued by the community of Bidache against the renting of the property of a certain Christian landlord who had persuaded a neighboring Jewish widow to undergo baptism and who was also suspected of homosexuality. A local Jew named Salazar had tried to circumvent this ban, however. In his decision up-

holding the communal excommunication, the rabbi expressed his amazement over the failure of the Jewish court of Bayonne to enforce the ban in one of its dependencies. See Sasportas' *Ohel Ya'aqob*, fols. 70 f. No. 65; and *supra*, Chap. LXIII, n. 71. See also G. Nahon's "Inscriptions funéraires hébraïques et juives à Bidache, Labastide-Clairence (Basses-Pyrénées) et Peyrehorade (Landes). Rapport d'une mission," *REJ*, CXXVIII, 349–75 (dating back to 1633).

10. S. Simonsohn, "Opinion of the Sorbonne Concerning the Settlement of Jews in France (1633)" (Hebrew), *Zion*, XXIII–XXIV, 98–101 (from an Italian translation of that opinion extant in MS in the Jewish communal archives of Mantua). In fact, in his inquiry addressed to the Paris theological faculty, the duke of Nevers had pointed out that he unquestionably had to tolerate Jews in his other, newly acquired, duchy of Mantua, where they had lived for many generations. See *infra*, n. 56. The Paris theologians naturally had to take cognizance of the long tradition of canon law, amply discussed in our earlier volumes. Nonetheless, France was not yet prepared for full-fledged religious toleration of Judaism, as was demonstrated by the intolerant act of 1615.

11. C. Roth, "Quatre Lettres d'Élie de Montalto. Contribution à l'histoire des Marranes," *REJ*, LXXXVII, 137–65, esp. pp. 141 ff., 148 ff. On Elijah Montalto's remarkable personality and works, see also *supra*, Vol. XIV, pp. 109 f., 347 n. 40; and *infra*, n. 34. The Rodrigues couple's staunch resistance to reconversion to Judaism was undoubtedly repeated in many other cases. Because an effective Inquisition was lacking, it is doubly difficult to ascertain the ratio of secret Jews to those who, in most French communities, continued to profess their Christian faith, whether out of conviction, inertia, or for some worldly advantage. See, however, *supra*, n. 4.

12. Duarte de Paz' letters to Bishop Jean de Bellay mentioned by A. Herculano in his *Da Origem e estabelecimento da Inquisição em Portugal*, I, 283 ff.; II, 85 ff., 143 ff., etc.; in J. C. Branner's English trans. entitled *History of the Origin and Establishment of the Inquisition in Portugal*, pp. 322 ff., 394 ff., etc.; and *supra*, Vol. XIII, pp. 50 ff., 329 f. nn. 53 ff.

13. Luis de Matos, *Les Portugais en France*, pp. 7 f., 208 ff.; J. Mathorez, *Les Étrangers en France*, esp. Vol. I dealing with "Les Orientaux et les extra-peuples"; Sir Henry Cobham's dispatch of September 19, 1581, in Public Record Office, *Calendar of State Papers, Foreign Series, 1581–82*, ed. by Arthur John Butler, p. 318 No. 340; the sultan's 1564 recommendation reproduced in my "Suleiman the Magnificent and Solomon ibn Ya'ish," which is to appear in the *Joshua Finkel Jubilee Volume*. The constant flow of information from the French agents residing in Constantinople is well illustrated by the dispatches published in particular by E. Charrière in his ed. of the *Négociations de la France dans le Levant*. French relations with Dom Antonio are treated, among others, by P. Durand-Lapie, "Un Roi détroné réfugié en France. Dom Antoine 1er de Portugal, 1580–1595," *Revue d'histoire diplomatique*, XVIII, 133–45, 275–307, 612–40; XIX, 113–28, 243–60; the pamphlet *Sommaire declaration des iustes causes et raisons qui ont meu et meuuent le treshault et trespuissant Prince Dom Anthoine Roy de Portugal*, published in Toulouse in 1582 under the name of Dom Antonio and reproduced in facsimile with an intro. by M. A. Soares de Azevedo in "Un Raríssimo opusculo

de D. António, Prior do Crato," *Boletim internacional de bibliografía lusobrasileira*, VII, 297–309; A. de Faria, *Descendance de D. Antonio, prieur de Crato, XVIIIème roi de Portugal. Extraits, portraits, notes et documents*, 2d ed.; and, more generally, H. Lapeyre, *Les Monarchies européennes du XVIe siècle. Les relations internationales* (with a good selected bibliography, pp. 20 ff.); and F. Braudel, *La Méditerranée et le Monde Méditerranéen*, 2d ed., *passim*. See also *infra*, nn. 16 and 67–68; Chap. LXV, nn. 12 and 22.

It is highly unlikely that Henry III was completely unaware of Alvaro Mendez' Jewish antecedents or the inquisitorial suspicions about his posssible heterodoxy. Nonetheless, with the characteristic mixture of personal piety and mundane pursuit of international political power which he often displayed in France—as he had during his short reign in Poland-Lithuania—he evidently did not hesitate to favor the Marrano's anti-Spanish activities. See J. Boucher, "Henry III, mondain ou dévot? Ses retraites dans les monastères de la région parisienne," *Cahiers d'histoire*, XV, 112–28. Moreover, such a mixture of *Realpolitik* with deep religious drives characterized that entire tense period of the French Wars of Religion. We certainly are justified neither in minimizing the religious factor in these wars nor in going to the other extreme and exaggerating the importance of messianic-utopian yearnings such as those represented by the maverick thinker Guillaume Postel. See J. H. Salmon, ed., *The French Wars of Religion: How Important Were Religious Factors*; F. Secret, "De quelques courants prophétiques et religieux sous le règne de Henri III," *Revue d'histoire des religions*, CXXVII, 1–32; and *infra*, n. 23.

14. See J. Weyl, "Les Juifs protégés français aux échelles du Levant et en Barbarie sous les règnes de Louis XIV et Louis XV. D'après des documents inédits tirés des archives de la Chambre de Commerce de Marseille," *REJ*, XII, 267–82; XIII, 277–94. See also G. Rambert, ed., *Histoire du commerce de Marseille*, esp. III, Part 2, ed. by J. Billioud, pp. 263 ff. (on the trade with Levantine seaports from 1515–1599; includes the names of successive French consuls); IV, Part 1, ed. by L. Bergasse, pp. 56 ff. (on the period from 1599 to 1660, stressing the administrative shortcomings of the French consulates in the Levant).

15. See J. Berger de Xivrey and J. Guadet, eds., *Recueil de lettres missives de Henri IV*, esp. III, 282 ff., 287, 320 f.; supplemented by B. Barbiche, ed., *Lettres de Henri IV concernant les relations du Saint-Siège et de la France, 1595–1609*, esp. pp. 94 ff. (illustrating both Henry's submissiveness to the Papacy and his ardent desire to promote France's trade with the Iberian Peninsula); Hardouin [de Beaumont] de Péréfixe, *Histoire du roy Henry le Grand*, Paris, 1662 ed.; or in the English trans. by John Dauncey, entitled *The History of Henry IV, surnamed The Great, King of France and Navarre*, pp. 338 ff. (inaccurately cited from the German trans. entitled *Lebensgeschichte des grossen Heinrich*, Leipzig, 1669, pp. 568 ff. by J. J. Schudt in his *Jüdische Merckwürdigkeiten*, IV, 85 ff., 109 f.); *infra*, n. 49; L. Brunschvicg, "Les Juifs de Nantes et du pays nantais," *REJ*, XIV, 80–91; XVII, 125–42; XIX, 294–305 (also reprint), esp. XVII, 125 ff. (incidentally citing also the text of a MS in the Bayonne Public Library concerning the expulsion of a number of Jews from St.-Espirit in 1636, because of "their continuous relationships with the Spaniards"; p. 131); J. Mathorez, "Notes sur les Espagnoles en France, depuis le XVIe siècle jusqu'au règne de Louis XIII," *BH*, XVI, esp. pp. 347 ff.; *supra*, Vol. XIV, pp. 56 f., 325 f. n. 53.

16. See J. Weyl, "La Résidence des Juifs à Marseille," *REJ*, XVII, 96–110, esp. pp. 99, 102 ff.; *supra*, n. 14; and more generally, A. Crémieux, "Un Établissement juif à Marseille au XVIIe siècle," *ibid.*, LV, 119–45; LVI, 99–123.

17. T. Malvezin, *Histoire*, p. 129; G. Cirot, "Les Juifs de Bordeaux; leur situation morale et sociale, de 1550 à la Révolution," *Revue historique de Bordeaux*, II, IV, VII–IX, XI–XII, XXIX, XXXI–XXXII, esp. II, 370 f.; I. S. Révah, "Le Premier établissement," *Annuaire* of the Institut de philologie et d'histoire orientales et slaves, XIII, 539–52, esp. pp. 543, 547 ff.; C. Roth's earlier study "Les Marranes à Rouen. Un chapitre ignoré de l'histoire des Juifs de France," *REJ*, LXXXVIII, 113–55; J. Mathorez, "Notes sur les Espagnoles," *BH*, XVI, 361 (citing, as a popular adage, the Rouen poet-satirist's simile referring to the Marranos' arrogance); and *infra*, nn. 29–33. On the commercial and political enmity between Rouen and Portugal, which intermittently jeopardized the very life of the Portuguese residents in the Norman capital, see, for instance, the report sent home on September 29, 1531, by the Portuguese representative Gaspar Vaz, as cited by M. Mollat in his "Quelques aspects de la vie économique et sociale de la France dans la première moitié du XVIe siècle vus à travers la correspondance des diplomates portugais," *BEP*, n.s. XII, 224–53, esp. pp. 248 f. See also, more fully, idem, *Le Commerce maritime normand à la fin du Moyen Age;* J. Mathorez, "Notes sur les rapports de Nantes avec l'Espagne," *BH*, XIV, 119–26, 383–407; XV, 188–206; idem, "Notes sur l'histoire de la colonie portugaise de Nantes," *ibid.*, XV, 316–39.

18. [André Maillard?] *La Fvlminante pour feu tres grand, et tres chrestien Prince Henry III, Roy de France et de Pologne. Contre Sixte V soy disant Pape de Rome et les Rebelles de la France*, n. p., n. d., pp. 5, 7, 19, 39; Anonymous, *Lettre d'vn Catholique François av Roy de Navarre, pour l'induire a se retourner à l'Église Catholique, Apostolique et Romaine*, n. p., 1586; Pierre de l'Estoile, *Journal . . . pour le règne de Henri IV*, ed. and annotated by L. R. Lefèvre, 5th ed., I, 68; L. Dorléans, *Premier et second advertissements des Catholiques anglais aux François, et à la Noblesse qui suit à présent le Roy de Navarre*, Paris, 1590, fol. 81, all cited by M. Yardeni in "The Attitude to the Jews in Literary Polemics during the Religious Wars in France" (Hebrew), *Zion*, XXVIII, 70–85, esp. pp. 76 and 80; J. Mathorez, "Notes sur les Espagnoles en France," *BH*, XVI, 371; R. Ródenas Vilar, "Ayudó Felipe IV a los hugonotes?" *Arbor*, LVII, 59–66 (shows on the basis of archival documentation for the years 1624–25 that the negotiations actually led to a Spanish promise to subsidize, with 100,000 ducats, a Huguenot assault on La Rochelle). The equation of Jews with Spaniards went so far that a well-known satirist compared the Habsburgs' preference for marrying within their own dynasty with the Jews' clannishness in opposing intermarriage. See V. Verger's ed. of *Satyre Ménippée; ou la vertu du catholicon d'Espagne et de la terme des états de Paris*, ed. with a Historical Commentary by C. Nodier, I, 156. Incidentally, a Parisian contemporary does not hesitate to use the term "ce Juif" for the non-Jewish commander responsible for the destruction of a beautiful church in a conquered village near Laval. See the text reproduced by the editor of the Ratisbon [Brussels], 1752, ed. of the *Satyre*, III, 268 ff., 325. See also C. Lenient's twin studies *La Satire en France au moyen âge*, esp. pp. 180 ff. (on Satan and his vogue in the fifteenth century); 188 ff. (on Jews and Lombards); and *La Satire en France ou, la littérature militante, au XVIe siècle*, esp. pp. 149 ff.; and, more

418 LXIV: FRENCH AND ENGLISH AMBIGUITIES

generally, H. Hauser, *Les Sources de l'histoire de France; XVIᵉ siècle*, III, 36 ff. and *passim; supra,* n. 15; and *infra,* nn. 35 and 38.

19. *Lettres patentes du Roy portant commandement à tous juifs et autres faisans profession et exercice de judaïsme, de vuider le Royaume, pays et terres de son obéyssance, à peine de la vie et de confiscation de leurs biens. Vérifiées en Parlement le 18 may 1615;* the bibliographical notes thereon in Z. Szajkowski's *Franco-Judaica,* p. 1 No. 1; L. Brunschvicg, "Les Juifs de Nantes," *REJ,* XVII, 125 ff.; T. Malvezin, *Histoire,* pp. 114 ff.; J. Mathorez, "Notes sur les Espagnols en France," *BH,* XVI, 346 ff. The ambiguity of the 1615 legislation is stressed, with a somewhat dubious interpretation, by R. Anchel in *Les Juifs de France,* p. 128, where the pertinent phrases are cited from the MSS preserved in the Bibliothèque Nationale. We shall see (*infra,* nn. 47 ff.) that from the outset the Jewish community of Metz was not included in that decree of expulsion. Yet, because this intolerant enactment was frequently invoked by anti-Jewish forces in the following generations, its influence in retarding the growth of the Jewish communities in France must not be wholly disregarded.

20. Jean Fontanier, *Trésor inestimable* (on the rapidly growing Metz Jewry of the period, see *infra,* nn. 47 ff.); Anonymous, *L'Ancienne nouveauté de l'Écriture sainte ou l'Église triomphante à cette terre,* cited from a Paris MS, together with other data, by R. Anchel in *Les Juifs de France,* pp. 149 ff. According to a contemporary pamphlet describing Jean Fontanier's life and death, the martyr had been converted to Judaism by Daniel Montalto in Constantinople. See the bibliographical entries in Z. Szajkowski, *Franco-Judaica,* p. 130 Nos. 1574–75; and L. Kahn, *Les Juifs à Paris depuis le VIᵉ siècle,* pp. 41 f. On the earlier interrelations between the Genevan and French Protestants, see esp. R. M. Kingdon, *Geneva and the Consolidation of the French Protestant Movement, 1566–1572: a Contribution to the History of Congregationalism, Presbyterianism and Calvinist Resistance Theory.* See also F. Secret's "Notes," *REJ,* CXXX, 227 f., referring to a physician Bassin in Paris who may likewise be counted among the local Judaizers.

21. Isaac de la Peyrère, *Du rappel des Juifs,* Amsterdam, 1643, pp. ii ff.; idem, I: *Prae-Adamitae;* II: *Systema theologicum, ex Praeadamitarum hypothesi,* Part I; idem, *Deprecatio . . . ad Sanctissimum Patrem nostrum Pontificem optimum maximum Papam Alexandrum VII;* Richard Simon, *Lettres choisies,* Amsterdam 1730 ed., II, 13 ff. No. ii; 26 ff. No. iv., esp. p. 28; and III, 41 f. No vii. Curiously, Simon thought that *Du rappel des Juifs* had remained unpublished. See L. Strauss's searching analysis of De la Peyrère's teachings in *Die Religionskritik Spinozas als Grundlage seiner Bibelwissenschaft: Untersuchungen zu Spinozas Theologisch-Politischem Traktat,* pp. 32 ff. See also H. J. Schoeps, *Der Philosemitismus des 17. Jahrhunderts (Religions- und geistesgeschichtliche Untersuchungen)* (also in the *Zeitschrift für Religions- und Geistesgeschichte,* I, 19–34, 245–69); and *infra,* n. 99. The numerous discussions of the period concerning the restoration of the Jews to Palestine are reviewed by Abbé J. Lémann in *L'Entrée des Israélites dans la société française,* 6th ed., pp. 262–84; and R. Anchel in *Les Juifs,* pp. 135, 149 f.

22. See the report by R. Bailly, summarized in the *Archives juives,* IV, 33; the list of *Noms, surnoms, âges, entrée, études, ordination, incorporation et demeure*

de ceux qui sont entrés à l'Institution de la congrégation des Prêtres de l'Oratoire de Jésus Christ nostre Seigneur à Paris depuis de mois de l'aoust 1641 (till 1695), preserved in the Archives Nationales, fasc. M M 610, fol. 76v No. 861; R. Anchel, *Les Juifs,* p. 139. An earlier convert from Judaism, likewise called Louis, is discussed by A. Dufour and F. Rabut in their "Louis de Nice, juif converti, filleul et médecin du duc Louis Savoie, et directeur des salines de Tarentaine. . . 1445–1447," *Mémoires et documents* of the Société savoyarde d'histoire et d'archéologie, XV, 5–28. The proliferation of converts named Louis (their original Hebrew names are often unknown) was doubtless owing to their adoption, at their baptism, of the names of their royal, princely, or other Christian patrons.

23. S. Krauss, "Le Roi de France Charles VIII et les espérances méssianiques," *REJ,* LI, 87–96; E. Dermenghem, *Thomas Morus et les utopistes de la Renaissance,* pp. 230 f.; F. Secret, "L'Humanisme florentin du quattrocento vu par un kabbaliste français, Guy le Fèvre de la Boderie," *Rinascimento,* V, 105–112; V. Baroni, "La Bible chez les controversistes catholiques du XVIIe siècle en France," *RHPR,* XIX, 97–129; M. Villain, "Le Message biblique de Lefèvre d'Étaples," *Recherches de science religieuse,* XL, 243–59. Guillaume Postel's considerable influence on his generation, despite the numerous oddities in his personal behavior, is well documented by F. Secret's "Notes sur Guillaume Postel," *BHR,* XXI–XXVI; his *Bibliographie de manuscrits de Guillaume Postel;* his comprehensive analysis *Les Kabbalistes chrétiens de la Renaissance;* C. G. Dubois, "Une Utopie politique de la Renaissance française: Rêveries de Guillaume Postel (1510–1581) autour l'unité européenne," *L'Information littéraire,* XX, 56–62 (Postel "does not think of forcible conversion or of integrating Muslims and Jews into Christian society; he rather tries to define certain lines of a religious ideology on which they all could agree"; p. 59); and *supra,* Vol. XIII, pp. 393 f. n. 6, 403 f. n. 20. Blaise Pascal's eloquence, which so greatly enhanced the impact of his thoughts on generations of readers, owed much to his frequent borrowings from the Bible. See, for instance, L. E. Seidmann, *Pascal und das Alte Testament.* See, on the other hand, M. Hay's strong condemnation *The Prejudices of Pascal concerning in Particular the Jesuit Order and the Jewish People.* On the general impact of biblical studies on the Renaissance and the Reformation, see *supra,* Vol. XIII, Chaps. LVII and LVIII. See also E. Droz, "Bibles françaises après la Concile de Trent (1546)," *Journal of the Warburg and Courtauld Institutes,* XXVIII, 209–222.

24. See A. L. Gabriel, "Les Étudiants étrangers à l'Université de Paris au XVe siècle," *Annales de l'Université de Paris,* XXIX, 377–400 (also reprint); and on the considerable influx of Portuguese students, L. de Matos, *Les Portugais à l'Université de Paris entre 1500 et 1550* (emphasizing the role of the Gouvéas; see *supra,* Vol. XIII, pp. 118 f., 367 f. n. 61), esp. pp. 74, 104, 112. See also, more generally, J. Beckmann, "Die Universitäten vom 16. bis 18. Jahrhundert im Dienste der Glaubensverbreitung," *Neue Zeitschrift für Missionswissenschaft,* XVII, 24–47, esp. pp. 26 ff. (on the Sorbonne); and M. Fournier's voluminous compilation *Les Statuts et privilèges des universités françaises depuis leur fondation jusqu'en 1789.* Not surprisingly, Old Testament symbolism also penetrated contemporary French art. See, for example, R. Trinquet, "L'Allégorie politique dans la peinture française au temps de la Ligue: *L'Abraham et Melchisédech* d'Antoine Caron," *BHR,* XXVIII, 636–67; the author considers the painting to be a brilliant, if

camouflaged, satire on the French *League* in its struggle against Henry IV before 1594, and Caron to be "one of the greatest satirical painters of his time." Other long-established artistic symbols derived from the arena of Judeo-Christian religious polemics. The Synagogue, in particular, had long appeared in various shapes, for the most part, like its counterpart the Church, in female form. But almost invariably the figure of the Church was resplendent in her victory, while the Synagogue was a woman downcast in defeat, with a broken scepter and eyes covered so that she could not see the truth. See B. Blumenkranz, *La Représentation de Synagoga dans les Bibles moralisées françaises du XIIIᵉ au XVᵉ siècle;* and *supra,* Vol. XI, pp. 131, 346 n. 11. This form of graphic apologia impressed onlookers of all classes deep into the sixteenth and seventeenth centuries and beyond.

The influence of the Hebrew Bible on the medieval French language, not only through various loan words but also in entire phrases and grammatical forms, is well illustrated by J. Trénel in *L'Ancien Testament et la langue française du moyen âge (VIIIᵉ–XVᵉ siècle).* A similar study on the pertinent later developments would likewise be of great interest. The bearing of such linguistic borrowings on the much-debated origin and evolution of a Judeo-French dialect will be discussed in a later chapter. See also, N. Gruss, "L'Imprimerie hébraïque en France (XVIᵉ–XIXᵉ siècles)," *REJ,* CXXV, 77–91; and, more generally, L. S. Halkin's succinct observations in "La Vie religieuse," cited *supra,* n. 5.

25. Jean Bégat, *Response contre la calumnieuse accusation publiée sous le titre de l'apologie de l'Édit de Roi sur la pacification de son Royaume pours les deputés des trois Estats de Bourgoingne* [Paris, 1564], fols. K 4v f.; Gentian Hervet, *Apologie ov défense, contre vne response des ministres de la nouuelle église d'Orléans, escripte en leur nom, par je ne sçay qui, se nommant, l'vn pour tous,* p. 88; and data supplied by M. Yardeni in her aforementioned essay in *Zion,* XXVIII. See *supra,* n. 18. See also Jean Bodin's arguments in favor of toleration, similar to those of Bégat, though more judiciously formulated, *infra,* nn. 26–27.

26. Jean Bodin, *Methodus ad facilem historiarum cognitionem,* Preface, and Chap. viii, Amsterdam, 1650 ed., pp. 4, 324 (also in the English trans. by B. Reynolds entitled *Method for the Easy Comprehension of History);* Hugo Grotius, *Epistolae ad Gallos,* the first Leiden, 1648 ed., esp. the lengthy letter No. cx, pp. 249 ff.; Gottfried Wilhelm Leibniz, Letters of 1669 to Gottleib Spitzelius and of 1671 to Antoine Arnauld, and other data, quoted by G. E. Guhrauer in his ed. of *Das Heptaplomeres des Jean Bodin. Zur Geschichte der Cultur und Literatur im Jahrhundert der Reformation,* pp. lxxx ff.; Jean Bodin's *Les Six Livres de la Republique* (1576), I.v, III. vii, VI. iv, in its first Paris, 1576 ed., pp. 46, 397 f., 697, etc.; Vladimir Lenin (Ulianov), "Socialism and Religion," in his *Selected Works,* XI, 658, 661; M. Yardeni, "Attitudes to the Jews" (Hebrew), *Zion,* XXVIII, 82 ff.; and particularly the comprehensive study by Jacob Guttmann, "Über Jean Bodin in seinen Beziehungen zum Judentum," *MGWJ,* XLIX, 315–48, 459–89, which offers the fullest analysis not only of Bodin's political views relating to Jews but also of the various Hebrew sources utilized by the French thinker in his diverse writings, especially the *Heptaplomeres.* See also G. Roellenbleck's study mentioned *infra,* n. 27. We must not overlook, however, Bodin's contribution to the widespread belief in demons and witches through his *Démonomanie,* published in French and in Latin, which played into the hands of the many Jew-baiters who

accused Jews of sorcery and alliance with Satan. See his *De la Démonomanie des sorciers*, Paris, 1580; *De magorum daemonomania libri IV*, Latin trans. by Lotarius Philiponus (pseud.) Basel, 1581; *supra*, n. 7; and Vol. XI, Chap. XLIX *passim*.

27. Pierre Daniel Huet, *Demonstratio evangelica ad serenissimum Delphinum*, Paris, 1679 ed., pp. 26, 284, 309 f., 335 ff., 351, 385, 387 ff., 405; C. Roth, *A Life of Menasseh ben Israel*, pp. 148 ff., 284 f. On Huet's moderately phrased attacks on Jews and Judaism in his *Demonstratio*, see F. Vernet's succinct remarks in his "Juifs (Controverses avec les)," *Dictionnaire de théologie catholique*, VIII, Part 1, col. 1902; A. Dupront, *Pierre Daniel Huet et l'exégèse comparatiste au XVIIe siècle*, esp. pp. 47 f., 123 ff., 268 f.; and, more generally, F. A. de Gournay's older biography, *Huet, évêque d'Avranches, sa vie et ses oeuvres avec des extraits de documents inédits*. The issue of Bodin's Jewish origins seems not to have been raised until some eighty years after his death, in the letter addressed on July 1, 1673, by the well-known critic and poet Jean Chapelain, to Professor Hermann Conring. See *Commercii epistolici Leibnitiani ad omne genus eruditionis*, ed. by J. D. Gruber, Hanover, 1745, Part 2, p. 1122, also cited by P. T. de Laroque in his "Lettres inédites à Peiresc par Salomon Azubi, rabbin de Carpentras (1632–1633)," *REJ*, XI, 103 n. 1. (Incidentally, from this essay, as well as from the "Notice complimentaire" thereto by J. Dukas, *ibid.*, pp. 105–125, 252–65; XII, 95–106, we also learn much about the close relations in the 1630s between the famous French scientist and archaeologist Nicolas Claude Fabri de Peiresc, lay abbot of the monastery of Guitres, and the Sofia-born Carpentras rabbi, Salomon b. Yehudah Ezobi or Azubi. This scholarly and personal exchange will be more fully discussed in connection with Ezobi's own work in a later volume.) The allegation of Bodin's Jewish descent was frequently repeated, by various authors, including Vogt Woldebrand in his *Apparatus litterarius singularia, nova, anecdota, rariora*, I, Wittenberg, 1717. Not unjustifiedly, a modern scholar has spoken of a conspiracy against Jean Bodin, which he attributes to the initiative taken by the historian Antoine Tessier in 1684. See P. Mesnard, "La Conjuration contre la renommée de Jean Bodin: Antoine Tessier (1684)," *Bulletin* of the Association Guillaume Budé, 4th ser. IV, 535–59; R. Berg, "Le Demi-juif Jean Bodin," *Revue juive de Lorraine*, XIII, 29–35.

On Bodin's high appreciation of biblical and rabbinic teachings, see also G. Roellenbleck, *Offenbarung, Natur und jüdische Überlieferung bei Jean Bodin. Eine Interpretation des Heptaplomeres* (with a good selected bibliography); and, more generally, J. Franklin, *Jean Bodin and the Sixteenth-Century Revolution in the Methodology of Law and History; P. Mesnard's succinct lectures in *Jean Bodin en la historia del pensamiento*, with an Intro. by J. A. Maravell; and other recent literature briefly analyzed by Mesnard in his lecture *État présent des études bodiniennes* (while admitting the great paucity of biographical data, Mesnard denies the Jewish ancestry of Bodin's mother on the basis of several French genealogical studies). On Bodin's contemporary Michel de Montaigne, see D. M. Frame, *Montaigne: a Biography; F. S. Brown, *Religious and Political Conservatism in the Essais of Montaigne; H. Friedenwald, "Montaigne's Relation to Judaism and Jews," *JQR*, XXXI, 141–48; other publications discussed *supra*, Vols. XIII, pp. 367 f. n. 61; XIV, p. 327 n. 57; and still others listed in S. A. Tannenbaum's *Michel Eyquem de Montaigne (a Concise Bibliography).* See also, more generally, S. Ettinger's pertinent remarks in his aforementioned succinct essay on "The

Beginnings of the Change in the Attitude of European Society towards the Jews," *Scripta Hierosolymitana*, VII, 193–219.

28. Theodor Beza (de Bèze), *Abraham Sacrifiant* (1550; in 1577 trans. into English by Arthur Golding under the title *A Tragedie of Abraham's Sacrifice*, ed. by M. W. Wallace); his *Correspondance*, ed. by F. Aubert and H. Meylan, esp. I, 200 ff. No. vi. See also Beza's introductory poem to his trans. of Psalms, reproduced *ibid.*, pp. 207 ff. No. ix. Several letters also reflect Beza's deep interest in Hebraic studies; for instance, his epistle of November 5, 1552, to Bullinger (*ibid.*, pp. 93 f. No. 28). His recommendation, of November 5, 1549, to Maclou Popon, that he enable a friend to inspect some Hebrew manuscripts in Dijon, is particularly intriguing because the books were located in the city's Cour des Comptes. As the editor suggests they might have come there in the aftermath of the government's confiscation of Jewish possessions. See *ibid.*, pp. 56 f. No. 13; and, more generally, P. F. Geisendorf's biography *Théodore de Bèze*. On Racine, see *supra*, Vol. XIII, pp. 456 f. n. 86; A. W. Ward, "Drama," *Encyclopaedia Britannica*, 11th ed., Cambridge, 1910, VIII, 475–546, esp. p. 511; J. Lichtenstein, *Racine, poète biblique;* B. L. Knapp, "Jean Racine's *Esther* and Two Hebrew Translations of the Drama," to appear in the *Salo Wittmayer Baron Jub. Vol.*, ed. by S. Lieberman *et al.;* and her more general study, *Jean Racine: Mythos and Renewal in Modern Theater;* as well as O. Ullmann, "Le Livre d'Esther et la tragédie de Racine," *Evidences*, 52, pp. 33–41; and A. Spire, "L'Ancien Testament dans la littérature française" in his *Souvenirs et bâtons rompus*, pp. 272–305. The 1549 suppression of the performance of Passion plays removed an important source of incitation of the masses against the Jews, since, with few exceptions (such as that mentioned *supra*, Vol. XI, p. 357 n. 28), the plays bore a strongly anti-Jewish message. See also S. Friedfertig, "La Littérature française et les lettres hébraïques," *Revue de littérature comparée*, XXII, 448–59 (briefly analyzing Racine's influence on later Hebrew letters, beginning with David Franco Mendes's paraphrase of *Athalie* entitled *Gemul 'Atalyah*). Cf. J. Melkman, *David Franco Mendes, a Hebrew Poet*, pp. 57 ff.; and *supra*, Chap. LXIII, n. 26; D. Seidman, "Les Sources 'Juifves' de R. Garnier," *BHR*, XXVIII, 74–77; and, more generally, C. Lehrmann, *L'Élément juif dans la littérature française*, I: Des origines à la Révolution, pp. 79 ff.

29. See M. Kayserling, *Sephardim. Romanische Poesien der Juden in Spanien*, pp. 153 ff.; João Pinto Delgado, *Poema de la reina Ester, Lamentaciones del Profeta Jeremias, Historia de Rut, y varias poesias*, reissued with an Intro. by I. S. Révah, esp. pp. xx f., xxx f.; and Révah's ed. of the "Autobiographie d'un marrane: Édition partielle d'un manuscrit de João (Moseh) Pinto Delgado," *REJ*, CXIX, 41–130, esp. p. 41; as well as the earlier essays by E. M. Wilson, "The Poetry of João Pinto Delgado," *JJS*, I, 131–43; A. D. H. Fishlock, "The Rabbinic Material in the 'Ester' of Pinto Delgado," *ibid.*, II, 37–50; idem, "La Plainte de João Pinto Delgado sur le pillage des trésors du Temple," *Revue de littérature comparée*, XXXVIII, 66–75; idem, "The *Lamentaciones* of João Pinto Delgado," *Atlante*, III, 47–61; idem, "Lope de Vega's 'La Hermosa Ester' and Pinto Delgado's 'Poema de la Reyna Ester,' a Comparative Study," *BHS*, XXXII, 81–97; idem, "The Shorter Poems of João Pinto Delgado," *ibid.*, XXXI, 127–40 (showing remarkable influences of the Aggadah, as well as of the Counter Reformation Spanish poetry, on the poet who as a member of the Marrano diaspora was removed from

direct contacts with either Jewish or Spanish literati). Of more specifically contemporary interest is C. Roth's ed. and analysis "An Elegy of João Pinto Delgado on Isaac de Castro Tartas," *REJ*, CXXI, 355–66 (extolling the martyrdom of the Brazilian Jewish poet; see *infra*, Chaps. LXV, n. 102 and LXVI, n. 91). See also, more generally, F. Secret, "Glanes pour servir à l'histoire des Juifs en France, à la Renaissance," *REJ*, CXV, 87–107.

30. See M. Kayserling, *Sephardim*, pp. 216 ff.; and especially the very well documented study by I. S. Révah, "Un Pamphlet contre l'Inquisition d'Antonio Enríquez Gómez: La seconde partie de la 'Política angélica' (Rouen, 1647)," *REJ*, CXXI, 81–168; *supra*, Chap. LXIII, n. 70; and *infra*, Chap. LXV, n. 61. That the Iberian inquisitors were quite disturbed that such criticisms were being disseminated in their home countries is not at all surprising. Despite the vigilance exercised by their agents, and the sharp penalties inflicted on all persons possessing books forbidden by Church censorship, they could not effectively stem the flow of such writings across the Franco-Iberian border. See the data assembled by M. Défourneaux in *L'Inquisition espagnole et les livres français aux XVIIe siècle*, which apply, in a slightly lesser degree, to the seventeenth century as well.

31. See the sources cited, *supra*, n. 30. On the conflicts between the central and the provincial, or local, administration of criminal justice, see the examples cited by M. Foucheux in *Le Procès de Cinq-Mars. Quelques procès criminels de XVIIe et XVIIIe siècle*, ed. by J. Imbert, pp. 77 ff.; P. Bastide in *Les Grands procès politiques de l'histoire;* and *infra*, n. 32. Of considerable interest also are certain related data offered by I. S. Révah in his study of the career and tragic end of Manuel Fernandes Villareal, an influential New Christian diplomat and a close friend to Enríquez Gómez. It was published under the title "Manuel Fernandes Vilareal, adversaire et victime de l'Inquisition Portuguese" in *Iberida, revista de filologia*, I, No. 1, pp. 33–54, No. 3, pp. 181–207. See also *supra*, Chap. LXIII, n. 73; and *infra*, Chap. LXV, nn. 103–104.

32. See C. Roth, "Les Marranes à Rouen," *REJ*, LXXXVIII, 113–55 (with an extensive documentary appendix from the archives of the Office Fiscal de Brabant); I. S. Révah, "Autobiographie d'un marrane," *ibid.*, CXIX, 58 ff.; idem, "Le Premier établissement," *Annuaire* of the Institut de philologie, etc., XIII, 539–52; *supra*, nn. 9 and 17.

33. Estebanillo González' reputed story in *Vida y hechos de Estebanillo González hombre de Navarrete*, ed. by E. Fernández in *BAE*, XXXIII, 287–368, reprinted in a popular volume, 3d ed., pp. 90 f., briefly summarized in French by M. Grunwald in his "Notes sur des Marranes à Rouen et ailleurs," *REJ*, LXXXIX, 381–84; R. Anchel, *Les Juifs*, pp. 150 f. On the beginnings of the Rouen community, and the role played by refugees therefrom in other cities, see *supra*, n. 17.

34. H. Friedenwald, "Montalto, a Jewish Physician at the Court of Marie de Medicis and Louis XIII," *Bulletin* of the Institute of the History of Medicine, III, 129–58 (reprinted in his *The Jews and Medicine*); P. Delaunay, *La Vie médicale aux XVIe, XVIIe, XVIIIe siècles*, pp. 359 f. The somewhat inconsistent records concerning Montalto's Jewish loyalties have been analyzed by C. Roth in his

"Quatre Lettres d'Élie Montalto. Contribution à l'histoire des Marranes," *REJ*, LXXXVII, 137–65; his "Élie Montalto et sa consultation sur le Sabbat," *ibid.*, XCIV, 113–36 (reproducing the text from a Leghorn MS, with a facsimile of the first and the last pages). Montalto's authorship of that Hebrew responsum need not be questioned, although he undoubtedly required for its composition some assistance from his rabbinic friends in Venice or Leghorn, and possibly from his Judaically better-trained sons, Moses, who later moved to Lublin, Poland, and Isaac, who seems later to have served as rabbi in Siena. It is very likely that this responsum was written in Italy, between Montalto's visits to France, in answer to criticisms voiced by some Italian coreligionists (hence the preservation of what may be its holograph copy in Leghorn). Despite his effective defense of riding on the Sabbath—apparently with a view toward his practice during a previous stay at the royal court in France—he may have been sufficiently impressed by his critics before his final return to Paris to demand that he be freed from attending patients on the Jewish Sabbath, as reported by Daniel Levi (Miguel) de Barrios in his *Relación de los poetas y escritores españoles de la Nacyon judayca Amstelodama*, p. 55, reprinted by M. Kayserling in "Une Histoire de la Littérature juive du Daniel Lévi de Barrios," *REJ*, XVIII, 283. Evidently backed by Léonora Galigaï and the queen-regent (see below), he felt that he could exact such promises despite the opposition of many court circles to the settlement of any New Christians in Paris. Montalto's position at Court is also illustrated by his reply to an apparent inquiry by the Queen Mother concerning the marriage of young Louis XIII. This reply was published in Paris in 1614 in a twelve-page pamphlet entitled *Lettre d'Espagne, présentée à la Royne régente*. It is available in three slightly differing versions at the Bibliothèque Nationale in Paris.

35. The D'Ancre-Galigaï affair, which immediately created a great sensation in France and abroad, has been amply analyzed in the modern historical literature. See esp. F. Hayem, *Le Maréchal d'Ancre et Léonora Galigaï* with a brief "Notice biographique" of the author by A. Lefranc (includes lengthy excerpts from the "Procès de Léonora Galigaï"; G. Mongrédien, *Léonora Galigaï. Un procès de sorcellerie sous Louis XIII* (esp. valuable for the chapter, characteristically entitled "L'Assassination de la Maréchale d'Ancre (8 juillet 1617)," describing on the basis of archival research the various phases of her trial, ending in a judicial murder; pp. 175 ff.); and the older, dramatic narrative of the rise and fall of the Concinis (though silent on the Jewish aspects) by L. Batiffol, under the descriptive title, "Le Coup d'état du 24 avril 1617," *RH*, XCV, 292–308; XCVII, 27–77, 264–86; M. Jacob, "L'Ascendance juive de Dacquin, médecin de Louis XIV," *Univers Israélite*, XXVI; I. S. Révah's intro. to his aforementioned ed. of João Pinto Delgado's poems, pp. xxxii ff. (citing a Paris MS); and other sources cited by Z. Szajkowski in his *Franco-Judaica*, p. 130 Nos. 1572–73 (with an extensive bibliography). On the D'Ancre-Galigaï excesses and tragic end, see also the numerous comments by the papal nuncio in his reports to Rome, ed. by L. de Stefani in *La Nunziatura di Francia del Cardinale Guido Bentivoglio. Lettere a Scipione Borghese*, esp. the entries listed in the Index Vol. IV, p. 558. All this did not prevent Philippe Dacquin's son, Louis Henri (who spelled his family name as D'Aquin, as his father had often done), from publishing in 1612 a Latin paraphrase of Rashi's commentary on the Book of Esther, together with some pertinent excerpts from the Talmud and the Yalqut.

36. See *supra,* Chap. LXIII, n. 76; J. Chalande, "La Rue des Juifs à Toulouse aux quinziéme, seiziéme et dix-septième siècles," *Bulletin* of the Société archéologique du Midi de la France, n.s. XXXVII–XXXIX, 367–72 (shows that the street persisted until it was built upon in 1669–79; on the other hand, his argument that the *maison de Juifs* of 1478 could not have been located in the earlier Jewish quarter, is not conclusive); R. Anchel, *Les Juifs,* pp. 141, 144 f.; Z. Szajkowski, "An Auto-Da-Fé against the Jews of Toulouse in 1685," *JQR,* XLIX, 278–81. On other southern French cities, see the noteworthy materials assembled by Szajkowski in his *Franco-Judaica,* pp. 27 f.

37. Royal edict of April 1778, registered by the Paris Parlement on Aug. 21, 1778, cited by Z. Szajkowski in his *Franco-Judaica,* p. 122 No. 1444; P. Browe, "Die Kirchenrechtliche Stellung der getauften Juden und ihrer Nachkommen," *AKKR,* CXXI, 169 f., 180; *supra,* Vols. XIII, pp. 79 f., 86 ff., 344 f. n. 16, 353 ff. nn. 25 ff.; XIV, 9 ff., 15 f., 32 ff., 303 ff. nn. 7 ff. and 14, 317 ff. nn. 29 ff., and the literature listed there. On the French use of the Spanish doctrine of *limpieza* to downgrade the whole Spanish nation, see *supra,* Vol. XIII, pp. 89 f., 355 n. 30. In connection with François Rabelais, mentioned there, see also M. Bastiaensen, "L'Hébreu chez Rabelais," *RBPH,* XLVI, 725–48; and L. Febvre, *Le Problème de l'incroyance au XVIᵉ siècle. La religion de Rabelais,* rev. ed., which includes, for instance, a summary of the interesting debate concerning the phrase *lamah hazabhthani,* borrowed from Matt. 27:46 by a lady for an inscription on a ring, and its medieval antecedents (pp. 164 f.). See Rabelais' *Oeuvres,* critical ed. by A. Lefranc *et al.,* IV, 253, with the comments thereon by J. Plattard in "L'Écriture sainte et la littérature scripturaire dans l'oeuvre de Rabelais," *Revue des études Rabelaisiennes,* VIII, 257–330, esp. pp. 268 f.

38. See the new data gathered from archival records of the Galigaï trial by J. M. Pelorson in "Le Docteur Carlos García et la colonie hispano-portugaise de Paris (1613–1619)," *BH,* LXXI, 518–76, esp. pp. 575 f.; Armand Jean du Plessis de Richelieu's letters to López from Nov. 7, 1627 on, reproduced in his *Lettres, instructions publiques et papiers d'état,* assembled and ed. by G. d'Avenel, II, 699 f. No. clxiii; III, 4 ff. No. ii, 11 f. No. vii, 57 No. xxxiv n. 2; IV, 90 ff. No. xlix (with the editor's note thereon); VI, 889 No. ccccxlvii (includes the epithet "le seigneur Hebreo" in the cardinal's letter to Mazarin on Dec. 3, 1641); VII, 303 (on March 20, 1642, orders the payment to "Loppès" of 327,000 livres "for advances in the service of the King"), etc.; H. Baraude (pseud. for Baron A. A. A. J. Tupinier), *López, agent financier et confidant de Richelieu,* p. 164; G. Hanotaux and Le Duc de la Forge, *Histoire du Cardinal de Richelieu,* IV, 360; *Recueil des testaments politiques du Cardinal de Richelieu, du Duc de Lorraine, de M. Colbert et de M. Louvois,* II, 76, elaborated with significant economic and fiscal data in all of sections vi and vii (pp. 76–135); R. Anchel, *Les Juifs de France,* pp. 146 f.; and, more generally, H. Hauser's analysis *La Pensée et l'action économiques du Cardinal de Richelieu;* and, from another angle, Duke George of Mecklenburg, *Richelieu als merkantilistischer Wirtschaftspolitiker und der Begriff des Staatsmerkantilismus.* To be sure, the authenticity of Richelieu's political testament has been heatedly debated ever since its publication. See the review offered by E. Boehm in his Leipzig dissertation, *Studien zum politischen Testamente Richelieu's. Der Streit um die Echtheit;* and L. André's more recent affirma-

tive observations in the intro. to his critical ed. of Richelieu's *Testament politique*, pp. 9 ff. In any case, however, the passage here quoted does reflect the statesman's otherwise well-documented concern for the development of his country's economic resources.

It appears that, despite the widely scattered body of evidence, a study of Richelieu's attitude to Jews and Judaism, with all its contradictions and compromises, would be eminently worthwhile. See, for instance, the vast array of primary and secondary sources reviewed in W. F. Church's "Publications on Cardinal Richelieu since 1945: a Bibliographical Study," *JMH*, XXXVII, 421–44; and in C. J. Burckhardt's comprehensive German biography, *Richelieu*, III, 213 f. (repeating almost verbatim the statement by Hanotaux and the Duke de la Forge); with the recent supplementary volume, *Richelieu. Nachwort, Anmerkungen, Literaturnachweise, Personenregister.*

39. The literature on the economic history of France in the early modern period is enormous. It can easily be consulted in such general works as the *Cambridge Economic History of Europe;* or S. B. Clough and C. W. Cole, *Economic History of Europe.* See also P. Jeannin's brief survey, *Les Marchands au XVIe siècle;* Braudel's penetrating observations on *Civilisation matérielle et capitalisme XVe–XVIIIe siècles*, Vol. I (Vol. II: *Capitalisme* is to follow); J. Meuvret, "Les Idées économiques en France au XVIIe siècles," and other essays in the same issue, dedicated to an analysis of "Aspects de l'économie française au XVIIe s.," *XVIIe siècle, Revue*, Nos. 70–71, pp. 1–130; various papers presented at the sessions of the *Conference internationale d'histoire économique*, held since 1960; and other studies annually listed in the *Bibliographie de l'histoire de France.*

40. Of the vast specialized literature pertaining to French domestic and international economic policies in the sixteenth and seventeenth centuries, we need but mention here a few monographs relating to the trade and navigation of Bordeaux, the major center of New Christian and Jewish life in the period before 1650, and particularly to its exchanges with Portugal and other centers of Jewish international trade. See J. Bernard's thoroughly documented *Navires et gens de mer à Bordeaux (vers 1400–1550);* J. Fayard, "Notes sur le trafic maritime entre Bordeaux et Hamburg à la fin du XVIIe siècle," *Annales du Midi*, LXXIX, 219–28 (showing that the number of vessels leaving Bordeaux for the Elbe city was, as a rule, about one-tenth the total of those departing for Holland, but it was nevertheless quite substantial); M. Mollat, "Quelques aspects de la vie économique et sociale de la France dans la première moitié du XVIe siècle vus à travers la correspondance des diplomates portugais," *BEP*, n.s. XII, 224–53, esp. pp. 248 f., 252. For other communities, even the rather readily available notarial archives have rarely been investigated from the Jewish point of view. For instance, J. B. Daranatz's "Autour de Bayonne du XVe au XVIIe siècle d'après Archives notariales bayonnaises," *Bulletin* of the Société des sciences, lettres et arts de Bayonne, n.s. XXV, 34–40, 130–38, 216–37, merely scratches the surface of the general economic life of Bayonne, and offers little with respect to Jewish trade and industry in the city. See, e.g., the 1743 document relating to the Jewish butcher shop in St.-Esprit; p. 35.

41. See W. Doyle, "Le Prix des charges anoblissantes à Bordeaux au XVIIIe siècle," *Annales du Midi*, LXXX, 65–77. Even in 1774 the acquisition by Moses Eliezer

Liefmann Calmer [ben Kalonymus] of the barony of Picquigny, "constituting one of the most ancient baronies and one of the most important territories in the realm on account of its size, its domains, its peculiar privileges, and notably on account of the number of its vassals amounting to more than 1,800," gave rise to a sharp conflict with the bishop of Amiens. See Z. Szajkowski, *Franco-Judaica*, pp. 103 ff.

42. The Rouen satirist, cited *supra*, n. 17; Z. Szajkowski, "Trade Relations of Marranos in France with the Iberian Peninsula in the Sixteenth and Seventeenth Centuries," *JQR*, L, 69–78; the vast array of primary sources assembled by him in his *Franco-Judaica*, pp. 55–116; and, with special reference to Metz, R. Anchel, *Juifs de France*, pp. 153 ff. Of interest also is A. Hertzberg's chapter "From Mercantilism to Free Trade" in *The French Enlightenment and the Jews*, pp. 78 ff., which, while concentrating on the conditions in the eighteenth century sheds occasional light on the earlier developments as well. Needless to say, economic factors also played a considerable role in shaping the political status of Jews and Marranos, and have frequently been mentioned in this chapter and in our earlier volumes. At times economic rivalries were complicated by the inner divisions among the "Portuguese" themselves. In describing how much he felt personally threatened because of the hatred of the Rouen burghers toward all Portuguese, the Portuguese agent Belchior Raposo reported in 1531 that "a certain Emmanuel Phillippe [a New Christian?] was about to construct a galleon of 80–100 tons; he is said to have averred that he was building it in order to attack Portuguese shipping in revenge for the death of his father, slain by the Portuguese in India or Brazil." See M. Mollat, "Quelques aspects," *BEP*, n.s. XII, 248 f.

43. The Dauphiny official's statement of 1486, cited by X. Gasnos in his *Étude historique sur la condition des Juifs dans l'ancien droit français*, pp. 214 f.; and more generally, A. Prudhomme, *Les Juifs en Dauphiné aux XIVe et XVe siècles* (reprinted from the *Bulletin* of the Académie delphinale; with Isidore Loeb's comments thereon in his "Revue bibliographique," *REJ*, VI, 287–307, esp. pp. 298 f.); idem, "Notes et Documents sur les Juifs du Dauphiné," REJ, IX, 231–63; *supra*, Vol. X, p. 338 n. 28; Jean Baptiste Colbert, *Lettres, instructions et memoires*, ed. by P. Clément, II, 722; De la Berchère's report of August 12, 1693, in A. M. Boislile, ed., *Correspondance des contrôleurs généraux des finances avec les intendants des provinces, d'après des documents conservés aux Archives Nationales* (Vol. III with P. de Brotonne), I, 292 No. 1103. See also Richelieu's *Testament*, cited *supra*, n. 38.

44. R. Anchel, *Les Juifs*, pp. 139 f.; C. Roth, "Les Marranes à Rouen," *REJ*, LXXXVIII, 113 ff.; T. Malvezin, *Histoire*, pp. 94 ff., 131 f.; Z. Szajkowski, "Trade Relations," *JQR*, L, 69–78 (largely based on numerous notarial records); and, more generally, the materials assembled in G. Cirot's long series in the *Revue historique de Bordeaux* (see *supra*, n. 17); J. Mathorez, *Les Étrangers en France sous l'ancien régime*; L. de Matos in *Les Portugais en France au XVIe siècle*; and W. Sombart, *Die Juden und das Wirtschaftsleben*, pp. 199 f. (in the English trans. p. 172; also citing the *Spectator* correspondence of September 27, 1712, in VII, No. 495 [1749], 88 f.). As we recall, despite its intolerance at home, the French government did not mind extending its protection to some Levantine Jews, an action which accrued to the political and economic advantage of both sides. Situations of this kind also inspired the French ambassador's report of 1618 to his home government

about the international cooperation among Jews, which, he said, was the foundation of the astounding prosperity of the leading Jewish circles in Amsterdam.
See *supra*, n. 14; Chap. LXIII, nn. 50 ff., 64.

45. Archives Nationales, Fascicles E 1704 fol. 12a, 1804, the former partially
excerpted by R. Anchel in *Les Juifs*, p. 134, where other similar intolerant moves
by administrative bodies during the late seventeenth and early eighteenth centuries
are mentioned. Although they invariably invoked Louis XIII's decree of 1615,
which had never been formally abrogated, they seem to have had no more than
a delaying effect. On the shortcomings of the older French welfare system, see, for
instance, such recent sudies as N. Z. Davis's "Poor Relief, Humanism and Heresy:
the Case of Lyon," *Studies in Medieval and Renaissance History*, V, 215–75; and
J. P. Gutton, "Les Mendiants dans la Société parisienne au début du XVIIIe
siècle," *Cahiers d'histoire*, XIII, 131–41.

46. V. Emanuel, *Les Juifs à Nice (1400–1860)*; J. Decourcelle, *La Condition des
Juifs de Nice aux 17e et 18e siècles* (Jur. diss. Marseilles), pp. 15 ff.; E. de Clermont-
Tonnère, *Histoire de Samuel Bernard et de ses enfants*, esp. pp. 3 ff. (noncommittal
with respect to Bernard's Jewish origin), 19 f., 24, etc.; L. Kahn, *Les Juifs à Paris
dépuis le VIe siècle*, pp. 37 ff.; P. Hildenfinger, *Documents sur les Juifs à Paris
au XVIIIe siècle: Actes d'inhumation et de scellés*; H. Monin, "Les Juifs de Paris
à la fin de l'ancien régime," *REJ*, XXIII, 85–98; Z. Szajkowski, *Franco-Judaica*,
esp. pp 1 ff. (with the exception of three items, the entire section dealing with Paris
lists entries dated 1759–80); Richard Simon, *Lettres choisies ou l'on trouve un
grand nombre des faits anecdotes de littérature*, Rotterdam, 1702–1705 ed., IV,
303 No. viii, with reference to Henri Sauval's aforementioned *Histoire et recherches
des antiquités de la ville de Paris*, which was not to appear in print until 1724
(see *supra*, n. 8); R. Anchel, "The Early History of the Jewish Quarters in Paris,"
JSS, II, 45–60, esp. pp. 57 ff., repeated with minor modifications in *Les Juifs*, pp.
59 ff., 74 ff. See also *ibid*, pp. 127 ff.

47. See the fully documented analysis by R. Clément in *La Condition des Juifs
de Metz sous l'ancien régime*, esp. pp. 19 ff., 232 ff. Nos. i–xvii; G. Zeller,
La Réunion de Metz à la France (1552–1648), esp. II, 133 f.; A. Cahen, "Le
Rabbinat de Metz pendant la période française (1567–1871)," *REJ*, VII, 103–116,
204–226; VIII, 255–74; XII, 283–97; XIII, 105–126; esp. VII, 111; the more popular
survey by N. Netter in his *Vingt siècles d'histoire d'une communauté juive (Metz
et son grand passé)*; J. de Fombusque, "Les Juifs de Metz," *La Question juive
en France et dans le monde*, II, Nos. 9, pp. 61–81; 10, pp. 32–45; other data,
cited by Z. Szajkowski in his *Franco-Judaica*, pp. 13 ff.; B. Blumenkranz's brief
survey, "Les Juifs de Lorraine," *Annales de l'Est*, 5th ser. XIX, 199–215; and,
more generally, Major Westphal's comprehensive *Geschichte der Stadt Metz*; and
J. Schneider's *Histoire de Lorraine*. See also M. Parisse's succinct survey "Vingt
ans des recherches d'histoire lorraine," *Annales de l'Est*, 5th ser. XVIII, 265–83.

48. R. Clément, *La Condition des Juifs*, pp. 231 f.; also X. Richard, "Deux
lettres de privilèges, et de franchises accordées aux Juifs de l'evêché de Metz (1427 et
1603)," *Annuaire (Jahrbuch) of the Société d'histoire et d'archéologie de la Lorraine*,
I, 201; II, 152–57. If true, the king's assertion concerning the Jews' fecundity is

doubly remarkable, as the general French population had suffered severely in those years from pestilences (in 1584 and 1598) and other demographically adverse factors. Recent population research, based on a detailed examination of local parish records, has shown that, after a period of fairly steady growth in the years 1500–1570, the last two or three decades of the century witnessed a considerable retardation and, in many areas, an actual decline in the number of inhabitants. See esp. P. Goubert, "Registres paroissaux et démographie dans la France au XVIe siècle," and F. Lebrun, "Registres paroissaux et démographie en Anjou au XVIe siècle," both in *Annales de démographie historiques*, II, 43–48 and 49–50. On Metz, see the earlier study by J. Rigault, "La Population de Metz au XVIIe siècle. Quelques problèmes de démographie," *Annales de l'Est*, 5th ser. II, 307–315.

49. V. J. Tapié, *La France de Louis XIII et de Richelieu*, p. 93; R. Clément, *La Condition, passim;* L. Daville, "Les Israélites de Lorraine sous le règne de Charles VI (1594–1608)," *Revue juive de Lorraine*, VI, 78–92. On Henry IV's threat to expel the Jews from Bayonne–St.-Esprit, see H. Léon, *Histoire des Juifs de Bayonne*, pp. 19 f.; and *supra*, n. 15.

50. See R. Clément, *La Condition*, pp. 32 ff.; B. Blumenkranz, "Les Juifs en Lorraine," *Annales de l'Est*, 5th ser. XIX, 207; J. Rigault, "La Population de Metz au XVIIe siècle," *ibid.*, II, 307–315; Jacques Bénigne Bossuet, *Discours sur l'histoire universelle*, II, xx–xxiv in *Oeuvres complètes*, ed. by F. Lachat, XXIV, 467 ff.; idem, *Méditations sur l'Évangile*, xxiv–xxxi, *ibid.*, VI, 131 ff., 137 ff., etc.; idem, *Politique tirée des propres paroles de l'Écriture Sainte*, new critical ed. with an intro. and notes by J. Le Brun; A. Cahen, "Le Rabbinat de Metz," *REJ*, VII, 226. On the Blood Accusation of 1669–70, see J. Reinach's detailed analysis in *Une Erreur judiciaire sous Louis XIV, Raphaël Levy* (also reprinting the *Abrégé du Procès*, the *factum* by Richard Simon, the translation of a Yiddish diary written by a contemporary Metz Jew, and two decisions of the Royal Council); and other sources, both primary and secondary, listed by Z. Szajkowski in his *Franco-Judaica*, p. 119, esp. Nos. 1419–20 (taking Richard Simon's authorship of the *factum* for granted), and 1424; and his "Mazarinades of Jewish Interest," *Studies in Bibliography and Booklore*, VI, 35 ff. On Simon's generally ambivalent attitude to Jews and Judaism, see also M. Yardeni, "La Vision des Juifs et du judaïsme dans l'oeuvre de Richard Simon," *REJ*, CXXIX, 179–203.

Some of these controversies with the burghers engaged the attention of the Parlement of Metz. The registration of the royal *lettres patentes* of 1632 actually took two years of extended deliberations. See J. L. C. Emmery de Grozyeuix, ed., *Recueil des édits, déclarations, lettres patentes et arrêts de Conseil enregistrés au Parlement de Metz;* (also the various catalogues of books and MSS in the private library he left behind on his demise; printed in Metz, 1849–50); the various "arrêts" of the Parlement in 1635–58, also listing the earlier governmental enactments, in Z. Szajkowski's *Franco-Judaica*, pp. 13 f.; and the eighteenth-century sources relating to Jews in Lorraine, listed *ibid.*, p. 20. The extent to which the burghers' resistance, abetted by the local Parlement, interfered even with ordinary Jewish commerce may be seen from the Parlement's attempt to limit the Jews' trading rights to secondhand articles (May 23, 1634); it later extended them to include dealing in cattle and meat (April 10, 1647). It was not until September

25, 1657, or almost a century after their formal admission to settlement in Metz, that Jews were expressly allowed to engage in all branches of commerce. See E. H. Perreau, "Condition des Juifs dans notre ancienne France," *Mémoires* of the Académie des Sciences, Inscriptions et Belles Lettres de Toulouse, 13th ser. IV, 295 f. Needless to say, religious disparity also played a major role in that tense period of the Wars of Religion, and there was a growing anti-Protestant reaction in Lorraine, including Metz, the population of which had originally evinced strong pro-Protestant sympathies.

51. N. Netter, "Les Anciens cimitières israélites de Metz près de la Porte Chambière," *REJ*, LI, 280–302; LII, 98–113; and M. Ginsburger, "Les Anciens cimitières israélites de Metz," *ibid.*, LII, 272–81 (bringing their number in the early modern period up to four). A similarly tolerant attitude was often displayed by French commanders elsewhere. When the French occupied Thionville in 1643, the municipal officials insisted on their long-observed exclusion of Jews. But the French military governor, Marshal De Grancey, in an ordinance of August 4, 1656, overruled their objections and admitted two Metz Jews, Olry (or Faist) Raphaël and Salomon Penel Levy, to settlement in Thionville "for the good of the public as well as of the garrison." See A. Cahen, "Les Israélites de Thionville," *Annuaire des Archives israélites*, II, 56–61. See also *supra*, Vol. XIV, pp. 257, 399 n. 33.

52. See esp. *supra*, Vols. XIII, pp. 107 ff., 170 f., 363 f. nn. 51–52, 398 f. n. 13; XIV, pp. 97 f., 322 n. 45; and the literature listed there and in the next note.

53. R. de Maulde, *Les Juifs dans les états français du Saint-Siège au moyen âge*, pp. 19, 24 ff., 33, 36, 39 ff., 86 (statute of 1532, Art. xxi), 143 (statute of 1558, Art. ix), 186 f. (giving the text of Clement VIII's renewal in 1592 of the laws of 1555 and 1556); I. Loeb, "Les Juifs de Carpentras sous le gouvernement pontifical," *REJ*, XII, 34–64, 161–235, esp. pp. 190 ff.; A. Mossé, *Histoire des Juifs d'Avignon*, esp. pp. 82 ff., 93 ff.; D. de Sainte Marthe *et al.*, eds., *Gallia Christiana in provincias ecclesiasticas distributa*, I, 884 ff., 955 f.; P. Browe in "Die Kirchenrechtliche Stellung der getauften Juden und ihrer Nachkommen," *AKKR*, CXXI, 170. Originally, Jews had been scattered throughout the Comtat, but with the progressive restrictions during the Middle Ages they were increasingly concentrated in the four cities of Avignon, Carpentras, Cavaillon, and Isle-sur-Sorgue. For this reason the entire area came to be known by the Hebrew designation *arba' qehillot* (the four communities). Elsewhere, individual Jewish visitors were given, at best, permission to sojourn for three days of any month. The reason given was that the Jews needed that much time to collect debts owed them by local debtors who used "excuses and subterfuges" in order not to pay. See, for instance, such a permit of November 13, 1567, included in the *Recueil des principaux règlements faits par les Eminentissimes Cardinaux Légats ou illustrissimes et excellentissimes Vice Légats . . . d'Avignon*, in French trans., Avignon, 1670, pp. 206 ff. (also cited by Z. Szajkowski in his *Franco-Judaica*, p. 32). Other interesting regulations are reproduced *ibid.*, pp. 175 f., 192 ff., 205 ff.

54. See R. Caillet, *Foires et marchés de Carpentras, du moyen âge au début du XIXe siècle; supra*, Vol. XII, p. 290 n. 36; G. Cirot, "Les Juifs de Bordeaux," *Revue historique de Bordeaux*, VII, 353 ff., 361; A. Hertzberg, *The French Enlightenment*, pp. 93 ff., and numerous other passages listed in the *Index*, p. 393

s.v. Avignonnais; Z. Szajkowski, "Relations among Sephardim, Ashkenazim and Avignonese Jews in France from the 16th to the 20th Centuries," *Yivo Annual of Jewish Social Science*, X, 165–96, reprinted in his *Jews and the French Revolutions*, pp. 235–66; idem, *Franco-Judaica*, pp. 32 ff., 74 ff., 115 f., etc. According to Caillet, foreign Jews helped their Carpentras coreligionists to defy the papal prohibition against their visiting fairs in Provence and Languedoc. In Carpentras itself Jewish traders faced the opposition of local non-Jewish merchants, who as late as 1715 offered 1,500 livres toward the rebuilding of their city hall, demolished by fire, in return for a restriction of Jewish trading to secondhand clothing as in Rome. The city council supported the demand, but failed to secure such an ordinance from the papal administration.

55. See L. Dulieu, "Les Relations estudiantines entre la Faculté de Médecine d'Avignon et l'Université de Médecine de Montpellier au XVIᵉ siècle," *BHR*, XXVIII, 91–108; and, more generally, V. Laval's *Histoire de la Faculté de Médecine d'Avignon, ses origines, son organisation et son enseignement (1303–1791)*, Vol I: *Les origines et l'organisation* (no more published), reproducing among other documents a candidate's certificate of baptism, as well as an attestation that he was "Catholic, apostolic and Roman Catholic, of good life and morals," signed by his local priests. Such an attestation had to be submitted by each applicant for admission or for a degree, from the 15th to the 18th century; pp. 403 f. Apps. v–vi.

56. S. Simonsohn, "Opinion of the Sorbonne Concerning the Settlement of Jews in France (1633)" (Hebrew), *Zion*, XXIII–XXIV, 98–101; *supra*, n. 10; Vol. XIV, pp. 98 ff., 267 f., 342 nn. 27–29, 402 f. n. 44; R. Anchel, *Les Juifs*, p. 148, citing documents of Nov. 10, 1631, and Sept. 25, 1649. The Sorbonne's favorable opinion in the Jewish case is doubly remarkable as in those years the faculty was for the most part intransigently conservative on other religious and ideological issues. See L. Thorndike, "Censorship by the Sorbonne of Science and Superstition in the First Half of the Seventeenth Century," *Journal of the History of Ideas*, XVI, 119–25; and, more generally, C. Jourdain, *Histoire de l'Université de Paris au XVIIᵉ et au XVIIIᵉ siècle*, in the revised 1888 ed., which does not include however, the valuable documentary appendix in the original edition. See esp. I, 245 ff., which shows that in 1536 the Paris theologians combined strong religious zeal with much patriotic fervor, doubtless enhanced by their country's involvement in the Thirty Years' War. Perhaps it was this patriotic feeling which made them more receptive to the *raison d'état* and a sober return to the trends prevailing in the mid-sixteenth century (contrary to the tendencies generated by the Counter Reformation and the Wars of Religion), when Chancellor Michel de l'Hôpital (Hospital) had viewed religious toleration in general as promoting the interests of the French state—an attitude which, understandably, was denounced by his opponents as bordering on Huguenot heresy. See his *Oeuvres complétes*, ed. by J. S. Duféy (with the editor's introductory "Essai sur la vie et les ouvrages de Michel L'Hospital," I, 3–311), esp. pp. 277 f.; and H. Schneier's Freiburg dissertation, *Beiträge zur Entwicklungsgeschichte der modernen Toleranzidee in Frankreich des XVI. Jahrhunderts*, esp. pp. 33 ff. See also *supra*, Vol. XIII, pp. 117 f., 367 n. 60.

57. The Jewish trader Joseph Abraham Charleville, mentioned in Amsterdam in 1705, doubtless derived his name from his previous residence in the French city. See H. I. Bloom, *The Economic Activities of the Jews of Amsterdam*, p. 68.

See also, more generally, the bibliographical notes on the "Origine et croissance d'une ville neuve Charleville aux XVIIᵉ et XVIIIᵉ siècles" in the *Orientations et recherches*, 1969, pp. 34–36, prepared for the 95ᵉᵐᵉ Congrès de Sociétés savantes in Rheims, 1970.

58. L. de Matos, *Les Portugais en France*, pp. 19 f.; Jean Baptiste du Tertre, *Histoire générale des Antilles habitées par les Français*, II, 462, cited by N. M. Crouse, *The French Struggle for the West Indies, 1665–1713*, pp. 3 f.; *supra*, Chap. LXIII, n. 79; and *infra*, nn. 59–60. Of interest also is M. L. Marchand-Thébault's study "L'Esclavage en Guyenne française sous l'ancien régime," *Revue française d'histoire d'outre-mer*, XLVII, 3–75. It shows that, while French colonists were recorded in the colony in 1613, the first Negro slaves appeared there only in 1652. By 1704, however, the 264 white settlers in Cayenne were vastly outnumbered by 1,137 (or 1,132) Negro, and 83 Indian, slaves. There is no evidence, however, that Jews had participated in the importation of those slaves or in the slave trade generally. See also J. Gazin [Gossel], *Éléments de bibliographie générale, méthodique et historique de la Martinique (Antilles françaises)* (listing early records, including travelogues); and the more recent "Bibliographie d'histoire de l'Amérique française" compiled by P. Aubin and P. A. Linteau for the *Revue d'histoire de l'Amérique française*, XXII, 493–515, 662–82; XXIII, 159–80.

59. Jean Baptiste Colbert, *Lettres, instructions et mémoires*, ed. by P. Clément, III, 522 f.; various ordinances and editions of the *Code Noir;* Moreau de Saint-Méry, *Lois et constitutions de colonies françoises de l'Amérique sous le Vent*, I, 9 f. (citing the generally favorable decrees issued for the Portuguese by Henry III on Nov. 11, 1574), 13 f. (reproducing Louis XIII's intolerant decree of April 23, 1615), 83 f. (contradictory edicts of 1656 and 1658), 180 ff. (antagonistic ordinance of 1669), 225 f. (a contrary egalitarian royal letter of May 23, 1671), 388 (royal decree expelling Jews from all French islands in America; dated May 2, 1684), 424 f. (repeated in March 1685); and Z. Szajkowski, *Franco-Judaica*, p. 38. Of the secondary literature, see esp. A. Cahen, "Les Juifs de la Martinique au XVIIᵉ siècle," *REJ*, II, 93–114; idem, "Les Juifs dans les colonies françaises au XVIIIᵉ siècle," *ibid.*, IV, 127–236; V, 68–92, 258–72; T. Malzevin, *Histoire des Juifs de Bordeaux*, pp. 241 ff.; J. Rennard, "Juifs et Protestants aux Antilles françaises au XVIIᵉ siècle," *Revue d'histoire des Missions*, 1933; J. Petitjean-Roget, "Les Juifs à la Martinique sous l'Ancien Régime," *Revue d'histoire des Colonies*, XLIII, No. 151; and I. S. Emmanuel, "Les Juifs de la Martinique et leurs coreligionnaires d'Amsterdam au XVIIᵉ siècle," *REJ*, CXXIII, 511–16. See also J. Rennard, *Histoire religieuse des Antilles françaises, des origines à 1914; d'après des documents inédits*, esp. pp. 39 ff., 67 ff.; and J. Adelaïde, "La Colonisation française aux Antilles à la fin du XVIIᵉ siècle," *Bulletin* of the Société d'histoire de la Guadeloupe, 1967–68; and the literature listed in the next note. On the dispersion of Brazilian Jews after the Portuguese reconquest of Recife, see *infra*, Chap. LXVI, n. 100, etc.

60. See H. Gradis, *Notice sur la famille Gradis et sur la maison Gradis et fils de Bordeaux;* H. Graetz, "Die Familie Gradis," *MGWJ*, XXIV, 447–59; XXV, 78–85; C. Schnakenbourg, "Note sur les origines de l'industrie sucrière en Guadeloupe au XVIIᵉ siècle (1640–1670)," *Revue française d'histoire d'outre-mer*, LV, 267–315; P. Butel, "Le Trafic colonial de Bordeaux de la guerre d'Amérique à la Revolution,"

Annales du Midi, LXXIX, 287–306; the literature cited *supra,* nn. 58–59; and, more generally, S. Daney's older *Histoire da la Martinique depuis la colonisation, justqu'au 1815,* esp. pp. 118 f.; L. P. May's Paris dissertation, *Histoire économique de la Martinique (1635–1763),* esp. pp. 24 ff. (stresses the difficulties of securing enough manpower, but fails to refer to Jews); W. A. Roberts's *The French in the West Indies,* esp. pp. 74 f., 150 ff.; L. Chauleau, *La Société à la Martinique au XVIIe siècle (1635–1713)* (includes a succinct, informative section on Jews, based largely on archival data; pp. 168 ff.); and J. Rennard's *Tricentenaire des Antilles: Guadeloupe-Martinique,* esp. pp. 116 ff. See also L. Ragatz, *Early French West Indian Reocrds in the Archives Nationales,* 2d ed.; A. P. Newton, *The European Nations in the West Indies, 1493–1688;* and G. Debien's critical comments on some recent publications in his "Antilles de langue française: Bibliographie," *Caribbean Studies,* VII, Part 2, pp. 53–70 (this is part of the meritorious general effort of editors of that journal to list current bibliographies relating to the entire Caribbean area); as well as the aforementioned, more comprehensive "Bibliographie de l'Amérique française (publications récentes)" by P. Aubin *et al.* in the *Revue d'histoire de l'Amérique française,* XXII–XXIII, which is likewise part of a recurring program. These developments, also important for the later French colonization in the Louisiana territory and Canada, became really significant after 1650, and particularly after 1685; they will be more fully analyzed in a later volume.

61. J. Amador de los Rios, *Historia social, política y religiosa de los Judíos en España,* III, 377; *The Statutes of the Realm. . . From Original Records and Authentic Monographs,* ed. by T. E. Tomlins for the Record Commission, IV, Part 1, p. 244, and reproduced in English by C. H. Williams in his ed. of *English Historical Documents* (in the series ed. by D. C. Douglas *et al.,* Vols. I–XII), Vol. V: 1480–1558, p. 834 No. 126; *The Wandering Jew Telling Fortunes to Englishmen* (1649), reprinted in J. O. Halliwell's *Books of Character, Illustrating the Habits and Manners of Englishmen from the Reign of James I to the Restoration,* pp. 1–71, esp. p. 17; L. Wolf, *Jews in Elizabethan England,* p. 19 and *passim.* On Cassidoro de Reina's group, see P. J. Hauben, "A Spanish Calvinist Church in Elizabethan London, 1559–1565," *CH,* XXXIV, 50–56.

62. L. Wolf, "Jews in Tudor England," in his *Essays in Jewish History,* ed. by C. Roth, pp. 84 ff. Other examples are cited by Roth in "The Inquisitorial Archives as a Source of English History," *TRHS,* 4th ser. XVIII, 107–122. Samuel Usque's work and its impact on the entire Marrano world will be analyzed in a later volume.

63. I. Abrahams, "Joachim Gaunse: a Mining Incident in the Reign of Queen Elizabeth," *TJHSE,* IV, 83–101; John Foxe, *A Sermon Preached at the Christening of a Certain Iew, at London. . . . Conteining an Explication of the XI. Chapter of St. Paul to the Romans.* Translated out of Latine into English by James Bell, London, 1578; C. J. Sisson, "A Colony of Jews in Shakespeare's London," *Essays and Studies by Members of the English Association,* XXIII, 38–51, esp. pp. 41 ff. Sisson also points out (p. 49) that his search through London parish registers yielded numerous records of Marrano marriages and deaths, but none of baptisms. Evidently less in fear of detection than those in Spain or Portugal, many secret Judaizers in England neglected to bring their children to church for that essential ceremony. Of course, in their adult life, these children could use Gaunse's argu-

ment as to why they were not obligated to adhere to Christian beliefs and rituals (such may have been the case with Ferdinand Alvares). On the development of the London Marrano community in the early decades of Elizabeth's reign, see A. M. Hyamson, *The Sephardim of England: a History of the Spanish and Portuguese Community 1492–1951*, pp. 8 ff.; *supra*, Vol. XIII, pp. 125 ff.; and *infra*, Chap. LXV, n. 2.

64. [Robert Parsons or Persons], *A Brief Discovrse Contayning Certayne Reasons Why Catholiques Refuse to Goe to Church*, Dedicated by Iohn Howlet to the queen, London, 1580 ed., fol. 5b; Laurence Vaux, *A Catechisme or Christian Doctrine, Necessary for Children and the Ignorant People* (1568, 1583) in the Collection of the Chatham Society, n.s. IV, p. 18; A. J. Loomie's careful archival study *The Spanish Elizabethans: the English Exiles at the Court of Philip II* (including "A Soldier: Sir William Stanley," pp. 129–81); and, more generally, O. Caraman, ed., *The Other Face: Catholic Life under Elizabeth I*, esp. pp. 56 ff., 60 f., 171; W. R. Trimble, *The Catholic Laity in Elizabethan England, 1558–1603* (describes "the dormant years of Catholicism" in 1559–73, its "attempted revivification" in 1574–83, and its "decline" in 1584–1603). Henry VIII's aforementioned consultation with Italian rabbis and converts in connection with his fateful divorce of Catherine of Aragon, and his intervention in behalf of such secret Judaizers as Diogo Mendes in Antwerp, may have added to Catholic resentment. See *supra*, Vols. XIII, pp. 123, 128, 371 f. nn. 66–67, 374 n. 73; XIV, pp. 101, 343 n. 31. To the literature listed there, add T. C. P. Zimmerman, "A Note on Clement VII and the Divorce of Henry VIII," *EHR*, LXXXII, 548–52 (arguing, on the basis of Paulo Giovio's [Paulus Jovius] report in his *Historiae sui temporis*, that the pope's changeable attitudes were owing to design, rather than vacillation); and, particularly, M. H. Albert, *The Divorce* (reviews anew the great Tudor controversy, but without any reference to the role in it of the Italian rabbis).

65. E. R. Samuel, "Portuguese Jews in Jacobean London," *TJHSE*, XVIII, 171–230; Public Record Office, *Calendar of State Papers*, Foreign, Turkey, p. 2; M. Hume, "The So-Called Conspiracy of Dr. Ruy Lopez," *TJHSE*, VI, 32–55 (also listing the main primary sources, p. 55); J. Gwyer, "The Case of Dr. Lopez," *ibid.*, XVI, 163–84 (although highly speculative, this essay offers a fairly plausible reconstruction of the intrigues and counterintrigues which led to Lopez' downfall); the older, but still informative, essay by S. L. Lee, "The Original of Shylock," *Gentleman's Magazine*, CCXLVIII, 185–200; F. Marcham's privately printed ed., *The Prototype of Shylock: Lopez the Jew, Executed 1594: an Opinion by Gabriel Harvey;* C. Roth in "The Inquisitorial Archives," *TRHS*, 4th ser. XVIII, 112; and, particularly, L. Wolf's *Jews in Elizabethan England*, pp. 24 ff., 31 n. 63, 56 ff. See also M. J. Kohler, "Dr. Rodrigo Lopez, Queen Elizabeth's Jewish Physician and His Relations to America," *PAJHS*, XVII, 9–25 (also referring to the strange episode of the English capture in 1592 of two Spanish ships containing, among other goods, one and a half million papal indulgences, which were to be sold in the New World and which the queen gave Lopez for sale in Spain's American colonies); and other sources discussed by J. de Araujo in his *Dom Antonio, Prior do Crato: Notas de bibliographia;* J. Albrecht's more recent sketch "Dom Antonio (Ein portugiesischer Kronprätendent des 16. Jahrhunderts)," *Abhandlungen und Vorträge* of the Bremer Wissenschaftliche Gesellschaft, VIII–IX, 42–58; the writings

cited *supra*, n. 13; and *infra*, n. 72; and, more generally, C. Roth, *A History of the Jews in England*, pp. 139 ff.; and W. K. Jordan, *The Development of Religious Toleration in England*.

66. See the noteworthy archival and printed data, assembled and analyzed by L. Wolf in his *Jews in Elizabethan England*, pp. 23 f., 47, 50 ff.; Bernardino de Mendoza's dispatch of April 1, 1582, to Philip II, reproduced in English trans. in Public Record Office, *Calendar of State Papers*, Spanish, 1580–86, pp. 321 f.; *Acts of Privy Council*, ed. by J. R. Dasent, VIII, 20 f., 80 f., 91 f., 127 f., 160, 217 f., 231 f., 269; IX, 79, 114, 168, 238, 327; C. Roth, *A History of the Jews in England*, pp. 140, 279 note c; and *infra*, n. 90.

67. See Public Record Office, *Calendar of State Papers*, Foreign, 1581–82, pp. 250 ff. Nos. 255–56; Spanish, 1587–1603, p. 92 No. 93; Venice, 1581–91, p. 399 No. 753, all cited together with many other documents by L. Wolf, *Jews in Elizabethan England*, esp. pp. 52, 57, 61, 85 f., 90. The extremely complicated international situation during the last two decades of the sixteenth century has often been discussed. See esp. F. Braudel, *La Méditerranée et le Monde Mediterranéen à l'époque de Philippe II;* R. B. Wernham, *Before the Armada: the Emergence of the English Nation, 1485–1588;* and G. Mattingly, *The Armada*, which also shows how slowly the news of the defeat of the "Invincible Armada" reached the European countries, even neighboring France.

68. Public Record Office, *Calendar of State Papers*, Foreign, Turkey, No. 2; Venice 1592–1603, pp. 188 ff. No. 412 and 416; L. Wolf, *Jews in Elizabethan England*, pp. 71 ff., 85 f., 90 and *passim*. On the situation in Milan, see *supra*, Vol. XIV, pp. 81 ff., 127 ff., 336 ff. nn. 9–12, 353 f. nn. 57–58. The dramatic careers of Alvaro Mendez and his associates in the Ottoman Empire will be reviewed *infra*, Vol. XVII.

69. See P. F. Mullany, *Christopher Marlowe's Doctor Faustus, Tamberlain I and II, The Jew of Malta* [and] *Edward the Second;* R. Ornstein, "Marlowe and God: the Tragic Theology of *Doctor Faustus*," *PMLA*, LXXXIII, 1378–85 (a new approach based upon the longer 1616 ed.); S. L. Lee, "The Original of Shylock," *Gentleman's Magazine*, CCXLVIII, 187; E. D. Coleman, *The Jew in English Drama: an Annotated Bibliography*, with a Preface by J. Bloch, pp. viii f.; *supra*, Vol. XI, pp. 176 f., 372 n. 72. See also the literature listed in the next note.

70. Robert Wilson, *The Three Ladies of London*, London, 1584, reprinted in R. Dodsley's ed. of *A Select Collection of Old English Plays*, and therefrom re-issued with additional notes by H. C. Hazlitt, VI, 245–502, esp. pp. 328 ff.; Christopher Marlowe, *The Jew of Malta*, Act ii, ed. by H. S. Bennett, in *The Works and Life*, ed. by R. H. Case *et al.*, III, 88 f.; William Shakespeare, *The Merchant of Venice*, in *The Comedies*, Oxford ed. by J. W. Craig, Oxford, 1915 ed., pp. 585–681, and many other editions. See also E. Rothstein, "Structure as Meaning in *The Jew of Malta*," *Journal of English and Germanic Philology*, LXV, 260–73 ("The play . . . is skillfully constructed, and effective, if not in stimulating our emotions, then in placing before us the image of a morally crippled world, a complex emblem of unChristian action"; p. 273); G. K. Hunter, "The Theology of Marlowe's Jew of Malta," *Journal of the Warburg and Courtauld*

Institutes, XXVII, 211–40; J. H. Sims, *Dramatic Uses of Biblical Allusion in Marlowe and Shakespeare;* and, more generally, J. L. Cardozo, *The Contemporary Jew in Elizabethan Drama;* M. F. Modder, *The Jew in the Literature of England to the End of the Nineteenth Century,* esp. pp. 17 ff.; and D. Bevington, *Tudor Drama and Politics: a Critical Approach to Topical Meaning.* Because of Shakespeare's great prestige, and because the intriguing personality of Shylock has through the ages been subjected to a large variety of interpretations by critics and outstanding actors in each generation, the bibliography on *The Merchant of Venice* is enormous. Here it will suffice to mention the following studies: H. Graetz, *Shylock in der Sage, im Drama und in der Geschichte,* 2d ed. (reprinted from *MGWJ*, XXIX); G. Friedlander, *Shakespeare and the Jew;* H. Sinsheimer, "Shylock—die Geschichte einer Figur," *JJGL*, XXXI, 137–66 (with special reference to B. V. Wenger's study cited below); E. E. Stoll, "Shakespeare's Jew," *University of Toronto Quarterly*, VIII, 139–54 (offering an almost line-by-line commentary); H. M. Flasdieck's informed, though Nazi-biased, "Jüdisches im und zum 'Merchant of Venice,'" *Neuphilologische Monatsschrift*, IX, 148–60, 182–89 (discusses, among other matters, Hebraic influences—such as the Passover Haggadah or some related Catholic liturgy—on the poet, as well as the various theories concerning the etymology of the names Shylock and Jessica). There have even been attempts to question Shylock's Jewishness altogether. See, for instance, A. Engle, "Was Shylock a Jew? New Thesis on the Origin of 'The Merchant of Venice," *Jewish Quarterly* (London), I, No. 2, pp. 13–18 (summarizing a venturesome theory by Shlomoh Schoenfeld in a MS in Haifa). Of some interest also is N. N. Holland's *Psychoanalysis and Shakespeare,* esp. pp. 231 ff., claiming that "perhaps because many psychoanalysts are Jewish, *The Merchant of Venice* has received a great deal of attention, more, proportionately, than some of Shakespeare's more important plays," and reviewing the theories advanced by Sigmund Freud and his successors. The story of the divergent interpretations of Shylock on the stage which began, some two months after Lopez' execution, with performances by the famed actor Richard Burbage, who with his beard and attire consciously imitated the Jewish physician, has been analyzed in T. B. Lelyveld's Columbia University dissertation, *Shylock on the Stage: Significant Changes in the Interpretataion of Shakespeare's Jew* (typescript and University microfilm).

Understandably, the background of Shakespeare's story, particularly of the trial of Shylock vs. Antonio with its dominant theme of the "pound of flesh," has attracted the widest attention. It is generally assumed that Shakespeare, here as in many other of his plays, borrowed the plot from an Italian novel; in this case, from Giovanni Fiorentino's *Il Pecorone* (about 1378), readily available in the collection *Classici italiani*, XXV, 68–96; and in the English trans. by J. P. Collier in the *Shakespeare Library*, I, 1319–53. It is less likely that the English dramatist had heard the aforementioned anecdote current in Rome about Pope Sixtus V's summary judgment in a similar case (except that the pound of flesh at issue there belonged to the Jewish moneylender), cited *supra*, Vol. XIV, p. 348 n. 42. Although this story did not appear in print until it was included in Giovanni Leti's biography of Sixtus almost a century later, it may have been bruited about widely enough to reach London, particularly in connection with Sir Francis Drake's attack on Santo Domingo. If that assumption were proved correct, it would be doubly significant that, Shakespeare, under the influence of the anti-Jewish atmosphere of London in the 1590s, reversed the roles so that it was the Jewish usurer who demanded the Christian's flesh, rather than vice versa.

On the proceedings during the trial, see J. D. Rea, "Shylock and the Processus Belial," *Philological Quarterly*, VIII, 311–13 (showing that Shakespeare borrowed many elements from the folkloristic descriptions of a trial in which the devil presented his claim to rule over all, or segments, of humanity, since man's fall, but was defeated by the Virgin, who opposed his insistence on justice by an appeal to mercy); and S. J. Sevin, "The Trial of Shylock according to Jewish Law" (Hebrew), *Sinai*, II, Part 1, Nos. 1–2, pp. 55–71, 246, which includes additional notes by the editor, Jehudah Leb Fischman (Maimon) and others, *ibid.*, pp. 70–71, 246. Sevin *et al.* emphasize that, according to Jewish law, no one has the right to dispose of his body or any limb thereof, which belong only to God; that is why, for instance, a defendant's confession does not suffice for a court to condemn him to severe physical punishment. This point had been clearly stated by the twelfth- and fifteenth-century rabbis Joseph ibn Megas and David ibn Abi Zimra. See also, from another angle, L. Kellner's "Shakespeare and the *Pirqe Abot* [*Sayings of the Fathers*]" (Hebrew), *Debir*, I, 285–88 (several examples persuaded Kellner, an authority on Shakespeare, that the poet's apothegms reveal astonishing similarity not only with some sayings of the ancient rabbis—which he might have read in Latin versions by Paul Fagius or Paul Weidner, though it is unlikely that he read them at all—but also with some statements in the Talmud, for which Kellner was unable to furnish any intermediary source). The specific motif of the pound of flesh has been comprehensively analyzed by B. V. Wenger in her "Shylock's Pfund Fleisch. Eine stoffgeschichtliche Untersuchung," *Shakespeare Jahrbuch*, LXV, 92–174; with the comments thereon by M. Schlauch, "The Pound of Flesh in the Germanic North," *Journal of English and German Philology*, XXX, 348–60; and by J. L. Cardozo in "The Background of Shakespeare's *Merchant of Venice*," *English Studies*, XIV, 117–86; all showing that, though this theme is not part of universal folklore (it has not been found in Chinese, Malayan, or Amerindian sources), it bears resemblance to tales widespread in Europe and the Middle East since Roman times; B. Nelson and J. Starr, "The Legend of the Divine Surety and the Jewish Moneylender," *Annuaire* of the Institut de philologie et d'histoire orientales . . . Brussels, VII, 289–338; and other sources listed by S. A. Tannenbaum in his *Shakespeare's The Merchant of Venice (a Concise Bibliography)*, esp. pp. 54 ff., 58 ff. See also more recent detailed bibliographies such as G. R. Smith, comp., *A Classified Shakespeare Bibliography 1936–1958;* P. Genzel, comp., "Shakespeare-Bibliographie für 1964–65," and "Shakespeare-Bibliographie für 1966," *Deutsche Shakespeare-Gesellschaft West Jahrbuch*, Supplement to CIII; and CIV, 333–423; R. E. Habenicht's annual compilation, in the *Shakespeare Quarterly*, "Shakespeare: an Annotated World Bibliography," XVII, 213–342; XVIII, 207–334; XIX, 213–313, etc., esp. XVII, 291–306, presenting a comprehensive listing on "Shakespeare in Israel: a Bibliography for the Years 1950–1965" consisting of some 250 entries (Nos. 1357–1606); and L. Prager, "Shakespeare in Yiddish," *Shakespeare Quarterly*, XIX, 149–63: Beginning with Bezalel Wischnipolski's Yiddish rendition of *Julius Caesar* in 1888, which followed I. E. Salkinson's Hebrew translation of *Othello* (*Itiel*, 1874) and *Romeo and Juliet* (*Ram ve-Ya'el*, 1878), both with introductions by Perez Smolenskin (with an informative Biographical-Bibliographical Appendix; pp. 159 ff.).

71. See Philip Henslowe, *The Diary*, ed. by W. W. Gregg, I, 13 ff., 21 ff., 187; II, 151, and other references listed in the Index, II, 389, with H. S. Bennett's comments thereon in his Intro. to *The Jew of Malta*, in Marlowe's *Works*, III, 1 f.; S. L.

Lee in his "Elizabethan England and the Jews," *Transactions* of the New Shakespeare Society, 1st ser., pp. 143–66, esp. p. 161. See also A. M. Levi, "Una Nobile figura di usuraio ebreo in un dramma inglese del 1584," *RMI*, XXI, 382–86 (from her thesis *L'Ebreo del dramma inglese fino a Shakespeare);* A. B. Stonex, "The Usurer in Elizabethan Drama," *PMLA*, XXXI, 190–210; H. Michelson, *The Jew in Early English Literature*, esp. pp. 66 ff.; E. D. Coleman, *The Jew in English Drama: an Annotated Bibliography*, p. viii nn. 3–4; E. Rosenberg, *From Shylock to Svengali: Jewish Stereotypes in English Fiction;* and *infra*, n. 72.

72. See *supra*, n. 61; A. J. Loomie, *The Spanish Elizabethans: the English Exiles at the Court of Philip II;* A. Tretiak, "The Merchant of Venice and the 'Alien' Question," *Review of English Studies*, V, 402–409; M. F. Modder, *The Jew in the Literature of England*, pp. 20 ff.; Petruccio Ubaldini, cited by G. Mattingly in *The Armada*, p. 344. After reviewing forty-seven Elizabethan plays, Louis Wann found that their authors generally evinced considerable hostility toward strangers, especially Orientals. In every one of the six plays in which a Jew plays a significant role, "he is *the* villain, or *one* of them. He is either a grasping miser or a treacherous tool, and no sympathy is ever shown to him." See Wann, "The Oriental in Elizabethan Drama," *Modern Philology*, XII, 423–47, esp. pp. 441–42. See also L. S. Brown's Duke University dissertation, *The Portrayal of Spanish Characters in Selected Plays of the Elizabethan and Jacobean Eras, 1585–1625* (typescript), summarized in *Dissertation Abstracts*, XXVII, 1779 A f.

The figure of 10,000 foreigners in London is probably correct, although the official record submitted by the mayor and alderman in 1571 counted only 4,631 aliens (some 80 percent of them Dutch; the number actually declined two years later). See E. N. Adler, *London* (Jewish Communities Series), pp. 80 ff. However, this report is manifestly incomplete; for instance, it included only 7 "Portugals," which was but a small fraction of the existing Portuguese group. See also C. W. Chitty, "Aliens in England in the Sixteenth Century," *Race, The Journal of the Institute of Race Relations*, London, VIII, 129–45, with reference to the antialien riots of 1517 and 1593 in London, and of 1570 in Norwich. Those of 1593, incidentally, help us explain the popular hostility toward New Christians during the Lopez trial.

73. See A. J. Loomie, *Toleration and Diplomacy: the Religious Issue in Anglo-Spanish Relations, 1603–1605 (Transactions* of the American Philosophical Society, n.s. LIII No. 6); *infra*, Chap. LXV, nn. 18 and 63; Thomas Wilson, *A Discourse upon Usury, By Way of Dialogue and Orations, for the Better Variety and More Delight of All Those That Shall Read This Treatise*, London, 1572, pp. 232, 257, 269, 283; new ed. with an Historical Intro. by R. H. Tawney, esp. pp. 115 ff.; C. H. George, "English Calvinist Opinions on Usury, 1600–1640," *Journal of the History of Ideas*, XVIII, 455–74; the reflection of these attitudes in A. B. Stonex's aforementioned study, "The Usurer in Elizabethan Drama," *PMLA*, XXXI, 190–210; and M. A. R. Lunn's more recent Birmingham thesis, *Attitudes to Usury in England in the 16th and 17th Centuries*. On the preferential treatment extended at the beginning of the sixteenth century to Spanish importers, see "The Rate of the King's Custom and Subsidy of Merchandises Registered in the Exchequer," reproduced in *The Tudor Constitution: Documents and Commentary*, ed. with an Intro. by G. R. Elson, pp. 48 ff.; and, in contrast thereto, H. Taylor's "Price

Revolution or Price Revision? The English and Spanish Trade after 1604," *Renaissance and Modern Studies*, XII, 5–32. See also R. W. Kenny's colorful description, "Peace with Spain, 1605," *History Today*, XX, 198–208; and, more generally, E. Schulin, *Handelsstaat England. Das politische Interesse der Nation am Aussenhandel vom 16. bis ins frühe 18. Jahrhundert.*

Toward the end of the sixteenth century, the growing interplay of England's political, economic, and religious factors; the need for religious solace among explorers and adventurers in their herculean empire-building tasks; and the pressures of international conflicts, offered many stimuli to religious intolerance toward all dissenters, including the New Christian merchants. See the pertinent observation by L. B. Wright in his *Religion and Empire: The Alliance between Piety and Commerce in English Expansion, 1558–1625;* and T. K. Rabb's *Enterprise and Empire: Merchant and Gentry Investment in the Expansion of England, 1575–1630.* See also F. J. Fischer, "London's Export Trade in the Early Seventeenth Century," *EcHR*, 2d ser. III, 151–61; and the pertinent essays included in Fisher's ed. of *Essays in the Economic and Social History of Tudor and Stuart England. In Honour of R. H. Tawney.*

74. [B.] L. Abrahams, "Two Jews before the Privy Council and an English Law Court in 1614–15." *JQR*, [o.s.] XIV, 354–58; H. I. Bloom, *The Economic Activities of the Jews of Amsterdam*, pp. 12 ff., 79 f.; and, particularly, D. Abulafia-Corcos, "Samuel Pallache and his Trial in London" (Hebrew), *Zion*, XXV, 122–33; *supra*, Chap. LXIII, n. 59; *infra*, nn. 75, 77. It may be noted, however, that the influence of the Privy Council on England's governmental affairs steadily declined under James I and Charles I. See J. D. Lind's recent University of Minnesota dissertation, *The Privy Council and Government Economic Policy in England, 1603–1637* (typescript). Pallache's difficulties must have been aggravated by the growing Anglo-Dutch commercial rivalries, which ultimately led to open warfare between those former anti-Spanish allies. See G. Edmundson, *Anglo-Dutch Rivalry in the First Half of the Seventeenth Century*, esp. pp. 21 ff., 36 ff. (on the fishery disputes which, beginning in 1609, greatly disturbed the relations between the two countries). Of minor interest are the observations, usually superficial and often erroneous, made by a twenty-two-year-old German tourist during a sojourn of seven weeks in England in 1616. See A. Ernstberger, "London und England in 1611. Ein Reisebericht des Nürnberger Jungpatriziers Hans Wilhelm I. Kress von Kressenstein," *Jahrbuch für fränkische Landesforschung*, XXIII, 139–53. See also Abraham Cohen's *An Anglo-Jewish Scrapbook, 1600–1840. The Jew through English Eyes*, esp. pp. 213 ff. (referring mainly to later periods).

75. See, for instance, M. Möring, "Die Englische Kirche in Hamburg und die Merchant Adventurers," *Hamburgische Geschichts- und Heimatsblätter*, XX, 93–112; H. Zins, *Anglia a Bałtyk w drugiej połowie XVI wieku* (England and the Baltic in the Latter Half of the Sixteenth Century: The Baltic Trade of English Merchants in Poland in the Elizabethan Age and the Eastland Company); F. Braudel, *La Méditerranée et le Monde Méditerranéen à l'époque de Philippe II*, 2d ed. rev., I, 560 ff.; H. M. Robertson, *Aspects of the Rise of Economic Individualism: a Criticism of Max Weber and His School*, new ed.; *supra*, Vols. XIII, pp. 295, 463 n. 104; XIV, p. 405; and *infra*, Vol. XVI. The tendency to treat Jews as individuals became even more marked with the progress of English mercantilism

in the Cromwellian age and after. It was to lead to the 1697 regulation of the Royal Stock Exchange in London, which reserved 12 out of 124 seats at the Exchange for Jews, and was the "First Stage of Anglo-Jewish Emancipation," according to L. Wolf's felicitous description in his *Essays in Jewish History*, ed. by C. Roth, pp. 115–43. For that period, see also R. Grassby's succinct analysis of "English Merchant Capitalism in the Late Seventeenth Century: the Composition of Business Fortunes," *Past and Present*, No. 46, pp. 87–107.

Needless to say, the bibliography of English economic history has been growing by leaps and bounds. See esp. the annual "List of Publications on the Economic History of Great Britain and Ireland," published by R. S. Craig and N. B. Harte; and the lists for 1966–69 which appeared in *EcHR*, 2d ser. XXI, 620–45; XXII, 323–41; XXIII, 352–79; XXIV, 267–91, respectively.

76. See J. P. Kenyon, ed., *The Stuart Constitution, 1603–1688. Documents and Commentary*, esp. pp. 91, 456 ff.; M. A. S. Hume, *The Great Lord Burghley, passim;* William Allen, *An Admonition to the Nobility and People of England and Ireland concerning the Present Wars;* F. Edwards, *Guy Fawkes: the Real Story of the Gunpowder Plot.* See also *The Letters and Memorials by William Cardinal Allen,* ed. by the Fathers of the Congregation of the London Oratory, with an Historical Introduction by T. F. Knox, esp. pp. 16 No. i, 299 ff. No. clxxvii, 332 f. No. cxcix; T. H. Clancy, *Papist Pamphleteers: the Allen-Persons Party and the Political Thought of the Counter-Reformation in England, 1572–1615;* and, more generally, P. McGrath, *Papists and Puritans under Elizabeth I.*

77. Sir Marmaduke Langdale's letter to Sir Edward Nicholas of Sept. 20, 1655, in *The Nicholas Papers*, ed. by G. F. Warner, III, 51; *Calendar of State Papers, Venice*, XI (1607–1610), ed. by Horatio F. Brown, pp. 319 f. No. 588; L. Firpo, ed., *Relazioni di ambasciatori veneti al Senato. Tratte dalle migliori edizioni disponibili e ordinati cronologicamente*, Vol. I: Inghilterra, pp. 471 ff., 586; C. Roth, *History of the Jews in England*, p. 280, citing the Tuscan dispatch from an archival document from Florence; Robert Parsons' [or Person's] 1580 letter to Acquaviva, cited by P. Caraman, ed., in *The Other Face*, p. 61; Sir Edward Coke, *The Second Part of the Institutes of the Laws of England Containing the Exposition of Many Ancient and Other Statutes*, 3d (London, 1669) ed., pp. 506 ff.; *supra*, n. 1. See C. W. Johnson, *The Life of Sir Edward Coke, Lord Chief Justice of England in the Reign of James I. With Memoirs of His Contemporaries*, esp. II, 389 f.

Other influential leaders may have been less discerning than Coke in economic matters. In fact, it has been shown that even before the end of Elizabeth's reign, the well-to-do Catholics had been largely eliminated, leaving behind a mass of poor and lower-middle-class "Papists." Under the circumstances, wealthy New Christians must have aroused the ire of Church of England extremists even more if they were genuinely professing Catholics than if they fit the Venetian envoy's description and were secret Jews at heart. See the data supplied by W. R. Trimble in *The Catholic Laity*, pp. 178 ff. On the other hand, Coke's "inconsistency" appears less surprising when one realizes that his general behavior earned him the characterization "myth-maker" in C. Hill's *Intellectual Origins of the English Revolution*, pp. 225 ff., 233 ff., 256 ff. Coke's general intolerance is well described by C. D. Bowen in *The Lion and the Throne: the Life and Times of*

Sir Edward Coke (1552–1634), esp. p. 257. On the justice's general repudiation of the validity of Jewish testimony, and his curious theory concerning the effects of the expulsion of the Jews from England in 1290, see H. S. Q. Henriques, *The Jews and the English Law*, pp. 58 f., 178 f., 186 ff. It was an example of the frequent use of historical arguments in support of political biases. See P. Styles, "Politics and Historical Research in the Early Seventeenth Century" in L. Fox's ed. of *English Historical Scholarship in the Sixteenth and Seventeenth Centuries*, pp. 49–72, esp. pp. 55 ff.; and *infra*, n. 99. Coke's religious narrow-mindedness could well go hand in hand with his general economic liberalism, which may have helped to determine his favorable decision in the case of Samuel Pallache. See *supra*, n. 74. The dichotomy in the famous jurist's personality, and its impact on the progress of capitalism on the British Isles, has been aptly reexamined by B. Melament in "The 'Economic Liberalism' of Sir Edward Coke," *Yale Law Journal*, LXXVI, 1321–58 (a "liberalism" of "a distinctly Tudor cast . . . as alien to the early nineteenth century as [it was] familiar to the sixteenth").

78. Joseph Wybarne, *Machiavellus* (1597); H. P. Stokes, *Studies in Anglo-Jewish History*, pp. 207 ff.; Christopher Marlowe, *The Jew of Malta*, The Prologue Spoken at Court, in *The Works*, ed. by A. Dyce, I, 230; H. Michelson, *The Jew in Early English Literature*, pp. 73 ff.; F. G. Fleay, *A Biographical Chronicle of the English Drama, 1559–1642*, II, 274; A. M. Hyamson, *The Sephardim of England*, p. 9.

79. William Tyndale, Preface to his trans. of Genesis, London, 1530, reproduced in C. H. Williams's ed. of *English Historical Documents* (in David C. Douglas's series, Vol. V), p. 820 No. 118; C. H. Williams, *William Tyndale*, esp. pp. 65 ff.; G. M. Trevelyan, *England under the Stuarts*, 15th ed., pp. 60 f.; *supra*, nn. 23 ff.; and Chap. LXIII, n. 32. See also, more generally, A. S. Herbert's *Historical Catalogue of Printed Editions of the English Bible, 1525–1961*, rev. ed.; and the pertinent chapters in *The Cambridge History of the Bible*, Vols. II and III, ed. by G. W. H. Lampe and S. L. Greenslade, respectively. On the Authorized Version, see *infra*, n. 80.

80. Philippus Ferdinandus, *Haec sunt verba Dei, . . . Praecepta . . . translata in linguam latinam*, Cambridge, 1597; Joseph J. Scaliger, *Epistolae omnes quae reperiri potuerunt*, pp. 208 No. lxvi, 594 No. ccxciii; S. Stein, "Philippus Ferdinandus Polonus; a Sixteenth Century Hebraist in England," *Essays in Honour of J. H. Hertz*, pp. 397–412; *supra*, Chap. LXIII, n. 47; and Vol. XIII, pp. 167, 209 f., 243, 396 f. n. 9, 406 n. 23, 416 f. n. 5. See also J. A. B. van den Brink, "Bible and Biblical Theology in the Early Reformation," *Scottish Journal of Theology*, XIV, 337–52; E. J. Rosenthal, "Rashi and the English Bible," *BJRL*, XXIV, 138–67 (includes twenty-one examples of Rashi's interpretation followed in the English versions, pp. 151 ff.; and a number of illustrations of its impact on English Bible commentaries, pp. 162 ff.); idem, "Edward Lively, Cambridge Hebraist," *Essays and Studies Presented to Stanley Arthur Cook*, ed. by D. W. Thomas, pp. 95–112. Despite the availability of these and numerous other studies, some of which are mentioned in the next note, Israel Baroway is right in stressing the present inadequacy of research in Christian Hebraism of the Tudor-Jacobean

Age and in pointing up a number of lacunae. See his "Toward Understanding Tudor-Jacobean Hebrew Studies," *JSS*, XVIII, 3–24 (with a rich bibliography).

The impact, however indirect, of the Jews in England on the preparation of the 1611 Authorized Version of the Bible, will be discussed more fully in a later chapter. For the time being, we need but refer to C. C. Butterworth, *The Literary Lineage of the King James Bible, 1340–1611* (considers 1534 and George Joye's translation of the Psalter to be "a critical point"; pp. 71 ff.); D. Daiches, *The King James Version of the English Bible: an Account of the Development and Sources of the English Bible of 1611 with Special Reference to the Hebrew Tradition;* H. W. Robinson, ed., *The Bible in Its Ancient and English Versions,* esp. pp. 128–45 ("The English Versions [to Wyclif]," by W. A. Craigie), 146–95 ("The Sixteenth-Century English Versions"), and 196–234 ("The Authorized Version and After"; both by J. Isaacs); and the works listed *supra,* n. 79; Vol. VI, pp. 272 ff., 462 f. nn. 51–52; XIII, pp. 160 ff., 209 ff., 390 ff. nn. 3–9, 416 ff. nn. 5–6. See also such monographs as Frank Rosenthal, "Robert Wakefield and the Beginnings of Biblical Studies in Tudor England," *Crozer Quarterly,* XXIX, 173–80; G. Gray, *William Tyndale and the English Bible;* R. H. Milner, "The English Bible 1611–1961; Some Literary Considerations" *Babel,* IX, 70–79.

Clearly, Bible translators were interested in Scriptural texts not merely from their philological and historical aspects but also, as a rule, to derive from them support for their own doctrinal beliefs. See, for example, W. E. Nix, "Theological Presuppositions and Sixteenth Century English Bible Translation," *Bibliotheca Sacra,* CXXIV, 42–50, 117–24; and, more generally, with reference to parallel efforts on the Continent, W. Schwarz, *Principles and Problems of Biblical Translation: Some Reformation Controversies and Their Background.* On James I's religiopolitical orientation, see, for instance, A. J. Loomie's *Toleration and Diplomacy: the Religious Issue in Anglo-Spanish Relations 1603–1605;* and H. Witte, *Die Ansichten Jakobs I. von England über Kirche und Staat, mit besonderer Berücksichtigung der religiösen Toleranz.*

Not surprisingly, biblical lore had an enormous influence on the poetry and drama of the period. See the comprehensive bibliography compiled by E. D. Coleman in *The Bible in English Drama: an Annotated List of Plays including Translation from Other Languages;* M. Roston, *Biblical Drama in England from the Middle Ages to the Present Day,* esp. pp. 49 ff., 87 ff.; and such more detailed monographs as C. Ackerman, *The Bible in Shakespeare.* Nor did the graphic arts escape the overwhelming impact of the Old Testament narratives and teachings. See esp. H. Heimann's notes on the 225 excellent reproductions assembled in *The Bible in Art. Miniatures, Paintings, Drawings, and Sculptures Inspired by the Old Testament,* with an Intro. by M. Brion.

81. See F. A. Patterson *et al.*'s comprehensive Columbia University ed. of *The Works of John Milton;* J. L. Blau, *The Christian Interpretation of the Cabala in the Renaissance,* with additional notes by him in "The Diffusion of the Christian Interpretation of the Cabala in English Literature," *Review of Religion,* VI, 146–68; and by R. M. Benbow in "Cabalism in Renaissance England," *Notes and Queries,* CCIII, 54–55; *supra,* Vol. XIII, pp. 180 f., 403 ff. nn. 20 and 23; and *passim.*

As with all other aspects of John Milton's work, the influence of his Hebraic studies on his outlook and writings has been discussed and rediscussed for generations. Suffice it to mention here the following more recent studies: A. D.

Hallam, "Milton's Knowledge and Use of Hebrew," *Milla wa-Milla; The Australian Bulletin of Comparative Religion*, V, 18–22; M. Boddy, "Milton's Translation of Psalms 80–88," *Modern Philology*, LXIV, 1–9 (describing its part in the 1648 war of propaganda over the fate of Charles I); J. M. Steadman, "Milton and the *Argumentum Paris*: Biblical Exegesis and Rhetoric," *Archiv für das Studium der neueren Sprachen und Literaturen*, CCII, 347–60 (with reference to the crucial difference between translating Isaiah's *Adameh le-'elyon* (14:14) as "I shall make myself *like* the most high," or "*equal* to the most high"); J. M. Evans, *Paradise Lost and the Genesis Tradition;* J. H. Sims, *The Bible in Milton's Epics* (understandably showing a vast preponderance of Old Testament passages and ideas; see the Indexes, pp. 259 ff., 279 ff.); H. S. Gehman, "Milton's Use of Hebrew in the *De Doctrina Christiana*," *JQR*, XXIX, 37–44 (with special reference to the divine names in the Bible; attributes "the serious errors in accentuation and vocalization" in the Hebrew words to an amanuensis, rather than to Milton himself); M. Kelley, *This Great Argument: a Study of Milton's De Doctrina Christiana as a Gloss upon Paradise Lost;* J. Z. Werblowsky, "Milton and the *Conjectura cabbalistica*," *Journal of the Warburg and Courtauld Institutes*, XVIII, 90–113; and, more generally, J. Bradshaw, *Concordance to the Poetical Works of John Milton*. See also such more specialized analyses as G. McColley's "The Book of Enoch and Paradise Lost," *HTR*, XXXI, 21–39 (claims that, "with the possible exception of Genesis, there is no single book in the Old and New Testaments or in apocryphal and pseudepigraphic literature, in which are concentrated more conceptions fundamental to Milton's epic"); and the "alternative hypothesis" suggested by A. Williams in "Milton and the Book of Enoch," *ibid.*, XXXIII, 291–99 (reviews, in particular, pertinent material in contemporary biblical commentaries by Andrew Willet and others); D. C. Allen, "Milton and Rabbi Eliezer," *Modern Language Notes*, LXIII, 262–63, offering four illustrations likely to have been borrowed directly or indirectly, from the *Pirqe de-Rabbi Eliezer);* D. M. Berry's dissertation, *The Doctrine of the Remnant 1550–1660. A Study in the History of English Puritanism and Paradise Lost;* and, particularly, H. F. Fletcher's twin books, *Milton's Semitic Studies and Some Manifestations of Them in His Poetry* and *Milton's Rabbinical Readings;* as well as his essays on the relations between Milton and Yosippon, Rashi, and Gersonides, listed in his Bibliography appended to the *Milton Studies* in his honor, pp. 240 f. Some repercussions in the American colonies are briefly pointed out by S. Bercovitch in "Cotton Mather Against Rhyme: Milton and the *Psalterium Americanum*," *American Literature*, XXXIX, 191–93; and, more generally, R. D. Havens's comprehensive study, *The Influence of Milton on English Poetry*. See also G. Qvarnström, *The Enchanted Palace: Some Structural Aspects of Paradise Lost*, emphasizing, in particular, the differences between the first edition, in ten books, of 1667, and the second edition, in twelve books, of 1674.

On other Christian Hebraists of the period mentioned in the text, see *supra*, n. 80; Frank Rosenthal, "Robert Wakefield," *Crozer Quarterly*, XXIX, 173–80; C. Roth, "Sir Thomas Bodley, Hebraist," *The Bodleian Library Record*, VII, 242–51; idem, "An Additional Note on the Kennicott Bible," *ibid.*, VI, 659–62; the scholars analyzed by S. Levy in his "English Students of Maimonides," *Miscellanies JHSE*, IV, 61–84 (includes interesting excerpts from Ralph Skynner's letters to Bishop James Ussher; in one letter, this translator of the first book of the Maimonidean Code expressed his bewilderment about Maimonides, "the ocean of all Jewish learning, the quarries of silver and gold whose . . . fame surpasses the Indies; [yet] his wine is mixed now and then with water, and his silver with some dross"); by I. Baroway in *JSS*, XVIII, 3–24; and, more fully, by A. Schper [Spears], in his London dissertation, *Christian Hebraists in Sixteenth-Century England* (typescript); and by H. Fisch, *Jerusalem and Albion: the Hebraic Factor in XVIIth-Century Literature*. See also various additional entries in Roth's *Magna Bibliotheca Anglo-Judaica*, esp. pp. 329 ff., 343 ff., 361 ff. (regrettably R. P. Lehmann's *Nova Bibliotheca Anglo-Judaica* does not update these particular sections); and those listed in my *Bibliography of Jewish Social Studies, 1938–39, passim*. Characteristically, interest in Hebrew carried over not only into the related Aramaic-Syriac (Chaldaic) texts but also, as with Edward Pococke, into Arabic letters. See, for instance, P. M. Holt, "The Study of Arabic Historians in Seventeenth-Century England: the Background and the Work of Edward Pococke," *BSOAS*, XIX, 445–55 (with a brief survey of other European countries). Many of these English Hebraists will reappear in various connections in our later chapters.

82. William Perkins, *A Treatise of the Vocations, or Callings of Men with the Sorts and Kindes of Them, and the Right Use Thereof*, in *The Workes*, London, 1612–13, I, 747–79; H. M. Robertson, *Aspects of the Rise of Economic Individualism*, pp. 15 ff.; R. M. Krapp, "A Note on the Puritan 'Calling,'" *Review of Religion*, VII, 242–51; House of Commons *Journals*, V, 512, cited and analyzed by I. Abrahams and C. E. Sayle in "The Purchase of Hebrew Books by the English Parliament in 1647," *TJHSE*, VIII, 63–77, esp. p. 67; C. Roth, "The Marrano Typography in England," *The Library*, 5th ser. XV, 118–28, with a few corrections suggested by I. S. Révah in his review of that essay in *REJ*, CXX, 400–401. See also, more generally, the literature listed *supra*, Vol. XIII, pp. 294 ff., 463 nn. 103–104.

Parliament's investment of £500 in a Hebrew library in the midst of a raging civil war and great fiscal stringency is doubly significant when it is compared with the prevailing market prices for books. See, for instance, I. Roy, "The Libraries of Edward, 2nd Viscount Conway and Others: an Inventory and Valuation of 1643," *BIHR*, XLI, 35–46 (with an Appendix: "Owners and their Libraries"); and, for the entire period to 1640, H. S. Bennett's noteworthy trilogy *English Books and Readers*, for the years 1475–1557, 1558–1603, and 1603–1640. Hebrew presses were also needed to provide the frequent Hebrew quotations and other inserts in English and Latin works. Such assistance was occasionally required even in the struggling English colonies in America. See W. Eames, "On the Use of Hebrew Types in English America before 1735," *Studies in Jewish Bibliography . . . in Memory of Abraham Solomon Freidus*, pp. 481–502. See also L. B. Wright, *Religion and Empire: The Alliance between Piety and Commerce in English Expansion, 1558–1625*.

83. [Robert Parsons], *A Brief Discovrse*, cited *supra*, n. 64; Thomas Draxe, *The Worlde's Resurrection, or the Generall Calling of the Iewes: a Familiar Commentary on the Eleventh Chapter of Saint Paul to the Romains*, London, 1608, esp. the opening paragraph; Leonard Busher, *Religious Peace: or, a Plea for Liberty of Conscience . . . Presented to King James and the High Court of Parliament*, reprinted in *Tracts on Liberty of Conscience and Persecution, 1614–1661*, ed. with an Historical Intro. by E. B. Underhill, pp. 1–81, esp. pp. 28, 30 f., 47, 70 f.; E. N. Adler, *London*, pp. 85 f.; and C. Roth, "Jews in Oxford after 1290," *Oxoniensia*,

XV, 63–80, esp. pp. 65 f. Perhaps Parsons was not the authentic voice of English Catholicism. A former Protestant and in 1580 a Jesuit expatriate, he was more a diplomat and pamphleteer than a man of God. In his secret mission to England of that year, he sought by all means at his disposal to subvert the Elizabethan regime. In this agitation he may have tried to captivate the benevolence of the small, but influential and wealthy, group of New Christian "Catholics." Yet there must have been many other Catholics in England who like Parsons, saw in Puritanism and the Church of England, rather than in Judaism, the chief enemy of their Church. On Casaubon, see also F. Secret's "Notes sur les Hébraïsants," *REJ*, CXXX, 223 f.

84. Sir Henry Finch, *The World's Greatest Restauration; or, The Calling of the Ievves, and (With Them) of All the Nations and Kingdomes of the Earth, to the Faith of Christ*, London, 1621. See F. Kobler's fine analysis in "Sir Henry Finch (1558–1625) and the First English Advocates of the Restoration of the Jews to Palestine," *TJHSE*, XVI, 101–120; and some other related pamphlets listed in C. Roth's *Magna Bibliotheca Anglo-Judaica*, pp. 372 ff. See also *supra*, nn. 20–21.

85. Bernardino de Mendoza's 1581–82 dispatches to Philip II, reproduced in an English trans. in Public Record Office, *Calendar of State Papers*, Spanish, 1580–86, pp. 179 No. 139, 287 No. 218, 306 No. 225; Ireland, 1574–85, pp. 467 item 67, 468 item 72, 472 item 4, 474 items 26–27, 483 item 17, 557 item 48; L. Wolf, *Jews in Elizabethan England*, pp. 14 and 16; James Harrington, *The Oceana and Other Works*, ed. by J. Toland, p. 36; ed. by J. B. Liljengren, p. 11; as well as Liljengren's analysis in his "Harrington and the Jews," *Årsberättelse* (Bulletin) of the Société royale de Lettres of Lund, IV, 65–92. Mendoza probably described William Ames' features in order to facilitate his detection by the Spanish police in Lisbon, where William had been sent by Dom Antonio with letters to some of his partisans. See also, more generally, the debate between C. B. Macpherson and J. F. H. New in the former's "Harrington's 'Opportunity State,'" *Past and Present*, No. 17, pp. 45–70; New's critique thereof in his "Harrington a Realist?" *ibid.*, No. 24, pp. 75–81; and Macpherson's "Harrington, a Realist: a Rejoinder," *ibid.*, pp. 82–85. On the Jews in Ireland, see *supra*, Vol. IV, pp. 82, 280 n. 108; and *infra*, n. 90.

86. John Weemes (or Weemse), *The Christian Synagogue. Wherein is Contained the Diverse Reading, the Right Poynting, Translation, and Collation of Scripture with Scripture, With the Customes of the Hebrews and Proselytes, and of All Those Nations, With Whom They Were Conversant*, London, 1623 (4th ed., 1635); idem, *A Treatise of the Four Degenerate Sonnes, viz., the Atheist, the Magician, the Idolater, and the Jew. Wherein are Handled Many Profitable Questions Concerning Atheisme, Witchcraft, Idolatry, and Iudaisme: and Sundry Places of Scripture Cleared Out of the Originall Tongues*, London, 1636. Among these questions is "whether the Jews are to be suffered in a Christian Commonwealth or not?"— to the airing of which the author devotes an entire chapter (VI) in the section dealing with Jews (pp. 337 ff.). On the title page of this book, as well as in both texts, the author frequently cited Hebrew passages, biblical and rabbinic. See also J. Bowman's analysis, "A Seventeenth-Century Bill of 'Rights' for Jews," *JQR*, XXXIX, 379–95. Incidentally, in arguing for the equality of rights of converts,

Weemes emphasized the great contributions many of them had made to Christian students of the Bible, from the days of St. Jerome on. He paraphrased the Jewish adage "from *Moses* to *Moses* [Maimonides] there arose no such a *Moses*" by stating: "from *Immanuel* Jesus Christ to Immanuel Tremellius there arose no such an Immanuel" (p. 343).

87. See H. E. I. Phillips, "An Early Stuart Judaising Sect," *TJHSE*, XV, 63–72 largely based upon the unpublished Pagitt papers; and, more generally, C. E. Whiting, *Studies in English Puritanism from the Restoration to the Revolution, 1660–1668*, esp. pp. 314 ff.

88. Samuel Richardson, *The Necessity of Toleration in Matters of Religion*, London, 1637, reprinted in *Tracts on Liberty of Conscience and Persecution, 1614–1661*, ed. with an Historical Intro. by E. B. Underhill, I, 233–85, esp. p. 265; Roger Williams, *The Bloudy Tenent of Persecution for Cause of Conscience. Discussed in a Conference between Truth and Peace* (printed anonymously in London, 1644); idem, *Hireling Ministry None of Christ's*, London, 1652, together with his other works reprinted in his *Complete Writings*, ed. by S. L. Caldwell *et al.*, VII, 147–91, with Perry Miller's "An Essay in Interpretation," *ibid.*, pp. 5–25; O. S. Strauss, *Roger Williams, the Pioneer of Religious Liberty*, p. 178; P. Miller, *Roger Williams: His Contribution to the American Tradition*, esp. p. 255; Hugh Peters, *A Word for the Armie and Two Words to the Kingdome. To Cleare the One, and Cure the Other*, Art. 10; idem, *Good Work for a Good Magistrate*, pp. 53, 90; Edward Nicholas, *Apology for the Honourable Nation of the Jews, and All the Sons of Israel*, pp. 14 f. (this pamphlet was soon translated into Spanish). Matching action with preachment, Roger Williams effectively applied his doctrines in the newly founded colony of Rhode Island. See also LeRoy Moore, "Religious Liberty: Roger Williams and the Revolutionary Era," *CH*, XXXIV, 57–76; idem, "Roger Williams and the Historians," *ibid.*, XXXII, 432–51; and, more broadly, I. H. Polishook, *Roger Williams, John Cotton and Religious Freedom: a Controversy in New and Old England;* and J. Garrett's recent biography, *Roger Williams, Witness beyond Christendom, 1603–1683*.

To be sure, neither Williams nor the other advocates of toleration ever abandoned the idea of the Jews' ultimate conversion to Christianity. "It is no civil injury for any man," he declared, "to disturb or oppose a doctrine, worship, or government spiritual. Christ Jesus and his messengers and servants did, and do, profess a spiritual war against the doctrine, worship, and government of the Jewish, the Turkish, and other pagan and anti-Christian religions of all sorts and sects, churches and societies." But he demanded that such purely spiritual conflicts should never lead to "civil injury" of either party. See his *Bloody Tenent Yet More Bloody*, written in Rhode Island and brought with him to England in 1651, and published there in 1652, as reprinted in his *Complete Writings*, IV, esp. p. 266. Some other data are summarized and partially excerpted by L. Wolf in his *Menasseh ben Israel's Mission to Oliver Cromwell*, pp. xviii ff. Of course, these pamphlets were but a tiny fraction of the vast polemical literature which dinned into the ears of the English public the need for basic legal and religious reforms in English society and government. See esp. S. E. Prall, *The Agitation for Law Reform during the Puritan Revolution, 1640–1660;* K. T. Erikson, *Wayward Puritans: a Study in the Sociology of Deviance;* J. F. H. New,

Anglican and Puritan: the Basis for Their Opposition, 1558–1640; C. Bridenbaugh, *Vexed and Troubled Englishmen, 1590–1642;* and C. H. George's suggestive analysis in "Puritanism in History and Historiography," *Past and Present,* No. 41, pp. 77–104 (with ample bibliographical references).

89. Joanna and Ebenezer Cartwright, *Petition of the Jews for the Repealing of the Act of Parliament for their Banishment out of England;* the Venetian envoy Gerolamo Agostini's report of March 13, 1643, reproduced in an English trans. in the Public Record Office, *Calendar of State Papers,* Venice, XXVI, (1642–43), ed. by Allen B. Hinds, pp. 251 ff.; H. I. Bloom, *The Economic Activities of the Jews of Amsterdam,* pp. 105 ff. On the general economic trends of the period and their effect on public opinion with respect to freer competition and encouragement of immigration, and on Carvajal's early career, see L. Wolf, "The First English Jews: Notes on Antonio Fernandez Carvajal, with Some Biographical Documents," *TJHSE,* II, 14–46, esp. pp. 16 ff., 26; Don Patinkin, "Mercantilism and the Readmission of the Jews to England," *JSS,* VIII, 161–78; and other sources cited by M. James in her *Social Problems and Policy during the Puritan Revolution, 1640–1660,* esp. pp. 147 f., 183 ff., 188 ff. In many ways the tracts written during the 1640s for and against the toleration of Jews were direct preliminaries to the negotiations for the readmission of the Jews to England, dramatized in 1655 by the mission of Menasseh ben Israel to Oliver Cromwell and the debates at the Whitehall Conference. Although ending without a definite conclusion, these negotiations opened a historic chapter in the destinies of English Jewry will be more fully treated in a later volume. For the time being, but refer to L. Wolf's well-documented *Menasseh ben Israel's Mission;* C. Roth's *A Life of Menasseh ben Israel;* H. S. Q. Henriques, *The Jews and the English Law,* pp. 49 ff.; and M. Wilensky, *Shivat ha-Yehudim le-Angliah* (The Jews' Return to England in the Seventeenth Century), which also includes a succinct review of the earlier debates.

90. *Supra,* n. 66; Paul Jacob's letter first published by M. Adler in "History of the Domus Conversorum from 1290 to 1891," *TJHSE,* IV, 16–75, esp. pp. 73 f. (reprinted in his *Jews of Medieval England,* p. 376); also reproduced in C. Roth's *Anglo-Jewish Letters (1158–1917),* pp. 43 f.; L. Wolf, *The Jews in the Canary Islands,* pp. 33 ff., 183, 197; B. Shillman, *A Short History of the Jews in Ireland,* pp. 10 ff.; L. Hyman, *The Jews of Ireland,* pp. 6 ff. On the Jews in Malta and Gibraltar, see *supra,* Vol. XIV, pp. 50 f., 323 n. 47; and *infra,* Chap. LXV, n. 80. See also W. Lawlor, *The Reformation in Ireland.*

91. E. S. Daniels, *Extracts from Various Records of the Early Settlement of the Jews in the Island of Barbados, W. I.* (privately printed); H. Friedenwald, "Material for the History of the Jews in the British West Indies," *PAJHS,* V, 45–101 (chiefly after 1660); I. S. Emmanuel, "New Light on Early American Jewry," *AJA,* VII, 3–64 (also of interest for the Jewish communities in the Dutch and French colonies). We possess an interesting record of the Jews in Barbados in the noteworthy collection of *Monumental Inscriptions in the Burial Ground of the Jewish Synagogue at Bridgetown, Barbados,* Transcribed with an Intro. by E. M. Shilstone with a Foreword by S. W. Baron and a Preface by W. S. Samuel; and Samuel's "Review of the Jewish Colonists in Barbados in the Year 1680," *TJHSE,* XIII, 1–111. See

also, more generally, M. J. Chandler, *A Guide to the Records in Barbados*, esp. p. 37, referring to parochial registers of marriages, etc.; particularly Vol. C2, listing Jews from 1660 to 1886; and H. Kellenbenz's review article, "Von den Karibischen Inseln. Archive und neuere Literatur, insbesondere zur Geschichte von der Mitte des 17. bis zur Mitte des 19. Jahrhunderts," *JGLA*, V, 378–404.

Our information about the history of Jamaica and about the much shorter, though no less important, history of the Jewish community on the island, is far more limited. See J. A. P. M. Andrade's comprehensive survey, *A Record of the Jews in Jamaica from the English Conquest to the Present Time*, ed. by B. Parks; C. V. Black, *History of Jamaica*, Rev. ed.; and the literature listed there. Andrade contends that "the friendship which subsisted between Columbus and the Jews continued with his descendants, and as their proprietary rights excluded the Inquisition and prevented the inclusion of Jamaica in the bishopric of Cuba, unavowed Jews were enabled to live in Jamaica in comparative safety, even during the Spanish period." But the really known history of Jewish settlers on the island begins only with the English conquest in 1655. It may be noted that some Jewish residents of the West Indies secured letters of endenization from the British government long before such letters were issued to Jews in the British colonies on the American mainland or in the mother country. In fact, as early as 1661, Daniel Bueno Henriques was granted such a privilege. See S. Oppenheim, "A List of Jews Made Denizens in the Reign of Charles II and James II, 1661–1687," *PAJHS*, XX, 109–113 (compiled by P. Carteret Webb, a supporter of Pelham's "Jew Bill" in 1753).

Most remarkably, in the mid-eighteenth century, Jamaican Jews see⬛⬛⬛⬛e outstripped their coreligionists on the American mainland in their ea⬛⬛⬛o benefit from the privileges conferred on Jews by the British Naturalization Act of 1740. The documents extant in the Public Record Office in London and examined by J. H. Hollander, though possibly not quite complete, have shown that of the 189 identifiable American Jews who secured naturalization in the first thirteen years the Act was in effect (1740–53), the large majority (151) were from Jamaica, as against a mere 24 from New York. See Hollander, "The Naturalization of Jews in the American Colonies under the Act of 1740," *PAJHS*, VIII, 102–117; and my recent collection, *Steeled by Adversity: Essays and Addresses on American Jewish Life*, pp. 94 and 595 n. 28. See also *supra*, n. 60; and Chap. LXIII, nn. 79 ff.; *infra*, Chap. LXVI, n. 81.

Because they had attained a degree of equality, some Jews were able to acquire plantations, which they, like their neighbors, cultivated with the aid of slaves. Probably there were also some Jewish slave traders in the British and other colonies. Naturally, such employment and trade are highly repugnant to present-day feelings. But this emotional reaction, which has colored much of the historical literature on the institution of slavery, should not blind us to the exigencies and realities of the situation then prevailing. Note, for instance, D. W. Thoms's pertinent observations concerning some of the West-Indian islands; they have equal validity in many other areas as well. See his "Slavery in the Leeward Islands in the Mid Eighteenth Century: A Reappraisal," *BIHR*, XLII, 76–85, contrasting with the long-accepted views, such as those expounded by E. V. Gouveia in her *Slave Society in the British Leeward Islands at the End of the Eighteenth Century*. See also other sources mentioned by E. C. Baker in *A Guide to Records in the Leeward Islands*.

92. William Bradford, *History of "Plimouth Plantation,"* ed. from the Original Manuscript for the Commonwealth of Massachusetts, p. viii; W. Eames, "On the Use of Hebrew Types in English America," *Studies in Jewish Bibliography . . Freidus,* pp. 481 ff.; J. H. Primus, "The Role of the Covenant in the Puritanism of John Hooper," *Nederlands Archief voor Kerkgeschiedenis,* n.s. XLVIII, 182–96 (referring to an early forerunner of Puritanism who died as a martyr under Mary Stuart in 1555).

93. John Winthrop, "A Modell of Christian Charity" (1630) in *Winthrop Papers,* ed. by S. Mitchell *et al.,* II, 282–95, esp. p. 295; John Cotton, *An Abstract of the Lawes of New England [Moses, His Judicials],* reprinted in P. Force's *Tracts and Other Papers, Relating Principally to the Origin, Settlement and Progress of the Colonies in North America, from the Discovery of the Country to the Year 1776,* Vol. III, Pt. 9. The story of the Hebraic element in the civilization of colonial New England has often been told. It may be noted, for instance, that, the oldest American college, Harvard, not only included instruction in the Hebrew language as part of its curriculum but also demanded from its first graduating class in 1642 that they write papers on such topics as "Hebrew is the Mother of Languages." See, more generally, D. de Sola Pool, "Hebrew Learning Among the Puritans of New England prior to 1700," *PAJHS,* XX, 31–83, esp. pp. 39 f.; I. S. Meyer, "Hebrew at Harvard (1637–1760). A Résumé of the Information in Recent Publications," *ibid.,* XXXV, 145–70; and other studies cited in my *From Colonial Mansion to Skyscraper: An Emerging Pattern of Hebraic Studies* (reprinted from *Rutgers Hebraic Studies,* Vol. I). See also my *Steeled by Adversity,* where this and other essays are somewhat revised and brought up to date.

However, seventeenth-century Christian Hebraism in the American colonies was more an augury for the future than a mirror of contemporary realities, on which see, for instance, J. R. Marcus, *Early American Jewry.* Nor did the experience of English colonizers in America necessarily influence public opinion in the motherland to favor Jews. On the contrary, businessmen who had encountered stiff competition from Jewish traders in the New World often turned into Jew-baiters of the first order. For one example, John Bland, who had acquired in America a passionate hatred of the Jewish people, in his tract *Trade Revived* (London, 1659), called Jews "the Horseleeches of every Commonwealth, State and Kingdom, having ingrossed into their hands the quintessence of our trade with all other people and Nations . . . filling all parts wherever they arrive or be admitted, with false Money and Commodities, Usury and such like." Bland referred, especially, to Antonio Fernandez Carvajal. He advocated another expulsion of the Jews from England (pp. 20 f.). See E. Schulin, *Handelsstaat England,* pp. 169 f., 249.

94. See B. L. Abrahams, "A Jew in the Service of the East India Company in 1601," *JQR,* [o.s.] IX, 173–75; W. J. Fischel, "Abraham Navarro, Jewish Interpreter and Diplomat in the Service of the English East India Company (1682–1692)," *PAAJR,* XXV, 39–62; XXVI, 25–39; idem, "The Jewish Merchant Colony in Madras (Fort St. George) during the 17th and 18th Centuries: a Contribution to the Economic and Social History of the Jews in India," *Journal of Economic and Social History of the Orient,* III, 78–107, 175–95; idem, *Ha-Yehudim be-Hodu* (The Jews in India: Their Contribution to the Economic and Political Life); and some of the other

monographs by that author on Asian Jewish communities and outstanding individuals, for the most part in later periods. See also S. Mendelssohn's general survey, *The Jews of Asia, especially in the Sixteenth and Seventeenth Centuries,* which furnishes little information on Jews in the colonies of the Western powers, however; and the literature listed *supra,* nn. 58–59; Chap. LXIII, nn. 78 ff.; and *infra,* Chap. LXVI, nn. 108 ff. The developments affecting the local Jewish populations in parts of Africa and Asia before and after the European Expansion will be more fully analyzed in a later chapter.

95. R. M. Kingdon, "Some French Reactions to the Council of Trent," *CH,* XXXIII, 149–56 (exemplified by Calvin, the jurist Charles Dumoulin, and the historian Innocent Gentillet); W. S. Maltby, *The Black Legend in England: the Development of Anti-Spanish Sentiment, 1558–1660* (Diss. Duke University); and, more generally, the literature listed by L. Willaert in his *Après le Concile de Trente. La Restauration catholique, 1563–1648* (in A. Fliche *et al., Histoire de l'Église,* XVIII), esp. pp. 361 ff. ("Les Élements de l'Antiromanisme"). See also *infra,* Chap. LXV, nn. 3 and 16.

96. See, for instance, M. Yardeni's recent observations in her *La Conscience nationale en France à l'époque des guerres de religion (1559–1589),* and the literature listed there; and *supra,* Vol. XI, Chapter L, *passim.*

97. J. Cornwall, "Evidence of Population Mobility in the Seventeenth Century," *BIHR,* XL, 143–152; L. Stone, *The Crisis of the Aristocracy, 1558–1641,* esp. pp. 36 ff. (on social mobility), 39 ff. (on preeminence of land), 769 App. xiv (on biological failure, 1559–1641); W. Euler's Nazi-oriented accumulation of genealogical data, authentic, dubious, and spurious, in "Das Eindringen jüdischen Blutes in die englische Oberschicht," *Forschungen zur Judenfrage,* VI, 104–252, 282–314. See also, more generally, H. Kellenbenz, *Der Merkantilismus in Europa und die soziale Mobilität;* and local studies such as T. C. Dale, ed., *The Inhabitants of London in 1638,* editing, with a brief introduction, a contemporary MS entitled "Settlement of Tithes, 1638," extant in the Lambeth Palace Library.

98. See *supra,* nn. 74, 77; William Prynne, *A Short Demurrer to the Jewes Long Discontinued Remitter into England. Comprising, An Exact Chronological Relation of Their First Admission into, Their Ill Deportment, Misdemeanors, Condition, Sufferings, Oppressions, Slaughters, Plunders by Popular Insurrections, and Regal Exactions in; and Their Total Final Banishment by Iudgment and Edict of Parliament, Out of England, Never to Return Again. Collected Out of the Best Historians. With a Brief Collection of Such English Laws, Scriptures, as Seem Strongly to Plead and Conclude against Their Readmission into England. . . . With an Answer to the Chief Allegation for Their Introduction,* 2d ed. enlarged, London, 1656. (Although this work was characterized by much "nonsense, railing, improper instances misunderstood and misapplyed Authorities," as were some of his earlier writings, according to a critic in *A Word to Mr. Wil. Prynn Esq. and Two for the Parliament and Army,* London, 1648, it was to exert considerable influence on the negotiations for the readmission of the Jews to England in the mid-1650s.) Sharing with Coke many highly disagreeable personal traits, Prynne was even more intolerant of religious dissent of any kind. To the end of his life in 1669,

he was frequently embroiled in controversy and was among the leading book burners in seventeenth-century England. See the data accumulated by C. R. Gillett in his *Burned Books: Neglected Chapters in British History and Literature,* in the numerous entries listed in the Index, *s.v.* Prynne. Among the French historians, see esp. François de Belleforest, *Les Grandes Annales et histoire générale de France dès la venue des Francs en Gaule jusqu'au reigne du Roy très chrétien Henry III,* Paris, 1579. The fairly numerous, though for the most part incidental, references to medieval Jews by early modern French historians, particularly when they wished to explain the recurrent instances of intolerance from Dagobert to Philip the Fair and beyond, are well analyzed and documented by M. Yardeni in "The Jews in French Historiography of the Sixteenth and Seventeenth Centuries" (Hebrew), *Zion,* XXIV, 145–88.

99. See *supra,* n. 56; Jacques Basnage, *L'Histoire et la religion des Juifs depuis Jésus Christ jusqu'à présent,* Rotterdam, 1706–1711; 2d ed. enlarged, The Hague, 1716–26 (with contemporary English translations); E. A. Mailhet's Geneva dissertation, *Jacques Basnage, théologien, controversiste, diplomate et historien: sa vie et ses écrits;* and, more generally, A. Klempt, *Die Säkularisierung der universalhistorischen Auffassung. Zum Wandel des Geschichtsdenkens im 16. und 17. Jahrhundert,* esp. pp. 89 ff. (showing how De la Peyrère's pre-Adamite theory helped to undermine the universal acceptance of biblical chronology). See *supra,* n. 21. See also the data analyzed by J. P. Bodmer, "Die Französische Historiographie des Spätmittelalters und die Franken. Ein Beitrag zur Kenntnis des französischen Geschichtsdenkens," *Archiv für Kulturgeschichte,* XLV, 91–118; R. Mandrou, "L'Historiographie française des XVIe et XVIIe siècles: Bilans et perspectives," *French Historical Studies,* V, 57–66; Y. M. Bercé, "Historiographie des temps modernes. Travaux parus depuis 1950 sur l'histoire et les historiens français du XVIe au XVIIIe siècle," *BEC,* CXXIV, 281–95; L. Fox, ed., *English Historical Scholarship in the Sixteenth and Seventeenth Centuries: a Record of the Papers at a Conference Arranged by the Dugdale Society to Commemorate the Tercentenary of the Publication of Dugdale's Antiquities of Warwickshire;* C. Read, comp., *Bibliography of British History: Tudor Period, 1485–1603,* 2d ed.; E. Lousse, ed., *Grundbegriffe der Geschichte. 50 Beiträge zum europäischen Geschichtsbild.* The attitude of the early English historians toward Jews and Judaism likewise merits monographic treatment.

LXV: IBERIAN DOWNGRADE

1. M. de [Oliveira] Lemos, *Zacuto Lusitano, a sua vida e a sua obra*, pp. 360 ff., here cited from the English rendition by C. Roth in *A Life of Menasseh ben Israel*, pp. 46 f.; C. J. Sisson, "A Colony of Jews in Shakespeare's London," in *Essays and Studies* by Members of the English Association (collected by S. C. Roberts), XXIII, 42 ff.; C. Roth, *The Spanish Inquisition*, pp. 138 ff.; the 1673 report cited by J. Lucio d'Azevedo, "Judeus portugueses na dispersão," *Revista de história* (Lisbon), IV, 105–127, 201–217, esp. p. 113 n. 2; and *supra*, Chap. LXIV, n. 32. On the southern French communities, see also E. Ginsburger, "Les Juifs de Peyrehorade," *REJ*, CIV, 35–69; and *supra*, Chap. LXIV, n. 9.

2. F. H. Lyon, *Diego de Sarmiento de Acuña, Conde de Gondomar*, pp. 7 ff.; Gondomar's dispatches published by the duke of Alba *et al.* in their ed. of *Documentos inéditos para la historia de España*, Vols. I–IV. See also A. J. Loomie, "Bacon and Gondomar: an Unknown Link in 1618," *Renaissance Quarterly*, XXI, 1–10, showing that, despite his "jest," Bacon expressed, in the summer of 1618, his "satisfaction" about the king's acceptance of Gondomar's proposal, and his own "affection" for the Spanish envoy. Sir Francis concluded: "Farewell and take care of your health which stands endangered by heavy cares" (pp. 1, 8 f.). In fact, the Spanish diplomat seems to have been an Old Christian of staunchly Catholic persuasion. See F. de P. Fernández de Cordoba, ed., "Testamento de Don Diego Sarmiento de Acuña, I conde de Gondomar, publicado ahora por primera vez," *Cuadernos de Estudios Gallegos*, XXII, 83–111. Of course, testaments worded in pious Catholic terms could have been written by descendants of Jews or even secret Judaizers. This seems to have been the case, for instance, with Don García de Yllan, the host of Queen Christina in Antwerp. See *supra*, Chap. LXIII, n. 14. It may have been done for more effective camouflage, in order to forestall posthumous confiscation of the testator's property. But in the case of Gondomar, all the evidence indicates that Bacon was merely applying to him the unwarranted generalization that all Iberians abroad were of Jewish descent. See also *supra*, Vol. XIII, pp. 89 ff., 118 f., 355 n. 30, 367 f. n. 61. Ironically, in Spain and Spanish America it was the "Portuguese" who were frequently identified with Marranos. See the numerous authorities cited by B. Lewin in *El Judío en la época colonial*, pp. 47 ff. This undoubtedly was a contributory factor in Spain's reluctance to admit Portuguese to the mother country or the overseas possessions. See *infra*, Chap. LXVI, nn. 47, 49, 51, and 53. On Leavis, see also *supra*, Chap. LXIV, n. 63.

3. F. Braudel, *La Méditerranée et le Monde Méditerranéen à l'époque de Philippe II*, pp. 522 ff.; 2d ed., II, 233 ff.; F. Cereceda, "El Nacionalismo religioso español en Trento," *Hispania* (Madrid), V, 236–85; G. L. Pinette, "Die Spanier und Spanien im Urteil des deutschen Volkes zur Zeit der Reformation," *ARG*, XLVIII, 182–91, esp. pp. 188, 190; A. Paz de Mélia, "El Embajador Polaco Juan Dantisco en la corte de Carlos V 1524–1527," *Boletín* of the R. Academia Española, XI, 54–69, 305–320, 427–44, 584–600; XII, 73–93, esp. XI, 429, 438 ff.; *infra*, n. 16; and *supra*, Chap. LXIV, n. 95. Philip's everlasting involvement in German affairs is well illustrated by his ex-

tensive correspondence with various German princes. See Marquis De la Fuensanta del Valle, ed., *Correspondencia de los príncipes de Alemania con Felipe II, y de los embajadores de éste en la corte de Viena (1556–1598)* in CODOIN, XCVIII, CI, CIII, CX, CXI (incomplete; stops with 1574). More justifiedly than a modern historian, could Philip's Spanish contemporaries speak of him as *Felipe II, rey de España y monarca del Universo*. See M. Tomás's pertinent monograph. See also, more generally, the older, but still very useful, comprehensive biography by H. Forneron, *Histoire de Philippe II;* and the more recent studies by B. Chudoba, *Spain and the Empire 1519–1643;* and M. Fernández Alvarez, *Política mondial de Carlos V y de Felipe II*, with an Intro. by V. Palacio Atard.

4. J. J. F. Gordo, "Memoria sobre os Judeos em Portugal," *Historia e memorias* of the Royal Academy of Science in Lisbon, VIII, Part 2, pp. 1–35, esp. pp. 10, 23 f., 29, 34 f.; M. Kayserling, *Geschichte der Juden in Portugal,* pp. 276 ff.; L. Serrano, ed., *Correspondencia diplomática entre España y la Santa Sede durante el pontificado de S. Pio V,* I, 47 f. No. 23, 199 ff. No. 79, 223 ff. No. 86, 256 ff. No. 100, 270 ff. No. 107; IV, pp. li ff.; A. Baião, "A Inquisição em Portugal y no Brasil. Subsidios para a sua história," *Archivo histórico português,* IV–X (was to be continued); F. de Almeida, *História de igreja de Portugal,* esp. III, Part 2, pp. 110 ff., 145 ff.; idem, *História de Portugal,* esp. III, 2, 112; *Corpo diplomático portuguez contenido os actos e relações políticas e diplomáticas de Portugal com as diversas potencias de mundo,* ed. by L. A. Rebello da Silva *et al.,* XII, 29, 91 ff., 166; and other sources listed by P. Browe in "Die Kirchenrechtliche Stellung der getauften Juden und ihrer Nachkommen," *AKKR,* CXXI, 3–22, 165–91, esp. pp. 20 ff. On the often precarious relations between Philip II and Pius V and other popes, as well as the king's domestic policies vis-à-vis the Spanish Church, see Sixtus V's 1589 instructions to Cardinal Enrico Caëtani, reproduced by A. de Boüard in *La Légation du Cardinal Caëtani en France 1589–1590,* p. 62 (from which the pope's observation cited in the text is quoted); G. Catalano, *Controversie giurisdizionali tra Chiesa e Stato nell'età di Gregorio XIII e di Filippo II,* in *Atti* of the Accademia di scienze . . . , Palermo, 4th ser. XV, Part 2, with a documentary appendix of 37 nos.; J. Lynch, "Philip II and the Papacy," *TRHS,* XI, 23–42; A. M. Rouco-Varela, *Staat und Kirche im Spanien des XVI. Jarhunderts.* See also *supra,* Vols. XIII, pp. 88 f., 354 f. n. 28; XIV, pp. 81 ff., 336 ff. nn. 9–12; and *infra,* n. 7.

5. See F. Cereceda, "El Nacionalismo religioso español en Trento," *Hispania* (Madrid), V, 236–85; I. Cloulas, "Le 'Subsidio de las galeras,' contribution du clergé espagnol à la guerre navale contre les Infidèles, de 1563 à 1574," *MCV,* III, 289–325, esp. the Table on the final page; supplemented by his "La Monarchie catholique et les revenus épiscopaux. Les pensions sur les 'mitres' de Castille pendant le règne de Philippe II (1556–1598)," *ibid.,* IV, 107–142; L. Serrano, ed., *Correspondencia diplomática,* I, 49, 224, 256, 271; and, more generally, the works listed *supra,* n. 4.

6. See *supra,* Vol. XIII, pp. 73 f., 79 f., 340 f. n. 11, 344 f. n. 16; R. Muños Garrido, *Ejersicio legal de la medicina en España (siglos XV al XVIII);* H. Ciria y Nasarre, *Santa Teresa y Felipe II. Concepto cabal de justo y de piadoso que se forma del Rey Prudente legendo las obras de Santa Teresa de Jesús;* A. Rodriguez-Moñino, "Las Justas toledanas a Santa Teresa en 1614 (Poesías inéditas de Baltasar Elisio de Medinilla)," *Studia philologica. Homenaje . . . a Dámaso Alonso,* III, 245–68; Efrén

de la Madre de Dios and O. Stegging, *Tiempo y vida de Santa Teresa;* A. de la Virgen del Carmen, *Historia de la reforma teresiana (1569–1962);* E. Llamas Martínez, "Santa Teresa de Jesús, gloria de España y doctora de la Iglesia," *Salmaticensis,* XV, 641–97; Philip II's statement, in his edict addressed to the military Orders of Santiago, Calatrava, and Alcántara, cited from a Madrid MS by A. A. Sicroff in *Les Controverses des statuts de "pureté de sang" en Espagne,* p. 138 n. 184. See *infra,* n. 49. Needless to say, not all New Christian physicians were allowed to pursue their careers peacefully; many either were tried by the Inquisition or else fled abroad. See *Médicos perseguidos por la Inquisición española;* P. A. d'Azevedo, "Medicos cristãos novos que se ausentaram de Portugal no principio do século XVII," *Arquivo de história de medicina portuguesa,* n.s. V, 153–72. Many examples of this kind have been, and will be, cited in other chapters. On the developments in Tudela, see A. Domínguez Ortiz, *La Clase social de los conversos en Castilla en la edad moderna,* pp. 50 ff.

The Tudela populace did not necessarily share the favorable sentiments of its spokesmen toward the New Christians; for generations thereafter, in fact, its majority held all Marranos in utter contempt. New Christian names were regularly entered in a large scroll, called *La Manta,* which was displayed in the Tudela Cathedral to the end of the eighteenth century. See J. Yanguas y Miranda, *Historia de Navarra,* II, 122; M. Kayserling, *Die Juden in Navarra,* pp. 109 f. On the ever-sharpening attitude toward "purity of blood," see *supra,* Vol. XIII, pp. 84 ff., 89 ff., 353 ff.; and *infra,* esp. nn. 46 ff. See also other data supplied in the documents reproduced by F. Díaz-Plaja in *La Historia de España en sus documentos, el Siglo XVI,* pp. 510 ff., 514, 530 f., 557 ff.

7. J. I. Tellechea Idígoras, *Fray Bartolomé de Carranza. Documentos históricos,* with a Foreword by G. Marañon y Posadillo (Archivo documental español, XVIII, XIX, XXII); idem, *Un "Sermon de tolerança" de Bartolomé Carranza?* (reproducing the text of the sermon and other documents); idem, *El Arzobispo Carranza y su tiempo.* Valdés' Index and that promulgated by Pius IV in the name of the Tridentine Council in 1564 are reproduced by H. Reusch in *Die Indices librorum prohibitorum des sechzehnten Jahrhunderts gesammelt und herausgegeben,* pp. 154 ff., 208 ff., with Reusch's comments thereon in *Der Index der verbotenen Bücher. Ein Beitrag zur Kirchen- und Literaturgeschichte,* I, 258 ff., 294 ff., 299 ff. See also J. I. Tellechea Idígoras, "La Censura inquisitorial de Biblias de 1554," *Anthologica annua,* X, 89–142 (pointing out some 130 "heretical" expressions found in Protestant Bibles published since 1528); idem, "Felipe II y el inquisidor general D. Fernando de Valdés. Documentos inéditos," *Salmaticensis,* XVI, 329–72; J. L. González Novalin, *El Inquisidor general Fernando de Valdés (1483–1568). Su vida e su obra;* I. S. Révah, "Un Index espagnol inconnu, celui édicté par l'Inquisition de Séville en novembre 1551," *Studia philologica. Homenaje . . . a Dámaso Alonso,* III, 131–46, esp. pp. 132, 136, 140 f., and 145 f.; *supra,* Vol. XIV, pp. 19 ff., 54 ff., 310 ff. nn. 15 ff., 325 f. nn. 51 ff.; and, more fully, my study "The Council of Trent and Rabbinic Literature," in my *Ancient and Medieval Jewish History: Essays,* ed. by L. A. Feldman, pp. 353–71, 555–64.

8. J. M. Madurell Marimón, "Licencias reales para la impresión y venta de libros, 1519–1705," *RABM,* LXXII, 111–248; F. J. Sánchez Cantón, ed., *Floreto de anécdotas y noticias diversas que recopiló un fraile dominico residente en Sevilla a mediados*

del siglo XVI (Memorial histórico español, XLVIII), pp. 125 f. No. 152; J. Caro Baroja, Los Judíos en la España moderna y contemporanea, I, 294. This must have been a bitter pill to swallow for men like the Coronels, who in 1492, at a fairly advanced age, had followed their octogenarian father to the baptismal font to escape the hardships of exile. On the earlier, less intolerant, period, see also F. J. Norton's Printing in Spain, 1501-1523.

9. See *supra*, n. 7; and Vol. IX, pp. 55 f., 266 n. 1; J. Enciso, "Prohibiciones españolas de las versiones bíblicas en romance antes el Tridentino," *Estudios bíblicos,* III, 523-60. The inquisitorial suspicions about all independent biblical studies, especially those by eminent New Christians like Luis de León and several other professors at the University of Salamanca, have been discussed *supra*, Vol. XIII, pp. 80 ff., 346 ff. nn. 17-18. In this respect Philip II rather reluctantly followed the lead of the inquisitors, although he evinced sufficient personal interest in biblical studies to promote the publication of the Antwerp Polyglot, often called the *Biblia regia.* See esp. Benito Arias Montano's *Correspondencia . . . con Felipe II, el secretario Zayas y otros sugetos, desde 1568 hasta 1580* in CODOIN, XLI, 127-418; B. Rekers's Amsterdam dissertation, *Benito Arias Montano 1527-1598: a Study of a Group of Spiritualist Humanists in Spain and the Netherlands, on the Basis of Their Correspondence* (Dutch); and J. A. Vásquez's *Arias Montano, "rey de nuestros escripturarios,"* 2d ed. See also *supra*, Vol. XIII, p. 392 n. 4.

Perhaps Philip's ego was flattered by the adulation emanating from the Plantin press, like *Une Ode à Philippe II, écrite, imprimée et reliée par Plantin.* Such odes were no rarity, however, in the flattery-prone Renaissance age. Even the official chronicler of the royal house of France once glowingly described Philip II's achievements and those of his New Christian counselor Antonio Pérez, before the latter's fall. See the *Breve compendio y Elogio de la vida del rey Felipe II, de felicisima memoria, escrito en francés por Pedro Matéo, Cronista Mayor del Reino de Francia, y traducido en castellano, con la muerte del Principe Don Carlos, causas de ella y los sucesos de Antonio Pérez,* preserved in a seventeenth-century MS. See *Indice de colección de Don Luis de Salazar y Castro,* ed. by B. Cuarteiy y Huerta *et al.,* XXXII, 241 No. 51, 554.

Even more remarkably, Philip actually preserved, in the Library of San Lorenzo founded by him at the Escorial, two medieval *Jewish* versions of the Bible in Spanish, forerunners of the famous Ferrara Bible. (Other copies may still have been in Marrano possession at that time.) One of the two Escorial MSS bears on its covers the king's coat of arms in gold. Philip also maintained close personal relations with such biblical scholars as the Jesuit Juan Bautista Villalpando, whose three-volume *Explanationes* on Ezekiel and the prophet's vision of the reconstructed Temple of Jerusalem, published in Rome, 1596-1604, left its imprint on general Spanish esthetics and architecture. See J. Llamas, "La Antigua Biblia castellana de los Judíos españoles," *Sefarad,* IV, 219-44; idem, "Nueva Biblia medieval judía e inédita, en romance castellano," *ibid.,* IX, 53-74; R. C. Taylor, "El Padre Villalpando (1552-1602) y sus ideas estéticas (Homenaje en su cuarto centenario)," *Anales y Boletín* of the Real Academia de Bellas Artes de San Fernando, 2d ser. I, 409-475. Not surprisingly, like other somewhat independent biblical scholars, Villalpando was suspected of heterodox leanings. See E. Zudáire, "El Maestro Juan de Villalpando, sospechoso de herejía," *Anuario de estudios atlanticos,* XIV, 443-96.

These biblical works, as well as the difficulties of the Antwerp Polyglot (to which brief allusions are made *supra*, Vol. XIII, p. 392 n. 4; Chap. LXIII, n. 66; and *infra*, n. 17), will be treated more fully in a later chapter. Here we need but mention the intense interest Spanish intellectuals showed in biblical studies, which could not be completely suppressed by inquisitorial threats. See, for example, F. Álvarez, "El Movimento bíblico en Sevilla durante el siglo XVI," *Archivo hispalense*, 2d ser. XXVI, 9–45, esp. pp. 22 ff. There is no way of telling to what extent the Marranos' vital concern about the availability of vernacular versions of the Bible had helped stimulate that interest among the Spanish public as a whole. Of special relevance also is a fascicle, preserved among the "Papeles de Inquisición" in the Archivo Histórico Nacional in Madrid (leg. 4470 No. 2), relating to the proceedings instituted by the Inquisition against Bibles *en romancio*, including the Alba Bible and one printed in Amsterdam.

10. See, for instance, R. Ricard's description in "Ibero-Africana II: Baptême d'un Juif de Fès à l'Escorial (1589)," *Hespéris*, XXIV, 136, with reference to L. Niño Azcona's *Felipe II y la villa de El Escorial a través de la historia*, esp. p. 95. The neophyte is described in the parish records as "a man of forty . . . called Moisen ucn Zamerro" (probably a variant of Ibn Zimra).

11. A. Baião, *A Inquisição, Documentos*, pp. 10, 24; and other sources summarized by P. Browe in "Die Kirchenrechtliche Stellung," *AKKR*, CXXI, 20.

12. J. Yanguas y Miranda, *Historia de Navarra*, II, 90, 120; M. Kayserling, *Die Juden in Navarra*, pp. 108 f.; Public Record Office, London, *Calendar of State Papers*, Foreign Series, 1579–1580, pp. 45 f.; C. Roth, *A History of the Marranos*, p. 89; J. Caro Baroja, *Los Judíos en la España moderne*, I, 458. Philip II's rather complicated attitude toward his newly acquired kingdom is succinctly analyzed by P. Rocamora y Valls in his "Portugal y Felipe II," in *El Escorial, 1563–1963*, published in beautifully illustrated vols. by the Concejo de Administración del Patrimonio Nacional, I, 647–56. See also J. Vidago, "Felipe II, Lusitanista," *Ocidente*, LXXV, 193–200 (showing that the king had a lifelong interest in Portuguese culture). On the Pretender's career, see M. Domingues, *O Prior do Crato contra Filippe II. Evocação historica*; and, more generally, the older studies by A. de [Portugal de] Faria, *D. Antonio, prieur de Crato, XVIIIème roi de Portugal (1534–1595). Extraits, notes et documents*, Vol. I; idem, *Descendance de D. Antonio, prieur de Crato, XVIIIème roi de Portugal. Extraits, portraits, notes et documents*, 2d ed.; idem, *D. Antonio I, prior de Crato, XVIIIème rei de Portugal (1534–95) e seus descendents. Bibliografia* (includes 719 entries and a number of documents); and the other literature listed *supra*, Chap. LXIV, n. 13. We have seen that, led by Alvaro Mendez, many New Christians in Paris, London, and Constantinople likewise sided for a time with Dom Antonio, though some of them were quickly disabused. Despite these "intrigues," Mendez apparently had no difficulty in securing for his envoy Judah Serfatim a rather friendly reception in Madrid in 1597. See *supra*, Vol. XIV, pp. 81 ff., 304 nn. 9–12; Chap. LXIV, nn. 13, 67–68.

13. A. Domínguez Ortiz, *La Clase social*, pp. 150 ff., 180 n. 58, 189, etc.; B. Chudoba, *Spain and the Empire*, p. 92; *supra*, Vols. XIII, pp. 74 f., 341 f. n. 12; XIV, pp. 77 ff., 335 f. nn. 6–7. It must be borne in mind, however, that Old Christian Spaniards, too, often found it difficult to travel abroad. Even Jesuit students wishing to

attend schools in Rome or elsewhere had difficulty securing the necessary exit permits. See J. I. Tellechea Idígoras, "Un Percance inquisitorial desconocido (1561). Los Jesuitas y la real pragmática del Felipe II de 1559," *AHSI*, XXXIV, 79–85.

14. Bishop Santa-Croce's letter to Cardinal Carlo Borromeo, the papal secretary of state, of May 23, 1561, summarized from a Roman document by A. Herculano in his *History of the Origin and Establishment of the Inquisition in Portugal*, pp. 630 ff. On Oleastro, see A. Vilela's biographical sketch, "Un Exegeta português do Concilio de Trento: Oleastro—No IV Centenario de sua morte (1563–1963)," *Brotéria*, LXXVIII, 16–28. See also, more generally, P. Monteiro, *Historia da Santa Inquisição do reyno de Portugal e suas conquistas*; F. de Almeida, *Historia de Portugal*, III, 134–62; and *supra*, Vols. XIII, pp. 44 ff.; XIV, pp. 18 f., 309 n. 17.

15. See the data, largely cited from archival sources, by H. C. Lea in *A History of the Inquisition of Spain*, I, 299 f., 485 f., 528 f., 538 f. After convicting a Judaizer, the Inquisition rarely reduced his sentence. This happened to Thomas Fernandes, however, who had been denounced to the Lisbon Inquisition for having been a practicing Jew in England. Perhaps he was thus rewarded for cooperating with the authorities and testifying in detail, as we recall, as to how he had observed the practice of Passover and other Jewish rituals at the home of his uncle in Bristol, England. He was first condemned to perpetual imprisonment and the permanent display of the sanbenito, but after a few months was allowed to leave prison and live in a designated suburb; later, even this restriction was relaxed and he was given special permission to travel without wearing the penitential garb. See L. Wolf, *The Case of Thomas Fernandes before the Lisbon Inquisition, 1556*," ed. by C. Roth, *Miscellanies, JHSE*, II, 32–56; and *supra*, Chap. LXIV, n. 62.

16. See A. Rodríguez Villa, "Los Judíos españoles y portugueses en el siglo XVII," *BAH*, XLIX, 98 f. See also the data cited in A. Domínguez Ortiz's review article, "Historical Research on Spanish Conversos in the Last 15 Years," *Américo Castro Jub. Vol.*, pp. 63–82. Opposing views on the "Black Legend" and its underlying assumption of cruelty as a national characteristic of the Spanish people have more recently been voiced by S. Quesada Marco in *La Legenda antiespañola* (denying the Legend's validity); and B. Keen, "The Black Legend Revisited: Assumptions and Realities," *HAHR*, XLIX, 703–719 (arguing for its essential correctness). See also *supra*, n. 3; Chap. LXIV, n. 95.

17. L. Pereña Vicente, *La Universidad de Salamanca, forja del pensiamento político español en el siglo XVI*, p. 17; *supra*, Vol. XIII, pp. 80 ff., 345 ff. nn. 17–18. On a similar *cause célèbre*, of somewhat later date, at the Portuguese University of Coimbra, see *infra*, nn. 88 ff. It may be noted that from the beginning Luis de León maintained that "in all matters which the General Council of the Inquisition had entrusted to the Theological Faculty of this university [Salamanca] he had served with more diligence, care, willingness, and perseverance than any other of the professors." Although this assertion was not contradicted by any witness, he languished in prison for several years (1572–76), merely because of his Jewish descent and his efforts to spread the reading of the Bible among the masses, and because, as one of his later admirers contended, "he knew more Hebrew than that era permitted."

Miguel de la Pinta Llorente not unjustly calls the prosecution of the Salamancan "Hebraists" the "major scandal perpetuated in cultural affairs on the Peninsula." See his *La Inquisición española*, I, 346 ff., 360. The chances are that, if they had known about it, the inquisitors would have been even more irked by the influence medieval Hebrew liturgical poetry exerted on De León's lyrics than by the frequent use he made of the medieval Hebrew Bible commentators in his biblical studies. See J. M. Millás Vallicrosa, "Probable influencia de la poesía sagrada hebráica española en la poesía de Fray Luis de León," *Sefarad*, XV, 261–86.

18. *Calendar of State Papers*, Foreign series, [V] 1562, ed. by J. Stevenson, pp. 77 f. No. 158, 98 f. No. 190, 106 f. No. 222; R. M. Kingdon in "The Plantin Breviaries: a Case Study in the Sixteenth-Century Business Operations of a Publishing House," *BHR*, XXII, 133–50. See also *supra*, n. 9.

19. Ḥayyim Vital Calabrese, *Sefer Shibḥe* (Laudations of Ḥ. V. C.; an autobiography), Lwów, n.d., pp. 51 ff., citing the story told him by a Marrano physician, Abraham ibn Ya'ish, allegedly a former Spanish courtier; J. J. F. Gordo, "Memoria sobre os Judeos em Portugal" (*supra*, n. 4), p. 34; Philip II's complaint, cited by A. González Palencia, in *La España del siglo de oro*, ed. by R. J. Michels, p. 30; E. Grierson, *The Fatal Inheritance: Philip II and the Spanish Netherlands*, p. 362; Count de Lerma's letter of September 16, 1605, cited from a Simancas MS by J. G. da Silva in his *Stratégie des affaires à Lisbonne entre 1595 et 1607. Lettres marchandes de Rodrigues d'Evora et Veiga*, p. 5 n. 27; A. Baião, "A Historia da Inquisição em Portugal," *Archivo histórico portugués*, VII, 241; M. Kayserling, *Geschichte der Juden in Portugal*, pp. 284 f.; Francisco Sorranzo's 1596 report published by N. Barozzi and G. Berchet in their ed. of *Relazioni degli stati europei lette al Senato dagli ambasciatori veneti nel secolo decimosettimo, raccolte e annotate*, I, Part 1, p. 156; also reproduced in a Spanish trans. by F. Díaz-Plaja in *La Historia de España en sus documentos; el siglo XVI*, pp. 805 f.; G. Marañón, *El Conde-Duque de Olivares (la pasión de mandar), passim;* and L. Pfandl's introduction to his German translation, *Olivares. Der Niedergang Spaniens als Weltmacht*, pp. 6 ff., 10, 23 f.; F. Braudel, *La Méditerranée et le Monde Méditerranéen*, pp. 522, 583, 1086; H. C. Lea, *A History of the Inquisition of Spain*, I, 471 f.

Despite C. H. Carter's legitimate reservations concerning the pervasive influence of the Council of State on the affairs of Philip III's regime (see "The Nature of Spanish Government after Philip II," *Historian*, XXVI, 1–18), the influence of royal favorites like Lerma appears undeniable. See Juan de Chumacero's *Acusación . . . contra . . . [el Duque de Lerma] por haber convertido todo el poder que tuvo en beneficio suyo y de sus deudos* (MS No. 2394 of the Biblioteca Nacional, Madrid); and J. Reglá, *Semblanza de un monarca y perfiles de una privanza.*

20. See the *Relacion de lo executado en la prision de D. Pedro Franqueza, conde de Villalonga, i de los bienes que se le embargaron por decreto de S. M.*, cited from a Madrid MS by A. Domínguez Ortiz in *La Clase social*, p. 85 n. 6; and, more generally, J. Judería's biographical sketch, "Los Favoritos de Felipe III: Don Pedro Franquesa, conde de Villalonga, Secretario de Estado," *RABM*, XIX, 309–327; XX, 16–27, 223–40, esp. XIX, 319 ff.; XX, 21, 228 ff., 240; Henry IV's letter to Nicholas de Neufville de Villeroy of May 16, 1601, in his *Lettres Missives*, ed. by J. Berger de Xivey and J. Guadet. It is not surprising that, along with other royal favorites,

Franquesa became the butt of contemporary satirists. See M. Herrero García, "La Poesía satírica contra los políticos del reinado de Felipe III," *Hispania* (Madrid), VI, 267–96.

On the general economic decline of Spain under Philip III and his successors, see the studies by A. J. Hamilton, "The Decline of Spain," *EcHR*, VIII, 168–79; and *American Treasure and the Price Revolution in Spain, 1501–1650*, esp. pp. 73 ff., 211 ff., 358 ff. Although superseded in many details by subsequent research, Hamilton's investigations still offer the most comprehensive picture of how prices went up while the general prosperity of the country was going down. On the contrast with conditions under Philip II, see the telling illustrations furnished by R. Altamira in *A History of Spain from the Beginnings to the Present*, trans. from the 2d Spanish ed. by M. Lee, pp. 389 ff. However, in overemphasizing the metallic factor, Hamilton and his followers have failed to pay attention to other, equally important, causes of Spain's decline, such as the growing flight of the upper bourgeoisie into the ranks of the landed aristocracy; the widespread unwillingness to work among the masses; the government's faulty import and export policies (similar policies were later the bane of Poland, often styled by her neighbors the "Spain of the North"); the demographic drain of warfare and excessive emigration to the colonies; and, last but not least, the long-range effects of the expulsion of Jews and Moors. See J. Polišensky's pertinent observations in his "Bohemia y la crisis política española de 1590–1620," *Historica*, XIII, 157–69; and, more generally, H. Kellenbenz, "The Impact of Growth on Government: the Example of Spain," *Journal of Economic History*, XXVII, 340–62; and other literature listed in the following notes.

21. J. Mendes dos Remedios, *Os Judeus em Portugal*, II, 84 f., 100 ff.; idem, "Os Judeus e os perdões gerais," *Biblos*, I, 631–55; J. Lucio d'Azevedo, *Historia dos Christãos Novos Portugueses*, 194 ff.; J. Amador de los Rios, *Historia social . . . de los Judíos*, III, 461; J. Caro Baroja, *Los Judíos en la España moderna*, I, 342 ff.

22. A. Danvila y Burguero, *Don Cristóbal de Moura primer Marqués de Castel-Rodrigo (1538–1613)*, esp. pp. 795 ff.; J. Caro Baroja, *Los Judíos*, I, 410 ff., 414 n. 37; III, 304 ff. On the Portuguese aspects of the Reubeni-Molkho episode, see S. Schwarz, "O Sionismo no reinado de don João III," *Ver e creer*, March, 1946, pp. 101–115 (includes the text of a previously unpublished letter from Reubeni to the king); and *supra*, Vol. XIII, pp. 109 ff., 364 ff. nn. 53–58. Some temporary rapprochement between the leading Jewish statesmen in Constantinople and the Spanish Court in the 1590s may also explain Judah Serfatim's aforementioned mission to Madrid in Ibn Ya'ish's behalf in 1597. This mission, the purpose of which was not publicly divulged, probably could not have taken place during the tense earlier relationship between Philip and his New Christian antagonist. See *supra*, n. 12; Chap. LXIV, nn. 13, 16, 67–68. Perhaps further research in both Spanish and Ottoman archives might shed some new light on this intriguing problem.

23. F. Cantera Burgos, "Dos escritos inéditos y anónimos sobre los Judíos y España durante el siglo XVII," *Scritti sull'ebraismo in memoria di Guido Bedarrida*, pp. 33–47; G. de Arriaga, *Historia del Colegio de San Gregorio de Valladolid*, ed. by M. Hoyer, II, 150; Agustín Salucio, *Discurso . . . acerca de la justicia y buē gobierno de España, en los estatutos de limpieza de sangre: y si conviene, o no, alguna limitación en ellos*, reed. by A. Valladares in *Semanario erudito*, XV; H. Sancho [de So-

pranis], "El Maestro Fr. Agustín Salucio, O. P. Contribución a la historia literaria Sevillana del siglo XVI," *Archivo Hispalense*, 1952, pp. 9–47; A. Domínguez Ortiz, *La Clase social*, pp. 87 ff. The fullest discussion of Salucio's tract, its authenticity and date of publication, is offered by A. A. Sicroff in *Les Controverses des statuts de "pureté de sang" en Espagne du XVᵉ au XVIIᵉ siècle*, pp. 186–209.

24. Gonzalo Fernández de Oviedo, *Las Quinquagenas de la nobleza de España*, I, 279. See also the numerous other examples cited *supra*, n. 2; Vol. XIII, pp. 89 f., 334 n. 64, 355 n. 30. The attempted suppression of Salucio's distinguished work by Philip II is mentioned by H. C. Lea in *A History of the Inquisition of Spain*, II, 306. As pointed out by Sicroff (in *Les Controverses*, p. 208 f. n. 101), neither the date of the outlawry nor its motivation are known. Yet it did not prevent the Cortes from studying the matter closely in 1600, nor did it deter many writers from taking cognizance of Salucio's arguments for decades thereafter. Excerpts from eleven such publicist tracts were published by A. Domínguez Ortiz in *La Clase Social*, pp. 225 ff. App. iv.

We shall see that the measures taken by the government did not put an end to the anti-Spanish generalizations abroad, or contribute to an amelioration of the status of the New Christians at home. A century and a half later, when the regime of Ferdinand VI (1746–59) undertook a number of moderate internal reforms, the incongruous position of the remnant of New Christians again came up for discussion. José de Carvajal, a leading royal counselor, ordered Don Joseph de Loyando of Saragossa to copy for him Salucio's tract and other liberal statements extant in the archives. He thus wished "to assemble as much as has been written against the cruel impiety with which those living outside the Christian religion were treated while all humane gates to enter and embrace it were shut against them." See his letter of 1751 to Loyando, cited from a Madrid archival document by A. Domínguez Ortiz in *La Sociedad española en el siglo XVIII*, with a Foreword by Carmelo Viñas y Mey, p. 230 n. 27.

25. J. de Olarra Garmendía and M. L. de Larramendi (Olarra's widow), eds., "Correspondencia entre la Nunciatura en España y la Santa Sede durante el reinado de Felipe III (1598–1621)," *Anthologica annua*, VII, 409–782; IX, 495–816; X, 451–730; XI, 367–666; XII, 323–607; XIII, 395–697; XIV, 499–630; esp. VII, 438 f. No. 145, 626 No. 1437, 631 No. 1468, 649 No. 1597, 654 No. 1628, 655 No. 1675, 662 No. 1685, 665 No. 1709; IX, 733 No. 1473 (also reprinted in separate volumes by the Instituto Español de Historia Eclesiástica in Rome); J. Mendes dos Remedios, *Os Judeus em Portugal*, II, 70 ff., 83 f. (giving the text of the decree of pardon); Fray Juan de Salazar, *Política española* (1617), new ed. by M. Herrero, p. 18; F. Braudel, *La Méditerranée*, pp. 408 ff.; 2d ed., 11, 39 ff. See also the detailed study by Mendes dos Remedios, "Os Judeus e a perdóes gerais," *Biblos*, I, 631–55. According to Fortunado de Almeida's computation of the figures given in the royal ordinances of Dec. 13, 1604; Feb. 1, April 23, May 30, June 8 and 21, 1605; and the two issued on Dec. 27, 1606, the New Christians were to pay the Treasury 1,700,000 cruzados, in addition to absolving it of its debts of 225,000 cruzados. There also appear to have been some substantial payments to the municipality of Lisbon. See J. J. de Andrade e Silva, comp., *Collecção chronologica da legislação portugueza*, Vol. I: 1603–1612, pp. 90, 105, 128, 139, 185 f.; and *Elementos para a história do município de Lisbôa*, II, 136 ff., both cited by F. de Almeida in his *Historia de Portugal*, III, 159.

It may be noted that, in the spirit of "forgiveness" characterizing the negotiations of 1604, the king defied both the public and the inquisitorial personnel by a cedula he issued on February 17 of that year (invoking Clement VIII's brief of May 24, 1603), in favor of Don Pedro Ossorio de Velasco, a descendant of Pablo de Santa María. Of course, everyone knew that Pablo had previously been called Solomon ha-Levi and had served as rabbi of Burgos, and that only after his conversion had he become a leading Castilian bishop, statesman, and controversialist. Nonetheless, the king now decreed that Ossorio and all other descendants of Santa María should be considered "Old Christians." See F. Cantera Burgos, *Alvar García de Santa María y su familia de conversos. Historia de la judería de Burgos y de sus conversos más egregios*, pp. 280 ff. A similar action by Emperor Ferdinand III in 1641 in the case of Jacob Rosales in Hamburg, who received through the Spanish ambassador a diploma freeing him from the blemish of Jewish ancestry, was mentioned *supra*, Vol. XIV, pp. 282 f., 408 f. n. 59. These acts are reminiscent of the conferral, in the 1930s, of the status of "honorary Aryans" on a few Jewish favorites of the Nazi rulers in Germany.

In the light of this extraordinary action by both pope and king, it may perhaps not be too venturesome to suggest that it was the influence of the powerful Santa María clan which accounted for a phenomenon found so puzzling by Nicolás López Martínez, a generally unsympathetic commentator on the *converso* "peril." In discussing the archive of the Cathedral of Burgos, López Martínez was surprised to find therein "the absence of the type of documentation which is most frequently and abundantly available in Spanish archives: proofs of the purity of blood." See "El Estatuto de limpieza de sangre en la catedral de Burgos," *Hispania* (Madrid), XIX, 52–81, esp. pp. 72 ff. Apps. 1–6 (1550), 7 (1585).

26. See Francisco de Torrejoncillo, *Centinela/ contra Ivdios,/ puesta en la torre de la/ Iglesia de Dios con el Trabajo caudal*; A. A. Sicroff's summary thereof in *Les Controverses*, pp. 167 ff.; H. Kamen, "Confiscations in the Economy of the Spanish Inquisition," *EcHR*, 2d ser. XVIII, 311–25, esp. p. 314; *infra*, n. 29; and *supra*, Chap. LXIII, n. 28; and Vol. XIII, pp. 32 ff., 319 ff. nn. 33–35. How unwilling Portuguese public opinion was to follow counsels of moderation may be seen in the example of Ierónymo de Mendonça, a nobleman and army officer turned historian. A participant in King Sebastian's disastrous North-African Crusade, Mendonça spent a long time in Moroccan captivity. While initially sharing his fellow-Crusaders' hatred of Jews, he soon learned that he was one of the lucky captives acquired by Jewish masters, who treated them with "flourish [*brandma*], affability, and courtesy." He especially admired the Moroccan Jewish women, their chastity, and their devotion in the care of wounded prisoners. He asserted that all Moroccan Jews spoke Spanish and that, when the time came for his return to Portugal, many of them had envied him for his ability to go back to their ancient Iberian homeland. Yet the keynote of Mendonça's presentation in his *Iornada de Africa*, published in 1607, was pity for the ever-oppressed North-African Jews, rather than a general emphasis (like that of many contemporary French writers) on the toleration extended by Muslim rulers to Jews and Christians, in contrast to the religious intolerance in many Christian lands. Moreover, even the purely humanitarian lessons and the appreciation of Jewish kindness which readers could derive from a perusal of Mendonça's *Jornada* were gravely distorted by later Portuguese writers. See E. Glaser, "Le Chroniqueur portugais Jerónimo de Mendonça et son esprit de tolérance," *BH*, LVI, 38–48.

27. M. F. Thomaz, *Repertorio Geral . . . das Leis Extravagantes do Reino de Portugal*, I, 188; A. Baião, "A Inquisição," *Archivo histórico portugués*, VIII, 241; M.

Kayserling, *Geschichte der Juden in Portugal,* pp. 284 f.; M. de la Pinta Llorente, "Orígenes y organización del Santo Oficio en Portugal," *RABM,* 4th ser. LIV, 73–102; A. Domínguez Ortiz, *La Clase social,* pp. 83 ff.; J. Caro Baroja, *Los Judíos,* I, 345 ff.; M. Mendez Bejarano, *Histoire de la juiverie de Séville,* pp. 175 ff.; J. A. de Figueiredo, *Synopsis Chronologica,* Lisbon, 1790, p. 286. Regrettably, the available documentation does not show clearly what role Pope Paul V played in the abrogation of the pardon, which had been enacted by his predecessor in 1604. But he evidently acquiesced in its formal cancellation by Philip III in 1610. See the exchanges between Rome and Madrid, as reflected in J. de Olarra Garmendía and M. L. de Larramendi's compilation of the "Correspondencia entre la Nunciatura en España y la Santa Sede," *Anthologica annua,* XI, 365–666 (reprint, Vol. IV). It is possible that the Iberian New Christians had overtaxed their resources in pledging the huge ransom to the Crown. Lack of funds may have accounted for both their lagging payments and their inability to "lobby" effectively in Rome against the revocation of the amnesty. Impoverishment of the Marrano community doubtless was also partly responsible for the sudden drop of 48 percent in the revenue of the Saragossan Holy Office in 1612, as compared with the income of 1608 and before. See H. Kamen, "Confiscations," *EcHR,* 2d ser. XVIII, 520.

It appears that, during the few years when the Portuguese inquisitors found themselves hampered by the negotiations for, and the proclamations of, the pardon, their Spanish counterparts were able to intensify their activities because many Portuguese descendants of Spanish Jews had returned to Spain. This movement, begun after 1580, was doubtless accelerated by the granting of the pardon (1604–1605). Two years later, disgruntled over the slowness of Marrano payments, the Cortes and, following it the government, decided that all instalments due from the Portuguese Marranos must be shared by those who had interveningly settled in Spain (Ordinance of February 14, 1607). The economic dislocations arising in Portugal itself from the accelerated Marrano emigration and the government's vacillating policies are partially reflected in the business correspondence published by J. G. da Silva in his *Stratégie des affaires à Lisbonne entre 1595 et 1607.*

28. K. Garrad, "La Inquisición y los moriscos granadinos, 1526–1580," *BH,* LXVII, 63–77, esp. pp. 74 ff.; C. Ron de la Bastida, "Manuscritos árabes en la Inquisición granadina (1582)," *Al-Andalus,* XXIII, 210-13 (listing 34 works, all of which, except for 4 medical and astrological MSS, were prohibited); *supra,* Vol. III, pp. 43, 249 n. 53; A. C. Hess, "The Moriscos: an Ottoman Fifth Column in Sixteenth-Century Spain," *AHR,* LXXIV, 1–25, esp. pp. 17 f.; B. Vincent, "L'Expulsion des Morisques du Royaume de Grenade et leur répartition en Castille (1570–1571)," *MCV,* VI, 211–46 (with five very informative maps). On the reports of the three Jewish envoys in France and the appeal of the North-African rulers to the Porte, regarding the Moriscos, see the diplomatic dispatches cited by F. Braudel in *La Méditerranée,* pp. 898 f.; 2d ed., II, 363. See also T. Halperin-Donghi, *Un Conflicto nacional: moriscos y cristianos viejos en Valencia,* reprinted from *CHE,* XXIII–XXIV, 5–115; XXV–XXVI, 83–250; idem, "Recouvrements des civilisations: les Morisques du Royaume de Valence au XVIe siècle," *Annales ESC,* XI, 154–82; and, more generally, the comprehensive studies by H. C. Lea, *The Moriscos of Spain: Their Conversion and Expulsion;* and by P. Boronat y Barrachina, *Los Moriscos españoles y su expulsión. Estudio histórico-crítico,* with a Foreword by Manuel Danvila y Collado (also reproducing 70 informative documents).

29. Agustín Salucio, *Discurso*, xi, cited by A. Domínguez Ortiz in *La Clase*, pp. 90 f.; J. P. Le Flem, "Les Morisques du Nord-Ouest de l'Espagne en 1594, d'après un recensement de l'Inquisition de Valladolid," *MCV*, I, 223–44; B. Loupias, "La Pratique secrète de l'Islam dans les évêchés de Cuenca et de Sigüenza aux XVIᵉ et XVIIᵉ siècles," *Hespéris Tamuda*, VI, 115–31; S. Cirac Estropañan, *Registros de los documentos del Santo Oficio de Cuenca y Sigüenza*, Vol. I.: Registro de los procesos de delitos y de los expedientes de limpieza; D. Mansilla, "La Reorganización eclesiástica española del siglo XVI, Part I: Aragón-Cataluña," *Anthologica annua*, IV, 97–238, esp. pp. 174 ff.; Felipe de Nájera's testimony at his trial, cited by J. Caro Baroja in *Los Judíos*, I, 392, 398.

30. The conflicting contemporary estimates of the number of Moriscos affected by the decree of 1609 were given by Jaime Bleda in his *Crónica de los Moros de España*, Valencia, 1618 (though the royal license printed therein is dated September 7, 1619), esp. pp. 867 ff.; and by P. Fernández Navarette in his *Conservación de monarquias, y discursos políticos sobre la gran consulta que el Consejo hizo al señor rey Felipe Tercero*, vii, reprinted in *BAE*, XXV, 449–546, esp. pp. 465 ff. The vast exaggerations have long been discounted by modern scholars. See J. Reglá Campistol, "La Expulsión de los Moriscos y sus consecuencias. Contribución a su estudio," *Hispania* (Madrid), XIII, 215–67, 402–479 (includes several quotations from archival sources, especially the explanation given by Count Lerma to the vice-chancellor of Aragon that the expulsion aimed at making "all these kingdoms as pure [*limpios*] and purged of these people as possible); idem, "La Expulsión de los Moriscos y sus consecuencías en la economía valenciana," *Studi in onore di Amintore Fanfani*, V, 525–45 (examining the impact on demography, agricultural production, concentration of land ownership, inflation, and decline of the middle class). The debates on that expulsion and the numbers affected by it are well summarized in H. Lapeyre's detailed analysis in his *Géographie de l'Espagne morisque;* and in P. Chaunu's observations thereon in his "Minorités et conjuncture: l'Expulsion des Morisques en 1609," *RH*, CCXXV, 81–98. Notwithstanding the numerous parallels between, and frequent interdependence of, the two groups, the impact of the expulsion of the Moriscos on the fate of the Iberian Marranos has yet to be studied in depth. Certainly, even more than other Spaniards and Portuguese, those of Jewish descent must have been importantly affected by this outbreak of racialism and its contribution to the demographic and economic decline of the two countries.

There is no question that the population of Spain and Portugal, which had been steadily increasing during the sixteenth century, declined rather speedily under Philip III and his successors. See, for instance, the data offered by A. Castillo in his "Population et 'richesse' en Castille durant la seconde moitié du XVIᵉ siècle," *Annales ESC*, XX, 719–33, esp. p. 726 (showing that in the half century 1541–91 the population of the major cities grew between 12 percent in Granada, depopulated by the intervening Morisco rebellions, and 139 percent in Madrid); C. and J. P. Le Flem, "Un Censo de moriscos en Segovia y su provincia en 1594," *Estudios segovianos*, XVI, 433–64; and J. Nadal and E. Giralt in "Ensayo metodológico para el estudio de la población catalana de 1553 a 1717," *Estudios de historia moderna*, III, 237–84, esp. pp. 261 ff.; and, more generally, J. Ruiz Almansa, "La Población de España en el siglo XVI: Estudio sobre los recuentos de vecindario de 1594, llamados comúnmente 'Censo de Tomás González,'" *Revista internacional de sociología*, III,

115–36, and J. de Smet, *Despoblación y repoblación de España (1482–1920)*. On the international repercussions of the expulsion of the Moriscos, prospects of which had deterred Philip II from banishing them in 1582, see also J. Reglá, "La Cuestión morisca y la coyuntura internacional en tiempos de Felipe II," *Estudios de historia moderna*, III, 217–34, esp. pp. 220 ff., incidentally showing that, not only in Valencia but also in the provinces of Aragon, the ratio of Moriscos before 1609 had exceeded 20 percent of the total population.

31. See B. Bennassar's comprehensive *Recherches sur les grandes épidemies dans le nord de l'Espagne à la fin du XVIᵉ siècle*. *Problèmes et documentation de la méthode* (asserts, on the basis of municipal records, particularly of Badajoz, that Spain lost some 10 percent of its population in the plague years of 1596–1602; and considers this decline a turning point in the country's historical evolution); J. Nadal and E. Giralt, "Ensayo metodológico," *Estudios de historia moderna*, III, 249 ff.; L. Sanchez Granjel, "Las Epidemías de peste en España durante el siglo XVII," *Cuadernos de historia de la medicina española*, III, 19–40; R. Baehrel, "La Haine des classes en temps d'épidemie," *Annales ESC*, VII, 351–60 (mainly dealing with phenomena which occurred after 1650, the author's observations also shed light on earlier tendencies to pin the blame on scapegoats, of which the allegations of well poisoning by medieval Jews is a classic example; see *supra*, Vol. XI, pp. 159 ff., 365 ff. nn. 48–53); I. A. A. Thompson, "A Map of Crime in Sixteenth-Century Spain," *EcHR*, 2d ser., XXI, 244–67 (though tentative and largely based on scattered records relating to those condemned to galley slavery who included other than ordinary criminals, this thought-provoking essay reveals a close correlation between the crime wave and the social unrest in the decaying urban centers and disaffected provinces); W. Brandis, "Die 'Santa Hermandad.' Ein Kapitel spanischer Rechtsgeschichte," *Archiv für Kulturgeschichte*, XLI, 302–41, esp. p. 341. Of course, the countries north of the Alps and the Pyrenees likewise suffered greatly from the recurring plagues, but their rapidly advancing, dynamic societies were able more speedily to make up for the ensuing demographic and economic losses.

32. Antoine de Brunel, *Voyage d'Espagne* (1655), reproduced by C. Claverie in *Revue hispanique*, XXX, 119–375, esp. p. 207; A. Domínguez Ortiz, "La Esclavitud en Castilla durante la edad moderna," *Estudios de historia social de España*, II, 367–428; R. Pike, "Sevillian Society in the Sixteenth Century: Slaves and Freedmen," *HAHR*, XLVII, 344–59. In the case of Moorish slaves, there was the further complication that many of them continued to profess their Muslim faith, be it in a diluted, syncretistic form. Although the Inquisition found it convenient to shut its eyes to this breach of religious conformity, the situation became so troublesome that it led to the total banishment of slaves of Moorish descent in 1712. See also A. Domínguez Ortiz, *La Sociedad . . . siglo XVIII*, pp. 225 ff.; and, regarding the *converso* slave trade, Martín González de Cellorigo's highly inflated estimates, mentioned *infra*, n. 38. The effects of both slavery and the slave trade on the socioeconomic status of Iberian Jewry merit special monographic treatment.

33. See I. S. Révah, "Sources peu connues de l'histoire de Portugal au XVIᵉ siècle," *BEP*, XI, 271–73; idem, "Les Marranes," *REJ*, CXVIII, 70 ff.; and *infra*, n. 35. See also Count de Lerma's statement of 1605, cited *supra*, n. 19.

34. C. Roth, "The Strange Case of Hector Mendes Bravo," *HUCA*, XVIII, 221–45, also reproducing, in an English trans., the archival record of the culprit's "Confession" (pp. 229 ff.). The lists of names presented by the self-confessed penitent have served C. Roth, I. S. Révah, and other scholars in good stead in partially reconstructing the membership of the burgeoning Jewish communities of Hamburg and Amsterdam in the early seventeenth century. See *supra*, Chap. LXIII, n. 4; and Vol. XIV, pp. 272 ff., 404 f. n. 48. Of course, these data can often be supplemented and corrected from internal Jewish sources, especially autobiographical and family records, such as those examined by I. S. Révah in his "Pour l'histoire des nouveaux chrétiens portugais. La relation généalogique d'I. de M. Aboab," *Boletim internacional de bibliografia luso-brasileira*, II, 276–88; and his essay mentioned *infra*, n. 35.

35. See I. S. Révah, "Autobiographie d'un Marrano. Édition partielle d'un manuscrit de João (Moseh) Pinto Delgado," *REJ*, CXIX, 41–130, esp. pp. 47 ff., 53, 93. See also *supra*, Chap. LXIV, nn. 29 ff.

36. See *Actas* of the Cortes, XXI, 378; XXXII, 539 ff.; XXXVI, 342 ff., in part summarized by A. Domínguez Ortiz in *La Clase social*, pp. 97 ff. Of interest also is an earlier review of the effects of the pardon of 1604–1605, by an unsympathetic contemporary, in a memorandum entitled *Pretenden los Christianos nuevos perdon general. Varios lançes que en esto sucedieron*, excerpted from a Madrid MS by J. Caro Baroja in his *Los Judios*, III, 304 ff. App. xiv. The unfounded denunciations mentiond by Cimbrón, not only affected New Christians but sometimes extended to all classes of the population. A noteworthy illustration is offered by the later report of an official of the French embassy in Madrid, concerning the behavior of a local priest. Although not a fiscal of the Holy Office, the priest had made it a practice after Easter to visit all houses in the parish to collect from the inhabitants their tickets showing that they had partaken of Holy Communion. Those who failed to produce a ticket were immediately denounced to the Inquisition. New Christians served as special targets for many such volunteer informers. Some confidence men pretended to be agents of the Holy Office, and used this stratagem to extort "bribes" from unwary victims. "Clever" extortions of this type are described with much relish in contemporary picaresque novels by Alonso de Castillo Solórzano and others. See that author's *Tardes entretenidas* (1625), Madrid 1908 ed., pp. 191 ff.; and *Lettres écrites de Madrid en 1666 et 1667 par [Jean] Muret attaché de l' ambassade de Georges d'Aubussen, archevêque d'Embrun*, ed. by M. A. Morel-Fatio, p. 78, both cited by J. Caro Baroja in *Los Judios*, I, 357 f.

37. See the extensive memorandum by Juan Pérez de Saavedra extant in a contemporary Spanish manuscript version, entitled *Verdades catholicas contra ficciones judaycas de la gente de la nacion hebrea*, reproduced by M. de la Pinta Llorente in his "Orígenes y organización del Santo Oficio en Portugal," *RABM*, LIV, 95 ff. A similar self-serving blindness toward the faults of Spain's foreign policy induced an anonymous memorialist of the early seventeenth century (probably either Hernando de Salazar or Diego Serrano da Silva of the Supreme Council of the Inquisition) to warn the king, "May your Majesty not ignore the perilous condition created by the people of the Hebrew nation who have moved from Portugal to these realms [the Low Countries] and the damage which this situation threatens to inflict upon the

LXV: IBERIAN DOWNGRADE

religion and the state of this monarchy." See the excerpt cited by A. Rodríguez Villa in "Los Judíos españoles y portugueses en el siglo XVII," *BAH*, XLIX, 90 ff.

38. Martín González de Cellorigo's memorandum of 1619, republished with an extensive introduction by I. S. Révah in "Le Plaidoyer en faveur des 'Nouveaux-Chrétiens' portugais du licencié Martín González de Cellorigo (Madrid, 1619)," *REJ*, CXXII, 279–398, esp. pp. 359 f., 375 f., 390 ff., 392. On this important socio-economic thinker see J. L. Pérez de Ayala, "Un teórico español de la política financiera: Don Martín de Cellorigo," *Revista de derecho financiero y de hacienda pública*, IX, 711–47. Although, having access to inquisitorial and other archives, González de Cellorigo was probably in a better position than most other scholars to satisfy his scientific curiosity about economic data, his estimate of the part played by the New Christians in Iberia's foreign trade was largely conjectural. His contention that the Marranos had a large share in the country's slave trade appears particularly dubious. It is certainly not borne out by other contemporary sources or by historical probabilities. See *supra*, n. 32. See also, more generally, J. Larraz López, *La Época del mercantilismo en Castilla, 1500–1700;* V. Palacío Atard, *Derrota, agotamiento, decadencia en la España del siglo XVII*, 2d ed. (especially interesting in his review of contemporary and more recent evaluations of the causes of Spain's amazingly rapid decline, pp. 111 ff.); and particularly J. Vicens Vives's comprehensive *Historia social y económica de España y América*, Vols. III–IV. Of interest also are A. Bermúdez Coñeta's observations on "La Decadencia económica de España en siglo XVI. Ensayo de una interpretación," *Revista de Economía política*, VII, 238–56 (also briefly reviewing the earlier approaches).

39. G. Marañon, *El Conde-Duque de Olivares (la pasión de mandar)*, pp. 379 f.; and in the less explicit German translation by L. Pfandl, esp. pp. 381 ff. Remarkably, even in that final controversy, few enemies seem to have raised the issue of Olivares' "impure" descent from his Aragonese *converso* great-grandfather Lope de Conchillos. See *infra*, n. 48. Except for Quevedo, who in his unbridled attack darkly hinted at this "blemish" of the hated count-duke, others were satisfied with deprecating Conchillos as a *papelista* (a term akin to "bookworm"). Perhaps, being largely recruited from the higher aristocracy and its associates, the opposition did not wish to raise an issue which might have cast a shadow on many other members of the mighty clan of Guzmán as well.

Not surprisingly, the great power in all Spanish affairs—including the changeability in the treatment of Marranos—exercised by the royal favorites, especially chief ministers like the Count de Lerma and Count-Duke Olivares, gave pause to contemporary Spanish political thinkers. See the interesting analysis of the position of the *valido* (royal favorite) as viewed by seventeenth-century political theorists and described by J. A. Maravall in *La Teoria española del Estado en el siglo XVII*, pp. 303 ff.; or in the French translation by L. Cazes and P. Mesnard, revised by Maravall and published under the title *La Philosophie politique espagnole au XVIIe siècle dans ses rapports avec l'esprit de la Contre-Réforme*, pp. 242 ff.

40. Matéo de Lisón y Biedma, *Discursos y Apuntamientos . . . En que se tratan materias importantes del gouierno y de la Monarquía*, Madrid, 1622 (?) and cited by M. Hume in *The Court of Philip IV: Spain in Decadence*, new ed., p. 50; the *Junta's* circular of October 28, 1622, published from a Madrid MS by A. González Palencia

in his documentary publication *La Junta de Reformación. Documentos procedentes del Archivo Histórico Nacional y del General de Simancas* (in *Archivo Histórico Español*, V), pp. 379 ff. No. lxii.

41. The *Pragmatica* of February 10, 1623, published in Madrid, and subsequently included in part in *Nueva Recopilación de leyes*, I, vii. 35; and in *Novísima Recopilación de leyes*, XI, xxvii. 22 (1805 ed., Vol. V, pp. 267 ff.). See A. Domínquez Ortiz, *La Clase social*, pp. 103 ff.; A. A. Sicroff, *Les Controverses*, pp. 218 ff. The burning of the "Green Book" is specifically recorded in Saragossa following a general order of Inquisitor-General Andrés Pacheco and the Supreme Council of the Inquisition dated November 22, 1623, and one addressed to Saragossa three days later. See C. Pérez Pastor, *Bibliografía madrileña o descripción de las obras impresas en Madrid, siglo XVI* (to 1625), III, 442, item 12.

42. See Duarte Gómes Solis, *Discurso sobre los Comercios de las dos Indias, donde se tratan materias importantes de Estado y Guerra, dirigido a la Sacra y Católica Majestad del rey Don Felipe Quarto nuestro señor*, Lisbon, 1622, esp. fols. 134 ff., 156 ff. (the British Museum copy of that edition is provided with extensive marginal comments by a later reader); reed. by M. B. Amzalak, pp. 21, 132; and Amzalak's brief study, *O Economista Duarte Gómez Solis* in his series *A Economia política em Portugal*, mentioning, among other matters, that on four journeys to India, Gómes had suffered three shipwrecks. Gómes' earlier approaches to the Duke de Lerma (his letters dated November 20, and December 12, 1602, are reproduced by Amzalak, *ibid.*), may have appeared to him more encouraging. See *Uma Carta de Duarte Gómes ao Duque de Lerma*, likewise ed. by Amzalak; and *Mémoires inédits de Duarte Gómes Solis (Décembre, 1621)*, ed. by L. Bourdon (publishes the pertinent reports thereon by Mendo da Mota de Valadares and Pedro Alvares Pereira of 1621). It may be noted that Américo Castro, with his usual ingenuity, presents Gómes' kind of managerial technocracy as part of "Un Aspecto del pensar hispano-judío" akin to the thought processes of diverse personalities like Santob de Carrión, Alphonso de la Torre, Luis Vives, and Baruch Spinoza. See his essay under this title in *Hispania* (America), XXXV, 161-72.

43. Joannes Jacobus Chifflet (or Chiflet), *Vindiciae hispanicae in quibus arcana regia publico pacis bono luce donantur*, Antwerp, 1645, dedication; Francisco Suárez' contention cited by an unnamed author in the texts, published with a French summary by E. N. Adler in his "Documents sur les Marranes d'Espagne et de Portugal sous Philippe IV," *REJ*, XLVIII, 1-28; XLIX, 51-73; L, 53-75, 211-37; LI, 97-120, 251-64; esp. XLIX, 66 f. Doc. vii; L, 211 ff. Doc. xii. We must bear in mind, however, that Suárez was anything but an extreme racialist. On one occasion, he approved the admission of a prominent descendant of the Moorish royal house of Granada to the Military Order of Alcántara. See J. A. de Aldama, "Un Parecer de Suárez sobre un estatuto de la O. M. de Alcántara," *Archivo teológico granadino*, XI, 271-85. See also, more generally, Suárez' *Defensio fidei catholicae . . . adversus Anglicanae sectae errores;* his "Contra Judaeos" cited *supra*, Vol. IX, p. 291 item 16; and F. P. Canarvan, "Subordination of the State to the Church according to Suarez," *Theological Studies*, 1951, pp. 354-64. Clearly, Suárez' relatively advanced political views, which, perhaps unwittingly, made him a forerunner of the modern doctrine of sovereignty and even of some elements of rationalism (see R. Labrousse,

Essai sur la philosophie politique de l'ancienne Espagne; politique de la raison et politique de la foi, pp. 17 ff., 90 ff.), did not prevent him from harboring some anti-Jewish and anti-Marrano prejudices. Remarkably, even he did not escape inquisitorial suspicions. See B. Llorca's twin essays, "El P. Suárez y la inquisición española en 1594: Memorial del mismo sobre la cuestión 'de auxiliis div. gratiae,'" *Gregorianum,* XVII, 3–52; and "La Inquisición española y el libro postumo del P. Francisco Suárez 'De vera intelligentia,'" *AHSI,* VII, 240–56.

On the general background of the new negotiations with the Marranos, see Matías de Novoa's comprehensive *Historia de Felipe IV* (the second part of his *Memorias,* the first of which described the reign of Philip III), ed. by the marquis de la Fuensanta del Valle, J. Sancho Rayon, and F. de Zaballuna (this is one of several contemporary histories of Philip's regime); and the more recent studies by J. Deleito y Piñuela, *El Declinar de la monarquía española* (Part 1 of *La España de Felipe IV);* idem, *La Vida religiosa española bajo el cuarto Felipe: Santos y pecadores,* which includes a description of an inquisitor and especially of the auto-da-fé of 1632, based on a contemporary *Relación* in a MS of the National Library of Madrid.

44. See the documents edited and summarized by E. N. Adler in his "Documents sur les Marranes d'Espagne," *REJ,* XLVIII, 1 ff. Nos. i and ii (French); XLIX, 55 ff. Nos. i and ii (Spanish); J. Espinosa Rodríguez, *Fray Antonio de Sotomayor y su correspondencia con Felipe IV;* and C. Sempedro y Folgar, ed., "Cartas familiares de Fr. Antonio de Sotomayor confesor de Felipe IV," *El Museo de Pontevedra,* II, 46–67. According to Adler (XLIX, 54), many other documents are preserved in the British Museum, including a large manuscript of 300 folio pages (Add. 28462), and another (marked Egerton 344), which in part duplicate the collection published by him, but also furnish much new information. Hence, there are significant gaps in our knowledge of the period between 1623 and 1630. Among the various reform projects of the time, mention may also be made of one submitted to the Suprema in 1623, demanding the rotation, every four months, of the provincial inquisitors who were in charge of trials. This measure was intended to expedite the proceedings and to prevent those accused of heresy from interminably languishing in prison while awaiting trial. See H. C. Lea, *A History of the Inquisition of Spain,* I, 509.

45. E. N. Adler, "Documents," in *REJ,* XLVIII, 10 ff. No. vii (French); XLIX, 67 ff. No. viii; L, 217 ff. No. xiv (Spanish). The opinion rendered by the inquisitor-general is undated, but from its location in the archival files it appears to have been written about 1630.

46. E. N. Adler, Docs. xxii and xxiii in *REJ,* XLVIII, 24 ff. (French); LI, 98 ff. No. xxvi (Spanish); M. de la Pinta Llorente in *RABM,* 4th ser. LIV, 98 f. (citing an anonymous Spanish archival document entitled "True Catholics against Jewish Fictions [advanced by] People of the Hebrew Nation").

47. João Pinto Ribeiro, *Discurso si es util, y justo de desterrar de los Reinos de Portugal a los Christianos Novos, convencidos do Judaismo por el tribunal del S. Officio, y reconciliados por èl con sus familias* (unpublished); Fernão Ximenes de Aragão, *Doutrina Catholica para instrucção e confirmação dos fieis, extinção . . . do Judaismo,* Lisbon, 1625 (this book was sufficiently popular to be reprinted within three years); idem, *Triunfo da religião Catholica contra a pertinacia do Judaismo,*

ou, *Compendio de verdaderia fe*, Lisbon, 1752; Vicente da Costa de Mattos, *Breue discurso contra a heretica perfidia do Iudaismo*, Lisbon, 1622 (reprinted in 1634); idem, *Honras christãs nas afrontas de Jesu Christo e segunda parte do primeiro discurso contra a heretica perfidia do Iudaismo*, Lisbon, 1625 (reprinted in 1634); The contrasting attitudes of Luis Vives and Alphonso de Zamora stemmed, of course, from their greater erudition and deeper penetration of the hoary Judeo-Christian dialogue, rather than from their own Jewish descent. Certainly, consciousness of that "blemish" often stimulated writers to become even more vociferous in their denunciation of Jews and Judaism. Alphonso de Spina himself offers a telling illustration of that "defense mechanism." On the two outstanding early sixteenth-century Christian apologists, see P. Graf, *Ludwig Vives als Apologet. Ein Beitrag zugleich zur Geschichte der Apologetik;* and *Luis Vives como apologeta; contribución a la historia de la apologética*, Spanish trans. from the German by J. M. Millás Vallicrosa (with Millás's additional comments thereon in "La Apologética de Luis Vives y el Judaismo," *Sefarad*, II, 293–323); Alphonso de Zamora, *Hokhmat Elohim* (Libro de la Sabiduria de Dios; or, God's Wisdom), trans. into Spanish with notes by F. Pérez Castro under the title *El Manuscrito apologetico de Alfonso de Zamora*. See *supra*, Vol. IX, pp. 97 ff., 287 ff.

Of course, Pinto Ribeiro was not the only author suffering from an enforced silence, since the Spanish Inquisition made extensive use of its power to outlaw "undesirable" books. Even its Portuguese sister institution published indexes of forbidden books from the beginning of its large-scale operations in 1547. See I. S. Révah, *La Censure inquisitoriale portugaise au XVIᵉ siècle*, Vol. I (includes facsimiles of Indexes of 1547, 1551, 1559). See also *supra*, nn. 7–8; Vols. XIII, pp. 76 f., 343 n. 14; XIV, p. 25, 314 n. 23.

48. Francisco Gómez de Quevedo y Villegas, *La Cueva de Meliso*, vv. 1466 ff. (in his Intro. to Quevedo's *Obras completas*, L. Astrana Marín denies Quevedo's authorship of that satire); *Isla de los Monopantos*, later included in Quevedo's major poetic work, *La Hora de Todos* (posthumously published in Madrid, 1650), and readily available in A. Fernández-Guerra y Orbe's ed. of his *Obras. Collección completa* (in *BAE*, XXIII and XLVIII), supplemented by a third vol. of Florencio Janer's ed. of his *Poesías* (in *BAE*, LXIX), I, 381–425, esp. pp. 414 ff. No. xxxix (the editor's fine explanatory notes include a reproduction of *La Cueva de Meliso* and the author's note thereon), here cited from John Stevens's 1709 English translation entitled "The Hour of All Men and Fortune in Her Wits," as revised by Charles Duff in his edition of Quevedo's *The Choice Humorous and Satirical Works*, pp. 293–379, esp. pp. 356 ff. No. xxxix; Fray Benito de Peñalosa y Mandragón, *Libro de las cinco excelencias del español que despueblan a España para su mayor potencia y dilatación*, Pamplona, 1629, pp. 35 f.; and the comments thereon by A. Domínguez Ortiz in *La Clase social*, pp. 116 f.; M. Herrero García in his *Ideas de los Españoles del siglo XVII*, 2d ed., pp. 604 ff.; and J. Caro Baroja in *La Sociedad criptojudia en la Corte de Felipe IV*, p. 40. Quevedo is aptly described by a modern historian as an "irrepressible defamer who venomously lashes out at anything within the reach of his pen and tongue." See J. Deleito y Piñuela, *El Declinar de la monarquía española*, 4th ed., p. 86. See also L. Astrana Marín's ed. of the *Epistolario completo de Don Francisco de Quevedo y Villegas* (with bibliography); and his *La Vida turbulenta de Quevedo*, 2d ed., esp. p. 482, citing Jean Camp's enthusiastic appraisal of *La Hora de Todos*.

The story of Olivares' alleged negotiations with the Salonican Jews was further elaborated by his enemies after his downfall. In a MS entitled *Noticia del nacimiento, vida y hechos de Don Gaspar de Guzmán, Conde-duque de Olivares, valido de la cathólica Magestad del señor don Felipe IV, el Grande,* circulated on February 8, 1643, ten days after the minister's retirement, the public was told that Olivares had overruled the Papacy's objections by claiming that the negotiations were necessary in the service of the king. He is said to have won over to his point of view not only the majority of the Council of State but also some highly respected theologians, and even a small number of officials of the Inquisition. Encouraged by this support, the minister supposedly conceived the plan of abolishing the Holy Office altogether. But at this point the king balked, "for he viewed the Holy Tribunal as a bulwark of the Catholic faith, and as a bastion for the preservation of good mores." See the summary of a copy of that *Noticia,* then in private possession, by J. Amador de los Rios in his *Historia social,* III, 546 ff. Needless to say, no one bothered to submit substantial evidence for the veracity of this rumor.

49. Juan Escobar del Corro, *Tractatus bipartitus de puritate et nobilitate probanda secundum statuta S. Officii Inquisitionis,* etc., 2 parts, Lyons, 1637, *passim;* and *supra,* nn. 23 and 41. See the fairly comprehensive analysis of this work by A. A. Sicroff in *Les Controverses,* pp. 223 ff. Sicroff also cogently argues that the book was written late in 1632 or in 1633, possibly even in 1628, although it was not published until 1637. He also points up certain data about inquisitorial practices, incidentally communicated by the inquisitor of Llerena. For example, Escobar defends the nonacceptance by the Spanish Inquisition of the ruling issued by Pope Gregory XIV in 1591 that all children abandoned by unknown parents automatically be considered *limpios.* He did not justify his repudiation of the papal ordinance on the ground that it gave preference to the children of únwed mothers and unknown fathers over the legitimate offspring of honorable citizens in whose veins may have coursed a few drops of Jewish or Moorish blood. He merely emphasized the curious legal technicality that the Statutes had, from the outset, been enacted as exceptional Spanish regulations, which could not be abrogated by general rulings applicable to the Church Universal. See also *supra,* Vol. XIII, pp. 85, 352 f. n. 23.

Incidentally, nonadmission to the military orders, of which some *conversos* had long been prominent members, was not a matter merely of prestige—a factor that itself could not be minimized in so honor-conscious a society as that of seventeenth-century Spain. It also barred some ambitious, highly-placed Marranos from positions of great practical influence on the country's political and economic life. See L. P. Wright, "The Military Orders in Sixteenth and Seventeenth Century Spanish Society: the Institutional Embodiment of a Historical Tradition," *Past and Present,* No. 43, pp. 34–70. To be sure, the statistical data of papal dispensations allowing the officers to disregard certain defects in the admission of candidates to the Order of Santiago (and probably other orders as well), which are supplied by Wright from records of the Consejo de las Ordenes in the National Archives in Madrid (pp. 60 f.), indicate that only a few such dispensations were granted in the case of "impurity of blood." Under Philip II, 3 dispensations were obtained by non-*limpio* applicants, as against 2 by persons lacking noble descent and 5 by persons of illegitimate birth; under Philip III, the ratio of non-*limpios* dropped to 1 out of 50; and under Philip IV, to none out of 208. The main reason probably was either the dearth of New Christian applicants who entertained any hope of securing such a dispensation or ultimate papal refusal to grant the exception. This paucity of New Christian members is the more remarkable as admission to one or another order could be secured for money, under the excuse of its being a contribution to Spain's conduct of the Thirty Years' War and other defense needs. The practice continued unabated, despite the equivocal opinion rendered by the special royal commission *(Junta de Hábitos)* on June 25, 1649, reproduced by A. Domínguez Ortiz in *La Sociedad española en el siglo XVII*, pp. 362 f. App. x. See also *infra*, nn. 50 and 62.

50. Escobar del Corro, *Tractatus bipartitus*, fols. 108b ff., esp. fol. 111a items 33–34; A. A. Sicroff, *Les Controverses*, pp. 230 f.; *infra*, n. 103. Escobar's general theory of the hereditary transmission of racial traits was mentioned *supra*, Vol. XIII, pp. 85 and 352 f. n. 23. Of course, even if the discovery that an individual was not *limpio* did not have any immediate effect on his business or professional activities, its impact on his and his family's *honor* often was very grave, indeed. We must not forget the high estimation of "honor" in Spanish society which some persons placed on a par with life itself. See *supra*, Vol. XIII, pp. 22 f., 67 f., 93, 314 n. 22, 337 n. 5, 306 f. n. 36; and the stimulating comparative study by J. G. Péristiany, *Honour and Shame: the Values of Mediterranean Society*.

51. Fray Jerónimo de la Cruz, *Defensa de los estatutos y noblezas españolas. Destierro de los abusos, y rigores de los informantes*, Saragossa, 1637. This tract, too, has been fully analyzed by A. A. Sicroff in *Les Controverses*, pp. 236 ff. The frequent inconsistencies, even a certain basic lack of logic in some of the major arguments in De la Cruz' treatise, induced Sicroff to suspect that the friar's real purpose was not to controvert Salucio's *Discurso*, but rather to underscore the validity of his predecessor's main contentions. Sicroff believes that, by attacking with undue sharpness the tract whose attribution to Salucio he impugned, and by heatedly defending the principle of *limpieza* (which Salucio had never denied), De la Cruz wanted to camouflage his own intention to reveal the shortcomings of inquisitorial procedures. This hypothesis appears to be a bit overspeculative. Inconsistent and illogical reasoning can easily be detected among many pamphleteers, without giving rise to suspicions of an intended double-talk. It must be borne in mind, nevertheless, that in periods of great religious or political intolerance with rigid thought control exercised by the authorities and backed by public opinion, many authors of distinction, even if writing nonpolemical treatises, had to conceal their innermost thoughts behind a screen of verbiage or apparently contradictory arguments. Evidence that such a method was employed by several famous philosophers, and that there is a need to read their works between the lines, is marshaled with considerable ingenuity by Leo Strauss in his *Persecution and the Art of Writing* (includes a study of "The Literary Character of the *Guide for the Perplexed*" by Maimonides, which had first appeared in the *Essays on Maimonides*, ed. by me, pp. 37–91). Hypotheses of this kind, even if they cannot enjoy universal acceptance, retain much heuristic merit.

52. J. Adam de la Parra's memorandum, known to H. C. Lea from a Bodleian MS, has been only partially excerpted in a summary thereof by A. Domínguez Ortiz in his "Una Obra desconocida de Adam de la Parra," *Revista bibliográfica y documental*, V, 97–115, esp. pp. 108 f. (see also his critique in *La Clase social*, pp. 118 ff.); Bartolomé Ximénez Patón, *Discurso en favor del santo y loable estatuto de la limpieza*, Granada, 1638.

53. Francisco Gómez de Quevedo y Villegas, *Historia de la Vida del Buscón*, v, in his *Obras*, ed. by A. Fernández-Guerra y Orbe (in *BAE*, XXIII), I, 493b; also in John Stevens's English trans. of 1709, revised by Pedro Pineda in 1743 and recast in C. Duff's ed. of Quevedo, *The Choice Humorous and Satirical Works*, p. 24; J. O. Crosby, *En torno a la poesía de Quevedo;* Tirso de Molina, *El Árbol del mejor fruto*, iii. 4 in his *Comedias*, ed. by E. Cotarelo y Morí (in *Nueva BAE*, IV and IX), I, 30–60, esp. pp. 52 f.; Félix Lope de Vega Carpio, *Lealtad en el agravio*, in his *Obras*, published by the R. Academia Española with a new biography of the author by C. A. de la Barrera, VIII, 489–520, esp. p. 495b; Luis Vélez de Guevara, *Hércules de Ocaña*, iii, in his *Ocho comedias desconocidas*, ed. by A. Schaeffer, II, 217–93, esp. p. 292. On Lope de Vega's strong influence on this play, see F. E. Spencer and R. Schevill, *The Dramatic Works of Luis Vélez de Guevara. Their Plots, Sources and Bibliography*, pp. 377 ff. Most of these, and many other, passages are cited with extensive documentation in M. Herrero García's *Ideas de los Españoles del siglo XVII*, pp. 597 ff., esp. pp. 606 ff., 614, 625 ff., 632 f.; and in E. Glaser's "Referencias antisemitas en la literatura peninsular de la edad de oro," *Nueva Revista de filología hispánica*, VIII, 39–62.

On the supposedly characteristic "Jewish" nose, see the proverb cited *supra*, Vol. XIII, pp. 33, 320 n. 34; and, more generally, M. Herrero García's "Los Rasgos físicos y el carácter según los textos españoles del siglo XVII," *Revista de la filología española*, XII, 157-77, esp. pp. 173 ff., also quoting Luis de León's literal trans. of the biblical phrase referring to God as *erekh-appa'im* (long-suffering; Exod. 34:6, etc.) by *ancho de narices* (broad-nosed). Nor did Quevedo hesitate to attack on this score his equally eminent literary confrere Luis de Góngora. He satirically addressed the latter: "Why do you criticize the Greek language/ Being only a rabbi of the Jewish [tongue]/A matter which your nose does not negate?" See his *Obras en verso del Homero español*, in the facsimile reproduction of the first ed. of 1627 by J. López de Vicuña, with an Intro. and Indices by D. Alonso, pp. 147, 179. Luis Góngora's brother, Francisco, indeed had some difficulties when he was called upon to prove his *limpieza*. See M. Arigas, *Don Luis de Góngora y Argote. Biografía y estudio crítico*, pp. 100 ff.; and E. Glaser's remarks thereon in "Referencias antisemitas," pp. 50 f. See also A. Collard, "La 'Herejía' de Góngora," *Hispanic Review*, XXXVI, 328–37, esp. pp. 333 ff. (showing how a purely literary feud quickly turned into a political struggle with vilification of Góngora's *converso* origin); D. Alonso, "El Pobre Cañizares," *Boletín* of the Academia Española, XLI, 413–24; idem and E. Galvarriato de Alonso, eds., *Para la biografía de Góngora: Documentos desconocidos;* and R. Jammes, *Études sur l'oeuvre poétique de Don Luis de Góngora y Argote.* Remarkably, even the ever-hostile Quevedo does not refer to the long-accepted medieval attibution of a special body odor to Jews, nor does he mention the frequent Spanish explanation thereof by the Jewish use of olive oil instead of lard. See *supra*, Vols. XI, pp. 136 f., 352 f. n. 18; XIII, pp. 322 f. n. 18.

Needless to say, derision of Jewish messianic expectations could well go hand in hand with the high appreciation of those Christian theologians who, like the Hebraists of Salamanca, greatly extolled the corresponding Christian hopes for ultimate redemption. See F. Sánchez-Arjona, "La Certeza de la esperanza cristiana en los teólogos de la escuela de Salamanca," *Scripta theologica* (Pamplona), I, 119–46. The admirers of that distinguished faculty were hardly aware of the extent to which its New Christian members, from Francisco de Vitoria to Luis de León, and their disciples were influenced in their teachings by the heritage of Hebraic messianism.

54. Francisco de Torrejoncillo, *Centinela contra Ivdíos*, p. 113; *supra*, n. 26. Numerous other statements of a similar nature are cited by M. Herrero García in his *Idéas de los Españoles, passim.*

55. Miguel de Cervantes Saavedra, *El Ingenioso hidalgo Don Quixote de la Mancha;* and *Il Retablo de las maravillas;* in the facsimile edition of *Obras completas*, published by the R. Academia Española, II, 91a; III, 27b; idem, *Novela del amante liberal* in his *Novelas exemplares, ibid.*, IV, 48a; D. Aubier, *Don Quichotte, prophète d'Israël*, esp. pp. 9 ff., 271 ff. (emphasizing the impact of the *Zohar*); P. Werrie's inconclusive discussion, "Cervantès, était-il juif?" *Écrits de Paris*, March 1968, pp. 92–97; and, more generally, the sources cited by J. A. Maravall in *La Philosophie politique espagnole au XVIIe siècle*, trans. from the Spanish by L. Cazes and P. Mesnard. The passages here quoted, and a few others, listed by C. Fernández Gómez in his *Vocabulario de Cervantes*, pp. 268 *s.v.* Cristiano, and 575 *s.v.* Judería and Judío, controvert Cervantes' alleged silence on the Jewish question, as claimed by R. Cansinos Assens in his *Cervantes y los Israelitas españoles*. See also A. Domínguez Ortiz, "Los 'Cristianos Nuevos,'" *Boletin . . . Granada*, XXI, 270; idem, *La Clase social;* and *infra*, n. 57.

The historical background of Velázquez' paintings and other contempory works of art is analyzed, for instance, by C. Justi in his *Diego Velázquez and His Time*, trans. by A. H. Keane, and revised by the author, esp. pp. 59 ff., 377 f. On Velázquez' possible Jewish antecedents, see J. Caro Baroja, "Sombras en torno a Velázquez," *Revista de Occidente* (Madrid), 2d ser. II, 222–28 (pointing out especially the coincidental presence in Madrid of a kinsman (?), Diego Rodriguez da Silva the royal historiographer, a New Christian and later a professing Jew; see *infra*, n. 75); M. B. Amzalak in the Intro. to his ed. of Ḥizqiyahu (Hezekiah) da Silva's *Del fundamento de nuestra ley. Sermon moral* (delivered in 1690), pp. v f.; and J. M. de Azcarate, "La Fuente de Cain y Abel del palacio de la Ribera," *Boletin* of the Seminario de Estudios de Arte y Arqueología (Valladolid), XXVIII, 263–64 (the fountain was transferred in 1654 to the Prado gardens).

56. See J. L. Flecniakoska, *La Formation de l'"auto" religieux en Espagne avant Calderón (1550–1635);* idem, "Le Rôle de Satan dans les 'autos' de Lope de Vega," *BH*, LXVI, 30–44, esp. pp. 42 ff.; J. Rodríguez Puértolas, "La Transposición de la realidad en los autos sacramentales de Lope de Vega," *ibid.*, LXXII, 96–112, esp. pp. 98 f., 102 f., 110 f., 112; A. M. Layuela, "Los Autos sacramentales de Lope, reflejo de la cultura religiosa del poeta y del su tiempo," *Razón y fé*, CVIII, 168–90, 330–49; other studies listed by R. L. Grismer in his *Bibliography of Lope de Vega*; A. A. Parker, "The Chronology of Calderón's Autos Sacramentales' from 1647," *Hispanic Review*, XXXVII, 164–88 (with a chronological table, 1647–81; pp. 187 f.); A. Valbuena-Briones, *Perspectiva crítica de los dramas de Calderón*, esp. pp. 73 ff. (analyzing Calderón's *Judas Macabeo*); and the mutually complementary essays by J. Corrales Egea, "Relaciones entre el auto sacramental y la contrareforma," *Revista de Ideas estéticas*, III, 511–14; and N. González Ruiz, "Fé, poesía y combate en el auto sacramental," *España eucaristica*, 1952, pp. 59–68. See also J. E. Varey's succinct survey, "La Mise en scène de l'auto sacramental à Madrid au XVIe et XVIIIe siècle," in *Le Lieu théatral à la Renaissance*, ed. by J. Jacquot *et al.*, pp. 215–26; and, in greater detail, N. D. Shergold and J. E. Varey, "A Problem in the Staging of 'Autos sacramentales' in Madrid 1647–48," *Hispanic Review*, XXXII, 12–35. On the ante-

cedents of this evolution, see J. P. W. Crawford, "The Devil as a Dramatic Figure in the Spanish Religious Drama before Lope de Vega," *Romanic Review,* I, 302–312, 374–83; and other data mentioned *supra,* Vol. XI, pp. 133 ff., 348 ff. nn. 13 ff.

57. See J. Ortega y Gasset, *Meditaciones del Quijote;* R. del Arco's twin essays, "La ínfima levadura social en las obras de Cervantes" and "La Crítica social en Cervantes," *Estudios de historia social de España,* II, 209–290, 291–326; A. Castro, *El Pensamiento de Cervantes,* p. 254; idem, "Cervantes y la Inquisición," *Modern Philology,* XXVII, 427–33, reprinted in *Semblanza y estudios españoles. Homenaje ofrecido a Don Américo Castro por sus ex-alumnos de Princeton University,* pp. 137–43; J. López Navio, "Sobre la frase de Duquesa: 'las obras de caridad hechas floja y tibiamente' (Don Quijote 2, 36)," *Anales Cervantinos,* IX, 97–112, arguing, in answer to Castro, that Cervantes' casual criticism of "good works" referred only to such as were performed in a careless and lukewarm fashion. This point of view is supported by M. Descouzis, who tries to prove that, on the whole, the great novelist strictly conformed with the decisions of the Council of Trent, especially with respect to the Council's opposition to duels, its doctrines of penitence and justification, the use of the term "dignity" as a synonym for "clergy," and the like. See Descouzis, *Cervantes a nueva luz,* Vol. I: *El "Quijote" y el Concilio de Trento,* esp. pp. 21 ff. However, Descouzis pays insufficient attention to the fact that the element of "intention" in good works was an integral part of meritorious deeds according to pre-Tridentine Church teachings as well, and that this idea had its roots in a long-accepted biblical and postbiblical Jewish emphasis, which had permeated the entire ramified Jewish social welfare system for ages. In this respect, the possible Jewish traditions, conscious or unconscious, in Cervantes' family, could have only reinforced the accepted views of Christian theologians. See also *supra,* Vol. XIII, pp. 97, 358 n. 41; and, more generally, P. Hazard, *Don Quichotte de Cervantès. Étude et analyse;* L. Astrana Marín, *Estudio crítico a la edición, IV Centenario del Quijote,* p. 40; his comprehensive biography, *Vida ejemplar y heróica del Miguel de Cervantes Saavedra con MII documentos hasta ahora inéditos y numerosas ilustraciones y grabados de época* (his excellent genealogical reconstruction nonetheless leaves many questions open).

From the enormous and ever-growing literature on Cervantes, we need but mention here the exploration of various pertinent aspects by the following authors: A. de Del Rio Agostini [Bonelli], "El Teatro cómico de Cervantes," *Boletín* of the R. Academia Española, XLIV, No. 172, pp. 223–307, No.173, pp. 475–539; XLV, Nos. 174–75, pp. 65–116, esp. XLIV, 276 ff. (description of various characters); C. Bernheimer, "Some New Contributions to Abraham Cardoso's Biography," *JQR,* XVIII, 97–129, esp. p. 112; H. Recoules, "Dios, el diablo y la sagrada Escritura en los Entremeses de Cervantes," *Boletín* of the Biblioteca Menéndez Pelayo, XLI, 91–106; J. Antonio Monroy, *La Biblia en el Cervantes,* esp. pp. 25 ff., 35 ff., and 41 ff.; and his list of biblical quotations in *Don Quixote, ibid.,* pp. 175 f. On Castro's general views of Cervantes see, among others, P. Garragorri's comments in his "Historia y literatura (hacia Cervantes)," *Cuadernos hispanoamericanos,* LXXII, 257–72. Yet, the doubts about the master's depth of piety have not been resolved. See also *supra,* nn. 9 and 55; and T. S. Tómor's "Cervantes y Lope de Vega (Un caso de enemistad literaria)," *Actas* of the Asociacíon internacional de Hispanistas, 1966–68, pp. 617–26. This enmity may have been intensified, in part, by Lope's hostile attitude to the *conversos.* It should be noted, however, that while study of the Bible by laymen was suspect, instruction in Hebrew at the university level was still being encouraged. In 1625 Philip IV actually established a chair for Hebrew and another for Chaldaic and Syriac out of a total of twenty-three chairs at the new Jesuit Colegio Imperial. See J. Simón Díaz, "La Cátedra de hebreo en los estudios de San Isidro de Madrid," *Sefarad*, VIII, 97–116.

58. See Lope de Vega's *La Hermosa Ester* in his *Obras* (published by the R. Academia Española), III, 307–345; his *Rimas sacras*, Madrid, 1614 (facsimile ed. with an Intro. by Joaquín de Estrambasaguas, Madrid, 1963), fol. 3r; his *Las Paces de los Reyes y Judía de Toledo*, in the critical ed. by J. A. Castañeda; De Barrios' ballad "De Jacob y Raquel" and a sonnet in his *Coro de las Musas*, Brussels, 1672, pp. 260 ff. See E. Glaser, "A Biblical Theme in Iberian Poetry of the Golden Age," *Studies in Philology*, LII, 524–48, esp. pp. 534 ff. and 542 ff.; idem, "Lope de Vega's 'La Hermosa Ester,'" *Sefarad*, XX, 110–35 (also listing other important studies of that "tragicomedy," which, "completed in 1610, constitutes a landmark in the history of the Spanish theater"); K. R. Scholberg, ed., *La Poesía religiosa de Miguel de Barrios*, with a lengthy intro. on the author's life and work; and the comments thereon by E. M. Wilson in his "Miguel de Barrios and Spanish Religious Poetry," *Bulletin of Hispanic Studies*, XL, 176–80. (The De Barrios collection includes several poems commemorating contemporary martyrs for the faith; pp. 240 ff.) See also M. R. Lida de Malkiel, "*La Infancia de Moisés* y otros tres estudios. En torno al influjo de Josefo en la literature española," *Romance Philology*, XXIII (=Ramón Menéndez Pidal Mem. Vol. I), 412–48 (showing how, through their borrowing of picturesque details from Josephus, a number of Spanish writers, including Lope de Vega, were indirectly indebted to the Aggadah); E. Segura Covarsi, "La 'Raquel' de García de la Huerta," *Revista de estudios extremeños*, VII, 197–234. On Lope's relation with the Holy Office, see the data analyzed by A. Castro and H. A. Rennert in their *Vida de Lope de Vega (1562–1635)*, (based on Rennert's original *The Life of Lope de Vega*), 2d ed., pp. 169 f., 272, 535; A. Castro, "Una Comedia de Lope de Vega condenada por la Inquisición," *Revista de filología española*, IX, 311–14; and D. J. Pamp, *Lope de Vega ante el problema de la limpieza de sangre*. The description of the functions of a familiar of the Holy Office is reproduced from a Brussels MS in J. P. Davos's ed. of the *Description de l'Espagne par Jehan L'Hermite et Henri Cock, humanistes belges, archers du Corps de la Garde royale (1560–1622)*, p. 127 n. 90.

In passing, we may also mention here the still-controversial problem of the extent to which Matéo Alemán's consciousness of his Jewish descent colored his famous picaresque novel, *Guzmán de Alfarache*. To the literature listed *supra*, Vol. XIII, pp. 67 f., 337 f. n. 51, add J. A. van Praag, "Sobre el sentido del *Guzmán de Alfarache*," in *Estudios dedicados a Menéndez Pidal*, V, 283–306; J. H. Silverman, "Plinio, Pedro Mejía y Matéo Alemán," *Papeles de Son Armadans*, LII, 30–38 (explains much of Alemán's pessimism as being an attempt to cover up his Jewish ancestry); D. McGrady, *Matéo Alemán*; and, more generally, A. A. Parker, *Literature and the Delinquent: the Picaresque Novel in Spain and Europe, 1599–1753*, esp. pp. 13 ff., 31. However, despite the obvious tensions of Marrano life, it remains questionable whether one may speak of "la peculiaridad literaria de los conversos," be they of the kind of Alemán, who tried to conceal his Jewish ancestry, or like De Barrios, who returned to Judaism in tolerant Holland. See the attempt to define such a peculiarity by E. Asensio in the essay with that Spanish title in *Anuario de estudios medievales*,

IV, 327–51. In any case, the attitude of the great Spanish writers of the Golden Age toward the New Christian problem, as well as toward Judaism as a religion, merits much more extensive monographic treatment than has hitherto been accorded to it.

59. See P. B. Gams, *Die Kirchengeschichte von Spanien*, III, Part 2, pp. 268 ff.; J. Caro Baroja, *Los Judíos*, II, 230 f.; *supra*, Vol. XIII, pp. 79 f., 344 f. n. 16. On St. Theresa's Jewish ancestry, see N. Alonso Cortés, "Pleitos de los Cepedas," *Boletín* of the Academía Española, XXV, 85–110; and H. Serís, "Nueva genealogía de Santa Teresa (artículo-reseña)," *Nueva Revista de filología hispánica*, X, 365–84. It may also be noted that Lope de Vega had earlier participated in the celebration of Theresa's beatification, on October 16, 1614. He was a member of a committee which judged the poems to be presented on that occasion. He also recited the opening panegyric extolling the saintly nun's virtues. See A. Castro and H. A. Rennert, *Vida de Lope de Vega*, 2d ed., p. 211. The 1519 statement of the municipality of Ávila that Theresa's grandfather Juan Sánchez of Toledo and his sons were "*conversos* and descendants of a Jewish lineage" was largely corroborated by the testimony of several witnesses. See, however, F. Cantera's reservations in his note thereon in *Sefarad*, XVII, 432; and his earlier remarks on "Santa Teresa de Jesús de ascendencia judía?" *ibid.*, XIII, 402–404, a review of the then newly published Vol. I of the Saint's *Obras completas: Nueva revisión del texto original, con notas críticas*, ed. by F. Efrén and F. Otilio, and Efrén's introductory "Biografía de Santa Teresa," esp. pp. 159 ff. Despite such reservations, Theresa's grandfather's appearance as a Judaizer before the Inquisition seems to be beyond doubt.

It is truly ironical, therefore, that in 1625, in a bellicose sermon on St. Theresa, the preacher Fray Hortensio Félix Paravicino invoked the shade of the gentle, other-worldly nun in exhorting his audience not only to improve their own moral conduct, since their sins were injuring God's cause, but also militantly to combat any manifestation of heresy. He exclaimed: "To think that, because of my wickedness, Thou, O God, findest Thy doctrine subverted! To the defense, Madrid! To the defense, lords and ladies! To the defense, ye commoners! To the defense, everyone!" See M. Herrero García, ed., *Sermonario clásico*, pp. 10 f.; here cited from the passage trans. into English by O. H. Green in his *Spain and the Western Tradition: the Castilian Mind in Literature from El Cid to Calderón*, IV, 147 f.

60. See Francisco López de Villalobos, *Los Problemas* (*BAE*, XXXVI), p. 444; his noteworthy work, *El Sumario de la medicina, con un Tratado sobre las pestíferas bubas*, ed. with an Intro. by E. García del Real, pp. 14 ff., 123, 321 f.; J. Caro Baroja, *La Sociedad criptojudía en la corte de Felipe IV*, pp. 89 f.; idem, *Los Judíos*, I, 289; II, 174 f., 290; C. Calamita, *Figuras y semblanzas del imperio. Francisco López de Villalobos médico de reyes y príncipe de literatos;* and H. Friedenwald's succinct sketch, "Francisco López de Villalobos, Spanish Court Physician and Poet," *Bulletin* of the Institute of the History of Medicine of Johns Hopkins University, VII, 1129–39. A number of other telling passages were long before culled from Villalobos' writings by A. M. Fabié *et al.* in their lengthy biographical intro. to their ed. of the physician's *Algunas obras*, published by the Sociedad de Bibliófilos españoles (in its collection, Vol. XXIV), pp. 5 ff. This volume includes a new ed. of the *Sumario* and a considerable number of Villalobos' "Cartas." In a letter, probably written sometime between 1535 and 1540, to Fray Vicente Lunel, prior-general of the Franciscan Order, Villalobos courageously complained about the maltreatment of certain

French Franciscans upon their arrival in Spain for no other reason than their being *conversos*. See his undated Spanish letter, *ibid.*, "Cartas castellanas," pp. 165 ff. No. xlv; also reprinted by A. Domínguez Ortiz in *La Clase social*, pp. 249 ff. App. vi. See also *supra*, Vol. XIII, pp. 73, 340 f. n. 11. The widespread allegation that Jewish physicians often tried to kill their Christian patients was echoed by such writers as Tirso de Molina in *La Prudencia en la mujer* in his *Obras dramáticas completas*, ed. by B. de los Rios, and many others. In connection with this passage, E. Glaser cites the later observation by the generally more enlightened, though no less anti-Jewish, Benito Jerónimo Feijóo y Montenegro, that such doctors would speedily lose their patients. See Glaser's "Referencias antisemitas," *Nueva Revista de filología hispánica*, VIII, 44 f.

Villalobos evidently was a daring exception. Perhaps he was too sure of his indispensability to Charles V [I]. However, most other New Christians, like many minority groups elsewhere, tended to become infected with the prejudices rampant among the hostile majority. A telling illustration is offered by the comparatively moderate writer Lucas Gracián Dantisco. In *El Galateo español* (a Spanish counterpart to the popular Italian *Il Galateo* by Giovanni della Casa) this author describes proper courtly behavior and, among other directions, advises the reader that he may appropriately ridicule someone's physical defects but must never deride one's family descent. Yet he cannot escape referring, albeit rather good-naturedly, to the word *judío* as a term of opprobrium. He tells of two New Christians who hurled the insulting epithets "Jew" and "drunkard" at each other yet subsequently became good friends. See L. de Pinedo, *Libro de chistes*, pp. 53 f.; Lucas Gracián Dantisco, *El Galateo español*, new ed. revised, Madrid, 1746, pp. 89, 128; or the new critical edition with Intro., Notes, and Glossary by M. Morreale, p. 148; E. Glaser, pp. 48 n. 22, 57 n. 48; J. Caro Baroja, *Los Judios*, I, 292; and M. Morreale's general analysis of "Una Obra de cortesanía en tono menor: el 'Galateo español' de Lucas Gracián Dantisco," *Boletín* of the R. Academia Española, XLII, No. 165, pp. 47–89.

61. I. S. Révah, "Un Pamphlet contre l'Inquisition d'Antonio Enríquez Gómez: La seconde partie de la 'Política Angélica' (Rouen, 1647)," *REJ*, CXXI, 81–168; *supra*, Chaps. LXIII, n. 70; LXIV, nn. 30 and 36; Balthazar (Isaac) Orobio de Castro, *Israel vengé, ou exposition naturelle des prophéties hebraïques que les Chrétiens appliquent à Jésus, leur prétendu Messie;* idem, *La Observancia de la Divina Ley de Mosseh*, ed. by M. B. Amzalak; Orobio de Castro's disputation with Philip van Limborch, reproduced by the latter in his *De veritate religionis Christianae amica collatio cum erudito Judaeo*, Amsterdam, 1687 (see *supra*, Chap. LXIII, n. 76); Isaac (Fernando) Cardoso, *Las Excelencias de los Hebreos*, Amsterdam, 1679, *passim*. Much apologetic material is also included in Cardoso's *Philosophia libera in septem libros distributa*, Venice, 1673, as analyzed by Y. H. Yerushalmi in his biography entitled *From Spanish Court to Italian Ghetto: Isaac Cardoso*, esp. pp. 271 ff. Among other former Marranos living in foreign lands, one might mention the prominent proselytizers Immanuel Aboab and Elijah Montalto (whose apologetic work is not available, however). See C. Roth, "Immanual Aboab's Proselytization of the Marranos: From an Unpublished Letter," *JQR*, XXIII, 121–62, reprinted in his *Gleanings*, pp. 152–73 (without the documentary appendix); and *supra*, Chap. LXIV, nn. 11 and 34. These and other works by Marrano controversialists constitute an important segment of Jewish literary activity of that period and will be more fully discussed in a later chapter.

62. Liudprand (Luitprandus), bishop of Cremona, *Opera quae extant, Chronicon et Adversaria,* ed. with notes by P. H. de la Higuera and J. L. Ramirez de Prado, Antwerp, 1640 (later also in Migne's *PL,* CXXXVI, 967 ff. [Chronica], 1133 ff. [Adversaria]; and in G. H. Pertz's *Monumenta Germaniae Historica,* V); Julian Petri, *Chronicon,* ed. by J. L. Ramirez de Prado, Paris, 1628, both analyzed by J. Godoy Alcántara in his *Historia crítica de los falsos cronicones,* esp. pp. 210 f.; and F. Martínez Marina, "Antigüedades hispano-hebreas, convencidas de supuestas y fabulosas. Discurso histórico crítico sobre la primera venida de los Judíos a España," *Memorias* of the R. Academia de la Historia, III, 317–468; as well as other sources cited by A. Domínguez Ortiz in *La Clase social,* pp. 213 ff. App. i; *supra,* n. 49; and Vol. XIII, pp. 95 ff., 357 ff. nn. 38–40. On the original editor of these chronicles, an erudite, if rather uncritical, bibliophile, see J. de Entrambagaguas's analysis in his *La Biblioteca de Prado.* Domínguez Ortiz goes a bit too far in attributing most of these falsifications to pro-Marrano bias, however. Many of them undoubtedly stemmed from the naive wish to glorify Spain—a phenomenon encountered in most other Christian countries, which also tried to associate the antiquity of their peoples with Old Testament personalities and events. On similar manifestations of Austrian super-patriotism, see *supra,* Vol. XIII, pp. 194 f. 411 n. 39. Needless to say, not everybody in Spain believed these tales. For example, the legend about the arrival of Jews in Spain after the first fall of Jerusalem was dismissed, on the authority of Orosius, St. Jerome, and Hegesippus, by Pedro de Salazar y Mendoza, as a "contrivance of the rabbis." See his *Crónica de el Gran Cardenal de España Don Pedro Gonçalez de Mendoça,* lxxii, pp. 246 ff.

We must also remember that the entire status of the Spanish nobility had long been under debate. The author of the tract discussed in the text undoubtedly belonged to the minority which extolled the virtues of the aristocracy, as opposed to the considerable number of literary detractors and the majority, who held an intermediary position. See A. Domínguez Ortiz, *La Sociedad . . . siglo XVII,* I, 315 ff. The relative silence in that debate about the *hidalguía*'s intermingling with the New Christian group may have been owing to the government's disapproval of any public discussion of the questionable Jewish ancestry of many noble families, a policy which found its clearest expression in the suppression of such works as the *Tizón de la nobleza.* On the other hand, the very compilation and dissemination of that genealogical work is said to have owed its origin to the fact that its purported author, Cardinal Francisco de Mendoza y Bobadilla, was himself the grandson of a *converso,* Andrés Cabrera of Segovia. Peeved by the difficulties encountered by his nephew Count De Chinchón in producing proofs of his "purity of blood" before he was admitted to a military Order, the cardinal thus wished to show that many Castilian nobles had such a "tainted" ancestry. See J. Caro Baroja, *Los Judíos,* II, 253 ff., 368 f.; M. Bataillon, "Benedotto Varchi et le cardinal de Burgos, D. Francisco de Mendoza y Bobadilla," *Lettres romanes,* XXIII, 3–62, esp. pp. 6 f.

63. A. Castillo, "Dans la monarchie espagnole du XVIIe siècle; les banquiers portugais et le circuit d'Amsterdam," *Annales ESC,* XIX, 311–16; F. Mauro, "Marchands et marchands-banquiers portugais au XVIIe siècle," *Revista portuguesa de historia,* IX, 63–78. On the increasingly chaotic situation in Spain during the reign of Philip IV, see especially the various studies by J. Deleito y Piñuela, esp. *El Declinar de la monarquia española; idem, La Mala vida en la España de Felipe IV,* with a foreword by G. Marañon, 2d ed.; and A. Domínguez Ortiz's basic study *Política y haci-*

enda de Felipe IV. See also A. Bermúdez Cañete, "La Decadencia económica de España en el siglo XVI. Ensayo de una interpretación," *Revista de Economia política*, VII, 238–56; and the other publications listed *supra*, nn. 20 and 38; and Chap. LXIII, n. 63. On the lopsided economic status and widespread indebtedness of the leading class of nobles, and their adverse impact on the national economy, see also A. Domínguez Ortiz's pertinent observations in *La Sociedad . . . siglo XVII*, I, 223 ff.

64. José de Pellicer (Joseph Pellizer) y Tobar, *Avisos históricos, que comprehenden las noticias y sucesos mas particulares, ocurridos en nuestra Monarquia desde el año de 1639*, ed. by A. Valladares de Sotomayor in *Semanario erudito*, XXXI, 3–288 (esp. pp. 21 f.); XXXII, 3–287; XXXIII, 3–288 (includes a number of other documents, pp. 259 ff.); A. Domínguez Ortiz, *La Clase social*, p. 119 n. 30. See also the highly informative twin studies by A. Girard, *Le Commerce français à Séville et Cadix au temps des Habsbourg. Contribution à l'étude du commerce étranger en Espagne aux XVI*ᵉ *et XVII*ᵉ *siècles;* and *La Rivalité commerciale et maritime entre Séville et Cadix jusqu'à la fin du XVIII*ᵉ *siècle.*

65. See H. Hauser, "Les Relations commerciales entre la France et l'Espagne et la politique de Richelieu," *Revue d'histoire, économique et sociale*, XXIV, 5–13, esp. pp. 8 f.; A. Domínguez Ortiz, "Guerra económica y comercio extranjero en el reinado de Felipe IV," *Hispania* (Madrid), XXIII, 71–110, showing that despite stringent laws against trade with enemy aliens, Spain continued to exchange goods with both Holland and France clandestinely, with the connivance of corrupt officials. It probably was easier for Marrano merchants, with their interterritorial connections, to carry on with that profitable trade. See also *infra*, n. 68; and, more generally, Juan Reglá's chapter on "La Época de los dos últimos Austrias" in J. Vicens Vives' ed. of *Historia social y económica de España y America* (also in *Historia de la España moderna*), III, 250 ff., 318 ff.

66. See José de Pellicer's *Avisos históricos*, in *Semanario erudito*, XXXI, 268; the anonymous *Noticias de Madrid 1621–1627*, ed. by A. González Palencia (see *infra*, n. 68); various letters from Sebastián González and others to their fellow-Jesuit Rafael Pereyra in 1637–46, published by P. de G[ayangos] in his ed. of *Cartas de algunos Padres de la Compañía de Jesús sobre los sucesos de la Monarquia entre los años de 1634 y 1648* (*Memorial histórica español*, XIII–XIX), esp. II, 39, 65; IV, 390; VI, 338; VII, 257, with the editor's notes thereon; and J. Caro Baroja, *La Sociedad criptojudia en la Corte de Felipe IV*, esp. pp. 65 ff. The banquet of 1637 is described in some detail by contemporaries. See esp. A. Rodríguez Villa, *La Corte y monarquia de España en los años de 1636-37. Colección de cartas inéditas y interesantes*. See also, more generally, A. Morel-Fatio, *L'Espagne au XVI*ᵉ *et au XVII*ᵉ *siècle. Documents historiques et litteraires, publiés et annotés;* and J. Caro Baroja, *Los Judíos*, II, 103 ff., summarizing, with extensive documentation, the inquisitorial and other records pertaining to Manuel Cortizos and his family. Here (p. 106 n. 11) Caro Baroja also confirms Cortizos' purported Jewish origins, against the strictures advanced by A. Domínguez Ortiz in his *Política y hacienda de Felipe IV*, pp. 136 f. However, we must also remember Gayangos's justified warning (I, p. x) concerning the general unreliability, sometimes outright falsehood, of many contemporary reports (comparable to the gossip columns in modern newspapers), except for a few semiofficial

and otherwise more-or-less dependable documents, like those by Rodrigo Méndez Silva. See *infra*, n. 75.

67. See J. García Mercadal, *España vista por los estranjeros*, III, 100 f. (based on reports by travelers and ambassadors from early times to the seventeenth century; here citing a MS report from the National Library in Madrid); A. Morel-Fatio, *L'Espagne au XVIe et au XVIIe siècle*, pp. 636, 661 ff., 667, 673; J. Caro Baroja, *Los Judíos*, II, 103 ff.; III, 347 ff. Apps. xxxiv–xxxv. On the doubts expressed by scholars concerning Cortizos' loan to the queen, as well as the authenticity of the subsequent exchange of letters between the queen and Olivares, see G. Marañon, *El Conde-duque*, p. 351.

68. F. Mauro, "Marchands," *Revista portuguesa de historia*, IX, 63 ff.; the detailed archival study by A. Domínguez Ortiz, "El Proceso inquisitorial de Juan Núñez Saravía, Banquero de Felipe IV," *Hispania* (Madrid), XV, 559–81; J. Caro Baroja, *La Sociedad*, pp. 43 ff. On Villadiego's mission, see *supra*, Chap. LXIV, n. 32. Under the circumstances, it appears unlikely that Juan was able to offer the Inquisition 12,000 ducats for the privilege of not having to appear in the auto, as was reported by Fray Sebastián González in his letter of December 16, 1637 (but three days after the event), to Rafael Pereyra in P. de G[ayangos]'s ed. of *Cartas*, II (*Memorial histórico español*, XIV), p. 272; and, more fully, in the anonymous *Noticias de Madrid*, fols. 117vo. Unfortunately, the part of the Madrid MS No. 2513 containing these valuable succinct *Noticias* was published by A. González Palencia only to the year 1627 and, of course, does not reproduce Sebastián González' letter of 1637. See his ed. of *Noticias de Madrid, 1621–1627*.

Illegal smuggling of precious metals out of the country, with the cooperation of corrupt Spanish customs agents and shipmasters, continued after Olivares, although ever since the decree of February 7, 1626, it had been under the sanction of capital punishment. The practice, complained of in the days of Philip II by the Dominican friar Tomás de Mercado, who said that "strangers despoil our country of its gold and silver and inflate their own holdings by employing all sorts of stratagems and deceits," was even more widespread in 1655, according to the keen French observer Antoine de Brunel. See the passages quoted by M. Defourneaux in *La Vie quotidienne en Espagne au siècle d'or*, pp. 91 f.

The general inefficacy of the government's economic policies was demonstrated, in particular, during the Thirty Years' War, when not only the corrupt lower bureaucracy but also the highest authorities of the realm often violated their own prohibitions against the importation of goods from hostile Holland, by granting special import licenses for much-needed merchandise. See the examples cited by A. Domínguez Ortiz in his "Guerra económica," *Hispania* (Madrid), XXIII, esp. pp. 95 f., 109 f. App. iv. On the other hand, disregard of the prohibition against certain exports, a ban intended to deprive the enemy of raw materials and industrial products required for their war effort, is rightly compared by Domínguez with the inefficacy of Napoleon's Continental Blockade. In the long run it only stimulated the growth of Atlantic piracy.

69. See Alonso de Santa Cruz, *Crónica de los Reyes Católicos*, ed. with an Intro. by J. de Matos Carriazo, p. 196. We have only a brief mention of Cansino's arrest in a letter addressed on October 23, 1646, by Sebastián González to Rafael Pereyra, in

which the friar describes Cansino as "a Jew by nationality and profession [who], they say, caused great inconveniences by his excessive dealings with some members of the *nación*, as they are called in Portugal." See P. de G[ayangos], ed. of the *Cartas de algunos Padres*, VI (*Memorial histórico español*, XVIII), p. 420; the summary in J. Caro Baroja, *Los Judíos*, II, 110 ff.; M. Kayserling, *Biblioteca española-portugueza-judaica*, pp. 10 f., 33. On the importance of the Levant trade to Spain, and its role in Franco-Spanish trade relations, see H. Hauser, "Les Relations commerciales," *Revue d'histoire économique et sociale*, XXIV, 11 f. This aspect will be more fully elucidated in connection with the economic activities of Levantine Jewry in a later chapter. The role which the Jews of Amsterdam, London, and Hamburg, too, played in the commercial exchanges with the Iberian Peninsula is well illustrated by H. Kellenbenz's archival study *Unternehmerkräfte im Hamburger Portugal- und Spanienhandel, 1590–1625*, esp. pp. 241 ff. (mentioning among other matters that Hector Méndez de Brito in Lisbon left an estate of 726,000 ducats in cash, real estate, and merchandise; pp. 246 f.). See also the other data mentioned *supra*, Vol. XIV, pp. 273 ff.; Chaps. LXIII, nn. 50 ff.; and LXIV, nn. 36 ff., 89, etc.

70. Moses b. Baruch Almosnino, *Extremos y grandezas de Constantinopla*, first composed in Hebrew characters by the author and then republished in Latin script by Jacob b. Ḥayyim Cansino, Madrid, 1638. The introductory material of 34 pages is devoted not only to the "translator's" dedication of the volume to Count Olivares, who supposedly had saved his life at a critical juncture, but also to all sorts of certificates attesting the services rendered by Cansino and his family to the Spaniards in Morocco. See also M. Kayserling, *Biblioteca espagnola-portugueza-judaica*, pp. 10 f., 33; S. A. Rosanes, *Dibre yeme* (or *Qorot*) *ha-Yehudim be-Togarma* (or *Turqiah*; a History of the Jews in Turkey), II, 91 ff. On Luis de Acosta, see J. Caro Baroja, *Los Judíos*, II, 110 ff., 334.

71. Francisco Vilches' letter to Rafael Pereyra of August 6, 1634, in the *Cartas*, I (Memorial histórico español, XIII), ed. by P. de G[ayangos], p. 85; Matéo de Novoa, *Historia de Felipe IV*, II (in CODOIN, LXXVII), 380; F. Cantera Burgos, "Dos escritos inéditos," *Scritti nell'ebraismo . . . Guido Bedarrida*, pp. 40 ff.; Adolfo de Castro, *El Conde-Duque de Olivares y el rey Felipe IV*, pp. 133 f.; Pedro Varela's memorandum mentioned by J. Amador de los Rios in his *Historia social*, III, 549 f., 552 f.; *Novísima Recopilación de las leyes* of 1802, XII, 1.5–6. An interesting report submitted by a spy to the inquisitor-general in Madrid in 1673, describing the entry of many judaizing residents of Bayonne and Peyrehorade into Castile for the purpose of persuading local *conversos* to emigrate north or to Islamic countries, is cited by J. Lucio d'Azevedo in his "Judeus portugueses na dispersão," *Revista de Historia* (Lisbon), IV, 113 n. 2. See also other data analyzed by A. Domínguez Ortiz in *La Clase social*, pp. 114 f.; and his *La Sociedad española en el siglo XVIII*, with an Intro. by C. Viñas y Mey, pp. 228 ff. The subject of the readmission of Jews to Spain continued from time to time to agitate the minds of statesmen and journalists into the nineteenth century (see, for instance, M. Fernández Rodríguez, "España y los Judíos en el reinado de Alfonso XII," *Hispania* [Madrid], XXV, 565–84), but nothing tangible was accomplished until after the upheavals in the first half of the twentieth century. This question, fully meriting an historical monograph, is, I understand, to be analyzed in a forthcoming Columbia University dissertation by Victor Mirelman.

72. See Ludwig von Pastor's *Geschichte der Päpste*, XIII, 728 f.; or *The History of the Popes*, English trans. from the German under the editorship of F. I. Antrobus *et al.*, XXIX, 196 f. Regrettably, Pastor does not supply his evidence for Pignero's Jewish ancestry. Nor is the Italian spelling of his name explained in any way, although he may be identical with, or the son of, the Thomé Pinheiro de Veiga who earlier in the century wrote a volume entitled *Fastigimia* (published in the *Collecção de manuscriptos inéditos* of the Municipal Public Library of Oporto, III). This local Lisbon conflict touched a sensitive nerve, since the Papacy might have seen therein a dangerous precedent to the constant flow of its financial collections from Spain—on the importance of which revenue, see N. García Martín's Madrid 1962 dissertation, summarized in his "Las Aportaciones económicas de España al Papa en tiempos del conde-duque Olivares (1621–1643)," *Revista de le Universidad de Madrid*, XI, 653–54.

Pignero's high-handed treatment of the papal collector was but one episode in the almost constant tensions between the Papacy and the Spanish regime generated by Spain's protracted efforts to secure far-reaching state controls over the Spanish Church, independently of the papal supremacy. In 1636 the Papacy must have been especially disturbed by Pignero's action, as its well-informed intelligence service had doubtless reported to it the contents of a Lisbon royal commission's opinion regarding "Rome's abuses and means to forestall them." The text of that *Parecer de la Junta que mandó Felipe IV para tratar de los abusos de Roma y medios de evitarlos* is still extant in MS 4181 of the National Library in Madrid. Even during the regime of pious monarchs like Charles V and Philip II, these tensions often threatened to bring about a break in diplomatic relations between the head of the Church and his main international supporter, the "Catholic king" of Spain. See, for instance, A. M. Rouco-Varela, *Staat und Kirche im Spanien des XVI. Jahrhunderts; supra*, Vols. XIII, pp. 28 ff., 106 f., 113 f., 317 ff. nn. 29–30, 363 n. 49, 365 n. 57, etc.; and *infra*, Chap. LXVI, nn. 17 and 37.

73. See H. Lapeyre, *Simon Ruiz et les "asientos" de Philippe II*; idem, *Une Famille de marchands: les Ruiz. Contribution à l'étude du commerce entre la France et l'Espagne au temps de Philippe II* (citing, among other matters, Yehiel Nissim da Pisa's explanation of the distinction between fees for the exchange of currency and interest charges, accepted by both Christians and Jews; p. 300); and, more generally, A. É. Sayous, "La Genèse du système capitaliste; la pratique des affaires et leur mentalité en Espagne du XVIe siècle," *Annales d'histoire économique et sociale*, VIII, 334–54; J. Larraz López, *La Época del mercantilismo en Castilla, 1500–1700*; and other literature listed *supra*, nn. 65 and 68; and *infra*, n. 85. Living as they did under the shadow of the Inquisition, and wholly dependent on the protection extended to them by the government, the New Christian merchants and contractors necessarily supported the government's policies, whether or not these were in the best interest of the country. Many weaknesses of the Spanish economy were, in any case, beyond the power of the authorities, which could use mere palliatives, often contributing more to the malady than to its healing. All this despite the realization by thoughtful political theorists of the period that Spain was speedily riding to a fall. Commenting on the critique of the country's economic imbalances by Pedro Fernández Navarette and others, E. J. Hamilton rightly observed: "History records few instances of either such able diagnosis of fatal social ills by any group of moral philosophers or of such utter disregard by statesmen of sound advice." See his "The Decline of Spain," *EcHR*, VIII, 168–79, esp. p. 179. See also *supra*, n. 63.

Despite much research done in recent years by Iberian and foreign scholars, great lacunae in our knowledge of the business transactions of the New Christian bankers have been well illustrated by F. Mauro's analysis of the data yielded by the inquisitorial prosecution of Fernão Martins in 1651–56. Although the officials conducted twenty-six interrogations about Martins' sequestered property, they could find assets of only 2,546,000 reals in immovables, shipping, etc., in addition to some 700,000 reals in outstanding loans. On the other hand, they were told that Martins' debts exceeded 22,000,000 reals. This kind of insolvency was doubtless often claimed by defendants who had been able to secrete important assets before they were seized by the inquisitorial fiscals. In contrast, Duarte da Silva's inventory showed debts of only 12,375,000 reals and assets of some 31,500,000 reals, in addition to large outstanding loans, of which two-thirds were owed by the Crown. See the interesting analysis in F. Mauro's "Marchands," *Revista portuguesa de historia*, IX, 63 ff., 70 f., 77 f.

74. See J. Caro Baroja, *Los Judíos*, I, 356 f.; idem, *La Sociedad cryptojudía*, pp. 63 f.; A. Domínguez Ortiz, *La Clase*, pp. 121 f. The considerable economic differentiation within the New Christian community is evident even from such inquisitorial records as were assembled by the Holy Office of Toledo. See especially H. Beinart, *Anusim be-din ha-Inqviziṣiah* (Conversos on Trial by the Inquisition), pp. 166 ff. On the commercial activities and life of Seville, see the various studies by H. Chaunu and P. Chaunu, esp. their voluminous *Séville et l'Atlantique;* and the shorter review by M. Moret, *Aspects de la société marchande de Séville au début du XVIIᵉ siècle,* with a Preface by P. Chaunu. On the lights and shadows of the remarkable social life of Seville—which adumbrated many of the social phenomena of modern urban progress and decay—see the stimulating chapter in M. Defourneaux's *La Vie quotidienne en Espagne au siècle d'or*, pp. 83 ff.; and R. Pike's essays cited *supra*, n. 32, where the serious uncertainties concerning the role played by the New Christian merchants in Spain's growing slave trade, or even their employment of slaves in business or domestic service, are also discussed.

75. J. de Mal Lara, *Filosofía vulgar*, cited by Américo Castro in his *De la edad conflictiva*, p. 169; I. S. Révah, "Le Procès inquisitorial contre Rodrigo Méndez Silva, historiographe du roi Philippe IV," *BH*, LXVII, 225–52. Rodrigo Méndez Silva further documented his patriotism and loyalty to king and dynasty by a funeral oration in memory of Emperor Ferdinand III, Philip IV's distant cousin. He also wrote a tract attacking Oliver Cromwell and his republican administration, a tract which appeared in Madrid in 1657 under the title *Parangon de los Cromueles de Inglaterra* (dedicated to the duke of Medinaceli). More than Charles V or Philip II, Philip IV needed an official chronicler to transmit to posterity a more favorable record of his reign than was conveyed by the often adverse judgments of contemporary publicists. While some of Philip's admirers, then and after, enthusiastically called him Philip the Great—an epithet he deserved neither by virtue of his talents nor as a mirror of his achievements—others, such as Matéo (Matías) de Novoa, wrote about him in a critical, even satirical, vein. On historians' differing evaluations of the king's reign, see the manuscripts and publications listed by B. Sánchez Alonso in his *Fuentes de la historia española e hispano-americana. Ensayo de bibliografía sistemática*, 3d ed., II, 308 f. In any case, despite his maltreatment by the Holy Office, Méndez Silva loyally refrained, even after his release and emigration to Italy, from

casting aspersions on either the Spanish governmental system or the personality of its head.

76. See Felipe Godínez, *Amán y Mardoqueo, Los Trabajos de Job,* and three other plays reprinted in the *Comédias escogidas,* ed. by Juan de San Vicente *et al.,* Madrid, 1652–81 (Vol. XLVIII added in 1704; possibly the two plays mentioned in the inquisitorial sentence of 1624 were for that very reason omitted from the original collection; see E. Cotarelo y Mori, *Catálogo descriptivo de la gran collección de Comedías escogidas*); A. de Castro, "Noticias de la vida del doctor Felipe Godínez," *Memorias* of the R. Academia Española, VIII, 277–83; Juan Pérez de Montalván (or Montalbán), ed., *Fama posthuma a la vida y muerte del Doctor Frey Lope Felix de Vega Carpio y elogios-panegyricos a la immortalidad de su nombre,* Madrid, 1636, reprinted in Lope's *Colección de las obras sueltas, así en prosa, como en verso,* XX, esp. pp. 147 ff.; and Lope's comment on *La Godina* in his letter reproduced by A. A. de la Barrera in Lope's *Obras* (published by the R. Academia Española), I, 654–56. See also the relatively full, though not carefully documented, description of Godínez' trials and tribulations by M. Méndez Bejarano in his *Histoire de la juiverie de Séville,* pp. 195 ff. (also enumerating Godínez' plays); J. Caro Baroja, *La Sociedad,* pp. 115 ff.

Not surprisingly, Francisco de Quevedo, who deeply hated Juan Pérez de Montalván (or Mantalbán), linked him with Godínez. In his *Perinola,* Quevedo accused Montalván of indiscriminately quoting eminent and mediocre writers and added: "He cites Godínez, not St. Benedict; nor does he cite him before God [*delante de Dios*], but rather [quotes him] with the same seriousness as he does the great Philo Judaeus or Leone Ebreo. However, I excuse him, for the doctor's [Godínez'] talent deserves it, and, I believe also, because he [Godínez] is his [Montalván's] relative." Quevedo thus succeeded in both damning Godínez with faint praise and insinuating that Montalván, too, was a New Christian—as usual without adducing any proof. See Quevedo's *Perinola. Al doctor Juan de Montalbán, graduallo no se sabe donde; en lo qué, ni se sabe ni el lo sabe,* in his *Obras,* ed. by A. Fernandez-Guerra y Orbe, II (*BAE,* XLVIII), 463–78, esp. p. 467, with the editor's note thereon. See also G. W. Bacon's comprehensive study of "The Life and Dramatic Works of Doctor Juan Pérez de Montalván (1602–1638)," *Revue hispanique,* XXVI, 1–474, esp. pp. 24 ff., 33; and Y. H. Yerushalmi, *From Spanish Court to Italian Ghetto: Isaac Cardoso,* pp. 151 ff., 161 f.

77. J. Caro Baroja, "El Proceso de Bartolomé Febos o Febo," *Homenaje a Don Ramón Carrande,* II, 59–92; Y. H. Yerushalmi, *From Spanish Court,* pp. 137 ff. In itself, Febos' trial and sentence had nothing unusual about it. In fact, his reconciliation after three years marked a relatively happy ending for him. Nor were his personality and his intellectual or economic resources in any way distinguished from that of the average defendant. Perhaps the most remarkable feature of his trial was its additional documentation of the intimate relationships between Peninsular and foreign Marranos, particularly those of Rouen, whose difficulties had embroiled French factions in a strife ultimately resolved by the intervention of Richelieu himself. See *supra,* Chap. LXIV, n. 32.

78. See A. Mira de Amescua (or Mescua), *El Caballero de Gracia;* Lope Félix de Vega Carpio, *El Niño inocente de La Guardia,* in his *Obras,* published by the R. Academia Española, V, 71–107, esp. pp. 74 f.; his *auto sacramental* devoted to *La*

Santa Inquisición, ibid., III, 149–64; and numerous other pertinent passages, cited by J. Rodríguez Puértolas in "La Transposición de la realidad," *BH,* LXXII, 98 ff. See also H. A. Rennert, "Mira de Mescua et la Judía de Toledo," *Revue hispanique,* VII, 119–40 (or under the more descriptive original title, *La Desgraciada Raquel y Rei Dⁿ Alphonso el 8°);* D. A. Murray's Stanford Univ. 1951 diss. *Mira de Amescua's La Judia de Toledo;* J. L. Flecniakoska, "*La Jura del Príncipe, auto sacramental* de Mira de Amescua, et l'histoire contemporaine," *BH,* LI, 39–44; E. Glaser, "Lope de Vega's *El Niño inocente de La Guardia," Bulletin of Hispanic Studies,* XXXII, 140–53; and *supra,* Vol. XI, 155 f., 362 f. n. 42. The story of the Madrid auto of 1632 was described in detail, immediately after the event, by Juan Gómez de Mora, "maestro de las obras de su magestad" (head of the royal building department), who was in charge of the necessary constructions. See his *Auto de Fe celebrado en Madrid este año de MDCXXXII,* and the analysis thereof, with the aid of additional archival data, by E. Meneses García in his "Construcción del tablado para el Auto de Fe de 1632," *RABM,* LXXII, 363–92, esp. pp. 367 ff., 377 ff., 386 f.

79. José Vicente del Olmo, *Relación historica del avto general de fé, que se celebró en Madrid este año de 1680. Con asistencia del rey N. S. Carlo II. y las magestades de la reina N. S. y la avgustissima reina madre. Siendo inquisidor general el excelent.^{mo} Sr. D. Diego Sarmiento do Valladaros,* Madrid, 1680, here largely quoted from the excerpts in English reproduced by J. Rivas Puigcerver in "How Jews Were Burnt in the Spain of the Seventeenth Century," *Menorah,* XXX, 72–77. There are a great many such descriptions by eyewitnesses of autos in various periods. These and other materials have long been part of the ever-proliferating bibliography on the Spanish and Portuguese Inquisitions. See esp. the literature cited *supra,* Vol. XIII, Chaps. LV and LVI. Also of much interest with respect to Jewish martyrs of the Holy Office during the seventeenth century, are M. Schwab, "Victimes de l'Inquisition au XVIIe siècle," *REJ,* XXX, 94–100 (referring to two 1627 autos in Seville and Cordova); E. N. Adler, "Auto de Fé and Jew," *JQR,* [o.s.] XIII, 392–437; XIV, 698–718; R. J. H. Gottheil, "Gleanings from Spanish and Portuguese Archives," *ibid.,* XIV, 80–95; idem, "The Jews and the Spanish Inquisition (1622–1721)," *ibid.,* XV, 182–250. These essays are more significant for their statistical data than for their interpretations.

80. C. Roth, *History of the Marranos,* pp. 85, 89; Treaty of Utrecht, Art. X in C. Freschot's ed. of *Actes, Mémoires et autres pièces authentiques concernant la paix d'Utrecht,* V, 167 (in Latin and French; this major exception to the full sovereignty which was to be enjoyed by Great Britain "absolutely with all manner of right, forever, without any exception or impediment whatsoever" is not mentioned by J. W. Gerard in his *The Peace of Utrecht: a Historical Review of the Great Treaty of 1713–14 and of the Principal Events in the War of the Spanish Succession,* pp. 292 f.); A. B. M. Serfaty, *The Jews of Gibraltar under British Rule,* with a Foreword by A. E. Beattie, pp. 5 ff.; J. Jacobs, *An Inquiry into the Sources of the History of the Jews in Spain,* pp. 7 f. No. 97; A. S. Turberville, *The Spanish Inquisition,* pp. 128 ff. On similar conditions in Lisbon, see *infra,* n. 102.

It may be noted in this connection that Gibraltar, the Arabic name of which still betrays its Moorish antecedents, had not always been an integral part of Castile. In fact, before the British occupation of 1704, it had belonged to Spain for little more than two centuries. See J. L. Cano de Gardoqui and A. de Béthencourt, "Incorporación de Gibraltar a la Corona de Castella, 1436–1508," *Hispania* (Madrid), XXVI, 324–81. The preponderance of Judaizers in inquisitorial trials is doubly remarkable as the Holy Office also continued to keep its vigilant eyes not only upon Protestants and Muslims but also upon the truly Catholic, although mystical and often licentious, Alumbrados. See B. Llorca, *Die Spanische Inquisition und die "Alumbrados" (1509–1667) nach den Originalakten in Madrid und in anderen Archiven;* and *supra,* Vol. XIII, pp. 25 f., 316 n. 26, 347 f. n. 18. In addition there also were a great many foreigners on the Peninsula who, in that religiously excitable age, were ready objects of suspicion.

81. B. Braunstein, *The Chuetas of Majorca: Conversos and the Inquisition of Majorca,* esp. pp. 56 ff., 64 ff., 92 f., 190 ff. App. v. In commemoration of the event, the Inquisition not only ordered the destruction of the house and garden in which the secret Judaizers had performed their divine services but also erected a pillar in the center of the open square thus created; for generations thereafter this monument bore the inscription: "In the year 1679 by order of the Inquisition this garden was uprooted, ploughed over, and sown with salt because here the Law of Moses was being taught. This column shall never be removed or broken up at any time under the sanction of major excommunication."

82. B. Braunstein, *ibid.;* H. Kamen, "Confiscations in the Economy of the Spanish Inquisition," *EcHR,* 2d ser., XVIII, 517; H. C. Lea, *A History of the Inquisition of Spain,* II, 315 ff., 386 f. That the royal Treasury had to be satisfied with such a tiny share of the spoils can in part be explained by local conditions, since the Majorcan Inquisition had long successfully fought for its independence. For example, in 1623 it had insisted on exclusive jurisdiction over its own personnel. When the viceroy protested, he was excommunicated. This incident produced a split between the civil and ecclesiastical authorities, which was healed only when the government conceded much of the autonomy desired by the local Holy Office. In part, however, this was a long-pursued conscious policy of the Suprema and many of its subdivisions to conceal from the civil authorities all that pertained to its finances, particularly its revenue from confiscations. Between 1610 and 1650, Philip III and Philip IV in vain tried time and again to get information concerning the financial yields of inquisitorial fines and confiscations. These matters were such well-guarded secrets that, for instance, the colonial branch offices often refused to submit the necessary data to their own Suprema in Madrid. See H. C. Lea, I, 332 f., 484 f.; and *infra,* Chap. LXVI, nn. 37 and 52 ff.

Needless to say, such constant living under the shadow of denunciation and ultimate loss of life and property affected not only the economic activities of talented New Christians. Its reflection, often oblique, yet unmistakable, in the work of many prominent *converso* writers and thinkers, has been illustrated by a number of telling examples in S. Gilman's perceptive essay "The 'Conversos' and the Fall of Fortune," *Américo Castro Jub. Vol.,* pp. 127–36.

On the subsequent intergroup relations on the island, the controversies which for several generations past have raged among scholars on the subject of the attitudes of both the majority and the minority, and the present-day number and position of the Chuetas, see M. Forteza, *Els Descendants dels conversos de Mallorca. Quatre mots de la veritat.* This volume also lists the fairly numerous novels and short stories describing the life of that intriguing minority, including Vicente Blasco Ibáñez' famous *Los Muertos mandan.*

83. The impact of the absolutist regimes of the three Philips made itself strongly felt also in the treatment of New Christians and other operations of the Holy Office. To begin with, there were borderline cases between the civil and ecclesiastical jurisdiction, like that of Pignero de Vega—which, we remember, was finally settled only by diplomatic negotiations between the Spanish ambassador and the papal organs in Rome. We also recall that of the numerous Portuguese New Christians living in Spain, some fell victim to the *Spanish* Inquisition, while others continued to play a considerable role in Spain's economic, political, and intellectual life. Regrettably, the later years of the Portuguese Inquisition have not yet been given the comprehensive treatment which its early beginnings received from Alexandre Herculano more than a century ago. However, much can be learned from the older and the more recent works by P. Monteiro, A. J. Saraíva, A. Baião, J. Lucio d'Azevedo, and others mentioned in our earlier volumes as well as in the forthcoming notes. See *supra*, Vols. XI, pp. 245, 407 n. 68; XII, pp. 23 f., 257 n. 21; XIII, pp. 44 ff., 327 ff. nn. 47-52.

84. Juan Adam de la Parra, *Pro cautione christiana in supremis Senatibus sanctae Inquisitionis et Ordinum, Ecclesia Toletana, et coetibus scholarium observata. Aduersus Christianorum proselytos, et sabbatizantes, nomine et specie christianorum Declamat*, Madrid, 1630 [1633], esp. fols. 30 ff., 33b f.; cited by H. C. Lea in *A History of the Inquisition of Spain*, III, 291 f.; and other passages in the anti-Jewish writings of the period, such as those by João Baptista de Este (the aforementioned Italian convert) in *Diálogo entre discipulo e mestre catequisante onde se resoluem todas as duuidas que os judeus obstinados costumam fazer contra a veridade da Fé Catholica. . . . Traducido mui fielmente da Ecritura et Rabbinos*, Lisbon, 1621; Vicente de Costa de Mattos (*or de Matos*) and Fernão Ximenes de Aragão (dean of Braga), quoted *supra*, n. 47.

85. See, for instance, J. S. da Silva Dias, *Correntes de sentimento religioso em Portugal (séculos XVI a XVIII)*, Vol. I. Of special interest with respect to those branches of the Portuguese economy in which the New Christians were particularly active, are the following publications: F. Mauro, *Le Portugal et l'Atlantique au XVIIe siècle, 1570–1670;* J. G. da Silva, *Stratégie des affaires à Lisbonne entre 1595 et 1607;* V. Rau, "Affari e mercanti in Portogallo dal XIV al XVI secolo," *Economia e storia*, XIV, 447-56; idem, "Feitores e feitorias—'Instrumentos' do comércio internacional português no século XVI," *Brotéria*, LXXXI, 458-78; M. Ramos de Oliveira, "Feiras e Judeus," *Beira alta Arquivo provincial*, XXVII, 195-213.

86. See Manuel Bocarro (Jacob) Rosales' didactic poem *Anacephaleoses de Monarquia Lusitana*, Lisbon, 1624; and, more generally, J. Lucio d'Azevedo, *A Evolução do Sebastianismo*, 2d ed.; H. Kellenbenz, "Dr. Jakob Rosales," *Zeitschrift für Religions- und Geistesgeschichte*, VIII, 345-54, esp. pp. 347 f.; *supra*, Vol. XIV, pp. 282 f., 408 f. n. 59. D'Azevedo minimizes the impact of Marrano messianism on Sebastianism. Yet his main argument—that "the persistence of [Portuguese] messianism for so long a time, the sameness of its expression, its suffusion of the mentality of the people, constitute a phenomenon which, except among the Hebrew race, has no parallel in history" (p. 7)—rather strengthens the assumption that the Old Christians had learned a good deal from their New Christian neighbors in this area. Needless to say, messianism was but one of the sociopolitical factors which opposed Portugal's integration into the Spanish Empire. See, for instance, M. E. Brook's

analysis of *A King for Portugal: the Madrigal Conspiracy, 1594–95*, describing, on the basis of a Simancas archival document, the trial and execution of Gabriel de Espinosa, a pastry maker of Madrigal de las Altas, who appeared as one of the four pretenders successively claiming to be the lost King Sebastian.

87. See the various, often complementary, editions of Gonçalo Annes Bandarra's works: (1) *Trovas*, esp. iii, strophes cix-lix, new ed. by J. L. da Silva, pp. 56 ff.; (2) *Trovas inéditas* . . . *que existão em poder de Pacheco, contemporaneo de Bandarra;* (3) *Bandarra descuberto nas suas trovas. Collecçam de Profecias mais notaveis respeito a felicidade de Portugal, e cahida dos maiores Imperios do mundo;* and J. Lucio d'Azevedo, *A Evolução do Sebastianismo*, 2d ed., pp. 123 f. While the easy apprehension and punishment of the several false Sebastians had probably lulled the Spanish authorities into a false sense of security, these messianic dreams helped to keep Portugal's nationalist feelings and subdued irredenta alive long enough for them to burst forth at the critical moment of 1640. See M. Martins d'Antas, *Les Faux don Sébastien: Étude sur l'histoire de Portugal;* H. Cidade, *A Literatura autonomista sob os Filipes*. On Trancoso as a center of New Christian life, see esp. Y. H. Yerushalmi's observations in his *From Spanish Court to Italian Ghetto*, pp. 55 ff. It may be noted that the great popular reverence for the memory of King Sebastian did not save the grandsons of the king's mathematics teacher, Pedro Nunes, from inquisitorial prosecution in 1623–32. See A. Baião, *Episódios dramáticos da Inquisição Portuguesa*, I, 163 ff.; idem, *O Matemático Pedro Nunes e sua familia à luz de documentos inéditos*. On the impact of the messianic movements on António Vieira and his associates, see the literature listed *infra*, nn. 97 ff.; and Chap. LXVI, n. 98. The conflicting messianic teachings of the brothers Abraham and Isaac Cardoso are brilliantly analyzed by Yerushalmi, pp. 302 ff. It appears that a careful comparative study of Portugal's Old and New Christian messianic ideologies and their likely interrelations would be a highly meritorious undertaking.

88. See the decrees of November 10, 1621, and February 23, 1623, in M. Fernandes Thomaz, comp., *Reportorio das leis extravagantes*, II, 392; J. Caro Baroja, *La Sociedad criptojudía*, p. 91; S. Leite, *Estatutos da Universidade de Coimbra, 1559*, esp. p. 94. The trial of António Hómem, which left a considerable imprint on the life of the New Christians in Portugal, is fully described by A. J. Teixeira in his *Antonio Homem e a Inquisição*, esp. pp. 41 ff.; and by A. Baião in his *Episódios dramáticos da Inquisição Portuguesa*, I, 109 ff. See also M. Kayserling, *Geschichte der Juden in Portugal*, pp. 291 f.; and *infra*, nn. 89 and 105.

89. The trials of the jurist Tomé Vaz in 1618–20; the mathematician André de Avelar in 1620 and 1621–23; and another jurist, Francisco Vaz (Velasco) of Gouveia, in 1626–31 are fully analyzed and documented by A. Baião in his *Episódios dramáticos*, I, 131 ff., 139 ff., 167 ff. See esp. pp. 147 ff., furnishing an excerpt from Avelar's sentence, from which my quotation in the text is translated.

90. Diogo de Assumpção's sentence is reproduced in A. J. Teixeira's *Antonio Homem*, pp. 218 ff. See J. Lucio d'Azevedo's *Historia dos Christãos Novos Portugueses*, pp. 159 f., 458 f. App. vii. See also, in general, the older but still useful comprehensive *Historia da Santa Inquisição do reyño de Portugal e suas conquistas* by P. Monteiro; and, of interest for future research, M. T. Geraldes-Barbosa's brief

comments on "Les Archives de l'Inquisition portugaise," *Mélanges . . . Charles Braibant*, pp. 163–73 (includes a valuable list of the pertinent fascicles; pp. 169 ff.).

91. The sermon of the Dominican friar António de Sousa is reproduced in A. J. Teixeira's *Antonio Homem e a Inquisição*, pp. 261 ff.; and cited by J. Lucio d'Azevedo in his *Historia*, pp. 176 f.; that of João de Ceita, in its Spanish version, is reprinted in E. Glaser's "*Convertentur ad vesperam*, on a Rare Spanish Translation of an Inquisitorial Sermon by Frei João de Ceita," *Américo Castro Jub. Vol.*, pp. 137–44. (In the Vulgate the verse is numbered 59:6). The generally incendiary nature of most of the lengthy sermons preached at the Portuguese autos, and their frequent indirect incitation to violence, are well described by E. Glaser in his twin essays, "Portuguese Sermons at Autos-da-Fé: Introduction and Bibliography," *Studies in Bibliography and Booklore*, II, 53–78, 96; and "Invitation to Intolerance: a Study of the Portuguese Sermons Preached at Autos-da-Fé," *HUCA*, XXVII, 327–85. Discounting the usual exaggerations, the localities enumerated by De Sousa indeed had a large number of secret Judaizers. The district of Beira, in particular, has preserved many Judaic traditions until the present day. See esp. J. Leite de Vasconcellos Pereira de Mello's chapter on "Cristãos-Novos do nosso tempo en Trás-os-Montes e na Beira; suas práticas judáicas" in his *Etnografia Portuguesa*, Vol. IV, ed. by Viegas Guerreiro, pp. 162–253; P. Amilcar, "Os Marranos nas Beiras. Tradições judio-portugueses," *Beira Alta*, 2d ser. XX, 101–114; and Y. H. Yerushalmi, *From Spanish Court to Italian Ghetto*, pp. 55 ff. Such differences in the character of various Portuguese localities are noticeable even today. See, for instance, the comparative study of the two leading cities by Luis de Pina *et al.* in their *Duas Citades ao servicio de Portugal. Subsidios para o estudo das relações de Lisboa e Porto durante oito seculos*, published by the municipality of Oporto on the 800th anniversary of the conquest of Lisbon. Dependent as we are mainly on inquisitorial sources relating either to the accused or to persons mentioned indirectly in some, often unreliable, testimony, we cannot ascertain the ratio of secret Jews in the New Christian population of the areas mentioned by Sousa. However, close investigations conducted by I. S. Révah in Oporto, have shown that in that locality the large majority of New Christians were really Marranos. See *supra*, n. 33.

92. Miguel Pais d'Almanza's letter to Queen Marianna of Austria, cited by J. Lucio d'Azevedo in *Historia*, pp. 198 f.; the revival of the accusation of host desecrations in 1614 and 1630, *ibid.*, pp. 202 f.; Menasseh ben Israel, *Vindiciae Judaeorum, or, a Letter in Answer to Certain Questions Propounded by a Noble and Learned Gentleman, Touching the Reproaches Cast on the Nation of the Jews; Wherein All Objections Are Candidly, and Yet Fully Cleared*, London, 1656, p. 11; Francisco Manuel de Melo (or Manoel de Mello), *Cartas familiares, escritas a varias pessoas sobre assumptos diversos*. Selected by A. L. de Azevedo. See also *infra*, n. 96. Folkloristic accusations of the alleged inveterate enmity of Jews toward all Christians retained wide circulation into the Enlightenment Era and beyond. Not even so rationalistic a writer as Benito Jerónimo Feijóo y Montenegro could avoid its impact. He wrote: "Some members of that canaille commit so skilled a homicide on Christians that it can be detected only with great difficulty. They do it especially on persons whom they consider useful to the Church. . . . This fact is sufficient to make us hate and abominate Jewish doctors." See his *Teatro crítico*

universal, o Discursos varios en tódo género de materias, para desengaño de errores comunes, Madrid, 1778 ed., V, 134 ff.; and, on his generally positive attitude toward the French Enlightenment, see G. Delpy, *Feijoo et l'esprit européen.* Feijóo's accusation is the more remarkable as the Portuguese must have known that some of the New Christian exiles abroad who had formally returned to Judaism, such as Amato Lusitano and Elijah Montalto, were much in demand as medical experts among royal and other distinguished Christian families in various lands.

It may be of interest to note that recently uncovered evidence confirms that these two doctors may have been related to each other. See J. Lopes Dias, "Laços familiares de Amato Lusitano e Felipe Montalto. Novas investigações," *Imprensa médica,* XXVI, 22–36. Amato, the more distinguished physician of the two, found an excellent biographer in Maximiano Lemos, himself an eminent Portuguese physician. See H. Monteiro, *Escorso biográfico duma grande figura da medicina portuguesa, Maximiano Lemos* (reprinted from *O Médico,* No. 489). Both Amato and Elijah have been mentioned here in various connections. A somewhat fuller analysis of their medical contributions will be included in a later volume in connection with the general evolution of medical studies among early modern Jews.

93. See the *Tratado sobre a gente da nação hebrea do Reyno de Portugal,* submitted in 1629 to the king by theologians then assembled at Tomar; and the licentiate Francisco Murcia de la Llana's memorandum, entitled *Discurso político del desempeño del Reyno* (extant in a MS in the Madrid National Library), which he presented to the king on May 21, 1624; both excerpted by J. Lucio d'Azevedo in his *Historia,* 462 f. App. ix, and 473 f. App. xvi. On the discussions concerning the reasons for the allegedly disproportionate proliferation of Jews and Moriscos as compared to the rather stagnant old Christian population, see *supra,* nn. 29–30, where the arguments presented by Felipe de Nájera are also cited. The extent to which the discrepancy in population growth between the two minority groups and the majority was but a figment of the overheated popular imagination cannot now be ascertained. Even the overall demographic trends in sixteenth- and seventeenth-century Portugal are highly problematic. See the pertinent methodological observations by V. Rau in her "Para a historia da população portuguesa dos séculos XV e XVI (Resultados e problemas de métodos)," *Do Tempo e da historia,* I, 7–46, esp. pp. 29 ff. (with reference to the communities in the region of Beira Alta, where a chance 1496 record in a small town counted 108 Jewish *moradores* in a total population of 2,372); and J. G. da Silva, "Au Portugal. Structure demographique et développement économique," *Studi in onore di Amintore Fanfani,* II, 491–510.

94. J. Albrecht, *Dom Duarte de Bragança. Ein Lebensschicksal aus dem Zeitalter des Dreissigjähren Krieges;* António Carvalho de Parada, *Justificação dos Portugueses sobre a acção de libertarem seu reino da obediencia de Castella,* Lisbon, 1643, Chaps. VIII and IX; Pantaleão Rodrigues Pacheco, *Manifesto do Reyno de Portugal presentado à Santidade de Urbano VIII,* Lisbon, 1643. The authorship of that *Manifesto* is uncertain; its attribution to Pacheco is made by J. Lucio d'Azevedo on the basis of an inconclusive letter dated Madrid, January 8, 1641; see D'Azevedo's *Historia,* pp. 236 f. On Pacheco's general role in Rome during the early 1640s, see L. von Pastor, *The History of the Popes,* XXIX, 206 ff. As proof that not the Portuguese but rather the Castilians favored the Marranos, another writer, Fray Francisco de Santo Agostinho de Macedo, argued that during the union of the

two countries many Portuguese New Christians had found a rather friendly reception in Castile, whereas no Spanish Marranos had settled in Portugal. See his *Philippica Portuguesa contra la invectiva Castellana a el rei nuestro señor Don Iuan IV*, Lisbon, 1645, xx, pp. 105 f.

Regrettably, we have no information about John's attitude, while he was still only duke of Braganza administering his own vast estates, to the local Inquisition and the New Christian residents, some of whose descendants retained their Marrano identity into the twentieth century. See J. Caro Baroja, *Los Judíos*, I, 182; III, 225 ff.; and the sources cited there. On the other hand, perhaps for commercial reasons, few New Christians had been attracted to Catalonia, once a major center of peninsular Jewish life. See J. H. Elliot, *The Revolt of the Catalans: a Study in the Decline of Spain (1598–1640)*; and other studies reviewed by A. Domínguez Ortiz in "The Revolt of Catalonia against Philip IV," *Past and Present*, XXIX, 105–111.

95. See the biographical essays on Rosales-Bocarro by H. Kellenbenz and I. S. Révah mentioned *supra*, Vol. XIV, pp. 282 f., 408 f. n. 59; further studies on that family by P. A. d'Azevedo, "O Bocarro Francês e os Judeus de Cochim e Hamburgo," *Arquivo Histórico Portuguêz*, VIII, 15–20, 185–98; and by C. R. Boxer, "Antonio Bocarro and the 'Livro do Estado da India Oriental,' " in *Garcia de Orta, Revista*, Special No. of 1956, pp. 203–219. It is possible, however, that Rosales' anti-Braganza activities were intended mainly to furnish him greater immunity from inquisitorial prosecution. We learn from the testimony of a witness in London in 1656 that Don Antonio Rodrigues Robles, who was to play an important role during the Jewish Resettlement in England, had lived ten years earlier in the Canary Islands. When asked how it was possible at that time for a Portuguese to live in the Spanish colony, the witness answered that Robles had been one of those Portuguese who had sided with Spain after 1640 and that "the King of Spaine gave them libty to lyve there." See L. Wolf, "Crypto-Jews under the Commonwealth," *TJHSE*, I, 84. Such liberty may not have been formally conferred upon the Spanish partisans by any royal order, but since Spain had not recognized Portugal's independence, it probably had some bearing in practice. Although removed from the direct reach of the Spanish Inquisition, Rosales, while living in Hamburg, had every reason to try to be on good terms with the Austrian Habsburgs.

On the frequently contradictory and confusing attitudes of the foreign powers toward newly independent Portugal, see the mutually complementary studies by E. Prestage, *The Diplomatic Relations of Portugal with France, England and Holland from 1640–1668;* K. Mellander and E. Prestage, *The Diplomatic and Communal Relations of Sweden and Portugal from 1641 to 1670;* M. B. Amzalak, *As Relações diplomáticas entre Portugal e a França no reinado de D. João IV (1640–1656);* C. Van der Haar, *Die Diplomátieke betrekkingen tussen de Republiek en Portugal, 1640–1661* (The Diplomatic Relations between the [Dutch] Republic and Portugal, 1640–1661); and M. E. Madeira Santos, *Relações diplomáticas entre Portugal e Veneza (1641–1649)*. None of these works sheds much light on the attitude of New Christians vis-à-vis the great international conflict. See also, more generally, the near-contemporary comprehensive work by L. de Menezes Conde de Ericeira, *Historia de Portugal Restaurado* (the printer's Preface to Volume III of the new edition, Lisbon, 1751, reproduces the grand duke of Tuscany's approval, dated April 30, 1680, of the first part of the *Historia*); and some additional documentary studies, presented by

A. Cánovas de Castillo in his "Revolución de Portugal; Textos y reflexiones," in his *Obras. Estudios del reinado de Felipe IV,* 2d ed. I, 9–244, 315–60.

96. Côrtes of January 28, 1641, Chaps. iv, x, xxiii, xxvii, xxix, lxxv, summarized by J. Lucio d'Azevedo in his *Historia,* pp. 238 f. Despite the great influence of the public on the policies of the new regime, King John IV was not prepared to approve these extreme measures. See, more generally, E. Prestage, *The Royal Power and the Cortes in Portugal;* M. F. de Barros Santarém, *Memorias e algumos documentos para a historia e teoria das Côrtes geraes que em Portugal se celebraram pelos tres estados do reino,* new ed. with a Foreword by A. Sardinha.

Nevertheless, it appears that many New Christians continued to encounter serious difficulties in admission to monastic orders. A curious inquiry on this score was addressed to Rabbi Saul Levi Morteira by one of his Amsterdam congregants, who had been asked by a Lisbon friend to use his good offices with his acquaintances in Rome to secure a papal brief to facilitate such admissions. Although assured that his intervention, if successful, would yield him a "huge annual profit," the prospective Amsterdam intermediary was concerned that the funds expended in Rome would belong to the category of subsidies to Gentile religious worship forbidden by Jewish law. In his reply Morteira declared that the Roman recipients were not at all likely to expend such douceurs on gifts for church services and the like, but would rather use them for food and other secular expenses. Characteristically, neither the rabbi nor his questioner was apprehensive that such intervention might help Marrano parents to place their children in monasteries and convents and thus indirectly contribute to the Catholic Church. Either they were both persuaded that they were dealing with families which had already become thoroughly Christianized, or else they tacitly assumed that the Lisbon parents were anxious to secure monastic habits for their children as a relatively effective safeguard against inquisitorial prosecutions. See the Hebrew text of that responsum, published with a Polish translation by F. (E.) Kupfer from a copy once in the possession of the famous eighteenth-century bibliophile Ḥayyim Yosef David Azulai and now in Warsaw, in "A Hebrew Document Relating to Affairs of the Church in the Seventeenth Century" (Polish), *Przegląd Orientalistyczny,* 1955, pp. 95–99. This responsum is undated; it could reflect conditions before as well as after 1640.

97. C. R. Boxer, *A Great Luso-Brazilian Figure Padre António Vieira, S. J., 1608–1697,* p. 4. On this extraordinary Jesuit father, whom we shall encounter again in connection with the history of Brazilian Jewry (*infra,* Chap. LXVI, nn. 96 ff.), see especially his own testimony before the Inquisition, *Defesa perante o Tribunal do Santo Oficio,* ed. with an intro. and notes by H. Cidade. Many insights may also be derived from Vieira's sermons and letters published in the respective editions by Gonçalo Alves of Vieira's *Sermões* (in *Obras completas*); and by J. Lucio d'Azevedo of Vieira's *Cartas, coordenadas e anotadas.* See esp. his letter to the Jews of Rouen of April 20, 1646 (in *Cartas,* I, 56 ff. No. ccxxx). D'Azevedo also wrote an excellent biography of the preacher-diplomat, entitled *Historia de António Vieira.* See also I. Lins's perceptive analysis in *Aspectos do Padre António Vieira,* with a Preface by M. P. Filho, esp. pp. 52 ff., 117 ff., 154 ff.; and *infra,* nn. 98–99; and Chap. LXVI, nn. 96 ff.

Apart from practical considerations, Vieira's attitude toward Jews and Judaism was also colored by his deep spiritual yearning for a messianic age. He envisaged a glorious future with a universal monarchy established under Portugal's leadership. A fine analysis of Vieira's dreams about these ultimate developments is offered by R. Cantel in his *Prophétisme et messianisme dans l'oeuvre d'Antonio Vieira*. It may be noted that the large majority of the biblical quotations cited from Vieira's works by Cantel were taken from the Old Testament, particularly Isaiah, the Psalms, and the Book of Daniel. Except for the Apocalypse, which was, of course, deeply indebted to the intertestamentary Jewish writings, passages from the New Testament are very sparsely used. See Cantel's "Index biblique," p. 269. At the same time, in some of his sermons Vieira made a special effort to convince Jewish and judaizing listeners of the truth of such Christian dogmas as the Trinity, often making use of the question and answer method to prove his points. See J. Barrento's detailed analysis of "Forma e função de Interrogação nos Sermões de Vieira," *Portugiesische Forschungen der Görresgesellschaft*, VII, 145–94, esp. the examples cited, pp. 189 ff. A comprehensive monograph on Vieira's biblical and Judaic interests should indeed prove to be very meritorious from the standpoint of both Luso-Brazilian and Jewish history.

98. Antonio Vieira's *Obras escolhidas*, ed. with an Intro. and Notes by A. Sérgio and H. Cidade, IV, 1–26, 67–71; J. J. Andrade e Silva, comp., *Collecção chronológica da legislação portuguesa*, Vol. VII: 1648–1656, pp. 27 ff.; E. Prestage, "Tres consultas do Conselho da Fazenda de 1656 e 1657," *Revista de Historia* (Lisbon), IX, 105–126; idem, "Ministros portugueses nas Cortes estrangeras no reinado de D. João IV e a sua correspondencia," *ibid.*, IV, 218–28, esp. p. 227; J. Lucio d'Azevedo, *Historia dos Christãos Novos*, pp. 252 ff.; and I. S. Révah's comprehensive analysis of "Les Jésuites portugais contre l'Inquisition: la Campagne pour la fondation de la Compagnie Générale du Commerce du Brésil," *Revista do livro*, I, Nos. 3–4, pp. 29–53 (see *infra*, n. 101). See also C. R. Boxer, "Padre António Vieira, S. J., and the Institution of the Brazil Company in 1649," *HAHR*, XXIX, 474-97 (extensively using MSS preserved in the British Museum); and G. de Freitas, "A Companhia Geral do Comércio do Brazil (1649–1720). (Subsidios para a História Econômica de Portugal e do Brasil)," *Revista de História* (São Paulo), II, Nos. 6, pp. 307–328; 7, pp. 85–110; 8, pp. 313–44.

99. See I. S. Révah, in *Revista do livro*, I; António Vieira, *Obras escolhidas*, IV, *passim;* idem, *Obras inéditas*, I, 215; idem, *Cartas*, III, 560 ff., etc. Vieira's remarkable project, apparently initiated by some of his Jewish acquaintances in Bahia, Brazil, was from the outset hampered by the great paradox in Dutch-Portuguese relations. On the one hand, after the expiration of its truce with Spain in 1621, Holland was locked in unrelenting battle with its former overlords and, therefore, together with France, was a staunch supporter of the Portuguese revolt against Philip IV. On the other hand, outside of Europe the Dutch consistently fought the Portuguese in Brazil, Angola, and the Far East. Economically, ever since 1602, when they entered the Indonesian territories and ended Portugal's spice monopoly, Dutch merchants became formidable competitors in what had long been a mainstay of the Portuguese economy. After 1648, when the Peace Treaties of Westphalia established more peaceful relations between the Netherlands and Spain, and the Portuguese were successfully trying to recapture Pernambuco from the Dutch (they completed this task in 1654), the new Company lost much of its importance. See *infra*, Chap. LXVI.

100. See António Vieira's *Cartas*, ed. by J. Lucio d'Azevedo, III, 556 ff. No. ccxxx (letter of May 2, 1689, to Count de Ericeira, referring to his earlier negotiations with

Duarte da Silva; pp. 562 ff.); 737 ff. App. ii (Carta apologética ao Padre Jácome Iquazafigo of April 30, 1686, esp. Proposición, xi; pp. 781 ff.); *Defesa perante o Tribunal do Santo Oficio*, II, 385 f. See also J. Lucio d' Azevedo's *Historia de António Vieira*, I, 139 ff.; II, 305 ff. App. i: Documentos relativos ao processo; C. Roth, *A Life of Menasseh ben Israel*, pp. 162 ff., 327 f. nn. 28–30; J. J. van den Besselaar, *Antônio Vieira en Holland (1624–1649)*, esp. pp. 23 f. We must also constantly bear in mind the frequent similarity of Portuguese names. For example, the Portuguese Jesuit António Vieira (styled in the document Ir[mão = Brother], rather than P[adre = Father]) who was listed among the passengers departing for India on April 17, 1647, cannot be identical with the eminent Luso-Brazillian preacher. See J. Wicki, "Liste der Jesuiten-Indienfahrer 1541–1758," *Portugiesische Forschungen der Görresgesellschaft*, VII, 252–450, esp. p. 298 No. 944; and *infra*, Chap. LXVI, n. 114. It may also be noted that, perhaps because of international tensions, the number of such departures greatly diminished in 1641, and none occurred in 1642, the first two years of the newly won Portuguese independence.

101. See especially I. S. Révah, "Les Jésuites portugais contre l'Inquisition," *Revista do Livro*, I. This fine analysis is based upon Révah's customary thorough archival research, although the popular journal in which it appears does not provide it with the necessary documentation. See also, more generally, J. Lucio d'Azevedo's *Historia de António Vieira*, I, 59 ff.; II, 345 ff. App. ii: Escritos satíricos contra Vieira, 353 ff. App. iii: Missões; and his *Historia de Christãos Novos*, pp. 246 ff., 252 ff., 477 ff. Apps. xix–xxi. The victory of the anti-Marrano forces arrayed behind the Inquisition, over the more tolerant Jesuits, was reminiscent of a similar struggle on the Peninsula a century earlier. Soon after the foundation of the Jesuit Order in Rome, a number of New Christians joined the Order in Spain at its establishment in 1546, as several of their confreres had done in the Roman headquarters. Yet the campaign for *limpieza* set in motion by Archbishop Silíceo in Toledo in 1547 ultimately led to the adoption of that criterion for the denial of admission to persons of Jewish descent, first in Iberia and finally, as we recall, throughout the Order. See I. S. Révah, "Les Origines juives de quelques Jésuites hispano-portugais du XVIe siècle," *Études ibériques et latinoamericaines* in the *Publications* of the Faculté des lettres of Poitiers, VI, 87–96 (a paper submitted to the IV Congress of the French Hispanistas in Poitiers, held on March 18–20, 1967); and *supra*, Vol. XIV, pp. 9 ff., 303 ff. As a result of its victory the Portuguese Holy Office was able to implement ever more strictly the statutory provisions of the *Regimento* formulated by its inquisitor-general Francisco de Castro on October 22, 1640, and enacted as part of the Portuguese legislation. See the text reproduced in J. J. Andrade e Silva's *Collecção chronológica de legislaçao portuguesa*, V, 251–378, esp. Livro III: Das penas (pp. 342 ff.). On the difficulties in Rome, even after the aforementioned affair with Castracani (*supra*, n. 72) had beeen allayed, see L. von Pastor, *The History of the Popes*, XXIX, 209 ff.; XXX, 72 ff. The extremely complex international relations of Portugal in the period just before and after the Peace of Westphalia, are discussed in the literature mentioned *supra*, n. 95.

102. See L. Cardozo de Béthencourt, "L'Auto de Fé de Lisbonne de décembre 1647," *REJ*, XLIX, 262–69; J. Lucio d'Azevedo, *Historia dos Christãos Novos*, pp. 268, 483 f. App. xxii. The noteworthy personality of Isaac Tartas, student of medicine and theology, poet, and a linguist said to have had good command of Spanish,

French, Hebrew, and Latin, as well as the impression made by his martyrdom on Jewish contemporaries, will be treated in later chapters. See *supra*, Chap. LXIV, n. 29; and *infra*, Chap. LXVI, n. 91. On Gibraltar, see *supra*, n. 80.

103. See Bishop Miguel of Lamego's letters to Count da Vidigueira of June 14 and August 10, 1642, in *Corpo diplomático portuguez*, ed. by L. A. Rebello da Silva *et al.*, XII, 291, 295; and especially J. Ramos Coelho, *Manuel Fernandes Villa Real e o seu processo na Inquisição de Lisbõa*; I. S. Révah, "Manuel Fernandes Vilareal, Adversaire et victime de l'Inquisition Portugaise," *Iberida, Revista de Filologia*, I, No. 1, pp. 33–54; No. 3, pp. 181–207. The titles of the two editions of Villareal's panegyric on Richelieu are *Epitomé genealógico del Eminentíssimo Cardenal Duque de Richelieu y discursos políticos sobre algunas acciones de su vida*, Pamplona [Paris], 1641; *El Político Christianíssimo o Discursos Políticos sobre algunas acciones del Eminentíssimo Señor Cardenal Duque de Richelieu*, Pamplona [Paris], 1642. The French, Italian, and German versions are discussed by Révah in No. 1, pp. 36 ff., Révah quoting extensively from the French translation, including the passages cited in our text, which are taken from that ed., pp. 95 ff.

104. See the sources quoted *supra*, n. 103; Chaps. LXIII, n. 73; LXIV, n. 31. It is noteworthy that the inquisitorial sentence condemning Villareal to "relaxation" was found sufficiently intriguing by the novelist Camilo Castelo Branco to be reproduced verbatim in his novel *O Ôlho de vidro* (The Eye of Glass), published in Lisbon, 1866. While in prison, Villareal had enough energy to compose a lovely sonnet, reproduced by I. S. Révah in *Iberida*, I, No. 3, pp. 206 f. Menasseh ben Israel unwittingly contributed to the martyr's ordeals, not only because his book was found in Villareal's possession but also because of a letter he had addressed to the "culprit"; the letter was included in the inquisitorial dossier, from which it seems to have been removed sometime after 1875. See C. Roth, *A Life of Menasseh ben Israel*, pp. 136 ff., 324 f.; and Révah's note thereon in *Iberida*, I, No. 1, pp. 34 f. n. 3. Roth identifies Menasseh's letter to Villareal as that published by E. N. Adler in "A Letter of Menasseh ben Israel," *TJHSE*, V, 174–83, reprinted in his *About Hebrew Manuscripts*. See also J. S. da Silva Días, "Seiscentesimo e Renovação em Portugal no seculo XVII. Estudo de um proceso inquisitorial," *Biblos. Revista de Facultade de Letras*, Coimbra, XXXVI, 201–264 (although dealing with the eighteenth-century trial of Padre Manuel de Santa María Teixeira, also sheds much light on earlier prosecutions of monks).

105. Miguel da Silveira (*or* Silveyra), *El Macabeo, poema heróico*, Naples, 1632; Antonio Enríquez Gómez, *Sansón Nazareno, poema heróico*, Rouen, 1656, esp. the Prologue; and other data analyzed by J. Amador de los Rios in his *Estudios históricos, políticos y literarios sobre los Judíos de España*, pp. 534–46; M. Kayserling in *Sephardim*, pp. 182 ff.; Sousa Viterbo in "Poesias avulsas do Dr. Miguel da Silveira," *O Instituto* (Coimbra), LIII, 378–82, 441–48, 494–503; J. Caro Baroja, *La Sociedad criptojudía*, pp. 93 ff. See also M. Kayserling, "Thomas de Pinedo. Eine Biographie," *MGWJ*, VII, 191–202; and particularly E. Glaser, "Miguel da Silveira's *El Macabeo*," *BEP*, XXI, 5–49. Although admitting that "the Biblical epic is in Iberia a genre almost exclusively cultivated by authors of Jewish ancestry or professing Jews," Glaser minimizes the "Jewish" content of the poem. Of course, even the most devoted Judaizer of seventeenth-century Spain knew very little about ancient Jewish history

according to Jewish sources. Even after Silveira's apparent flight to Naples, and the publication of *El Macabeo,* we hear of no suspicions publicly voiced regarding his orthodoxy. This is the more remarkable as the poet took occasion to glorify his Portuguese homeland but failed to refer to any Christian doctrines or to the traditional Christian predilection to refer to the Maccabeans as religious martyrs, rather than as freedom fighters. The very selection of this theme may have stemmed, consciously or unconsciously, from the secret observance of Ḥanukkah in certain Marrano circles in Portugal as was charged by the Inquisition in the famous trial of António Hómem. See *supra,* n. 88; and Y. Yerushalmi, *From Spanish Court to Italian Ghetto,* pp. 143 f. n. 14. The sole instance, quoted by Caro Baroja, in which the poet purportedly alludes to Christian teachings—namely, the phrase "the Holy Ghost consecrates it"—is inconclusive. After all, Jewish tradition had long glorified the inspiration given by the "holy spirit" (*ruah ha-qodesh*). See the passages quoted by Caro Baroja, pp. 95 and 99.

106. See Antonio Enríquez Gómez, "Poesías," ed. by Alfonso de Castro in his collection *Poetas líricos de los siglos XVI y XVII,* ed. with an Intro. (*BAE,* XXXII, XLII), II (XLII), 363–91, esp. his *Epistolas de Job* (pp. 585 ff.), which have strong autobiographical overtones; M. Kayserling, *Sephardim,* pp. 216 ff.; idem, *Biblioteca,* pp. 49 ff.; *supra,* Chaps. LXIII, n. 70; and LXIV, n. 30. The identity of Enríquez Gómez with Fernando de Zárate was originally suggested in the biographical note by Alfonso de Castro, II (*BAE,* XLII), pp. lxxxix–xci, also referring to the inclusion of the poet's comedy in the seventeenth-century Index of Prohibited Books, which explicitly gives this identification. Though the hypothesis was subsequently denied by several scholars, it was revived by I. S. Révah and J. Caro Baroja. See Révah, "Les Marranes," *REJ,* CXVIII, 50 f.; Caro Baroja, *La Sociedad criptojudía,* pp. 119 f. However, a residuum of uncertainty still lingers. See also *supra,* n. 61; Chaps. LXIII, n. 70; LXIV, n. 30.

107. A. Domínguez Ortiz, *La Clase social,* pp. 226 f. App. ivb (the attribution, in the margin of the Madrid MS, of the tract to Francisco de Uceda, is highly uncertain, as the writer includes in his discourse two apparently contradictory dates, 1586 and 1637, although the handwriting indicates a composition in the first half of the seventeenth century); A. Marx's brief description of the Portuguese MS in his "Report" in the *Register* of the Jewish Theological Seminary of America of 1926, p. 127 (the MS also reproduces laws, regarding the Portuguese Inquisition, enacted in 1613, 1640, and 1774); M. Kayserling, *Die Juden in Navarra,* pp. 188 f.; *supra,* n. 101.

108. P. S. Lachs, "An English Account of an Auto da Fé: Lisbon, 1669," *JQR,* LVII, 319–26. See also V. Brant's "Une Page de Sémitisme diplomatique et commercial: Incidents de la vie d'Amsterdam au XVIIᵉ siècle, d'après des pièces inédites," *Bulletin* of the Académie r. de Belgique, Classe des Lettres, 1905, pp. 573–96; and A. Rodríguez Villa's comments thereon in "Los Judíos españoles y portugueses en el siglo XVII," *BAH,* XLIX, 87–103. Rodríguez Villa quotes lengthy excerpts from an anonymous memorandum submitted to the king early in the seventeenth century. It includes the assertion—which the memorandist considers, out of his thorough knowledge of the inquisitorial records, as certain beyond any doubt—that "the crime of Judaism, and all the others accompanying it, are not committed by one or another individual, but rather by the whole people or nation, in which those who

have been acquitted of grave suspicions of having committed it enjoy the widest respect" (p. 94). This undated memorandum is attributed in a later marginal note to Padre Hernando de Salazar, but is ascribed by others to Diego Serrano da Silva. However, if Serrano da Silva was indeed the author, he must have changed his mind by the time he submitted another opinion, probably to Olivares. Here he argued, on the contrary, that most of the families, tainted by Jewish ancestry, "are at heart most faithful Christians, devout and pious, sending their daughters to live in convents and their sons to the priesthood." See the quotations from a Madrid MS by A. Domínguez Ortiz, *La Clase social*, pp. 243 f. App. iv i.

109. See T. Herrero del Collado, "El Proceso inquisitorial por delito de herejía contra Hernando de Talavera," *Anuario de historia del derecho español*, XXXIX, 671–702, esp. pp. 701 f.; *supra*, Vol. XIII, pp. 75 f., 342 f. n. 13; J. Gentil da Silva's succinct observations in "L'Autoconsommation au Portugal (XIVe–XXe siècles)," *Annales ESC*, XXIV, 250–88; A Bermúdez Coñeta, "La Decadencia económica de España," *Revista de Economía política*, VII, 238–56; and other studies mentioned *supra*, nn. 38, 43, etc.

CHAPTER LXVI: IBERIA'S COLONIAL EMPIRES

1. See L. Amabile, *Il Santo Officio della inquisizione in Napoli. Narrazione con molti documenti inediti,* esp. I, 84 ff., 218 f., 242 f., 326 ff., 342 ff.; II 5 f., 24 ff. In their opposition to the Spanish-type Inquisition, the Neapolitan leaders did not hestitate to appeal to the pope and even sent in 1563 a delegation to the Council of Trent. Similarly, they strenuously objected to the right of the Holy Office to confiscate goods of the accused; perhaps they were taught by the experience of the Iberian Peninsula, where the confiscations served as a major incentive to prosecution. See *ibid.,* I, 226 ff., 260 ff.; *supra,* Chap. LXV, n. 26; Vols. X, pp. 245 f., 408 f. n., 32; XI pp. 257 ff., 413 ff. nn. 82 ff.

2. L. Amabile, *Il Santo Officio,* II, 5 ff., 23 ff.; *Documenti* (Appendix to Vol. II), pp. 12 No. iii, 28 ff. No. viii; N. Ferorelli, *Gli Ebrei nell'Italia meridionale dall'età romana al secolo XVIII,* pp. 241 ff. and the sources cited there. The number of women sentenced in 1571 is variously given in the sources as 2, 4, or 12; they supposedly were members of a judaizing sect. The paucity of Neapolitan condemnations is doubly remarkable, as the city had long been the seat of Juan de Valdés, the purportedly heretical leader of Jewish descent. See *supra,* Vol. XIII, pp. 78 f., 343 f. n 15.

3. L. Amabile, *Il Santo Officio, Documenti,* pp. 12 No. ii, 28 ff. No. viii; N. Ferorelli, *Gli Ebrei,* pp. 242 f. Apparently the family of Odoardo Váez had Jewish connections even before 1657; one of its allegedly judaizing members, Don Francesco Váez, had died in Cremona in 1636. See F. Capacelatro, *Degli annali della città di Napoli,* pp. 69 ff. On other vestiges of Judaism in the Neapolitan provinces, see also the aforementioned works by O. Dito, *La Storia calabrese e la dimora degli Ebrei in Calabria dal secolo V alla seconda metà de secolo XVI;* G. Summo, *Gli Ebrei in Puglia dal XI al XVI secolo; supra,* Vol. X, p. 398 n. 2; G. Sorgio, "Note sul Tribunale dell'Inquisizione in Sardegna dal 1492 al 1563," *Studi sardi,* XII–XIII (= Studi . . . B. R. Motzo), 313–20; and H. C. Lea, *The Inquisition in the Spanish Dependencies,* pp. 70 ff.

4. C. Marciani, "Ebrei a Lanciano dal XII al XVIII secolo," *Archivio storico per le provincie neapolitane,* LXXXI, 167–96, esp. pp. 180 ff., 183 ff.; N. Ferorelli, *Gli Ebrei,* pp. 241 f. It may be noted that while coming to the fairs the Jewish visitors engaged in various forms of money transfer. No fewer than 11 successive documents in the archival records refer to their *lettere di cambio* during the three years of June 16, 1638, to September 11, 1641. In one case the Jew Isacco Pacifico, "moved by compassion" for a debtor who had already been imprisoned on account of insolvency, voluntarily reduced, on November 1, 1641, the amount due him, from 110 denarii to 55, payable partly in kind by clothing valued at 15 denarii, and by seven yearly instalments of 6 denarii each and a final sum of 4 denarii in the eighth year. Evidently the surplus was intended to cover nominal interest and service charges. See Marciani, pp. 187 ff. Nos. 24 ff., 192 ff. Nos. 82–93.

On the more significant developments in Milan and the southern Netherlands, see *supra*, Vol. XIV, pp. 81 ff., 336 ff. nn. 9–12, etc.; and Chap. LXIII, nn. 1 ff.

5. The Gospel of Matthew 5:17 (on the relation between this saying and its corresponding Aramaic version in Bab. Talmud Shabbat 116b, see *supra*, Vol. II, pp. 67 f., 356 f. n. 15); *The Jews in the Canary Islands Being a Calendar of Jewish Cases Extracted from the Records of the Canariote Inquisition in the Collection of the Marquess of Bute*, trans. from the Spanish and ed. with an Intro. and Notes by L. Wolf, esp. pp. 80, 100 ff., 106, 113 f.; and, more generally, the older, but still indispensable, voluminous works by A. Millares Torres, *Historia de la Inquisición en las Islas Canarias* and *Historia General de las Islas Canarias;* as well as the other literature listed *supra*, Vol. XIII, pp. 130 ff., 374 ff. nn. 75–76, to which may be added S. A. Zavala, "Las Conquistas de Canarias y América," in his *Estudios Indianos*, pp. 7–94.

6. A. Domínguez Ortiz, "Absentismo eclesiástico en Canarias," *Anuario de estudios atlánticos*, X, 235–47, esp. App ii; A. Cioranescu, *Thomas Nichols, mercader de azúcar, hispanista y hereje. Con la edición y traducción de su Descripción de las Islas Afortunadas;* L. Wolf, *The Jews in the Canary Islands*, pp. xxvi ff., xxxi f., 115 ff., 126 ff., 129 ff., 133 ff. On the De Fonseca and Pinto families in Holland, see *supra*, Chap. LXIII, n. 70. Needless to say, such interterritorial dispersion of merchant families was not limited to Jews and New Christians. For instance, the Espinosa clan, originating in Medina de Rioseco, and in the sixteenth century consisting of some 250 members, spread out over many countries in Europe and the Indies. See G. Lohmann Villena, *Les Espinosa, une famille d'hommes d'affaires en Espagne et aux Indes à l'époque de la colonisation.* Although the name De Fonseca was not infrequent among Old Christians, it is possible that the Pedro de Fonseca who, in 1583, had secretly secured from the Spanish inquisitor-general, Cardinal Gaspar Quiroga, an appointment to serve as notary of the sequestrations of the property of the accused before the Mexican Inquisition, was himself a New Christian. In their objections to this commission, the two Mexican inquisitors emphasized that they far more needed the services of a constable and that they had selected Don Pedro de Villegas, a *limpio*, for that post. See H. C. Lea, *The Inquisition in the Spanish Dependencies*, pp. 139 ff., 213 f.

7. L. Wolf, *The Jews in the Canary Islands*, pp. 119, 126 ff., 129 ff.; H. C. Lea, *The Inquisition in . . . Dependencies*, pp. 158 f. Of some interest also is the comprehensive monograph by A. Millares Carlo, *Ensayo de una bio-bibliografía de escritores naturales de las Islas Canarias (siglos XVI, XVII y XVIII).*

8. See L. Wolf *The Jews in the Canary Islands*, p. 114; H. C. Lea, *A History of the Inquisition of Spain*, I, 471 f. One must also bear in mind that our general information about Portuguese settlers on the islands, whether of *converso* or Old Christian stock, still is very limited. See J. Pérez Vidal, "Aportación portuguesa a la población de Canarias. Datas para su estudio," *Anuario de estudios atlánticos*, XIV, 41–106; and, more generally, J. Vidago, "Os Portugueses e a sua situação de estrangeiros no Império dos Felipes (1580–1640)," *Brotéria*, LXXVIII, 149–57; H. H. Keith, "New World Interlopers: the Portuguese in the Spanish West Indies, from

the Discovery to 1690," *The Americas*, XXV, 360–71. We must always bear in mind that the term "Portuguese" was at that time often used as a synonym for New Christian.

9. Martín Fernández de Navarrete, *Colección de los viajes y descubrimientos que hicieron por mar los Españoles desde fines del siglo XV*, I, 294; Philip II's rescripts of February 21, and August 7, 1596, to the audiencia in Santo Domingo, respectively summarized by S. B. Liebman in *The Jews in New Spain: Faith, Flame and the Inquisition*, p. 160; and reproduced by R. Konetzke in his *Colección de documentos para la historia de la formación social de Hispanoamérica*, II, 42 No. 21 (see also *ibid.*, I, 57 ff. No. 26, 192 f. No. 117); Pedro de Valdéz' report of December 15, 1605, cited from an archival document by H. H. Keith in his "New World Interlopers," *The Americas*, XXV, 370; C. Adler, ed., *Trial of Gabriel de Granada by the Inquisition in Mexico 1642–1645*, translated from the original by D. Fergusson and ed. with notes by C. Adler (= *PAJHS*, VII), p. 19; J. T. Medina, *Historia del Tribunal del Santo Oficio de la Inquisición de Cartagena de las Indias;* M. Kayserling, *Christopher Columbus and the Participation of the Jews in the Spanish and Portuguese Discoveries*, English translation from the German by C. Gross, esp. pp. 90 ff.; P. G. Guitéras, *Historia de Isla de Cuba*, 2d ed. rev.; and *supra*, Chaps. LXIII, nn. 78 ff.; LXIV, nn. 58 ff., 90 f. Sometimes Cuba served as a way station for passengers to Spain's continental possessions in North and South America. For example, Sebastián Rodríguez, who in 1642 was arrested for judaizing and six years later was reconciled by the Inquisition of Cartagena in an auto-da-fé of May 24, 1648, had come to Mexico after a four-month stay at the fort of Havana. See L. García de Proodian in *Los Judíos en América. Sus actividades en los Virreinatos de Nueva Castilla y Neuva Granada s. XVII*, with a Foreword by M. Ballesteros Gaibrois, pp. 27, 540 No. 230. The paucity of information concerning New Christians in Spain's West Indian islands has been but slightly alleviated by the growing literature on their general history. See the "Current Bibliography" regularly published in the periodical *Caribbean Studies*. From the listings there it appears, however, that contemporary scholars are principally interested in more recent periods. Even H. Kellenbenz's study of archival and published resources concentrates on the period after 1650. See his "Von den Karibischen Inseln. Archive und neuere Literatur, insbesondere zur Geschichte von der Mitte des 17. bis zur Mitte des 19. Jahrhunderts," *JGLA*, V, 378–404; VI, 452–69. It is not astonishing, therefore, that few new data have been coming to light concerning the New Christians or Jews living on these islands before 1650.

10. C. Miralles de Imperial y Gómez, "Censura de publicaciones en Nueva España (1576–1591). Anotaciones documentales," *Miscelanea Americanista* of the CSIC Instituto "Gonzalo Fernández de Oviedo," II (= *Homenaje a D. Antonio Ballesteros Beretta*), 219–48, esp. pp. 221 f., 230 App. iii; R. E. Greenleaf, *Zumárraga and the Mexican Inquisition, 1536–1543;* J. García Icazbalceta, *Don Fray Juan de Zumárraga primer obispo y arzobispo de México*, new ed. rev. by R. Agnayo Spencer and A. Castro Leal.

11. P. Chaunu, "Inquisition et vie quotidienne dans l'Amérique espagnole au XVIIᵉ siécle," *Annales ESC*, XI, 228–36, esp. p. 230. The main material pertaining

to the Mexican Inquisition, still available in the Mexican National Archives, has found numerous investigators since J. T. Medina's pioneering works, *La Primitiva Inquisición americana (1493–1569). Estudio histórico;* and *Historia del Tribunal del Santo Oficio de la Inquisición en México* (now available in a thoroughly revised ed. by J. J. Rueda); and H. C. Lea's *The Inquisition in the Spanish Dependencies.* Among the most meritorious workers in this field one ought to mention Alfonso Toro and, more recently, Seymour B. Liebman. Their numerous monographs have in part been mentioned *supra,* Vol. XIII, pp. 380 f. n. 81; they will also be cited frequently in the following notes, together with contributions by numerous other scholars. Here we need but mention that, despite all the difficulties enumerated by himself, Liebman has succeeded in identifying in the archives no less than 1,100 names of Jews who had lived in Mexico during the colonial period. See his *A Guide to Jewish References in the Mexican Colonial Era: 1521–1821;* his "The Jews of Colonial Mexico," *HAHR,* XLIII, 95–108; his "Los Judíos en la historia de México," *Cuadernos americanos,* XXVI, Part 1, pp. 145–56; and particularly his comprehensive study, *The Jews in New Spain.* Although subject to numerous corrections in detail, such as those suggested by H. P. Salomon in his exceedingly negative reviews in *SR,* V, 277–80; and *AJHS,* LXII, 190–201. Liebman's volume still offers the most up-to-date Jewish history in colonial Mexico.

However, in addition to the Mexican National Archives, one must investigate many local public and private collections. See, for instance, S. Williams, "The G. R. G. Conway Collection in the Library of Congress: a Checklist," *HAHR,* XXXV, 386–97 (containing Mexican inquisitorial documents of 1559–77); and Liebman's "The Abecedario and a Check-List of Mexican Inquisition Documents at the Henry E. Huntington Library," *ibid,* XLIV, 554–67, referring to that collection's forty-seven volumes, the partial description of which previously offered by E. N. Adler related mainly to records that pertained to Mexican trials of 1601–1692 and were brought by E. Nott Anable to New York. See E. N. Adler's *Auto de Fé and Jew,* pp. 156 ff.

Yet even a full coverage of the inquisitional materials would reveal only a few aspects of Jewish life in the Spanish colonies. In one of his major works on this subject, Alfonso Toro has rightly pointed out that the paucity of prosecutions for the observance of Jewish rituals, particularly in the period before 1571, may have been owing largely to the judges' ignorance. The inquisitors had at that time but a few guidelines at their disposal to identify specific Jewish rituals, whereas other manifestations of heterodoxy stemming from Jewish teachings and customs were often classified by them under a generic heading such as blasphemy, which was subject to milder punishment. See Toro, ed., *Los Judíos en la Nueva España. Selección de documentos del siglo XVI, correspondientes al ramo de Inquisición,* pp. xxvii, 191 ff. Only a systematic search through the extant contemporary chronicles and travelogues by visitors to the country, as well as through the materials available in foreign archives and libraries, may help round out the picture of a group whose life was deliberately hidden behind a thick screen of secrecy. See, for instance, Á. M. Garibay K., "Los Historiadores de México antiguo en el Virreinato de la Nueva España," *Cuadernos americanos,* XXIII, Part 1, pp. 129–47; W. Mayer, *Early Travelers in Mexico, 1534–1816;* B. Flores Salinas, *México visto por algunos de sus viajeros (siglo XVI y XVII);* E. Guzmán, *Manuscritos sobre México en Archivos de Italia;* supplemented by such special listings as E. J. Burrus's "Mexican Historical Documents in the Central

Jesuit Archives [in Rome]," *Manuscripta*, XII, 133–61; L. Liagre and J. Baerten, *Guide des sources de l'histoire d'Amérique Latine conservées en Belgique;* P. de Gayangos y Arce, *Catalogue of Manuscripts in the Spanish Language in the British Museum* (plus numerous acquisitions of the last eighty years); J. P. Harrison, *Guide to Material on Latin America in the National Archives [Washington, D. C.]*, Vol. I (concerned mostly with the nineteenth and twentieth centuries). Of course, equally important are the scattered materials in other Latin American archives, on which see R. R. Hill, *The National Archives of Latin America;* and L. Gómez Canedo, *Los Archivos de la historia de América. Período colonial.* On Luis Carvajal the Younger, see *infra*, nn. 28–30.

12. See C. H. Haring, *Trade and Navigation between Spain and the Indies in the Time of the Hapsburgs;* and the papers submitted to the Twelfth International Congress of Historical Sciences and published under the title *Les Grandes voies maritimes dans le monde, XVe–XIXe siècles.* The great difficulties of travel to and through Spanish America even a century after the establishment of the colonial regime are well illustrated by A. Alvarez's story of *Fray Diego de Ocaña (1599–1606). Un viaje fascinante por la América Hispana del siglo XVI.* See also S. Zavala, "La Utopía de América en el siglo XVI," *Cuadernos americanos, XXIV,* Part 4, pp. 130–38; J. B. Lynch, "Apocalyptic, Utopian and Aesthetic Concepts of Amerindian Culture in the Sixteenth Century," *Comparative Literature Studies,* IV, 363–70; V. A. Neasham, "Spain's Emigrants to the New World, 1492–1592," *HAHR,* XIX, 147–60; and *supra,* Vol. XIII, pp. 196 f., 412 n. 42.

13. See E. N. van Kleffens, *Hispanic Law until the End of the Middle Ages. With a Note on the Continued Validity after the Fifteenth Century of Medieval Hispanic Legislation in Spain, the Americas, Asia and Africa,* esp. pp. 255 ff.; R. Konetzke, "Legislación sobre inmigración de extranjeros en América durante la época colonial," *Revista internacional de Sociología,* III; and his "Grundzüge der spanischen Gesetzgebung über die Auswanderung nach dem amerikanischen Kolonialreich," *Festschrift Percy Ernst Schramm,* II, 105–113. On these discriminatory laws, especially Charles V's important decree of 1539, and the various methods of evading them, see *supra,* Vol. XIII, pp. 136 ff., 379 f. nn. 79–80. See also B. Lewin, "The Struggle against Jewish Immigration into Latin America in Colonial Times," *Yivo Annual of Jewish Social Science,* VII, 212–28 (English trans. of his Yiddish essay published in *Yivo Bleter*), which, however, deals almost exclusively with the situation in South America. Regrettably, the comprehensive list of passengers to the Indies, ed. by C. Bermúdez Plata, covers only the period of 1509–1559, and even for that period mentions only a fraction of the actual émigrés. See Bermúdez Plata's ed. of *Catálogo de pasajeros a Indias durante los siglos XVI, XVII y XVIII;* J. Friede's comments thereon in his "The *Catálogo de Pasajeros* and Spanish Emigration to America to 1550," *HAHR,* XXXI, 333–48; and *infra,* n. 14.

14. See J. Friede, "Algunas observaciones sobre la realidad de la emigración española a América en la primera mitad del siglo XVI," *Revista de Indias,* XII, 467–96; *supra,* n. 13; R. E. Greenleaf, "The Inquisition and the Indians of New Spain: a Study in Jurisdictional Confusion," *The Americas,* XXII, 138–66. On the theory of humane treatment of the Indians, and the frequent deviations therefrom, see especially the comprehensive works by J. Höffner, *Christentum und*

-50. The paucity of European women naturally led to an increase of the population.

The literature on the cultural evolution of Mexico is enormous. See, for example, the publication by Mexico's Archivo General de la Nación of the *Documentos para la historia de la cultura en México; una biblioteca del siglo XVI: catálogo de libros expurgados a los Jesuítas en el siglo XVIII*. There exist that many specialized bibliographies of the literature relating to various branches of intellectual endeavor. A substantial compilation of such bibliographies long ago prepared by C. K. Jones under the title *A Bibliography of Latin American Bibliographies*. Even its revised 2d ed. is now some thirty years old, thus does not cover the period of greatest qualitative and quantitative work in this field. On the general impact of the Jesuit Order on Mexican culture and its attitude toward *limpieza*, see F. J. Alégre, *Historia de la provincia de la Compañia de Jesús de Nueva España*. New ed. by E. J. Burrus and F. Zubillaga; P. Decarme, *La Obra de los Jesuitas mexicanos durante la época colonial, 1572–1767 (compendio histórico)*; and *supra*, Vol. XIV, pp. 13 ff., 306 ff. nn. 12–14. However, there seems to be no way of ascertaining how many New Christians were allowed to join the American sections of the Order even in the less restrictive sixteenth century. A casual review of the biographical data furnished by F. Zambrano in the two volumes of his *Diccionario bio-bibliográfico de la Compaña de Jesús en México* has yielded no satisfactory results. This is the less surprising as the Marrano settlers bore, for the most part, widely used Spanish names, and that none of the nearly 180 prominent members of the Order treated by Zambrano bore a name which could be identified as being of distinctly Jewish origin.

Of special interest to New Christians must have been the inquisitorial censorship of books, particularly of vernacular Bibles, which were their main source of information concerning what they considered their Jewish heritage. See, for example, C. Miralles de Imperial y Gómez, "Censura de publicaciones en Nueva España" (*supra*, n. 10), esp. p. 222; J. Friede, "La Censura española del siglo XVI y los libros de historia de América," *Revista de historia de América*, No. 47, pp. 45–94; and, more generally, A. Flores, ed., *The Literature of Spanish America: a Critical Anthology* (Vol. I is devoted to the colonial period). Understandably, the Church still played a great role in the intellectual evolution of the country. However, there also was a slowly growing lay intelligentsia among both the government bureaucrats and the private citizens. Only thus was the government able to control the Mexican Church to the extent it did.

22. See Pedro Moya de Contreras' *Cinco cartas*, ed. with a Biographical Introduction by S. C. Gutiérrez and F. Sosa; H. C. Lea, *The Inquisition in the Spanish Dependencies*, pp. 534 f. App. No. xi (reproducing a Spanish extract from the Edict of Faith extant in a Riva Palacio MS); *supra*, Vols. III, 194 f., 222 n. 28; XIII, pp. 35 ff., 322 f. n. 37. As usual, the Edict also enumerated certain behavioral patterns by which laymen could recognize their judaizing neighbors. During the subsequent investigation, the phyical examination of male defendants often produced the "incontrovertible" proof of their having at some time submitted to Jewish ritualistic circumcision. True, some American Indian tribes had also practiced circumcision. A graphic representation of such a ceremony on a piece of gold jewelry is briefly described by H. Feriz in "Die Darstellung einer Beschneid-

Menschenwürde. Das Anliegen der spanischen Kolonialethik des goldenen Zeitalters, or its Spanish translation by F. de Asis Caballero entitled *La Ética colonial española del siglo de oro. Christianismo e dignidad humana*, with an Intro. by A. Truyol Serra; and by K. S. Latourette, *A History of the Expansion of Christianity*, Vol. III: *Three Centuries of Advance A. D. 1500–1800*, pp. 83 ff. See also *infra*, nn. 63–64.

15. IV Esdras 13:40 ff., here cited from the English trans. by G. H. Box in R. H. Charles's ed. of *The Apocrypha and Pseudepigrapha of the Old Testament in English*, II, 619; Gregorio García, *Origen de los Indios de el Nuevo Mundo e Indias Occidentales*, Valencia, 1607.

16. Thomas Thorowgood, *Jewes in America; or Probabilities that the Americans are of that Race*, London, 1650; Menasseh ben Israel, *Miqveh Yisrael Spes Israelis*, Amsterdam, 1650, or the English trans. by Moses Wall entitled *The Hope of Israel*, London, 1650; with the comments thereon and related texts by M. Kayserling in *Christopher Columbus and the Participation of the Jews in the Spanish and Portuguese Discoveries*, esp. pp. 95 ff., 153 ff. App. viii; L. Wolf, *Menasseh ben Israel's Mission to Oliver Cromwell*, pp. xxiv ff., 1 ff., 7 ff.; C. Roth, *The Life of Menasseh ben Israel*, pp. 176 ff., 330 ff., 353; L. E. Huddleston, *Origins of the American Indians: European Concepts, 1492–1729*, pp. 33 ff., 118 ff., 128 ff., 138 ff. See also J. Miranda's succinct observation on "Los Indígenas de América en la época colonial; teorías, legislación, realidades," *Cuadernos americanos*, XXIII, Part 1, pp. 153–61.

The historicity of the "myth" of ancient Israelitic connections with the pre-Columbian population of the Americas has for a long time been curtly dismissed by modern critical historians. However, slowly accumulating new archaeological and other evidence—which would take me too far afield to describe even briefly—has raised some serious questions in the minds of reputable scholars concerning the early presence of peoples of Mediterranean, as well as of Negro and Mongolian, stock, perhaps especially connected with the Phoenician circumnavigation of Africa in the days of Pharoh Necho (609–595 B.C.E.) reported by Herodotus. Nor are direct vestiges of ancient Israelitic influences to be ruled out. See now C. H. Gordon, *Before Columbus: Links between the Old World and Ancient America*, which, however, raises more questions than it answers; the general survey by R. Sanders in his "Who *Did* Discover America?" *Midstream*, XVII, No. 7, pp. 9–21; and J. Lear's succinct reservations against the regnant skepticism on this score in his review of S. E. Morison's recent work, *The European Discovery of America: the Northern Voyages, A.D. 500–1600*, in the *Saturday Review* of Sept. 4, 1971, pp. 61–62. Whatever one thinks of the realities of these East-West contacts in ancient times, however, there is no doubt that the debate about the ancient Israelitic origins of the American Indians had an impact on the readmission of the Jews to England, a matter which will be analyzed in a later volume.

Of the fairly extensive literature relating to the allegedly Indian Jewish tribe living in Mexico today, which consists largely of travelogues and popular essays rather than of rigorously documented studies, we need but mention the following: the older romantic notions well summarized by M. Behar in "Les Sefardís du Mexique: les Juifs indiens," *Les Cahiers Sefardis*, September, 1947; the more restrained observations by some modern anthropologists—for instance, R. Patai's report on "Venta Priesta Revisited," *Midstream*, XI, No. 1, pp. 79–92; and, more decisively, S. B. Liebman, "Mexican Mestizo Jews," *AJA*, XIX, 144–74. See also *infra*, nn. 18 and 63.

17. See the *Recopilación de Leyes de los Reynos de las Indias*, I, vi; VI; *supra*, Vol. XI, pp. 198 ff.; J. L. Mecham, *Church and State in Latin America*; and, more generally, L. Lapétegui and F. Zubillaga, *Historia de la Iglesia en la América Española desde el Descubrimiento hasta comienzos del siglo XIX* [Vol. I]: México, América Central, Antillas; A. de Engaña, [Vol II]: *Hemisferio Sur*. Although deficient in many respects, and particularly inadequate bibliographically, these two volumes offer a fair review of the general evolution.

Most remarkably, the Mexican clergy was so impressed by the royal absolutism that, on its own, it tried to stave off the interference of the papal see. This attitude came clearly to the fore in the resolutions adopted by the Third Mexican Council of 1585. Although convoked for the purpose of introducing the canons of the Tridentine Council into Mexican Church doctrine and practice (these canons became known in Mexico too late to be implemented by the Second Council, which had met in 1565), the resolutions often ran counter to both the Tridentine decisions and earlier canonical legislation. Not surprisingly, when they were submitted to the Roman Congregation on the [Tridentine] Council, they underwent a far-reaching revision. Among other matters, the Papacy insisted upon extending greater protection to the natives than was given them in the earlier formulation. In practice, however, the papal wishes were again disregarded. See L. Hanke, "Pope Paul III and the American Indians," *Harvard Theological Review*, XXX, 74–81 (with an extensive bibliography of earlier studies); E. J. Burrus, "The Third Mexican Council (1585) in the Light of the Vatican Archives," *The Americas*, XXIII, 390–407; and, more generally, P. Leturia, *Relaciones entre la Santa Sede e Hispanoamérica*, rev. by A. de Engaña *et al.* Among other aspects, Leturia also tries to answer the intriguing question of "why the nascent Spanish-American Church was not represented in Trent" (I, 495 ff.).

18. See R. E. Greenleaf, "The Inquisition and the Indians of New Spain: a Study in Jurisdictional Confusion," *The Americas*, XXII, 138–66; Velasco's report of February 7, 1554, reproduced in M. Cueva's ed. of *Documentos inéditos para la historia de México*, p. 190; and, more generally, the mutually complementary studies by R. Konetzke, "El Mestizaje y su importancia en el desarrollo de la población hispano-americana durante la época colonial," *Revista de Indias*, VII, 7–44, 215–37; and by M. Mörner, *El Mestizaje en la historia de Iberoamérica*. A fuller study of Jewish-mestizo relations going beyond S. B. Liebman's essay mentioned *supra*, n. 16, and extending to the South-American countries as well, would be of considerable importance.

From different angles a reexamination of Negro-Jewish relations in the colonial period would likewise be meritorious. For the time being, we must be satisfied with such general studies of the psychological attitudes and sociopolitical realities in both Spain and its colonies as are offered by H. M. Jason in "The Negro in Spanish Literature to the End of the Siglo de Oro," *College Language Association Journal*, IX, 121–31; and esp. F. Tannenbaum in *Slave and Citizen: the Negro in the Americas*, and the literature cited there. See also *supra*, n. 14; and *infra*, nn. 63–64.

19. A. Domínguez Ortiz, *La Clase social*, p. 129 (cites the proverb "Ni judío

necio ni liebre perezosa"); S. B. Liebman, *The* Lohmeyer Lobo, *Aspectos de influência dos homer. ibero-americana. Século XVII* (Diss. Guanabara), reinterpretation of "La Influencia del mercantilism de América Latina," *Técnicas financieras*, XXXI, 2 also is the pioneering effort by S. F. Cook and W. la stratification sociale au Centre du Mexique duran siècle?" *Annales ESC*, XVIII, 226–58. See also, more *La Organización financiera de las Indias (siglo XV* voluminous work by H. Chaunu and P. Chaunu, *Séville* See also *infra*, nn. 50–51.

20. See the twin studies by W. Borah and S. F. C *Central Mexico in 1548: an Analysis of the* Suma de v *Americana*, XLIII); and by Cook and Borah, *The Indian Mexico 1531–1610* (Ibero-Americana, XLIV); S. B. Liebman, p. 145; and *infra*, n. 24. To be sure, some of Borah and Coo criticized by other scholars, and the exact figures given questionable. The uncertainties begin with the very estima population before Columbus. See A. Rosenblatt, *La Población Viejos y nuevos cálculos.* Yet there is no doubt about the am native population.

It should be noted, however, that this extraordinary excess natality was more a result of the natives' inability to adjust to t (including the protracted, all-year-round labor, contrasted with a 60–70 working days in the cultivation of maize in the precolonial of newly imported communicable diseases; and the great plague of of any deliberate genocidal tendencies on the part of the conqu even the Iberian immigrants had to overcome tremendous difficultie their methods of industrial production and the use of Europe exchange and commercial instruments to the exigencies of the new See the plausible arguments presented by A. E. Sayous in "L'Ada méthodes commerciales des pays chrétiens de la Méditerranée occi Amérique pendant la première moitié du XVIe siècle," in *Wirtschaft u Festschrift . . . Alfons Dopsch*, pp. 611–25. In vain did the Church try upon the entrepreneurs, as well as upon the government agents, to exacting with respect to the aboriginal population than they had been treatment of employees in their home country. See, for instance, S. Poole Church and the Repartimientos in the Light of the Third Mexican Council, *The Americas*, XX, 3–36; and other data assembled by K. S. Latourette aforementioned, somewhat overapologetic, analysis of that subject in *A Histo the Expansion of Christianity*, III, 83 ff. Not surprisingly, however, Soviet scho although generally concerned with more recent, rather than colonial, deve ments, have had a field day in describing the oppressive nature of Spanish colon ism. See some of their writings listed by L. Okinshevich and R. G. Carlton in the *Latin America in Soviet Writings: a Bibliography*, Vols. I: 1917–1958; II: 1959 1964. On the small share of women in the Old Christian migratory movemen from Spain to the New World, see R. Konetzke, "La Emigración de mujeres españoles a América durante la época colonial," *Revista internacional de Sociología*, ungsszene auf einem Goldschmuck aus Panama," *Zeitschrift für Ethnologie*, XC, 293–94. (An allegedly related practice among some Mexican Marrano women will be discussed *infra*, n. 40.) But Indians were not subject to inquisitorial trials.

In general, the Edicts of Faith not only tended to resemble one another in their general tenor but often were mere duplicates, despite the passage of generations. See, for instance, the almost identical formulas included in the Edicts of 1639 and 1795, as reproduced in facsimile and an English trans. in S. B. Liebman's *The Jews in New Spain*, pp. 96 ff. It may be noted that, in their report to Spain on October 20, 1574, the new inquisitors, the Licentiates Alphonso Fernández Bonilla and Alonso Granero de Avalos (later archbishop of Mexico and bishop of Charcas, respectively) referred to Hernando Alonso and Jerónimo de Morales as the only Judaizers "relaxed" before that date. See the text reproduced by J. T. Medina in *La Primitiva Inquisición americana*, II, 106 ff. Doc. xxiv. In addition to the literature listed in the preceding notes, see M. Y. Ibañez, *La Inquisición en México durante el siglo XVI*.

23. H. C. Lea, *The Inquisition in the Spanish Dependencies*, pp. 199 ff., 245; Fernández del Castillo, *Libros y libreros del siglo XVI*, p. 584; A. Wiznitzer, "Crypto-Jews in Mexico during the Sixteenth Century," *AJHQ*, LI, 175 ff., 214; S. B. Liebman, "The Jews of Colonial Mexico," *HAHR*, XLIII, 100; idem, "Los Judíos en la historia de México," *Cuadernos americanos*, XXVI, Part 1, pp. 146, 149.

24. See the literature listed *supra*, nn. 21 and 23. Needless to say, despite the sharp decline of the native population before 1650, the European colonists of all kinds still were but a small minority of the country. See also S. F. Cook and L. B. Simpson, *The Population of Central Mexico in the 16th Century* (Ibero-Americana, XXXI); W. Borah and Cook's more recent "Conquest and Population: a Demographic Approach to Mexican History," *Proceedings* of the American Philosophical Society, CXIII, 177–83.

25. C. Adler "The Trial of Jorge de Almeida by the Inquisition in Mexico," *PAJHS*, IV, 29–79, esp. pp. 74 f. (an English summary with extensive quotations from a Spanish MS in the possession of the American Jewish Historical Society); Ludovico à Paramo, *De origine et progressu Officii Sanctae Inquisitionis*, fols. 241 f., in the excerpt reproduced by G. A. Kohut in his "Jewish Martyrs of the Inquisition in South America," *PAJHS*, IV, 122, 159 ff. App. 1; *Trial of Gabriel de Granada by the Inquisition in Mexico 1642–1645*, trans. from the original [Spanish] by D. Fergusson and ed. with notes by C. Adler (= *PAJHS*, VII). Of some interest also is the rare description of the living conditions of a New Christian family by a contemporary visitor. Jorge de Almeida's house, he noted, was "very beautiful and well decorated, located in a lane and accoutred with many silver utensils. In it were served many well-prepared food delicacies, such as chicken roasted in earthenware and pot roasts, as well as magnificent fruits." See A. Toro's comprehensive study of the Carvajal family, cited in the next note, I, 115; and *supra*, Vol. XIII, pp. 322 f. n. 37.

26. Our main source, the inquisitorial record, and the background of the Carvajal family, have been carefully examined especially by A. Toro in *La Familia Carvajal; estudio histórico sobre los Judíos y la Inquisición de la Nueva España*

en el siglo XVI basado en documentos originales en su mayor parte inéditos. Despite S. B. Liebman's strictures and numerous corrections in detail, this still is the standard work on the subject. See Liebman's *The Jews in New Spain,* pp. 141 ff., 349 f., esp. n. 9. The provisions of the 1579 contract are cited here from P. W. Powell's English trans. in his *Soldiers, Indians and Silver,* p. 172. See also B. Lewin's earlier summary in his *Mártires y conquistadores judíos en la América hispánica,* pp. 20 ff. (also available in a Yiddish trans. in his "Don Luis de Carvajal y de la Cueva. Governor General and Conqueror of the New Kingdom of León (1539–1590)," *Davke,* IV, 310–18).

27. The royal rescript of August 8, 1587, is reproduced in R. Konetzke's *Colección de documentos,* I, 583 f. No. 441. The trial of Luis de Carvajal the Elder has been extensively recorded and commented on. See "Proceso integro de Luis Carvajal el Viego, Gobernador del Nuevo Reino de León, por judaizante," in A. Toro's aforementioned ed. of *Los Judios en la Nueva España,* pp. 205–372, esp. pp. 211, 369. An English translation of these proceedings is available among the manuscripts of the Cambridge University Library and in the Library of Congress; see J. Street, "The G. R. G. Conway Collection in Cambridge University Library: a Checklist," *HAHR,* XXXVII, 73 f. Nos. 45–46. The date of 1583, often given for Carvajal's first arrest, appears to be rather dubious, however.

If the reports underlying the 1587 rescript were right, they served as a telling illustration of the ineffectiveness of *The Spanish Struggle for Justice in the Conquest of America* on the part of the central administration, as described by L. Hanke in his book under this title. However, the allegation that Carvajal mistreated peaceful Indians is controverted not only by the stipulation of the original contract but also by the statement of another viceroy, Martín Enríquez, that the governor had always "tried harder to make a peace treaty with the Indians than to drink their blood." Moreover, Tampico appears to have been intermittently under Indian attack, and it had to be defended by stern measures. At least we learn from the English traveler John Chilton, who had visited that area sometime between 1568 and 1578, that the Indians had slain 14 of the town's 40 Christian settlers. See F. Benítez, *The Century after Cortés,* trans. from the Spanish by J. MacLean, p. 114; John Chilton's travelogue in R. Hakluyt's ed. of *The Principal Navigations, Voyages, Traffics, and Discoveries,* as summarized by W. Mayer in his *Early Travelers in Mexico, 1534–1816,* pp. 17 ff., 21.

Not surprisingly, it was the mistreatment of the natives by Spanish patroons (Carvajal was, if anything, one of the least cruel among them), rather than by the Inquisition or governmental autocracy, which has attracted the attention of Soviet scholars. Among the relatively few historical studies of Latin America in the sixteenth and seventeenth centuries published in Russia since the Revolution of 1917, one might mention the fairly typical interpretation by M. S. Alperovich, "Character and Forms of Exploitation of Indians in Spain's American Colonies in the XVI–XVII Centuries" (Russian), *Novaia i noveishaia istoria,* 1957, No. 2. pp. 49–68, and particularly the twin essays by G. I. Ivanov, "The *Encomienda* in Mexico and the Indian Revolts in the Sixteenth Century" and "The *Repartimiento* in Mexico in the XVI–XVII Centuries. From the History of the Feudal and Colonialist Exploitation of the Indian Population" (both in Russian), *Uchenye Zapiski* (Scholarly Studies) of the Gosudarstvennye Pedagogichevstkii Institut (the Governmental Pedagogical Institute) in Ivanovo, XXXV, 99–157, and 158–95, respectively. See also, more generally, J. A. Ortega y Medina, *Historiografía soviética iberoamericanista 1945–1960; supra,* n. 20; and *infra,* nn. 63–64.

28. The fascinating personality and writings of Luis de Carvajal the Younger have long intrigued Mexican scholars and have more recently attracted the attention of several United States historians as well. Our main sources of information is the text of the *Procesos de Luis de Carvajal (El Mozo).* This publication, collated by R. Gómez and arranged and selected by L. González Obregón under the direction of R. López, includes in its Appendix Carvajal's *Memorias* (pp. 461 ff., esp. pp. 464 f.) and the *Cartas* (pp. 497 ff., esp. pp. 500 f., 518, reproducing the passages quoted in our text). Many additional data had been previously supplied by J. T. Medina in his aforementioned work on Mexico, based largely upon the Mexican Inquisition's reports to the Suprema in Madrid, and further supplemented by A. Toro in *La Familia Carvajal.* A good summary of Carvajal's trial may be found in A. Wiznitzer's "Crypto-Jews in Mexico during the Sixteenth Century," *AJHQ,* LI, 168–214, esp. pp. 189 ff.; and F. Benítez's *The Century after Cortés,* pp. 115–38. The subject has been treated again more fully by S. B. Liebman in a special monograph, *The Enlightened: The Writings of Luis de Carvajal, el Mozo,* with a Preface by A. Nevins, which includes a complete English translation of Carvajal's *Memoirs* (pp. 53 ff.), his *Letters* (pp. 87 ff.), and his *Last Will and Testament* (pp. 123 ff.). The quotations in our text are taken from this translation, pp. 90 f., 107 f. Simultaneously and quite independently M. A. Cohen undertook to write a book on the same subject. In the meantime he published a translation of "The Autobiography of Luis De Carvajal, the Younger," and "The Letters and Last Will and Testament of Luis De Carvajal, the Younger," *AJHQ,* LV, 277–318 and 451–520, respectively; and analyzed "The Religion of Luis Rodríguez Carvajal: Glimpses into the Passion of a Mexican Judaizer," *AJA,* XX, 33–62. Both Liebman and Cohen list the earlier publications in this field.

29. Report of the 1596 auto-da-fé reproduced by J. García Icazbalceta in his *Bibliografía mexicana del siglo XVI,* ed. by A. Millares Carlo, p. 449; Alonso de Contreras, "Ultimos momentos y conversión de Luis de Carvajal, 1596," *Anales* of the Museo Nacional de Arqueología, III, 64–78, both cited in an English trans. by S. A. Liebman in *The Jews in New Spain,* pp. 160, 182, 350 f. nn. 1 and 15. See also the literature listed *supra,* n. 28. Contreras' assertion of Luis' last-moment surrender to the inquisitors' pressure to kiss the crucifix in order to be garroted before being burned appears questionable. We have only the belated testimony of this single witness, who may have felt constrained to justify his undisguised sympathy for the martyr to himself and his superiors. See A. M. Carreño, "Luis de Carvajal, el Mozo," *Memorias* of the Academia mexicana de la historia, XV, 87–101, esp. p. 101; S. B. Liebman, *The Enlightened,* pp. 32, 35 f., 146 f.; and the observations by M. Berger in his Yiddish translation and analysis of "Letters of a Marrano (Carvajal, 1595)" *Yorbukh Amopteil* (Annual of the American Branch of the Yiddish Scientific Institute), I, 185–216.

30. See the *Procesos,* pp. 481 f.; S. B. Liebman, *The Enlightened,* p. 72; M. A. Cohen in *AJHQ,* LV, 302 f.; *supra,* Vol. XIV, pp. 19, 309 f. n. 17; my "The Council of Trent and Rabbinic Literature," in my *Ancient and Medieval Jewish History: Essays,* ed. by L. A. Feldman, pp. 353–71, 555–64; and A. Vilela, "Un Exegeta

português do Concilio de Trento: Oleastro—No IV Centenario da sua morte (1563–1963)," *Brotéria*, LXXVIII, 16–28. The story of Luis' primitive self-circumcision is graphically told in the *Procesos*, pp. 464 f.; and in Liebman's translation in *The Enlightened*, p. 57; or Cohen's version in "The Autobiography," *AJHQ*, LV, 284 f.

Under those circumstances, it would be amazing if Luis' brother Miguel (Jacob Lumbrozo) were able, after relatively few years of sojourn outside the Spanish Empire, to compose a lexicon of difficult Hebrew terms from the Bible with a Spanish translation and to publish it under the title *Ḥesheq Shelomoh* (Solomon's Desire) in Venice in 1617. It is almost certain that someone else compiled this lexicon, since, as M. Kayserling has shown, the book had previously appeared in Venice in 1588, when Miguel was still living in relative obscurity in Mexico. See Kayserling's *Biblioteca española-portugueza-judaica*, p. 64; A. Ya'ari, *Reshimat sifre ladino* (Catalogue of Judeo-Spanish Books in the Jewish National and University Library), p. 6 No. 36; and particularly, I. Sonne, "Jacob Lumbrozo and the *Ḥesheq Shelomoh*" (Hebrew), *KS*, XI, 499–506, categorically denying the authorship of Lumbrozo, who in fact objected to many of its assertions. See also M. Lazar, "The Judaeo-Spanish Translations of the Bible after the Expulsion of the Jews from Spain" (Hebrew), *Sefunot*, VIII, 333–75, esp. pp. 351 ff. (includes an excerpt in fascimile). Miguel's connection, if any, with another Jacob Lumbrozo, an early Jewish settler in Maryland, will be discussed in a later chapter.

31. See J. Jiménez Rueda, *Herejías y supersticiones en la Nueva España (Los Heterodoxos en México)*; R. Ricard, "Pour une étude du judaïsme portugais au Mexique pendant la période coloniale," *Revue d'histoire moderne*, XIV, 516–24, esp. p. 523; *supra*, n. 30.

32. Gregorio López' *Tratado del* [or *Exposición al*] *Apocalipsis*, reproduced in Gregorio de Argaiz' *Vida y escritos del Venerable Varón Gregorio López*; his other works, and his biography of Bishop Francisco Losa, first published in Mexico City in 1613, are all cited by M. A. Cohen in his "Don Gregorio López: Friend of the Secret Jew. A Contribution to the Study of Religious Life in Early Colonial Mexico," *HUCA*, XXXVIII, 259–84. Cohen also convincingly argues here against the attribution of secret judaizing to López.

33. B. Lewin, "Luis de Carvajal, primer poeta y místico judío en Hispano-América," *Comentario*, XV, No. 62, pp. 7–14; Hernando de Ojéa's *La Venida de Cristo y su vida y milagros, en que se concuerdan los dos Testamentos divinos, Viejo y Nuevo*, analyzed by C. Perez Castro in *La Imprenta en Medina del Campo*, pp. 322 ff. No. 252; and by R. Ricard in his "Fray Hernando de Ojéa, apóstol de los Judíos mexicanos," *Abside*, I, Part 8, pp. 23–28. See also R. Heliodoro Vale, "Judíos en México," *Revista chilena de historia*, LXXXI, 215–36; and R. Ricard's succinct observations "Pour une étude du judaïsme portugais au Mexique," *Revue d'histoire moderne*, XIV, 516–24. Although New Spain extended into many territories which are now part of the United States, and Marranos settled in many outlying townships and villages, there is thus far no evidence of inquisitorial prosecutions of Judaizers in these peripheral regions. See, for instance, F. V. Scholes, "The First Decade of the Inquisition in New Mexico," *New Mexico Historical Review*, pp. 195–241, which describes trials for bigamy, witchcraft, and a variety

of native ceremonies during the years 1626–36, but does not mention cases of secret practice of Jewish rituals.

34. A. Wiznitzer, "Crypto-Jews in Mexico during the Seventeenth Century," *AJHQ*, LI, 222 ff.; S. B. Liebman, "The Jews of Colonial Mexico," *HAHR*, XLIII, 102 f. The switch to the more serious charge in the course of the investigation—circumcision, for instance, could not easily be concealed—is illustrated by the case of one Juan Franco. First accused of sorcery, he was later prosecuted as a Judaizer. See Liebman, *The Jews in New Spain*, p. 140. See also *ibid.*, pp. 309 ff. (listing the names of Judaizers among the accused in the auto of 1601).

35. F. Rodríquez Marín, "Documentos hasta ahora inéditos referentes a Matéo Alemán, y a sus deudos más cercanos (1546–1607)," *Boletín* of the Real Academia Española, XX, 167–217, esp. pp. 216 f.; *infra*, n. 49; J. T. Medina, *Historia del Tribunal del Santo Oficio de la Inquisición en México*, revised by J. Jiménez Rueda, Chap. x–xiv, pp. 169 ff., esp. pp. 185, 204 f.; H. C. Lea, *The Inquisition in the Spanish Dependencies*, pp. 226 ff.; L. González Obregón, *México viejo; noticias históricas, tradiciones, leyendas y costumbres*, new ed. enlarged, pp. 675 ff., 685 ff. (giving a list of "heretics" tried in the sixteenth and seventeenth centuries). The relative moderation of the inquisitors in the first decades of the seventeenth century and its continuation beyond the era of the "General Pardon" was in part owing to economic factors. Pierre Chaunu, in particular, has strongly stressed the impact of the business cycles on the number and severity of the sentences meted out by the Holy Office. He asserted that "in the Spanish world purged of religious dissent, Judaism played, in Mexico as in Madrid, the indispensable role of scapegoat, a catalyst for the popular resentments accompanying long-range economic readjustments." That is why the number of condemned was greatest at the beginning and the end of each such period of adaptation to economic contraction, while it declined during the period of stability on the lower level of the economy. See, especially his "Pour un tableau triste de Mexique au milieu du XVIIe siecle. Le 'Diario' de Gregorio Martin de Guijo," *Annales ESC*, X, 78–85, esp. pp. 83 f.; and his related statements cited with approval by I. S. Révah in "Les Marranes," *REJ*, CXVIII, 39. To be sure, in this particular case, the assumption that the 1640s marked the end of the economic slowdown in Mexico is rather dubious. Many scholars prefer 1580 as the final date. See *infra*, n. 37. Yet even the sixty-year recession postulated by Chaunu may have had some temporary upswings.

36. J. T. Medina, *Historia del Tribunal . . . en México*, rev. by J. Jimínez Rueda, pp. 185 f.; the English translation of Almeida's sentence in C. Adler's aforementioned study of "The Trial of Jorge de Almeida," *PAJHS*, IV, 74 f. See *supra*, n. 25; and the list of alleged Judaizers who appeared at the Mexican autos in 1625–35 in S. B. Liebman's *The Jews in New Spain*, App. pp. 312 ff. Nor were defendants acquitted once by inquisitorial courts and released from prison safe from "double jeopardy." After suffering the loss of their property and employment, many were banished from New Spain. However, they were not provided with transportation, and the ship captains, defying the express orders of the Holy Office, usually refused to take on passengers unable to pay. Such banished

"criminals" were subsequently liable to prosecution for their continued presence in the country. See also the literature listed *infra*, n. 44.

37. See J. T. Medina, *Historia del Tribunal . . . en México*, rev. by J. Jiménez Rueda, pp. 180, 210 with the notes thereon; H. C. Lea, *The Inquisition in the Spanish Dependencies*, pp. 212 ff.; H. and P. Chaunu, *Séville et l'Atlantique, passim;* and H. Lapeyre's comments on this voluminous work in his review, "De l'Atlantique au Pacificque. Les trafics maritimes de l'Empire colonial espagnol," *RH*, CCXXVIII, 327–38, esp. pp. 336 f. Much new light on the internal bickerings between the secular and inquisitorial authorities on both sides of the Atlantic Ocean was shed by M. Birckel's detailed archival study, "Recherches sur la Trésorerie inquisitoriale de Lima, Part 1: 1569–1610; Part 2: 1611–1649," *MCV*, V, 223–307; VI, 309–357. Based upon detailed examination of the reports of the Lima Holy Office to the Supreme Council of the Inquisition, still preserved in the National Archive in Madrid, Birckel's analysis presents a vivid picture of the financial dealings of the South-American branch over the first three-quarters of a century of its operations. See *infra*, nn. 52 ff. One wishes that a similar careful study of the *cuentas de receptorias* stemming from the Mexican Holy Office—despite the admitted weaknesses of the original bookkeeping in Mexico, as well as in Lima—would be published in the near future.

38. See C. E. P. Simmons, "Palafox and His Critics: Reappraising a Controversy," *HAHR*, XLVI, 394–408; the literature cited there; and on Simón Váez Sevilla, *infra*, nn. 42–43.

39. B. Lewin, *La Inquisición en México. Impresionantes relatos del siglo XVII*, esp. pp. 40 f. The fiscal Juan Saenz de Mañozca, who prepared the lengthy indictment against Solomon Pacheco-Macharro, soon became one of three chief inquisitors. Together with his two colleagues, he was later condemned for a variety of unethical and illicit practices. But as a first cousin of Juan de Mañozca y Zamora, archbishop of Puebla de Los Angeles (1643–53), he seems to have enjoyed special protection during the Pacheco-Macharro trial. When in 1645 the archbishop, whose predecessors had included such leading prosecutors of heretics as Juan de Zumárraga (1527–48) and Pedro Moya de Contreras (1573–91), was appointed *visitador* of the Mexican branch of the Holy Office by the Spanish Suprema, the three inquisitors seem to have escaped immediate censure. But their evasions did not save them in 1654 from a severe reprimand by the *visitador* Pedro de Medina Rico. Yet Saenz' fine of 1300 pesos and his suspension from office for nine years did not prevent his appointment as bishop of Cuba after but two years. See S. B. Liebman, *The Jews in New Spain*, pp. 278 f. (where some details require correction). The rumors about Jews supporting the Portuguese rebellion in 1640 were, as usual, vastly exaggerated. See *supra*, Vol. XIII, pp. 69 ff., 338 f. nn. 7–8; Chap. LXV, n. 94.

40. B. Lewin, *La Inquisición en México*, pp. 60, 84, 92, etc. The trial of Pacheco de León-Macharro and the other defendants of the 1640s produced a number of unexpected, in fact almost unbelievable, testimonies. For instance, in connection with the accusation against María de Zárate, condemned in 1659 to a fine and obligatory hospital service as a nurse for four years, we hear of feminine circum-

cision allegedly practiced among some Mexican Marranos, an observance unknown in the annals of Jewish law or folklore elsewhere. This accusation is slightly related, however, to another fantastic story told in 1635 by the imprisoned daughters of Duarte de León Jaramillo. They claimed that, when their father had initiated them into Judaism, he had cut off a piece of flesh from the left shoulder of each, roasted and eaten it. These incredible testimonies were gladly picked up by the inquisitors; and Padre Mathias de Bocanegra, to whose description of the subsequent auto-da-fé we owe much of our information on the subject, joyfully reported this evidence of Jewish cannibalism. See *ibid.*, pp. 142 f.; J. T. Medina, *Historia . . . México*, pp. 184, 204; A. Wiznitzer, "Crypto-Jews," *AJHQ*, LI, 226 f. The idea of circumcising females may have stemmed from the initiation rites practiced among certain North-American Indian tribes, where the "circumcision" consisted of removal of the young girl's hymen and the shortening of her clitoris. See G. Hernández de Alba, "The Highland Tribes in Southern Colombia," and "The Betoi and Their Neighbors" in J. H. Steward, ed., *Handbook of South American Indians*, II, 947; IV, 407; and H. Feriz's aforementioned essay "Die Darstellung einer Beschneidungsszene," *Zeitschrift für Ethnologie*, XC, 293–94.

More reliable is some further documentation of the persistence of Jewish allegiance in many families, despite all their trials and tribulations. This phenomenon is well illustrated, for instance, by the descendants of Blanca Enríquez. Her daughter, Doña Catalina de Silva, was burned in 1649. In the same auto, Catalina's son Pedro Tinoco, aged twenty-nine, bachelor of philosophy and medicine, as well as a practicing physician, was reconciled, but not without receiving two hundred lashes in public, being ordered to wear a sanbenito, and being subsequently deported to Spain. His academic diplomas were canceled. See A. Wiznitzer, "Crypto-Jews," *AJHQ*, LI, 250.

41. H. C. Lea, *The Inquisition in . . . Dependencies*, pp. 236 ff.; L. González Obregón, *Rebeliones indigenas y precursores de la independencia de México*, pp. 238 f.; B. Lewin, *La Inquisición en México*, pp. 96 ff.

42. B. Lewin, *La Inquisición en México*, pp. 34 f.; idem, " 'Las Confidencias' of Two Crypto-Jews in the Holy Office Prison of Mexico (1654–1655)," *JSS*, XXX, 3–22, esp. pp. 12 f. These "confidences" offer a remarkable illustration of the spying by inquisitorial agents among the prisoners. See also *infra*, n. 43.

43. H. C. Lea, *The Inquisition in the Spanish Dependencies*, pp. 231 f. On the trial of Francisco Botello, see especially the data analyzed by J. T. Medina in his *Historia . . . México*, pp. 247 f.; A. Wiznitzer in *AJHQ*, LI, 252 ff.; B. Lewin, *La Inquisición en México*, pp. 114 ff., partly in connection with the trial of Botello's wife, María de Zárate.

44. [L. González Obregón *et al.*, eds.], "Causa criminal contra Tomás Treviño de Sobremonte, por judaizante, [1625]," *Boletín* of the Archivo General de la Nación, Mexico, VI, 99–148, 305–308, 420–64, 578–620; ["Segundo proceso, 1642"], *ibid.*, pp. 757–77; VII, 88–142, 256–72, 402–436, 596–99; VIII, 1–172; A. Wiznitzer in his "Crypto-Jews," *AJHQ*, LI, 229 ff., 252 ff. (also referring to the controversial records concerning Botello's execution); B. Lewin's succinct description of "Tomás Treviño de Sobremonte, 'santo de la ley judía' en México, 1592–1649," in his

Mártires y conquistadores judíos, pp. 116–76 (also in his Yiddish essay, "Tomás Trebiño de Sobremonte, the 'Martyr for the Jewish Faith' in Mexico," *Davke,* XVI, 166–204); H. C. Lea, *The Inquisition in . . . Dependencies,* pp. 232 ff.; J. Jiménez Rueda, *Herejías y supersticiones,* pp. 132 ff.; S. B. Liebman, *The Jews in New Spain,* pp. 237–51, etc. On the auto-da-fé of 1659 we possess the interesting eyewitness report of November 26, 1659, submitted by the viceroy, the duke of Albuquerque, to the king, and reproduced, with comments, by A. Rodríguez Villa in his *Artículos históricos,* pp. 71 ff. (also describing the difficulties in assigning seats to the various dignitaries according to their rank). See also the older, but still valuable, studies by G. García, *La Inquisición en México;* and R. Heliodoro Valle, "Judíos en México," *Revista chilene de historia y geografía,* LXXXI, 215–36, referring, among other matters, to the sixteenth-century Flemish painter Simón Perínez (Pereyns), who, when arrested by the Inquisition in Mexico, secured permission to paint in his cell. He spent his time between hearings in painting a picture of the Virgin of Pardon (doubtless expecting this painting to influence his judges), which still hangs in the Cathedral of Mexico City, according to M. Toussaint, *Iglesias de México,* Vol. II: *La Catedral de México.* Heliodoro Valle also briefly analyzes the hypothesis current before and after Menasseh ben Israel, about the American Indians' descent from the Lost Ten Tribes of Israel. See *supra,* nn. 15–16.

45. See S. B. Liebman, *The Jews in New Spain,* esp. pp. 57, 135 ff.; and, on other American areas, hitherto less carefully explored, the literature listed *infra,* nn. 68–69. It is immaterial for our purposes whether we call Spain's overseas possessions "colonies" or "dependencies." Since in this generation "colonialism" has become a dirty word—a curious reversal of the lofty Kiplingian emphasis on the "white man's burden"—Ricardo Levene has argued: *Las Indias no eran colonias.* But whatever one thinks of this basically semantic issue, there is no question that the long-accepted chronological division between the "colonial" and "independence" periods of the Latin-American countries still is the most telling line of demarcation between the two epochs.

46. J. T. Medina, *Historia del Tribunal de la Inquisición de Lima,* new ed., I, 39, 283 ff., 293 ff., followed by H. C. Lea, *The Inquisition in the Spanish Dependencies,* pp. 419 ff. Remarkably, not all the cases studied by these distinguished pioneers in this area of research appear in the comprehensive records examined by L. García de Proodian in *Los Judíos en América.* For example, the stories of Juan Álvarez and of several other defendants mentioned by Medina and Lea are not included in her presentation. See *infra,* n. 47. In one case, that of Francisco Rodríguez, there is an outright contradiction. According to Medina and Lea, "he was pertinacious to the last and was burned alive" in the auto of 1595, whereas according to Proodian, he was reconciled at the auto of 1600 (p. 488 No. 7). Of course, reconciliation may have involved life imprisonment or condemnation to many years of galley slavery, penalties which were sometimes worse than death. For other defendants, see *ibid.,* pp. 487 ff. No. 1–16, mainly listing those reconciled in the auto of 1600. Additional weaknesses of Proodian's monograph have been stressed by several reviewers, including S. B. Liebman (*JSS,* XXXIII, 63–67). But they ought not to discourage serious students from utilizing the materials assembled by the author from Madrid and other archives, including numerous transcripts of

Lima inquisitional records which have long since been destroyed. On the financial administration of the Lima Inquisition, see *infra*, n. 52.

47. See B. Lewin, *Los Judíos bajo la Inquisición en Hispanoamérica*, pp. 31 f.; *Recopilación de Leyes* . . . *de las Indias*, VII, v.29; R. de Lafuente Machain, *Los Portugueses en Buenos Aires, Siglo XVII*. Despite the usual pioneering weaknesses, J. T. Medina's standard works, *El Tribunal del Santo Oficio de la Inquisición en las provincias de la Plata;* idem, *Historia del Tribunal del Santo Oficio de la Inquisición de Lima* (including its Documentary Appendix, II, 453 ff.); idem, *Historia del Tribunal del Santo Oficio de la Inquisición en Chile;* and idem, *Historia del Tribunal del Santo Oficio de la Inquisición de Cartagena de las Indias,* are still the basic tools for research in this area. See the well-deserved praises showered on this dedicated early historian in the essays ed. by M. A. Bromsen, *José Toribio Medina, Humanist of the Americas: An Appraisal,* which includes a study by A. A. Neuman, "Medina, Historian of the Inquisition," pp. 79–95. However, many new data and insights have been accumulating in recent decades. See also E. N. Adler, "The Inquisition in Peru," *PAJHS*, XII, 9–37 (translating in full and summarizing the instructions of the Lima Holy Office from a MS; for instance, the description of how one could detect a secret Jew, pp. 22 ff.); B. Lewin, *El Judío en la época colonial; un aspecto de la historia rioplatense,* with a Foreword by E. P. Muños (chiefly concerned with Argentina and Uruguay, both of which became important only in the eighteenth century, from which period date the various archival documents included in the appendices); and several other studies by him mentioned in my previous and forthcoming notes. Of some interest still are the lists of autos-da-fé staged in Lima in the years 1573–1806 and in Cartagena from 1614 to 1782 in E. N. Adler's *Auto-de-Fé and Jew,* p. 152; A. Guimarães, "Os Judeus portugueses e brasileiros na America hespanhola," *Journal de la Société des Américanistes de Paris*, n. s. XVIII, 297–312; and some noteworthy data relating to individual New Christians included in Diego de Cordova's *Crónica franciscana de las provincias del Perú,* reprinted by the Academy of American Franciscan History, Washington.

48. Difficulties of travel in most South American lands were but partially mitigated by the fairly extensive network of good roads built by the Incas in their realm before the Spaniards' arrival. However, there was little improvement in communications even after a century of Spanish rule, when a horse and carriage were still considered a luxury. The normal beasts of burden were mules or donkeys, the counterparts of the slow ships, averaging 200–300 tons, which at long intervals sailed between Spain and the New World. See E. Schäfer, "Der Verkehr Spaniens mit und in seinen amerikanischen Kolonien," *Ibero-Amerikanisches Archiv*, II, 435–55. See also W. Borah, *Early Colonial Trade and Navigation between Mexico and Peru* (Ibero-Americana, XXXVIII).

49. *Ordenanzas Reales para la Contratacion de Sevilla* . . . , Valladolid, 1604, cited by G. A. Kohut in "Jewish Martyrs of the Inquisition in South America," *PAJHS*, IV, 106; J. T. Medina, *El Tribunal del Santo Oficio de la Inquisición en las provincias de la Plata,* p. 61 (citing Gutiérrez de Ulloa's letter of April 8, 1580), 155 (quoting De Trejo's report of 1619), and 200 ff. (reproducing Manuel de Frías' memorandum of the same year); idem, *Historia del Tribunal de la Inquisición*

de Lima, II, *passim;* B. Lewin, *El Judío en la época colonial,* pp. 34, 54 ff. (reproducing the lengthy memorandum by De Frías); idem, *Mártires y conquistadores judíos;* idem, *La Inquisición en Hispanoamérica (Judíos, Protestantes y Patriotas);* and *infra,* n. 50. Of great interest is the description of the entire area written by a Portuguese New Christian at the beginning of the seventeenth century. See *infra,* n. 55. On Cervantes' intention to travel to Latin America and his derogatory description of these far-off lands, see his *El Caloso extremeño* in his *Obras (BAE,* I, 172); R. Levene, *Investigaciones acerca de la historia económica de Virreinato del Plata* in his *Obras* ed. with biographical introductions by C. Heras and A. Cornejo and a bibliography compiled by R. Rodríguez Molas (published by the Argentinian Academia Nacional de Historia), I, 65; E. Cros, "La Vie de Matéo Alemán. Quelques documents inédits, quelques suggestions," *BH,* LXXII, 331–37; *supra,* n. 35; and Vol. XIII, pp. 337 f. n. 5, 358 n. 41. See also P. Garagorri, "Historia y literatura (hacia Cervantes)," *Cuadernos hispanoamericanos,* LXXII, 257–72 (analyzing Américo Castro's writings on Cervantes, though neglecting the Jewish and American aspects).

A great many other documents relating to "Portuguese" tried by the Lima Inquisitions are still dormant in the Peruvian archives, from which no publications comparable to those of Mexico have thus far been issued. Even García de Proodian's archival researches, her large Documentary Appendix (pp. 259–483), and her "Documentary Index" recording individual cases (pp. 485–549) leave considerable room for further investigation. See the examples culled from a single collection, the *Catálogo de la Biblioteca Corbacho* available in the Bolivian Biblioteca Nacional, by L. Hanke in *The Portuguese in Spanish America,* pp. 13 f. Although in only two of these cases (those of Gaspar López de Agueto and Juan Rodríguez Estela of Potosí) the record specifies, somewhat tautologically, that each was a *Judío judaizante,* the chances are that many of the others were likewise accused of judaizing. García de Proodian mentions Rodríguez Estella as arrested in Buenos Aires in 1673 and transferred to Lima in the following year. But later the defendant was transferred back to Buenos Aires, and we do not know the final outcome. See her *Los Judíos,* p. 547 No. 257. However, Gaspar López de Agueto is not mentioned. See also the various reference works to the Latin-American archives, cited *supra,* n. 11.

50. See Konetzke, *Colección de documentos,* I, 142 f. No. 117, 370 ff. No. 255; and, in general, F. Chevalier, *La Formation des grandes domaines au Méxique. Terres et sociétés aux XVIe–XVIIIe siècles,* or in his *Land and Society in Colonial Mexico: the Great Hacienda,* English trans. by A. Eustis, ed. with a Foreword by L. B. Simpson (much of what is said here applies also to other parts of the Spanish-American empire); and J. Lockhart's succinct observations on "Encomienda and hacienda: the Evolution of the Great Estate in the Spanish Indies," *HAHR,* XLIX, 411–29. See also S. de Maxo's comparative study of "Feudalismo europeo y feudalismo español," *Hispania* (Madrid), XXIV, 123–33 (with special reference to F. Formosa's Spanish trans. of F. L. Ganshof's *El Feudalismo* and particularly to L. G. de Valdeavellano's Prologue and Epilogue thereto); and M. Aymard's brief summary of a round-table discussion held at the Casa de Velázquez in Paris on April 13–14, 1967, in his "Á propos d'une table ronde: les transformations du latifundio en Espagne et en Amérique latine," *MCV,* IV, 417–21.

In many areas, moreover, New Christian traders themselves may have regarded the conditions as too primitive for the display of their enterprising energies. In long stretches of Spanish America the money economy was still operating side by side with a medieval kind of barter. See, for example, C. Garzón Maceda, *Economía del Tucumán, economía natural y economía monetaria, siglos XVI–XVII–XVIII;* and, more generally, C. Verlinden, "Modernità e medioevalismo nell'economia e nella società coloniale americana," *Annali di storia economica e sociale,* IV, 1–60; and other studies reviewed by M. E. Rodrigues Vincente in *Los Estudios sobre la sociedad y la economía de Hispanoamérica durante el periodo colonial. Desde 1950 a 1960. Orientaciones bibliográficas.* Regrettably, because of obvious difficulties, the economic aspects of Jewish life in colonial Spanish America have been almost totally neglected in the existing historical literature. See also *supra,* nn. 19–20.

51. G. Friedländer, *Los Heroes olvidados,* pp. 22 ff.; B. Lewin, *El Judío . . . en la época colonial,* pp. 89 f.; H. H. Keith, "New World Interlopers," *The Americas,* XXV, 369 f. The presence of four Jewish miners in the Friedländer list is not at all surprising, since Potosí was under the Lima Inquisition's jurisdiction and we have other evidence for the presence of Portuguese New Christians in that mining community. See Bartolomé Arzáns de Orsúa y Vela, *Historia de la villa imperial de Potosí,* ed. by L. Hanke and G. Mendoza; L. Hanke's *The Imperial City of Potosí: an Unwritten Chapter in the History of Spanish America;* and the brief comments thereon by J. L. Phelan, "The History of Potosí of Bartolomé Arzáns de Orsúa y Vela," *HAHR,* XLVIII, 532—36.

Perhaps because of the industrial importance of Potosí, located about 14,000 feet above sea level, the numerous "Portuguese" were treated with relative leniency by the inquisitorial commissioners; for instance, the Jesuit father Juan de Vega in the early seventeenth century. Of course, he had no decisive jurisdiction; like other commissioners, he had to follow orders from Lima, transfer all arrested culprits there, and leave the ultimate decision to the Lima tribunal. However, it has been estimated that in 1610 about half the foreign residents (including temporary sojourners) consisted of Portuguese, and of all heretics arrested by the Potosí branch, Judaizers amounted to about one-third. See I. Wolff, "Zur Geschichte der Ausländer im spanischen Amerika. Die Stellung des extranjero in der Stadt Potosí vom 16. bis 18. Jahrhundert," *Europa und Übersee. Festschrift für Egmont Zechlin,* ed. by O. Brunner and D. Gerhard, pp. 78–108, esp. pp. 88 f., 94 f. Among these crypto-Jews was one Antonio Rodríguez Correa, a grocer. A native of Celorico de la Beira, which, as we recall, was the birthplace of many distinguished Judaizers, he had emigrated to Potosí. To his misfortune, having made some money in Potosí, he moved to Lima, where his secret was speedily discovered. Despite his "rebellious" behavior, he was condemned in 1604–1605 to a prison term of but three years and deportation to Spain. Remarkably, there he became a monk, joined the Capuchin monastery in Osuna, assumed the new name of Antonio de San Pedro, and lived an exemplary Christian life to his death in 1633 at the age of fifty-three. The fame of his great humility, his pious works, his charitable treatment of prostitutes and beggars, and particularly of his miraculous healings spread far and wide, and is still remembered by the populace of Osuna today. He became the subject of three successive edificatory biographies later in the seventeenth century. While the first two biographers remained silent on his Jewish antecedents, the third, Fray Juan de San Damaso, made a special point of extolling the achievement of the Inquisition in turning a Jew into a pious "servant of the Lord." Another interesting case was that of a hidalgo named Fulgencio Orozco, who in 1610, at the age of fifty, settled in Potosí. Unlike many other immigrants, he did not prove financially successful; and, falling ill, he blasphemed a great deal against Jesus for not having helped him to acquire a fortune. Perhaps for this reason he was considered a Judaizer, but under the influence of a popular friar he died as a repentant Christian. See Arzáns de Orsúa, *Historia*, I, 241, 288 ff.; J. Caro Baroja, *Los Judíos en la España moderna*, II, 240 ff.

52. These financial data are based upon the official accounts, the so-called *cuentas de repertorias*, submitted by the Lima Holy Office to the Suprema. Briefly mentioned by J. T. Medina in various contexts, and presented in a somewhat more organized fashion by H. C. Lea, they have been systematically reexamined and carefully analyzed by M. Birckel in his aforementioned "Recherches sur la Trésorerie inquisitoriale de Lima" in *MCV*, V–VI. See *supra*, n. 37. These figures not only elucidate the financial management of the Lima and other inquisitorial offices but also shed considerable light on various other phases of their activities. They are doubly welcome in the case of Lima, whose archives have preserved but a small fraction of the original documents. It has long been assumed that most of the inquisitorial records were destroyed by the mob on the occasion of the closing of the Holy Office in 1813, but it now appears that a great many of them were still extant on October 12, 1825, when the Council of Government issued a strict order that all its documents relating to religion be burned "absolutely, unreservedly, and without any distinction." Only records relating to pious works, genealogy, and the like were to be preserved. Moreover, whatever materials may have survived the 1825 bonfires, were doubtless included in the second burning of 1943. See A. Tibesar, "The Peruvian Church at the Time of Independence in the Light of Vatican II," *The Americas*, XXVI, 349–95, esp. pp. 373 ff. App. ii.

53. See J. T. Medina, *Historia del Tribunal de la Inquisición de Lima*, II, esp. pp. 45 ff.; B. Lewin, *El Santo Oficio en América y el más grande proceso inquisitorial en el Peru*, reproducing in his Documentary Appendix (pp. 155 ff.) the full contemporary account by Fernando de Montesinos in his *Auto de la Fé celebrado en Lima a 23. de Enero de 1639*, Madrid, 1640; L. García de Proodian, *Los Judíos en América*, pp. 316 ff. App. xviii, 503 ff. Nos. 76–89. On the weakness of the evidence for any consciously "conspiratorial" activity by the New Christian community in Lima, see S. B. Liebman's recent reexamination of "The Great Conspiracy in Peru," *The Americas*, XXVIII, 21–42. See also *infra*, nn. 78–79. Evidently, even the highly developed spy system employed by the Inquisition to monitor conversations between prisoners, who were unaware that such occasional "confidences" would ultimately be used against them, did not produce any supporting evidence for this accusation. See, for instance, the excerpts published in English by B. Lewin in "'Las Confidencias' of Two Crypto-Jews in the Holy Office Prison of Mexico (1654–1655)," *JSS*, XXX, 3–22; *supra*, n. 42.

All these descriptions of the Lima trial, its preliminaries, and its aftermath, basically go back to the reports submitted by the Lima Inquisition to Madrid. They were carefully reviewed in Simancas by Medina and were more recently reexamined by García de Proodian. Although most of the testimonies relating to the "great conspiracy," originally kept in Lima, had been destroyed (see *supra*, n. 52), the inquisitorial reports to the Suprema were quite full and, except for some details, the Lima archives, if preserved, would very likely not have yielded any startlingly new information.

54. See the sources cited *supra*, n. 53. Dependent as we are mainly upon inquisitorial records relating to the Portuguese under investigation, it is difficult to ascertain to what extent the New Christian "men of business" at the court of Philip IV influenced the mercantile transactions of their secret coreligionists in Latin America. Some background information on the subject was assembled by E. M. Lohmeyer Lobo in her Guanabara dissertation, *Aspectos de influência dos homens de negócio na política comercial ibero-americano. Século XVII*. See also the complementary studies by A. Guimarães, "Os Judeus portugueses e brasileiros na America hespanhola," *Journal de la Société des Americanistes de Paris*, XVIII, 297–312; L. Hanke, *The Portuguese in Spanish America*; J. Vidago, "Os Portugueses e a sua situação de estrangeiros no Imperio dos Felipes (1580–1640)," *Brotéria*, LXXVIII, 149–57; G. de Reparaz, "Os Portugueses na Perú nos séculos XVI e XVII," *Boletim* of the Sociedade de Geografía de Lisbõa, LXXXVa, Nos. 1–3, pp. 39–55; R. de Lafuente Machain, *Los Portugueses en Buenos Aires. Siglo XVII;* and, more generally, R. Vargas Ugarte, *Historia general del Perú*, esp. Vol. III.

55. See the anonymous memorandum first published from a Paris MS by J. de la Riva Agüero in his "Descripción anónima del Perú y de Lima a principios del siglo XVII, compuesta por un Judío portugués y dirigida a los Estados de Holanda," in *Actas y Memorias* of the Congreso de Historia y Geografía hispanoamericanas held in Seville, April 1914, pp. 347–84, and in his *Obras completas*, ed. with an Intro. by G. Lohmann Villena and revised with Notes by C. Pacheco Vélez, VI, 73–118. This text was reprinted in the *Revista del Archivo Nacional del Perú*, XVII, 3–44; and again in the *Revista Histórica* (Lima), XXI, 9–36. It also was republished by B. Lewin, with an extensive intro. and notes, under the title *Descripción del Virreinato del Perú. Crónica inédita de comienzos del siglo XVII*. On the pervasive fear of Negro uprisings and even of individual attacks by fugitive slaves, see I. Wolff, "Negersklaverei und Negerhandel in Hochperu 1545–1640," *JGLA*, I, 181 ff.; and F. P. Bowser III's Univ. of California, Berkeley, dissertation, *Negro Slavery in Colonial Peru, 1529–1650*, summarized in Dissertation Abstracts, XXIX, 205A–206A (believes that "by 1620, the volume of the Peruvian slave trade was probably more than triple what it had been in 1560"). On contemporary Lima, see also *infra*, n. 59.

56. H. C. Lea, *The Inquisition in the Spanish Dependencies*, pp. 421 ff., 427 ff.; B. Lewin, *El Judio en la época colonial*, pp. 24 ff.; L. García de Proodian, *Los Judíos*, p. 516 No. 126; other literature cited *supra*, nn. 37 and 53; F. J. H. Hernández, *Colección de bulas, breves* (photo offset), II, 370 f.; M. Birckel, "Recherches," *MCV*, VI, 337 ff., 348 ff. (also promising a more precise future examination of the total yield of the "great conspiracy" to the Inquisition; p. 349 n. 3). That the Holy Office greatly underestimated (at least in its reports to the Suprema) the wealth of the Lima business community, is evident from the anonymous Jewish "Description of Peru" (see *supra*, n. 55), which, though doubtless exaggerated, claimed that some merchants were worth more than a million pesos each, while several others owned half a million, and many had property valued at 100,000–200,000 pesos.

57. R. A. Molina, "Don Jacinto de Laríz 'el Demente,' Gobernador del Rio de la Plata," *Boletín* of the Academia Nacional de la Historia in Buenos Aires, XXXIII, Part 2, pp. 463–88, esp. pp. 481 f. In another context, Lewin quotes a lengthy excerpt from an Edict of Faith which was even more specific on how Jewish practices might be discovered by the uninitiated. See his *Los Judíos bajo la Inquisición en Hispanoamérica*, pp. 43 ff.; and *supra*, n. 22. If Lewin is right and the total number of alleged Judaizers prosecuted by the Lima Inquisition before the auto of 1639 was as high as 108, then evidently more defendants were acquitted than the seven expressly designated as such. On the other hand, we must bear in mind that, whenever the inquisitors had insufficient evidence, they often delayed the sentence while keeping the defendants in prison for years on end. We have indeed a note relating to such cases pending in 1641 at the Inquisition of Cartagena, cases which remained unresolved for years. Curiously, among such defendants held back in 1641, appears the name of Antonio Montesinos, probably the same individual who later went to Amsterdam and, as we recall, under the name of Aaron Levy made the famous deposition stating that the American Indians were descendants of the Ten Tribes of Israel. See García de Proodian, *Los Judíos*, pp. 532 f. No. 196 bis; *supra*, nn. 15–16; and *infra*, n. 63.

58. See García de Proodian, *Los Judíos*, pp. 521 ff. Nos. 146, 155–56; G. Céspedes del Castillo, "La Sociedad colonial americana en los siglos XVI y XVII" in J. Vicens Vives, *Historia social y económica de España y América*, III, 387–578, esp. pp. 394 f.; R. Konetzke's more detailed analysis of "La Emigración de mujeres españolas a América durante la época colonial," *Revista internacional de Sociología*, III, 123–50; and *supra*, n. 20.

59. See the documents published by J. T. Medina and B. Lewin cited *supra*, n. 53; L. García de Proodian, *Los Judíos*, pp. 112 f. (uncritically accepting Francisco de Vergara's testimony), 400 ff. App. xxxiii (esp. pp. 450 f.), 459 f. App. xxxvi, 520 No. 139; B. Lewin's *Mártires y conquistadores judíos*, pp. 208 ff. It may be noted that, although the "House of Pilates" was still known to the populace as late as the nineteenth century, little folklore seems to have been attached to it or to the "Street of Merchants" as a whole. At least, in a chapter on the streets of Lima in his *Leyendas y curiosidades de la historia nacional*, pp. 37 ff., L. A. Eguiguren briefly discusses a number of other streets in that "city of kings," but does not mention the *Calle de Mercaderes*. On the University of San Marcos, and its Marrano connections, see idem, *Alma Mater. Orígenes de la Universidad de San Marcos (1557-1579)*; idem, *Historia de la Universidad* (Publicaciones del Cuarto centenario de la Universidad Nacional Mayor de San Marcos), Vol. I, Parts 1–2; La Universidad en el siglo XVI; and *infra*, n. 65.

60. The dramatic story of Francisco Maldonado de Silva has frequently been told. See the documentation in J. T. Medina's *El Tribunal del Santo Oficio de la Inquisición de las provincias del Plata*, pp. 171 ff.; the transcript of the "Report to the Supreme Council of the Holy Inquisition, relative to the trial of Francisco de Silva, Bachelor, alias 'Sun of Nazareth' [Heli Nazareo], unworthy of the God of Israel" in Medina's *Historia del Tribunal del Santo Oficio de la Inquisición en Chile*, II, 71 f.; and, based thereon, in G. A. Kohut's analysis of "The Trial of Francisco Maldonado de Silva," *PAJHS*, XI, 163–79. Some additional documentation from

the Madrid National Archive is reproduced in L. García de Proodian's *Los Judíos*, pp. 340 ff. App. xxvi, which includes 9 facsimile reproductions of Maldonado de Silva's autograph writings. See also B. Lewin, *Mártires*, esp. pp. 177 ff., 208 ff.; idem, *El Santo Oficio*, pp. 142 ff.; and G. Böhm, *Nuevos antecedentes para una historia de los Judíos en Chile colonial*, pp. 39 ff., 128 ff. nn. 25–29.

Among other matters, Böhm mentions the remarkable library of sixty selected volumes found in Maldonado's Concepción home at the time of his arrest in 1627. Apart from a series of medical and pharmacological works, the library included books by Pliny, Luis de León, and Lope de Vega. To be sure, according to the existing laws, New Christians were barred from medical practice. Because of the shortage of qualified physicians, however, and in the absence of objections from an interested party, this difficulty was frequently overlooked by the authorities, or was overcome by the purchase of a special certificate of exemption, the fees for which the Inquisition found quite remunerative. See J. T. Lanning, "Legitimacy and *Limpieza de Sangre* in the practice of Medicine in the Spanish Empire," *JGLA*, IV (1967 = Richard Konetzke Jub. Vol.), 37–60. On Paul of Burgos' *Scrutinium scripturarum*, see *supra*, Vol. IX, pp. 102 f., 292 f. n. 6 item 2. Needless to say, information derived from such sources, however ingeniously interpreted, was hardly sufficient to convey to the reader an adequate knowledge of true Judaism. As a result, many Marranos, especially in the vast reaches of the New World, unless they were instructed by visitors from the old Jewish communities, were led to adopt strange doctrines and peculiar practices even more unconsciously syncretistic than those of their European coreligionists. These new religious trends, and their impact on Jewish culture in the entire Marrano dispersion, will be discussed in a later chapter.

61. See G. Friedländer, *Los Héroes olvidados*, pp. 68 ff.; and *supra*, n. 55. These possibilities bear further careful investigation.

62. L. Wolf, "American Elements in the Re-Settlement," *TJHSE*, [III] 1896–98, pp. 76–100, esp. pp. 96 f. App. vii; idem, "Cromwell's Jewish Intelligencers" reprinted in his *Essays in Jewish History*, pp. 91–114, esp. pp. 107 f.; G. A. Kohut, *Simon de Caceres and His Plan for the Conquest of Chili in 1655: a Contribution to the Tercentenary of Oliver Cromwell*, reprinted from the *American Hebrew*, LXV, 201–203. See also G. Böhm, *Nuevos antecedentes*, pp. 60 ff. Regrettably, we know very little about Simon's antecedents and his specific connections with Chile. A substantial New Christian settlement had existed there since the days of the Spanish conquest, in which some Marranos had actively participated. We cannot even tell whether there was any family connection between him and the eminent Chilean pioneer Diego García de Cáceres, a Spanish hidalgo of partial Jewish descent. See *supra*, Vol. XIII, pp. 139 f., 381 f. n. 82.

63. See L. Hanke, *Aristotle and the American Indians: a Study in Race Prejudice in the Modern World;* R. Barón Castro's succinct observations in "Le Problème de l'Indien en Amérique Espagnole," *Journal of World History*, VIII, 76–92. Most of the various writings by Bartolomé de las Casas are assembled in his *Obras Escogidas*, ed. with an Intro. by J. Pérez de Tudela Bueso in collaboration with E. López Oto, *BAE*, XCV–XCVI, CV–CVI, CX; see esp. Pérez's 180-page critical introductory essay "Significado histórico de la vida y escritos del Padre Las Casas" in Vol. I [XCV]

and the "Opusculos, Cartas y Memoriales" in Vol. V [CX]. These writings include his *Apologética Historia sumaria*, recently republished in a critical ed. from a microfilm of a Paris MS by E. O'Gorman; together with the comments thereon by A. Losada in "La 'Apología,' obra inédita de Fray Bartolomé de las Casas; actualidad de su contenido," *BAH*, CLXII, 201–248; and by J. L. Phelan, "The 'Apologetic History' of Fray Bartolomé de las Casas," *HAHR*, XLIX, 94–99. The date and the circumstances leading up to the composition of this major work by Las Casas are still controversial. Following a suggestion by Marcel Bataillon, O'Gorman rejected the then prevailing view represented by Lewis Hanke and the earlier editors and proposed a later, nonapologetic origin for that work. But this view has not been generally accepted. On Las Casas' Jewish antecedents, see Américo Castro's twin essays, "Fray Bartolomé de las Casas," *El Libro español*, IX, 231–56; and "Fray Bartolomé de las Casas o Casaus," *Mélanges à la mémoire de Jean Sarrailh*, pp. 211–43, also in his *Cervantes y los casticismos españoles*, pp. 255–312. While Castro's arguments about Las Casas' Jewish descent have not yet been confirmed by solid documentary evidence—as have been some of his earlier "guesses" about other leading Spanish figures (we still know too little about the prominent preacher-statesman-historian's family background)—they offer a highly reasonable working hypothesis.

There is an enormous recent literature on Las Casas, including a number of essays by M. Bataillon which were assembled in his *Études sur Bartolomé de las Casas*, ed. by R. Marcus. Numerous other early studies were listed by L. Hanke and M. Giménez Fernández in their *Bartolomé de las Casas (1474–1566). Bibliografía crítica y cuerpo de materiales para el estudio de su vida, escritos, actuación y polémicas que suscitaron durante cuatro siglos.* The debate was stimulated not only by the general antiracialist reaction of recent years but also by the repeated attacks on "the Apostle of the Indies" by the distinguished Spanish historian R. Menéndez Pidal, who especially emphasized Las Casas' alleged paranoia and megalomania. See, for instance, his *El Padre Las Casas, su doble personalidad;* and an early reply thereto by M. Giménez Fernándes in his "Sobre Bartolomé de las Casas" in *Actas y memorias* of the XXXVI International Congress of Americanists, held in Seville, 1964, pp. 71–129. The four-hundredth anniversary of Las Casas' death in 1966, in particular, gave rise to an outpouring of studies on his life and work. See esp. L. Hanke, "Don Ramón Menéndez Pidal and Fray Bartolomé de las Casas" in *Documenta Revista de la Sociedad Peruana de Historia*, IV, 345–58; other writings by that author analyzed in S. Serov's "Bartolomé de las Casas. Su vida y su obra en los estudios de Lewis Hanke," *Historia y Sociedad, Revista*, V, 7–19; J. Cómas, "Los Detractores del protector universal de indios y la realidad histórica," *ibid.*, pp. 20–39, and other essays in that issue (all opposed to Menéndez Pidal's views, mainly from the Marxist point of view); and the essays in the special anniversary issue of the *Revista de historia de América*, LXI–LXII, 1–186. Also noteworthy from different angles are V. D. Carro's analysis of "Bartolomé de las Casas y la lucha entre dos culturas: Christianismo y Paganismo," *Ciencia tomista*, XCIV, No. 298, pp. 89–126; No. 299, 161–232; his detailed comparative study of "Los Postulados teológico-jurídicos de Bartolomé de las Casas; sus aciertos, sus olvidos y sus fallos, ante los maestros Francisco de Vitoria y Domingo de Soto," *Anuario de estudios americanos*, XXIII, 109–246 (stressing Las Casas' relative weaknesses: his emotionalism, his failure to emphasize the Indians' duties as well as their rights, and even his factual errors); and J. A. Ortega y Medina, "Bartolomé de las

Casas y la historiografía soviética," *Historia Mexicana*, XVI, 320–40. None of these writers in any way connects Las Casas' (or Vitoria's) teachings with his Jewish antecedents. See also *supra*, nn. 14 and 18; Vol. XIII, pp. 80 f., 345 ff. n. 17; and *infra*, n. 65.

64. See E. H. Korth's *Spanish Policy in Colonial Chile: the Struggle for Social Justice, 1535–1700*, pp. 174 ff., 181 ff., 188; G. Böhm, *Nuevos antecedentes*, pp. 53 ff.; R. Latcham, *El Tesoro de los Piratas*. Böhm also refers in this connection to a later raid on Chile, headed by a Marrano, Carlos Henriques, who served under the English captain Sir John Narborough. Some additional data and insights may also be obtained from a careful perusal of the forty volumes of contemporary and near-contemporary accounts assembled in the *Colección de Historiadores i de documentos relativos a la independencia de Chile*, published by the Chile Biblioteca Nacional. See also, more generally, the older, but still very useful, comprehensive *Historia general de Chile* by D. Barros Arana; and the *Crónica de la Araucania*, by H. Lara. For data relating to the Chilean Inquisition and its Marrano aspects, we are still in the main dependent on the materials assembled by J. T. Medina in his volumes on the Inquisition in Chile and Lima and the other studies listed *supra*, nn. 53, etc.

65. See Antonio Rodríguez de León Pinelo, *Discurso sobre la importancia, forma y disposición de la Recopilación de Leyes de las Indias Occidentales* (1623), ed. by J. T. Medina in his *Biblioteca hispano-americana (1493–1810)*, Vol. II (esp. the numerous entries listed in the *Index*, p. 530); Medina, *Historia del Tribunal . . . de Lima*, II, 154 ff.; León Pinelo, *El Paraiso en el Nuevo Mundo. Comentario apologético, historia natural y peregrina de las Indias Occidentales Islas de Terra Firma del Mar Oceano*, reed. by R. Porras Barrenechea, esp. I, iii, xii, xvii f.; idem, *Anales de Madrid. Reinado de Felipe III años 1598 a 1621*, ed. with a critical Intro. of Manuscript No. 1255 of the National Library in Madrid by R. Martorell Téllez-Girón. Although Lope de Vega reflected many notions prevailing among his Spanish intellectual confreres about the New World's enormous wealth, and repeated some of the current clichés about certain exotic articles arriving therefrom, he also betrayed some more detailed knowledge of conditions there, which probably was communicated to him by friends like León Pinelo. See his *Dos obras con tema americano*, ed. by J. W. Hamilton; M. A. Morínigo, *América en el teatro de Lope de Vega*, esp. pp. 26 ff., 55 ff., 64 ff.; and A. Moramón, "El Nuevo Mundo en el universo dramático de Lope de Vega," *Revista de Indias*, XVIII, 169–77.

On Antonio's life and family antecedents, see L. G. Martínez Villada, *Diego López de Lisboa* (the diploma of Diego's appointment as *regidor* of Cuzco, issued by Philip IV on October 11, 1630, is still extant in the National Archive in Madrid); A. Larrouy, "La Familia de Antonio de León Pinelo en el Rio de la Plata," *Actas* of the XVII International Congress of Americanists, Buenos Aires, 1912, esp. pp. 607 f.; R. Molina, "Antonio de León Pinelo y su vida en América. Su testamento y su obra," *Boletin* of the Academia Nacional de Historia in Buenos Aires, XXIV–XXV, 453–76; M. del Carmen Pescador del Hoyo, ed., *Documentos de Indias siglos XV–XIX. Catálogo*, esp. pp. 117 No. 330, 126 No. 353, 179 f. Nos. 474–75; J. Caro Baroja, *Los Judíos*, II, 340 f.; and other sources cited by B. Lewin in *Los León Pinelo. La ilustre familia marrana del siglo XVII ligada a la historia de la Argentina, Perú, América y España; his Martires y conquista-*

dores judíos, pp. 216 ff., 236 ff.; and by L. Hanke in *The Portuguese in Spanish America,* pp. 10 ff.

To be sure, the identification of Juan and Diego López with the victim of the Lisbon Inquisition and his American son has sometimes been questioned. Under the peculiar system prevailing in Spain, even a far less common name like Gutiérres de Cetina was borne by three contemporaries, only one of whom was a distinguished poet. See J. Moreno de Guerra, "Datos para la biografía del poeta Gutiérres de Cetina," *Revista de Historia y de Genealogía española,* III, 49–60. Yet the weight of evidence favors an affirmative assumption in the López case. In addition to the literature here listed, see the observations by such leading scholars in this field as G. Lohman Villena and A. Millares Carlo in their introductions to their respective eds. of Antonio de León Pinelo's works: *El Gran Conciller de las Indias: Estudio preliminar y Notas,* esp. pp. xviii f., xxi, 1, 3 ff.; and *El Epítome de Pinelo: Primera bibliografía del Nuevo Mundo* (includes a facsimile reproduction of the first 1629 ed. of that work). His remark on Hebrew is cited in the text from the second impression of the *Epítome,* Madrid, 1737, fol. 5b.

Of the vast literature on the *Recopilación,* we need but mention here J. Torre Revello, *Noticias históricas sobre la Recopilación de Leyes de las Indias (Publicaciones* of the Faculdad del Instituto de investigaciones históricas in Buenos Aires, Filosofía, XLVI); M. M. Martínez, "En el cuarto centenario de las Nuevas Leyes de Indias," *Ciencia Tomista,* LXV, 39–58 (discussing the predecessor of the *Recopilación* which had first been promulgated in Valladolid in 1543, as well as its subsequent editions). Consciously or unconsciously, this recodification of the existing laws included many provisions designed to safeguard the rights of the Indian population, provisions which were in danger of falling into partial oblivion because of their persistent violation in practice. See R. Zorraquin Becù, "Aspectos fundamentales del derecho indiano" in *Libro jubilar de Victor Andrés Belaunde,* I, 445–58; A. Romulo Gamaitan's Madrid dissertation, *La Condición jurídica del Indio en el derecho indiano,* summarized in the *Revista de la Universidad de Madrid,* XII, 916–18; and particularly the analysis by the eminent student of Argentine's legal history, Ricardo Levene, in his *Introducción a la historia del derecho indiano,* reproduced in his *Obras,* III, 1–265, esp. pp. 188 ff., 201 ff. (On this outstanding historian and his impact on Argentinian historiography, see L. Gianello's succinct comments in his "Ricardo Levene y los estudios históricos en la Argentina," *BAH,* CLXIV, 189–98.) On the University of San Marcos, see Diego de León Pinelo, *Semblanza de la Universidad de San Marcos,* trans. from Latin by Luis Antonio Eguiguren (a trans. of Diego's *Hypomnema apologeticum pro Regali Academia Limnensi in Lipsianam periodum);* and *supra,* n. 59. See also G. Lohmann Villena, *El Conde de Lemos, Virrey del Perú,* esp. pp. 279 ff.

Significant contributions by Antonio de León Pinelo to the history and bibliography of all of Latin America—including Mexico, which he had apparently never visited—are analyzed, for example, by J. Quiñones Melgoza in "Los Cronistas de órdenes religiosas mencionados en el Epítome de León Pinelo," *Boletín* of the Bibliotéca Nacional in Mexico, 2d ser. XVII, Nos. 3–4, pp. 17–40; G. Baudot in "La *Memoria* de Antonio de León Pinelo; unos títulos de historiografía mexicana," *Historia mexicana,* XVIII, 227–43 (referring to the author's study in preparation for the *Epítome);* and A. Muro Obrejón in his "Antonio de León Pinelo 'Libros reales de Gobierno y Gracia . . .' Contribución al conocimiento de los cédularios del Archivo General de Indias (1492–1650)," *Anuario de estudios americanos*, XVII, 539–602 (also reprint; it offers in its 30-page appendix a fascimile reproduction of León Pinelo's work). On León Pinelo's private library, see also G. Lohman Villena's analysis of "El Testamento de Don Antonio de León Pinelo," *Revista de Indias*, VI, 33–72.

Among other studies by the outstanding jurist one ought to mention his curious two-volume work, *Velos antiguos y modernos en los rostros de las mujeres; sus conveniencias y daños*, in which he defends the idea of complete coverage of feminine faces on moral, historical, and legal grounds; and his *Relación sobre la pacificación y población de las Provincias del Marché y Lacandón*, ed. with an Intro. by J. Delgado, in which he reproduced the official report he had presented to the Council of the Indies in 1638. Perhaps it may not be too venturesome to suggest that, like his younger brother Diego and Bartolomé de las Casas, he became so deeply interested in Indian affairs because of his New Christian antecedents and an understandable affinity to any other group oppressed on racial grounds. Both brothers evinced, indeed, an unusual familiarity with the conditions of many Indian tribes. See also *supra*, n. 63. In this connection one must bear in mind that, despite frequent segregation of the Indian population, both topographically and socioeconomically, there was some acculturation between the races, not only through intermarriage and free sexual relations but also through cultural exchanges. An outstanding example of an Inca imbued with Spanish culture was the poet Garcilaso de la Vega, "el Inca," whose admiration for the philosophy of Leone Ebreo was mentioned *supra*, Vol. XIII, pp. 193 f., 410 f. n. 38. To the literature cited there, add the Inca Garcilaso de la Vega's *Obras completas*, ed. with an Intro. by C. Saenz de Santa María (*BAE*, CXXXII–XXXV); J. de Riva Agüero's "Estudios de literatura peruana: Del Inca Garcilaso a Eguren," revised with notes by C. Pacheco Vélez and A. Varillas Montenegro, in Riva's *Obras completas*, II, 1–62, esp. pp. 36 ff.; and J. G. Varner, *El Inca: the Life and Times of Garcilaso de la Vega*.

66. See M. Serrano y Sanz's Intro. to his new ed. of *La Ovandina de D. Pedro Mexía de Ovando* (Colección de libros y documentos referentes a la historia de América, XVII), Vol. I, pp. ix–cxxxv, and the text, pp. 415 ff. Chap. xlvi; J. Godoy Alcántara, *Historia crítica de los falsos cronicones;* and *supra*, Vol. XIII, p. 381 n. 82. In Chap. viii, pp. 71 ff., Mexía de Obando discusses the problem whether Jews living in Spain and their descendants were entitled to enjoy the rights of nobility. He answers this question in the negative by arguing, especially, that by repudiating Christ they had forfeited their privileged position among peoples. In this connection he indirectly rejected the legend of the Spanish Jews welcoming Jesus as a messiah. "I hold it for most certain that the Jews who had entered Spain [at that time] had consented to the death of Christ our Redeemer, which I find evidenced by the infidelity of all those who lived under the reign of the Visigothic king, Chintila." See *La Ovandina*, I, 75; *supra*, Vol. III, pp. 41 f., 248 f. n. 52.

Other works by Mexía de Obando included *Crónica de la Nobleza civil o política, su divino origen, grandezas, grados y méritos; como son los Príncipes distribuydores della; de sus privilegios y dignidades, con alyunas casas de caualleros que fueron ylustres y títulos en tiempo de los godos,* of which the *Obandina* was supposed to have been the first volume; *Memorial práctico;* and *Epítome del Gobierno de Indias.* Written in the same vein, they seem to have found no willing publisher. According to Serrano, their genealogies are "full of errors or, more correctly, of falsehoods." On the other hand, apart from his mercenary proclivities, Mexía de Obando revealed a certain populist, muckraking interest. In his critique of the existing ruling classes, he often felt impelled to defend the rights of the subject Indian population. In this respect he followed in the footsteps of Bartolomé de las Casas and Francisco Vitoria, probably quite unaware that both these distinguished political thinkers had some Jewish antecedents. See M. Serrano y Sanz, "Un Discípulo de Fr. Bartolomé de las Casas. Don Pedro Mexía de Ovando (siglo XVII)," *Archivo de Investigaciones históricas* (Madrid), I, 195–312 (incomplete); and *supra*, nn. 63 and 65. Together with the somewhat more reliable inquisitorial records, some of the genealogical data preserved by Mexía de Obando have proved useful to reputable modern scholars, such as G. Lohmann Villena in his study *Informaciones genealógicas de Peruanos seguidos ante el Santo Oficio.*

67. The story of the Cartagena Inquisition has also been told in a pioneering way by J. T. Medina in his *Historia del Tribunal del Santo Oficio de la Inquisición de Cartagena de las Indias.* His findings have been supplemented by H. C. Lea in his *Inquisition in the Spanish Dependencies*, pp. 453 ff., 466 ff.; L. García de Proodian, *Los Judíos*, esp. pp. 501 No. 67, 512 ff. Nos. 111–24, 533 ff. Nos. 198–222; and particularly by M. Tejado Fernández in his *Aspectos de la vida social en Cartagena de Indias durante el seiscientos*, esp. pp. 147 ff., 323 ff. (on the "plague of Jews who had invaded New Granada"); and in his "Un Foco de judaismo en Cartagena de Indias durante el seiscientos," *BH*, LII, 55–72 (both studies offer interesting biographical sketches and documents). The acquisition of a public office through open purchase was not uncommon. See J. H. Parry, *The Sale of Public Office in the Spanish Indies under the Habsburgs* (Ibero-Americana, XXXVII).

68. See the studies listed *supra*, n. 67. Tejado Fernández's emphasis on the quest for money rather than religious liberty as the main incentive to the Portuguese settlers in South America, as well as I. S. Révah's response thereto in his "Les Marranes," *REJ*, CXVIII, 59 f., with special reference to Luis Franco Rodríguez, are both a bit pointless. Quite apart from the fact that motivations for human actions are generally very mixed, it is well known that major migratory movements are for the most part determined by economic factors. This has been true from the days of the early nomads to the present. However, religious persecution has not only added strong incentives of a spiritual nature but has also usually involved economic discrimination and has certainly helped to build up the desire to leave for areas of relative freedom at whatever cost. True, religious liberty was hardly greater in the Spanish colonies than in the mother country; but, because of the New World's vast open spaces and the multiracial composition of its population, many a heterodox person found it easier to escape detection there. See also such more recent monographs on specific Spanish-American regions hitherto neglected by modern research, as E. Chinchilla Aguilar, *La Inquisición en Guatemala*, esp. pp. 180 ff. (describing the prosecutions of individual Judaizers, beginning in 1572 with Diego Andrada Pardo, denounced to the Mexican Inquisition in Nicaragua), 187 ff., 299 ff. (on inquisitorial censorship of books and periodicals—among the prohibited books were an English and several Spanish Bibles; a book entitled *Elieser y Naptali* by Florian, "intended to offer a complete apology for Judaism"; criticisms of the Holy Office; and politically subversive writings); and R. Villaseñor Bordes, *La Inquisición en la Nueva Galicia. Recopilación y comentarios.*

69. François René, Viscount de Chateaubriand, *The Genius of Christianity*, IV, iv. 4, in the English trans. by C. I. White, p. 571; J. Pfotenhauer's well-documented older study of *Die Missionen der Jesuiten in Paraguay;* G. Otrube, *Der Jesuitenstaat in Paraguay. Idee und Wirklichkeit;* L. Baudin's brief sketch of *Une Théocratie socialiste: l'état jésuite du Paraguay;* P. W. Conzelmann, *Wirtschaftswachstum und entwicklung im Jesuitenstaat von Paraguay;* G. V. O'Neill, *Golden Years on the Paraguay: a History of the Jesuit Missions from 1600 to 1767;* R. E. Valásquez, *La Rebelión de los Indios de Arecaya, en 1660. Reacción indigena contra los excesos de la encomienda en el Paraguay;* and *supra,* Vol. XIV, pp. 15 f., 307 f. n. 14. See also, more generally, the comprehensive work by F. J. Alégre, *Historia de la provincia de la Compañia de Jesús de Nueva España,* new ed. by E. J. Burrus and F. Zubillaga. Needless to say, the involvement of the Paraguayan Jesuits in secular affairs often created resentment. It doubtless was a contributory factor in Pope Clement IX's bull of June 17, 1669, which, harking back to ordinances enacted by Pius IV in 1563 and Urban VIII in 1633, forbade all priests to engage in business. See *Bullarium romanum,* Turin ed., XVII, 798 ff.; L. Pastor, *The History of the Popes,* XXXI, 411 f.; and P. Conzelmann's observations, p. 78.

Nor should we underestimate the influence of canon law and of the Church generally on the state legislation in the other Spanish possessions, particularly in so far as they found expression in the *Recopilación de Leyes . . . de las Indias.* See esp. R. Gómez Hoyos's *La Iglesia de America en las leyes de Indias* (slightly rev. ed. of his dissertation at the Gregorian University in Rome in 1945, entitled *Las Leyes de Indias y el Derecho eclesiástico en la América española e Islas Filipinas*). In other Spanish-American colonies, too, the Jesuit Order played a major role, though its members did not concentrate primarily on the extirpation of heresy through inquisitorial methods. They rather devoted themselves to the more humane forms of missionizing among Indians and Negroes. See F. Mateos, ed., *Historia general de la Campañia de Jesús en la provincia del Perú; crónica anónima de 1600 que trata del establecimiento y misiones de la Campañia de Jesús en los paises de habla española en la América meridional;* R. Vargas Ugarte, *Historia de la Compañia de Jesús en el Perú,* esp. Vols. I–II (to 1640; mentioning, among other matters, that Juan de Altienza, who served as the provincial head of the Peruvian branch of the Society of Jesus in 1585–92, had originally been a protégé of Diego Jacobus Laynez, whose Jewish antecedents must have been known to him; I, 171); and J. Höffner's volume in both German and Spanish, cited *supra,* n. 14. Although these authors, like Alégre, rarely refer to the New Christian members of the Order, it seems more than likely that the Jesuits' great concern for social justice, their emulation of biblical models, and their concentration on education, owed a great deal to the numerous influential New Christians who, as in the early Roman headquarters, played a considerable role in the formative stages of the Order's Latin-American sections. See esp. the data quoted by A. Castro in his essays cited *supra,* n. 63. This different approach to life, even more than the inquisitors' suspicions of the lack of *limpieza* of some Jesuit leaders, was doubtless responsible for the frequent friction between the Order and the Holy Office. Of the first seven Jesuit fathers who landed in Peru in pursuit of their missionary ideals, no fewer than four become involved in a bitter controversy with the Inquisition. One of them, Miguel de Fuentes, was banished from the Indies, although in 1587 he was allowed to return. See M. Birckel, "Le P. Miguel de Fuentes, S. J. et l'Inquisition de Lima," *BH,* LXXI, 31–139. On a similar conflict in Brazil, see *supra,* Chap.

LXV, n. 98. However, the efforts of these men to ameliorate the position of the native population reflected the humanitarian, if formally Christian, theory more than the administrative practice. Much as one may wish to discount the so-called Black Legend, there is no question that the native population suffered severely and declined sharply under the new regime. See *supra*, n. 20.

70. See G. Freyre, *The Masters and the Slaves: a Study of Brazilian Civilization*, English trans. by S. Putnam, 2d ed.; idem, *O Luso e o Trópico: Suggestões em torno dos métodos portugueses de integracão de povos autóctonos e de culturas diferentes da europeia num complexo novo de civilização: o lusotropical*, or in the English trans. by H. M. D'O. Matthew and F. de Mello Moser, entitled *The Portu-- guese and the Tropics;* and his other writings collected in *Obras Reunidas* (see also *infra*, nn. 76 and 88); with the comments thereon by H. Kellenbenz in his "Einige Aspekte der frühen Wirtschafts- und Sozialgeschichte des Nordostens von Brasilien: Ergebnisse und Anregungen neuer Forschungen," *JGLA*, I, 27–71; C. R. Boxer, *Race Relations in the Portuguese Colonial Empire, 1415–1825*. See also, more generally, C. Wagley, *An Introduction to Brazil*, rev. ed.

71. A. Baião, "A Inquisição em Portugal e no Brasil," *Archivo histórico português*, V, 423 f.; S. Leite Filho, *Os Judeus no Brasil* (reproduces in the Appendix the letters of authorization for Barreiros and Furtado de Mendoça; pp. 113 ff. Nos. iv–v); J. Lucio d'Azevedo, *Historia dos Christãos Novos Portugueses*, pp. 212 f., 224 ff.; C. R. Boxer, *Salvador de Sá and the Struggle for Brazil and Angola, 1602–1686*, p. 15; and A. Novinsky, *Cristãos Novos na Bahia (1624–1654)* (typescript; this informative volume appeared in print while the present MS was in press). The high ratio of New Christians in the Brazilian population was, understandably, vastly increased under the Dutch rule of Recife. See *infra*, n. 87. The early functioning of the Brazilian Inquisition is documented in the reports of the *visitador* Heitor Furtado de Mendoça in *Primera visitação do Santo Oficia ás partes do Brasil: Confissões de Bahia, 1591–92*, ed. with an Intro. by J. Capistrano de Abreu; continued in *Denunciações da Bahia, 1591–1593*, likewise ed. with an Intro. by Capistrano de Abreu; *Denunciações de Pernambuco, 1593–1595*, ed. with an Intro. by R. García; "Livro das Denunciações que se fizerão na Visitação do Santo Oficio a Cidade do Salvador da Bahia de Todos os Santos de Estado do Brasil, no anno de 1618. Inquisidor e Visitador o Licenciado Marcos Teixeira," ed. with an Intro. by R. García in the *Annaes* (Anais) of the Bibliotheca Nacional do Rio de Janeiro, XLIX, 75–198; A. Novinsky, "A Inquisição na Bahia. Um Relatório de 1632," *Revista de História* (São Paulo) XXXVI, No. 74, pp. 417–23; and other sources quoted by A. Wiznitzer in his *Jews in Colonial Brazil*, pp. 12 ff. The relatively high percentage of New Christians in the white population of Brazil is not controverted by the figures derived by Tarcizio do Rêgo Quirino from the records of visitations in the northern provinces in 1591–93. The Portuguese New Christians were, of course, not counted among the "foreigners," as were even the Spaniards, who constituted the largest contingent (37.8 to 55 percent) of all aliens. We recall that after 1580 many Portuguese Marranos settled in Spain. Some of them doubtless found that environment equally inhospitable and emigrated to America, where they may well have been counted as Spaniards, especially before inquisitorial authorities. See Rêgo Quirino's computations in *Os Habitantes do Brasil no fim do século XVI*, esp. pp. 29 f.

The Vieira trial by the Inquisition is recorded in his *Defesa perante o Tribunal do Santo Oficio*, ed. with an Intro. and Notes by H. Cidade; and analyzed with special reference to the foundation of the new Company by I. S. Révah in "Les Jésuites portugais contre l'Inquisition: la campagne pour la fondation de la 'Compagnie Générale du Commerce du Brésil' (1649)," *Revista do livro*, I, Nos. 3–4, pp. 29–53; E. Sluiter, "Report on the State of Brazil, 1612," *HAHR*, XXIX, 518–62 (publishing the text of the *Rezão de Estado do Brasil*, probably written by Diogo de Campos Moreno), esp. pp. 520 and 547 ff. (referring to Pernambuco); other literature listed *supra*, Chap. LXV, nn. 98–101; *infra*, nn. 97–98; and, more generally, Leite's comprehensive work, *Historia da Companhia de Jesus no Brasil*, esp. IV, 1 ff.; IX, 192 ff., 402 ff.; and R. Ricard, "Algunas enseñanzas de los documentos inquisitoriales de Brasil (1591–1595)," *Anuario de estudios americanos*, V, 705–715, emphasizing that the largest source of Portuguese emigration to Brazil was northern Portugal, including Tras-os-Montes and Beira Baixa, the main New Christian foci.

Of special interest for Recife, which became the center of Jewish life during the Dutch regime, is the publication by F. Rustico of *Cartas sobre a Campanhia de Jesus, dirigidas aos Rvds. Padres do Collegio de San Francisco Xavier da cidade do Recife*. The appearance of António Vieira, the outstanding Jesuit thinker and statesman, before the Inquisition was rightly compared with that of António Hómem by J. Lucio de Azevedo, who called these confrontations the two major *causes célèbres* in the entire history of the Portuguese Inquisition. Of course, for the Brazilian preacher, the investigation and trial consituted merely a series of unpleasant episodes, whereas Hómem's prosecution entailed years of suffering and a tragic end. See his comprehensive biographical study, *História de António Vieira*, 2d ed.; A. Baião, *Episódios dramáticos da Inquisição portuguesa*, I, 255–363; the pertinent remarks by L. Avelino, "Vieira—Govêrno, Politica e Eleições," *Verbum*, XVIII, 41–50; idem, "Vieira eo Hómem," *Brotéria*, LXXII, 550–61; and *supra*, Chap. LXV, nn. 88 ff.

72. See the comprehensive studies by H. Wätjen, *Das Holländische Kolonialreich in Brasilien: Ein Kapitel aus der Kolonialgeschichte des 17. Jahrhunderts*, esp. pp. 40 ff.; and C. R. Boxer, *The Dutch in Brazil 1624–1654*, pp. 20 ff.; as well as such detailed monographs as idem, "Piet Heyn and the Silver Fleet," *History Today*, XIII, 398–406.

73. See Manoel Themudo's report in A. Novinsky's "A Inquisição de Bahia. Um Relatório de 1632," *Revista de História* (São Paulo), XXXVI, No. 74, 417–23; that of the Évora Inquisition of 1641, cited by J. Lucio d'Azevedo in his "Judeus portugueses na dispersão," *Revista de História (Lisbon)*, IV, 214 n. 1; the Portuguese soldier's Diary cited by F. A. Varnhagen in his *História geral do Brasil*, II, 223; H. Kellenbenz, "Einige Aspekte," *JGLA*, I, 31 f. n. 13; A. Wiznitzer, *Jews in Colonial Brazil*, pp. 51 ff.; E. Marco Dorta, *La Recuperación de Bahia por Don Fadrique de Toledo (1625)*. It may be noted that the Lisbon authorities were forewarned by Brazilian officials about Dutch schemes in 1622 and even earlier. Yet they did nothing to strengthen Bahia's defenses. Nor was there any intimation on either side of the ocean about the political unrealiability of the New Christian population. See, for instance, [A. da Silva Rego *et al.*, eds.], "Papeles varios de Portugal, 1619–1626," *Documentação ultramarina portuguesa*, II (Gulbenkiana, IV),

263–560 (reproduced from an Egerton MS in the British Museum), esp. pp. 287 ff. On the Marrano role in the Dutch invasions of Brazil, see *infra*, nn. 76–77 and 82. See also F. Mauro's economic study *Le Portugal et l'Atlantique au XVIIe siècle, 1570–1670;* S. B. Schwartz, "Lûso-Spanish Relations in Hapsburg Brazil, 1580–1640," *The Americas,* XXV, 33–48; and the numerous older writings listed by J. H. Rodrigues in his *Historiografia e bibliografia do domínio holandés no Brasil,* esp. pp. 373 ff.

74. See A. Wiznitzer, *Jews in Colonial Brazil,* pp. 25, 32 ff.; H. Kellenbenz, "Einige Aspekte," *JGLA,* I, 32 ff.; *supra,* nn. 53, 62–63; and *infra,* n. 78. The events during the apogee of Dutch power in Brazil were described by a contemporary, Kaspar van Baerle (Barlaeus) in his *Rerum per octennium in Brasilia et alibi gestarum, sub praefectura illustrissimi Comitis I Mauritii Nassaviae &c. Comitis Historia* (also translated into Portuguese by C. Brandão, under the title *História dos feitos recentemente practicados durante oito anos no Brasil e noutras partes sob o governo do illustrissimo João Mauricio Conde de Nassau).* See also L. Driesen's *Leben des Fürsten Johann Moritz von Nassau-Siegen.*

75. Dierick Ruiters [or Dirck de Ruiter], *Toortse der Zeevaart* (Torch of Navigation) [1623], ed. by S. P. L'Honoré Naber, pp. 35 ff.; Willem Usselinx, quoted by J. F. Jameson in his *Willem Usselinx, Founder of the Dutch and Swedish West-India Companies,* pp. 75 f., both also cited by C. R. Boxer in his *Salvador de Sá,* pp. 44 ff. Boxer emphasizes that the Dutch public confidently expected the forth-coming conquest of Brazil and some Dutch leaders feared that too much talk on this subject might imperil the whole enterprise by alerting the Portuguese to the immediacy of the attack. See also idem, *The Dutch in Brazil;* H. Wätjen, *Das Holländische Kolonialreich in Brasilien;* and *supra,* Chap. LXIII, n. 52.

76. P. Prado, *Paulistica Historia de São Paulo,* together with other data cited by J. Gonçalves Salvador, in "Os Cristãos-novos nos capitanias do Sul (Séculos XVI°–XVII°)," *Revista de História* (São Paulo), XXV, 49–86; and by G. Freyre in *The Masters and the Slaves: a Study in the Development of Brazilian Civilization,* trans. from the Portuguese of the Fourth and Definitive Edition by S. Putnam, esp. pp. xii and 36 n. 90. In the second edition, revised and enlarged, Prado defended, against critics of his first edition, his views on the significant role played by New Christians and Jews in the upbuilding of the present Brazilian metropolis. See pp. 91 ff. See also A. Wiznitzer, *Jews in Colonial Brazil,* pp. 138 f.; the vast general bibligraphy (mainly for the period after 1650) compiled by A. Leite in his *História da civilização paulista; supra,* Vol. XIII, pp. 142 f., 383 f. n. 85; and *infra,* n. 77.

77. C. Adler, "A Contemporary Memorial Relating to Damages to Spanish Interests in America Done by Jews of Holland (1634)," *PAJHS,* XVII, 45–51, esp. pp. 48 ff.; Duarte de Albuquerque Coelho, *Memorias diarias de la Guerra del Brasil por discurso de nueve anos empecando desde de MDCXXX,* Madrid, 1654, p. 18; A. Wiznitzer, *Jews in Colonial Brazil,* pp. 51 ff., 57 ff. On Fernando de Noronha Island and the early New Christian role in its discovery and colonization, see J. F. de Almeida Prado, *Pernambuco e as Capitanias de Norte do Brasil (1530–1630). História da formação da sociedad brasileira,* II, 104 ff.; and *supra,* Vol. XIII, pp. 141 f., 383 n. 84. Relations between the Brazilian "Portuguese" and their counter-

parts in the European dispersion, as well as in the Spanish possessions in the New World, have been amply documented by several scholars. See also *supra*, Chap. LXIII, nn. 51–52.

78. J. T. Medina, *Historia del Tribunal . . . de Lima*, II, 114 f.; B. Lewin, *Il Santo Oficio en América y el más grande proceso inquisitorial en el Perú*, pp. 135 ff., 171; García de Proodian, *Los Judíos*, pp. 316 ff., 503 ff.; and *supra*, nn. 53 and 74.

79. Félix Lope de Vega Carpio, *El Brasil restituído* in his *Obras*, published by the Spanish Academy in Madrid (large edition), XIII, 75–106; A. P. Canabrava, *O Comércio português no Rio da Prata (1580–1640)*; A. Novinsky, *Cristãos Novos na Bahia*, pp. 66 ff., 100, 108, 115. See also, more generally, A. Miramón, "El Nuevo Mundo nel universo dramático de Lope de Vega," *Revista de Indias*, XXVIII, 169–77; and *supra*, n. 6. Curiously, the original manuscript of Lope's play, signed by the author on October 23, 1625, has found its way into the New York Public Library. See A. Wiznitzer, *Jews in Colonial Brazil*, p. 184 nn. 48–49; and G. de Solenni's comments on his new ed. of *Lope de Vega's "El Brasil Restituído," Together with a Study of Patriotism in His Theater*, esp. pp. xii ff., 10 ff. On Themudo's investigation, see *supra*, n. 73. Lope de Vega's generally anti-Jewish stance has been discussed *supra*, Vols. XI, pp. 155 f., 362 f. n. 42; and Chap. LXV, nn. 76 and 78.

Regrettably, the issue of New Christian and Jewish participation in the Dutch invasions of Brazil in 1624 and 1630 have become a subject of heated controversy on nationalistic grounds. Among seventeenth-century Brazilian writers and politicians trying to explain the initial defeat of their Portuguese forces, it was the line of least resistance to place the entire blame upon alleged New Christian collaboration with the Dutch conquerors. This theme was frequently repeated in modern historical literature, particularly by Jew-baiting authors. On the other hand, Dutch patriots, especially among Jews, felt it incumbent upon themselves to extol such collaboration as a contribution to the memorable Dutch overseas expansion. A more balanced view, taken by such historians as C. R. Boxer and A. Wiznitzer, has found good support in special investigations devoted to this subject by A. Novinsky in her introduction to "Uma Devassa do Bispo Dom Pedro da Silva, 1635–1637," *Anais do Museu Paulista*, XXII, 217 ff.; and especially in the paper which she submitted to the 1969 World Congress of Jewish Studies in Jerusalem entitled "An Historical Bias: The New Christians' Collaboration with the Dutch Invaders of Brazil (XVII Century)," which is to appear in that Congress's *Proceedings*.

80. See Kaspar van Baerle (Caspar Barlaeus), *Rerum per octennium in Brasilia et alibi gestarum . . . Historia* (also in the Portuguese trans. cited *supra*, n. 74); R. Ródenas Vilar, "Un Gran proyecto anti-holandés en tiempo de Felipe IV. La destrucción del comercio rebelde en Europa," *Hispania* (Madrid), XXII, 542–58 (with reference to the events of 1626, the negotiations with Poland and the Hanse, and Wallenstein's campaign). On this abortive scheme by Philip IV and Olivares, as well as on the generally declining fortunes of the West India Company, see esp. the studies by W. J. van Hoboken and J. G. van Dillen, cited *supra*, Chaps. LXIII, nn. 11 and 52. See also E. K. Kerler, "The Jews in the Holland and Zeeland Colonization of South America" (Dutch), *Historia*, V, 125–32.

81. See *infra*, n. 89; the extensive data assembled by A. Wiznitzer in "The Jews in the Sugar Industry of Colonial Brazil," *JSS*, XVIII, 189–98; the arguments pro and con aired in G. Freyre's *The Mansions and the Shanties: the Making of Modern Brazil*, trans. from the Portuguese and ed. by H. de Onís, with an Intro. by F. Tannenbaum, pp. 10 ff.; H. Kellenbenz in "Der Brasilienhandel der Hamburger 'Portuguesen' zu Ende des 16. und in der ersten Hälfte des 17. Jahrhunderts," *Actas* of the III Colóquio Internacional de Estudos luso-brasileiros, Lisbon, 1957, II, 277–96; or in its revised and enlarged form under the same title in *Portugiesische Forschungen der Görresgesellschaft*, I, 316–34; idem, *Sephardim an der unteren Elbe, passim;* L. Becker, *Die Geschichte des Hamburger Zuckerhandels von seinen Anfängen bis zum Weltkrieg;* H. Pohl, "Die Zuckereinfuhr nach Antwerpen durch portugiesische Kaufleute während des 80-jährigen Krieges," *JGLA*, IV (= Richard Konetzke Jub. Vol.), 348–73. Understandably, Pernambuco with its numerous sugar cane plantations and refineries, as well as its greater proximity to Europe, had even before the Dutch occupation attracted numerous New Christian settlers. Its conquest also loomed large to the enterprising Dutchmen. On the importance of sugar cane for that entire region, see esp. G. Freyre's *Nordeste: Aspectos de influencia de cana sobre a vida e a paisagem do Nordeste do Brasil.* The great impoverishment of that province in recent generations has also been largely the result of the changing world technology in sugar production and distribution.

Obviously, the New Christian and Jewish merchants in Amsterdam likewise took an active part in this developing branch of world commerce. Although their direct share in the Dutch West India Company was at first very moderate—they may have exerted more influence on it through their role in the Bank of Amsterdam— it was significant enough to give rise to exaggerated rumors about their special interest in the conquest of the area of primary sugar production in the Brazilian northeast. See H. I. Bloom, "A Study of Brazilian Jewish History, 1623–1654, Based Chiefly upon the Findings of the Late Samuel Oppenheim," *PAJHS*, XXXIII, 43– 125; idem, *The Economic Activities of the Jews of Amsterdam*, esp. pp. 36 ff., 124 ff., 128 ff. The leading New Christian merchant in Lisbon, Duarte da Silva, is also known to have been a major distributor of both Brazilian sugar and tobacco throughout western Europe. In 1646 he is recorded to have sold these wares through agents in Rome, Venice, Leghorn, Rouen, Antwerp, London, Hamburg, and many lesser cities. See A. Baião, *Episódios dramáticos da Inquisição portuguêsa*, 2d ed., II, 266; F. Mauro, *Le Portugal et l'Atlantique au XVIIᵉ siècle (1570–1670). Étude économique*, esp. pp. 480 f. See also, more generally, B. de Magalhães, *O Açúcar nos primórdios do Brasil Colonial;* N. Deerr, *The History of Sugar*, with the comments thereon by L. M. Friedman in his "Some References to Jews in the Sugar Trade," *PAJHS*, XLII, 305–309; A. Pereira da Costa, "Origens históricas da indústria assucareira em Pernambuco," *Arquivos* (Recife), 1945–51, pp. 257–329; H. Rabe, "Aktienkapital und Handelsinstitutionen im Überseehandel des 17. Jahrhunderts," *VSW*, XLIX, 320–68; C. Furtado, *The Economic Growth of Brazil: a Survey from Colonial to Modern Times*, trans. from the Portuguese by W. de Aguilar and E. C. Drysdale; other recent works on Dutch and Brazilian economic history, listed *infra*, n. 92; and *supra*, Chap. LXIII, nn. 52 and 62; LXIV, n. 60.

82. C. Cau *et al.*, eds., *Groot Placaatboek* (The Great Broadside Book, etc.), II, 1236 f. (Art. x); H. I. Bloom, "A Study of Brazilian Jewish History," *PAJHS*, XXXIII, 54 ff.; G. A. Kohut's somewhat one-sided "Sketches of Jewish Loyalty,

Bravery and Patriotism in the South American Colonies and the West Indies" in Simon Wolf, *The American Jew as Patriot, Soldier and Citizen*, ed. by L. E. Levy, pp. 443–84. If some overbearing Dutch officials or the generally intolerant Calvinist clergy from time to time infringed on the rights of Jewish individuals, the latter had open channels of communication with the Amsterdam headquarters of the West India Company, through their Dutch coreligionists, including the growingly influential Jewish shareholders. When, for instance, some Dutch officers unlawfully appropriated 70–80 barrels of wine belonging to the Jew Simon Drago, a personal visit to Amsterdam seems to have secured some compensation for him. See A. M. Vaz Dias, "A Look at Marrano History" (Dutch), *De Vrijdagavond*, IX, April 1939, pp. 77 ff., esp. p. 79.

83. Duarte de Albuquerque Coelho, *Memorias diarias de la Guerra del Brasil*, p. 18; Manoel Calado, *O Valeroso lucideno e o triunfo da liberdade*, Lisbon, 1648, esp. Recife 1942 ed., II, 26 ff.; L. Wolf, ed., *The Jews in the Canary Islands*, p. xxvii (also citing some interesting statistical data relating to 625 persons convicted of judaizing in thirteen autos-da-fé of 1683–1746); *supra*, n. 77. True, Wolf's sweeping declaration is not borne out by other European evidence. See, for instance, the conclusions reached by I. S. Révah in "Les Marranes," *REJ*, CXVIII, 50 f.; and the Hebrew sources cited *supra*, Vol. XIII, pp. 149 ff., 386 n. 93. But it is possible that in the isolated Marrano settlements in the vast expanses of the Spanish and Portuguese empires, many individuals followed the example of their Old Christian neighbors and, in view of the usual paucity of women of their own stock, chose mates outside the fold. There probably was a kernel of truth in the 1640 accusation of the Consistory of the Reformed Church that the Brazilian Jews "not only marry Christian women, but also employ them as servants in their household and frequently live in concubinage with them." See H. Wätjen, *Das Holländische Kolonialreich in Brasilien*, pp. 230 f. On the far from negligible manifestations of xenophobia and the incipient awakening of a new Luso-Brazilian nationalism, see the pertinent data cited by P. Calmon in *Historia social do Brasil*, I, 254 ff., 264 ff.; and M. de Oliveira Lima, *Formação histórica da nacionalidade brasileira*, trans. from the French by A. Domingues, with Forewords by G. Freyre, M. E. Martinenche, and J. Verissimo, esp. pp. 47 ff., referring especially to the *Prosopopeia* and the *Diálogos das Grandezas do Brasil*, both probably of New Christian authorship, as the early voices expressing the nascent Brazilian national sentiment. See *infra*, n. 89.

84. C. Cau *et al.*, eds., *Groot Placaatboek*, II, 1236 f., 1252 f.; the petition of the Amsterdam Jewish elders of November 27–28, 1645, and the directives of the States General of December 7, 1645, published in Dutch and in an English trans. by I. S. Emmanuel in his "New Light on Early American Jewry," *AJA*, VII, 3–64, esp. pp. 9 ff., 38 ff. Apps. E. and F. (see also the earlier English trans., from a document in the *Notulen van Staten General* of September 26, 1653, by H. I. Bloom in "A Study of Brazilian Jewish History," *PAJHS*, XXXIII, 103 f. App. A); and other sources listed by A. Wiznitzer in *Jews in Colonial Brazil*, esp. pp. 57, 63, 100 f., 184 n. 51, 185 n. 1, 189 n. 17.

85. K. van Baerle, *Rerum per octennium in Brasilia et alibi gestarum*, 2d ed., pp. 526 f. (in the Portuguese trans., pp. 327 ff., 346 f., 398 n. 142); the discussions at the Recife Assembly of 1640, reproduced in a Portuguese trans. of the Dutch

text published in the *Kroniek* of the Historisch Genootschap of Utrecht, 6th ser. IV by P. de Souto-Maior in his "A Religião christã reformada no Brasil no século XVII (Actas dos synodos e classes do Brasil no século XVII, durante o dominio holandez)," *Actas* of the First Congresso de Historia Nacional held on September 7–16, 1914 (= Special 1915 Supplement to the *Revista do Instituto Histórico e Geográfico Brasileiro*), pp. 707–780, esp. p. 759 item 7; the governor's reply cited by Souto-Maior in his "Fastos pernambucanos," in that *Revista*, LXXV, Part 1, pp. 259–504, esp. pp. 305 f.; the Jewish petition of May 1, 1642, reproduced in facsimile by A. Wiznitzer in his "Nova luz sobre a petição dos Judeus brasileiros a Mauricio de Nassau, em 1642," *Aonde Vamos?* XIII, No. 589, cover and pp. 8, 18; idem, *Jews in Colonial Brazil*, pp. 64 ff., 82, 88; and C. R. Boxer, *The Dutch in Brazil*, pp. 118 ff., 123 f. On the "Cortes" of 1640 which, convoked by the Dutch administration, anxious to listen to the grievances of the earlier, Catholic settlers, ended in utter futility, since few of their resolutions had any practical effect; see the brief comments by M. de Oliveira Lima in his *Pernambuco, seu desenvolvimiento histórico*, pp. 108 ff.; and by C. Brandenburger in his *Pernambuco und die Entwicklung Brasiliens zur Selbständigkeit. Studien zur brasilischen Geschichte*, I, 75 ff.

86. Menasseh ben Israel, *Conciliador o de la convenencia de los lugares de la S. Escriptura, que repugnantes entre si parecen*, Part 2, Amsterdam, 1641, pp. 87 f.; C. Roth, *A Life of Menasseh ben Israel*, pp. 57 ff.; A. Wiznitzer, *Jews in Colonial Brazil*, pp. 83 ff. The contention of the Recife burghers that the Jewish immigrants included arrivals from Poland and Germany is not confirmed by any direct evidence. The two lists of members of the congregation of Recife in 1648–53, published by Wiznitzer, have only three names (among 171) which may reflect Ashkenazic provenance: Simson Guzdorff, David Loeb, and Isaque Seboff. Of course, some Hebrew family names, like Cohen, Levy, or Serfatty, may have been borne by Ashkenazim, too. Yet, unless we believe that, after settling in the preponderantly Sephardic community, some of the German Jews who had left their war-ravaged country, preferred to adopt Sephardic or neutral names—few had done it upon arrival in Amsterdam—we must assume that the authors of the burghers' petition were merely trying to underscore the "foreignness" of many of their Jewish compatriots. See A. Wiznitzer, *The Records of the Earliest Jewish Community in the New World*, with a Foreword by S. W. Baron, pp. 11, 50 ff., 75 ff.

87. A. Wiznitzer, *The Records* (with some corrections by I. S. Emmanuel in his "New Light," *AJA*, VII, 61 n. 35); Wiznitzer, "The Number of Jews in Dutch Brazil (1630–1654)," *JSS*, XVI, 107–114 (includes citation from Willem [Guilelmus] Piso's *Historia naturalis Braziliae*, Amsterdam, 1648, p. 33; pp. 110 f. n. 20); C. Porto, "Povoamento e ocupação do interior pernambucano na fase colonial," *Arquivos* (Recife), 1945–51, pp. 241–56. See also *supra*, n. 71. The prevalent practice of entire Jewish families to either join or follow their heads in emigrating to new lands came most clearly to the fore in the Jewish mass migrations to the United States in the late nineteenth and early twentieth centuries. See the data cited in my *Steeled by Adversity*, ed. by J. M. Baron, pp. 280 ff., 630 nn. 19–20. On the other hand, the exodus of Jews from Recife in 1645 is well illustrated by the merchant Abram Fereira, who paid 252 florins for himself, his wife, an adult daughter and two minor children on the ship Zeelandia returning to Middelburg, Holland. See H. Wätjen, *Das Holländische Kolonialreich in Brasilien. Ein Kapitel aus der Kolonialgeschichte des 17. Jahrhunderts*, p. 347.

88. See Jacob de Andrade Velozino's as yet unpublished *Theologo religioso contra o theologo politico de Bento de Espinosa que de Judeo se fe atheista;* G. Freyre, *The Mansions,* p. 213; M. Kayserling, *Biblioteca española-portugueza-judaica,* pp. 12 f., 108. On Freyre's personal attitude to Jews and Judaism, with which he must have become better acquainted during his studies under Franz Boas at Columbia University, see the somewhat overapologetic note by S. Putnam, translator of Freyre's *The Masters and the Slaves,* p. 561 f. He may also have been influenced by some living traditions about Jewish life in Recife under Dutch domination during the years of his residence in that city and region, in which he always maintained a lively interest. See esp. M. Mota, "Gilberto Freyre e o Recife," in [G. Amado *et al.,* eds.,] *Gilberto Freyre, sua ciência, sua filosofia, sua arte. Ensayos sobre o autor de Casa-Grande y Senzala e sua influencia na moderna cultura do Brasil,* pp. 367-75, and other admiring essays in that volume, esp. pp. 544 ff., 561 f. On the Brazilian Jews' difficulties in gaining admission to the local bar, see A. Wiznitzer, "Michael Cardoso, o primeiro advocato judeo no Brasil e no Novo Mundo," *Aonde Vamos?* 2d ser. XVI, 65.

89. Bento Teixeira (Pinto), *Prosopopeia,* ed. by A. Peixotto; [Ambrósio Fernándes Brandão], *Diálogos das Grandezas do Brasil,* ed. with an Intro. by J. Capistrano de Abreu and Notes by R. Garcia; additional observations by Capistrano de Abreu in his "Diálogos das Grandezas do Brasil," reprinted from the *Jornal de Commercio* of 1900-1901 in his *Ensaios e estudos* (crítica e história), 3d ser. I, 297-336. Further comments on both the *Prosopopeia* and the *Diálogos* are offered by the careful student of Pernambucan history J. A. Gonsalves de Mello in his *Estudos pernambucanos. Crítica y problemas de algumas fontes da história de Pernambuco,* emphasizing that Teixeira employed in his *Prosopopeia* a good deal of Christian camouflage, and editing a theretofore unpublished portion of the *Diálogos* from Leiden and Lisbon manuscripts. Gonsalves de Mello, after discussing the various theories concerning the authorship of that early Brazilian classic, strongly argues in favor of Brandão as the author. See also his new "integral" edition of the *Diálogos das Grandezas,* according to the Leiden manuscript, published by the University of Recife, esp. the detailed intro. and pp. 57 ff., from which the quotations in our text are taken. About the same time as Gonsalves de Mello, A. Wiznitzer has reached substantially similar conclusions in his *Jews in Colonial Brazil,* pp. 26 ff. See also I. S. Révah's review of Gonsalves de Mello's book in *REJ,* CXX, 405-406; and G. Freyre, *The Mansions and the Shanties,* p. 222 n. 7. See also *supra,* n. 83.

90. Isaac b. David Aboab da Fonseca, *Zekher 'asiti le-nifleot El* (I Have Made a Memorial for God's Wonders; a poem), ed. by M. Kayserling in *Ha-Goren,* III, 155-74; idem, *Melekhet-ha-diqduq* (The Art of Grammar; unpublished); idem, *Bet Elohim* (House of God) and *Sha'ar ha-Shamaim* (Gate of Heaven), Hebrew trans. of Abraham Cohen Herrera's respective kabbalistic tracts, *Casa de Dios* and *Puerto del Cielo,* both published in Amsterdam, 1655; Moses Raphael de Aguilar, *Compendio de Epitome Hebraica,* Amsterdam, 1660. The biographical and further data on these and other writers were analyzed by M. Kayserling, "Isaac Aboab, the First Jewish Author in America," *PAJHS,* V, 125-36; idem, *Biblioteca española-portugueza-judaica,* pp. 4 f., 9; G. A. Kohut, "Early Jewish Literature in America," *PAJHS,* III, 103-147. Additional material has been presented by J. S. da Silva Rosa in his *Iets over den Amsterdamschen Oppenrabbijn Isaac Aboab* (Something about the Amsterdam Chief Rabbi Isaac Aboab); A. Wiznitzer, *Jews in Colonial Brazil,*

esp. pp. 169 ff. and App. end, including a facsimile excerpt from Aboab's poem, as well as the sources cited there. See also *supra*, Chap. LXIII, n. 73. Of interest also is Aboab's portrait on the frontispiece of Wiznitzer's volume; and the letter sent to Amsterdam by Aboab and his assistant, Aharon Serfatty, published in Portuguese with an English trans. by I. S. Emmanuel in his "New Light," *AJA*, VII, 24 ff. App. A. Less significant aesthetically and from the standpoint of literary history, Aboab's poem has the epochal merit of being the first fruit of the Hebrew muse in the New World.

91. See M. Kayserling, *Sephardim*, pp. 204 ff.; and, more fully, A. Wiznitzer, "Isaac de Castro, Brazilian Jewish Martyr," *PAJHS*, XLVII, 63–75; idem, *Jews in Colonial Brazil*, pp. 110 ff., 195 n. 5; and C. Roth, "An Elegy of João Pinto Delgado on Isaac de Castro Tartas," *REJ*, CXXI, 355–66. See also *supra*, Chap. LXIV, n. 29; LXV, n. 102. Kayserling (pp. 296, 360 nn. 490–91) also mentions a *ḥakham*, Jacob Lagarte, and a poet, Eliahu Machorro, among the Brazilian Jews briefly alluded to by Daniel Levi (Miguel) de Barrios, but supplies no further information. Neither is listed among the members of the two Jewish congregations in Wiznitzer's *Jews*, pp. 137 f. See also H. A. Cidade, *A Literatura portuguesa e a expansão ultramarina; as ideias—os factos—as formas de arte*, which furnishes some comparative insights for the Portuguese Jewish authors, whether they wrote in an Iberian or a Hebrew idiom. These personalities and their works will be discussed somewhat more fully in our later chapters, in connection with the general communal and intellectual history of early modern Jewry.

92. The 1637 Memorandum of the Olinda Chamber, reproduced by F. A. Pereira da Costa in his "Rehabilitação histórica do Conde de Nassau," *Revista do Instituto Histórico e Geográfico Brasileiro*, LXXI, Part 2, pp. 1–105, esp. pp. 32 f.; the 1640 resolution of the Recife "Cortes," cited by P. de Souto-Maior in "Fastos pernambucanos," *ibid.*, LXXV, Part 1, pp. 305 f.; Martim Moreno Soares' letter to King John IV, published by C. R. Boxer in "The Recovery of Pernambuco," *Atlanta* (London), II, 3 n. 2; A. Wiznitzer, *Jews in Colonial Brazil*, pp. 122 f.; J. Lucio d'Azevedo, "Judeus portugueses na dispersão," *Revista de história* (Lisbon), IV, 105–127, 201–217, esp. pp. 214 f.; and *supra*, n. 86. Not surprisingly, Jews often had greater difficulties in this respect with their Dutch friends than with their Portuguese enemies. As interested and experienced traders, the Dutch were far more resentful of Jewish competition than were the Portuguese or Spanish colonials, among whom the characteristic Spanish contempt for business (if not for its fruits), and general deprecation of hard work, rubbed off also on their leading officials and colonial burghers. On the regional differences in Brazil and the difficulties of communication between the various cities, see the contemporary data published by A. da Silva Rego from a Madrid MS in "Descripción de la Provincia del Brasil" and other contemporary memoranda in *Documentação ultramarina portuguesa*, II (Gulbenkiana, IV), pp. 1–39. See also, more generally, C. Prado, Jr., *História económica do Brasil*, 6th ed.; idem, *Formaçao do Brasil contemporaneo*, Vol. I, 7th ed.; in the English trans. by S. Macedo entitled *The Colonial Background of Modern Brazil*; and V. de Magalhães-Godinho, *L'Économie de l'Empire portugais aux XVe et XVIe siècles*; and *supra*, n. 81.

93. See A. Wiznitzer, *Jews in Colonial Brazil*, pp. 122 ff., 171, 191 nn. 74–76 (on

the basis of archival documents); F. A. de Varnhagen, *História geral de Brasil*, III, 82.

94. Luis de Menezes, conde de Ericeira, *Historia de Portugal restaurado*, I, 839; A. Wiznitzer, "Jewish Soldiers in Dutch Brazil (1630–1654)," *PAJHS*, XLVI, 40–50; S. Oppenheim, "The Early History of the Jews in New York (1654–1664)," *ibid.*, XVIII, 1–91, esp. pp. 9 ff. The military valor of Jews, who had been unaccustomed to military service in the European countries may be explained, in part, by their new sense of freedom and equality, as well as by the absence of practical alternatives. As a German, Johann (John) Nieuhof, who had spent nine years in Dutch Brazil (1640–49), observed in his travelogue, published in 1682, "the Jews more than anyone else were in a desperate situation and preferred, therefore, to die sword in hand than face their fate under the Portuguese yoke: the flames." See his *Gedenkweerdige Brasiliaense See- en Lant-Reize*, Amsterdam, 1682 (in the English trans. entitled *Voyages and Travels into Brasil and the East-Indies*, London, 1703, pp. 146b, 155 f.). The Jewish soldiers did not anticipate, and certainly could not rely upon, the subsequent Dutch-Portuguese agreement, which was to extend to Jewish prisoners protection equal to that given to Christian Dutchmen. See *supra*, Chap. LXIII, n. 84; and *infra*, n. 100.

95. The report in the *Augsburger Zeitung* of August 30, 1646 (via Cologne), cited by K. H. Oberacker, Jr., in his "Presse-Nachrichten über Brasilien im 17. Jahrhundert," *Staden-Jahrbuch*, XIII, 143; H. I. Bloom, "A Study of Brazilian Jewish History," *PAJHS*, XXXIII, 87; A. Novinsky, "An Historical Bias." See *supra*, nn. 79 and 87.

96. John IV's decree of February 7 [6], 1649, in J. J. de Andrade e Silva's *Collecção chronologica da legislação portugueza, 1648–1656*, pp. 27 f.; C. R. Boxer, *The Dutch in Brazil*, pp. 204 ff., 209 ff.; F. Mauro, *Le Portugal et l'Atlantique*, pp. 480 f.; I. S. Révah, "Les Jésuites portugais contre l'Inquisition," *Revista do livro*, I, Nos. 3–4, pp. 29–53; his "La Troisième proposition du P. António Vieira en faveur des nouveaux-chrétiens," *Boletim internacional de bibliografía luso-brasileira*, III, 267–83 (a minute examination, on the basis of the extant MSS of that important article of Vieira's pro–New Christian memorandum of May 25, 1647); and other studies listed *supra*, Chap. LXV, nn. 97 ff.; and G. de Andréa Frota's "Padre António Vieira. Ensayo bibliográfico relativo ao Brasil," *O Ocidente*, LXVI, 76–96.

97. G. de Freitas, *A Companha Geral do Comércio do Brasil (1649–1720)*; C. R. Boxer, "Padre António Vieira, S. J., and the Institution of the Brazil Company in 1649," *HAHR*, XXIX, 474–97, esp. pp. 481. The Lisbon New Christian merchants doubtless viewed their heavy investment in the new Company as insurance against inquisitorial inroads on their lives and property, rather than as a promising business venture. In fact, in the first fifteen years of its existence, the Company was able to pay only one dividend, of 15 percent, to its stockholders. See also J. Lucio d'Azevedo's biographical study, *História de António Vieira*, 2d ed., I, 136 ff., 140 ff., 160 ff.

98. António Vieira, *História do Futuro. Livro anteprimeyro prologomeno a toda a historia do futuro*; J. Lucio d'Azevedo, *Historia de António Vieira*, II, 168 ff.;

Vieira's *Defesa perante o Tribunal de Santo Ofício,* ed. by H. Cidade, II, 371 ff. (24th examination); M. Bataillon, "Le Brésil dans une vision d'Isaïe selon la Père António Vieira," *BEP,* n.s. XXV, 11–21; R. Cantel's comprehensive analysis *Prophétisme et messianisme dans l'oeuvre d'Antonio Vieira;* A. J. Saraíva's recent observations on "António Vieira, Menasseh ben Israel et le Cinquième Empire," *SR,* VI, 25–56; and other studies mentioned *supra,* Chaps. LXIV, n. 21 (on De la Peyrère); LXV, esp. n. 87 (on Bandarra), and nn. 97–100 (on Vieira). Raymond Cantel has also called attention to the related messianic yearnings of one of Vieira's contemporaries, in his "Le P. Jorge de São Paulo, témoin de Portugal en 1658," *Revista portuguesa de historia,* VI (= Pierre David Jub. Vol., I), 265–73; and to the survival until today of certain messianic yearnings among the Pernambucan populace in his "Les Prophéties dans la littérature populaire du Nordeste," *Caravelle,* XV, 57–72. See also M. I. Pereira de Queroz's more general sketch "Messianism in Brazil," *Past and Present,* 31, pp. 62–86. By dramatically mentioning the historic coincidence that in 1666, the very year of the expected redemption, both Vieira and Shabbetai Zevi found themselves in prison, Saraíva has also alluded to the great historic upheaval created in Jewish life by the appearance of the "messiah of Izmir." This climactic episode in the perennial Jewish messianic hope will be treated here in later volumes.

At the same time, Vieira was realistic enough to conclude that Brazil could not be developed by the small number of white settlers alone. Therefore, while preaching humane treatment of the Amerindians, he also insisted that the government increase the shipment of West-African slaves to its American possessions. It has been pointed out that in this respect he was far less progressive than Las Casas or even his fellow-Jesuit Alonso de Sandoval. See Vieira's letter of April 20, 1567, to King Affonso VI in his *Cartas,* ed. by J. Lucio d'Azevedo, I, 460 ff.; C. R. Boxer, *A Great Luso-Brazilian Figure, Padre António Vieira,* esp. pp. 22 ff.; M. Haubert, *L'Église el la question des "Sauvages." Le Père Antoine Vieira au Brésil;* A. J. Saraíva, "Le Père António Vieira S. J. et la question de l'esclavage des Noirs au XVIIᵉ siècle," *Annales ESC,* XXII, 1289–1309 (showing that Vieira's libertarian demands concerning the treatment of Amerindians, which had brought down on him the wrath of the Portuguese colonists and were later partially responsible for the expulsion of the Jesuits from the region, caused him to advocate the importation of Negro slaves to appease the local landowners); and L. Avelino, "Vieira—Governo, Política e Eleições," *Verbum* (Rio de Janeiro), XVIII, 41–50.

It should be noted, however that the idea of finding a more effective way to protect Portuguese shipping had long been discussed among the royal advisers in Lisbon. One proposal was to concentrate all arrivals and departures of ships to and from Brazil in one locality, as was long practiced in Spain; it was seriously debated in 1627. See H. Kellenbenz, "O Projeito duma 'Casa de Contratação' en Lisboa," *Atas* of the Fifth Congresso internacional do história do descobrimentos, Lisbon, 1961. Nor was Vieira the first to initiate an informal alliance between Jesuits and New Christians against the Inquisition. Such an alliance started soon after the establishment of the Jesuit Order in Portugal's American possessions in the middle of the sixteenth century. See S. Leite Filho, *Os Judeus no Brasil,* pp. 85 ff.; and *supra,* n. 71.

99. See G. Thomas's well-documented monograph, *Die Portugiesische Indianerpolitik in Brasilien 1500–1640,* esp. pp. 125 ff.; H. I. Bloom, "A Study," *PAJHS,*

XXXIII, 105 f. App. B.; A. Wiznitzer, *Jews in Colonial Brazil*, pp. 109 f., 143 ff.; idem, "The Synagogue and Cemetery of the Jewish Community in Recife, Brazil (1630–1654)," *PAJHS*, XLIII, 127–30. According to J. Lucio d'Azevedo, however, despite the Dutch intervention, three Recife Jews seized in the Rio de São Francisco area were actually burned. See his "Judeus portugueses na dispersão," *Revista de história* (Lisbon), IV, 215. See also the biographical studies by P. Calmon, *Francisco Barreto, restaurador de Pernambuco;* J. A. Gonsalves de Mello, *João Fernandes Vieira, mestre de campo do têrço de infantaria da Pernambucco;* and, more generally, M. de Oliveira Lima's older review *Pernambuco, seu desenvolvimento histórico.*

100. H. I. Bloom, "A Study," *PAJHS*, XXXIII, 106 f., App. C; the terms of the Dutch capitulation of Taborda in January, 1654, most readily available in the Portuguese text reproduced by F. A. Varnhagen in his *Historia geral do Brasil antes da sua separação e independencia de Portugal*, 3d ed., III, 141–46 (also listing earlier eds. in both Portuguese and Dutch), esp. Arts. 6, 8, and 14; Saul Levi Morteira, *Provvidencia de Dios con Ysrael, y Verdad, y Eternidad da la Ley de Moseh y Nulidad de los demas Leyes* (The Providence of God with Israel, and the Truth and Eternity of the Law of Moses, and the Nullity of the Other Laws), cited in the original and in an English trans. from several MSS by A. Wiznitzer in "The Number of Jews," *JSS*, XVI, 112 f., 114 App. ii. The events of 1646–47 are analyzed by Wiznitzer in his *Jews in Colonial Brazil*, pp. 106 ff. See also the graphic description of the gradual decline of Dutch power in Brazil, in C. R. Boxer's "The Recovery of Pernambuco," *Atlanta*, II, 1–17; and V. Brant's aforementioned communication to the Belgian Academy of 1905, referring to the then unpublished correspondence between the Dutch and Spanish diplomats (*supra*, Chaps. LXIII, n. 69; LXV, n. 108).

After the 1654 evacuation, the few Jews or Marranos who remained in the country reverted to their earlier status of a suspect minority, under the constant surveillance of the Inquisition. See Wiznitzer, *Jews in Colonial Brazil*, pp. 143 ff., almost totally superseding the earlier studies by S. Leite Filho, *Os Judeus no Brasil;* and by J. Lucio d'Azevedo, "Notas sobre o Judaismo e a Inquisição do Brasil," *Revista do Instituto Histórico e Geográfico Brasileiro*, CXLV, 680–97. Needless to say, the Dutch occupation, however brief, and the Jewish role in the economy of the country during that period, also left a permanent imprint on Brazil's subsequent evolution. See J. A. Gonsalves de Mello, *Tempo de Flamengos. Influência da ocupação holandesa na vida e na cultura do Norte do Brasil*, with a Foreword by G. Freyre, esp. pp. 290 ff.; S. Leite Filho, *Da influência do elemento judaico no descobrimento e comércio do Brasil (séculos XVI e XVII).*

101. See the illuminating summary by C. R. Boxer, *Four Centuries of Portuguese Expansion, 1415–1825: A Succinct Survey;* and the older, but still very valuable, work by António Baião *et al.*, eds. *Historia da expansão portuguesa no mundo.* On the antecedents, see P. Chaunu's *L'Expansion européenne du XIIIe au XVe siècle.* Regional surveys are offered by R. Coupland, *East Africa and its Invaders, From the Earliest Times to the Death of Seyyid Said in 1856;* R. W. Howe, *Black Africa: Africa South of the Sahara from Prehistory to Independence;* P. J. M. McEvan, *Africa from Early Times to 1800;* and R. Brentjes, *Uraltes junges Afrika; 5000 Jahre afrikanischer Geschichte nach zeitgenössischen Quellen.*

Regrettably, our sources of information for the precolonial period are extremely limited. See the judicious analysis by R. Mauny *et al.* of "Le Problème des Sources de l'histoire de l'Afrique noire jusqu'à la colonisation européenne," *Rapports* of the XI International Congress of Historical Sciences, Vienna, 1965, II, 177–232. The valuable efforts by Patricia Carson and others to offer *Guides to Materials for West African History in European Archives* are for the most part limited to modern documents. Volumes I and IV (comp. by Carson) deal with *Materials for West African History in the Archives of Belgium and Holland* and *France;* while Vols. II (comp. by A. F. C. Ryder) and III (comp. by J. R. Gray and D. S. Chambers) describe such *Materials* in Portuguese and Italian archives, respectively. See also B. Davidson, *The African Past, Chronicles from Antiquity to Modern Times;* idem, *Guide to African History;* and H. Brunschwig's survey of recent publications in his review article, "L'Afrique occidental," *RH,* CCXXXIX, 379–412. Like most other writers, Brunschwig refers mainly to studies dealing with the better-known developments in the nineteenth and twentieth centuries. This neglect of the earlier periods, characteristic of the large majority of both extant sources and modern research is doubly regrettable, as J. P. Chrétien has rightly, if somewhat exaggeratedly, answered in the affirmative his query, "Le Moyen Âge, âge d'or de l'Afrique?" *L'Information historique,* XXVII, 185–95. Quite useful also is A. M. Lewin, comp., *A Bibliography of African Bibliographies, Covering Territories South of the Sahara,* 3d ed. (supplies entries dated up to 1955). Of considerable interest also are the reflections of the extraordinary Portuguese ventures in the literature of the mother country. See the analysis in H. A. Cidade, *A Literatura portuguesa e a expansão ultramarina* (Vols. I: Séculos XV e XVI; II: Séculos XVII e XVIII), esp. II, 77 ff., describing the reactions to "the fanaticism of the Inquisition" in the colonies.

Valuable as this literature is for the background of the life and status of the few Jews who made sporadic appearances on the African continent south of the Sahara, it rarely refers directly to them or to New Christians. However, since the reconstruction of the past of the "Dark Continent" has but recently become the subject of intensive research in many lands, it may be hoped that some new light will also emerge on the Jewish settlement there before the nineteenth century. See *infra,* n. 104.

102. Paulo Dias de Nováis' Charter of September 19, 1571, reproduced by A. Brásio in his compilation of *Monumenta Missionaria Africana, África Ocidental,* III, 36 ff. (see *infra,* n. 107); and analyzed in A. da Silva Rego's *Portuguese Colonization in the Sixteenth Century: a Study of the Royal Ordinances (Regimentos),* pp. 97 ff.; the Jesuit Joseph de Anchieta's letter of April 23, 1563, cited by C. R. Boxer in his *Four Centuries,* p. 30 n. 6; Boxer, *Salvador de Sá,* pp. 231, 279. The estimates of the annual averages of slave exports to 1730 are given by D. Birmingham in *The Portuguese Conquest of Angola.* The key position in Portugal's African empire was held by Angola. See M. Valabru's pertinent remarks in his *Angola, clef de l'Afrique.* On its conquest and administration, see esp. A. de Oliveira Cadornega, *História Geral das Guerras Angolanas,* reprinted from the original Luanda, 1681–83, ed. (Vols. I–II, ed. and rev. with notes by J. Matias Delgado; III, ed. and rev. with notes by M. Alves da Cunha), with the comments thereon by G. M. Childs in "The Peoples of Angola in the Seventeenth Century according to Cadornega," *Journal of African History,* I, 271–79 (esp. pp. 277 f. on trade relations). See also

W. G. L. Randles's succinct summary, "Les Portugais en Angola," *Annales ESC,* XXIV, 289–304.

103. See Muḥammad ibn ʿAbd Allah ibn Baṭṭuṭa's *K. Tuḥfat an-Nuẓẓar* (Voyages), ed. with a French trans. by C. Defrémery and B. R. Sanguinetti, IV, 407 f. (Arabic and French), and in the English *Travels in Asia and Africa 1325–1354,* trans. and selected with an Intro. and Notes by H. A. N. Gibbs, p. 327; M. Palau Marti, *Le Roi Dieu au Bénin, Sud Togo, Dahomey, Nigeria occidental,* with a Foreword by H. Deschamps; P. Verger, "Mouvements de navires entre Bahia et le golfe de Bénin (XVIIᵉ–XIXᵉ siècles)," *Revue française d'histoire d'outre-mer,* LV, 5–36; A. J. Saraíva, "Le Père António Vieira S. J. et la question de l'esclavage des Noirs au XVIIe siècle," *Annales ESC,* XXII, 1289–1309; C. Sempat Assadourian, *El tráfico de esclaves en Córdoba de Angola a Potosí, siglos XVI–XVII;* J. Pope-Hennessy, *Sins of the Fathers: a Study of the Atlantic Slave Traders, 1551–1807.* It should also be noted that even the leader of the Portuguese revolt in Recife, João Fernandes Vieira, although himself of partial Negro descent, was an enthusiastic advocate of the importation of Negro slaves to Brazil. See also *supra,* nn. 98–99.

Understandably, the growth of the slave trade made the European missionaries suspect in the eyes of many Africans. Even in modern times, when slavery had ceased to be an issue, Christian missionaries suffered from the prevailing feeling among the natives that the promotion of Christian missions by the colonial powers was but a part of their exploitation of the colonial peoples. See, for instance, H. W. Mobley, *The Ghanaian Image of the Missionary: an Analysis of the Published Critique of Christian Missionaries by Ghanaians, 1897–1915.* How much more were such suspicions justified in the sixteenth and seventeenth centuries, when conversion of the native populations to Christianity was an avowed aim of the conquerors! See also the Marxist interpretation of "Les Fondements de l'expansion européenne en Afrique au XVᵉ siècle. Europe, Maghreb et Soudan occidental" by M. Małowist in *Acta Poloniae historica,* XVIII, 155–79.

104. See *supra,* Vol. III, pp. 91, 116 f., 271 f. n. 24, 286 f. nn. 52–53; Muḥammad ibn Muḥammad ash-Sharif al-Idrisi (Edrisi), *Description de l'Afrique et de l'Espagne,* Arabic text, ed. with a French trans. and notes by R. Dozy and M. J. de Goeje, pp. 29 f. (Arabic), 4 and 35 ff. (French); *Tarikh al-Fettâch,* by Maḥmud ben Al-Haj al-Mutawakkīl Kāti, ed. by O. V. Houdas and M. Delafosse, pp. 119 ff.; N. Slouschz, "Étude sur l'histoire des Juifs au Maroc," *Archives Marocaines,* IV, 345–411; VI, 1–107; idem, "Hébréo-Phéniciens et Judéo-Berbères," *ibid.,* XIV; idem, *Travels in North Africa,* esp. Part II: The Three Jewels of the Sahara, pp. 115 ff., 191 ff. (or in the expanded Hebrew edition, entitled *Sefer ha-Massaʿot);* and particularly H. Z. (J. W.) Hirschberg, *Toledot ha-Yehudim be-Afriqah ha-ṣefonit* (A History of the Jews in North Africa: From Antiquity to Our Time), esp. II, 2 ff. On the frequently transitory Islamization of the native tribes, see the interesting data supplied by N. Levtzion in his *Muslims and Chiefs in West Africa: a Study of Islam in the Middle Volta Basin in the Pre-Colonial Period.*

105. See the literature listed *supra,* n. 104; G. S. Colin, "Des Juifs nomades retrouvés dans le Sahara marocain au XVIᵉ siècle," *Mélanges d'études luso-marocaines* dedicated to the Memory of David Lopes and Pierre de Cénival,

pp. 53–66 (includes a French trans. of the second part of an interesting private letter by Yahuda ben Zamirro in 1527); and R. Mauny, "Le Judaïsme, les Juifs et l'Afrique occidentale," *Bulletin* of the Institut français d'Afrique noire, XI, 354–78, esp. pp. 366, 371 ff., 374. On the contrasting attitudes of Muslims and Jews, see also *infra*, n. 108.

106. See *supra*, Vol. XI, p. 247; C. A. Garcia, "A Ilha de S. Tomé como centro experimental do comportamento do Luso nos trópicos," *Studia* of the Centro de Estudos históricos ultramarinos in Lisbon, XIX, 209–221; J. J. Williams, *Hebrewisms of West Africa from Nile to Niger with the Jews*, esp. p. 22. There is a vast literature on the Jews in North Africa from pre-Islamic and Islamic days. Together with Berbers and "Arabs," some Arabic-speaking Jews must have penetrated both East and West Africa. However, the evidence is limited largely to oral recollections, and even those do not speak of Jews directly, but rather reveal a certain impact of biblical and, to a lesser extent, postbiblical Judaism. Here again, as in the case of the Amerindians, the "Lost Ten Tribes" of Israel have given rise to an endless recourse to hypotheses. An example of the extreme use of these materials is A. H. Godbey's *The Lost Tribes, A Myth—Suggestions Towards Rewriting Hebrew History*. Despite its methodological weaknesses, some of the ramified data assembled by Godbey are worthy of further consideration. From another angle, one may suggest that the trade with Africa, carried on by merchants of many nationalities, must have also attracted Jewish and New Christian traders. See, for example, J. Denucé, *L'Afrique au XVIe siècle et le commerce anversois;* the incidental suggestions offered by N. Slouschz in his *Travels in North Africa;* and the data assembled by S. Mendelssohn in *The Jews in Africa*.

107. See A. Brásio's ed. of *Monumenta Missionaria Africana*, III, 48 and n. 13, citing the decree of 1574 from an archival document; D. R. Barrett, "Two Hundred Independent Church Movements in East-Africa," *Social Compass*, XV, 101–116. We have little information about inquisitional activities in Africa. Apart from the small number of white residents (including suspected Calvinists and Lutherans), which discouraged the establishment of a large inquisitorial apparatus, discrimination against New Christians on racial grounds made little sense in a civilization where the vast majority of inhabitants were Negroes. The relative few who adopted Christianity syncretized its teachings with some of their tribal traditions and rituals, if they did not revert to their ancient paganism altogether. To prosecute such "heresies" would have made even less sense than in America, where the Holy Office in Mexico, Lima, and Cartagena had long been told to close their eyes to Amerindian transgressions. To be sure, the much-vaunted tolerance of the Portuguese in their colonial possessions has been seriously questioned by recent students of Portugal's imperial policies. The English scholar C. R. Boxer has rightly quoted the 1694 statement by a white Portuguese in Luanda describing the Negroes as "brutes without intelligent understanding" and "irrational beings," as fairly representative of the attitudes of many colonizers toward the black subjects. See Boxer's "The Colonial Question in the Portuguese Empire, 1415–1825," *Proceedings* of the British Academy, XLVII, 113–38; and his *Race Relations in the Portuguese Colonial Empire, 1415–1825*. Nonetheless, the maintenance here of a major agency for the persistent surveillance of New Christians, who were distinguishable from other white settlers only by their lack of

limpieza, if it could be proved at all at such distance from the home offices, would have been quite anomalous.

108. See García de Silva y Figueroa, *Comentarios de la embajada que de parte del Rey de España Don Felipe III, hizo al Rey Xa Abas de Persia,* [ed. by M. Serrano y Sanz], II, 530; and the excerpt therefrom trans. by C. R. Boxer in his *Four Centuries,* p. 35. See also the searching, yet still tentative, *Études sur l'Islam et les tribus maures,* relating to Senegal, the Braknas, Guinea, the Ivory Coast, and Dahomey, published about half a century ago by P. Marty; the more general review by M. Brelvi, *Islam in Africa,* with a Foreword by M. M. Sharif and an Intro. by I. H. Qureishi; R. B. Serjeant, *The Portuguese of the South Arabian Coast. Hadramis Chronicles with Yemeni and European Accounts of Dutch Pirates of Mocha in the Seventeenth Century;* E. Sancau, "Uma Narrativa do expedição portuguesa de 1541 ao Mar Roxo," *Studia* of the Centro de Estudos históricos ultramarinos, XI, 199–234 (analyzing João de Castro's report); various papers submitted to the Fifth International African Seminar at Ahmadu Bello University in Zaria in January 1964, and ed. with an Intro. by I. M. Lewis and a Foreword by Daryll Forde, under the title *Islam in Africa,* esp. pp. 5 ff. and 216 (showing the distribution of Islam south of the Sahara and on the eastern seaboard of Africa, principally in the vicinity of long-established Muslim settlements); J. B. McKenna, *A Spaniard in the Portuguese Indies, the Narrative of Martin Fernández de Figueroa* (reproducing Fernández' *Conquista d'las Indias* in a facsimile of the first print, a critical ed. of the Spanish text and an English trans. with notes). Despite the author's strongly anti-Jewish bias, his occasional observations on the early years 1505–1511 are worthy of note; see esp. pp. 24 ff. Title ii, 86 f. Title xxii, 124 f. Title xl, 165, 180 f. On the Portuguese contacts with Ethiopia, see *supra,* Vol. XIII, pp. 110, 114 f., 364 ff. nn. 53 and 58. Fuller light on medieval Jews and their trade relations with countries along the Indian Ocean may be expected from the comprehensive publication of the pertinent Genizah sources by Shlomoh Dob Goitein. See his preliminary study published as far back as 1954, "From the Mediterranean to India. Documents on the Trade to India, South Arabia and East Africa from the Eleventh and Twelfth Centuries," *Speculum,* XXIX, 181–97; and other studies listed in his comprehensive work, *A Mediterranean Society: the Jewish Communities of the Arab World as Portrayed in the Documents of the Cairo Geniza,* Vols. I–II.

109. See Gaspar Corrêa, *Lendas da India* (Legends from India), II, 134 f.; M. Kayserling, *Christopher Columbus and the Participation of the Jews in the Spanish and Portuguese Discoveries,* trans. by C. Gross, pp. 119 ff.; the reports by Barzaeus and other Jesuit missionaries, reproduced by J. Wicki, ed., in *Documenta indica,* Vols. I–XI. After the publication of Wicki's first volume W. J. Fischel culled the main items relating to the Jews of Ormuz and, with the aid of a few additional data obtained from other sources, described the events of 1549–51 in Ormuz in his "New Sources for the History of the Jewish Diaspora in Asia in the 16th Century," *JQR,* XL, 379–99. See also his broader Hebrew monograph, *Ha-Yehudim be-Hodu* (The Jews in India: Their Contributions to the Economic and Political Life), esp. pp. 52 ff. Gaspar Barzaeus' numerous reports and letters also fill most of Wicki's Vol. II, esp. pp. 71 ff. Doc. 26, items 4–5; 215 ff. Doc. 56; 445 ff. Doc. 104. Still young upon his arrival in Ormuz in 1549, the Flemish missionary

died four years later, at the age of thirty-eight. But he established a great reputation for himself both in Asia and among his Flemish compatriots. In fact, next to St. Francis Xavier, he ranked as the leading contemporary Jesuit missionary in Asia. In 1610 the Belgian province of the Society of Jesus actually suggested to Rome that he be canonized; one of its members, Nicolas Trigault, wrote at that time a full-length *Vita Gasparis Barzaei Belgae e Societatis Iesu, B. Xaverii in India socii.* After Barzaeus' departure from Ormuz in 1551, our sources concerning Jewish life in that community dry up. Needless to say, the missionary activities of Barzaeus and his confreres' were not limited to Jews, but rather extended to the entire motley of races and ethnic groups which constituted the population of that flourishing emporium. See also A. da Silva Rego, ed., "Do Principio do Reyno de Ormus," *Documentação ultramarina portuguesa,* II, 79–95, esp. pp. 90 ff. (reproducing a contemporary Portuguese description of Ormuz); and *infra,* nn. 112 and 117.

110. See Nicholas Lancillottus' report to Loyola of January 27, 1550, and that by Ludovicus Frois to the Portuguese Jesuits of December 1, 1560, in J. Wicki, *Documenta indica,* II, 13 ff. Doc. 8; IV, 721 ff. Doc. 94, esp. p. 739 item 35. We are not informed about Barzaeus' library. However, it may not have greatly differed from that brought to Asia by Francis Xavier a few years earlier. We are told that Xavier had taken along books (a gift from King John III) valued at 100 cruzados. Similarly, Melchior Nunes Barreto, who in 1555 succeeded Xavier as the leading missionary in Japan, brought with him a substantial library, which included Thomas Aquinas' *Summa contra gentiles* and *Summa theologica,* the *Summa silvestrina* by Silvester Mazzolini de Prierias (which at that time ranked, next to the works of Aquinas, as the outstanding theological reference work of the Catholic Restoration), and many other classics. See *supra,* Vols. IX, pp. 101 ff., 290 ff. nn. 4 item 3, 6 item 2; XIII, p. 409 n. 33. While neither library specifically mentions Nicholas de Lyra or Paul of Burgos, the likelihood is that Barzaeus and the others had at their disposal either the actual works of these leading Catholic apologists, or at least notes from them, with which to argue for their point of view.

On the other hand, we know very little about any Jewish apologetical literature available to the local rabbis. Even Rabbi Solomon, who before settling in Ormuz had traveled widely and had been trained in a Jewish academy of Cairo (which still retained some of the glory of the days of the Maimonidean "princes" and David ibn abi Zimra), may have had few opportunities to acquaint himself with the sparse and scattered records of medieval Muslim-Jewish debates. He probably was even less well informed about Jewish replies to Christian polemics. Since we have no Jewish sources relating to Barzaeus' debates with the rabbis, we cannot judge to what extent the Jesuit's early sanguine reports about forthcoming Jewish conversions were superficially justified. The summary of the disputation of November 24, 1550, is given in Nicholas Trigault's *Vita Gasparis Barzaei,* II, 13; that of the discourse held in the synagogue on the Sabbath of December 10, 1549, in the same volume. These summaries may have undergone some changes in the half a century between Barzaeus' demise and the publication of Trigault's biography. See also the text, republished and fully commented on by G. Schurhammer in "Die Trinitätspredigt Mag. Gaspars in der Synagoge von Ormuz," *AHSI,* II, 278–309; and Wicki's ed. of *Documenta indica,* I, 610 ff. Doc. 87A, esp. 625 ff. items 50 ff.; 639 ff. Doc. 87B, esp. 660 item 22, and 677 f. items 50–51; 698 ff. Doc. 88. See also *infra,* n. 118.

111. Zechariah b. Saadiah ad-Dāhri (or az-Zahiri), *Sefer-ha-Musar* (Book of Moral Conduct); ed. by Y. Ratzaby, esp. pp. 28, 90, 145; Pedro Teixeira, *The Travels*, trans. and annotated by W. F. Sinclair, with further Notes and an Intro. by D. Ferguson, p. 168; García de Silva y Figueroa, *Comentarios* (see *supra*, n. 108); or in the earlier incomplete French trans. by A. de Wicqfort, entitled *L'Ambassade de Don Garcia de Silva Figueroa en Perse*, pp. 41 f.; other sources cited by W. J. Fischel in "The Region of the Persian Gulf and Its Jewish Settlements in Islamic Times," *Alexander Marx Jubilee Volume*, pp. 203–230, esp. pp. 216 ff.

112. St. Francis Xavier, *Epistolae aliaque eius scripta*, ed. by G. Schurhammer and J. Wicki, II, 418 f. (with the editors' n. 4 thereon); Nicholas Lancillottus' report to Loyola of December 22, 1550 in J. Wicki's ed. of *Documenta indica*, II, 132 ff. Doc. 35 item 4. Yet, as usual among Jew-haters, some of Xavier's "best friends were Jews." He and Loyola not only resisted the Portuguese opposition to the admission of Henry Henriques to the final vows on account of Henriques' Jewish ancestry, but also appointed him superior of all Jesuits in the Cape Comorin region. See Wicki, *ibid.*; and J. Brodrick, *Saint Francis Xavier (1506–1552)*, pp. 479 f. The paucity of Jewish conversions to Christianity is evidenced by Barzaeus' and his colleagues' own correspondence. Despite his high expectations, Barzaeus could mention only the conversion of a single girl. Notwithstanding their allegedly great friendship with the Jesuit father, the rabbis merely resorted to the pious excuse that they could not see their way to abandoning the religion of their forefathers. See *supra*, n. 110; and Wicki, *Documenta indica*, I, 610 ff. Doc. 87A, 625 ff. items 50–57 (curiously, items 51–52 are omitted, although they doubtless also relate to Barzaeus' grand debate with Rabbis Solomon and Joseph).

113. See João de Barros, *Asia. Dos feitos que os Portugueses fizeram no descobrimento e conquista dos mares, e terras do Oriente*, in 4 *decadas* (1552–63), 6th ed. in modern orthography and with notes by H. Cidade and with "final historical notes" by M. Múrias, Vols. I–IV; E. do Couto Lupi, *A Emprêsa portuguesa do Oriente, conquista e sustentação de senhorio do mare (século XVI)*; M. A. H. Fitzler [K.], "Der Anteil der Deutschen an der Kolonialpolitik Philipps II von Spanien in Asien," *VSG*, XXVIII, 243–81; and the collection of informative essays ed. by A. Baião, in *Historia da expansão portuguesa no mundo* (including esp. his own, II, 101–127; and those by H. Cidade and G. Sousa Dias, III, 97–106, 199–212). A good selection of contemporary sources is offered by G. Schurhammer in *Die Zeitgenössischen Quellen zur Geschichte Portugiesisch-Asiens und seiner Nachbarländer (Ostafrika, Abessinien, Arabien, Persien, Vorder- und Hinterindien, Malaischer Archipel, Philippinen, China und Japan) zur Zeit des hl. Franz Xaver (1538–1552). 6080 Regesten und 30 Tafeln*, new impression with a complete Index and supplements up to 1962. On the background, see J. Manuel Pacheco de Figueiredo (Junior), "Goa pre-portuguesa," *Studia* of the Centro de Estudos históricos ultramarinos, Lisbon, XII, 139–259; XIII–XIV, 105–225.

Of course, there were numerous Jewish settlements both before the arrival of the Portuguese in Asia and outside the Portuguese possessions in the sixteenth and seventeenth centuries. These Jewish communities, whose history still is full of obscurities, will be analyzed in connection with general Jewish developments in the late medieval and early modern Muslim world and its neighboring lands. Suffice it to refer, for the time being, to W. J. Fischel's *Ha-Yehudim be-Hodu* (The

Jews in India: Their Contribution to the Economic and Political Life), Hebrew trans. from the English by J. Hason (with extensive bibliographical notes); and *supra*, Vol. III, esp. pp. 114 ff., 284 ff. nn. 49–51. On the economic aspects, see also *infra*, n. 117.

The promotion of the use of the Portuguese language was from the outset part of the mother country's colonial policy. Its persistence throughout southeast Asia, even after the displacement of the Portuguese by Dutch rule is well illustrated by the following comment of the Dutch governor-general Johann Maetsuycker in 1659: "The Portuguese language is an easy language to speak and easy to learn. That is the reason why we cannot prevent here from the slaves brought here from Arakan who have never heard a word of Portuguese (and indeed even our own children) from taking to that language in preference to all other languages and making it their own." See K. W. Gunawardena, "A New Netherlands in Ceylon," *The Ceylon Journal of Historical and Social Studies*, II, No. 2, p. 242; F. J. Hopffer Rego, "A Língua portuguesa, entre outras, como instrumento a parte de uma política ultra-marina," *Boletim* of the Sociedade de Geografía de Lisbõa, LXXXVIa, pp. 35–44. See also D. Lopes, *A Expansão da lingua portuguesa no Oriente nos séculos XVI, XVII e XVIII*; C. R. Boxer, *Four Centuries*, pp. 36 ff., 54 ff.; and his *Portuguese Society in the Tropics: the Municipal Councils of Goa, Macao, Bahia and Luanda, 1510–1800*. As elsewhere, some Jewish émigrés from Spain and their descendants, continued to cultivate Spanish as their daily language. In his report from India in 1605 the Dominican friar Diego Aduarte noted with amazement that "there are Jews here [in India] with their own synagogues. They are white men who understand and also speak Spanish as well as any man born in Spain." Cited from a MS in C. R. Boxer's possession by J. S. Cummins in his English trans. of Antonio de Moya's *Sucesos de las Islas Filipinas*, p. 323 n. 2.

114. See M. A. P. Meilink-Roelofsz, *Asian Trade and European Influence in the Indonesian Archipelago, between 1500 and about 1630*, esp. pp. 131 f., 181 f., 297, 332, 361, 371, with the comments thereon by P. Chaunu in "Les 'Cristãos Novos' et l'effondrement de l'Empire portugais dans l'Océan Indien au début du XVIIe siècle," *REJ*, CXXII, 188–90; P. S. S. Pissurlencar, *Agentes da Diplomacia Portuguesa na India (Hindus, Muçulmanos, Judeus e Parses). Documentos coordenados, anotados e prefaciados*; C. G. F. Simkin, *The Traditional Trade of Asia*; J. Lucio d'Azevedo, *História de António Vieira*, II, 125 ff.; and *supra*, nn. 96 ff. Such an infusion of 20,000 cruzados annually would have been very helpful to the Portuguese trade with Asia. Despite all criticism from a mercantilist-minded public, the lack of demand for European goods in Asia forced the Western traders to export much silver to the Asian colonies in payment for the Oriental wares greatly coveted in European markets. See the illustrations offered on the example of the Anglo-Asian trade by K. N. Chandhuri in "The East India Company and the Export of Treasure in the Early Seventeenth Century," *EcHR*, n.s. XVI, 23–38. On the Portuguese decree of 1568, see *supra*, Chap. LXIII, n. 51.

One speaks with considerable diffidence, however, about the number of white settlers in Southeast Asia and, even more, about the ratio of New Christians among them. Apart from the general paucity of relevant sources and the difficulty in distinguishing between white settlers of common background and language, there is the basic deficiency of the onomatological criteria, which often have served us in good stead to separate the Jewish or crypto-Jewish segment from the majority of its neighbors. It appears that here, even more than elsewhere, the New Christians frequently bore the same names as their Old Christian compatriots, whether for purposes of better camouflage or by mere coincidence. Even Old Christians unrelated to one another frequently had exactly the same names. We recall the António Vieira who appeared on the list of travelers to the East Indies; he apparently had no relationship at all to his famous Luso-Brazilian namesake. See *supra*, Chap. LXV, n. 100; and numerous other examples, cited by G. Schurhammer in his "Doppelgänger in Portugiesisch-Asien," *Portugiesische Forschungen der Görresgesellschaft*, 1st ser. I, 192–224. Nonetheless, all signs seem to point to a very small New Christian population in Goa and other centers of the Portuguese domain in Asia.

115. The great mortality of passengers on the crowded vessels is attested, among many other sources, by the report of the Jesuit Joannes Baptista Ribera to Rector Alphonso de Zarate of the Jesuit College in Cordova, dated Goa, October 27–November 20, 1565. According to this eyewitness, of 650 passengers who embarked in Portugal, 80 had died before reaching the Cape of Good Hope, while many others had fallen ill. R. P. Rao claims that an average of 40 percent of all passengers from Portugal passed away before reaching India. It is understandable, therefore, that despite Goa's beauty (it became proverbial that "whoever hath seen Goa, need not see Lisbon"), and its tremendous economic opportunities, not too many Portuguese émigrés embarked in that direction. These hardships were doubly discouraging to the "weaker sex." See also *infra*, n. 116. It is truly astonishing, therefore, that under Portuguese rule Goa, nicknamed "the Rome of India," could develop as well as it did. Even an English visitor, Dr. Fryer, observed in 1675 that the city "looks well at a distance—stands upon seven hills: everywhere colleges, churches and glorious statues; but many houses disgracing it with their ruins." See J. Wicki, ed., *Documenta indica*, VI, 530 ff. Doc. 84; R. P. Rao, *Portuguese Rule in Goa 1510–1961*, pp. 35 f., 37, 39 (written in the period of India's annexation of that Portuguese colony, this book understandably betrays a moderately anti-Portuguese bias).

116. See the standard work by A. Baião, *A Inquisição de Goa. I: Tentative de história da sua origem, estabelecimento, evolução e extinção*, esp. pp. 17 ff., on the establishment of the institution; the earlier developments described by G. Corrêa in *Lendas da India*, II, 131 ff.; III, 274 ff.; the 1569 auto mentioned by J. Wicki in his ed. of *Documenta indica*, VIII, 35 ff. Doc. 12, esp. pp. 51 ff.; and his biographical sketches of the chief ecclesiastical leaders, "D. Jorge Temudo O. P.: 1, Bischof von Cochin, 2, Erzbischof von Goa, 1558–1567–1571," *Neue Zeitschrift für Missionswissenschaft*, XXI, 172–83, 243–51; idem, "D. Henrique de Távora, O. P. Bischof von Cochin, 1567–1578, Erzbischof von Goa, 1578–1581," *ibid.*, XXIV, 111–21, esp. p. 114 relating to his role in the conversion of Joseph de Ataíde. Baião's analysis is definitely incomplete. For instance, neither the death by burning of Catharina de Orta in 1569 nor a number of other trials are mentioned. See A. da Silva Carvalho, *Garcia d'Orta*, pp. 72 ff., 204; I. S. Révah, "La Famille de Garcia de Orta," *Revista da Universidade de Coimbra*, XIX, 407–420 (containing an extensive genealogical table); idem, "J. Cointa, Sieur des Boulez, exécuté par l'Inquisition de Goa en 1572," *Annali* of the Istituto Universitario Orientale, Sezione Romanza, Naples, 1961, pp. 71–75; Pedro de Azevedo, "O Bocarro Francês e os Judeus de Cochim e Hamburgo," *Archivo histórico português*, VIII, 186; J. Wicki,

ed., *Documenta indica*, VI, 103 ff. Doc. 24, esp. p. 113 item 15; VIII, 35 ff. Doc. 12, esp. pp. 51 f.; and *supra*, Vol. XIII, pp. 83 f., 351 f. n. 21. To the literature listed there concerning the famous scientist Garcia de Orta, we may now add a great many further monographs, particularly those appearing in the journal bearing his name. See esp. A. da Silva Rego's "Garcia de Orta e a idea de tolerancia religiosa," *Garcia de Orta*, XI, 663–76. See also, more generally, the fuller "Listas das Pessõas, prezas nos carceres do Goa, 1649" and similar other lists preserved in the Torre de Tombo Archive in Lisbon, No. 16,700 of the files of the Inquisition, etc.; as well as the *Repertorio geral de tres mil e oito centos procesos que sam todos os despachados neste Sancto Officio de Goa*, compiled in 1623 by José Delgado Figueira, extant in MS in the National Library in Lisbon, Codex 203. See also J. Lucio d'Azevedo, *Historia dos Cristãos Novos Portugueses*, pp. 231 f.

117. See *Bullarium Patronatus Portugalliae Regum in ecclesiis Africae, Asiae, atque Oceaniae*, ed. by L. M. Jordão [Paiva Manso] *et al.*, App. I, pp. 12–33, cited by J. Wicki, ed., *Documenta indica*, VIII, 35 ff. Doc. 12; Francisco de Porres' report reproduced by Wicki, *ibid.*, IX, 644 ff. Doc. 120, esp. pp. 646 f., item 2; his other data, *ibid.*, VIII, 437 ff. Doc. 58; 574 ff. Doc. 86; IX, 2*, 78 ff. Doc. 20, esp. p. 91 item 35; X, 228 ff. Doc. 16; his ed. of "Dokumente und Briefe aus der Zeit des indischen Vizekönigs D. Antão de Noronha (1563–1568)," *Portugiesische Forschungen der Görresgesellschaft*, 1st ser. I, 225–315 (also reproducing the important *Ferman*, granted in April 1541 by King Salghar of Ormuz to the king of Portugal in a contemporary Portuguese trans.; pp. 309 ff. App. 1); A. da Silva Rego, ed., *Boletím da Filmoteca ultramarina portuguesa* of the Centro de Estudos históricas ultramarinos in Lisbon, I, Part 2, pp. 164 No. 45, 234 f. No. 54, 311 Nos. 12–13.

Evidently being unable to implement the intolerant royal ordinances, some officials suggested economic measures. For instance, in an extensive memorandum addressed to the king on December 18, 1615, Viceroy Jerónimo de Azevedo suggested that in the sale of victuals for the journey (*viagems*) the first option be given to nobles. Only if the latter refused to buy, an offer under the same conditions would be made to the burghers, "with the exception of the plebeians and the New Christians." *Ibid.*, p. 780 No. 115 item 29. Remarkably, by 1589 the Portuguese authorities were so entrenched in Ormuz that the king asked his viceroy in India whether one Isaac, a Babylonian Jewish merchant, should be given a permit to settle in Ormuz and sell sun umbrellas there. See his letters of February 22, 1589, summarized *ibid.*, No. 2, p. 298 Nos. 1–2. See also M. A. P. Meilink-Roelofsz, *Asian Trade and European Influence in the Indonesian Archipelago*, esp. pp. 131 f.; and J. Kieniewicz, "Le Commerce en Asie et l'expansion portugaise vers l'Océan Indien au XVIe siècle," *Acta Poloniae historica*, XVIII, 180–93. Noronha, who had left Lisbon in 1564, generally sided with the inquisitors. He piously attended the autos-da-fé and, in his reports home, rarely indicated the friction which had gradually developed between the ecclesiastical and secular authorities in Goa. He also remained remarkably silent on the subject of the Goa Inquisition, at least in so far as can be seen from J. Wicki's ed. of "Dokumente und Briefe" in *Portugiesische Forschungen*, I.

118. See Alessandro Valignano's message to Mercurian, dated January 13, 1574, and reproduced by J. Wicki, ed., *Documenta indica*, IX, 78 ff. Doc. 20, 90 ff. items 21–22; X, 360 ff. Doc. 18, 586 ff. Doc. 4; Diego Laynez' letter to Barreto, dated

Trent, December 10, 1562, *ibid.*, V, 652 ff. Doc. 93, esp. pp. 655 f. item 8; *Sententia superiorum ecclesiasticorum Indiae* of April 9, 1579, *ibid.*, XI, 562 ff. Doc. 75; and *supra*, Vol. XIV, pp. 14 f., 25, 306 f. n. 13, 314 n. 23. Valignano naturally spoke as a recent Italian arrival, rather than as a Portuguese. Nevertheless he became the early historian of the Jesuit missions in Asia; most of the subsequent historiography of that period has strongly relied on his account. See his *Historia del principio y progresso de la Compañía de Jésus en las Indias Orientales (1542–64)*, ed. and interpreted by J. Wicki (includes a very laudatory description of Barzaeus' activities in Ormuz). By way of contrast to Valignano, we need but cite the report on the general state of affairs in the East Indies submitted in 1646 by the Augustinian Fray Augustinho d'Azevedo to the king, in which the friar warns against admitting to the Portuguese possessions not only Jews and Moors but also Venetians and other Italians, because they were likely to set a bad example for the natives. See *Documentação ultramarina portuguesa*, I, 5 ff. No. 2.

119. St. Francis Xavier, *Epistolae*, I, 344 ff. Ep. 57 item 2; A. Valignano, *Historia del principio*, II, 343; and other sources cited by J. Wicki, ed., *Documenta indica*, III, 758 ff. Doc. 16; IV, 1 ff. Doc. 1; XI, 641 ff. No. 89 item 42; L. A. Rebello da Silva *et al.*, eds., *Corpo diplomático portuguez*, IX, 12.

120. J. Wicki, ed., *Documenta indica*, VII, 318 ff. Doc. 68; VIII, 132 ff. Doc. 22; X, 228 ff. Doc. 16; Claude de Dellon, *Voyages avec sa Relation de l'Inquisition de Goa, augmentée de diverses pièces curieuses et l'Histoire des dieux qu'adorent les gentils des Indes*, I, 118. An English trans. of Vol. I by H. Wharton entitled *The History of the Inquisition as It Is Exercised at Goa* was published in the same year, 1688, as the French version. On the other hand, the Portuguese rendition by M. V. de Abreu (*Narração da Inquisição de Goa*) did not appear until 1866 in Nova Goa, but it was provided with extensive notes by the translator.

121. A. Valignano, *Historia*, pp. 393, 469 f.; J. Wicki, ed., *Documenta indica*, I, 352 ff. Doc. 55, esp. pp. 367 item 15, 376 f. item 27 (in this report of December 4, 1548, Pérez also emphasized the presence in Malacca of both white Jews from Turkey and Malabar Jewish natives of the area); 771 ff. Doc. 2, esp. p. 782 Art. 10; IV, 1 ff. Doc. 1, esp. item 6; V, 155 ff. Doc. 29; X, 316 ff. Doc. 17A, esp. p. 334 item 20. In his report of November 1569 to the general of the Order, Francisco Borgia, Sebastian Fernandi described the early House of Catechumens in Goa. It evidently was a very small undertaking, having room for only fifteen inmates. It appears that, as in Europe, the missionaries had bad experiences with some prospective Jewish (and Muslim) converts, who either disappeared shortly before the baptismal ceremony or were baptized and subsequently relapsed. The Jesuits therefore restricted actual baptism to catechumens who had undergone a three-month training period. See Fernandi's report *ibid.*, VIII, 35 ff. Doc. 12. Much new and valuable documentation on the catechumens and converts is presented by J. Wicki in his recent ed. of *O Livro do "Pai dos Cristãos."*

122. See Gregorius de Castro's report to Antonio Possevino, secretary-general of the Society in Rome, submitted in the autumn of 1574, and that of Antonio Monserrate to the general of the Order, E. Mercurian, dated January 12, 1579, both reproduced in J. Wicki's ed. of *Documenta indica*, VIII, 739 ff. Doc. 101, esp. pp.

751 ff. item 15; XI, 505 ff. Doc. 65, esp. p. 515 item 15; M. de Faria y Sousa, *Asia portuguesa*, Lisbon, 1666–75; in the English version entitled *The Portuguese Asia; or The History of the Discovery and Conquest of India by the Portuguese*, trans. by J. Stevens, I, 117 f.; II, 505; III, 111 (this work, covering the period 1412–1640, is based upon personal observation, as well as upon documentary evidence). This narrative is effectively supplemented by the description of events by the sixteenth-century Arab chronicler Zain ad-Din al-Ma'bari. See the text and Portuguese trans. published by D. Lopes under the title *Historia dos Portugueses no Malabar por Zinadim. Manuscripto árabe do século XVI.*

The remarkable Jewish community of Cochin, the foundations of which go back to the eleventh century or earlier (see *supra*, Vol. III, pp. 114 f., 284 f. n. 50), will be discussed more fully in a later volume. See also L. A. Noonan, "The Portuguese in Malacca: a Study of the First Major European Impact on East Asia," *Studia* of the Centro de Estudos históricos ultramarinos, XXIII, 33–103 (Diss. Univ. of Western Australia); A. M. Mundadan, *The Arrival of the Portuguese in India and the Thomas Christians under Mar Jacob, 1498–1552;* F. M. Rogers, *The Quest for Eastern Christians: Travels and Rumor in the Age of Discovery*, esp. pp. 114 ff.; N. J. Thomas, *Die Syrisch-orthodoxe Kirche der südindischen Thomas-Christen. Geschichte—Kirchenverfassung—Lehre* (Diss. Marburg). In his aforementioned letter from Trent (*supra*, n. 118), Diego Laynez also suggested the exclusion of Syrian priests from service as bishops of the St. Thomas devotees in Malabar. Although Jewish contacts with that region may have reached back to remote antiquity, the real history of the Jews in most of its parts is better known only after the Dutch occupation. See *supra*, n. 113; Vol. I, p. 321 n. 3; and, more generally, T. I. Poonen, *A Survey of the Rise of Dutch Power in Malabar, 1603–1678*. Related to these endeavors is the Dutch occupation of Ceylon and parts of Indonesia, on which see, for instance, K. W. Goonewardena, *The Foundation of the Dutch Power in Ceylon, 1638–1658;* and, more generally, I. Prins, "Did the Dutch on Arrival in Java Encounter Jews?" (Dutch), *Nieuw Israelietisch Weekblad* of June 7, 1929, and briefly summarized in *BMGJW*, V, 68–69. See also *supra*, Chap. LXIII, n. 51.

123. See Ferdinand de Meneses' estimate in his letter to Mercurian of November 15, 1579, in J. Wicki's ed. of *Documenta indica*, XI, 727 ff. Doc. 97, esp. p. 731 item 6; H. C. Lea, *The Inquisition in the Spanish Dependencies*, pp. 304, 311; P. Chaunu, *Les Philippines et le Pacifique des Ibériques (XVIe, XVIIe, XVIIIe siècles); introduction méthodique et indices d'activité;* P. Torres y Lanza, "Catálogo de los Documentos relativos a las Filipinas existentes en el Archivo de Indias de Sevilla (1573–1611)," *Boletím de Filmoteca Ultramarina Portuguesa*, IX, 91–154.